HENRY FLOOD

JAMES KELLY

Henry Flood

PATRIOTS AND POLITICS IN
EIGHTEENTH-CENTURY IRELAND

UNIVERSITY OF NOTRE DAME PRESS
Notre Dame, Indiana

Published in the United States in 1998 by
UNIVERSITY OF NOTRE DAME PRESS
Notre Dame, Indiana, 46556
All Rights Reserved.

and in Ireland by
FOUR COURTS PRESS LTD
Fumbally Lane, Dublin 8.

ISBN 0-268-01114-1 (cloth)

A CIP catalog record for this book
is available from the Library of Congress.

Printed in Great Britain by
the Martins Printing Group, Bodmin, Cornwall.

For Judith, Eva and James

Contents

Abbreviations

B.L., Add. Ms	British Library, Additional Manuscript
B.L.,O.C.	Beinecke Library, Osborn Collection
C.H.O.P.	*Calendar of Home Office Papers 1760–72*
D.C.	*Dublin Chronicle*
D.E.P.	*Dublin Evening Post*
D.P.L.	Dublin Public Library, Pearse Street
D.N.B.	*Dictionary of National Biography*
E.H.R.	*English Historical Review*
F.D.J.	*Faulkner's Dublin Journal*
F.J.	*Freeman's Journal*
F.L.J.	*Finn's Leinster Journal*
G.O.	Genealogical Office, Dublin
H.J.	*Hibernian Journal*
H.M.C.	Historical Manuscripts Commission
I.H.S.	*Irish Historical Studies*
J.C.H.A.S.	*Journal of the Cork Historical and Archaeological Society*
J.R.S.A.I.	*Journal of the Royal Society of Antiquaries of Ireland*
Ms(s)	Manuscript(s)
N.A.	National Archives of Ireland
N.L.I.	National Library of Ireland
N.L.S.	National Library of Scotland
N.M.A.J.	*North Munster Antiquarian Journal*
P.C.	Privy Council
P.O.	*Pue's Occurrences*
P.R.O.	Public Record Office
P.R.O.N.I.	Public Record Office of Northern Ireland
Q.U.B.	Queen's University, Belfast
R.I.A.	Royal Irish Academy
R.I.A. proc.	Royal Irish Academy, proceedings
R.O.	Record Office

R.S.A.I.	Royal Society of Antiquaries of Ireland
S.C.L.	Sheffield City Library
T.C.D.	Trinity College, Dublin
U.C.D.	University College, Dublin
V.J.(D).	*Volunteer Journal (Dublin)*
V.E.P.	*Volunteer Evening Post*

Acknowledgements

This biography would not have been possible but for the generosity of the owners and trustees of the manuscripts on which it is primarily based or the help and goodwill of archivists in Ireland, Britain and the USA. I wish to express by grateful thanks to the Earl and Countess of Rosse for their kindness and hospitality when I consulted the Rosse Papers at Birr. I wish also to express gratitude to the Duke of Rutland, and to the custodians, archivists and keepers of manuscripts in the Boston Public Library, British Library, Cambridge University Library, Dublin Public Library, East Sussex Record Office, Genealogical Office (Dublin), Harvard University Library, Hampshire Record Office, Henry Huntington Library, Ipswich and East Suffolk Record Office, Keele University Library, Kent Archives Office, Registry of Deeds and Land Commission of the Land Registry (Dublin), Library of Congress (Washington), Limerick Archives Office, Linenhall Library (Belfast), National Archives (Dublin), National Library of Ireland, National Library of Scotland, Norfolk Record Office, Northamptonshire Record Office, North Yorkshire Record Office, Oireachtais Library (Dublin), Pennsylvania Historical Society (Philadelphia), Public Record Office, Public Record Office of Northern Ireland, Royal Dublin Society, Royal Irish Academy, Royal Society of Antiquaries of Ireland, Sheffield City Library, West Sussex Record Office, Trinity College Dublin, the Beinecke, Sterling and Lewis Walpole Libraries of Yale University and the Warwickshire Record Office for facilitating access to collections in their care.

On a personal level, I would like to express my gratitude to Dr Pauric Travers, Fr Patrick O'Donoghue and Dr Dáire Keogh, departmental colleagues past and present, for their fellowship and support. Dr O'Donoghue's and Dr Keogh's comments on the text and Dr Travers' help with the proofs are deeply appreciated. The contributions of Judith Brady, Eva and James Kelly in the appearance of this book are less easy to describe. It was from them that I stole much of the time it took to write it; for this and for many other reasons it is they who deserve the profoundest acknowledgement.

Introduction

A noted Irish scholar once compared that task awaiting him when he undertook to write a 'general history' of modern Ireland to that of the 'ancient Israelite condemned to make bricks without straw'.[1] His unease derived from the thinness of the published work on the period with which was his concern. In the case of Henry Flood, it is less the sparseness of the published work, than the paucity of personal papers that is the source of difficulty. The main reason for this is that his lifelong friend, Ambrose Smith, and his agent 'occupied themselves for several days' shortly after his death destroying his papers.[2] A small bundle of letters was saved from incineration, but neither these nor the larger collection of Flood manuscripts in the papers of his friend, Lawrence Parsons, compensates for what was destroyed. The problems this cause are intensified by the fact that Flood did not confide easily in others, as two of his long-term counsellors, Lord Charlemont and Archbishop William Markham, were obliged to accept.[3] As a consequence, any attempt at a biography must be uneven and incomplete. Certain aspects of Flood's political career and his relationship with his friends and family can be pieced together with some confidence from the parliamentary record, legal documents, his own surviving papers and occasional references in those of friends, acquaintances, opponents and critics. But others – his relationship with his wife, friends and political acquaintances, his intellectual activities, and, most importantly, his political strategy at key points in his life – are either opaque or totally obscure.

In many respects, this is how Flood preferred it. Though convinced he possessed the commitment and ability to govern in a principled and virtuous manner, he proved incapable of working in concert with others for long periods. He made no lifelong political allies, and though his political skill, personal courage and formidable intelligence won him many admirers, he was too independent and individualistic to embrace power when the opportunity came his way. This may derive from the

---

1 F.S.L.Lyons, *Ireland since the famine* (London, 1973), p. 7.   2 T[homas] R[odd], ed., *Original letters to the right hon Henry Flood* (London, 1820), p. ii.   3 Flood's correspondence with Charlemont is in the Charlemont Papers in the Royal Irish Academy. His request, in April 1775, to Markham to return his letters (Birr Castle, Rosse Papers, C/2/2/3) partly accounts for the survival of their correspondence.

fact that he lived his life under the shadow of the circumstances of his birth. Flood's 'illegitimacy' was not used in an overtly confining or threatening way during his lifetime, but it is significant that it was commented upon by people other than family members who privately queried the legality of his inheritance.[4] The destruction of Flood's papers may mean we will never be able to measure its full impact on his outlook and behaviour, but a psychologist might suggest that it contributed to his personal reserve, to his obsessive concern with his reputation and to his incapacity to subordinate his freedom of action to the demands of a group, both as an opposition MP and as an officeholder. These characteristics are most readily identifiable from the late 1770s when his acceptance of office cost him the acclaim he had earned when he spearheaded the patriots' challenge to government policy in the House of Commons in the 1760s and early 1770s. His radical patriot stand following his dismissal from office in 1781 restored him to popular favour for a time, but it did not make him many political allies or cause him to temper his resolutely independent will. Privately, by contrast, as his small circle of close friends and his wife knew well, Flood could be most attentive to the needs of those for whom he cared deeply; he could also be an engaging and informed conversationalist, but he was not a 'hail fellow well met'. Indeed, he was frequently cavalier in his dealings with others, and while this provoked a number of well-documented altercations in Britain as well as Ireland, it did not make for informed gossip or fond remembrance. As a result, one has to rely more heavily than a biographer would wish on his public utterances and on the reports of others to reconstruct his life.

In most studies of the eighteenth century, Flood is indivisibly linked with Henry Grattan, his one time friend, who succeeded him as the leading spokesman of the patriot interest in the House of Commons. There was, it is true, much on which they were at one, but Flood's acceptance of office drove them apart, and their sharp political and personal disagreements in 1782–3 opened a deep fissure that was never closed. Despite their shared patriot principles, they were, in other respects, politicians of different generations, as their contrasting attitudes to the subject of Catholic relief testifies. Grattan's eventual embrace of emancipation places him securely among the small group of late eighteenth-century Irish Protestant politicians who were prepared to admit Catholics to political power. Flood, by contrast, throughout his career resisted the dilution of the penal disabilities which upheld the security of the Protestant interest. Within the eighteenth-century patriot tradition which he helped to define, Flood's was a liberal, reformist voice, but he drew a firm line at the admission of Catholics to the political process.

If Flood's conviction that it was essential that Irish Protestants perpetuated their dominant position represents an important reference point by which one can locate

4 Lill to Macartney, 29 Dec. 1773 in Thomas Bartlett, ed., *Macartney in Ireland 1768–72* (Belfast, [1978]), p. 252; William Hunt, ed., *The Irish parliament, 1775* (London, 1907), pp 20–1; Notes on Flood v Flood [1792] (N.A., Langrishe Papers, B.R.,KK, 38/16); List of Flood papers, 17 Oct. 1815 (T.C.D., MUN/P/1/1383/ 10); Earl of Rosse, 'Henry Flood' (Rosse Papers, C/12/1).

him on the political map of eighteenth-century Ireland, his commitment to affirming that the kingdom of Ireland was equal to England and that Irish Protestants
were entitled to the same rights and freedoms as Englishmen is another. It is also
significant that he embraced the traditional whig/patriot antipathy to crown patronage and large standing armies. However, he was not persuaded by the emerging
patriot argument that the political system was so irredeemably corrupt that no genuine patriot could take crown office, though his abject failure to advance his political
programme as an officeholder served, ironically, to affirm it. Indeed, some contemporaries were of the view that this was the primary significance of his political career.[5] This is unsustainable. Flood's was one of the most talented and important
voices in the eighteenth-century Irish parliament; and while his story, like that of
any prominent historical figure, is significant for itself, it offers a particularly fine
insight into the individualism that was a feature of Irish political patriotism as it
pursued the aspirations of a reformed Irish political system which afforded them
the same legal and constitutional rights as Englishmen, and a reconstituted Anglo-
Irish nexus based on the constitutional and commercial equality of the kingdoms of
Ireland and England. Furthermore, his life well illustrates the ostensibly paradoxi-
cal (and under-acknowledged) capacity of the Protestant elite, both individually
and collectively, to challenge the exercise of British authority in Ireland while re-
joicing in the existence of a close British political connection; to preserve their social and political ascendancy from dilution while encouraging economic development and antiquarian investigation that contributed in the long term to their dis-
placement; and, not least, to combine intellectual erudition, social sophistication
and aesthetic appreciation with a capacity for murderous violence in defence of
their political interests and their honour.

---

5 It undoubtedly influenced Henry Grattan's decision to decline office in 1783 and 1795 (James Kelly,
Henry Grattan (Dundalk, 1993), pp 21, 31).

PART ONE
EARLY YEARS AND LOCAL POLITICS

Henry Flood was a member of only the third generation of his family to live in County Kilkenny. This was not uncommon in a county in which the transfer of land to the New English, who emerged as the dominant interest in the seventeenth century, was prolonged due to the unique role of the Butlers of Ormonde in Irish life. The bulk of the Floods' lands, which were centred on Burnchurch (renamed Farmley by Henry Flood's father) in Shillelogher barony, were acquired during the 1650s long before the collapse of Ormonde power, and though their holdings were added to by a number of significant acquisitions in the eighteenth century, none were of Ormonde lands. Henry did not share the enthusiasm for land acquisition displayed by earlier generations, but he was as eager as they to attain political eminence. The Floods' involvement in Irish politics commenced with his grandfather, Francis Flood, who became MP for Callan in 1703. He subsequently forged a strong interest in the borough, which Warden, his son and heir, consolidated and extended. As was the case with other emerging families, such as the Fosters of Dunleer, a local power base established by one generation provided a springboard to national eminence by the next. Warden was neither an outstanding politician nor an exceptional jurist, but he was sufficiently attentive and adroit to attain a succession of high offices. Moreover, he never lost sight of his family responsibilities or of the importance of Callan to the family's eminence, and while he was more subtle and refined in his methods than his father, neither he nor his brothers, with whom he remained close, were averse to taking the law into their own hands or using the legal process for their own ends if other means failed. Recourse was made to such tactics to resist the efforts of the wealthier and better-connected Agars to wrest control of the borough of Callan in the late 1750s and 1760s. This provided Henry Flood with his first major political test, and he entered into the contest with typical family resolve, because the outcome would determine whether the Floods would continue to be one of the dominant families in County Kilkenny and whether Henry would have a safe parliamentary seat as he aspired to eminence at imperial as well as at national level.

I

Background and early years

Henry Flood's early years are shrouded in obscurity. There is even doubt about his year of birth. Most standard reference works concur that it was 1732;[1] but this cannot be accepted without discussion because Lawrence Parsons, who was his closest political ally during the last decade of his life, maintained that he 'was born about the [year] 1730'. Parsons' imprecision probably derived from a pietistic wish not provide Flood's estranged relatives with evidence with which to sustain their challenge to his controversial last will and testament. Certainly, the fact that the inscription on his coffin read 'aged 61' or 'aged 63 years', depending on whose recollection you choose to believe, indicates that this was a matter about which Flood possessed tender feelings. This attempt to convey a different impression, notwithstanding, the weight of evidence points to the conclusion that Flood was indeed born in 1732; the most persuasive source is the admission records of Dublin University which indicate that he was fifteen years old when he entered Trinity College in December 1747.[2] By this date also, the Floods seemed finally to have established themselves as a family of consequence among the Irish Protestant elite, due to the combined efforts of Henry's grandfather and father.

ORIGINS

According to the account of the family's origins provided by Henry's nineteenth-century biographer, Warden Flood, the 'Kilkenny branch' of the Floods traced its ancestry to Sir Thomas Fludd of Kent who was receiver-general and treasurer-at-war to Queen Elizabeth.[3] Some doubt has been cast over the authenticity of this

---

1 *DNB*, xix, 331; A.J. Webb, *A Compendium of Irish biography* (Dublin, 1878), p. 207; Sir Bernard Burke, *A genealogical and heraldic history of the landed gentry of Ireland* (London, 1912), p. 236.   2 Rosse Papers, C/12/1; Notes on Flood v Flood [1792] (N.A., Langrishe Papers, BR K.K./38/16 p. 19); Rosse to Provost Elrington, 18 Oct. 1815 (T.C.D., MUN/P/1/1383/2); Entrance book 1725–58 (MUN/V/23/3).   3 Warden Flood, *Memoirs of the life and correspondence of the right hon. Henry Flood* (London,

eminent lineage, and the most one can say positively is that the Kilkenny Floods' immediate ancestry can be traced not to Kent but to County Longford, to Thomas Flood of Newtown, who is listed as a 'titulado' in the 1660 poll tax returns for that county.[4]

Thomas Flood's son Francis, who was the founder of the Flood dynasty in County Kilkenny, was an ambitious, able soldier. A 'volunteer' in 1688, he was imprisoned by the Jacobites, but he made his 'escape early enough to be one of the first and the last in the field' during the Williamite war and to attain the rank of major in the Royal Cavalry Regiment. In circumstances that are unclear, but which are almost certainly connected with his marriage in 1692 to Anne Warden, the sixteen year-old daughter and heiress of John Warden of Burnchurch, he settled in County Kilkenny in the early 1690s.[5]

Anne Warden's grandfather, Colonel William Warden, was also a soldier. He had served with distinction in the Cromwellian army, arising out of which he acquired an estate of several thousand acres of expropriated land centring on the parish of Burnchurch.[6] Like many Protestants, Warden became disenchanted with the radicalism of the Protectorate, and he was sufficiently free with his opinions to be threatened with arrest in 1659. It is no surprise, therefore, that he supported the restoration of the Stuart monarchy, or that he benefitted thereby. He was appointed sheriff of County Kilkenny in 1660, and was elected to represent the borough of Gowran in the Irish parliament in the 1660s. He contrived at first to retain his military commission, but he was obliged to surrender it by the duke of Ormonde in 1663. However, he was confirmed in his property in 1666, and he appears to have devoted his life thereafter to the management of his estates.[7]

William Warden's high public profile was not emulated by his son John. He married Ann Otway of Westmorland, by whom he had a son and a daughter, but the premature death of the former left his daughter, Anne, as sole heir. Family tradition suggests that following her attainder by the Jacobite parliament in 1689 and the

1838), pp 2–3; G.D. Burtchaell, *Genealogical memoirs of the members of parliament for the county and city of Kilkenny* (Dublin, 1888), pp 100–1.   4 Seamus Pender, ed., *A census of Ireland, circa 1659* (Dublin, 1939), p. 458.   5 Flood to Southwell, 11 Sept. 1703 (B.L., Southwell Papers, Add. Ms 34773 f 128); Burtchaell, *Kilkenny members*, pp 100–2; Mary Kenealy, 'Henry Flood of Farmley', *Old Kilkenny Review*, (1983), p. 518.   6 According to the Books of Survey and Distribution for County Kilkenny, Warden Flood secured 2374 acres in the county, forty-nine of which were within the liberties of Kilkenny, and 331 held in joint ownership (William Healy, *History and antiquities of Kilkenny* (Kilkenny, 1893), appendix, pp 30–31, 77, 93, 95). He was confirmed in possession of 1737 acres by letters patent in 1666 (Abstract of title of Flood-Hanford estate, 1917 (Land Commission, Flood-Hanford estate Papers, Box 5555 (E.C., 10055)); R. Dunlop, *Ireland under the Commonwealth* (2 vols, Manchester, 1913), p. 208; Flood, *Memoirs*, pp 390–2; Kenealy, 'Henry Flood', p. 518.   7 Dunlop, *Commonwealth*, p. 701; Fergus O'Donoghue, 'Parliament in Ireland under Charles II' (M.A.thesis, U.C.D., 1970), p. 321; John O'Hart, *The Irish and Anglo-Irish landed gentry* (London, 1884), p. 422.

restoration of her lands on the victory of the Williamite army in 1690–1, the Cuffes of Castle Inch cast covetous glances at her and the Warden estates, and may even have sought to betroth her to one of their family. If so, they were frustrated by the entry on the scene of the ebullient Francis Flood.[8]

From the little we know of Francis Flood's life and deeds, it is clear that he was an ambitious man. He may even have anticipated that his marriage into the Warden family would have enabled him to secure the representation for the local borough of Callan, but the constituency was dominated in the 1690s by Major Samuel Booth and Henry Wemys. Like the Wardens, the Booths had secured lands in the area in the 1650s, and Samuel Booth's earlier marriage into the Warden family (his wife Hannah was Anne Warden's aunt) effectively meant that the interest that might otherwise have favoured Francis Flood was spoken for. Moreover, Booth was a figure of consequence in his own right. He served as High Sheriff of the county on three occasions (1679, 1680, 1692), and was seneschal to the duke of Ormonde who owned the manor of Callan and who ensured his return for the borough. Henry Wemys of Danesfort also possessed a stronger local profile than Flood. His father had represented Gowran in the 1630s and 1640s and Knocktopher in the 1660s, and his family's continuing influence in the area (which was reinforced by the lease of a large tract of Ormonde land at Danesfort) assured him of the second seat in the Callan constituency throughout the 1690s.[9] With no prospects there, or elsewhere in County Kilkenny, Francis Flood turned his attention to his native Longford and offered himself as a candidate to the electors of the borough of Granard in 1695. His defeat at the polls caused him to petition the House of Commons to overturn the return on the grounds that his opponents presented unqualified voters, but the result was allowed to stand.[10]

Francis Flood's failure to secure the representation for Granard set back but did not deflect his political ambitions. In 1703, when Samuel Booth was no longer a factor and Henry Wemys opted to pursue the representation for Kilkenny county, Flood countered the 'design' of the Cuffes to establish a strong presence in Callan by securing his return for the constituency in the general election held that year.[11] However, his hold on the seat proved short-lived for in June 1705 Agmondisham Cuffe petitioned the House of Commons for relief from 'several oppressive and

---

8 Flood, *Memoirs*, pp 3–4; Kenealy, 'Henry Flood', pp 518–19.   9 Flood to Southwell, 11 Sept. 1703 (B.L., Southwell Papers, Add. Ms 34773 f 128); Abstract of lands belonging to the duke of Ormonde, c.1700 (N.L.I., Ms 23787); Monica Brennan, 'The changing composition of Kilkenny landowners 1641–1700', T.P.Power, 'Parliamentary representation in county Kilkenny in the eighteenth century', in W. Nolan and K. Whelan, eds, *Kilkenny: history and society* (Dublin, 1990), pp 179, 325; Burtchaell, *Kilkenny members*, pp 82–3; N.A., Shelly Papers, Ms 999/462 p. 31; Longford to Ellis, 10 Oct. 1692 in P. Melvin, ed., 'Letters of Lord Longford and others 1689–1702' in *Analecta Hibernica*, 32 (1985), p. 101.   10 *Journals of the House of Commons of the kingdom of Ireland* (19 vols, Dublin, 1796–1800), ii, 57.   11 Return for the Irish parliament in 1703 (B.L., Southwell Papers, Add. Ms 34777 f 33).

undue practices perpetrated' by Flood and his representatives. According to Cuffe, Flood and his serjeant, John Roberts, the high constable of the barony, enlisted Catholics, returned false musters for personal financial gain, billeted soldiers on Cuffe's tenantry for prolonged lengths of time, compelled the same tenants to build walls and roads and to assemble bearing arms, and enforced their will by condemning recalcitrants to punishments which included terms in Burnchurch dungeon, spells in the stocks and public whippings. The House of Commons did not uphold all twelve charges, but they were sufficiently persuaded of the merits of the accusations of fraud, intimidation, oppressive billeting and illegal recruiting to deem them incompatible with membership of parliament. Francis Flood was expelled from the House of Commons and dismissed from holding a commission of the peace.[12]

This damning judgement might have caused a less resilient figure to forsake public life, but Francis Flood was not easily cowed. He contrived to take advantage of the opportunities that came his way and his extensive lands in the vicinity to build up an interest in Callan. His pro-government Toryism may also have been useful. But the decimation of the extensive interest of the duke of Ormonde through financial mismanagement and political misjudgment was the most decisive factor. It enabled him to acquire 'that interest in the management of [Callan's] municipal affairs which was usually exercised by the Lord of the manor' by providing him with the opportunity to convince the Wemys family that they could consolidate their influence in the borough by concluding an alliance with him and James Agar.[13]

Henry Wemys occupied the key office of borough sovereign between 1706 and 1715. During this time its electorate contracted sharply because of his disinclination to create new burgesses and freemen. Wemys' reasons for doing this remain unclear, but it worked to the advantage of Francis Flood who came a close second to Sylvester Cross in the poll to determine the two MPs to represent the constituency in 1713.[14] Two years later, when a further general election was called, Flood's position was even stronger. In the interval, he, Patrick Wemys, who had succeeded his father as sovereign of the borough in 1715, and James Agar, whose family built up an extensive interest in the county through marriage, lease and the purchase of forfeited Ormonde and other lands,[15] had concluded a formal agreement to share the

12 N.A., Shelly Papers, Ms 999/462 p. 21; Agmondisham Cuffe, *Petition to the honourable the knights, citizens and burgesses in parliament assembled... on behalf of himself, his tenants and other inhabitants of the County of Kilkenny* [Dublin, 1705]; *Commons Jn. (Irl.)*, ii, 473, 475–7, 478, 506; Burtchaell, *Kilkenny members*, pp 100–2.   13 Power, 'Parliamentary representation', p. 325; David Hayton, 'Ireland and the English ministers, 1703–15', (D.Phil., Oxford University, 1975), p. 326; Return for the Irish parliament in 1703 (B.L., Southwell Papers, Add. Ms 34777 ff 43, 67); N.A., Shelly Papers, Ms 999/462 f 31.   14 N.A., Shelly Papers, Ms 999/462 p. 22; Joe Kennedy, 'Callan 1700–1800', Power, 'Parliamentary representation' in Nolan and Whelan eds, *Kilkenny: history and society*, pp 296, 325; *Commons Jn. (Irl.)*, iii, 20–1. The poll was 53 votes for Cross, 47 for Flood, 23 for Thomas Candler and 7 for John Cuffe.   15 N.A., Landed Estates Courts, vol. 10, no. 2; Clifden deeds, D 20,038–150 *passim*; Land Commission, Estate Records, Box 1151; Mary Moran, 'The Agars of Gowran' in *In the shadow of the*

representation. According to the only surviving account, this was inaugurated by Patrick Wemys convening a number of 'clandestine [and] illegal assemblies' at Callan at which he oversaw the admission of 'sixty or seventy burgesses and freemen' who were committed to vote for Flood and Agar. In return, Agar undertook to ensure Wemys, who had represented Gowran borough between 1703 and 1714, was returned for that constituency. It cannot be affirmed beyond doubt that this was the basis of their agreement, but it is significant that Flood and Agar were elected to represent the borough of Callan following a tense and violent election. Wemys did not secure the return for Gowran on this occasion. However, this did not cause any long-term problems because James Agar was married to Wemys' sister Mary, and in 1721 he claimed the more glittering prize of the county representation in the by-election caused by the elevation of William Ponsonby to the peerage.[16]

If the precise terms of the agreement concluded by Francis Flood with Patrick Wemys and James Agar are beyond recovery, the absence of controversy suggests that it operated smoothly through the reign of George I. It was undoubtedly aided by the fact that Francis Flood and James Agar enjoyed a harmonious relationship. As a consequence, the three families had little difficulty withstanding the challenge offered by Maurice and John Cuffe, and securing the return of Warden Flood and Henry Wemys – the eldest sons and heirs of Francis Flood and Patrick Wemys – in the 1727 general election.[17]

The decision of Francis Flood not to stand for re-election for the borough of Callan in 1727 was prompted by age; he was in his late sixties and had, as it happened, only three more years to live. It also reflected his wish that Warden, who was already in his thirties and destined to inherit the family estates and the annual rental of £1,500 they produced, took charge of family affairs.[18] As the eldest of Francis Flood's and Anne Warden's nine children, it was his responsibility to take over from his father as 'head of the family'.[19] It was a role for which he was well-qualified; following some years at Kilkenny school, he attended Trinity College from where he graduated with a BA in 1714. He then read law at the Inner Temple to which he was

steeple 2 (1990), pp 110–11; W.G.Neely, 'The Ormonde Butlers of County Kilkenny 1515–1715', Brennan, 'Kilkenny landowners' and Kennedy, 'Callan' in Nolan and Whelan, eds, *Kilkenny*, pp 124, 183–4, 296; N.A., Shelly Papers, Ms 999/462 pp 22–3. **16** *Commons Jn. (Irl.)*, iii, 20–1, 40; Power, 'Parliamentary representation', p. 325; Burtchaell, *Kilkenny members*, pp 103–4, 116, 120–1; N.A., Shelly Papers, Mss 999/462 pp 22–3, 31. **17** N.A., Clifden deeds, D 20068; Power, 'Parliamentary representation', p. 235; Burchaell, *Kilkenny members*, p. 126; N.A., Shelly Papers, Ms 999/462 p. 23. The poll was Warden Flood 92, Henry Wemys 84, John Cuffe 52 and Francis Duggan 1. **18** Notes on Flood v Flood, p. 1; Lockington's brief, [1815] (T.C.D., MUN/P/1/1386/13); E. Hayes and T. Jones, *Reports of cases argued and determined in the Court of Exchequer* (Dublin, 1843), appendix, p. xxi. It should be noted that the Flood estates were charged with a debt of £2500 in 1727. **19** The phrase is John Flood's (T.C.D., MUN/P/1/1383/10); a similar term was used by Charles Flood in his will (Land Commission, Flood-Hanford estate Papers, Box 5555 (E.C. 10055)).

admitted in 1715. Five years later, he was called to the Irish bar, and embarked on a legal career that was to bring him right to the heart of Irish government.[20]

His seven brothers and sister are more elusive. Indeed, it is possible only with difficulty to establish the order in which they were born. Two of the brothers, Richard and William, have left such little trace that it is unlikely they reached maturity. Of the others, John, Francis and Charles actively supported the efforts of Warden and, when it was his turn, of Henry to uphold the family's control of Callan borough. John (1698–1774) possessed an estate of approximately 1,600 acres at Floodhall and became high sheriff of the county in 1726. Francis served as high sheriff on two occasions (1735, 1746), and resided at Paulstown Castle on a somewhat larger estate which he assembled through purchase and advantageous long term lease from, among others, the Agars.[21] He married Frances Hatton of Great Clonard, County Wexford. Charles never married but, like his brothers, he too carved out an estate in the county by lease and purchase, and resided at Ballymack on land leased to him by his eldest brother. He took a particularly active interest in the affairs of Callan borough, and was a spirited if unsubtle upholder of the family interest there.[22] Neither Henry nor George, who took orders, chose to involve themselves with Callan.[23] But their only sister, Anne, played a pivotal role because her husband, Henry Candler, who was successively curate and rector of Callan which was one of 'the best livings in Ireland', aligned the Candler political interest he inherited in south Kilkenny with the Floods in the constituency.[24]

As its most capable and best-connected member, Warden Flood was expected to use his influence and position to advance the standing of the Flood family and, when opportunity arose, to advantage the interests of his less well-placed relations.[25] He effectively consolidated the Floods' influence in the borough of Callan by ensuring the election of Henry Candler as borough sovereign on twenty-three successful occasions between 1735 and 1759. No less importantly, he pursued an active

---

20 R.A. Roberts, ed., *A calendar of the records of the Inner Temple* (5 vols, London, 1896-1936), iv, 23; E. Keane, P. Beryl Phair and T.U. Sadleir, eds, *King's Inns admission papers 1607–1867* (Dublin, 1982), p. 171; G.D.Burtchaell and T.U. Sadleir, eds, *Alumni Dublinenses* (London, 1924), p. 293; F.E. Ball, *The judges in Ireland 1221–1921* (2 vols, London, 1926), ii, 211.   21 Registry of Deeds, 214/102/140477, 205/28/134789; Memorials, May 1751 (Land Commission, Keogh estate Papers, Box 13 (E.C.,2272)). According to U.U. de Burgh, *Landowners of Ireland* (London, 1878) his descendants possessed an estate of 3852 acres; W.S. Mason, *A statistical account or parochial survey of Ireland* (3 vols, London, 1814-17), ii, 335–6.   22 *Burke's Irish landed gentry*; Registry of Deeds, 83/77/57624, 91/106/63541, 199/300/ 132274; Henry to Warden Flood [post 11 Nov. 1771] (R.I.A., Burrowes Papers, 23/K/53/10); Memorials of 17 and 18 Dec. 1745, 22 May 1759, Will of Charles Flood, 1770 (Land Commission, Keogh estate Papers, Box 13 (E.C.2272)); below pp 45–55.   23 Both held a variety of church livings; see J.B.Leslie, *Ossory clergy and parishes* (Enniskillen, 1933), pp 205, 209, 335; *Alumni Dublinenses*, p. 293; Warrant of appointment, 15 Sept. 1747 (N.A., Calendar of miscellaneous letters and papers prior to 1760, f 268).   24 Leslie, *Ossory clergy*, p. 107; Michael Quane, ed., 'Tour in Ireland by John Harden in 1797' in *J.C.H.A.S.*, 58(1953), p. 28; N.A., Shelly Papers, Ms 999/462 ff 31–2. Callan living was worth a reputed £2,300 per annum.

policy of land acquisition, and he made the first of a number of valuable purchases in 1729 when he paid £2,400 (£400 of which he provided in cash and the balance with a loan from James Agar) for an estate in Kilkenny.[26] At the same time, he did not neglect the interests of the county, as his exploration of improving navigation on the river Nore, or his career, as his rising legal reputation attests.[27] Only his personal life appeared problematic because of his attachment to Isabella Whiteside, who corresponded neither to society's nor to his family's image of an ideal partner for a rising lawyer and politician.

Like so many of the Flood family of her generation, Isabella Whiteside's biographical details are tantalisingly elusive. Henry's biographer, Warden Flood, claimed that he was 'not in possession of any account' of her. Lawrence Parsons was better informed. He maintained in an unpublished memoir that she 'was an English lady who had lived in the neighbourhood of Chester', and that Warden and she met at Finglas 'where she was on a visit with some friends' shortly after he was called to the Irish bar. Warden was soon 'enamoured' of her, but was unable to press his suit because his father, who had 'some higher connection in view for him', wished him to marry Ellis Agar, the eldest daughter of James Agar and Mary Wemys, in order to consolidate his alliance with both families and to advance further his family's profile in County Kilkenny.[28] This is plausible, but Parsons' account cannot be accepted without qualification because of his eagerness to refute the damaging imputations that Isabella Whiteside was not 'a woman of strict virtue and propriety of conduct' and that Henry Flood was born outside wedlock. Parsons maintains that Warden and Isabella were 'married ... privately' before Henry's birth but kept their relationship secret in order not to discommode his father. However, this conflicts with the account offered in 1792 when the question of Henry Flood's legitimacy was argued before the courts. According to the advocate representing those family members who challenged Henry's will, Warden Flood first met Isabella Whiteside two years after his father decided to bequeath him the Burnchurch estate. We know that Francis wrote his will in 1727, which would suggest Warden and Isabella's acquaintanceship dates from 1729, and not the early 1720s as suggested by Lawrence Parsons; counsel for Flood's wife maintained in 1792 that 1731 or 1732 were more likely dates.[29]

25 See, for example, Warden Flood to Bedford, 31 Aug. 1761 (Bedford Papers, P.R.O.N.I., T2915/12/8).   26 Notes on Flood v Flood, p. 1 and loose leaf (which notes he spent £3000 in 1759); List of Flood papers, 17 Oct. 1815 (T.C.D., MUN/P/1/1383/10 pp 1–3). Some indication of his land activities in Kilkenny and Dublin can be gleaned from Registry of Deeds 62/501/43861, 65/488/4577, 98/129/67899, 153/90/101766, 178/585/120969, 201/120/132029, 299/353/198599; N.A., Keneflick donation, Ms 999/355/2/2; Shee genealogy (N.A., Prim Collection, no 84). Among his purchases was Maiden Hall near Bennetsbridge (L.E.O'Hanlon, 'Testamentary records', *Irish Genealogist*, 2 no. 5 (1947), p. 142).   27 [Colles] to [Flood], 2 Nov. 1737 (N.A., Prim Collection. Ms 687/9); *Dublin Daily Post*, 25 May; Potter to Devonshire, Nov. 1740 (P.R.O.N.I., Chatsworth Papers, T3158/164).   28 Flood, *Memoirs*, p. 4; Rosse Papers, C/12/1; see also Rosse to Elrington, 18 Oct. 1815 (T.C.D., MUN/P/1/1383/2).   29 Notes on Flood v Flood, pp 1, 25.

If Parsons is undependable, what then can we say for certain of Isabella Whiteside, and of her relationship with Warden Flood? As far as can be established, her family background was mercantile, and following her parents' death she spent her formative years with relations at Whitehaven (not Chester, as Lawrence Parsons maintains). She also had relations named Hutchinson in trade in Dublin, who possessed a 'good house' in Hawkins Street (Lazar's Hill) and property in Rathfarnham, and it was while she was staying with them that Warden met and fell in love with this attractive, graceful person who 'had received the education of a gentlewoman'.[30] The early history of their relationship remains obscure, but at some point in the early 1730s, Warden and Isabella set up home together in Donnybrook Castle where Warden had lived since 1724. To outsiders, particularly the respectable women of the city and locality, she was his mistress, and they had few visitors as a consequence.[31] Isabella did have a carriage, but she seldom used it. She appears to have devoted her time to her children – to Henry who was born in 1732 and to his sister Arabella, who was born some years later.[32] In one of the very few details we possess of their childhood, we know that they were both wetnursed locally.[33]

Warden and Isabella lived together as common-law partners during the 1730s. Warden's renown as a lawyer continued to grow during these years, and in 1739 he secured the plum position of counsellor to the commissioners of the revenue. It was about this time also that his friend and *confidante*, Robert Jocelyn, who became lord chancellor in 1739, persuaded him to legitimise his connection with Isabella Whiteside. According to family history, Warden was hesitant, but on Jocelyn promising that his wife would confer social respectability on the couple by visiting them, Warden's reluctance was overcome. The absence of any record of their marriage in the Church of Ireland register of Donnybrook parish, in the registry of licences in the prorogation office or in the possession of the keeper of archives of the Dublin diocese frustrated subsequent efforts by the Flood family to establish precisely when the marriage took place; this suggests that it may have been conducted privately at some date between 1739 and 1742 and not officially registered. Anyhow, in 1746, the couple had another child, a son, whom they named Jocelyn after the Lord Chancellor. Since the marriage of their parents did not confer legitimacy retrospectively on Henry and Arabella, he was their only legal offspring.[34]

30 Notes on Flood v Flood, pp 23, 25, 32, 33 and *passim*; List of Flood papers, Oct. 1815 (T.C.D., MUN/P/1/1383/10 pp 1–3); 'Lockington's brief' [1815] (MUN/P/1/1386/13); Case note, [1815] (MUN/P/1/1386/14); Rosse Papers, C/12/1; Burrowes to Beresford, 6 Mar. 1793 in William Beresford, ed., *The correspondence of John Beresford* (2 vols, London, 1854), ii, 11–12.   31 One exception was Mrs Fitzgibbon, the aunt of John Fitzgibbon, who became Earl of Clare in 1793 (Notes on Flood v Flood, p. 29); Burrowes to Beresford, 6 Mar. 1793 in *Beresford Corres.*, ii, 12.   32 There was much speculation in 1792 as to whether Arabella was born in wedlock or not; the evidence points to the conclusion that she was not (Notes on Flood v Flood, pp 11, 16).   33 Notes on Flood v Flood, pp 17–19, 21, 24, 29, 30; List of Flood papers [1815] (T.C.D., MUN/P/1/1383/10).   34 Notes on Flood v Flood, pp 5–6, 8, 9, 14, 15, 22, 25, 28, 35, 39–40, loose leaf; Hayes and Jones, *Report of cases*, p. xxi; T.C.D., MUN/P/1/1383/ 10 p. 4.

The regularisation by Warden and Isabella of their relationship enabled the family to move from Donnybrook to a centre city location. In the mid-1740s, Henry lived with his father in Cuffe Street just off Stephen's Green.[35] This was a more appropriate residence for a family of their station, since Warden had been promoted to the solicitor generalship in December 1741. Ten years later he was made attorney general.[36] Despite his elevated office, Warden kept the intrigue and manoeuvring that was the dominant feature of Irish politics in the 1740s and 1750s at a distance. It is instructive, for instance, that though his sympathies and allegiance lay with the duke of Dorset, Primate Stone and John Ponsonby, he went to Spa in Germany to drink the waters in 1754 when the money bill dispute was at its height.[37]

Flood's pro-government stance was only to be anticipated since he owed his position to official favour. Besides, it made little sense in local terms to discommode the powerful Kilkenny-based Ponsonby interest. In this respect, it is perhaps significant that, compared with the Ponsonbys, Warden Flood used his position sparingly to secure rewards for his family and friends.[38] At the same time, he did not support either Dublin Castle or the Ponsonbys unconditionally, but when Commons' divisions were called, he was always more likely to vote with rather than against the administration. He was also faithful in his performance of his duties at the Privy Council.[39] Such commitment continued to serve him well, for when a further shuffle of legal and judicial offices took place in 1760, he surrendered the office of attorney general to Philip Tisdall in return for promotion to the vacant chief justiceship of the Court of King's Bench.[40] By this date Warden Flood was 65, and nearing the end of a legal career that had brought him status, influence and not inconsiderable financial reward. This provided him with a strong incentive to ensure his eldest son received the best possible start in life to compensate for the disadvantage arising from the circumstances of his birth.

35 'Lockington's brief' [1815] (T.C.D., MUN/P/1/1386/13); Notes on Flood v Flood, p. 9.   36 Warrant of appointment of Warden Flood, 24 Dec. 1741 (P.R.O., S.P., 67/20 ff 80–1); Duncannon to Wilmot, 7 Jan. 1742 (Wilmot Papers, P.R.O.N.I., T3019/357); An account of fiants sealed from the 27 Dec. 1741 to 24 June 1742 (B.L.,O.C., Southwell Papers, Box 2).   37 Potter to Devonshire, Nov. 1740 (Chatsworth Papers, P.R.O.N.I., T3158/164); *P.O.*, 10 Aug.; Stone to Sackville, 29 Aug.1754 in H.M.C., *Stopford-Sackville Mss*, pp 53–4.   38 Sir John Ponsonby, *The Ponsonby family* (London, 1929), pp 39–62; C.Snoddy, 'Some notes on parliament and its Limerick members 1767–71', *N.M.A.J.*, ix (1962-5), pp 172–3; N.A., Forfeited estates Ireland: 1641: undisposed land and plus acres (Kilkenny, Knocktopher barony, 6 July 1759); Ponsonby to Rigby, 4–18 May 1760 (P.R.O.N.I., Bedford Papers, T2915/9/47).   39 R.E. Burns, *Irish parliamentary politics in the eighteenth century* (2 vols, London, 1989–90), ii, 232–3; Memorandum of Charles O'Hara about Irish MPs, 1753 (N.L.I., O'Hara Papers, (microfilm p. 1576/68)); *A letter from a gentleman in the city to a member of parliament in the north of Ireland* ([Dublin], 1757), p. 15; earl of Belmore, *Parliamentary memoirs of Fermanagh and Tyrone from 1613–1885* (Dublin, 1887), p. 355; P.R.O., Privy Council Papers, P.C.1//7/15–88.   40 Flood to Bedford, 10 July 1760 (Bedford Papers, P.R.O.N.I., T2915/9/67); see also T2915/10/3, 8; Ball, *The judges*, ii, 144; Bedford to Pitt, 17 July, 11 Aug. 1760 (P.R.O., S.P., 63/418). He was also appointed a commissioner for making the River Nore navigable (P. Watters, 'The history of the Kilkenny canal', *J.R.S.A.I.*, 4th series, 2 (1872–3)).

EDUCATION

Henry Flood's early schooling was entrusted to private tutors before he was transferred to the care of a Mr Butler 'where he was but imperfectly taught the learned
languages'. Despite the limitations of his teachers, Henry learned easily, and in
December 1747, aged 15, he was admitted to Trinity College as a fellow commoner
(*socius comitatus*).[41] As a fellow commoner, Flood was in a privileged position in the
university. Students were graded according to their social rank. At the top of the
order were the *filii nobilis*, the sons of noblemen, who numbered two (out of eighty-
one) in Flood's class, and the fellow commoners, who numbered ten. They enjoyed
special privileges which were symbolised by their right to wear luxuriant gowns
(those worn by fellow commoners had velvet collars and sleeves), and by their entitlement to dine with the fellows of the college. They could also graduate in three
rather than four years, though they paid higher fees for this privilege; noblemen
paid £30 half-yearly and fellow commoners £15.[42]

One of the two noblemen's sons in Flood's year in Trinity was John Cuffe, the
heir of Lord Desart who had purchased the manor of Callan from the earl of Arran
in 1735, but considering their rivalry in Callan it is hardly surprising that they did
not become friends. Nor, as far as one can tell, did Flood socialise with Lucius
O'Brien or Hercules Langrishe, who were in the year behind him though they later
became friends as well as political colleagues. Indeed, the person with whom Flood
established his closest bond during his years in Trinity – Ambrose Smith of Dublin
city – had no identifiable political ambitions then or later in life. Their friendship
was probably influenced by the fact that they were nearly the same age and that they
shared comparable life experiences. Like Flood, Smith spent most of his formative
years in Dublin or its environs, where his father Thomas was a merchant.[43]

Henry Flood was probably familiar with the physical contours of Trinity College before he enrolled there as a student. As an institution, the College had grown
considerably in the thirty years since his father and uncles had taken their degrees.
The most impressive new building was the library (constructed between 1712 and
1723), but the College also possessed a new printing house (completed in 1734) and
a dining hall (completed in 1745), while just prior to Flood's matriculation, a bell
tower was added to the front of the Old Hall which jutted into the Old Square.[44]

In keeping with the positive impression created by the new buildings, Trinity

---

41 Rosse Papers, C/12/1; Entrance book 1725–58 f 177 (T.C.D, MUN/V/23/3); Flood, *Memoirs*, pp
10–11. 42 Constantia Maxwell, *A history of Trinity College Dublin 1591–1892* (Dublin, 1946), p. 132;
R.B. McDowell and D.A. Webb, *Trinity College Dublin 1592–1952: an academic history* (Cambridge,
1982), pp 114–15; Examination returns 1719–49, (T.C.D., MUN/V/27/1 f 118v). 43 Entrance Book
1725–58 (T.C.D, MUN/V/23/3 f 177); Examination returns 1719–49, (MUN/V/27/1 f 120v); *The
records of the Honourable Society of Lincoln's Inns 1420–1799* (London, 1896), p. 438. 44 J.W. Stubbs,
The history of the university of Dublin from its foundation to the end of the eighteenth century (Dublin, 1889),
pp 176–91.

College put the sharp factional antagonisms involving Whigs and Tories that were a feature of life in the university in the early eighteenth century behind it during the lengthy provostship of Richard Baldwin (1717–58). Dublin city continued to offer tempting distractions to the student body, but their behaviour improved visibly under Baldwin's 'arbitrary and at times harsh rule' till by the time Henry Flood embarked on his university career the violent *emeutés* involving students that were common-place during the first forty years of the century were rare. For all that, the dynamics of town and gown were such that undergraduates did not shirk confrontation with the notorious Catholic faction, the Ormonde boys, or with the city authorities if they perceived that one of their number was being abused or mistreated.[45] There is no evidence that Henry Flood partook in any such escapade, but as he moved into his late teens he was as prone as most young men of his age to savour the delights and distractions of the city.

The area where Provost Baldwin had least impact was scholarship. Academically, Trinity experienced one of its most lethargic periods in its history in the first half of the eighteenth century. It has been pointed out that 'during a period of thirty-two years, from 1722 to 1753 (that is to say, for three quarters of Baldwin's term as Provost)' no fellow of the College produced a 'single publication'. The quality of the teaching on offer was also uninspiring, though there were a number of energetic fellows who did not want for application and ideas. Henry Flood's tutor, Francis Andrews, was not one of them. As Provost (1758–74), Andrews oversaw further improvements to the physical fabric of the university and a number of important academic reforms, but he was more interested in politics, his law practice and in living the life of a *bon viveur* than in academic matters.[46]

Francis Andrews' deficiencies as a tutor to the young Flood were at least partially compensated for by the teaching of John Lawson and Thomas Leland. Lawson was a junior fellow of fifteen years standing when he became Professor of Oratory and History in 1750. He stressed the importance of closely studying classical orators because of the intimate relationship he perceived between oratory and liberty. He identified Demosthenes' opposition to the tyranny of Philip of Macedon as a particularly fine illustration of his thesis, and Thomas Leland, who shared his views, published an account of this episode as well as other work on the Greek orator. Through these and other publications, but most vividly through their teaching, Leland and Lawson imbued in their student charges the conviction that good oratory was essential to liberty. It was a view that was to have immense influence on the way in which several generations of Irish politicians – Flood included – conducted themselves in the Commons' chamber.[47]

45 Stubbs, *The University of Dublin*, pp 152–68; McDowell and Webb, *Trinity College*, pp 37–8; Maxwell, *Trinity College*, pp 111, 113–14, 134. 46 McDowell and Webb, *Trinity College*, pp 38–9, 52–3; Stubbs, *The university of Dublin*, pp 211–30 *passim*; Entrance book 1725–58 (T.C.D., MUN/V/23/3 f 177). 47 J.V. Luce, *Trinity College Dublin: the first four hundred years* (Dublin, 1992), p. 48; W.B. Stanford, *Ireland and the classical tradition* (Dublin, 1984), pp 52–4, 209–11.

The humanities course pursued by undergraduates at Trinity in the mid-eighteenth century followed a four-year cycle involving two courses of study in each year – one in science, the other in classics. The first-year course in classics was dominated by Homer's *Iliad* and Virgil's *Aeneid*, though Horace's *Odes*, Xenophon's *Cyropaedia*, Sallust and Terence also featured; the science course consisted of a systematic introduction to logic.[48] Flood was a diligent and attentive student during his first year. He and five others were voted the thanks of the house at the spring quarterly examinations in April 1748 for their faithful attendance at Greek lectures, though it is noteworthy that he was not among the twelve students singled out for special mention for their attendance 'at morning lectures'. Three months later, he was awarded a premium arising out of his attainments in the summer examinations in which he secured two *valde benes* and two *benes*.[49] Examinations were oral not written, and were conducted by the Provost and fellows in front of the assembled student body. This could be a forbidding experience, but the question and answer format of lectures was good preparation for this, as well as for careers in politics, the law and the church.

The abundant promise Flood demonstrated in his first year at Trinity was not maintained in his second and third years. In his second year, he took further courses in logic and studied Juvenal, Xenophon, Caesar's *Commentaries*, Cicero's select orations, Lucian, Horace's satires, epistles, and art of poetry and a selection from Plutarch's lives, but he did not elicit any mention (good or ill) for attendance or for his performances at examination. The third-year programme of study in science included courses in physics, geography and astronomy; that in the classics consisted of Virgil's *Georgics*, Cicero's *Offices*, twelve books of Livy, some Aschines and extensive selection of Demosthenes. This ought to have been more to Flood's liking. But, once again, he earned no special mention in the College examination returns which would suggest that he was not taking his academic work seriously. One of his obituarists observed that while at Trinity, Flood 'was more distinguished for ... the gaiety of his manners than for [his] application to study.[50] He was a handsome figure who 'attracted as many eyes as a man, as the Miss Gunnings ... did as women', so it may be that he found the distractions of the city of Dublin more to his liking than the discipline of study.[51]

Flood's disinclination to apply himself was evidently a source of family concern because it was decided that he should leave Trinity degree-less at the end of his third year and resume his studies at Christ Church, Oxford University. Oxford had the reputation of offering fewer distractions to students than Dublin, and it was

48 Examination returns 1750–70 (T.C.D., MUN/V/27/2 f 1).   49 Examination returns 1719–49 (T.C.D., MUN/V/27/1 ff 117v, 119).   50 Examination returns 1719–49 ff 121–2; *idem* 1750–70 f 1 ff; Luce, *Trinity College*, pp 50–1; *Gentleman's Magazine*, 61 (1791), p. 1224; Flood, *Memoirs*, p. 11.   51 *Gentleman's Magazine*, 61(1791), p. 1224; Rosse Papers, C/12/1; R[odd], ed., *Letters to Flood*, introduction; Mairead Dunleavy, *Dress in Ireland* (London, 1989), p. 121.

possibly this that resulted in his being sent there. Having paid his caution money (i.e. his deposit) on 24 October 1750, Flood entered Christ Church as a gentleman commoner in December. This was the equivalent of a Trinity fellow commoner, and if this eased his entry into this new environment, it was aided further by Ambrose Smith's decision to join him there in 1751.[52]

Like Trinity, the Oxford of which Flood became a part had enjoyed better times. Following the Glorious Revolution, the university became a haven of Toryism. This was too moderate to provide a milieu in which Jacobitism could flourish, but it played a part in creating an academic environment characterised by caution and conservatism. Had he been fully aware of this and of the power struggle that was taking place within the University between an 'aggressive if despairing Toryism' and 'resurgent' Whiggery, Warden Flood might have been less eager to send his eldest son there, but he was to have no cause to regret his choice on these grounds as Christ Church was one of the four securely Whig colleges in the university. Moreover, as far as we know, Henry was little interested in the machinations of Jacobites and Whigs.[53]

If the struggle between Whig and Tory for pre-eminence ensured that university politics at this moment were of more than local import, the mediocre academic instruction offered was of palpably greater consequence for the student body.[54] Christ Church was the largest and wealthiest college in the university, but its student numbers were at an historic low at this time. Total enrolment in the university in the 1750s (992) was more than 40 per cent below its early eighteenth-century level. In the case of Christ Church, this meant that the annual student intake in the late 1740s and 1750s hovered between the high teens and low thirties. A total of twenty-four undergraduates were admitted in 1750 along with Henry Flood, of whom just over half (52 per cent) were commoners; the remainder were equally divided between gentlemen commoners, servitors (poorer students who paid no fees) and Westminster students.[55]

As one of the small number of gentlemen commoners, Henry Flood was one of the Oxford student élite. As at Trinity, gentlemen commoners were distinguishable within the university from other student ranks by their dress and their right to dine

52 *Gentleman's Magazine*, 61(1791), p. 1224; Joseph Foster, *Alumni Oxonienses: the members of the University of Oxford 1715–1886* (6 vols, Oxford, 1888), ii, 471, iv, 1310; Notes on Flood v Flood, p. 9; Joseph to Samuel Stock, 11 Apr.1773 (T.C.D., Stock Papers, Ms 3762 f 43); Maxwell, *Trinity College*, p. 107.
53 Paul Langford, 'Tories and Jacobites 1714–51', L.S. Sutherland,'Political respectability 1751–1771', L.G. Mitchell, 'Politics and revolution 1772–1800' in L.S. Sutherland and L.G. Mitchell, eds, *The history of the university of Oxford, v: the eighteenth century* (Oxford, 1986), pp 120–7, 129–33, 164; E.G.W. Bill, *Education at Christ Church Oxford 1660–1800* (Oxford, 1988), pp 51–3.   54 M.L. Clarke, 'Classical studies' in Sutherland et al., eds, *History of the university of Oxford*, v, 520–4; Bill, *Christ Church, passim*.
55 Mitchell, 'Politics and revolution', J.P.D. Dunabain, 'College estates and wealth 1660–1815', V.H.H. Green, 'The University and social life' in Sutherland, et al., eds, *History of the University of Oxford*, v, 164, 300, 309–10; Bill, *Christ Church*, pp 167–70, 174–5.

at high table. They also had access to the senior common room and possession of reserved places in chapel, though these privileges were not always availed of because students of this rank were seldom called upon to attend chapel or hall.[56] Oxford required its students to become resident, but once they took possession and paid for their rooms, they were allowed plenty of freedom. Gentlemen commoners were at liberty, for the most part, to suit themselves, and since they had an estimated £160–200 to spend annually, they possessed the means to engage their physical appetites rather more than their intellects if that was their preference. This did not appeal to Flood. He received rooms, along with the other gentlemen commoners, commoners and students in Christ Church in Peckwater Quadrangle, but rather than resume the academically lethargic life he had embraced during his second and third years at Trinity, he determined to make more productive use of his time.[57]

As at Trinity, the classics constituted the core of the programme offered to students at Oxford but the commitment required was distinctly less. At Christ Church, the list of prescribed books had remained unchanged since 1717; more significantly, 'the range of reading in the classics was very narrow and two of the books in the list, the *Aeneid* and the *Iliad*, were likely to have been already familiar, in part at any rate, from schools' reading'.[58] This state of affairs derived from the poor academic stewardship provided the College by successive deans. John Conybeare, who was in charge when Flood was a student, had secured the office because of 'his combination of Whig and Anglican orthodoxy' rather than his intellectual qualities. This was of benefit to the College politically, but its academic reputation fell as a result of Conybeare's neglect. He is one of the main reasons why the number of 'matriculations in the College in the 1740s and 1750s fell to their lowest level since the reign of James II' and why his successors, David Gregory (1756–67) and William Markham (1767–77), sought to modernize the programme of study pursued by students and to curtail the exemptions traditionally granted to noblemen and gentlemen commoners whereby they did not have to take exams to graduate with a degree.[59]

Henry Flood had, of course, left Oxford by the time these reforms came on stream, and the College 'resumed its role as the nursery of the governing classes, and the great landed families, who for a generation had ignored the university'.[60] However, he was not untouched by the emerging impulse which encouraged academic excellence, because he encountered more committed intellectuals there than he did at Trinity. Among the most formidable was Thomas Tyrwhitt,[61] but the figure of greatest consequence was his tutor William Markham (1719–1807).

56 Green, 'The university and social life', pp 311, 315–21, 323–4, 328; Bill, *Christ Church*, p. 174.   57 Green, 'The university and social life', pp 319–21, 328–30; Bill, *Christ Church*, pp 241 n; letter of Mark Curthoys (archivist of Christ Church) to author, 11 Nov. 1993.   58 Clarke, 'Classical studies', p. 523. 59 Bill, *Christ Church*, pp 51–64, 180.   60 Bill, *Christ Church*, p. 56.   61 Clarke, 'Classical studies', pp 529–30, 532, 147; Sutherland, 'Political respectability', p. 133. Tyrwhitt (1730–86) came to Oxford in

Markham was born in Kinsale, County Cork (where his father eked out his scanty military half-pay by keeping a school), but was educated at Westminster school and Christ Church. When Flood arrived at Oxford, Markham, who was completing his studies in civil law in which he had already taken a BA (1742) and an MA (1745), was regarded as one of the finest minds in the university.[62] His study of the law caused some to conclude that he aspired to a legal career,[63] but, like Flood, he had other ideas. His appointment to a college lectureship in rhetoric at Christ Church (1747–50) and to the position of junior censor in 1751 persuaded him to take orders and to commit his life to education, and he left a deep mark, as a specialist tutor, on those gentlemen commoners and students who benefited from his guidance, as his son-in-law observed:

> It is difficult to say whether he most excelled in the manner of conveying knowledge, or in exciting youth to laudable pursuits. His knowledge of Grecian and Roman literature was universal; his taste pure. His geography was of such extensive range that it descended to all the minuteness of topographical accuracy; so that he never failed to secure the attention of his scholars by enlivening his lectures with the most pleasing descriptions and the most interesting anecdotes. He was at the same time so perfectly master of different incentives for different dispositions that the studious were ever ambitious of his praise, and the idle feared his rebuke.[64]

Henry Flood certainly profited from Markham's guidance, but the relationship they forged in 1750–1 went beyond the routine one of student and teacher. In Markham, Flood had an imaginative and stimulating teacher; in Flood, Markham had an able and interested student.

In many ways, Markham was just the tutor a student of Flood's 'great abilities' needed at this time. At Christ Church, the realisation that 'his attainments were far inferior' to those of the 'small literary group' to which he was introduced convinced him of the importance of serious study. According to one account, 'he felt himself so much distressed' by his lack of knowledge he resolved not to contribute to any discussion on literary subjects for six months, but 'to read intensely ... in order to put himself on a par with the other members'. Lawrence Parsons maintained he kept quiet for a year. Whatever the precise duration, the experience cured Flood of his

---

1747 where secured a fellowship and took an MA at Merton. He went on to serve as under-secretary to the duke of Newcastle, to become curator of the British Museum, clerk of the House of Commons and editor of Aristotle's *Poetica*.   62 For an outline of his career see C.R. Markham, *Memoir of Archbishop Markham* (London, 1906); *D.N.B.*; G.G. Cunningham, *Lives of eminent and illustrious Englishmen* (Glasgow, 1837), vii, 447–50; 'Some account of ... Dr William Markham', *Annual Register*, 1807, pp 789–90.   63 *Annual Register*, 1807, p. 789.   64 Markham, *Archbishop Markham*, p. 22 and Nicholls, *Literary anecdotes*, ii, 368; see also *Annual Register*, 1807, p. 789.

intellectual indolence and encouraged him to study with 'great ardour and unre-
mitting attention' for the duration of his time in Oxford. It is not clear what precisely he read. The academic programme presented to undergraduates at Christ
Church did not have a lot to offer someone with his educational history; but since
he did not have to take examinations to graduate it is not unlikely that he pursued a
course of study which reflected his own and Markham's interests and enthusiasms.
This would certainly corroborate the subsequent claim that he familiarised himself
with mathematics as well as 'Greek and Roman historians he had not before pe-
rused', since they were among the wave of innovations Markham made during his
decade as dean.[65] The result was striking. In 1751, Flood had some verses on the
death of Frederick, Prince of Wales, written under Markham's careful supervision,
published in *Epicedia Oxoniensia*.[66] And in the following December, having completed the two-years which gentlemen commoners spent on average in the university, he graduated with an honourary MA degree. This was unusual. Though the
granting of honourary MAs to gentlemen commoners had been revived by Francis
Atterbury when he was dean (1710–13), they were not generally awarded. The decision to bestow one on Henry Flood in 1752 may not be unconnected with the high
station held by his father, but it is equally likely that it was an acknowledgement of
his intellectual achievements while at the university.[67]

Before he graduated from Oxford, Flood registered in the Inns of Court in London where he was admitted to read law in January 1751. Following in his father's
footsteps, he enrolled in the Inner Temple, while Ambrose Smith was admitted to
Lincoln's Inn. As well as Smith, there were many other Irishmen (such as Nicholas
Osborne of Newtown Anner, County Tipperary, Matthias Earbery of County Cork,
Richard Welch of Newtown, County Kilkenny, Ambrose Power from County Tipperary, and Edward Bellingham Swan of County Dublin) at the Inns of Court at
this time, but Flood did not forge any lasting friendships.[68] It appears, indeed, that
he was satisfying his father's rather than his own wishes. As Warden's career had
amply illustrated, the law represented a reliable route to wealth and to high office in
Ireland, and he evidently hoped that his son would emulate, if not exceed, his attainments.[69] Henry was less than enthusiastic about this prospect. He reputedly
spent more time studying mathematics and reading Greek than reading law while
he went through the motions of completing the eight terms at the Inns of Court

---

65 Bill, *Christ Church*, 61; *Gentleman's Magazine*, 61(1791), pp 1124–5; Rosse Papers, C/12/1; Flood,
Memoirs, pp 11–13; *D.N.B.*   66 *Epicedia Oxoniensia* (Oxford, 1751). It should be noted that verses on
the same theme attributed to George Browne were written by Markham (Clarke, 'Classical studies', p.
520).   67 Foster, *Alumni Oxoniensis*, ii, 471; *P.O.*, 26 Dec. 1752; Flood, *Memoirs*, p. 14; Bill, *Christ
Church*, pp 180–1.   68 Roberts, ed., *Inner Temple records*, v, 9; *Lincolns' Inn admissions*, pp 438-40;
H.A.C. Sturgess, ed., *Register of admissions to the honourable Society of the Middle Temple* (3 vols, Lon-
don, 1949), i, 340.   69 Rosse Papers, C/12/1; for the usefulness of the law to ambitious men see
Sunderlin to Malone, 10 Nov. 1777 (Malone Papers, N.L.I., microfilm p. 1561); Marianne Elliott, *Wolfe
Tone: prophet of Irish independence* (Yale, 1989), p. 43.

necessary to enable him to become a lawyer. The experience was not made any the more pleasant by the fact that it was during this period that he was struck down by a serious illness (probably smallpox), which may have threatened his life and which certainly left his face permanently disfigured. Undaunted, Flood persisted because, according to Sir Lawrence Parsons, it was 'the cast of his mind to love struggling with difficulties, by which he was excited not dismayed'. He may even have practised law in England for a time before his return to Ireland but, if so, it was not an experience he found fulfilling, and his failure to seek admittance to the King's Inns in Dublin on his return indicates that he had by then determined that the law was not for him.[70]

ELECTION

It is not clear precisely when Flood returned to Ireland. But he was certainly back in Dublin on 6 December 1757, because he was one of a large body of notables who gathered at the Great Room in the Music Hall in Fishamble Street to hear Thomas Sheridan, the colourful manager of Smock Alley theatre who had, the previous year, published a treatise called *British education: or, the source of the disorders of Great Britain*, expound his controversial views on the deficiencies of the Irish educational system and his plans for their correction. Sheridan's basic thesis was that 'irreligion, immorality and corruption' in society could be remedied through the pursuit of an educational programme that concentrated on useful studies – specifically the art of oratory and the study of the English language.[71] His views were afforded a mixed reception by a sceptical public; the select audience that heard his presentation at Fishamble Street on 6 December was more sympathetic. There was, it is true, some resentment at his criticisms of the predilection of Irishmen to go to England for their eduction on the grounds that it diminished Trinity College and other Irish educational institutions, and to his claim that it encouraged the injurious practice of absenteeism. But his scheme for the enhancement of education in Ireland through the foundation of a second-level academy which placed oratory and the study of English at the centre of its curriculum was warmly welcomed because of the advantages he forecast it would bring the kingdom:

> Let it be the glory, let it be the boast of this country, that of the British dominions, Ireland first led the way, in an institution the best calculated to revive the

70 Rosse Papers/C/12/1; Keane, et al., eds, *King's Inns admission papers, passim.* 71 Sheridan's views are outlined at length in *British education; or the source of the disorders of Great Britain* (London, 1756). Another edition was published in 1769 and a limited facsimile edition in 1987. The work is discussed by W. Benzie, *The Dublin orator: Thomas Sheridan's influence on eighteenth-century rhetoric and belles lettres* (Leeds, 1972), pp 4–16 and E.K. Sheldon, 'The Hibernian Academy: an eighteenth-century group experiment in modern education', *Long Room*, 11 (1975), pp 23–4.

antient honour of these realms; to prevent the shame, as well as ruin which an acknowledged superiority in our rivals must in time bring upon us, to disappoint the ambitious views of our ancient avowed enemies.

This was a message well-calculated to impress the large numbers present who embraced the patriot ideal of improvement and, galvanized by the prospect, they agreed to 'form themselves into a society, for the improvement of education, and particularly for examining and carrying Mr Sheridan's scheme into execution if, when explained and considered, it should appear to deserve encouragement'.[72] Sheridan was insistent that an academy was necessary to put his educational theories into effect. Most of those present were less than sure, but they were so eager to ensure that the education of 'young gentlemen of fortune' was enhanced, they constituted themselves into the Hibernian Society for this specific purpose in 1758.[73]

The Society's inaugural membership comprised a broad range of Irish Protestant political and religious interests. Among the forty-one members of 'the committee' established to conduct its business were six peers (the earls of Kerry and Shelburne and Lords Strangford, Tullamore, Farnham and Newtown), three bishops (Clogher, Derry and Killala) and nine clergy (of whom Samuel Madden, John Leland, Francis Hutcheson and Anthony Marley are the best known). The leading laymen were mainly politicians (Sir Arthur Gore, Thomas Adderley, Charles Gardiner, Kean O'Hara, Hercules Langford Rowley, William Brownlow and William Scott, the prime serjeant), but it also included academics and writers like Dr Thomas Leland and Gorges Edmund Howard. Henry Flood was one of the committee's younger and lesser lights.[74]

The committee gave Sheridan's scheme 'their utmost attention', but it quickly emerged that, in common with the public at large, there were conflicting views on its merits.[75] Flood possessed deep reservations. He was as unimpressed by Sheridan, whom he described as 'crazy', as he was by the committee's chairman, John Tickell, whom he described as 'frantic'. He had contributed to the success of Sheridan's presentation on 6 December by his presence, but he regarded the breakfast Sheridan hosted to popularise his ideas as embarrassing and inappropriate. Sheridan's 'best pretence to part', he confided to Ambrose Smith in January 1758, just two weeks

72 Thomas Sheridan, *An oration pronounced before a numerous body of the nobility and gentry assembled at the Musick Hall in Fishamble Street* (Dublin, 1757); *The proceedings of the Hibernian Society* (Dublin, 1758), p. 4; Sheldon, 'Hibernian Academy', p. 25.   73 Michael Quane, 'Aspects of education in Ireland 1695-1795', *J.C.H.A.S.*, 73 (1968), p. 129.   74 Quane, 'Aspects of education', p. 129; *F.D.J.*, Jan-Feb., 8 Apr. 1758; Benzie, *The Dublin orator*, p. 17; E.K. Sheldon, *Thomas Sheridan of Smock Alley* (Princeton, 1967), p. 237.   75 [William Dennis], *A second oration to the Hibernian Society* (Dublin, 1758); *idem, An address to the Hibernian Society with a plan of education ...* (Dublin, 1758); *A critical examination of the sense, style and grammar of Mr Sheridan's printed oration* (Dublin, 1758); *A letter to a school master in the country from his friend in town relative to Mr Sheridan's scheme of education* (Dublin, 1758); Sheldon, 'Hibernian Academy', pp 25-6.

before the committee reported in favour of his plan, 'is a sort of pruriency of imagination and fermentation of the brain'. He was particularly critical of Sheridan's decision to submit his scheme piecemeal, with merely an 'abstract' of the whole, and he was taken aback by its author's arrogant expectation that 'we were unanimously to approve every tittle of it and to express our just admiration and astonishment at Sheridan's penetration'.[76] If implemented unaltered, Flood was convinced the scheme would pave the way 'for the extirpation of British education' which, he believed, had more going for it than Sheridan allowed. A majority of his fellow committee members were more positive, and at a meeting on 8 February they appointed officers and a standing sub-committee to set matters in train to raise finance for the funding of an educational academy which would be managed by Sheridan and nominated a delegation to lobby the lord lieutenant. Flood was chosen for none of these tasks. But he was not displeased that Sheridan's crucial absence in London (supposedly to hire instructors) during much of 1758 ensured the academy was modelled on more pragmatic principles than its author favoured.[77]

Though the enthusiasm for educational reform manifested at the meetings of the Hibernian Society in the early months of 1758 did not produce an educational institution along the precise lines advocated by Sheridan, the Society was busy nonetheless. By January 1759, it had its 'academy' in place, and instruction was already being offered in 'the learned languages' to youths and in history, geography, mathematics and French to older adolescents at their headquarters on the Little Green. The main organizers of these educational activities were Thomas Leland and Gabriel Stokes of Trinity College. Flood and others contributed behind the scenes by running the Society. He chaired one of the Society's meetings in January 1759, and was elected to the Committee of Guardians that chose Lord Charlemont as their president on 1 November 1759. His involvement diminished thereafter, as control passed to office holders and government supporters, and the society redefined its role to that of maintaining, educating and apprenticing the orphans and children of soldiers in Ireland.[78] Flood's withdrawal would suggest that he was unhappy with the direction the Academy was taking, but the lure of politics was more consequential. The attraction of the Hibernian Society certainly paled when compared with that of the House of Commons.

The absence of a provision for regular general elections in Ireland between the death of monarchs meant that such changes as occurred in the representation in the

---

76 Flood to Smith, 11 Jan. 1758 (Historical Society of Pennsylvania, Drew Collection, letters of English statesmen); *Proceedings of the Hibernian society*, pp 8–9.   77 Ibid.; Sheldon, 'Hibernian Academy', pp 27–9; Benzie, *The Dublin Orator*, pp 18–19; Quane, op. cit, pp 129–30; Sheldon, *Thomas Sheridan*, pp 247–8.   78 *F.D.J.*, 6 Feb., 3 Nov.; *Universal Advertizer*, 6 Nov. 1759, 26 Feb. 1760; Benzie, *The Dublin orator*, pp 18–19; Sheldon, 'Hibernian Academy', pp 29–31; McDowell and Webb, *Trinity College*, p. 56; *The charter for incorporating the Hibernian Society in Dublin ...* (Dublin, 1769); *By-laws agreed to and confirmed by the Hibernian Society according to the rules prescribed by their charter* (Dublin, 1775).

House of Commons between 1727 and 1760 arose from by-elections occasioned by the death of incumbents or their elevation to the peerage. In County Kilkenny, for instance, the death in 1751 of Henry Wemys had resulted in the return of his younger brother, James, to represent the constituency of Callan in tandem with Warden Flood.[79] Eight years later, the death of Brabazon Ponsonby, the Earl of Bessborough, and the accession to the peerage of his eldest son William (Lord Duncannon), who had represented the county since 1727, created a vacancy in the county constituency. County seats were the most prestigious in the Irish representative system, and news of Bessborough's demise instigated intense lobbying as prospective candidates assayed their chances.

Circumstances were ideal for one of the smaller interests in the county to secure the representation because with Patrick Wemys occupying one of the two seats, the Ponsonbys and the Agars unable to agree on a mutually acceptable candidate, and Lord Castlecomer, who, between his own and the eighty promised by James Agar senior, controlled 180 votes, unable to stand, the outcome depended on whom the major interests could be persuaded to back.[80] Three candidates emerged. The individual with the narrowest support base was John Blunden, who directed his appeal at those of 'the blood of the House of Desart', to whom he was related. None of their number had represented the county since the 1690s, but Blunden claimed optimistically that if the Cuffes endorsed him as 'a proper person to represent the county', he stood a good chance of securing the return. John Healy, a large and wealthy landowner, who was nominated at a meeting of the 'principal gentlemen and independent freeholders' who had grown weary of the domination of the county representation by the Ponsonbys and Wemys, was a more weighty candidate. But the most consequential of all was Henry Flood because of the willingness of Speaker Ponsonby to act, in Flood's words, 'the part of a thorough friend', the decision of the main branch of the Agars not to oppose his candidacy, and the broad support-base forged by his father in the country. Indeed, it was the conclusion of Flood's family and friends that Warden deserved most of the credit for setting Henry up for the representation for the county.[81] If so, his hard work brought him the result he desired. Blunden withdrew from the contest, and though Patrick Wemys sought to encourage the 'Independent gentlemen', who supported Healy, to force a contest, it was clear when the writs were issued that Healy could not sustain a poll and he withdrew from the contest on 26 October.[82] The election was fixed for 6 November, but as there were no candidates other than himself this was a mere formality, and

79 Burtchaell, *Kilkenny members*, pp 127, 131, 140–1.   80 Flood to Langrishe, 17 Apr. 1759 in Burtchaell, *Kilkenny members*, p. 145; Ellis to Devonshire, 20 Dec. 1755, 5 Sept. 1756, 20 Aug. 1758, Devonshire to Ellis, 30 Dec. 1755, Bessborough to Devonshire, 18 Aug. 1758, Ponsonby to Devonshire, 1 July 1756 (Chatsworth Papers, P.R.O.N.I., T3158/1036, 1049, 1275, 1344, 1591–2).   81 Burtchaell, *Kilkenny members*, pp 145, 153–4; Power 'Parliamentary representation', p. 309; Notes on Flood v Flood, pp 9, 25. 82 *F.D.J.*, 9, 16, 18 Sept. 1758, 30 Oct. 1759; *Universal Advertiser*, 2, 23 Jan., 13, 16, 20 Oct. 1759.

Flood was 'elected unanimously'. In celebration, he hosted 'a very grand entertainment and a ball at the Castle of Kilkenny' for the ladies and gentlemen who had supported his candidacy.[83] It was a great moment in the history of the Flood family. Their political aspirations had long centred on the borough of Callan; now they could add the county to their objects. Ironically, at this very moment, their command of Callan corporation was under serious threat, and because this was central to their continued political eminence, Henry, his father and uncles were determined to repulse this challenge to their continued control.

83 *F.D.J.*, 30 Oct., 10 Nov. 1759.

2

The politics of Callan, 1758–76

To travellers who visited it, eighteenth-century Callan was either 'a poor dirty town' or 'a wretched village' of 'mean appearance' interesting only because of the medieval and early modern ruins dotted about the area. However, politically, Callan was more than just another undistinguished settlement.[1] It was a parliamentary borough with a corporate government consisting of a sovereign, town clerk, thirteen burgesses and a fluctuating number of freemen who had the power to return two members to parliament.[2] Moreover, because parliamentary seats were, in the words of one contemporary, 'so honourable and such distinctive marks of intrinsic worth and virtue' that 'every gentleman of fortune aspired to either establish or to retain whatever hold he could on such prized possessions', Callan possessed a status its modest appearance belied.[3] This was vividly illustrated in the late 1750s and 1760s when the Agars mounted a determined challenge to displace the Floods, who had benefited most from the agreement they, the Wemys and Agars had entered into in the 1710s to share the representation of Callan. Of course, Callan was not the only constituency in which this happened, but the lengths to which the contending parties there were prepared to go to uphold their ambitions was greater than in Galway, Clonmel or any other constituency characterised by fiercely oppugnant rivalries.[4] Indeed, it was alleged that the Floods' determination was so total that they resolved *en famille* to go 'knee deep in blood' to overcome their rivals, and events bear out the allegation.[5]

---

1 Thomas Campbell, *A Philosophical survey of the south of Ireland* (London, 1778), p. 116; Michael Quane, ed., 'Tour in Ireland by John Harden in 1791', *J.C.H.A.S.*, 58 (1953), p. 28; *Richard Pococke's Irish Tours*, ed., John McVeagh (Dublin, 1995), pp 107, 192; Michael O'Flanagan, ed., *Letters of the Ordnance survey: Kilkenny* (2 vols, Dublin, 1928), ii, 36; William Tighe, *Statistical observations relative to the County Kilkenny in 1800 and 1801* (Dublin, 1802), p. 464. 2 *Municipal Corporations Report*, 8 (Ireland), 28 (1835), pp 451–4; ibid., 7 (Ireland), 27 (1835), p. 52. 3 J. Mockler, 'Mallow district in 1775', *J.C.H.A.S.*, xxi (1915), p. 23. 4 James Kelly, 'The politics of Protestant ascendancy in County Galway 1660–1832' in G. Moran, ed., *Galway: history and society* (Dublin, 1996), pp 248–51; P.R.O., Kings Bench Papers, KB7/5 (Clonmel), KB7/9, 10, 11 (Galway). 5 Brief for the prosecution in the trial of ... Henry Flood, (N.A., Prim Collection, PRI/37).

THE BREAK-UP OF THE FLOOD – AGAR – WEMYS COMPACT

By the late 1750s, a loose coalition involving representatives of the Agar, Mountgarret, Wemys and Cuffe families had come together to wrest command of the corporation of Callan from the Flood family, which had established itself as the most powerful interest in the borough during the twenty plus years that Henry Candler was sovereign.[6] The precise course of events is not easily reconstructed, but a central factor was the emergence of new personalities and new priorities as the generation that concluded the agreement to share Callan gave way in the 1730s to younger, more ambitious men to whom such arrangements were confining. In particular, the Agars and Cuffes became resentful of the Floods' monopoly of the office of sovereign.

As the leader of a family that had suffered more than most by the emergence of the Floods as a political force in south Kilkenny, John Cuffe (who was ennobled as Baron Desart in 1733) gave expression to his ambition to restore the fortunes of his family by building an elegant mansion at Castle Inch and by purchasing the Ormonde estate in the town and liberties of Callan from the earl of Arran in 1735 for £11,120. Both these undertakings necessitated expenditure the Cuffes could fund only by borrowing, and the heavy debt they built up was all the more burdensome because their status as lords of the manor of Callan did not bring them commensurate political influence on the corporation as a result of the tight control exercised by the Flood family. This unsatisfactory state of affairs remained unaltered when John Cuffe succeeded his father in 1749. Like the first baron, the second Lord Desart (1730–67) was anxious to extend his family's interest in Callan and with this in mind he had no hesitation in joining the anti-Flood interest that emerged in the late 1750s. He also had a financial imperative; the Cuffe's finances were now in a parlous condition because of the heavy outlay of the first baron, and there seemed little prospect of their being improved other than by political means since the first baron had reduced the revenue raising options open to his successor by granting his tenants generous long-term leases.[7]

The efforts of the first and second barons Desart to challenge the Floods' authority in Callan did not excite especial concern at Farmley as long as they remained on good terms with the Agars and the Wemys. However, the security of their position was undermined in the 1750s as the spirit of cooperation that had hitherto existed between them and the Agars gave way to rivalry, and cracks developed in their relations with the Wemys.[8]

6 Kennedy, 'Callan', p. 296; Power, 'Parliamentary representation', p. 326; R.S.A.I., Callan Court book', *passim.* 7 Kennedy, 'Callan', pp 302–3; William Carrigan, *The history and antiquities of the diocese of Ossory* (4 vols, Dublin, 1905), iii, 317; G.E.C., *The complete peerage*, v, 227 ff; Lease of Lord Desart and Mark Sherman, 21 Oct. 1737 (N.A., L.E.C., vol. 34 no. 49); N.A., Shelly Papers, Ms 999/462 p. 32. 8 It is significant that Mary Agar was party to the sale of land in Gowran barony to Charles Flood in 1745 (Land Commission Papers, Keogh estate, Box 13 (E.C.2272)), and that James Agar was one of the three lives in a three life lease made by Warden and John Flood in 1748 (Registry of Deeds, 153/47/101577).

Following his death in 1733, James Agar's sons, Henry and James, continued his policy of adding to the family's estates.[9] Their avaricious appetite for land was equalled by their political ambition to control the boroughs of south Kilkenny where the bulk of their landed property was located. In the process, differences emerged within the family which led them first to conclude that they need no longer co-operate with the Floods, and then to seek to displace them in Callan. The first hint of the troubles to come for the Floods can be identified in the power struggle that took place within the Agar family for control of Gowran.

Henry, the eldest of the two Agar brothers, followed his father by becoming MP for Gowran in 1727. The corporation of the borough was vested in a portrieve, twelve burgesses and an unlimited number of freemen who were nominated by the burgesses.[10] It was thus tailor-made for control by an ambitious politician, which is precisely what Henry Agar set about achieving. The absence of corporation records for the 1720s and early 1730s obscures his strategy, but it reached a critical point in 1736 when Henry's attempt to take control of the office of portrieve provoked his brother James, who resided at Ringwood and who was a burgess on the corporation, to accuse him of exceeding his authority by seeking to act as portrieve for two consecutive years.[11] The dispute went to law, and judgement went in Henry's favour, as a result of which he retained sole control of the borough until his premature death in November 1746. This provided James with the opportunity he had long awaited. Following Henry's death, he orchestrated matters to ensure that his nominee, George Forster, was elected portrieve and that he himself was returned for the vacant parliamentary seat. However, Henry's eldest son, who was also named James, was unwilling to accept this outcome. He forged an alliance with Francis Flood, Henry Flood's uncle, who had been elected a freeman and burgess of the borough in 1741, and supported him when, in 1748, he stood against George Forster in a premature and ill-judged attempt by James the younger to gain control of the portrieveship. Flood was defeated by 25 votes to 14, and in the years that followed every attempt James Agar and he made to increase their influence on the corporation by nominating well-disposed candidates as freemen and burgesses was frustrated by their opponents.[12]

As this suggests, Francis Flood was a figure of consequence in Gowran borough for a time after his failure to become portrieve in 1748, but the mutual need that united him and the younger James Agar, and that ensured that the Floods retained the goodwill of at least one branch of the Agar family was not destined to last. When David Chaigneau, whose father had purchased part of Gowran in 1715, died in

9 N.A., L.E.C., vol. 10, no. 2; N.A., Clifden deeds, nos 20038–20150.   10 Burtchaell, *Kilkenny members*, pp 114–15, 135, 139; *Municipal Corporations Report*, 8 (Ireland), 27 (1835), pp 517–18; Carrigan, *Ossory*, iii, 401.   11 A Statement of the case relative to the borough of Gowran, 23 June 1736 (N.A., Agar Papers, Ms 3239).   12 R.S.A.I., Corporation book of Gowran 1736–1800 (unfoliated); *Dublin Courant*, 22, 25 Nov. 1746.

1753 and James Agar was elected to represent the borough in his place, Francis Flood became dispensable. In 1756, Agar acquired the corporation's lands in lieu of money's owed and had the borough securely under his control by the time writs were issued for a general election in 1761.[13]

The break-up of the alliance between John Flood and the younger James Agar, following the latter's success in Gowran, had serious implications for the Floods. In the first place, it meant that the main branch of the Agars, which now controlled Gowran and Thomastown,[14] no longer needed their electoral support. Secondly, and more significantly, it caused James Agar of Ringwood, who had lost out in the struggle with his nephew for control of Gowran to target Callan, and to look to his cousins, the Wemys, who controlled the nomination to one of the borough's two parliamentary seats, as potential allies. The readiness of Henry Agar to nominate Wemys's to act as burgesses in the boroughs of Thomastown and Gowran demonstrates that relations between the two families were sufficiently amicable to permit political co-operation. Indeed, they even entered into an agreement in the mid-1750s to support each other in County Kilkenny. This proved short-lived, but the increasing closeness of the Agars and Wemys compromised the Floods' ability to control Callan corporation.[15] Despite this, the Floods still retained the upper hand as they demonstrated when they withstood the initial attempts by their opponents to take advantage of Henry Candler's death to seize control of the office of sovereign.

The death of Candler in January 1758 posed the Floods a serious problem. Though it is not possible to reconstruct the precise strength of the interested parties on the borough corporation at the time of his demise, Candler's authority derived from the standing of his family in the area as well as from his connection with the Floods. His departure inevitably weakened the Candler interest, and this combined with the intrigues of the Cuffe, Wemys, James Agar and other interests to make the annual election of a sovereign in 1758 exceptionally fraught. Initially, the Floods seemed set fair to retain long-term control since they contrived to have Charles Flood of Ballymack elected and sworn as sovereign for the remainder of Candler's annual term shortly after his death. However, they may have had the advantage of surprise, as their opponents had as many, if not more, supporters on the corporation; when an election was held in June to determine who should serve for the following year,

13 Corporation book of Gowran; *P.O.*, 16 Dec. 1755; *Public Gazetteer*, 2 May 1761; Power, 'Parliamentary representation', pp 321–2; Burtchaell, *Kilkenny Members*, pp 124–5; N.A., Shelly Papers, Ms 999/462, p. 32.   14 Henry Agar gained control of Thomastown from Sir William Fownes, who was allied with the Ponsonbys; Agar was made sovereign in 1743 and following this, he and James consolidated their command to ensure against a Ponsonby resurgence and the Agars were in sole control by 1760 (R.S.A.I., Minutebook of Corporation of Thomastown (unfoliated); Ellis to Hartington, 7 Oct., 15, 22 Nov. 1755, 15 June, Conway to Devonshire, 15 July, Ellis to Devonshire, 5 Sept. 1756 (Chatsworth Papers, P.R.O.N.I., T3158/ 923, 984, 989, 1266, 1286, 1344)).

the Floods were obliged to have recourse to extraordinary measures to ensure Charles Flood victory. On the day of the election, the Flood interest prevented their opponents from entering the court house where the poll was held by packing it with their friends and by creating an impassable human barrier composed of 'tenantry and retainers'. Supporters of the Agar and other anti-Flood interests congregated in a nearby house to protest against the Floods' actions, but it did not alter the outcome.[16] Buoyed up by this, the Floods maintained publicly that their control of the borough was as firm as ever, but this was wishful thinking. They were able to repulse James Agar's subsequent attempt to be made a burgess by rejecting several freemen voters presented by him on the grounds that they were 'papists' or 'married to papists', but they were unable to consolidate their own authority by electing freemen loyal to their cause with the result that the gathering tensions within the corporation exploded violently in the election for sovereign in 1759.[17]

The Floods were at serious risk of losing control of Callan borough in 1759 because, among other reasons, the laxness of their organization compared with that of their opponents. This greatly disquieted Henry, who ruefully described the discipline of the family's interest in April 1759 as 'careless and supine: every man is left to follow his own fancies and caprice whereas the opponents act upon one common plan, and all concur heart and hand in the prosecution of it'. Indeed, he was so worried by the strength and intensity of the Agar challenge that he was prepared to contemplate recourse to force: 'violence must be counteracted, if not by violence, at least by firmness and vigour', he observed ominously. In the meantime, he embarked on a canvas to keep the Ponsonbys on side, to minimise difficulties with other local interests, and to win back the allegiance of those freemen who had defected. His intervention was not without impact. By May, he had won over two crucial votes and was hopeful of more when he appealed to Sir William Fownes, who was enmeshed in a similar power struggle in the borough of Inistioge, to intercede on his behalf with another.[18] Sir William did as requested, for a price, but despite this and the acquisition of William Phillips' vote, allegedly by the administration of a bribe by Henry and his uncle John,[19] the outcome was uncertain when the burgesses and freemen of the borough assembled on 25 June, 'the day appointed for the election of a sovereign', to determine whether the Floods' nominee, Charles Flood, or Agar's nominee, James Wemys MP, had the most support. According to

15 Blennerhassett and Eager (Agar) pedigree (N.L.I., Ms 4112); R.S.A.I., Minutebook of Thomastown corporation, Corporation book of Gowran 1736–1800, (both unfoliated); Ellis to Devonshire, 23 Dec 1755, 5 Sept. 1756, Devonshire to Ellis, 30 Dec.1755 (Chatsworth Papers, P.R.O.N.I., T3158/ 1038, 1049, 1344).   16 N.A., Shelly Papers, Ms 999/462 pp 36–7.   17 Carrigan, *Ossory*, iii, 296; N.A., Shelly Papers, Ms 999/462 pp 32; M. Brennan, 'The making of the Protestant ascendancy in County Kilkenny' (Ph.D., State University of New York, 1983), p. 279.   18 Flood to Langrishe, 7 Apr. in Burtchaell, *Kilkenny members*, pp 45–6; Flood to Fownes, May 1759 (N.L.I., Fownes Papers, Ms 8470/3); Power, 'Parliamentary representation', p. 324.   19 Petition against John Flood, 29 Sept. 1767 (N.A., Shelly Papers, Ms 999/462 pp 26–8).

one report, Wemys won by 'a very considerable majority', but this is contradicted by others that maintain that Charles Flood was the victor. What is certain is that the election was marked by violent exchanges involving Henry's uncle, Francis and his son, an army ensign, also named Francis, and three supporters of James Agar, two of whom (Richard Littlejohn and Michael Money) died as a result. Violence on this scale could not be allowed to go unprosecuted, and Francis Flood senior and junior were ordered to trial. Though the two deaths arose out of duelling *rencontres*, which were generally treated indulgently by the law, the Floods left nothing to chance. They employed eight counsel for the trial which took place at Kilkenny on 10 August, and the verdict, which was returned after a marathon sitting of eleven hours, vindicated their careful preparation; both defendants 'were honourably and wholly acquitted' by the jury after only a few minutes consideration.[20]

There remained the crucial matter of who was the legal sovereign of the corporation. The fact that James Wemys took the oaths of office, as per custom, on 28 September suggests that he possessed the strongest claim, but when he sought to assume the duties of the office, he was blocked by Charles Flood who maintained that he alone was rightfully elected. Neither man would back down, so the matter was referred to the courts. The Irish Court of King's Bench found against Charles Flood, but the Floods appealed the judgement by bringing a writ of error to the English King's Bench thereby neutralising the decision of the Irish court *pro tem*, and, more importantly, prolonging their control of the corporation. Charles Flood continued to act as sovereign meantime; he was re-elected in a further acrimonious contest in June 1760 following which he was brought to trial for killing Matthew Keogh in a dispute arising out of his election, but, like his brother and nephew a year earlier, he too was acquitted.[21]

The rightful occupant of the office of sovereign of Callan thus remained a point of contention when writs were issued in April 1761 for an election to determine the parliamentary representation of the borough. Pending a decision to the contrary by the English Court of King's Bench, the Flood family maintained that Charles Flood should oversee the election. But to their dismay, the high sheriff of the county, Benjamin Kearney, who was aligned with the Agar interest, transmitted the precept authorising a poll to James Wemys who returned his elder brother, Patrick, and James Agar of Ringwood.[22] This was a result the Floods simply could not allow to stand and Henry petitioned the House of Commons in November 1761 to declare the poll invalid on the grounds that Sheriff Kearney had acted illegally by transmit-

20 Notes re election [1759] (N.L.I., Fownes Papers, Ms 8470/8); N.A., Calendar of presentments etc 1698-1813 ff 165-6; *F.D.J.*, 30 June, 3 July, 14 Aug.; *Universal Advertizer*, 30 June 1759; *Commons. Jn. (Irl.)*, vii, 30–1. 21 *Universal Advertizer*, 2 Oct. 1759; Brief for the prosecution in the trial of ... Henry Flood, 1769 (N.A., Prim Collection, PRI/37). 22 *Commons Jn. (Irl.)*, vii, 30–1; Francis Flood to Bagshawe, 24 Jan. 22 Apr. in J.A. Guy, ed., *Colonel Samuel Bagshawe and the army of George II, 1731–62* (London, 1990), pp 232–3, 238; *Public Gazetteer*, 21, 25 Apr.; Burtchaell, *Kilkenny members*, pp 140–1; Power, 'Parliamentary representation', p. 326; *Public Advertiser*, 4 July 1761.

ting the precept to James Wemys because he was not the legal sovereign. The committee of privileges and elections afforded the case a thorough scrutiny; it called for
and examined the corporation books and the affidavits lodged by the contending
parties in the Court of King's Bench, and was sufficiently persuaded by Flood's
case to uphold the petition. A new election was ordered, and when the precept for
holding it was transmitted to Charles Flood he oversaw the return on 2 January
1762 of Henry Flood and Patrick Wemys.[23]

If the final outcome of the general election polls for Callan in 1761–2 resembled
the return made in 1727 in that a member of both the Flood and Wemys families
were returned to represent the constituency, the standing of the Flood interest in
the borough was decidedly less assured. In 1727, the Floods held *secure* possession
of one of the borough's two seats and were able to ensure the sovereign was well-
disposed because of their agreement with the Agars and Wemys; in 1761, by contrast, their command of the office of sovereign was at risk, their alliance with the
Agars in tatters and their relations with the Wemys strained. More seriously, it was
James Agar, who was admitted to the corporation at about this time in Warden 'Flood's
interest', in what one can only conclude was a despairing attempt to buy him off,
and not they who commanded the fastest growing and, possibly, the largest interest
in the constituency, and who was deemed by the Irish courts to possess the stronger
claim in law to be regarded as the borough's patron.[24]

To Henry Flood's relief, the reversal of the election return for Callan made in
1761 obscured the decline in his family's influence on the borough corporation.
This was a matter of great personal import because he had failed to retain his seat
for County Kilkenny. In truth, this was no surprise. In contrast to 1759, when he
did not have to outpoll a prominent or well-connected opponent, both the Agars
and the Ponsonbys fielded leading family members. Flood did commence a canvass,
but when it became clear that his rivals could draw on a wider network of supporters, he withdrew and allowed James Agar of Gowran and John Ponsonby, the Speaker
of the House of Commons, the pleasure of being 'unanimously elected' on 20 April
1761.[25]

As well as the basic lack of freeholder support, one of the reasons Henry Flood
could not hope to compete with James Agar and John Ponsonby in an electoral
contest in an open constituency like County Kilkenny was his lack of funds. Elections were costly undertakings, and though *several* branches of the Flood family
were placed in the same income bracket as the Flowers of Ashbrook, the Blundens

23 *Commons Jn.(Irl.)*, vii, 30–1, 67, 73, 76, 91–2, 178; Power, 'Parliamentary representation', p. 326;
Public Gazetteer, 5 Jan. 1762; Burtchaell, *Kilkenny members*, p. 139; N.A. Shelly Papers, Ms 999/462 p.
23. Henry thus succeeded his father who became *de facto* a member of the House of Lords as a consequence of his promotion to the lord chief justiceship.   24 *The case of Henry Flood and John Flood esqrs
upon the petition of Thomas Matthew and John Echlin* [Dublin, 1768].   25 Below pp 129; *Public Gazetteer*, 28 Apr., 2 May 1761; Power, 'Parliamentary representation', p. 307.

of Castle Blunden, and the Bushe's of Kilfane in a tabulation of the wealth of the major landowners of County Kilkenny made in 1775, they were decidedly inferior to the Ponsonbys, Wandesfords, Butlers and Agars of Gowran.[26] Henry Flood's estimated annual income at that date was £2–3,000, and while this may understate the true figure, it was considerably more than he had at his disposal in the early 1760s. Indeed, even if one adds his father's legal income into the equation, the Floods were not in a position to sustain a long and, by implication, costly campaign to retain the representation for the county when candidates in boroughs were willing to spend as much as £500 and £1200 'buying votes'.[27] This conclusion is vividly corroborated by the admission by Francis Flood junior to a creditor in 1761 that it was pointless applying at this time to his father, whom it was reckoned in 1775 enjoyed a larger annual income than Henry Flood, to repay money owing because of the heavy cost of sustaining the family's interest in Callan.[28] There were, as this implies, financial as well as a political reasons why the Floods were determined to retain control of Callan. The prospect of having to borrow the estimated £2-4,000 it cost in the 1750s and 1760s to purchase a parliamentary seat was an option they also had good financial reason to avoid.[29]

THE STRUGGLE FOR CONTROL

The contending parties were fully aware that the result of the 1761–2 general election left the contest for control of Callan unresolved. Despite the setbacks he had already experienced, James Agar was determined not to give up the struggle, though the death of Patrick Wemys on 20 January 1762, a mere eighteen days after his election, came too soon to permit him to renew his challenge at the first opportunity. Charles Flood received the precept and, as he had done a few weeks previously, he oversaw the election of a Wemys – Patrick's brother James, who had previously represented the borough between 1751 and 1760.[30] The absence of a petition against the return suggests the election went off smoothly, but if the Floods interpreted this as indicating they had finally seen off the Agars, they were mistaken. James Agar could identify no advantage in appealing the result to the House of Commons given their decision in 1761. Instead, he authorised the initiation of legal proceedings in

---

26 G.O., Ms 443; Power, 'Parliamentary representation', p. 309.   27 Wyndham to Wyndham, 15 Nov. 1759 (B.L.,O.C., Wyndham letters, no. 14); John Ainsworth, ed., *Inchiquin manuscripts* (Dublin, 1943), p. 650; Guy, ed., *Bagshawe*, pp 203–4; N.A., Miscellaneous letters and papers prior to 1760, f 166; Ronayne to Grandison, 9 Apr. 1730 (P.R.O.N.I., Villiers-Stuart Papers, T3131/C/5/58); Mason to Mason, 24 Dec. 1739 (T3131/B/4/5).   28 Guy, ed., *Bagshawe*, pp 232–3.   29 Maurice Craig, *The Volunteer earl* (London, 1948), p. 98; H.M.C., *Charlemont*, i, 330–1; Lill to Townshend, 10 July 1768 (N.L.I.,Townshend Papers, Ms 394); J.L. McCracken, 'Irish parliamentary elections 1727–68', *I.H.S.*, v (1947), p. 211.   30 Burtchaell, *Kilkenny members*, pp 139, 140–1; *The Corke Journal*, 4 Mar. 1762; *The case of Henry Flood and John Flood*, p. 1.

the Court of Common Pleas against Charles Flood for illegally acting as sovereign of Callan since June 1758. It was an inspired move. A 'judgement of ouster' was sought and given on 13 May 1762 by Judge Christopher Robinson against Charles Flood for exercising 'without any lawful warrant or authority or legal grant the privileges and franchises of sovereign'. This meant that the office was now officially 'vacant' and six days later a writ of mandamus was issued in the name of the king authorising the burgesses and freemen of Callan to hold a new election on 8 June at the town tholsel.[31]

This was a potentially critical moment for the Flood interest in Callan, but they remained as determined as ever to ensure it did not cause them to forfeit control of the corporation. With this in view, Charles, his elder brother John and five of their closest allies on the corporation assembled on 8 June to elect a new sovereign. The meeting was chaired by John Flood and it chose to confirm Charles in the position for the remainder of the annual term.[32] However, in their haste to produce the desired result, Charles and John Flood overlooked a number of procedural requirements they were bound by law to observe which, in the long term, cost the family dear both in money and in effort, as Henry conceded some years later.[33] In the first place, they did not observe the instruction in the writ of mandamus that the town clerk should 'affix' a 'publick notice ... in the market place or any other publick place within the town or borough of Callan' at least six days before the election of a new sovereign. Secondly, they did not follow the 'antient usage and custom' of offering a list of three burgesses from which the assembled burgesses and freemen were requested to chose their sovereign. And, thirdly, Charles Flood did not take 'the oaths by law required' before John Flood, the presiding officer. These were precisely the sort of grounds on which a successful legal challenge could be mounted and Charles Flood was not long in office when George Huson applied to the Court of King's Bench to invalidate his election on the grounds that he was 'using and exercising without any lawful warrant the office, privileges and franchises of sovering[*sic*]'.[34] It is not clear on whose behalf Huson was acting, but since a George Huson is described in Henry Flood's will as his 'faithful servant', it is possible that these proceedings were initiated by the Floods in a desperate attempt to head off a court action to dispossess them of the borough. If this seems too fanciful, it is undeniable that the effect of Huson's intervention was to buy the Floods time since the case did not come before the Irish Court of King's Bench for final adjudication until 24 June 1764. In the meantime, relations between the Floods and the Agars, and the Floods and the Wemys continued to deteriorate.

---

31 Writ of error from Ireland, Huson vs Charles Flood, 27 June 1767 (P.R.O., KB 7/7, parchments 7–10); N.A., Shelly Papers, Ms 999/462 pp 36–7.   32 Writ of error from Ireland, Huson v Flood, parchments 9–16, 34.   33 Henry to Warden Flood [post Nov.1770] (R.I.A., Burrowes Papers, 23/K/53/10).   34 Writ of error from Ireland, Huson v Flood, parchments 31–5.

Responsibility for overseeing the Floods' efforts to retain control of Callan passed to Henry Flood following his marriage to Lady Frances Beresford in April 1762. As a result of this, and the decision of the Chief Justice to make him his principal heir, Henry took up residence at Farmley. He so obviously enjoyed what the countryside had to offer, that some of the Beresfords, who hoped that he would join their 'political party', feared he would forsake politics for rustic seclusion.[35] There was little prospect of this, as Callan continued to demand his attention. Indeed, he was taught a hard lesson when, in an attempt to align the Wemys (who had played off both contending parties to advantage since the late 1750s) firmly behind the Flood interest, he agreed that James Wemys should be elected sovereign of Callan in succession to Charles Flood in June 1762. It proved a costly error of judgement because Wemys was not long in office when he 'transferred his interest to Mr Agar' and initiated what Flood described as 'an unprecedented attack ... upon me behind my back'. Wemys' intentions are unrecorded, but he inflicted a critical blow upon the Floods' authority on the corporation on 4 October when, in the absence of Thomas Walton (a Flood loyalist), he authorised John Cole to act as town clerk and admitted twenty-seven new freemen, virtually all of whom were in the Agar interest, to membership. Flood was enraged by Wemys' actions. They threatened to swamp his family's interest among the freemen and burgesses of the corporation. However, since there was nothing he could do to reverse the decision, he chose wisely to avoid confrontation.[36]

Flood was less restrained in his dealings with James Agar, with whom his relations were now so bad that Ellis, Lady Brandon felt the need to mediate.[37] Her intervention proved unsuccessful. Indeed, relations continued to disimprove, and James Agar was bound over on 5 January 1763 'to keep the peace towards all his Ma[jes]ties subjects and in part[icu]lar Henry Flood Esqʳ for one whole year' arising out of an 'information' sworn against him. None of the Floods was similarly constrained and, taking advantage of the opportunity, Charles Flood accosted and set upon James Agar with an 'oak cudgel' in 'a dark entry or passage in the city of Kilkenny' about a month later. Flood's object was to provoke Agar into a duel, but his actions then and on a subsequent occasion, when Charles' alleged that 'he was a scoundril rascal' and that 'he (Flood) wou'd have Agar's blood before he shou'd have Callan', did not elicit the desired response. Charles was prosecuted for threatening conduct, convicted on his own admission at Kilkenny assizes in August, and fined £20.[38]

35 Rosse Papers, C/12/1; Flood, *Memoirs*, pp 21–2.   36 Flood to Stratford, 28 [ ] 1762 (N.L.I., Stratford Papers, Ms 18794/1); Writ of error from Ireland on *quo warranto* against John Flood, 1772–3 (P.R.O., King's Bench Papers, KB 7/8); Griffith to Agar, 2 May 1768 (Normanton Papers, P.R.O.N.I., T3719/C/2/4).   37 Kildare to Kildare, 23 Dec.[1762] in Brian Fitzgerald, ed., *The correspondence of Emily, Duchess of Leinster* (3 vols, Dublin, 1949–57), i, 163. It will be recalled that as Ellis Agar, Lady Brandon was identified by Francis Flood in the 1720s as a suitable marriage partner for his son Warden. 38 Brief for the prosecution in the trial of Henry Flood ..., 1769 (N.A., Prim Collection, PRI/37).

In the light of these events and, particularly, the increase in the number of free-men and burgesses in the corporation in the Agar interest, the election for sovereign on 27 June 1763 assumed a critical importance. It is difficult to establish precisely what took place because the rival corporations in the Flood and Agar interests now possessed different town clerks and separate corporation books.[39] But what appears to have happened is that when the rival interests assembled, Warden Flood proposed Eland Mossom, John Flood and Issham Baggs as suitable candidates and that this elicited a counter-proposal by Morris Cuffe, on behalf of James Agar who was present, in favour of Arthur Webb, Samuel Bradstreet of Saintsgrove and Robert Shearman. In accordance with precedent, the burgesses determined there should be a ballot between Samuel Bradstreet and John Flood which resulted in 'victory' for Flood, 26 votes to 8. However, since this outcome was only secured by the rejection of 'the new votes' of those freemen accepted by James Wemys the previous October, the Agar interest challenged its validity and, when this was rebuffed, with-drew and held their own election in which Bradstreet was declared elected by thirty-three votes to twenty-six.[40] Three months later, on 29 September, when the time came for the new sovereign to be instituted by the outgoing officer, both Bradstreet and Flood claimed the office. James Wemys, expectedly, acknowledged Bradstreet, but the Floods refused to be bound by his decision. Henry Flood had already pub-licly affirmed the legitimacy of his uncle's claim in a press advertisement asserting the propriety of his election in June, and as far as he and the rest of the Flood family were concerned this remained the case because, they alleged, the freemen and bur-gesses accepted by James Wemys in 1762 were not 'duly admitted or sworn'.[41]

James Agar, not surprisingly, thought otherwise, and encouraged by the success of his previous efforts he commenced legal proceedings (formally pursued on his behalf by William Costello, a gentleman resident in Dublin) in the Court of King's Bench against John Flood for illegally exercising the office of sovereign of the cor-poration of Callan.[42] While this joined the growing queue of legal cases against the Floods now in the court system, John Flood completed his term as the Flood corpo-ration's sovereign when he was succeeded by his brother Charles in 1764; the rival Agar corporation re-elected Samuel Bradstreet for another year.[43] This was neither a satisfactory nor a sustainable state of affairs, and it led in 1765 to a further applica-tion from Agar to the Court of King's Bench 'for liberty to exhibit an information against [Charles Flood] for ... usurpation'. Charles had little stomach for this. The

---

39 According to one source, 'there were three clerks each with a corporation book' – one (Thomas Walton) represented the Floods, another (James McClean) represented James Agar and still another (John Cole) represented James Wemys; *Public Gazetteer*, 2, 9, 23 July 1763. 40 Writ of error from Ireland on *quo warranto* against John Flood, 1772–3 (P.R.O., KB 7/8). According to the Shelly Papers (Ms 999/462 pp 36–7) the vote was 33 to 19 for Bradstreet. 41 Ibid.; *F.J.*, 4 Oct. 1763. 42 Writ of error ... against John Flood (P.R.O., KB 7/8). 43 *F.J.*, 3 July 1764; *The case of Thomas Matthew and John Echlin*, p. 1.

quo warranto case taken by George Huson to overturn his election as sovereign on 8 June 1762 had finally been determined in Agar's favour in June 1764. Charles had denied the charges of Huson's counsel that he and his brother had infringed the terms of the writ of mandamus of 19 May 1762, and the direct conflict of evidence to which this gave rise had obliged the court to direct the sheriff of County Kilkenny to assemble a panel of twelve grand jurors to determine the truth. They upheld Huson's claim. The grand jury accepted Flood's contention that he had taken the oaths of office in the manner prescribed, but they found against him on the other points at issue. As a result, the court directed that he should 'be absolutely fore-judged and excluded from exercising ... the office, libertys and franchise' of sovereign of Callan. He was also ordered to pay Huson's costs.[44] This was not to the Floods' liking, but encouraged by the fact that their decision to appeal the verdict of the Irish Court of Common Pleas in 1759 to the English Court of King's Bench had proved advantageous, they determined to appeal this judgment also.[45] This bought them more time (the case was not finally determined until 1767), and meant that Charles Flood had little reason to worry about the charge of usurpation levelled against him in 1765 but he ran scared. He swore an affidavit, which he later sought to recant, disclaiming 'all right, title and interest' in the office of sovereign. It did not help his cause and the verdict went against him once again.[46]

For Henry Flood, who bore most of the costs of these frequent court appearances as well as the responsibility for orchestrating the campaign to retain Callan, this was another depressing setback. The sudden death of his father, aged 69, in April 1764,[47] had increased his personal income fivefold, but the state of the Floods' finances overall disimproved as a consequence of the loss of Warden's salary and the heavy costs incurred defending Callan. Relations between the Floods and the Agars also continued to disimprove. As a consequence, Callan acquired an unenviable reputation as a place of 'tumult and disorder' where rival factions 'went armed into the town of Callan on the days when there was to be an election for magistrates or representatives'.[48] The only thing that seemed to unite the rival parties was their opposition to the Whiteboys who were active in the vicinity in the mid-1760s.[49]

If he was able to regard these events dispassionately, which is unlikely, it ought to have been clear to Henry Flood by this point that he was engaged in an energy-sapping and expensive war of legal attrition that he was unlikely to win. Certainly,

---

44 Writ of error from Ireland, Huson v Flood, 1767 (P.R.O., KB 7/7), parchment 52. Huson's costs were £125 4s. 3d.   45 The absence of a full legal record prohibits a definite explanation of what happened in this case, but it may be that the Flood's arguments were upheld because the House of Commons accepted Charles Flood was the legal sovereign in 1761.   46 *The case of Thomas Matthew and John Echlin*, p. 1.   47 *F.J.*, 17 Apr. 1764; Northumberland to Halifax, 18 Apr. 1764 (P.R.O., S.P.63/423). 48 'Notes on places of antiquarian interest', *J.R.S.A.I.*, 5th ser. xvi(1906), p. 275; Rosse Papers, C/12/1.   49 *Dublin Gazette*, 16 Apr. 1765; *F.J.*, 16 Oct. 1764; James Donnelly, 'The Whiteboy movement 1761–65', *I.H.S.*, xxi (1978), pp 20–54.

little seemed to go in his favour in 1764–5, and his hopes were dealt a further critical blow when James Agar purchased the manor of Callan from Lord Desart for £17,120 in 1765. This gave Agar control of most of the lands in the borough, which significantly improved his prospects of winning over a majority of burgesses and freemen. Enraged by this, Flood assaulted Agar 'in an inhuman manner openly in the street' when he encountered him by chance at Essex Bridge in Dublin on 12 May. This was a *casus duello* and Agar issued a challenge. However, before the two men could proceed to an exchange of shots in the Phoenix Park, the sheriff of Dublin 'interposed' and bound them over. This angered Flood, who maintained that Agar could easily have avoided being bound over, and his irritation was intensified ten days later when he received a request from Agar's second, Thomas Adderley, that he should accompany Agar out of the country to settle the matter in a foreign jurisdiction. Flood declared he was ready 'at an hour's notice' to go wherever necessary, though he had been advised by 'the most punctilious in duelling' that he was no longer bound even to respond to such messages because Agar had, by his carelessness, facilitated the imposition of the recognizance to keep the peace. However, instead of interpreting Flood's affirmative response as reason to press on with arrangements to bring the dispute to an expeditious conclusion, Agar and Adderley, procrastinated. Matters remained in limbo for a number of days until Agar determined that 'Calais or somewhere out of his majesty's dominions' was a suitable location. Flood's second, Sackville Gardiner, demurred, preferring, like Flood, to go to England. The two principals did embark finally for Holyhead in early June where they proceeded to an exchange of shots, arising out of which, one source maintains, Agar was slightly wounded.[50]

The preparedness of Henry Flood and James Agar to risk their lives in a duel indicates just how bitter and how personalised the battle for control of Callan had become. In the absence of a final decision on the two law cases still outstanding, the Floods retained the initiative in the borough and they took advantage of this when the writs issued in 1765 authorizing a by-election to fill the vacancy created by the death of James Wemys were delivered to George Flood rather than to Philip Savage, who acted on behalf of the Agars. With their arrangement with the Wemys now a thing of the past, Henry Flood determined to replace James Wemys with a member of his own family. Jocelyn, his younger brother, who was a student at Trinity, was returned to represent the constituency though he was still a minor.[51]

The election of Jocelyn Flood ushered in a short period of relative calm in the borough of Callan, though the fact that the rival camps maintained separate corpo-

50 Flood to Burke, 30 May (S.C.L., Wentworth Woodhouse Manuscripts, Burke Papers, P.1/47); *Dublin Gazette*, 8 June 1765; J.L. Clifford, ed., *Dr Campbell's diary of a visit to England in 1775* (Cambridge, 1947), pp 35–6, 109–10.   51 *Commons Jn. (Irl.)*, viii, 11; *Dublin Gazette*, 6 July, 19, 26 Oct.; *The case of Henry Flood and John Flood*, p. 1; Burtchaell, *Kilkenny members*, p. 160; *F.J.*, 12 Nov. 1765; *Alumni Dublinenses*, p. 293.

rations indicates that there was no relaxation in the suspicion with which each regarded the other. In 1766, Charles Flood was elected sovereign once again to represent the Flood interest and the Rev Arthur Webb to represent that of James Agar.[52] This is how matters stood on 19 May 1767 when Jocelyn Flood died unexpectedly after a 'few days illness at his seat at Marsdale'. This necessitated another by-election; and James Agar was determined there would be no repeat of 1765 when the Floods were allowed an obstacle-free opportunity to return one of their family. Encouraged by the fact that the *quo warranto* case against John Flood for illegally exercising the office of sovereign had commenced what were to prove protracted proceedings in the Irish Court of King's Bench in the spring of 1766 and that the writ of error against Charles Flood appealed to the English Court of King's bench was decided in his favour, Agar tightened the screw.[53]

Writs were issued for an election to choose a second MP for the borough of Callan on 21 October.[54] Before this, Agar signalled his determination to prevail at the poll when four burgesses loyal to him presented a petition to the corporation complaining that John Flood had, in June 1759,

> bribed and unduly influenced William Phillips gent., one of the burgess ... to promise ... to give his vote at the borough of Callan to the then attorney-general and his family in return for John and Henry Flood agreeing to indemnify Phillips from the covenants in his lease from Lord Mountgarret, and to get him a place worth £30 per annum or to pay him £30 per annum until they got him such a place'.

The petition was heard by the Agar controlled corporation at Callan on 19 and 20 October in the absence of Philips and John Flood, and the decision was that both should be removed from the register of burgesses.[55] If there had been only one corporation authority this would have dealt a further blow to the Flood interest. However, because they maintained their own corporation, they could and did choose to ignore it. Indeed, they were more disturbed by James Agar's attempt to induce supporters in the Flood interest to transfer their allegiance to him.

The best documented case is provided by the approach to Richard Griffith, the impecunious author who tried in vain 'to earn a living as a gentleman farmer', who was bound to Henry Flood by the ties of a financial debt as well as affection. Griffith was approached on Agar's behalf by the Rev Thomas Bushe with an offer to pay off his debt to Henry Flood and to make him an income of £30 per annum until such times as 'Mrs Griffith's £15 which she has from government can be made £50 in some shape or other'.[56] No agreement was arrived at as far as can be ascertained, but

52 *Dublin Mercury*, 8 July 1766; Kennedy 'Callan', p. 296.   53 *F.L.J.*, 23 May 1767; P.R.O., King's Bench Papers, KB7/7 and /8.   54 *Commons Jn.(Irl.)*, viii, 163; *F.L.J.*, 28 Oct. 1767.   55 Petition against John Flood, 29 Sept. 1767 (N.A., Shelly Papers, Ms 999/462 pp 26–30).   56 D.H. Eshelman,

Flood was sufficiently worried by the attempts to poach his supporters that he brought a number, Griffith among them, to live 'in his house at Farmley'. This was not without its funny side, as Lawrence Parsons recalled:

> Mr Flood had much difficulty often in conveying him [Griffith] to Callan at the time of elections in such a manner that he might escape from being arrested for debt. On one ... occasion ..., Griffith was brought into Callan by night and placed in a loft over the court house, in the ceiling of which a hole was cut, and when it was Griffith's turn to vote, he put his head through the hole and gave his vote, the bailiffs looking up at him, but could not reach him.[57]

Such bizarre measures may not have been necessary at the October 1767 poll to determine who should succeed Jocelyn Flood. Despite this, the election was tense. The essence of the problem for James Agar was the refusal of Henry Flood and his uncles to accept that they were acting illegally by continuing to nominate one of their number to serve as sovereign of Callan. The fact that they publicly trumpeted their possession of the corporation seal in support of their contention that they were the legal corporation merely added to Agar's irritation, and in an attempt to affirm their position, his officers commissioned a new seal in September. This prompted an ill-tempered exchange in the columns of *Finn's Leinster Journal* in which the Agars had the better of the argument, because they were able to adduce the 'absolute judgement of ouster' obtained in the Court of King's Bench in 1767 excluding Charles Flood from acting as sovereign and to cite his affidavit of 1765 in which he 'swears and admits he was not sovereign of Callan'.[58]

Victories in the public prints were of minor consequence, however, when the Flood corporation continued to be afforded official recognition. This was highlighted by the delivery to Charles Flood of the precept to hold a poll in October 1767. Frustrated by their inability to prevent Charles Flood overseeing the election of his nephew, John Flood junior of Floodhall, eleven of Agar's supporters 'did way-lay and attack' Henry Flood and one of his retainers at Shankill turnpike to prevent them attending the election, but it did not affect the outcome.[59] James Agar went through the motions of appealing against the return to the House of Commons, but in the absence of a *final* decision by the courts as to who was the legal sovereign, he had little prospect of success and he subsequently withdrew his petition.[60]

Elizabeth Griffith: a biographical and critical study (Philadelphia, 1949), pp 27–47; P.H. Highfell et al., eds, *A biographical dictionary of actors, actresses ... and other stage personnel in London 1660–1800* (Carbondale, 1978), vi, 374–80; Brandon to Bushe, 25 Oct., Note, 26 Oct., Note, late Oct. 1767, Griffith to Agar, 2 May 1768 (Normanton Papers, P.R.O.N.I., T3719/C/1/1–4).   **57** Rosse Papers, C/12/1.   **58** *F.L.J.*, 24 Oct. 1767.   **59** Burtchaell, *Kilkenny members*, p. 161; *F.L.J.*, 4 Nov. 1767; *Commons Jn.(Irl.)*, viii, 166, 175, appendix, ccix–ccx.   **60** *Commons Jn.(Irl.)*, viii, 181, 184–5, 186, 206; *The case of Henry Flood and John Flood*, p. 1; *F.L.J.*, 5 Dec. 1767.

This was not the end of the matter. A complaint for 'breach of privilege' was taken against those who had 'threaten[ed] and insult[ed]' Henry Flood and 'assault[ed] one of his domestics' at Shankill turnpike. The House of Commons ordered that those responsible should be taken into custody by the sergeant at arms. However, the person delegated to execute the instruction was 'opposed by a violent mob' and sent on his way prisonerless by 'seven or eight men armed with spades and shovels, who threatened to take away his life if he should attempt to come near them'. A subsequent attempt by a number of Henry Flood's retainers to serve summons on those responsible and to detain others, most of whom lived in 'a scattering village behind Ringwood House', met with an equally hostile reception and the matter was dropped.[61]

This was an opportunity lost by Henry Flood to embarrass James Agar before the whole kingdom, but it was more than compensated for by his triumph at the polls. He had little opportunity to savour the victory, however, because the ratification by the Irish parliament in 1768 of an Octennial Act meant that general elections would henceforward occur at eight year intervals, and that the first would take place immediately rather than in 1774 as he favoured.[62] Anticipating this event, James Agar intensified his efforts to secure control of Callan corporation in the summer of 1768. He revived his overtures to Richard Griffith by increasing the sum he undertook to pay him and his wife, and tightened his legal noose still further by initiating a new prosecution of Charles Flood at the Kilkenny assizes for illegally exercising the office of sovereign of Callan corporation in 1767–8.[63] He had pursued this strategy with success at the spring assizes when cases against Henry Flood's three uncles (Charles, John and George) for illegally serving as sovereign of Callan produced verdicts effectively precluding John and George from serving as sovereign ever again.[64] This left only the case against Charles Flood and the *quo warranto* appeal to the Court of King's Bench in England to be determined, and if the absence of a verdict in both allowed the Floods to sustain their authority in the borough in the very short term, Henry was acutely aware of the increasing precariousness of their position. His 'ground' in Callan was, he confided to Lord Charlemont in May, 'more ticklish than I could wish'. He was so desperate he even appealed to Charlemont to get Lord Shannon to suggest to John Ponsonby that James Agar of Gowran and he should 'join ... against' James Agar of Ringwood and 'secure ... Callan to' Flood.[65]

The nightmare outcome from the Floods' point of view – that neither Henry nor John would be returned for Callan – receded when the precept authorising the

61 *Commons Jn. (Irl.)*, viii, 166, 175, 199, 207, 211, 212–13, appendix, ccix-ccx; Burtchaell, *Kilkenny members*, pp 147–8.   62 See below, pp 125–6.   63 Griffith to Agar, 2 May 1768 and papers by Agar re proposal to Mrs Griffith (Normanton Papers, P.R.O.N.I., T3719/ 2/2/4, C/5/3).   64 *The case of Thomas Matthew and John Echlin*, p. 1; Brief for the prosecution of Henry Flood (N.A., Prim Papers, PRI/37). 65 Flood to Charlemont, 30 May [1768] in H.M.C., *Charlemont*, ii, 390.

holding of a poll in the constituency was transmitted by the well-inclined High Sheriff, Charles Kendal Bushe, to their uncle Charles. Despite this, James Agar presented his own candidates – Thomas Matthew of Thomastown, County Tipperary, and John Echlin of County Carlow – with the result that the poll which ensued in July was, even by Callan's unique standard, remarkably fraught:

> the avenue leading to the Court-House, where the election was held, was surrounded by several armed persons (strangers in that country) on horseback; the stairs leading to the Court-House were lined on both sides with numbers of obscure persons who had swords and pistols partly concealed under their coats and partly exposed to view; and many persons who did not claim any right to vote appeared armed in like manner in said court-house.

If it is difficult to say whom this advantaged most; but the outcome certainly pleased the Floods. Both Henry and John were returned by 'a fair and large majority of legal voices'.[66] James Agar, inevitably, contested this. James McClean, his town clerk, published an account of the poll in which he accused Charles Flood of usurping the office of sovereign and of declaring his nephews elected when the vote was to the contrary. This elicited a denial from Francis Knapp, who described himself as 'deputy-sovereign', on behalf of the Flood interest. But of greater consequence was the decision of Matthew and Echlin to appeal the outcome to the House of Commons, because it compelled Henry Flood to purchase a parliamentary seat in the borough of Longford as insurance in case the petitioners' objection was upheld.[67]

This was a commonplace precaution, but it was also the first public acknowledgement by Henry Flood that his family's ascendancy in Callan hung by an increasingly slender thread. This was confirmed in September when the Kilkenny assizes found Charles Flood 'guilty of usurping the magistracy of the borough for this year'. Charles sought to overturn the judgement by challenging 'the whole array', but this failed. He then sought a 'bill of exception', though he must have known this stood little chance because the English Court of King's Bench had previously upheld the verdict of its Irish counterpart in a similar case.[68] This meant that all that stood between James Agar and control of the borough was the increasingly remote possibility that the English Court of King's Bench would find in the Floods' favour in the cases still before them.

---

66 *The case of Matthew and Echlin*, p. 1; *The case of Flood and Flood*, p. 1; *F.L.J.*, 20, 23 July 1768. In the gross poll the Floods polled 22 as against their opponents 19. However, the poll of 'allowed voices', which excluded the 'new' freemen and burgesses admitted by James Wemys in 1762 and those ruled ineligible on the grounds that they were 'papists' or 'married to papists', gave them a 13 to 2 majority. 67 *F.L.J.*, 20, 23 July, 13 Aug.; O'Hara to O'Hara, 20 July (N.L.I., O'Hara Papers, Ms 20393); *Commons Jn. (Irl.)*, viii, 303, 343; Flood to Charlemont, 30 May 1768 in H.M.C., *Charlemont*, ii, 390. 68 *F.L.J.*, 24 Sept. 1768.

Given these circumstances, the Floods' moral as well as actual authority in the borough depended more than ever on their ability to preserve the support of those burgesses who had remained loyal. Every vote was vital, so when it emerged in September 1768 that Francis Knapp, the 'deputy sovereign', who 'usualy voted in the interest of Mr Flood', was contemplating leaving Farmley for a farm on James Agar's estate, Flood did not stint in his efforts to convince him to maintain his traditional allegiance. Knapp vacillated, but his wife was less accommodating, and she invited James Agar to their home to reassure her husband. Persuaded by his friends of the inadvisability of entering what was, in effect, enemy territory, Agar requested the landlord of the Red Lion Inn in Callan, a Catholic named Michael Keogh, go in his place. He even gave him his pistols though it was illegal for a Catholic to possess arms without a licence. However, when Keogh, accompanied by Bridget Knapp, arrived at Burnchurch on 28 September they were forced from the chaise in which they travelled by some of Flood's retainers who smashed it to pieces. Keogh drew and fired Agar's pistols in self-defence and was slightly wounded in the hand by a ball fired by his assailants, but he managed to escape serious injury by fleeing the scene – abandoning Agar's pistols in his way. This was potentially embarrassing, but Agar sought to turn the incident to his advantage. He directed Keogh to place advertisements in *Finn's Leinster Journal* in October offering a £40 reward for the discovery and prosecution of those who assaulted him. Not to be outdone, Henry Flood had George Huson publish a counter-advertisement a few days later in which he claimed that Keogh was hurt attempting to break and enter Knapp's house in pursuit of 'a corrupt bargain' he had entered into with 'a certain gentleman [James Agar] and a person belonging to Francis Knapp' [his wife]; that there had been attacks on Knapp's house 'in the dead of night'; and that 'bribes and threats' had been issued against those 'best acquainted with the said corrupt transactions [to prevent them] from bringing it to light'. Huson also appealed for information as to the ownership of the pistols Keogh had abandoned, and offered a reward of £40 to any person who would 'prosecute to conviction' those whom, the notice alleged, had attacked Francis Knapp's house. Keogh responded by alleging the whole incident was part of a plot devised by 'some persons of note' (Henry Flood and others of his family) to lure James Agar into a trap 'in order to murder him'.[69]

Using the breakdown in the administration of Callan's toll system caused by the existence of two rival corporations as a pretext, the grand jury of County Kilkenny appealed in October to 'the two contending parties to prevent rioting and bloodshed', but it made no impression.[70] James Agar was determined to press the matter

69 Brief for the prosecution ... of ... Henry Flood (N.A., Prim Collection, PRI/37); J.Prim, 'Documents re Flood duel', *Journal of the Historical and Archaeological Association of Ireland*, 3rd series, 1(1868–9), pp 234–41; *idem.*, 'Kilkenny inns and taverns', *Journal of the Kilkenny and south-east of Ireland Archaeological Society*, n.s.,4 (1862–3), pp 166–7 and notes; N.A. Shelly Papers, Ms 999/462 pp 33–4; *F.L.J.*, 9, 22, 29 Oct.; *P.O.*, 8 Oct. 1768. **70** *F.L.J.*, 12 Oct. 1768.

to a resolution. He began by appealing in January 1769 to the lord lieutenant, Lord Townshend, not to accept Henry Flood's nominee for the shievralty of County Kilkenny;[71] he subsequently filed an information with the Court of King's Bench against Flood and others in relation to events at Burnchurch the previous September, and on 22 August he instructed Richard Roth to visit Flood to demand his pistols back. Flood denied they were in his possession. Agar refused to accept his word and demanded that Flood meet him to settle the matter like a man of honour. Given Agar's offensive attitude and determination to provoke a duel (he repulsed all suggestions by Roth that he should let the matter drop), Flood had little alternative but to agree a time and a place if he was to avoid being ridiculed publicly by his rival as a liar and a coward. Dunmore in south Kilkenny was the agreed location and, with their seconds, Gervaise Parker Bushe and Richard Roth in attendance, the two principals lined up at fourteen paces at two in the afternoon on Friday 25 August. As had been the case throughout this phase of the dispute, Agar was also the more aggressive of the two protagonists on the field. He declined all suggestions of mediation, and once he had been cautioned by Bushe against using his free arm as a 'rest' for his pistol, he was the first to fire. Having missed with his first shot, he took up his second pistol in readiness to use it if Flood was also off-target. He was not. With Agar's words 'Fire, you scoundrel' echoing round the ground, Flood's ball penetrated Agar's left breast; he slumped to the ground and was dead within minutes.[72]

Because the duel had been conducted in the presence of seconds, and because Agar had issued the challenge, there was little prospect that Flood would be penalised should the case go to court. Gervaise Parker Bushe, for one, was convinced that 'no man ever was more compelled to defend his honour and his person, and no man ever did it with more temper and steady courage than Mr Flood'. Lord Townshend, who had planned to visit Flood at his seat at Farmley on his return from his Munster tour, was also convinced that 'Flood stands fair'.[73] Inevitably, the Agars disagreed, and they had supportive legal opinion from Theobald Wolfe and the attorney General to encourage them in their views.[74] They were determined James Agar's death should not pass unprosecuted, and the coroner's inquest gave them grounds for believing that they might even secure a capital sentence. Instead of returning a verdict of 'manslaughter in self defence', the coroner simply recorded the facts as they were presented and left the rest to the courts. Flood was 'charged with the

71 Agar to Townshend, 9 Jan. 1769 (N.L.I., Townshend Papers, Ms 8009/3); McCracken, 'Irish parliamentary elections', p. 216.   72 As note 69; *F.L.J.*, 26 Aug.; 'Findings of an inquest on death of James Agar in duel with Henry Flood', 1769 (N.A., Prim Collection, PR1/36);'An affair of honour a hundred years ago', *Dublin University Magazine*, 78 (1871), pp 376–7; 'A letter on a fatal duel', *Journal of Royal Historical and Archaeological Society of Ireland*, 4th series, ii (1870–71), pp 13–14; Bushe to Grattan, Sept. 1769 in Henry Grattan Jr, *Memoirs of the life and times of Henry Grattan* (5 vols, London, 1839–46), i, 140–2.   73 Bushe to Charlemont, 26 Aug.in H.M.C.,*Charlemont*, i, 294–5; Townshend to Macartney, 31 Aug. 1769 in Bartlett, ed., *Macartney*, p. 41.   74 'Findings of inquest on death of James Agar' (N.A., Prim Collection, PRI/36).

killing of ... James Agar ... in defence of the life of ... the said Henry Flood which ... James Agar had attempted and was again prepared and about to attempt'. This was unusual, but considering the previous history of the two men it was not wholly unanticipated. There was no question of Flood being held in custody despite the Agars' wishes to the contrary. He was bound by his own recognizance and those of his uncles, John and Charles, to the tune of £20,000 to present himself for trial at the spring assizes in 1770.[75]

Because of the national profile of the protagonists, the Flood –Agar duel excited enormous interest. It was the talk of the salons as well as of the coffee houses, the subject of private correspondence and public discourse. Counsel for the Agars alleged in court that the Floods manipulated press coverage in order 'to intimidate magistrates from doing their duty', but this was unnecessary. The press was eager to publish every scrap of information on the duel that came their way to satisfy the enormous public interest in the dispute and its outcome.[76]

Flood found the publicity so trying he appealed to Townshend 'for a special commission to be tried immediately'. Lord Charlemont also interceded on his behalf with the Lord Chancellor, but Lord Lifford rejected the application on the grounds that it would set an unwelcome precedent.[77] Counsel for the Agars, meanwhile, prepared as strong a case as they could. They had little with which to work, except the long-standing animosity of the combatants, because Flood had conducted himself impeccably on the duelling field, and fulfilled every legal requirement expected of him in its wake. The outcome was never in question; Flood surrendered himself on 21 March 1770 for trial and was found guilty of manslaughter in his own defence and 'most honourably acquitted' at the Kilkenny assizes a few days later.[78] To add to the Agars' woes and to Flood's satisfaction, the petition presented by Matthew and Echlin against the return of Henry and John Flood for Callan was rejected by the new House of Commons in December 1769, with the result that Henry Flood was able to resign the representation for the borough of Longford, and take his seat for Callan.[79]

Following on the death of James Agar, the fervour with which the contest for control of Callan was waged eased, though neither side showed any willingness to abandon the struggle. The death of Charles Flood of Ballymack in November 1770 was a blow to the Flood interest, as he was the most actively involved of Henry's three uncles in the affairs of the borough. He had, during his lifetime, made a number of serious 'involuntary errors' which, Henry maintained later, were responsible for

75 'Flood's bail bond, 1 Sept. 1769' in *Journal of the Kilkenny and South East of Ireland Archaeological Society*, 3 (1854–5), pp 316–17 and N.L.I., Walsh newscuttings, Ms 14023.   76 *F.L.J.*, September 1769– May 1770.   77 Flood to Townshend, 29 Aug. (N.A., Townshend Papers, Ms 724); Waite to Macartney, 11 Sept (B.L., O.C., Waite-Macartney Letters); Charlemont to Flood, 6 Sept., late Sept., 1 Oct. Lifford to Charlemont, 10 Sept. 1769 in R[odd], ed., *Letters to Flood*, pp 49, 50, 53–5; N.A., Shelly Papers, Ms 999/462 p. 35.   78 Brief for the prosecution of Henry Flood (N.A., Prim Papers, Ms 37); *F.L.J.*, 28 Mar., 18 Apr. 1770.   79 *Commons Jn. (Irl.)*, viii, 303, 315, 320, 322, 333, 341, 343.

the Floods losing control of Callan, but it is unfair to blame the outcome on him.[80] The truth was that the Agars collectively were more powerful than the Floods.

The primary locus of the conflict between the Floods and the Agars shifted to the courtroom in the early 1770s as the legal proceedings initiated by James Agar ground on remorselessly after his death. The Court of King's Bench in Ireland did not finally get round to hearing the case taken against John Flood by William Costello in 1763 until 1771, when it upheld the judgement arrived at in previous related cases and determined that John Flood should 'be absolutely forejudged and ex- cluded from exercising or using [the] office, privileges and franchises of sovereign ... of Callan'.[81] As he had done on previous occasions, Henry appealed the decision to the English Court of King's Bench, but this was only postponing the inevitable. He now realised that he had devoted 'ten years of health and time' and £12,000 to support a cause that had all but failed.[82] He continued to maintain a separate bor- ough corporation and, on the demise of his surviving uncles in the early 1770s, transferred the duties of sovereign to his devoted friend Ambrose Smith. He still indulged hopes he might regain the initiative in the borough and he was temporar- ily encouraged by the fact that when a general election was called in 1776, the pre- cept authorizing the election was delivered to Smith. He returned Henry Flood and Sir Hercules Langrishe following a poll held on 8 May in which he rejected a number of votes offered in support of their opponents, Pierce Butler and George Agar. How- ever, when the return was appealed to the House of Commons, Butler and Agar were deemed duly elected. This effectively decided the contest for control of the borough of Callan in favour of the Agars. Henry Flood no longer possessed a sus- tainable claim, though he refused to acknowledge this publicly or to give up the contest.[83]

What happened in Callan in the 1750s and 1760s was not typical of what took place in Irish parliamentary boroughs then or at any other point in the eighteenth century, but it well-illustrates the passions a 'no holds barred' tussle for pre-emi- nence could engender. In the process, both the Floods and the Agars acquired a national reputation for aggressiveness neither can have relished.[84] The episode also vividly demonstrates, at an individual level, the ambivalence towards the law that was a feature of mid-eighteenth century Irish society. Chief Baron Edward Willes noted on one occasion that 'it is not in ... [judges] power to procure the laws to be duly administered' because local officials, such as sheriffs, were expected to put

---

80 *F.L.J.*, 14 Nov. 1770; Henry to Warden Flood, post 11 Nov. 1771 (R.I.A., Burrowes Papers, Ms 23 K/ 53/10).   81 Writ of error from Ireland on *quo warranto* against John Flood (P.R.O., KB 7/8 (1772– 3)).   82 Henry to Warden Flood, post 11 Nov. 1771 (R.I.A., Burrowes Papers, Ms 23 K/53/10).   83 *Commons. Jn.(Irl.)*, ix, 297, 312, 337, 342, 357, 360, 377; Library of Congress, Cavendish's parliamen- tary diary, v, 1–3; below pp 231–6.   84 Jonah Barrington, *Personal sketches of his own time* (3 vols, London, 1827–32), i, 147–8 note; M. Bodkin, ed., 'Irish parliament in 1773', *R.I.A. proc.*, 48C (1942), p. 192.

their allegiance to their kin and to their friends above their allegiance to the law.[85] This was repeatedly illustrated in the case of Callan at election times when the presence of a friend in the office of high sheriff proved critical to the destination of electoral precepts. It is even more emphatically attested to by the necessity of having a loyal ally as sovereign because this was the key to maintaining control of a borough. It was so critical, in fact, that families like the Floods, Agars and Wemys in Callan and the Blakes and the Dalys in Galway, who did not want for legal knowledge or advice, were prepared to abuse due political and legal process in an attempt to get their way.[86] When this did not prove sufficient, the principals in these power struggles displayed little reluctance to have recourse to weapons if there seemed no other alternative and if a point of honour could be invoked. The law, in other words, was neither the final nor, always, the respected arbiter in borough disputes as the Floods demonstrated by the quite blatant way they used it to prolong their control of Callan.

In overseeing such a determined effort to keep Callan corporation under family control, Henry Flood displayed personal bravery as well as an unbending determination to get his own way. The impersonal nature of the sources on which one must rely for information on the dispute makes it impossible to monitor his attitude through the various stages of this labyrinthine affair, but he manifested little inclination to compromise or to take much notice of the sensibilities of others. This reflected his temperament as well as the fact that failure would set back his own political career which, following a quiet beginning, blossomed in the mid and late-1760s.

85 P.R.O.N.I., T2855/1 pp 45–6; Sean Connolly, *Religion, law and power* (Oxford, 1992), pp 203–30 *passim*. 86 James Kelly, *'That damn'd thing called honour': duelling in Ireland 1570–1860* (Cork, 1995), pp 139–47; Kelly, 'The politics of Protestant ascendancy: County Galway', pp 248–51.

PART TWO
PATRIOT POLITICIAN

Henry Flood first attracted national notice during the 1763–4 parliamentary session. This was his third as a member of parliament, and the dramatic impact he made was all the more resounding since he did not speak during the 1759–60 session and he was prevented by electoral complications from making his maiden speech until the 1761–2 session was well underway. No record of what he said on that occasion survives, but the issues he chose to comment on then and in other contributions suggests that his intention was to distance himself from Dublin Castle with which he had aligned himself on becoming an MP. At the same time, he was not prepared as yet to join with the small but vigorous patriot connection in the House of Commons because he had no wish to upset his father and because he was content to operate on his own. The rarity of his public utterances and the complete absence of personal papers for this period in his career means it is impossible to analyse the evolution of Flood's political thinking with any confidence, but the content of his speeches in the 1763–4 session makes it clear that his political sensibilities were both broadened and radicalised in the early 1760s, and that he found the arguments of patriots like Edmond Sexten Pery increasingly congenial. Their appeal was reinforced by the fact that the patriots did not constitute an organized political connection which meant the small number of MPs who actively espoused this point of view possessed enormous freedom of action. It was a position in which Flood flourished. His views struck a chord with the public, while his exceptional oratorical talent enabled him to become the leading patriot voice in the House of Commons by the mid-1760s. Despite this, and the kudos that came his way, Flood was not content with opposition. His political hero was William Pitt (from 1766 earl of Chatham) and, stimulated by his example and by the wish to advance his own whig-patriot programme of constitutional reform, he actively contemplated becoming part of a reforming Irish administration that was part of a Chatham government before the arrival of Lord Townshend in 1767 threw Irish politics into ferment and him firmly back into the bosom of the opposition. Flood came to perceive that Townshend was embarked upon the same form of despotic government of which the English Whigs accused Lord Bute, and the American colonists Lord Grenville and Charles Townshend. His strong opposition to Lord Townshend's policies in the Commons and his imaginative propaganda sorties in the press were insufficient to deflect the Lord Lieutenant, but it further enhanced Flood's reputation as the most capable patriot of the day, so that when Townshend returned to England in 1772 the public and political expectation of him was higher than ever.

3

The emergence of a patriot, 1759–66

Henry Flood took his seat in the Irish House of Commons for the first time on 20 November 1759.[1] Though Irish politics seemed bound fast in the ineluctably factional mould into which it had been poured during the early Georgian era, the mould was, in fact, showing signs of cracking open. The money bill dispute of the mid-1750s ensured that Henry Boyle, the greatest parliamentary manager of the century, was never to enjoy the same political authority he had possessed in the 1730s and 1740s when the undertaker system was at its most effective, while the emergence of an invigorated patriot connection critical of both the undertaker system and of government policy towards Ireland ensured both that political discourse was more animated and the disposition of MPs more fluid than they had been during Warden Flood's early career. At the same time, the fact that the kingdom was at war (the Seven Years War began in 1756) aroused traditional anxieties among the Protestant population that France might extend the conflict to Ireland by mounting an invasion or by encouraging disaffected Catholic interests to rebel.[2] The Floods were as activated by this as every other Protestant family. Three of Henry's uncles, John, Francis and Charles, became officers in an independent militia regiment of dragoons arrayed in County Kilkenny in 1756 as part of the civil response which caused tens of thousands of Protestants throughout the country to take up arms in readiness to support the regular military should their services be needed.[3] Henry did not make himself available for similar duty but, since he may not have been in the country, nothing can be read into this. His involvement with the Hibernian Society prior to his election indicates that he possessed broadly patriot inclinations, but his failure to align himself with this connection in the House of Commons on being sworn in is a warning against making too many claims or assumptions on this

---

1 *F.D.J.*, 4 Dec. 1759.   2 For evidence of Protestant susceptibilities on the latter point see, *inter alia*. Caldwell to Newtown, 7 Nov. 1757 (B.L., Lansdowne Ms 773 ff 68–81); James Kelly, ed., 'The Whiteboys in 1762: a contemporary account', *J.C.H.A.S.*, 94 (1989), p. 25; Thomas Reynolds, *The life of Thomas Reynolds* (2 vols, London, 1839), ii, 532–41.   3 A list of officers in the several regiments and independent troops and companies of militia in Ireland (G.O., Ms 608); Henry MacAnally, 'The militia array of 1756', *Irish Sword*, i (1949-53), pp 94–104.

point. The fact that his father was Attorney General when he was first elected was obviously important in determining how he conducted himself in the early years. But there is also reason to suggest that he developed the patriot opinions with which he is most intimately identified in the early 1760s, and that it was only when he had done so that he began to contribute actively to political debate.

THE IRISH POLITICAL SCENE IN 1759

As the most recent addition to the three hundred strong membership of the Irish House of Commons, Flood wisely declined to make an early 'trial of his oratorical powers' during the 1759–60 session. He had much to learn about the operation of the House. And, as he had done to such advantage at Oxford, he chose first to familiarise himself with the procedures and personalities of the Commons' chamber.[4]

The matter of most concern to the peers and commoners of the Irish parliament in 1759 was the report that the French planned an invasion of the British Isles in a strategic move to negative the impact of the gains registered by British forces overseas. The implications for Ireland of the global conflict between the two powers were underlined in the autumn of 1758 when the embargo introduced in 1756 was extended, without prior consultation, to 'all ships in Ireland laden with beef and pork' in an attempt to prevent 'houses in Cork ... victualling' the French navy.[5] Embargoes, ministers realised, were 'disagreeable to the people of Ireland'; but Irish unease was tempered in this instance by the realisation that the spectre of a French invasion was not conjured up for political reasons and that their 'dependency' on what many defined their 'mother country' was vital to their continued security.[6] Indeed, though reverses at sea in the summer of 1759 dealt a disabling blow to French plans, further reports in October of a multi-pronged descent by a large force of French troops, 18,000 of which were destined for Ireland, obliged the Lord Lieutenant, the duke of Bedford, to alert both houses of parliament.[7] This engendered 'a

---

4 *Gentleman's Magazine*, 61(1791), p. 1225; Rosse Papers, C/12/1.   5 Jeremy Black, *A system of ambition: British foreign policy 1660–1793* (London, 1991), pp 193–4; A.P.W. Malcomson, ed., *Eighteenth-century Irish official papers in Great Britain* (2 vols, Belfast, 1973–90), ii, 197–8, 201; Lord John Russell, ed., *The correspondence of John, fourth Duke of Bedford* (3 vols, London, 1842–6), ii, 369–71.   6 Malcomson, ed., *Irish official papers*, ii, 56, 198, 228; Charles to Mary O'Hara, 18 Apr. (N.L.I., O'Hara Papers, Ms 20389); Molyneux to Acheson, 19 Apr. 1755 (N.L.I., Gosford Papers, Ms 8018/1); Marcus de la Poer Beresford, 'Ireland in French strategy 1691–1789' (M.Litt thesis, T.C.D.,1975), chapter 5; Burns, *Irish parliamentary politics*, ii, 256–9; G.R.B. and J.H. Owen, eds, *The private papers of the Earl of Sandwich* (4 vols, London, 1935–8), ii, 3–10, 268–9; Bedford to Lords Justice, 8 Sept., Waite to Wilmot, 13 Sept. (N.A., Irish correspondence 1697–1798, Ms 2446); *Bedford Corres.*, ii, 377–82; Thomas Bartlett, 'A people made rather for copies than originals": the Anglo-Irish 1760–1800', *The International History Review*, xii (1990), pp 11–24.   7 Earl of Albemarle, *Memoirs of the Marquis of Rockingham and his contemporaries* (2 vols, London, 1852), i, 20; Burns, *Irish parliamentary politics*, ii, 259–60; Malcomson, ed., *Irish official papers*, ii, 228; Bedford to Lords Justice, 8 Sept., Waite to Wilmot, 13 Sept., Beys to Beauclerk,

greater spirit for the defence of their King and country' than 'at any time appeared' and ensured a ready response from both houses of parliament to an official request that additional money should be made available for the defence of the kingdom. The worst of the public and political panic was over by 20 November, when Flood took his seat in the Commons, but the mood remained anxious.[8]

Public and political unease was heightened by the country's ongoing economic travails. Like most harvests during Henry Flood's adult life, those of 1758 and 1759 were sufficient to ensure there was no repetition of the horrendous famine that had taken such a heavy demographic toll in 1740–1. However, bad weather and epidemic disease had reduced the country to 'near famine' in 1756–8, and if the associated mortality was modest, the population remained acutely aware of its vulnerability. This was due in part to the fact that the country was dependent on grain imports from abroad even during good years. Influenced by this, Flood was to make the increase in Irish grain production one of his political priorities; but he was in no position in 1759 to do anything to ease the immediate problems caused by the wartime contraction in trade and the embargo on designated agricultural exports that, it was alleged, advantaged only the 'idle'.[9] As a consequence, the economy remained susceptible to crisis in 1759, a point underlined by the action of two hundred nobles, gentlemen and merchants who responded on 5 November to a 'great run' on the private banks in the capital with a declaration of their confidence in the banking system.[10]

Economic difficulties did not automatically register in the political arena in the eighteenth century. But it is significant that on this occasion both the lord chief baron, Edward Willes, and the visitor, Henry Penruddocke Wyndham, linked the banking crisis to a rise in 'public clamour and distress' and to increased public resentment towards those who were perceived to be responsible.[11] The public was

20 Oct.(N.A., Irish correspondence 1697–1798, Ms 2446); Walpole to Mann, 13 Sept.,16 Oct. in W.S.Lewis et al., eds, *The correspondence of Horace Walpole* (48 vols,Yale, 1937–83), xxi, 328, 336; Forbes to Mitchell, 9 Oct. (B.L.,Add. Ms 6857 f 47v); Pitt to Beresford, 10 Oct. (B.L., Lansdowne Papers, Ms 1235 f 50); Lord Lieutenant's address, 29 Oct. 1759 (P.R.O., S.P.63/417). 8 Commons' and Lords' addresses, 30, 31 Oct. (P.R.O.,S.P., 63/417); Wyndham to Wyndham, 30 Oct., 25 Nov., 11 Dec. (B.L., O.C., Wyndham Letters, no 13); *Bedford Corres.*, ii, 386–91; Lady Llanover, ed., *The autobiography and correspondence of ... Mrs Delany* (3 vols, London, 1861), iii, 575; Malcomson, ed., *Irish official papers*, ii, 230; Caldwell to Shelburne, 29 Nov. (B.L., Kings Ms 439 ff 7–11); Bedford to Pitt, 30 Nov. (B.L.,Lansdowne Ms 1235 ff 56–8); *Universal Advertizer*, 27 Nov.; *F.D.J.*, 18 Dec. 1759. 9 L.M.Cullen, *An economic history of Ireland since 1660* (London, 1972), pp 68; P.A. Worthington, 'Dearth, death and disease: an analysis of mortality crises in five Lagan Valley parishes' (M.A. thesis, Q.U.B., 1991), pp 129–54; D- to Pitt, 12 Nov. 1759 (B.L., Mackintosh Collection, Add. Ms 34523 f 72). 10 Malcomson, ed., *Irish official papers*, ii, 230; Bedford to Pitt, 17 Nov. (B.L.,Lansdowne Ms 1235 f 55); Chief Baron Willes, Memorandum on debates ... 1759–60' (Warwickshire R.O., Willes papers, pp 12–18); Printed notice supporting banks, 5 Nov., Meeting of gentlemen, merchants etc at Tholsel, 8 Nov. (T.C.D., Crosbie Papers, Ms 3821/234–5); Wyndham to Wyndham, 15 Nov. 1759 (B.L.,O.C., Wyndham letters, No 14); *Bedford Corres.*, ii, 397; L.M. Cullen, *Anglo-Irish trade 1660–1800* (Manchester, 1968), p. 197. 11 Willes' Memorandum on debates ..., pp 14–18; Wyndham to Wyndham, 15 Nov. 1759

certainly more politically aware by the late 1750s than it had been even a decade
earlier. The challenge Charles Lucas posed the oligarchical elite that dominated
Dublin Corporation in the late 1740s and the efforts of the speaker, Henry Boyle, to
rally public opinion to his side during the money bill dispute had raised the political
consciousness of the Dublin crowd and the urban middle classes to new heights.[12]
Actions such as those undertaken in December 1753 when the 'mob' stopped coaches
in the street to compel the 'people [in them to] declare for England or Ireland' bear
witness to the fact that by the early 1750s, Protestant opinion perceived its identity
as having an Irish dimension.[13] But it is equally significant that it was in Britain that
most reference was made to Ireland's shaking off its 'dependency'. British politicians articulated alarmist fears that the money bill dispute was an act of 'direct
defiance of England' aimed ultimately at asserting the kingdom's independence,
though Henry Boyle expressly denied this was his object.[14] Boyle was responsible
for no resolutions asserting the aspiration of Ireland 'to shake off their dependency
upon' Britain because, like most Irish Protestants, Warden and Henry Flood included, this was not his object.[15]

Boyle's artful presentation of himself 'as the protector of the liberties of Ireland'
enabled him to survive the money bill dispute with his influence substantially intact. The fact that he could do so indicates that the most powerful politician in the
land did not regard office-holding and patriotism as incompatible. This is a matter
of central importance to an understanding of eighteenth-century patriotism, and
since this was the ideology to which Henry Flood subscribed, to an understanding
of his political career.

There was a strong and gathering current of opinion (as yet mainly articulated
by commentators and opinion makers) in the mid-eighteenth century which held
that it was impossible, given the corruption endemic in the political system, for a
genuine patriot to hold office. The implication – that patriotism implied 'constant
opposition to the measures of government' – was rejected by most practising politicians who were fully aware that office was the key to influence. In doing so, they

(B.L.,O.C., Wyndham letters, no 14); M.L. Legg, 'Money and reputation: the effects of the banking
crises of 1755 and 1760' in *Eighteenth-Century Ireland*, 11 (1996), pp 80–2.   12 David Dickson, *New
foundations: Ireland 1660–1800* (Dublin, 1987), pp 88–9; Sean Murphy, 'The Lucas affair' (M.A. thesis,
U.C.D. 1981), 192 ff; Jim Smyth, 'Dublin's political underground in the 1790s' in Gerard O'Brien, ed.,
Parliament, politics and people (Dublin, 1989), p. 131.   13 [ ] to Orrery, 19 Dec. 1753 (Harvard Univer-
sity Library, Orrery Papers); Thomas Bartlett, 'The Townshend viceroyalty 1767–72' (Ph.D. thesis,
Q.U.B., 1976), p. 13; [Malcomson], ed., *Irish official papers*, i, 88; *Bedford Corres.*, ii, 143.   14 Pelham to
Dorset, 28 Feb. 1754 in H.M.C., *Stopford Sackville*, p. 50; Rigby to Bedford, 25 Dec. 1753 in *Bedford
Corres*, ii, 143; Sir Dudley Ryder's diary, 13/4, 23 Jan. [1754], 3 Jan. 1755 (Harrowby Papers, P.R.O.N.I.,
T3228/1/62, 65, 68); Yorke, *The life and correspondence of Philip Yorke, Lord Chancellor Hardwicke* (3
vols, Cambridge, 1913), ii, 51–2; Malcomson, ed., *Official papers*, i, 81; Boyle to Gore, 27 Jan. (T.C.D.,
Arran Papers, Ms 7576); Sackville to [ ], ca 8 Nov.in H.M.C., *Stopford Sackville*, p. 49; [ ] to Orrery, 15
Dec. 1753 (Harvard University Library, Orrery Papers); Declan O'Donovan, 'The Money bill dispute
of 1753' (Ph.D. thesis, U.C.D., 1973).

were not being more venal than their better-known later eighteenth-century successors, just being more pragmatic. Space does not permit one to trace the application of the term 'patriot' from describing the 'commonwealthmen' who advocated a balanced constitution in the mid-seventeenth century to its embrace in the mid-eighteenth century by politicians who trumpeted their commitment to resisting the perversion of the system of limited constitutional monarchy inaugurated in 1688. In England, where this occurred, it resulted in the equation of a patriot with someone who opposed ministerial patronage, long parliaments, large standing armies and other potential threats to the successful operation of mixed government, but there was also another 'less politically partisan meaning' which defined a patriot as a 'good citizen' who was committed to the 'disinterested service' of his country.[16] In the Irish context, which is what primarily influenced Henry Flood's thinking, patriotism represented a tendency within the 'Protestant interest' that embraced both these points of view, since it defined political virtue, responsible parliamentary government, the economic betterment of the kingdom, and constitutional equality with Britain under the crown as its objects. It was, as Colin Kidd has argued, first and foremostly an 'emulative' identity, 'directed towards the replication of English freedoms in [a] "colonial" setting'; it was not in any respect proto-nationalist or ethnocentric for, as Henry Flood's career demonstrates, its adherents, in the main, possessed a deep and abiding reverence for England and for the English constitution.[17] Of course, the campaign by Irish Protestants to secure the same legal and constitutional rights as Englishmen did not commence in the eighteenth century. The 'Protestant interest' in Ireland was long exercised by the form of government most appropriate to its particular circumstances. The discourse on this subject in the mid-seventeenth century left an important legacy, but it was the contribution of William Molyneux, whose 1698 tract *The Case of Ireland ... stated* became the textbook of Irish political patriotism in the eighteenth century, that had the greater influence on Henry Flood.[18]

Molyneux was impelled to publish his famous text, in which he invoked Locke to affirm the desire of Irish Protestants to be afforded equal status with English-

15 *Bedford Corres.*, ii, 143; Sackville to Wilmot, 18 Dec. 1753 (Wilmot Papers, P.R.O.N.I., T3019/2227); Grandison to Villiers, 16, 31 Jan. 1754 (Villiers-Stuart Papers, P.R.O.N.I., T3131/D/6/2, 4); Countess of Cork and Orrery, ed., *The Orrery papers* (2 vols, London, 1903), ii, 8–11; Conway to Walpole, 8 May. 1755 in Lewis et al., eds, *Walpole Corres.*, xxxvii, 392–5. 16 J.R. Hill, *From patriots to unionists: Dublin civic politics and Irish Protestant patriotism 1660–1840* (Oxford, 1997), pp 10, 56–7; J.G. McCoy, 'Court ideology in mid-eighteenth century Ireland: an examination of political culture' (M.A., St Patrick's College, Maynooth, 1990), pp 95–6; J.G.A. Pococke, *The Machiavellian moment* (Princeton, 1975), pp 371–2; J.T. Leerssen, 'Anglo-Irish Patriotism and its European context: notes towards a reassessment', *Eighteenth-Century Ireland*, 3 (1988), pp 7–21. 17 Colin Kidd, 'North Britishness and the nature of eighteenth-century British patriotism' in *Historical Journal*, 39 (1996), pp 362, 378. 18 Aidan Clarke, 'Colonial constitutional attitudes in Ireland 1640–60', *R.I.A. proc.*, 90C (1990), pp 357–75; J.G. Simms, *Colonial nationalism 1698–1776* (Cork, 1976); Patrick Kelly, 'William Molyneux and the spirit of liberty in eighteenth-century Ireland', *Eighteenth-Century Ireland*, 3 (1988), pp 133–48.

men, by the readiness of the contemporary English parliament to confine Ireland's economic and constitutional freedoms. Indeed, like Molyneux, many contemporary Irish Protestants felt so aggrieved that they were being treated as subject colonists by those whom they regarded as their kinsmen that they concluded that a legislative union was the most likely way to ensure the constitutional and commercial equality with England they believed was also their birthright.[19] As this suggests, the agenda of Irish patriots at this time was essentially political and its focus Anglo-Irish relations, but the rage for party during Queen Anne's reign and the complex constitutional, judicial and economic problems that shaped political discourse in the 1720s and 1730s facilitated the elaboration of a more explicitly economic patriotism which emphasised domestic economic improvement.[20] This was not uninfluenced by contemporary developments in England, because it was during these years that the term 'patriot' became more popular in both kingdoms. More pertinently in terms of what it came to represent in Ireland, patriotism embraced a political programme which held not just that Ireland was entitled to equal treatment with England under the crown, but that this should occur in a context in which Ireland retained its own parliament, in which all averse discriminatory economic and constitutional regulations were repealed and due attention was devoted to fostering domestic economic development. The latter took the form of improving initiatives by landlords and organizations like the Dublin Society (of which Henry Flood became a member in 1775) and the Hibernian Society (in which, as we have seen, he was active for a time in the 1750s).[21] But patriotism also contributed to the acceleration in the volume of publications on Ireland past and present, and the foundation of bodies like the Physico-Historical Society (1744–52) which fostered such research, in which Flood was later to take a positive interest.[22]

Parallel with the elaboration of this broader definition of patriotism, the reflexive disposition of Irish politicians to attribute the kingdom's economic ills exclusively to the restrictions on its freedom to trade and, in particular, to the ban on woollen exports imposed in 1699 remained alive. Both Robert Deane of Dublin and

19 William Molyneux, *The case of Ireland ... stated*, ed., J.G. Simms (Dublin, 1977), *passim*; James Kelly, 'The origins of the Act of Union 1660–1800', *I.H.S.*, 25 (1987), pp 243–4.   20 Isolde Victory, 'Colonial nationalism in Ireland 1692–1725: from common law to natural right' (Ph.D. Thesis, T.C.D., 1984); James Kelly, 'Swift and the Irish economy in the 1720s', *Eighteenth-century Ireland*, 6 (1991), 7–36; Leerssen, 'Anglo-Irish patriotism', pp 10–11.   21 Above pp 35–7; *The royal charter of the Dublin Society to which are added the society's by-laws and ordinances* (Dublin, 1825), p. 59; Minutes of Royal Dublin Society 1775–91 (Royal Dublin Society); F.G. James, 'The Church of Ireland and the Patriot movement in the late eighteenth century', *Eire-Ireland*, 17 (1982), p. 47; Acheson to Dodington, 23 Oct. 1735, 2 Apr. 1737 in H.M.C., *Various collections, vi, Eyre Matcham papers*, pp 65–6; Grandison to Villiers, 21 Mar. 1754 (Villiers-Stuart Papers, T3131/D/6/11).   22 Ann de Valera, 'Antiquarian and historical investigation in Ireland in the eighteenth century', (M.A. thesis, U.C.D., 1978), pp 17–95; G.L. Herries-Davies, 'The Physico-Historical society', *Irish Geography*, 12 (1979) pp 92–8; J.C. Beckett, 'Literary life in eighteenth century Ireland' in S. Dyrvik, et al., eds, *The satellite states in the seventeenth and eighteenth centuries* (Bergen, 1979), p. 159.

contributors to the Historical Society, which Henry Flood may have attended while
a student at Trinity, expressed such opinions in the 1740s while acknowledging, at
the same time, that 'England is the centre of our gains and must ever be so'.[23] Inevitably, there was also continuing criticism of the restrictions on the Irish parliament's
freedom to legislate. The existence of Poynings' Law (1494), which gave the British
Privy Council the right to veto or to amend legislation ratified by the Irish parliament; the Declaratory Act (1719), which affirmed the primacy of the British parliament over that of Ireland and empowered the Westminster assembly to legislate for
Ireland if it saw fit; and the extensive recourse to patronage to ensure a secure working majority in the House of Commons and the Irish administration a strongly
Anglophile character provided continuing tangible evidence to Irish Protestants of
their dependent position. This was compounded by the condescension inherent in
English attitudes and actions, as observed by personalities as diverse as Mrs Delany
and Robert Deane, which increased the appeal of patriotism across the political
spectrum. As a result, the term 'patriot' figures more prominently in conversation
and discourse from the 1750s.[24]

   If the growing appeal of patriotism to which this attests can largely be accounted
for by the allure of a viewpoint which extolled good citizenship and fostered what
Bishop Berkeley termed 'public prosperity',[25] there was an overlapping constituency, which was more activated by the wish to attain the same constitutional rights
and privileges enjoyed by Englishmen, and which achieved voice by advancing criticisms of those aspects of government policy towards Ireland which deprived them
of these rights. This vexed supporters of English government in Ireland like Archbishop John Ryder of Tuam, who simplistically accused the 'patriots, as they call
themselves, [of doing] everything that can be done ... to irritate the people against
the government'.[26] This was unsustainable. But because the most articulate and
aspersive exponents of political patriotism were seen by supporters of the *status quo*
to encourage popular unruliness and anti-English sentiment, as well as to create
difficulties in the Commons, it is hardly surprising that those who shared Ryder's
outlook challenged their opponents' appropriation of the label, or countered with
the claim 'that government service is the epitome of patriotism'.[27]

23 L.M. Cullen, 'Economic development 1691–1750' in T.W. Moody and W.E. Vaughan, eds, *A new history of Ireland iv: eighteenth century Ireland 1691–1800* (Oxford, 1986), pp 138–9; Deane to Wood, 10 Sept. 1746 (B.L.,O.C., Deane Files); A.P.I. Samuels, *The early life, correspondence and writings of Edmund Burke* (Cambridge, 1923), pp 233–7, 251–2. 24 Delany to Dewes, 5 Nov. 1750 in Llanover, ed., *Delany Corres*, iii, 612; Deane to Wood, 10 Sept. 1746 (B.L.,O.C., Deane files); H.M.C., *Stopford-Sackville*, i, 52, 53, 55; Ryder to Ryder, 30 Nov. 1754, 20 May 1755 (Harrowby Papers, P.R.O.N.I., T3228/1/66, 69); Waite to Wilmot, 15 Mar. 1755 (Wilmot Papers, P.R.O.N.I., T3019/2529); Darnley to Crosbie, 1 Apr. 1755 (T.C.D., Crosbie Papers, Ms 3821/228); Henry to Archbishop of Canterbury, 13 May 1755 (B.L., Sloane Ms 4164 ff 23-5); Spencer to Price, 24 Jan. 1752 in H.M.C., *Puleston*, p. 339. 25 Leerssen, 'Anglo-Irish patriotism', p. 10. 26 Malcomson, ed., *Irish official papers*, ii, 54. 27 Ibid.; [Henry] to Canterbury, 20 Sept. 1755 (B.L., Sloane Ms 4164 f 31); McCoy, 'Court ideology', p. 95.

The emergence of a more vigorous, and as Lord Charlemont famously observed, more confident, patriot disposition in the 1750s combined with the failure of the attempt by the Lord Lieutenant, the duke of Bedford, in 1757–8 to free himself from 'party and faction' by constructing a 'broad bottom[ed] and balance[d]' administration placed greater pressure on Warden Flood, the Attorney General, and other officeholders who were expected to steer legislation through the Irish parliament.[28] Both he and Philip Tisdall, the Solicitor General, actively defended Bedford and his policies during the tough 1757–8 session.[29] That of 1759–60 was less demanding in this respect, with the result that Henry Flood had little opportunity to observe his father in the House of Commons following his election. However, the public mood was, if anything, more volatile as he was to learn two days after he took his seat when the populace rose in protest against a rumoured plan to bring about the union of the British and Irish legislatures.

The 1759 anti-union riots were a product of a conjuncture of factors which convinced the Dublin 'crowd' that a legislative union was in contemplation. One of these was the placement in the late summer by an enterprising London publisher of an advertisement in the Dublin press for Malachy Postlethwayt's *Britain's commercial interest*, a two-volume analysis of British trade first published in London in 1757, in which the author argued that a 'proper union' with Ireland would enhance Britain's prospects of success in the ongoing struggle for dominance with France.[30] This prompted an anxious debate in Ireland, but it was not until MPs assembled in parliament that the public felt any reason to conclude that this was more than the controversial opinion of an economic commentator. On 7 November, the Chief Secretary, Richard Rigby, sought and was given leave to introduce the heads of a bill to permit the convening of the Irish parliament at fourteen days' notice. This was prompted by concern over French military intentions, and since it was only marginally different to a similar provision in the British mutiny bill of 1756, it met with no resistance in the House of Commons.[31] Public opinion was less equanimous, however, and

28 H.M.C.,*Charlemont*, i, 6–7; A.T.Q. Stewart, *A deeper silence: the hidden origins of the United Irishmen* (London, 1993), pp 33–4; 'A short sketch of the political history of Ireland' (N.L.I., Joly Ms 29 ff 36–8); Fitzgerald, ed., *Leinster Corres.*, i, 34–6; Kildare to Fox, 3 Nov. 1757 (B.L., Holland House Papers, Add. Ms 51426 ff 129–31); Willes' 'Legal and political reminiscences', pp 9–13 (Warwickshire R.O.); Burns, *Irish parliamentary politics*, ii, 227–49; *Bedford Corres.*, ii, 287–98; Malcomson, ed., *Irish official papers*, ii, 178; Bedford to Pitt, 17 Nov. 1757 (B.L., Lansdowne Abstracts, Add. Ms 24137).   29 Willes' legal and political reminiscences, pp 9–13 (Warwickshire R.O., Willes Papers); Bedford to Pitt, 17 Nov. 1757 in *Bedford Corres.*, ii, 287–98.   30 Kelly, 'Origins of the Act of Union', pp 246–7, 249; Sean Murphy, 'The Dublin anti-union riot of 3 December 1759' in O'Brien, ed., *Parliament, politics and people*, p. 52; Malachy Postlethwayt, *Britain's commercial interest explained and improved ... also the great advantage which would accrue to this kingdom from an union with Ireland* (2 vols, London, 1757), i, 61–5, 268–393; *Universal Advertizer*, 21 July, 4, 7 Aug. 1759.   31 Kelly, 'Origins of the Act of Union', p. 247; *Universal Advertizer*, 27 Nov., 14 Dec. 1759.

the rumour was spread that this bill was intended to destroy the constitution of Ireland, that a parliament might be pack'd by surprise, who might consent to an union w[i]th England, [and] that no more parliam[en]ts w[ou]ld be held in Ireland etc etc. This rumour (however groundless) occasioned a great ferment. 'Twas s[ai]d this mo[tion] was only a prelude to an union and that certain of the members w[ou]ld be p[art] of the English parliam[ent].[32]

As a consequence, when the heads of Rigby's bill came up for discussion on 22 November, 'a riotous mob', estimated at about a thousand, 'assembled ... at the door of the parliament house' and 'mightily insulted the known courtiers, affronted those whom they suspected to be so, strictly examined all the members and erected a gallows and swore destruction to Mr Rigby ... and to the Provost of the College who, the mob thought, were the origins of the scheme'.[33] There is no evidence to suggest that Flood was among the MPs targeted by the crowd on this occasion, or what he thought of their intervention, but he was to have greater cause for concern two weeks later when the crowd rose again.

Though the crowd was persuaded to disperse on 22 November by the early adjournment of parliament, and by assurances from the Speaker that there was no plan to introduce a union and from Richard Rigby that he would withdraw his controversial bill, public unease was not allayed. Dublin remained undisturbed in late November, but when MPs reconvened on 3 December, a crowd variously estimated at between three and ten thousand, marched from Weavers' Square in the earl of Meath's Liberty to the houses of parliament. Their emotions stoked by fiery speeches, the assembled throng invaded the houses of parliament and promptly insulted the dignity of both by putting a blacksmith on the speaker's chair in the Commons and 'an old woman' in the chair in the Lords. They also compelled every parliamentarian they encountered to swear 'a solemn obligation never to consent to an union'. According to reports, the Lord Chancellor, John Bowes, the Chief Justice of the King's Bench, St George Caulfeild and the Solicitor General, Philip Tisdall, were among the nearly fifty members of both houses who were compelled 'to take an illegal oath by a mob administered'. They might have fared worse. A number of peers and commoners (including some 'English bishops', the postmaster general Sir Thomas Prendergast and Hercules Langford Rowley, the MP for County Londonderry) were assaulted.[34] But, most perturbingly for Henry Flood, his father was

32 Willes' 'Memorandum on debates', p. 3.   33 Wyndham to Wyndham, 25 Nov. (B.L.,O.C., Wyndham letters, no 15); Murphy, 'Anti-union riot', pp 53–4; Delany to Dewes, 24 Nov. in *Delany corres.*, iii, 577; Ryder to Ryder, 7 Dec. 1759 (Harrowby Papers, T3228/2/4).   34 Willes' 'Memorandum on debates', pp 4–5; 'A short sketch of the political history of Ireland' (N.L.I., Joly Ms 29 f 39); Wyndham to Wyndham, 4 Dec.(B.L.,O.C., Wyndham letters, no. 16); Ryder to Ryder, 7 Dec. (Harrowby Papers, P.R.O.N.I., T3228/2/4); Bedford to Pitt, 5 Dec. (B.L., Lansdowne Ms 1235 ff 58–60); B.M. to Seagrave, 11 Dec. 1759 in C.W. Seagrave, *The Seagrave family* (London, [1936]), pp 164–5; Murphy, 'Anti-union riot', pp 54–5; Grey to Wharton, 23 Jan. 1760 in Paget Toynbee and Leonard Whibley, eds, *Correspondence of*

set upon in his coach, which was 'cut to pieces, the harness thereof demolished, his wig destroyed, himself beat very well with good Irish cudgels ... [and] obliged to swear on a book that he would be true to his country and suffer no union'. He was not seriously hurt, but it was a poor reflection on the dignity of the law and of parliament that the Attorney General should be subject to such abuse, and that he should be compelled to abandon his coach and to take refuge in Trinity College.[35]

As with the earlier riot, there is no record how Warden or Henry Flood responded to these events, but it is hardly insignificant that it was the Solicitor rather than the Attorney General who took charge of the investigation that followed. Henry may not have shared the general readiness to attribute the episode to the machinations of 'papists and French emissaries',[36] but it is unlikely that the episode aroused doubts in his mind about the propriety of his decision to align himself with the Castle interest in the House of Commons. As the son of the administration's leading law officer in that chamber, this was expected, but it was his inclination in any case and his family biographer is incorrect therefore to state that 'he took his seat on the opposition side' from the moment he entered the House of Commons. MPs possessed considerable freedom as to how they conducted themselves, but Henry's later statement that he 'voted more often with than against the secretary of the day' during his early years in parliament indicates that he did not become an MP with opposition in mind.[37] In the light of this, his decision to concentrate on 'the forms and orders of proceeding in the house' was logical as well as perspicacious. 'He attended the house diligently every day, but resolved not to speak there during that entire session, wishing to observe the manner and powers of the members'. There was much to learn, but he 'studied the journals indefatigably, till he became a perfect master of parliamentary order'; he read Shakespeare, and translated Demosthenes (his favourite author), Aschines and Cicero 'with uncommon diligence' in order 'to embellish his style' and he 'practised speaking prepared and *ex tempore* speeches' with his brother Jocelyn.[38]

While Flood schooled himself in the arts of oratory, Dublin Castle took advantage of its commanding majority (described with only slight exaggeration by Henry Penruddocke Wyndham as 'more than five to one'), and the patriotic mood engendered by renewed fears of a French invasion to press ahead with its legislative pro-

Thomas Gray (3 vols, Oxford, 1935), ii, 657–9; Bowes to Secker, 6 Dec. 1759 (Lambeth Palace Library, Secker Papers, vol 2 f 210). I wish to thank Dr M.L. Legg for the latter reference.   35 Seagrave, *The Seagrave family*, p. 164; Rigby to Pitt, 5 Dec. 1759 in W.S. Taylor and J.H. Pringle, eds, *The correspondence of William Pitt, Earl of Chatham* (4 vols, London, 1838–40), i, 469–70.   36 Pitt to Bedford and reply, 20, 25 Dec. 1759 (B.L., Lansdowne Ms 1235 ff 60–4); *Bedford corres.*, ii, p. xxviii; Bedford to Pitt and reply, 16, 19 Feb. 1760 (P.R.O., S.P.,63/418).   37 Flood, *Memoirs*, p. 17; S.A. Cummins, 'Opposition and the Irish parliament 1754–71' (M.A. thesis, St Patrick's College, Maynooth, 1978), p. 114.   38 Flood, *Memoirs*, pp 4, 17–18; *Gentleman's Magazine*, 16 (1791), p. 1225; Rosse Papers, C/12/1.

gramme.[39] Circumstances were unconducive to opposition activity, but the egregious John Hely-Hutchinson, whose career intersects with Flood's at so many points, determined this was an ideal opportunity for him to showcase his talents. Like Flood, Hely-Hutchinson was a new figure on the political horizon; he had secured the return for Lanesborough in January 1759 but, unlike Flood, who was anxious to be seen to behave in a principled manner, Hely-Hutchinson's lodestone was preferment and with this in mind he calculated that a commanding performance on the opposition benches represented the shortest route to lucrative office. Indeed, he was the dominant opposition MP during the 1759–60 session – as is borne out by the fact that he was a teller in no less than eight of the nine divisions that the opposition pressed in November and December 1759. As a result, he attracted the notice he craved.[40]

Hutchinson's emergence was seen by some to signal the eclipse of Edmond Sexten Pery as the leading spokesman of the independent interest in the House of Commons. During the mid-1750s, Pery had virtually single-handedly agitated the issues – an abatement in the pension list, curtailing the expenditure of public money on 'jobbs', the inauguration of a regime of greater fiscal responsibility and accountability, annual rather than biannual parliaments, the development of the economy, the ratification of a *habeas corpus* act and the amendment of Poynings's Law – that were central to patriot concerns during the next three decades. As a result, he was regarded in some quarters as the embodiment of the 'new' patriot opposition.[41] The fact that he declined the prime serjeancy in the spring of 1759 only enhanced his credibility and popularity, until Hely-Hutchinson set about stealing his thunder.[42] It is not clear why Pery allowed this, but it may reflect his conclusion that active opposition served no purpose given the current Commons' alignment. His reserve certainly suggested that opposition offered little to a new MP like Flood whose background linked him with the Castle rather than with the opposition.

This was a matter of comfort for the Bedford administration which concentrated its energies in the winter of 1759–60 on a vain attempt to identify those responsible for the anti-union riots and to making contingency arrangements to safe-

---

39 Wyndham to Wyndham, 15 Nov. 1759 (B.L.,O.C., Wyndham letters, no. 14). According to chief Baron Willes the opposition could rely on no more than 20 to 25 votes (Willes, 'Memorandum on debates', p. 1). The divisions of November/December listed in Cummins ('Opposition and the Irish parliament', p. 54) show that the opposition never divided more than 41; Burns, *Irish parliamentary politics*, ii, 262–6. 40 Burns, *Irish parliamentary politics*, ii, 266–7, 317; Willes, 'Memorandum on debates', pp 1–2, 34–9; Cummins, 'Opposition and the Irish parliament', pp 52–4, 64, 187–8; Bowes to Dodington, [Dec. 1759] in H.M.C., *Reports on various collections, vi: Eyre Matcham Mss*, p. 71. 41 A.P.W. Malcomson, 'Speaker Pery and the Pery papers', *N.M.A.J.*, 16 (1973–4), pp 46, 48; Conway to Wilmot, 26, 29 Oct., 3 Nov. 1755, 29 Apr. 1756, Hartington to Wilmot, 11 Nov.(Wilmot Papers, P.R.O.N.I., T3019/2696, 2698, 2705, 2809, /6457/428); Ryder to Ryder, 15 Dec. 1755 (Harrowby Papers, P.R.O.N.I., T3228/1/73); Willes' 'Legal and political reminiscences', p. 8; *Ossory letters*, ii, 129–30; H.M.C., *Emly*, i, 174–88; Pery to Chatham, 20 Dec., Sackville to Pery, 29 Dec. 1757 (Emly (Pery) Papers, P.R.O.N.I., T3087/1/15).

guard the country against invasion. Bedford's principal Irish adviser and the 'usefullest servant the Crown has in the House of Commons' was not Warden Flood, though this was a role filled by a succession of attorneys general, but his friend and successor as solicitor general, Philip Tisdall. Indeed, Warden Flood appears to have been content to cede the limelight as he did not take a prominent part either when news reached Dublin on Friday 22 February, that Francois Thurot, the intrepid French privateer, and three shiploads of men had captured Carrickfergus.[43]

Thurot's invasion was brief and unsuccessful, and it had the positive consequence for the Irish administration of ensuring that opposition to their request for an extraordinary subsidy to fund further expensive additions to the army melted away and that the session was brought to an early and successful conclusion.[44] From Bedford's vantage point, this was a fitting end to a successful session, but there were others, like Lord Chancellor Bowes, who felt that 'the old machine [the undertaker system] by which the country was governed as a province' was 'almost destroyed' and that it had either to be 'restored or another formed' if political stability was to be ensured.[45] In fact, 'the old machine' was more robust than Bowes appreciated. At the same time, rising pride in what Henry Penruddocke Wyndham termed 'being an Irishman' and the identification of a definable programme of reform by the patriots in the House of Commons, indicated that they also had grounds for confidence in the future.[46] Their prospects were considerably enhanced by the acquisition in the early 1760s of a number of new recruits, of whom Henry Flood proved the most able. First, there was a general election to be fought.

THE 1761 GENERAL ELECTION AND ITS AFTERMATH

Coming so soon after the alarm caused by Thurot's occupation of Carrickfergus, the death, in October 1760, of George II prompted an emotional outpouring of monarchist sentiment from Protestant Ireland. In common with so many of his background, Henry Flood was a willing participant. He joined with a group of

---

42 Sackville to Pery, 24 Mar. 1758, Rigby to Andrews, 31 Mar. (Emly (Pery) Papers, P.R.O.N.I., T3087/ 1/15, 16); Pery to Bedford, 24 Mar. 1759 (Bedford Papers, P.R.O.N.I., T2915/7/28); Malcomson, ed., *Irish official papers*, ii, 218, 222; Malcomson, 'Speaker Pery', p. 54, note 43.   43 Malcomson, ed., *Irish official papers*, ii, 233; Willes' 'Memorandum on debates', pp 46–59; Burns, *Irish parliamentary politics*, ii, 282–5; P.R.O., S.P., 63/418 *passim*.   44 Burns, *Irish parliamentary politics*, ii, 284–5; 'News from Dublin', 5 Feb. in C. Giblin, ed., 'Catalogue of Nunziatura di Fiandra, pt 6', *Collectanea Hibernica*, x (1969), p. 119; Rigby to Wilmot, 27 Feb. 1760 (Wilmot Papers, P.R.O.N.I., T3019/6762/ 592).   45 Bowes to Dodington, 17 Apr.in H.M.C., *Eyre Matcham Mss*, p. 75; see also Kingsbury to Price, 22 May 1760 in H.M.C., *Puleston Mss*, p. 339.   46 *F.D.J.*, 24 June 1758; Wyndham to Wyndham, 30 Oct. 1759 (B.L.,O.C., Wyndham letters, no 13); 'News from Dublin', 8 Feb. 1760 in Giblin, ed., 'Nunziatura de Fiandra, part 6', pp 118–19; Walpole to Montagu, 2 Jan. 1762 in Lewis et al., eds, *Walpole Corres.*, x, 1.

more than a hundred peers and eminent commoners who put their name to a declaration of loyalty and obedience to his successor, George III, on 1 November.[47]

The demise of the monarch meant not just a new king but a new parliament, which was a matter of transcending consequence for Flood, as it was for all politicians, because George III was a young man and the absence of legislation providing for the dissolution of the Irish parliament at regular intervals implied the election would determine the character of representation in the kingdom for the duration of his reign. This was an unwelcome prospect for the small number of political radicals like Charles Lucas whose object was to make the representative system more responsive to public opinion, and they made it a central issue in their electoral campaign. As the prospective head of a family caught up in an increasingly tense struggle to control a parliamentary borough, a beneficiary of the support of major interests in County Kilkenny in 1759 and the son of a major officeholder, Flood showed no enthusiasm for constitutional innovation. In this, he was typical of a majority of parliamentary candidates who eagerly concluded private bargains to share and apportion representation in open county as well as closed borough constituencies.[48]

General election fever hit the country in the late autumn of 1760. In the absence of the duke of Bedford, who had returned to his seat at Woburn, the lords justice nominated to oversee the administration of the kingdom observed the 'fermentation' which the impending election prompted with unease. Their wish was to minimise the 'animosities, ... idleness and riot' which the election promised to engender if it was not 'began and ended as soon as possible' and, with this in mind, they advised Bedford to dissolve the existing parliament before Christmas because this would permit election writs to be distributed before 12 February and the election to be held within the terms of the current sheriffs.[49] Bedford was disposed to concur, but before he could act he had first to revolve a dispute over the application of Poynings' Law.[50] This was precipitated by the failure of the Irish Privy Council to observe the custom and practice of transmitting a money bill with the selection of bills it was obliged, by Poynings' Law, to submit to the British Privy Council to provide the king with due cause to authorise the convening of an Irish parliament. The Lords Justice justified their action on the grounds that because they were not specifically enjoined to include a money bill in the transmiss, it was unwise to do so when it was bound to create difficulties with MPs who were ultra-sensitive to any trespass upon their power to inaugurate money bills.

As the son of a privy councillor who was scrupulous in his attention to his duties

---

47 *Universal Advertizer*, 4 Nov. 1760.   48 *Universal Advertizer*, 1 Nov.; Charlemont to [Brownlow], 30 Oct. 1760 in H.M.C., *Charlemont*, i, 63.   49 *Bedford Corres.*, ii, 421–3; Chester to Bowen, 29 Nov. 1760 in E.A.McLysaght. ed., 'Reports on private collections: the Bowen papers', *Analecta Hibernica*, xv (1944), p. 17.   50 *Universal Advertizer*, 13 Dec. 1760; Malcomson, ed., *Irish official papers*, ii, 252–3.

on the Council Board,[51] it is reasonable to assume that Henry Flood was better informed on this constitutional controversy than most. His attitude is unrecorded, but the dispute offered him a vivid illustration of the reality of the subordination of the Irish legislature to the Privy Council on both sides of the Irish Sea, and it can be suggested, based on his later opinions, that he did not much like what he saw. Ideally for the harmonious operation of the Anglo-Irish connection, the difference should have been resolved expeditiously; but neither the cabinet nor the Privy Council in London was prepared to make any gesture to mollify Irish feelings. They regarded the action as a barefaced attempt to assert the independency of the Irish parliament and they expressed their strong wish that customary practice was followed without deviation. With such an important constitutional issue at stake, positions quickly hardened, and with this went all hopes of an early general election.[52] Meanwhile electioneering proceeded as if nothing was amiss. Debate was at its most vibrant in the constituency of Dublin city where Charles Lucas was a candidate, and where the contest threw up several political issues that were to feature prominently on the reformist agenda pursued by Flood in the 1760s.

Lucas conducted the early stages of his election campaign from England lest he was prosecuted under the outlawry proceedings that had obliged him to flee Ireland in 1749. He advertised his candidature with a series of pamphlets and addresses in which he offered himself to the 'free and independent electors of the city' as an 'HONEST NATIONAL REPRESENTATIVE' committed to the cause of 'reviv[ing] your expiring body politic'. This could only be achieved, he argued, if the political system was reformed, and one of the most urgent matters in need of reformation was the duration of parliaments. Lucas made no attempt to conceal his dismay at the prospect of 'another long reign with such a stupid, corrupt and perennial parliament as the last' because another such experience would, he warned his (and Flood's) friend Lord Charlemont, who facilitated his return to Ireland in March 1761, 'prepare the people for any yoke'. Few were quite so apocalyptic, but meetings of freemen and freeholders convened in Dublin in November and December 1760 to endorse his candidature gave rise to a campaign to invite electoral candidates to commit themselves publicly to support a septennial bill and, if returned, to vote against 'any money bill of longer duration than six months' until legislation was ratified limiting the Irish parliament to between six and eight years.[53]

---

51 This conclusion is based on his attendance in 1762–64 at the meetings of the Council to consider Irish bills prior to their transmission to the British Council (P.R.O., P.C.1/7/15, 17, 68, 75, 77–8, 80, 82–4, 87–8). 52 'A short sketch of the political history of Ireland' (N.L.I., Joly Ms 29 ff 39–40); Lord Justice to [Bedford], 23 Nov., 27 Dec. 1760 (N.A., Irish Correspondence, 1697–1798, Ms 2446); P.D. Brown and K.W. Schweizer, eds, 'The Devonshire diary', *Camden*, 4th series, 27 (1982), pp 61–2; Malcomson, ed., *Irish official papers*, ii, 63, 250–65. 53 Murphy, 'The Lucas affair', pp 226–7; *Universal Advertizer*, 1, 29 Nov, 9, 16 Dec; Lucas to Charlemont, 22 Nov. in H.M.C.,*Charlemont*, i, 265–6; Chester to Bowen, 11 Nov. 1760 in McLysaght, ed., 'Reports on private collections', p. 27.

The central contention of those who advocated parliamentary reform was that they wanted to restore the constitution to its original purity. In order to achieve this, septennial parliaments (which were the norm in England) were deemed essential. So too was the curtailment of the capacity of the executive to grant places, pensions and peerages to secure the allegiance of MPs because the unrestricted use of patronage paved the way for the exercise of arbitrary power which, some maintained, ministers were intent on advancing though the country groaned 'under the complicated evils of oligarchy and aristocracy'.[54] However, this trend could be reversed, reformers contended, if, as well as the above, limits were placed on the power of the crown to raise and dispose of revenue, and the constitutional initiative was fixed, where it belonged, in the House of Commons.[55] It is difficult to measure the appeal of these arguments, but the efforts of commercial and mercantile interests, and of the guilds in particular, to advance them were not unimpressive. They also paved the way for the foundation of groups like the Patriot Club and the Society of Free Citizens who urged a similar programme of reform.[56] Their emergence may not have made a significant mark on the composition of the House of Commons in 1761, but they certainly helped give parliamentary reform a national profile as it drew support from candidates in counties Dublin, Armagh, Westmeath, Antrim and Meath.[57]

Henry Flood was not among their number. As a recently elected representative for a large county constituency, George II's death came before he had an opportunity to build a support base among a sufficiency of freeholders to be perceived as a strong candidate. His fate was sealed when it emerged that the Agars and the Ponsonbys both intended nominating leading family members. Flood's disappointment in County Kilkenny was softened by his success at Callan, but the fact that he only secured this seat after a second poll meant he missed much of the 1761–2 parliamentary session.[58] As a result, he found, when he finally took his place in the House of Commons in January 1762, that he did not figure in the calculations either of the administration or of the enlarged and invigorated patriot interest.

Guided by Edmond Sexten Pery, Charles Lucas, Lucius O'Brien, MP for Ennis, and William Brownlow, MP for County Armagh (John Hely-Hutchinson had defected to the Castle in return for a promise of the prime serjeancy and an additional salary of £500[59]), the opposition's attacks on the Privy Council money bill, the pen-

---

54 *The Corke Journal*, Mar.-Apr. 1762.   55 Cummins, 'Opposition and the Irish parliament', pp 129–38; R.B.McDowell, 'Colonial nationalism and the winning of parliamentary independence, 1760-82' in Moody and Vaughan, eds, *A new history of Ireland iv*, pp 197-8.   56 *F.J.*, 4, 18 Oct., 1763; *Public Gazetteer*, 22 Dec. 1761.   57 *Universal Advertizer*, 6, 16, 20 Dec. 1760; *Dublin Gazette*, 1 Jan. 1761; James Kelly, 'Parliamentary reform in Irish politics 1760-90', in David Dickson, et al., eds, *The United Irishmen* (Dublin, 1993), p. 75; Chester to Bowen, 11, 29 Nov. 1760 in McLysaght, ed., 'Reports in private collections', p. 27.   58 Above pp 45–6.   59 Stone to Hely-Hutchinson, 3 Sept. in H.M.C., *Donoughmore Mss.*, pp 231–2; Halifax to Egremont, 16 Nov. (P.R.O., S.P., 63/ 419); Hertford to Walpole, 14 Dec. 1761 in Lewis et al., eds, *Walpole Corres.*, xxxviii, 147–50.

sion list, and their advocacy of legislation to limit the duration of parliaments to seven years caused the administration more than a few anxious moments in 1761.[60] However, the Castle profited from the eagerness of MPs to rally to the aid of the crown following Spain's decision to join France in the Seven Years War in December 1761, and it was this, and not Chief Secretary William Gerard Hamilton's oratorical skill (as is so often claimed) that ensured the Irish parliament's ready approval for the administration's request for extra funds to finance the addition of five battalions of troops to the Irish army establishment.[61] Flood was as caught up by this mood as everybody else, because in January 1762 he accepted a captain's commission in a regiment Lieutenant-Colonel James Gisborne undertook to raise to aid in the defence of the country.[62] It is unlikely that Flood or the regiment, if it ever came into being, saw service, but his readiness to partake in the defence of the kingdom reinforces his later contention that his disposition during the 1761–2 session was to support the administration.

The excitement engendered by the entry of Spain into the Seven Years War and the consequent extension of the embargo on Irish exports, enlivened what had, by the end of 1761, become a tame session.[63] Had he been present, Flood might have felt obliged to contribute to the debate on the pension list initiated early in the session by the opposition since his father was promoted to the chief justiceship of the Court of King's Bench by the duke of Bedford, whose ready resort to patronage so angered the patriots, but he offered no public comment on the matter then or following his swearing in.[64] However, he had discovered the power of oratory. According to Lawrence Parsons 'the ... speaker that seems to have raised Mr Flood's ambition most at this time, and gave him the highest idea of the power of eloquence, was Mr Gerard Hamilton'. Hamilton was not a ready speaker, but he prepared so meticulously for those rare occasions when he addressed the Commons that he generally 'produced an astounding sensation'. This encouraged Flood, though the absence of reference to him in the reports sent from Dublin Castle to London and the fact that he was not invited to any of the *soirées* of MPs hosted at Dublin Castle by Lord Halifax indicates that he remained an unknown quantity.[65] At the same time,

60 P.R.O., S.P., 63/418–9 *passim*; Fragments of a journal by Lord Halifax, 4, 19 Nov. 1761 (N.L.I., Ms 8064/7); Murphy, 'The Lucas affair', pp 227–8; Lucas to Halifax, 19 Sept. (N.A., Calendar of miscellaneous letters and papers 1760–89, f 2); *Public Gazetteer*, 22 Dec. 1761.   61 Halifax to Egremont, 18 Dec. 1761, 16, 28 Jan. 1762, Egremont to Halifax, 26 Dec., Rothes to Hamilton, 15 Dec. 1761 (P.R.O., S.P., 63/419); Horace Walpole, *Memoirs of the reign of George III* (4 vols, London, 1894), i, 111–12; Joel Gold, 'In defence of single-speech Hamilton', *Studies in Burke and his times*, x (1968–9), pp 1144–9; Montagu to Walpole, 6 Feb. 1762 in Lewis, et als, eds, *Walpole Corres*, x, 8; H.M.C., *Charlemont*, i, 18. 62 Halifax to Egremont, 16 Jan. 1762 (P.R.O.,S.P.,63/421 ff 15–9).   63 Egremont to Halifax, 5 Feb. 12 Mar., Halifax to Egremont, 15 Feb.1762 (P.R.O., S.P., 63/421).   64 Gore to Hely-Hutchinson, 20 Mar. (T.C.D., Donoughmore Papers, C/3/6); Stone to Pery, 21 Mar. 1761(P.R.O.N.I., Emly (Pery) Papers, T3087/1/21); Yorke, *Hardwicke*, ii, 51–2.   65 Parsons biography of Flood (Rosse Papers, C/12/1); A list of the Lords and Commons etc who have dined with Lord Halifax, Oct. 1761–February 1762 (N.L.I., Ms 1467).

the elevation of his father to the bench allowed him increasing freedom of action and, extrapolating from his subsequent behaviour, it is clear that the energy and arguments marshalled by patriots like Edmond Sexten Pery weighed more heavily with him than his father's obligations to Dublin Castle.

Pery resumed his place as the dominant opposition figure in the House of Commons in 1761–2. Though described by one observer as 'a nervous reasoner', he was the *de facto* leading spokesman of the 'flying squadron' – a connection of patriot and independent-minded MPs that voted according to issues and that was not averse to supporting measures sponsored by the administration when they perceived merit in them.[66] The precise composition of this 'squadron' is unclear, but there is no evidence that Flood joined it at any point in the 1761–2 session though the issues he addressed in his maiden and subsequent speeches reflected patriot concerns. According to one of the few reliable insights we possess into his political behaviour at this time, the first 'important point ... he attempted to effect in parliament' appertained to Poynings' Law which, he alleged, was misconstrued to permit the Irish Privy Council 'interfere with' the legislative deliberations of the Irish parliament. Subsequently, he 'addressed the house [of Commons] from the opposition side on the national embarrassments' and discommoded the Primate with 'the poignancy of his sarcasm'.[67] It is not possible to amplify these sketchy reports, but the fact that, on the latter occasion, Flood spoke from the 'opposition benches' indicates that he was no longer a Castle loyalist by the end of the 1761–2 session. At the same time he was not a reliable patriot either. He was still finding his way, and building up confidence as he went, because as well as the oratorical skills he learned from observing the likes of W. G. Hamilton and Edmond Pery at College Green, Lord Chatham and Charles Townshend at Westminster and actors at the theatre, he also developed his voice. According to Lawrence Parsons:

He ... overcame by great application the deficiency of his voice, for though it continued deep and a little too nasal, it had surprising flexibility and uncommon strength and energy. His modulation, when he declaimed, was exquisitely beautiful and captivating, and by such delicate strokes as our great actors are distinguished by, he used to produce extraordinary effects.

He spoke with what was deemed a 'provincial accent' when he argued, but 'this disappeared when he declaimed; for then his tones were those of the best public speakers and tragedians' he had studied.[68]

---

66 Henry MacDougall, *Sketches of Irish political characters* (Dublin, 1799), p. 72; Flood, *Memoirs*, p. 66; Curran, *Life of Curran*, i, 155–6; *Public Gazetteer*, 7 Feb. 1761. 67 *Gentleman's Magazine*, 61 (1791), p. 1225; Flood, *Memoirs*, p. 20. 68 Parsons' biography of Flood (Rosse Papers, C/12/1); Moira to Huntingdon, 26 Jan. 1765 in H.M.C., *Hastings*, iii, 144.

These qualities were to be fully revealed when the Irish parliament reconvened in October 1763. In the meantime, Flood had matters other than politics on his mind for in the late spring of 1762 he married Lady Frances Beresford.

MARRIAGE

The history of Flood's relationship with Frances Maria Beresford, the seventh daughter of Marcus, earl of Tyrone, and the sister of George the second earl, is one of the most obscure aspects of his often tenebrous biography. Frances Beresford was born in either August or September 1731 which meant that she was a year older than the man who was to become her husband.[69] When or how they became acquainted is unknown, but their attachment did not win the approval of Lady Frances' parents for she and Flood were married in a private ceremony on 13 April 1762 without their prior consent or a marriage settlement.[70] It is understandable that the Beresfords should have entertained reservations about the connection; Henry Flood's illegitimacy hardly qualified him as an eligible partner for the daughter of an earl. The Floods, by contrast, had less grounds for unease, and there is no evidence to suggest that they were other than pleased. Marriage into a noble family palliated the stigma caused by Henry's extra-marital birth by linking him and them with one of the most powerful families in the kingdom.

If the surreptitious marriage ceremony was unusual, the two families reconciled themselves to the event with commendable rapidity. The only exception was Lady Tyrone who, according to one source, displayed her displeasure with the union by refusing to call on Isabella Flood. This was a pointer to the ill-feeling that later developed between the Floods and the Beresfords but, in the short term, emotions were kept in check by the readiness of the couple's fathers to agree a marriage settlement. As befitted the daughter of an earl, Lady Frances was well provided for. Some estimates put her marriage portion as high as £10,000, which was the sum the earl of Tyrone agreed should be charged on his Cavan and Derry lands to provide for his 'younger children' in 1726, whereas the actual sum was £4,000 less. Six thousand pounds was more than adequate to secure Lady Frances against financial worry for life. However, though the earl of Tyrone authorized the payment of £4,000 to the young couple on 14 May, neither Henry nor his wife gained access to the money because they promptly 'assigned' it (minus minor transaction costs) to Warden Flood who had it earmarked for another purpose.[71]

69 Pedigree of Sir Frederick Flood (G.O.,Ms 112 f 30); Burtchaell, *Kilkenny members*, p. 151.   70 Notes on Flood v Flood, p. 2; *Public Gazetteer*, 20 Apr. 1762; Hayes and Jones, *Reports of cases*, p. xxi.   71 James Prior, *Life of Edmond Malone* (London, 1860), p. 102; Memorials of deeds, 15 May 1762, 28 Jan. 1769 (Registry of Deeds, 214/595/142635, 258/456/174146); Copy of public bill in case of Wallis v Flood, 20 Feb. 1778 (N.L.I., Inchiquin Papers, no. 2951).

Stimulated by the marriage of Henry and Frances and by his own increasing age, Warden Flood chose this moment to settle his affairs. To this end, he executed a settlement in May 1762 vesting the fee simple lands he possessed in County Kilkenny, which produced an annual rental of £3,000, in trustees and allocated them to his own use for life, subject to an annuity of £600 to be paid to Henry and an annuity, by way of a jointure, also of £600 to be paid to Lady Frances with a remainder to Henry for his life. This was unusual. Warden had been bequeathed the same lands by his father in fee, but because Henry was not his *legal* heir, Warden had no option but to inaugurate such an arrangement to protect his son from predatory relatives by awarding him a life interest only. However, anticipating that a regular and legal succession would be established during Henry's lifetime, Warden directed that the lands should be granted in tail male to Henry's first or other sons or, in their absence, to his own 'right heirs'. Warden's own 'right heir' was his second son, Jocelyn, who, possibly to draw attention away from what was being proposed in Henry's case, was to inherit on the same basis should Henry die heirless. These terms were reiterated by Warden in his will two months later. With Henry provided for and the destiny of the patrimonial estate mapped out, Warden availed of the 'full [and] absolute power of disposing' of Lady Frances' portion to provide for Isabella, his daughter; £2,000 was allocated towards financing her immediate needs and £4,000 reserved 'for her sole and specific use'. Jocelyn, who was currently at Westminster school, was bequeathed the house and lands at Marsdale.[72]

Though well-intentioned, Warden Flood's settlement and will were to cause much ill-feeling within the Flood family. Henry's possession of the Farmley estate was sufficiently secure to ensure him against legal challenge during his lifetime, but his moral authority was so compromised in the eyes of his relations that it led to complications over his sister's will in the 1770s and his own in the 1790s. Warden's inventiveness may also have contributed to the animus that came to characterise relations between the Floods and the Beresfords, despite Lawrence Parsons' suggestion that their differences were political.[73]

Following his marriage and the decision of his father to grant him a life interest in the lands there, Henry Flood made Farmley his home. It was a modest house compared with the palatial residences of some Irish grandees, but despite this and his primarily urban upbringing Henry took to rural life. He did not, at the same time, ape the lifestyle of a rural squire. He staged amateur dramatics, and occupied himself translating the classics and composing lyrical poetry. He also maintained an active interest in politics, proving that the concern voiced by some of the Beresfords that he might forsake politics following his marriage was very wide of the mark.[74]

72 Deed of trust, 14 and 15 May 1762 (Registry of Deeds, 214/592/142634); Hayes and Jones, *Reports on cases*, appendix pp xxi-ii, xxiv-v; O'Hanlon, 'Testamentary records ...', p. 142; Public bill ... Wallis v Flood, 1778 (N.L.I., Inchiquin Papers, no. 2951); Notes on Flood v Flood, p. 3. 73 Rosse Papers, C/12/1; Beresford to Allan, 27 Apr.1778 in *Beresford Corres.*, i, 30. 74 Below pp 171–8; Rosse Papers, C/12/1; Flood, *Memoirs*, pp 21–2, 23–5, 199–200; *F.L.J.*, 14 Apr. 1770.

THE 1763-4 SESSION

Flood's marriage to Lady Frances Beresford opened up to him the option of joining the Beresford 'political party' in the House of Commons. Given their fundamentally different political trajectories and attitudes in later decades, it is tempting to dismiss the wish of at least some of the Beresfords that this might take place as mere fantasy. However, in the early and mid-1760s, both Flood and the Beresford interest were sufficiently flexible politically to allow the contemplation of co-operation to take place. Indeed, according to Lawrence Parsons, 'a political party composed of [Henry] and Warden Flood, his cousin, and the Beresfords' was established, but 'it was of short duration' as unbridgeable differences emerged between Flood and Lord Tyrone.[75]

As the very brief existence of this 'political party' intimates, Flood was temperamentally as well as attitudinally too independent to subordinate his freedom of action for any length of time to the will of a group. It is instructive that, unlike most Protestants in Munster and south Leinster, he did not believe that the peasant agrarian movement, the Whiteboys, which was at its peak in this region in 1762–3, were Jacobites instigated by French *agents provocateur*.[76] This did not cause any ripples since members of the Flood family participated actively in the prosecution of Whiteboys in County Kilkenny, but his disinclination to co-operate with others inevitably became a matter of greater consequence when he pushed himself to the fore in the House of Commons.

The Lord Lieutenant in charge of the administration of Ireland when Flood embraced an active independent-patriot stance in 1763 was Hugh, earl of Northumberland. He was wrongly perceived in some quarters to be 'weak' and entirely subordinate to his Chief Secretary, William Gerard Hamilton, who retained the chief secretaryship.[77] Hamilton was a self-interested schemer, and he found an Irish soulmate in John Hely-Hutchinson, who encouraged him in his endeavour to weaken the patriots in the House of Commons by bringing its leading performer, Edmond Sexten Pery, over to the administration in the summer of 1762.[78] Pery was too canny a politician to become enmeshed in Hamilton's web. He was committed to opposing for another session, and he was to find an able ally in Henry Flood who had concluded that the independent patriot stand taken by the likes of Pery, Lucas, Lucius

75 Rosse Papers, C/12/1.   76 Halifax to Egremont, 13, 17 Apr. (P.R.O., S.P., 63/421); Seymour to Mitchell, 23 Apr. 1762 (B.L., Mitchell Papers, Add. Ms 6839 ff 244–5); Flood's speech, Oct. 1765 (Rosse Papers, F/21).   77 Halifax to Egremont, 13 Apr. 1762 (P.R.O., S.P.63/421); O'Hara to Burke, 26 July in Hoffman, ed., *Edmund Burke*, pp 311–12; Walpole to Montagu, 14 Apr. in Lewis, et al., eds, *Walpole Corres.*, x, 65; Romney Sedgwick, ed., *Letters from George III to Lord Bute* (London, 1939), pp 221–2; Kildare to Holland, 26 Apr. (B.L., Holland House Papers, Add. Ms 51426 f 194); Northumberland to Lords Justice 28 Apr. 1763 (N.A., Irish correspondence 1697–1798, Ms 2446).   78 Hamilton to Hely-Hutchinson, 26 June, 11 Nov., 4 Dec. in H.M.C., *Donoughmore*, pp 232, 240–2; Hamilton to Pery, 16 Aug. 1762 in H.M.C., *Emly*, p. 189.

O'Brien[79] and others was right for him. For Flood, as for all inexperienced politicians, this was not without risk, but he rose triumphantly to the challenge. Before the year was out he and Lady Frances were guests of the Lord Lieutenant at Dublin Castle.[80] Northumberland may have calculated, given his father's position and his broad support for the Castle during his first four years in parliament, that Flood could be won over, but having decided to take up the standard of opposition, Flood was to demonstrate that he was less amenable than Hely-Hutchinson to official blandishment.

The independent interest in the House of Commons to which Flood gravitated was better circumstanced to make an impression in 1763–4 than it had been for some time. Part of the reason for this was the failure of the Castle's attempts to fortify its own ranks by recruiting Pery and two other key opposition figures – Lord Charlemont and Sir William Osborne. But the galvanizing impact of the newly formed *Freeman's Journal*, which embraced the patriot slogans of virtue and liberty, and which strongly advocated septennial legislation and the curtailment of the power of the Castle to distribute a sufficiency of 'posts and pensions ... so as to have always a majority in each house under the absolute direction of the prime minister' was also significant.[81] Given that the conventions of opposition demanded that the agitation of an individual issue was left to the MP who was most closely identified with it, and septennial legislation was Charles Lucas' preserve, ministerial patronage provided Flood with his most obvious target. It was an opportune moment for him to take up the issue because the Irish civil list had grown by £17,000 in the first three years of the reign of George III. The earl of Halifax had made fewer nominations than the duke of Bedford, but his recommendation that W.G. Hamilton should be made chancellor of the exchequer by patent rather than 'during King's pleasure' provoked disquiet.[82] In an attempt to deflect criticism, the Prime Minister, George Grenville, authorised Northumberland to inform the 'principal members' of parliament that the King would grant no further 'places and pensions for lives or years on this kingdom', but though the Lord Lieutenant was convinced initially that this assurance 'made the most favourable impression upon the minds of all disinterested people', Flood and others were unimpressed. They determined to avail of every opportunity the session offered to draw attention to the corruption they believed lay at the heart of government.[83]

---

79 O'Brien to O'Brien, 21 Oct. 1761 in Ainsworth, ed., *Inchiquin Mss*, p. 224.   80 A list of Lords and commons who have dined with the Lord Lieutenant in 1762–3 (N.L.I., Ms 1468).   81 H.M.C., *Charlemont*, i, 142–3; Northumberland to Halifax, 13 Oct. in *C.H.O.P.*, i, 314–5; Grenville to Northumberland, 22 Sept. in W.J. Smith, ed., *The Grenville Papers* (4 vols, London, 1852–3), ii, 126–8; *F.J.*, 10, 13, 20, 24, Sept., 8, 18, 22 Oct. 1763.   82 Yorke, *Hardwicke*, iii, 378 note 4; P.R.O., S.P., 63/421 *passim*; Lords Justice to Northumberland, 6, 24 May, Tisdall and Gore to Lords Justice, 5 May, Northumberland to Lords Justice, 17 May (N.A., Irish Correspondence 1697–1798, Ms 2446).   83 Grenville to Northumberland, 22 Sept. in *Grenville Papers*, ii, 126–8; Northumberland to Grenville, 3 Oct. 1763 in J.R.G. Tomlinson, ed., *Additional Grenville papers 1763–5* (Manchester, 1962), pp 48–9.

Northumberland opened the 1763–4 parliamentary session on 11 October with
a king's speech which, despite its conciliatory tone, provided Flood, Pery and the
other patriots with an ideal opportunity to press for a reduction of the bloated pension list. The Lord Lieutenant expressed his wish that MPs would take advantage of
the conclusion of hostilities with France to reduce public expenditure but did not
refer specifically to patronage,[84] so when the House was debating its response to the
address on the following day, Edmond Pery drew attention to the absence of any
disapprobation of the size of the pension list in the draft under discussion, and
recommended the incorporation of a declaration that was 'definite and certain'.
This suggestion was greeted with scorn by the supporters of the administration
who accused him of fomenting 'distrust' of the crown. But it won the support of
Henry Flood, who endorsed Pery's call in a hardhitting speech in which he made it
clear that as far as he was concerned the only honourable course open to an MP was
opposition to the government of the day.[85]

As this suggests, Flood's first major recorded speech was both a personal testament and a political statement; it represented an affirmation by him that his decision to align himself with the independents and patriots in the Commons was
prompted by motives which were principled and proper:

> It is a melancholy reflection that those who distinguish themselves by their in-
> dependence, disinterestedness and public spirit, those who make the advantage
> of their country their only object, are too often branded by the name of *faction*,
> and under that opprobrious appellation held forth to public obloquy and re-
> proach, merely because they will not concur with the mean, interested and self-
> ish views of those who implicitly adopt the measures of a court ... Those are
> certainly a faction, in this sense, who unite upon any selfish or contracted views
> against the public or general interest, whether they are many or few; those who
> insidiously endeavour to extend the prerogative under the specious pretence of
> supporting it, those who encourage the exercise of unconstitutional power, as-
> sumed by a minister under the colour of strengthening the hands of govern-
> ment, and those who concur in the distribution of pecuniary gratification to
> individuals, at the expence of the nation as a compliment to royal munificence,
> those and those alone deserve to be stigmatized by the name of *faction*.

If this was combative, it palled when compared with his withering condemnation of
'the narrow minded, selfish court sycophant, who in the wickedness of his folly
sacrifices the many for the few ... and ... involves those for whom he is willing to
betray his country in the ruin which his treachery is bringing upon it'. Such people,

---

84 James Caldwell, *Debates relative to the affairs of Ireland in the years 1763 and 1764* (2 vols, London,
1766), i, 1–6; *F.J.*, 15 Oct. 1763.   85 Caldwell, *Debates*, i, 23.

he maintained, were 'vermaine' basking in the 'court sunshine' who would be swept away once 'virtue and wisdom' triumphed, and he urged to MPs to hasten the day because it was in their country's interest that they did so:

> It behoves those who are not yet circumscribed by the enchanted circle, those who have still the use of unperverted reason, and who still estimate the blessings of life by their just value to exert themselves in behalf of their native country and like its Guardian angel "to watch over it for good".

With this powerful appeal, Flood approached the end of his first speech of the 1763–4 session. It was a bold and confident contribution, and he brought it to an appropriate close with a motion requesting that the 'proper officer do attend and inform this house, whether any patents, granting pensions at will ... are enrolled'.[86]

Though he did not mention him by name, Flood's object was to prepare the way for a parliamentary debate on the appointment of W.G. Hamilton as Chancellor of the Exchequer. Anxious to protect the Chief Secretary, the Speaker, John Ponsonby, attempted to prevent the motion being put on a technicality, but he was over-ruled by a majority of MPs and it was approved.[87] This was a most encouraging outcome for Flood and, indeed, for the other independents in the Commons. They cannot have anticipated a victory on such a sensitive issue so early in the session, though motions critical of increases in expenditure on patronage had succeeded in the past. The administration, for its part, made light of the outcome. In his report to London, Northumberland simply described the 'question concerning pensions' as a traditional 'subject of opposition to discontented people'. He was, with good reason, more perturbed by his failure to perpetuate the arrangement, initiated by the duke of Bedford (and continued by the earl of Halifax), by which the Castle assured itself of a strong working majority in the Commons by drawing on the combined interests of Primate Stone, Lord Shannon and Speaker Ponsonby. Both the Primate and Lord Shannon had offered their support, but the Speaker, who did not wish to be seen to support the administration because of the opposition of 'his connexion in England' to the Grenville ministry, was less forthcoming.[88] This problem defied early resolution, and caused the Lord Lieutenant to request permission from London to signify *publicly* that it was the King's intention that 'no [future] grants either of offices or pensions for lives or for years should be made upon the establishment of Ireland, unless upon the most extraordinary occasions'. London was unhappy with this, but Northumberland persisted on the grounds that it would help his administration as well as ease his difficulties on the pensions issue.[89]

---

86 Caldwell, *Debates*, i, 30–7.   87 Caldwell, *Debates*, i, 37–8; Cummins, 'Opposition and the Irish parliament', p. 197.   88 Northumberland to Stone, 18 July, Northumberland to Shannon, 4 Aug. (Alnwick Papers, P.R.O.N.I., T2872/8, 17); Northumberland to Halifax, 13 Oct. 1763 in *C.H.O.P.*, i, 314–5; McDowell, 'Colonial nationalism', pp 198–9.   89 Northumberland to Halifax, 20 Oct., Halifax to

While Dublin Castle contrived to devise a strategy to negate Flood's and Pery's attempts to curtail its freedom to bestow patronage, it also kept a wary eye on the opposition's enthusiasm for legislation to limit the duration of parliament. As he had done during the 1761–2 session, Charles Lucas moved and was given permission to prepare the heads of a bill to this effect.[90] This was anticipated; what was unexpected was the instruction that Henry Flood should assist him since Flood had given no public signal to date that he supported septennial legislation.

Flood and Lucas were under no pressure to draft a septennial bill quickly as the business of the House of Commons between mid-October and late-December was primarily taken up with patronage and financial matters. Because of our dependence on the parliamentary record for information on the way the opposition conducted itself, it is hazardous to comment in detail on their *modus operandi*, but the visibly inchoate manner with which individual MPs pursued issues throughout October and November indicates that there was nothing of the nature of a formal structure and little by way of pre-planning or co-operation involved. This suited Flood, who found the cutting and trimming such engagement involved uncongenial. Moreover, he had every reason not to want to leave things as they were since most of what the opposition attempted on the subject of patronage flowed from his motion of 12 October. Thus on 27 October, John Eyre, the MP for Galway, secured approval for the publication of a list of the pensions on both the civil and military establishments. On the following day, Anthony Malone, who had been dismissed as Chancellor of the Exchequer in controversial circumstances in 1761, queried why the 'inrollments of the patents' called for by Flood earlier in the session had not appeared and, when he did not secure the desired response, raised the political temperature on the matter by claiming that recent appointments by patent were illegal and by requesting all the rolls of appointment 'from the Revolution'.[91] And on the 29th, Flood himself opposed a motion that the House should adjourn early on the grounds that an assembly which met for only six months every two years could not afford to lose a day's debate when 'very interesting and important questions concerning the pensions' remained unresolved.[92]

Flood's intervention on this occasion did not prevent an adjournment, but these contributions, and others in early November by Richard Cox on the fees paid to vice-treasurers and by Charles Lucas on the appointment to the exchequer, secured the opposition information which Castle officials had hoped not to make public.[93] The patriots were unable to make any impression on budgetary and other issues, but despite this the Castle was ill-at-ease and, on 8 November, in response to fur-

Northumberland, 27 Oct.(P.R.O., S.P., 63/422, *C.H.O.P.*, i, 318–9); Northumberland to Grenville, 20 Oct., Halifax to Grenville, 20, 22 Oct. 1763 in Tomlinson, ed., *Additional Grenville papers*, pp 56–7, *C.H.O.P.*, i, 317.   90 Cavendish to Wilmot, 18 Oct. 1763 (P.R.O.N.I., Chatsworth Papers, T3158/1651).   91 Caldwell, *Debates*, i, 86–107; Cavendish to Wilmot, 18 Oct. 1763 (P.R.O.N.I., Chatsworth Papers, T3158/1651).   92 Caldwell, *Debates*, i, 109–10.   93 Caldwell, *Debates*, i, 147–61, 167–83.

ther forceful criticism of the cost of the pension list, the Attorney General, Philip Tisdall, announced that George III had determined not to grant further pensions upon the Irish establishment for life or years 'except upon very extraordinary occasions'.[94]

This was a morale-boosting announcement for the patriots, and for Flood in particular, and his value to them was highlighted further on 9 November during the debate on a proposal by John Fitzgibbon, the MP for Newcastle, that the House of Commons should prepare an address to the King on the size of the national debt and the legality of expending so large a sum on the pension list. This proposition elicited a number of diverse contributions, but when discussion came to focus on the royal prerogative, upon which the motion was deemed to trespass, the Castle interest gained the initiative. Indeed, the debate appeared to be running away from the opposition when Henry Flood took the floor and advanced a coherent case for referring the matter to the courts for adjudication. In debating terms, this was a more impressive performance than his speech in support of his motion on 12 October because it was an *ex tempore* contribution to an evolving discussion. What Flood manifested on 8 November was that he possessed the facility to isolate the key points in a debate and the confidence to respond skilfully on his feet to an unfolding argument.[95] His verbal address was insufficient to win approval for Fitzgibbon's motion, but it consolidated his claim to be regarded, with Edmond Sexten Pery, Charles Lucas and Fitzgibbon as one of the handful of truly formidable independent voices in the House of Commons. Moreover, the fact that the opposition mustered 75 votes (as against the administration's 114) in the division that concluded the debate encouraged them to persist with their anti-patronage campaign. Flood seems to have had reservations about the wisdom of this because he left the running to others. It is not clear if he did so because he could see no advantage in pursuing the issue further at this time but he was correct if this was so. Motions by Pery and Richard Longfield on 16 November to initiate further inquiries disquieted Lord Northumberland, but he successfully appealed to the King's commitment not to increase the pension list to neutralise his critics.[96]

The seventy-eight votes cast against the administration on 11 November represented the optimum achieved by the opposition during the 1763–4 session. By then, Flood's focus had shifted to financial matters. Both Edmond Pery, who had sharply criticised the prodigality of 'public money' on 'jobbs' in early November, and Robert French, who maintained the size and expense of the army was 'extremely dangerous

94 Caldwell, *Debates*, i, 186–206.   95 Caldwell, *Debates*, i, 206–58; Northumberland to Halifax, 8, 10 Nov. 1763 (P.R.O., S.P.63/422, *C.H.O.P.*, i, 322–4).   96 Caldwell, *Debates*, i, 266–7, 273–91, 321–44; Waite to [ ], 10 Nov. (P.R.O., S.P.,63/422 ff 105–7); Northumberland to Halifax, 10 Nov. in *C.H.O.P.*, i, 323–4; Northumberland to Halifax, 12, 17 Nov. (Alnwick Papers, P.R.O.N.I., T2872/36); Division list for 16 Nov. (P.R.O., S.P., 63/422 f 167); Northumberland to Grenville, 8 Nov. 1763 in Tomlinson, ed., *Additional Grenville papers*, pp 65–7; Cummins, 'Opposition and the Irish parliament', pp 201–2.

to the constitution' on 12 November, had identified two possible targets. But it was not until 19 November when debate commenced in the committee of supply, and Flood joined with Pery in challenging the administration's economic policies, that opposition MPs offered a sustained critique of the national debt. Pery took the lead. He graphically highlighted the deterioration in the kingdom's finances by comparing the current national debt of £520,000 with the situation in the late 1740s, when the treasury ran a surplus, and cited the augmented pension and secret service lists, 'new and useless employments' and their associated salaries, absenteeism, a decline in revenue and the increased army establishment as the cause.[97] Most of these were sufficiently well-known patriot targets not to generate surprise or excitement. More significantly, Pery's critical allusion to the army establishment gave Chief Secretary Hamilton an ideal opportunity to seize the high ground and he availed of the opportunity to affirm that defence expenditure was proportionate to what was spent in England. This was the cue for Flood to enter the debate. He was eloquently dismissive of Hamilton's attempt to analogise the Irish military establishment with that of England – 'the most flourishing and most opulent nation under heaven' – and sought to refocus discussion on the size and cost of the Irish army establishment. What he said was in keeping with traditional patriot thinking on large standing armies, but he gave it an Irish twist by alleging the excessive size of the Irish army establishment was a direct result of the Castle's dependence on patronage to govern the country.[98] This was hardly sustainable, but it is a measure of Flood's rising reputation that his observations attracted hostile replies from a number of military men which he dealt with in an assured and confident manner. He also convincingly repulsed John Hely-Hutchinson's attempt to shift the focus of debate away from the army and pension list by attributing Ireland's financial problems to the consumption of foreign imports, by reminding his audience of the poverty and 'real grievances' of the five-sixths of the three million people he estimated lived in the country. These were not sentiments MPs were used to hearing in the Commons' chamber, and they may have contributed to the loss, by 122 votes to 74, of Pery's motion urging fiscal restraint.[99] However, the debate further illustrated Flood's prodigious facility as an *ex tempore* speaker. It also demonstrated that his opinions on many issues were intrinsically more radical than those of most of his parliamentary colleagues – a point emphasised five days later when the cost of the pensions paid to foreigners to the Irish exchequer was the subject of discussion.

Flood felt strongly about the size of the pension list and, on 24 November, when Pery's proposal that the Commons inform the King that the kingdom could not afford 'the great and continual increase of pensions' met with querulous objections from supporters of the administration, he rounded on its critics. Angry and disap-

97 Caldwell, *Debates*, i, 362–76.   98 Caldwell *Debates*, i, 377–92; Cummins, 'Opposition in the Irish parliament', p. 202.   99 Caldwell, *Debates*, i, 392–400.

pointed by what he defined as the inexplicable readiness of a majority of MPs 'quietly and tamely to acquiesce in a grievance without complaint' he accused them of being immobilized by 'slavish fear', and importuned them not to

> sink into voluntary slavery, by a supine timidity that will render us contemptible even to our tyrants and odious to the magnanimous nation which gloriously maintains that independence and freedom, that honour, and those privileges of which we seem not to know the value.

Given the sensitivity of the guardians of the Anglo-Irish nexus to any observations that reflected negatively on the British connection, it was not a surprise that these and other remarks about the country being reduced to abject 'slavery' by 'British tyrants' provoked an outcry. The Solicitor General, John Gore, was so disturbed he interposed to reprove him for uttering 'improper remarks ... most fatal to us and most injurious to Great Britain'. Flood was unrepentant, and when he continued in the same vein, he was interrupted again, this time by the Attorney General. Still Flood refused to alter his tone. Indeed, he warned his auditors defiantly that by the yardsticks of 'public liberty and national independence'

> a silent and implicit acquiescence in the grievance, which is universally allowed to accrue from pensions, is a prostitution of our character and a breach of our trust; an injury to the public, a dishonour to the King, and a disadvantage to *Great Britain*.

These defiant remarks consolidated Flood's growing reputation as the most assertive patriot voice in the House of Commons, but his outspokenness and independence troubled many on the opposition as well as government benches. Edmond Sexten Pery, for instance, had virtually as much cause as Castle officials to be displeased with Flood's behaviour on 24 November because he refused to support his motion on the grounds that it would not have any impact, and that the King's promise not to increase the pension list except in 'extraordinary circumstances' rendered it redundant.[100]

As this indicates, the patriot MPs in the House of Commons in 1763 were far from united tactically. Had they concerted their policies and co-ordinated their tactics, they may well have exerted greater impact because they were more than a match intellectually for the administration's spokesmen in the House of Commons. However, they continued to cut across each other. Thus less than two weeks after Flood's refusal to support Pery's motion on 24 November, Lucas and Pery clashed on the provision of a subsidy for a granary, while others waxed hot and cold on Lucas's bill to exclude civil and military office holders from sitting in parliament.[101]

100 Caldwell, *Debates*, ii, 497–510.   101 Caldwell, *Debates*, ii, 555.

As matters stood at the end of November 1763, the administration was content to allow opposition MPs an occasional triumph on minor matters such as Flood's motion of 28 November against requests for financial support for 'private undertakings', so long as the supply and money bills were not endangered.[102] The mounting confidence to which this gave rise in Castle circles contrasted with the growing discontent of the opposition. But if this contributed to their inability to produce more than fifty in Commons' divisions in December, it also worked to Flood's advantage because he was seen by many to articulate a purer vision of patriotism than Pery.[103] This was highlighted publicly on 13 December when Pery appealed once more to the House to address the King on the need to curtail the military establishment and the pension list. Flood endorsed the suggestion and proposed that a committee of the whole house be established to draw up such an address. Pery agreed, but Sir William Osborne, the MP for Carysfort, an able man and 'a distinguished speaker' who was disinclined to act 'in concert with anyone' and who had recently been flirting with the Castle, was unimpressed. Because Pery had supported an application for public funding for the construction of a granary and the enhancement of the navigation of the river Shannon, Osborne accused him of inconsistency; he was, he sneered, a 'mock patriot' motivated by 'self-interest' when compared with Flood:

> Steadiness and uniformity of conduct give a sanction to his [Flood's] proposals and a confidence in his professions. Uniformity of conduct is a proof of integrity, and there is no reason to suspect him of prostituting his parts to private purposes, under the specious appearance of patriotism and public spirit, who steadily opposes the destructive projects of jobbers and the friends of jobbers, whether they affect in general to show their oratory for the court or against it.

Flood may well have found these comments gratifying, but this does not obscure the fact that they were rhapsodic and invidious. Moreover, they diminished rather than improved the chances of the two proposals before the house being received. The result, when it was announced, was decisive. Flood's motion was defeated by 126 to 54 votes, and Pery's by 139 votes to 43. Too much ought not to be read into the difference in these divisions, but when taken in tandem with Osborne's hyperbole, it does suggest that before the end of 1763 there were perhaps ten MPs who believed Flood possessed a stronger claim than Pery to be regarded as the leading patriot in the House of Commons.[104]

102 Northumberland to Halifax, 23, 24, 28 Nov. (P.R.O., S.P. 63/422, *C.H.O.P.*, i, 329, 331); Halifax to Northumberland, 26 Nov. 1763 in *C.H.O.P.*, i, 330; Caldwell, *Debates*, ii, 522, 528–46; see also Poutt to Arran, 7 Jan.1764 (T.C.D., Arran Papers, Ms 7576). 103 Northumberland to Grenville, 20 Dec. in Tomlinson, ed., *Additional Grenville papers*, pp 72–4; Northumberland to Halifax, 8 Dec. 1763 in *C.H.O.P.*, i, 334; Caldwell, *Debates*, i, 345, 364–6, 417–9; Malcomson, ed., *Irish official papers*, ii, 64; Cummins, 'Opposition in the Irish parliament', p. 201. 104 Caldwell, *Debates*, ii, 577–604; Northumberland to

Flood certainly did nothing to dissuade them on 20 December when the House debated a proposal from Lord Sudley, MP for County Wexford, for a loyal address to George III in which MPs avowed their 'duty and loyalty to the best of sovereigns' for the successful conclusion to the Seven Years War and their 'utter abhorrence and detestation of the late seditious and treasonable libels maliciously' propagated by John Wilkes, the English radical. This proposition was positively received by most MPs but Pery and Flood were ill-at-ease. Both found reason to criticise what the former termed a 'most dishonourable and disadvantageous peace', but Flood was also opposed to the attempt to align the House of Commons with those who were persecuting Wilkes. He was, as this suggests, better disposed than most of those present towards Wilkes' wish to reform the representative system, and follow-ing hostile remarks by William Henry Fortescue on the danger to stable govern-ment posed by 'popular factions', he offered a stout defence of the participation of the public in political life: 'It was from the voice of the people, he said, that he and every gentleman in that House derived their legislative capacity, and their constitu-ents had an undoubted right to their attention'. Indeed, he continued, attention to the 'complaints ... and ... grievances' of the people was the essence of good govern-ment because it prevented 'licentiousness and riot', whereas the enforcement of

> bad measures ... was the worst of tyrannys, for ... nothing could more radically strike at the natural rights of mankind than first to oppress them, then by refus-ing to redress their grievances [to] compel them to attempt redressing them-selves, and finally making that attempt a pretence of subjecting them to new exile under the specious profession of punishing a seditious and turbulent spirit'.[105]

Flood's preparedness to articulate such advanced views on the relationship of government and people placed him firmly among the select number of liberal voices in the Irish House of Commons who identified their cause with that of Wilkes. Flood's attitude was almost certainly influenced by the supportive coverage accorded the 'Wilkes affair' in the Irish liberal press. However, antipathy in official circles to Wilkes' efforts to commit the Crown and the English political establishment to ac-cept his election for Middlesex ran deep in Ireland as well as Britain. This was emphasized on 3 February 1764 when William Henry Fortescue alleged that Sir Arthur Brooke, the M.P. for County Fermanagh, had been libelled by Peter Wilson, the editor of the *Dublin Magazine*, because Wilson had connected him in a *jeu d'esprit* with Wilkes' controversial *North Briton*. Determined to make an example of Wilson for what was, he contended, a grave insult, Fortescue moved that he should be taken

---

Halifax, 13 Dec. 1763 (Alnwick Papers, P.R.O.N.I., T2872/40).   **105** Caldwell, *Debates*, ii, 606–45; Northumberland to Halifax, 20, 22 Dec. 1763 in *C.H.O.P.*, i, 337–8.

into custody by the sergeant at arms for a breach of parliamentary privilege. The weight of parliamentary opinion supported the motion despite Pery's caution against infracting the freedom of the press, and Wilson was about to be consigned to an open term in Newgate prison when Flood called on MPs to reconsider. He initially contended that MPs should do so on the grounds that the punishment did not fit the crime, but when this did not produce the desired response, he switched his focus to the actions of the printer, and he was able by this means, as Anthony Malone acknowledged, to present Wilson's libel in a less serious light and, thereby, to have his sentence commuted to a week's incarceration.[106]

'The fire and imagination' Henry Flood demonstrated during the Wilson libel debate proved to be his last major contribution of the 1763–4 session. We know he also spoke during the debate on John Monk Mason's bill to empower 'papists to lend money on the mortgages of real estates' on 3 February, but there is no record of what he said. However, since he voted against the bill it is clear that he was unimpressed by the arguments of its supporters that it would make money in Catholic possession available to Protestants and give Catholics a stake in the maintenance of 'stable and orderly government' in the country. The worry of the bill's opponents was that it would strengthen the Catholic interest, and it was this that led the patriot MP for County Wexford, Thomas Le Hunte, who was at one with Flood in criticising the pension list, to offer a spirited defence of the penal laws. Flood was not as strident as Le Hunte on the Catholic question, but he was also not as accommodating as patriots like Pery and Robert French or courtiers like Philip Tisdall who had no difficulty with such a modest proposal for Catholic relief, and he was relieved when the measure was comprehensively defeated by 138 votes to 53.[107]

If the absence of any record of Flood's speech on Catholic relief in 1764 is disappointing, the lack of any contribution by him to the debates on the bill to limit the duration of parliaments which Lucas and he were instructed to draft in October is puzzling. This bill wound its way slowly through its various stages in the House of Commons in February where it was changed from a septennial to a decennial bill before it was finally respited by the Irish Privy Council. This was not an unexpected outcome given the antipathy of most privy councillors to the idea, but Flood's silence is curious, particularly as he was already being described in some quarters as 'the first speaker in the House'.[108] Perhaps he was at odds with the irascible Lucas,

---

106 *F.J.*, 20 Dec. 1763, 24 Mar.; Caldwell, *Debates*, ii, 673–700; Northumberland to Halifax, 8 Feb. 1764 (P.R.O., S.P.63/423). 107 Caldwell, *Debates*, ii, 511–15; John P. Day, 'The Catholic question in the Irish parliament 1760-82' (M.A. thesis, U.C.D., 1973), pp 59–64; Matthew O'Connor, *The history of the Irish Catholics from the settlement in 1691* (Dublin, 1813), pp 303–10; Lane to Barker, 4 Feb. (T.C.D., Barker-Ponsonby Papers, P1/9/20); Northumberland to Halifax, 8 Feb. 1764 (P.R.O., S.P.63/423). 108 Martin to Wynne, 10 Feb., 22 Mar. (N.L.I., Wynne Papers, Ms 22252/2,3); Caldwell, *Debates*, ii, 705, 709–13, 718–30; Lane to Barker, 7 Feb. (T.C.D., Barker Ponsonby Papers, P1/9/21); Northumberland to Halifax, 8, 11, 24, 28 Feb. 10 Mar. (P.R.O., S.P.63/423, *C.H.O.P.*, i, 387-8, 390-91, 393); [Chester] to [Bowen], 11 Feb. 1764 in *Analecta Hibernica.*, 15 (1944), p. 28.

but it is possible also that he simply was not in attendance. What is clear is that whereas Pery, O'Brien, Lucas and a number of other opposition stalwarts soldiered on as the session drew to its prolonged and uneventful close, Flood was not to be heard.[109]

If Flood had withdrawn from the House of Commons before the session was over, which is likely, he did so in the knowledge that it had been a triumph for him personally and a watershed in his public life. Before the session commenced, he was a little known backbencher more inclined to vote with the administration than against it; on its conclusion he was heralded as one of the most combative and talented patriot voices of his generation. Towards the end of March 1764, the one time chief secretary, Richard Rigby, queried of Edmond Sexten Pery 'how much above par patriotism' ended the session.[110] There is no record of Pery's reply; but if he did respond he ought to have mentioned that he now had a serious rival for the accolade of the leading patriot voice in the House of Commons, and that that was Henry Flood.

THE HERTFORD ADMINISTRATION

Flood spent the summer of 1764 in England from where he returned in late August.[111] During the months he was away, Irish politics slipped into the lull that was a feature of the intervals between parliamentary sessions. The duke of Northumberland did, it is true, replace his Chief Secretary W.G. Hamilton, with whom he did not get along, with the Irish peer, Lord Drogheda.[112] But neither this, the sympathetic coverage in the liberal press of John Wilkes' trials and tribulations, nor the suggestion emanating from the Grand Jury of County Tipperary that all masshouses should be closed by proclamation in those areas prone to Whiteboyism disrupted the essential calm that prevailed.[113] The kingdom was administered quietly and capably by the Lords Justice (Shannon, Stone and Ponsonby) until late 1764 when Stone and Shannon died. This intensified speculation as to who would wield the reins of power in Ireland since it was already common knowledge that the popular Northumberland would not be returning.[114] Lord Hertford, who had canvassed for the position in 1761, was widely perceived as his most likely successor, but a number

---

109 Northumberland to Grenville, 2 Mar. in *Grenville papers*, ii, 275.   110 Rigby to Pery, 25 Mar. 1764 (Emly (Pery) Papers, P.R.O.N.I., T3087/1/32).   111 *F.J.*, 28 Aug. 1764.   112 Lewis et al., eds, *Walpole Corres.*, xxxviii, 235; Hamilton to Oswald, 5 Dec. 1763, 10, 11 Jan. 1764 in *Memorials of the public life of James Oswald* (Edinburgh, 1825), pp 450–75.   113 Northumberland to Lords Justice and reply, 22, 29 May, 25 Aug. 1764 (N.A., Irish Correspondence 1697–1798, Ms 2446); P.R.O., S.P., 63/423 *passim*; *F.J.*, 21 Aug. 1764; Cummins, 'Opposition and the Irish parliament', pp 65–8; Walpole, *Reign of George III*, i, 332.   114 Monck Mason to Fitzgerald, 25 Dec. 1764, Pery to Fitzgerald, 31 Jan. 1765 in M.A. Hickson, ed., *Old Kerry records* (2 vols, London, 1872–4), second series, pp 275–6, 279–80.

of cabinet ministers had other ideas.[115] They had become increasingly uneasy with the practice whereby non-resident lords lieutenant handed over the reins of power to Irish lords justice for the long stretches that they did not reside in that kingdom. The deaths of Shannon and Stone provided them with an ideal opportunity to address this problem, and with three former lords lieutenant (Bedford, Halifax and Northumberland) among their number in favour of 'the lord lieutenant tak[ing] everything under his own management', it was decided at cabinet on 1 February 1765 to appoint only one lord justice to fill the vacancy created by Shannon and Stone, and

> to advise the King that whenever a new lord lieutenant should be appointed ... he should be directed to reside ['almost' (deleted)] constantly and in case of necessity that there should be a short leave of absence given to him and a lord deputy appointed to the government during that absence.[116]

It was a decision that proved easier to make than to implement. The cabinet did not get round to nominating a successor to Northumberland until 29 May, when they chose the necessitous Lord Weymouth in preference to the earl of Hertford. It was envisaged in some quarters that Weymouth would spend five years as a resident lord lieutenant, but he never even set foot in Ireland because the Grenville ministry fell before he could take up his posting. Instead, the earl of Hertford was appointed to succeed him in July.[117]

Flood was able to follow these events at close hand because he spent the summer of 1765 with his wife in London observing proceedings at Westminster in an attempt 'to improve his parliamentary style and manner'. This was hardly necessary since it was acknowledged by experienced observers that he was a finer orator than W.G. Hamilton and he was already being described as a future 'lead[er of] th[e Irish] parliament'.[118] It was during this time that he struck up an acquaintance with Edmund Burke. Burke was close to the Whig hierarchy, but Flood gained little politically from the connection. Burke provided him with some up-to-date political gossip and some newly-published works of Irish relevance, but the brevity of their correspondence demonstrates that for all their protestations of friendship they were

115 Brown and Schweizer, eds, 'The Devonshire diary', p. 78; Walpole to Hertford, 10 Jan., 18 Apr. and reply, 18 Jan. 1765 in Lewis et al., eds, *Walpole Corres.*, xxxviii, 489, 491, 533–4.   116 Moira to Huntingdon, 26 Jan. 1765 in H.M.C., *Hastings*, iii, 144–5; Tomlinson, ed., *Additional Grenville Papers*, pp 335–5.   117 Walpole to Mann, 25 May, 30 July in Lewis, et al., eds, *Walpole corres.*, xxii, 302–3, 315–6, *idem*, xxxix, 4–5; John Cannon, ed., *The letters of Junius* (Oxford, 1978), pp 121–2; Halifax to Lords Justice, 4 June (P.R.O., S.P., 63/423); C. Giblin, ed., 'Catalogue of Nunziatura di Fiandra', part 7, *Collectanea Hibernica*, xi (1970), p. 54; Bunbury to O'Brien, 22 June in Countess of Ilchester, ed., *Life and letters of Lady Sarah Bunbury* (2 vols, London, 1902), i, 168–70; O'Hara to Burke, 19 July in Hoffman, *Burke*, pp 321–2; Hertford to Lords Justice, 9 Aug. 1765 (N.A., Irish correspondence 1697–1798, Ms 2446).   118 *F.J.*, 18 May; Moira to Huntingdon, 26 Jan. 1765 in H.M.C., *Hastings*, iii, 144.

never close. They exchanged pleasantries, made mutually affirming noises, inquired after acquaintances (notably W.G. Hamilton and Lord Charlemont) and interesting events (notably Flood's duel with Agar). Most of all they discussed English politics, with which Flood was fascinated. He possessed unbounded admiration for William Pitt, only slightly less esteem for the 'bright genius' of Charles Townshend and 'the most favourable impressions' of Lord Rockingham.[119]

If Flood gleaned from his contacts in England that Ireland was soon to 'have a permanent lord lieutenant', he was encouraged by others to take advantage of the uncertainty to press urgently for a limitation of parliament lest the present 'unsettled state of Ireland' disimproved.[120] Like Lord Charlemont, with whom he was now on close terms, Flood was prepared to accept that, as a nominee of Lord Rockingham, the earl of Hertford merited their confidence.[121] Edmond Sexten Pery likewise indulged 'sanguine expectations' that a new era of 'good government' was imminent because he authorised Sir William Meredith, the English Whig, to convey a message on his behalf to Hertford that if he 'came over with *fair intentions* to conduct his administration on *fair principles*' he would support the Castle in the Commons.[122] He may have been prompted to offer this by his realisation that, over time, the parliamentary ranks of the patriots were destined to be 'reduced to a small minority as a result of patronage', though it grieved many of a patriot outlook that this was so. The *Freeman's Journal*, for example, expressed its hope that 'true patriots', among whom Henry Flood figured prominently, would not flinch from pressing the causes of a septennial act and the reform of the pension list, and it trumpeted supportive resolutions approved by bodies of citizens, and the defiant examples of John Wilkes and the American colonists, in anticipation that they might spur them to greater things in the new session.[123]

Such hopes were soon dashed. The opening of the 1765–6 session of parliament was delayed until 22 October because Hertford was held up at Holyhead by contrary winds,[124] but his King's speech contained nothing to encourage the patriots in the Commons. Flood was deeply disappointed. It was customary, he knew, for MPs 'to echo back ... the speech from the throne' but, as in 1763, he was unwilling to go

119 Flood to Burke, 9 May, Burke to Flood, 18 May in T.W. Copeland, et al., eds, *The correspondence of Edmund Burke* (10 vols, Cambridge, 1958–78), i, 191; Burke to Flood, 21 May, 18 July (Rosse Papers, C/1/1, 2); Flood to Burke, 30 May (S.C.L., Wentworth Woodhouse Manuscripts, Burke Papers, P.1/47); Flood to Burke, 27 July 1765 (Northamptonshire Record Office, Fitzwilliam Papers, A.viii.17). 120 [Nicolson] to Flood, 24 Aug. 1765 (R.I.A., Burrowes Papers, Ms23K.53/10). 121 Maurice Craig, *The Volunteer earl* (London, 1948), p. 149; H.M.C., *Charlemont*, i, 2, 23. 122 Meredith to Pery, 5 Oct. 1765 (Emly(Pery) Papers, P.R.O.N.I., T3087/1/35). 123 *F.J.*, 5, 8, 19 Jan., 23 Feb., 19, 22 Oct., 1765; *Dublin Gazette*, 26 Oct. 1765 and 1764–5 *passim*. 124 C. Giblin, ed.,'Nunziatura di Fiandra part 7', *Collectanea Hibernica*, xi (1968), p. 54; Waite to Bourke, 18 Oct.(N.A., Irish Correspondence 1697–1798, Ms 2446); Conway to Lords Justice, 17 Oct., Hertford to Conway, 22 Oct. 1785 (P.R.O., S.P., 63/424).

along with the practice of 'congratulatory repetition'. It was unacceptable to him that successive lords lieutenant opened parliament with mellifluous 'promising speeches' and did not govern accordingly, and he pointed to the broken promises which had not prevented 'any of those multiplied jobs which have [financially] exhausted, [and] those unconstitutional measures which have degraded and injured this country' in support of his contention.[125]

Despite these specific criticisms, Flood was not content simply to rehearse the well-known patriot criticisms of the deficiencies of the administration of Ireland. His object was to deepen and to extend both the political appeal and the intellectual foundations of Irish patriotism, and given the highly public forum in which he chose to do so, to enhance his own reputation as the most outspoken patriot in the Irish House of Commons. Flood's basic thesis was that 'tyranny and oppression' were engrained features of English government in Ireland. In the distant past, he claimed, citing 'the weighty and candid' Sir John Davies, it had prompted 'many rebellions' and the 'prostitut[ion]' of 'the sacred name of religion'. More recently, it had taken the form of the Wood's halfpence patent, of lords lieutenant lining their own pockets and of unkept promises to curb the pension list. He was particularly scathing about the latter, and he used it as his point of departure for a fierce attack on government in England and Ireland and the argument that it was necessary to sustain the English connection:

> thin and airy as it was, this shabby and inapparent, this subtle and fugitive security, was sufficient to pacify the suspicious and to lull the patriotism of some men. But to you who mean well I speak – beware of government. Their instrument is dissimulation, their views are not Irish, and their end is deception. They trade in deceit and traffic in seduction. Love and reverence your King. He is patriotic and beneficent. Love and reverence the people of England. They are free and magnanimous. But with respect to the ministers of England and their under-ministers here and elsewhere, be cautious, circumspect, suspicious. Remember your past unmanly injuries, and beware of [the] future.

Flood supported his conclusion by criticising the attempt by the Lord Lieutenant to use the Whiteboy disturbances to justify indefensible policies. Because of his Kilkenny connexion, he was better informed than most about Whiteboyism, and he singled out the Lord Lieutenant's description of the region as 'rebellious' for especial criticism. Ministers would not describe England or Englishmen as rebellious, he observed pointedly, because there were riots in the Spitalfields or violent protests against an increase in the excise on cider. Such interpretations, he averred, were exploited by politicians like Sir Robert Walpole to justify the implementation

125 Flood's speech of October 1765 survives in manuscript in the Rosse Papers (F/21).

of harsh and unjust laws in order to retain government in the hands of 'a faction'
though there was overwhelming evidence that 'such proscriptions and persecutions
... are of fatal consequence':

> They exacerbate and embitter. They make the prevailing side insolently insuf-
> ferable, and the inferior dangerously desperate. They are always suspicious and
> almost always proceed, the infatuation of a few zealots excepted, from the crooked
> views and interested malignity of a few operating on the indolent and ignorant
> credulity of the many.

In Flood's view, it was more appropriate to respond in the 'prudent' and restrained
way that had proved successful in Ulster. Regrettably, 'the same measures' were not
'taken in the south'. Instead, 'persecution only has been tried and the rod of iron
extended' with the inevitable result that 'the beast has been goaded into greater
resistance, and kicks'.

Flood's opposition to a simple law and order response to Whiteboyism was informed by his realisation that those who contended that mobs, sometimes 20,000
strong, 'were regularly exercised by night in ... the southern counties of this kingdom' were egregiously misinformed; it was impossible, he pointed out, to gather so
many people in such a 'thinly peopled' area. Such misleading claims were symptomatic of what he termed the 'virulence and ignorance and so little sober examination into this subject'. He was fully aware of the conviction of many Protestants that
a Catholic 'rebellion' was imminent, but he was sure that the Whiteboy disturbances posed no threat to the constitution, which is why, he explained, he had opposed a resolution presented to the County Kilkenny grand jury which sought

> to destroy the distinction and total separation of the petty from the grand jury,
> to subject the latter to the former, to make the two trials by these two distinct
> juries but one, contrary to the wise intention of the law, and to give to the grand
> jury, generally struck on motives of rank or favour rather than on strictly judicial
> considerations, a power of revision with regard to the characters of petty jurors,
> which is not endured by the constitution.

Flood's conviction that this was the correct stand to take derived primarily from his
anxiety to repudiate anything that smacked of arbitrary power. It was also guided by
his conviction that the mob cry of 'down with the Sassanaghs' did not mean 'down
with the Protestants' but down with Englishmen; 'it is a term of national, not religious distinction', he concluded.

This was a controversial contention, but then his views on Whiteboyism collided with the instinctive inclination of Irish Protestants to respond with *force majeure*
to disorder perpetrated by Catholics. Indeed, in a remarkable passage, he deemed
this disposition incompatible with 'patriotism':

Can you call the country free in which these things are done? Or shall men be called patriots for being forward on such an occasion? Is oppression become patriotism? Shall a man be called a patriot because he can drag his chariot wheels over the necks of miserable men, because he takes the cause of the strong against the weak, of an oligarchy against the whole? It is a cheap patriotism. Patriotism in general has been supposed to be a laborious virtue which encountered power in defence of weakness and prevented the tyranny of the few from overwhelming the many. Patriotism consists in relief, not in oppression, in moderation with respect to self-benefit, and a warm benevolence in promoting the benefit of others. It is a mild, a generous and a beneficent, not a narrow, persecuting, vindictive spirit.

This was highly idealistic, but it reflected Flood's conclusion that it was the government and not the Whiteboys that posed the real threat to the civil liberties of Protestants; by wrongly 'magnifying a false terror [the Whiteboys], we have diminished a real one ..., we have relinquished the civil power, abandoned magistracy and thrown ourselves into the arms of the *military*'.

Though he did not state so explicitly, Flood was of the opinion that the reflexive recourse to repression to deal with the Whiteboys attested to the failure of the Irish House of Commons to assert its rights 'to exert all its powers'. This was a conclusion of major personal as well as political significance because it indicated that Flood had embraced the English Whig argument that there was a ministerial plan, currently being implemented in the American colonies, 'to enslave' Ireland further by denying the right 'to tax' to the 'representatives of the people'. Claiming rights dating back 'near 600 years', to Magna Charta, Flood rehearsed with his audience what they had already lost:

We set out in the thirteenth century in every constitutional right equal to Britain, in some superior. We are now in the decline of the eighteenth century but, alas, how different. In Henry vii's time, where our declension commences, our judges were made dependent on the crown and their tenure changed into a tenure at will by statute instead of being for life, as they were originally. Our parliament at the same time, according to the construction of that act which seems prevalent, was made dependent on a dependent council ... The era of liberty, the Revolution, came. But, instead of an era of liberty to this unfortunate country, as it was to Great Britain, it forms the second and grand point of its declension. Since that time, we have seen one House of Parliament deprived of its judicature, and both, so far as a declaration of another body has validity, deprived of their independence and divested of their supremacy. We hoped that the reign of a patriot prince would restore to us the independence of our judges ... We hoped that the favourable period was on the wing for which we had long waited with patience and resignation. And what do we now hear of – an aggravation of everything grievous, an annihilation of our parliamentary rights, a deprivation of the last and most precious jewel remaining to us after former usurpations and an accumulation and completion of all that is ignominious and servile.

This was a pessimistic assessment, but Flood had no intention of conceding defeat; he instead used it to rally his audience to oppose what he described as an ongoing and systematic attempt to 'enslave' them:

It is at length time to show some sensibility, to awaken out of the turbid state of inattention in which we seem to have been congealed, to remember that we are men, and to act as such. We see that there is occasion for it. Every year takes something away from us. If we do not put a stop to it, we shall soon have nothing left. Nothing can be objected to this but a supposed impracticability and a want of power to prevent it. And here indeed we have an old prejudice to contend with, artfully propagated by a few and ignorantly received by many. But entrenched though it is in antiquity, it is so weak by its absurdity and so contradicted by fact, that when it is examined it must instantly give way to purer, nobler and more manly ideas. What? When Sir Robert Walpole sent over his patentee to debase the brass currency of this kingdom in order to indemnify for the bribes by which he had obtained his patent. Did the people suffer it to be crammed down their throats, or did they wisely, honestly and bravely reject it?

As well as the Wood's halfpence, Flood cited the money bill dispute in support of his contention that a 'national opposition' alone would defeat whatever 'court stratagem and corruption [is] employed in order ... to undermine the strength of the nation. Let us show all ministers, past, present and to come, that they are not to take these liberties wantonly with two millions and an half of men with impunity.' If the Irish parliament demonstrated the necessary resolve, he pronounced defiantly, 'the wiser and more intelligent of the people of England', who apprehend 'the decay of liberty in the dependencies of Britain as a melancholy presage of their own slavery', would be both appreciative and supportive.

With this optimistic affirmation, Flood approached the end of his lengthy oration. He concluded strongly with a profession of his resolve to commit himself to defending the liberties of the kingdom, and a ringing appeal to the serried ranks of parliamentarians to unite in support of this noble cause:

I have but a short life to promise to myself or to my country, but such as it is, it shall not be ignobly occupied; such as it is it shall be dignified with freedom; and, weak as we are, we are not so weak but that we can defend the liberties of our country and consequentially the liberties of Great Britain, and consequentially those of mankind. The idea is captivating and the practice glorious. We

have heard of men who have defied danger, death, poverty, reproach, pain – who
have defied all evils of nature or of accident – in a magnanimous pursuit; and
shall we think that this virtue is extinct – I ask you, and your eyes answer me that
it is not – I ask my own heart, and it replies in the negative. We have heard of the
freeman of Athens. We have heard of the freemen of Rome. We hear of those in
America. Why should we not hear of the freemen of Ireland? Come then, my
countrymen, let us be united.

As this stirring exhortation testifies, this was a speech of great energy and conviction. It was also Flood's longest, most ambitious and most assertive speech to date
and it indicates that he was drawn to take this radical patriot stand by his disapproval of government policy in Britain and America as well as Ireland.

Because Flood's views were so much more radical than those of the bulk of his
parliamentary colleagues, Dublin Castle had little difficulty negotiating his rhetoric
and securing approval for appropriately modulated addresses in October 1765.[126]
However, the root cause of the opposition's poor showing was not the unpopularity
of Flood's sentiments but the good-will shown the earl of Hertford by 'the chief
leaders of opposition', Edmond Pery included, who calculated that because the Lord
Lieutenant owned extensive estates there that he would 'do all [his] situation will
allow to promote the interest of Ireland'. As a consequence, the patriots started the
session in an extremely weak position 'with a minority of about ten' headed by
Henry Flood and Sir William Osborne.[127]

With such a large majority, the Castle interest was able to advance its legislative
programme without difficulty in the early weeks of the 1765–6 session. The absence
of a contemporary report on the debates that took place makes it extremely difficult
to assess Flood's engagement, but it can be established that he was among the most
active proponents of projects for public funding. On first glance, this may not appear consonant with his advocacy of restraint in public expenditure, whereas it was
a deliberate opposition tactic. Flood was joined by Lucas, Osborne, William Brownlow
and Sir Lucius O'Brien, each of whom supported a multiplicity of projects, as the
patriots sought to limit the amount of money available to the administration for
political jobbery and patronage.[128] This rather crude strategy was not without effect, but it registered less impact than their unanticipated attack on Poynings' law.

The opposition was provided with a gilt-edged opportunity to make political

---

126 Conway to Hertford, 31 Oct. (N.A., Irish correspondence 1697–1798, Ms 2446); Hertford to Walpole,
1 Nov. 1765 in Lewis, et al., eds, *Walpole corres.*, xxxix, 26.   127 Hertford to Walpole, 1 Nov. in Lewis, et
al., eds, *Walpole Corres.*, xxxix, 26–7 and note 20; Hertford to [Andrews], n.d., Hertford to [Pery], 3
Nov. 1765 (Emly (Pery) Papers, P.R.O.N.I., T3087/1/36, 37); Walsh to Townshend, 5 June 1766 in
H.M.C., *Marquess Townshend Mss*, p. 402.   128 Cummins, 'Opposition in the Irish parliament', pp 202;
F.J., 28 Dec. 1765; S.J. Fanning 'The King's purse and the absentee's pocket in eighteenth-century
Ireland' in G.L. Vincitorio ed., *Crisis in the 'Great Republic'* (New York, 1969), pp 51–2; P.R.O., S.P., 63/
424 *passim*; Rigby to Bedford, 23 Nov. 1765 in *Bedford Corres.*, iii, 322.

capital out of Poynings' Law in December when an Irish bill providing for a ban on corn exports in order to alleviate distress caused by a poor harvest in 1765 was amended by the British Privy Council. In the ordinary course of events this would have occasioned no more than a minor stir, but the outcome was complicated on this occasion by the fact that the amendment made to the measure extended the power of suspending and repealing it (reserved in the heads transmitted from Ireland to the Lord Lieutenant and Irish Privy Council) to the King and Privy Council in London. This bothered the Irish executive which had specifically requested that the legislation should be accorded a favourable reception, and their unease proved well-founded when the change was made an issue of in the House of Commons.[129] Credit for this belongs to Flood, for it was 'his sagacity penetrated the danger; he dragged the subject unexpectedly into disquisition ... and made us understand and believe the effects that are attributed to it'.[130] The Irish parliament was notoriously sensitive to anything that impinged upon its truncated legislative authority, and Flood's assertion that to grant to the British Privy Council the right to suspend the corn bill represented a threat to the 'National constitution' because it increased the power of the executive over parliament precipitated the administration into a debate on Poynings Law it could not win. Charles Lucas certainly did what he could to fan a storm of protest with three pugnacious addresses to his Dublin constituents in which he outlined what he saw as an underhand attempt to tilt the balance in the constitution in favour of the 'prerogatives of the prince'.[131] The earl of Hertford was taken aback by the deeds of those 'malevolent or ungrateful spirit[s] working to do mischief', but he had no cause for prolonged concern. The opposition, headed by Lucas, and with Flood and Pery supporting, were defeated in each of the five divisions they called on the grain bill in December–January.[132]

In the midst of this, Hertford invited Flood to one of his *soirées* on 18 December, but the Lord Lieutenant had nothing to offer him that would deflect him from the path of opposition.[133] Indeed, Flood, it appeared, could but gain by continuing to oppose the administration, as his public profile was visibly enhanced by his 'patriotic conduct' on Poynings' Law. The Corporation of Sadlers had signalled their approval of his actions by presenting him with the freedom of their body for 'his strenuous endeavours in parliament to promote a septennial bill' before the session commenced in October. Following his stand on the corn bill, he was admitted to the freedom of the weavers and merchants guilds, while he was awarded the freedom of

129 Cummins, 'Opposition and the Irish parliament', pp 138–42; Hertford to Conway, 30 Nov., 1765 (P.R.O., S.P.,63/424); Privy Council register, 1765 (P.R.O., P.C., 2/111 ff 440–1); Hertford to Winchelsea, 4 Dec. 1765 (N.A., Irish Correspondence 1697–1798, Ms 2446). 130 *H.J.*, 1 Dec. 1773. 131 Cummins, 'Opposition and the Irish parliament', pp 138–42. 132 O'Hara to O'Hara, 10 Dec. 1765 (N.L.I., O'Hara Papers, Ms 20393); Hertford to Walpole, 13, 20 Jan. 1766 in Lewis, et al., eds, *Walpole Corres.*, xxxix, pp 45, 49; Sackville to Irwin, 31 Jan. 1766 in H.M.C., *Stopford Sackville*, i, 22. 133 Hertford to Walpole, 13 Jan. 1766 in Lewis et al., eds., *Walpole Corres.*, xxxix, 45; A list of the lords and commoners who dined with the Earl of Hertford, 18 Dec. 1765 (N.L.I., Ms 1469).

the city for his attention to the rights and liberties of the subject on the initiative of the lower house of Dublin Corporation in January 1766.[134]

Flood shared the popular limelight with Charles Lucas, who was accorded a similar public fêting in the winter of 1765–6,[135] but he was the more active parliamentarian. This was amply demonstrated in early November when he upstaged Lucas by securing leave (with Alexander McAulay, MP for Thomastown) to brings in heads of a bill to limit the duration of parliament. He also signalled his support for a citizen's militia by securing leave to draft a bill (with William Talbot, MP St Johnstown) for the better regulation of the militia. The former measure was presented to the House of Commons on 23 January, and after completing the necessary stages it was sent to a committee of the whole house for consideration. The committee completed its deliberations before the 28th, when there was a debate in the House on the measure and on a wrecking amendment presented during the committee stage that the bill should provide for fourteen rather than seven-year parliaments. The leading protagonists were Henry Flood, who spoke in favour of the bill, and John Hely-Hutchinson who spoke against. It was the conclusion of one observer that Hutchinson had the better of the exchanges because he was able to bring a greater 'variety of precedents' to bear and because Flood had recourse to arguments 'not equally defensible'. However, Flood had more grounds to feel pleased since the bill was approved.[136] This, of course, had happened in 1763 and 1761, but there was optimism on this occasion that the bill would finally reach the statute book. The measure passed the Irish Privy Council on 6 February, but when it came before the British Privy Council it was 'postponed' to the great satisfaction of many MPs who, their public affirmations to the contrary notwithstanding, did not want the bill to become law.[137]

In the light of his ongoing efforts to perpetuate the Flood family's control of Callan, self-interest might suggest that Henry shared the reservations felt by many Irish MPs with the proposed septennial legislation, but his active role in forwarding the measure indicates that this was not so. He certainly had little time to dwell on the outcome, because no sooner had the septennial bill completed all stages in the House of Commons than he was called upon to present his heads of a bill for the better regulation of the militia. Significantly, Flood's initiative in this area was prompted by a chance remark by William Pitt that Ireland needed a militia law and his measure was grounded on the bill Pitt had guided through the Westminster parliament in 1758. Indeed, Flood sought to enhance his bill's prospects by appeal-

134 *Dublin Gazette*, 8 Oct. 1765; *F.J.*, 4, 14, 18, 21 Jan. 1766; Lady Gilbert, ed., *Calendar of ancient records of Dublin*, *xi* (Dublin, 1904), pp 472–5; for further evidence of his high standing see *F.J.*, 4 Jan., 18 Feb., 1766.   135 *F.J.*, 31 Dec. 1765, 4, 7, 14, 21 Jan. 1766; Sean O Dalaigh, ed., *Corporation book of Ennis* (Dublin, 1990), pp 216–7.   136 *Commons Jn. (Irl.)*, viii, 23, 26, 74, 76–7; O'Hara to O'Hara, 29 Jan. 1766 (N.L.I., O'Hara Papers, Ms 20393).   137 *F.J.*, 28 Jan., 8 Feb., 22 Mar.; Hertford to Conway, 22 Feb. 1766 (P.R.O., S.P., 63/424); Malcomson, ed., *Irish official papers*, ii, 66–7; P.R.O., P.C.2/111 f 576.

ing to Pitt for his endorsement, and while the latter was disinclined 'to hazard a judgement how far the militia laws of England would, with propriety and effect, apply to Ireland', he did 'applaud' the idea.[138] It was not enough to secure its passage, however. Flood's speech in support of the legislation was a further illustration of his 'brilliant and impressive eloquence', but despite difficulties within their own ranks, the Chief Secretary, Lord Beauchamp, and his main parliamentary manager, John Hely-Hutchinson, trumped Flood's efforts to move 'heaven and earth to get and to keep people away' so that the bill could progress beyond the committee stage. It was lost on a motion to vacate the chair by 78 votes to 30.[139]

If the loss of the militia bill disappointed Flood, he had reason to be pleased with the improvement in the opposition's vote in the Commons as the session progressed and with the fact that as well as the septennial legislation, heads of bills to extend the right of habeas corpus to Ireland and to alter the tenure of judges to *quamdiu se bene gesserint* were received and debated.[140] Neither of the latter two reached the statute book, and there is no record of Flood's sentiment's on either, but both were part of his and the patriots' legislative programme. His support for legislation backing the request of Protestant corporations to have the custom of quarterage on non-freemen afforded the sanction of law (the courts decreed in 1764 it was without statutory authority) was also popular. Flood's thoughts on this matter are also elusive, but the fact that he and James St.John Jeffryes were given leave on 13 February to prepare heads of a bill to confirm the disputed right of levying quarterage on non-freemen in Cork city indicates that he supported the claim of Protestant freemen to perpetuate their elitist position in towns and cities, though no bill was presented.[141]

By the mid-spring of 1766, there was a general expectation that the session would soon be over. At the same time, the comfortable control the administration enjoyed in the House of Commons at the beginning of the session had dissipated as Lord Hertford failed to fulfil the high hopes held of him and his personal popularity plummeted because of the perception that his primary motivation was to provide for his family. The opposition was in no position to exploit this disenchantment to advance a programme of reforms, but Flood and William Osborne were the dominant voices in the 'bustle, ... altercation, false reckoning and good deal of exclamation in the philippic style addressed to the passions of men' that passed for debate in the House of Commons in 1766. They frequently had the best of the argument, but

138 Flood to Pitt, 31 Dec. 1765 in Taylor and Pringle, eds, *Chatham correspondence*, iii, 1–5; R[odd] ed., *Letters to Flood*, pp 18–20; Basil Williams, *The life of William Pitt, Earl of Chatham* (2 vols, London, 1913), ii, 129.   139 *Commons.Jn.(Irl.)*, viii, 26, 78, 92, 98, 101, 112, 114, 120, 125, 126; H. Grattan Jr., *Memoirs of the life and Times of the right hon Henry Grattan* (5 vols, London, 1839–45), i, 203; Flood to Charlemont, 27 Mar. 1766 in H.M.C.,*Charlemont*, i, 277–80.   140 R.B. McDowell, 'Colonial nationalism and the winning of parliamentary independence' in Moody and Vaughan, eds, *A new history of Ireland*, iv, 199; B.L., Hardwicke Papers, Add. Ms 35892 ff 44–57.   141 *F.J.*, 21 Jan. 1766; Day, 'Irish Catholics', p. 43, 76–8.

it was not enough to win in the division lobbies, as Charles O'Hara conceded in March: 'The labouring oar was in the hands of administration; ... we succeeded by numbers only'.[142]

Ruffled by the attack by Flood and his patriot allies, the priority of the Lord Lieutenant before the end of March was to conclude the session quickly and without fuss.[143] The one major matter outstanding was the septennial bill which the public continued to hope would be returned from London. Their expectations were sustained by supportive resolutions approved at county meetings (including County Kilkenny where Henry Flood was among the signatories) in April and May,[144] and by a series of impressive minorities on constitutional points appertaining to Poynings Law pressed by Edmond Sexten Pery. By the beginning of May, MPs had become so impatient with the failure to return the septennial bill that a committee of which Flood was a member was directed to draft an address to the king requesting its return. The address was approved by the slim margin of just two votes, but it was too little and too late to allow the opposition to make political capital out of either the septennial bill or Poynings' Law.[145]

These were the last major events of the 1765–6 session which finally concluded in early June. Despite the cabinet's decision of February 1765, there was no question of Hertford remaining in the country while the parliament was not in session. He appointed three lords justice in June and did not tarry setting sail for England.[146] Hertford's eagerness to leave mirrored his experience in Ireland; he had not enjoyed the posting and was widely seen not to have acquitted himself well.[147] Henry Flood, by contrast, emerged with his reputation enhanced. He was never less than impressive during the session and the range and variety of measures he had proposed and supported indicated that the promise he had shown in 1763–4 had been amply fulfilled. He was now generally regarded as the country's 'leading patriot', whose 'principles and abilities would do honour to any country'; he was, with Sir William Osborne, 'the chief in the opposition'. Moreover, he was highly popular, as the presentation of further freedom boxes in the summer of 1766 highlights.[148]

142 Leland to Charlemont, 11 Mar. in H.M.C.,*Charlemont*, i, 278–9; O'Hara to O'Hara, 8 Mar. 1766 (N.L.I., O'Hara Papers, Ms 20393). 143 Hertford to Conway, 30 Mar. (P.R.O., S.P.63/424); Conway to Grafton, 7, 12 Apr. 1766 (Ipswich and East Suffolk Record Office, Grafton Papers (P.R.O.N.I., T2959/2/2,3)). 144 *F.J.*, 15, 29 Mar., 1, 19, 22, 29 Apr., 20, 24 May 1766. 145 Charlemont to Flood, 13 Mar. in R[odd], ed. *Letters to Flood*, p. 14; Cummins, 'Opposition and the Irish parliament', pp 211–13; A short sketch of the political history of Ireland (N.L.I., Joly Ms 29 f 41); *F.J.*, 6 May; Hertford to Conway, 7 May (P.R.O., S.P.63/424); Hertford to Walpole, 10, 21 May in Lewis, et al., eds, *Walpole Corres.*, xxxix, 67–8, 70–71; Sackville to Irwin, 27 June 1766 in H.M.C.,*Stopford-Sackville*, p. 24. 146 Hertford to Richmond, 6, 7, 11 June 1766 (P.R.O., S.P.,63/424). 147 Lewis, et al., eds, *Walpole Corres.*, xxxix, 71 note 8; Sackville to Irwin, 27 June 1766 in H.M.C., *Stopford-Sackville*, p. 24. 148 Walsh to [Townshend], 5 June (B.L.,O.C., Townshend Papers, Box 14); H.M.C., *Townshend Mss*, p. 402; *F.J.*, 21 June, 25 Oct. 1766.

4

Office or opposition? 1766–72

Like most patriots who achieved eminence on the opposition benches, Henry Flood was not content with the applause and admiration his oratory brought. He possessed a political agenda, and he was prepared to work with the Irish administration if it agreed to support his demands. Office offered a firmer prospect of influencing policy than opposition, and a steady stream of patriots accepted government employment for this reason. Indeed, some embraced power with such relish that they merged seamlessly into the Castle apparatus which sustained British interests in Ireland. Others, compelled by financial need, contented themselves with the monetary rewards of office and eschewed active political involvement. Neither of these options appealed to Flood. It was not that he had no use for the fruits of office. The high cost of sustaining his family's influence in the borough of Callan made any additional income welcome, but the allure of monetary reward was less compelling than his desire to reshape the pattern of government. Political achievement rather than financial covetousness fuelled Flood's ambition, and he was sufficiently confident in his abilities not to confine his horizons to Ireland. Like many of the Irish Protestant elite,[1] he was both at home in England and *au fait* with English politics, and he indulged a dream of sharing the imperial stage at Westminster with his political hero, the English patriot William Pitt, Earl of Chatham.

FLOOD AND CHATHAM

Henry Flood's admiration of Lord Chatham was widely shared by Whigs and patriots in Ireland as well as Britain in the 1760s.[2] The liberal peer, Lord Charlemont,

---

1 Romney Sedgwick, ed., *The history of parliament: the House of Commons 1715–54* (2 vols, London, 1970), i, 156–8; L.B. Namier and John Brooke, eds, *The House of Commons 1754–90* (3 vols, London, 1964), i, 156. An estimated 146 Irishmen were MPs at Westminster between 1715 and 1790.   2 See, *inter alia*, Giblin, ed., 'Nunziatura di Fiandra, part 6', pp 127–8; *F.L.J.*, 26 Aug. 1767, 2 Jan. 1768; A. Brooke Tyrell, 'Homage to Grattan 1746–1820', *Dublin Historical Record*, xxxvii (1983), p. 37; Richard Caulfeild, ed., *Council book of the Corporation of Cork* (Guildford, 1876), p. 808.

was also an admirer, and this and his eagerness to act as a mentor to the most promising patriot voice in the House of Commons provided the basis for a friendship that
deepened in the mid-1760s.[3] They also shared other interests. Like Flood, who visited London annually in the early and mid-1760s, Charlemont was passionately
interested in British politics. He maintained a town house in London between 1764
and 1773, and his encomiastic reports to Flood of Pitt's celebrated speeches in favour of the repeal of the Stamp Act in January 1766 reinforced Flood's positive
image of the former Prime Minister and animated the hopes he entertained that he
might be able to govern according to the patriotic design of his hero.[4] Such a prospect seemed remote in the spring of 1766. But the collapse of the short-lived
Rockingham administration which caused George III to invite Chatham to form a
new government with Charles Townshend, whom Flood regarded as the only genuine 'orator' in the House of Commons, meant his annual visit to England in the
summer of 1766 was more eventful than usual.[5]

Chatham nominated the earl of Bristol to succeed Hertford. One of the stipula-
tions insisted upon by George III, when he accepted Bristol's nomination, was that
the new lord lieutenant should reside in Ireland for the duration of his vice-royalty
which, it was reported, was for three years. This caused considerable unease among
the undertakers who feared that it would hasten their political eclipse, but it was
welcomed by reform-minded patriots like Flood who harboured strong hopes that
the new administration would govern Ireland in a more virtuous manner. Bristol's
nomination certainly sent the right signals to those who believed the case for administrative reform in Ireland was compelling, though informed voices queried his
aptitude for such a challenging task.[6]

As was normal, the appointment of a new lord lieutenant was the signal for the
commencement of a campaign of intense personal lobbying. The most pertinent,
because of the fear he entertained that Flood sought to displace him in the affections of government, was that undertaken by the Prime Sergeant John Hely-

---

3 Charlemont addressed him as 'my dearest friend' and 'my dearest Flood'.   4 Craig, *Volunteer earl*, p.
134; Flood, *Memoirs*, pp 44–5; A.T.Q. Stewart, *A deeper silence*, p. 34; I.R. Christie, 'William Pitt and
American taxation, 1766: a problem of parliamentary reporting', *Studies in Burke and his times*, 17 (1976),
pp 167–8; Charlemont to Flood, 13, [2]8 Jan. in R[odd], ed., *Letters to Flood*, pp 5–6, 8–9; *F.J.*, 29 Mar.
1 Apr. 1766.   5 Charlemont to Flood, 13 Mar., Flood to Charlemont, [ ] in R[odd], ed., *Letters to
Flood*, pp 14–17, 22–9; P.D.G.Thomas, *British politics and the Stamp Act Crisis 1763–67* (Oxford, 1975),
p. 285n; *Chatham Corres*, iii, 144n; Stock to Stock, 22 Feb. 1767 (T.C.D., Stock Papers, Ms 3762/20);
Flood, *Memoirs*, p. 47.   6 Bartlett, 'Townshend', pp 24–5; J.L. McCracken, 'The Irish viceroyalty
1760–73' in H.A. Cronne, T.W. Moody and D.B. Quinn, eds, *Essays in British and Irish history* (London,
1949), pp 157–8; Hervey to Grenville, 13 Aug. (Bristol Papers, P.R.O.N.I., T2960/1/5); George III to
Chatham, 22 Aug., Chatham to Bristol, 26 Aug., Bristol to Chatham, 27 Aug., in Taylor and Pringle, eds,
Chatham Corres, iii, 51, 55–7; Bowes to Willes, 3 Sept., Clayton to Willes, 12 Sept (Warwickshire R.O,
Willes Papers 8); Bowes to Hely-Hutchinson, 17 Sept. in H.M.C., *Donoughmore*, p. 259; Williams,
William Pitt, ii, 221–2; Walpole to Mann, 9 Sept. 1766 in Lewis, et al., eds, *Walpole Corres.*, xxii, 450.

Hutchinson. Determined not to be eclipsed, he requested the earl of Hertford to appeal on his behalf to Chatham that he should be considered for government office in England and a parliamentary seat at Westminster. Chatham was not prepared to indulge Hely-Hutchinson's hopes. But the palpable relief with which Hertford reported back that 'Lord Chatham did not mention Flood, nor do I think he has any thoughts of bringing him into parliament here' captures the anxiety of the current powerbrokers in the Irish parliament, as well as the suspicion and jealousy with which Hely-Hutchinson regarded Flood.[7]

By instinct and inclination, Flood was less forward than Hely-Hutchinson. However, he delayed his return to Ireland to strike up an acquaintance with the earl of Bristol. News of this quickly reached Ireland, and the political rumour-mill soon had it that Flood dined regularly with Bristol and had consented 'to take the lead' for the administration in the House of Commons. Such reports were wide of the mark.[8] Bristol was so wholly in awe of Chatham that he confined his discussions with Flood and Charlemont to generalities. However, he did make encouraging noises about altering the basis of English government in Ireland:

> I meant not to govern by any faction or party, but would rely on the support of those who had the national interest at heart, and should seek to distinguish those who were eminent for their integrity and their abilities; and therefore I would hope to have him [Flood] my friend.

Such sentiments were music to Flood's ears. He made the Lord Lieutenant no commitment, but he was certainly attracted by the legislative possibilities and, in particular, by the prospect of securing government support for septennial legislation which Chatham was reputed to favour, if he supported the new administration. So when he was ready to return to Ireland in December he requested and was given a letter of introduction to Chatham, who was taking the waters at Bath, in order that 'he should know from the fountainshead what system was intended and what measures would be pursued'.[9]

Flood's trip to Bath prolonged his journey home. But he deemed it a matter of urgency that he met with Chatham before he offered any assurances that his support would be forthcoming. Bristol, for his part, was so convinced Flood was 'well inclined' he concluded that 'some conversation' with Chatham would suffice to secure a binding commitment. The two men met on Saturday, 2 January 1767, and though reports of the meeting are sketchy it is clear that it did not go as Flood

---

7 Hertford to Hely-Hutchinson, 15 Sept. (T.C.D., Donoughmore Papers); Hely-Hutchinson to Chatham, [Sept.] 1766 in H.M.C., *Donoughmore*, pp 259–60. 8 Waite to Wilmot, 3 Jan. 1767 cited in Bartlett, 'Townshend', p. 33. 9 Bristol to Chatham, 29 Dec. 1766 in Taylor and Pringle, eds, *Chatham corres.*, iii, 144–7.

intended. He was carrying 'a severe feverish disorder' which, he maintained later, rendered him 'wholly incapable of explaining myself with any degree of exactness or propriety', but since it did not prevent him listing the four issues which were his price for supporting the administration – a septennial act, a *habeas corpus* act, the recognition of the independency of the Irish judiciary and the reform of the pension list – this alone does not account for his negative perception of the meeting.[10] Chatham who, according to one of his biographers, had no great opinion of Flood, was non-committal. However, he sent Bristol a sufficiently upbeat report of what he concluded was Flood's readiness to support the administration, that the Lord Lieutenant expressed himself 'perfectly apprized of his [Flood's] inclination to promote the King's service'.[11] This was going too far. Flood's account of the meeting has not survived, but from Lord Charlemont's reply to a letter from him, it is clear that he was deeply disappointed by Chatham's refusal to discuss his plans for the government of Ireland and by his failure to pronounce explicitly in favour of the four points he had raised:

> Your interview with the Patagonian [Chatham] has turned out pretty much as I expected. It is easier for a camel to go through the eye of a needle, or for a rich man to enter into the kingdom of Heaven, than for a politician to lay aside disguise, or for a Minister *here* [England] to think as we would with regard to our affairs.[12]

Charlemont's philosophical reaction was informed by his own encounter with Chatham. This was such a disappointment, Charlemont sought to convince Flood that opposition was the only honourable political course for a patriot:

> My disappointment of last year was no way inferior to your's at present. The highest and best founded esteem ... made me entertain the most sanguine hopes. But my friend was a M[iniste]r. Indeed, my dearest Flood, we must depend upon ourselves alone. *Firmness*, as you well observe, *may gain, or the want of it lose everything* ... What I am proud to call *our* way of thinking, may be of the greatest advantage.[13]

Flood was not convinced, and he provided Chatham with an opportunity to initiate further contact when he wrote from Ireland on 17 January apologising for his being out of sorts when they had met at Bath. Chatham did not reply.

---

10 Chatham to Flood, 1 Jan., Flood to Chatham, 8 Jan. 1767 in Taylor & Pringle, eds, *Chatham Corres*, iii, 147; Williams, *William Pitt*, ii, 221–2; P.D. Brown, *William Pitt, Earl of Chatham* (London, 1978), pp 339–40.   11 Williams, *William Pitt*, ii, 222; Bristol to Chatham, 8 Jan. 1767 in Taylor and Pringle, eds, *Chatham Corres.*, iii, 166–7; Charlemont to Flood, 13 Jan. 1767 in R[odd], ed., *Letters to Flood*, pp 7–10. 12 Charlemont to Flood, 13 Jan. 1767 in R[odd], ed., *Letters to Flood*, pp 7–10.   13 Ibid.

If Chatham was disinclined to provide Flood with the assurances he wanted on the four points he raised on 2 January, others were less coy and Edward Thurlow, the MP for Tamworth, and the earl of Bristol raised the matter of Flood's disposition with Lord Charlemont towards the end of January. Charlemont sought to dampen their expectations by stating that he was not prepared to give a commitment to support the administration because of his uncertainty about the policies they would pursue. However, he did not rule out the possibility completely, as he informed Flood:

> The utmost reserve for the present, and a steady resolution to keep watchfully upon our guard, and to wait till events should elucidate the nature of the present system, and clearly demonstrate that *real* good was intended, were the points upon which I chiefly insisted.[14]

If ministers possessed a clear and coherent plan for the government of Ireland which they believed Flood could support, they should have revealed it now, but no further overtures were made. In fact, Chatham's continued absence in Bath and the inability of Bristol to display any initiative ensured that the prospects of Flood supporting the administration continued to recede. Flood manifested little regret with this turn of events. At the same time, he did not accept it with equanimity, for he instructed a reluctant Charlemont to explore the possibility of his purchasing a seat for the Westminster parliament. As requested, Charlemont approached John Pitt, Chatham's cousin, a man of dubious reputation, who claimed to be in a position to return Flood for the Dorset constituency of Wareham for £3,000.[15]

While Flood's political focus oscillated in the winter and spring of 1766–7 between the prospects of influence at Dublin Castle and the prestige of a Westminster seat, he kept such a low profile that Charles Lucas complained to Charlemont 'that he never sees him'.[16] It was 'universally' maintained that he was the author of the controversial pamphlet *A letter to J[ohn] P[onsonby]*, which was published in London as well as Dublin in January 1767, but this is unlikely. Despite this, the tract is of more than passing interest because of Charles O'Hara's claim that he had heard Flood use 'some of the [same] expressions in private'. O'Hara did not like the pamphlet personally because of what he termed 'the meanness of the style, the no-arrangement of the matter, and total want of spirit and elegance' of its content, but this is a more accurate measure of his aversion to Flood's views rather than of his critical insight. A recent commentator has described it as 'witty and easy to read'.[17]

---

14 Charlemont to Flood, 29 Jan. 1767 in R[odd] ed., *Letters to Flood*, p. 10.   15 Charlemont to Flood, 19 Feb, 18 Apr. 1767 in R[odd], ed., *Letters to Flood*, pp 29–32, 43–5; Sedgwick, ed., *The House of Commons 1715–54*, ii, 350–51; Namier and Brooke, eds, *The House of Commons 1754–90*, i, 272.   16 Charlemont to Flood, 9 Apr. 1767 in R[odd], ed., *Letters to Flood*, p. 39.   17 The pamphlet is generally ascribed to Dr William Jackson; manuscript note by R.R. Madden on National Library copy

The basic thesis of *The letter to J[ohn] P[onsonby]* was that when the earl of Bristol took up permanent residence in Ireland, Ponsonby's power would be much diminished. He would be obliged, the author contended, to revert to the position of 'an honest country gentleman' which would be more advantageous to him personally and to Ireland politically than his continuing as 'not only a minister, but a dictator in the affairs of Ireland'. To the author, this prospect was potentially as significant as the Glorious Revolution and he waxed lyrical on the advantages to the British government and the Irish administration of a resident lord lieutenant providing stable and efficient administration, and putting an end to the 'mismanagement, corruption, knavery and blundering' that had been a feature of government in Ireland 'for these many years'. When Bristol, whom he portrayed very positively, became lord lieutenant, the kingdom could, he contended, anticipate a septennial act, a *habeas corpus* act, a judges bill, perhaps even a place bill, a qualification bill, and a militia bill. Equally consequently, there was even reason to believe that the restrictions on Irish trade (especially woollens) would be ameliorated, and that the practice of appointing Englishmen to Irish civil and ecclesiastical office curtailed.[18]

As Charles O'Hara observed, the opinions expressed in this tract accurately captured the eagerness of Flood and the other patriots to reduce 'the scheming undertakers' to 'the condition of servants who have been hired because the old liveries in the wardrobe fitted them', and to inaugurate a 'golden period' in which 'the whole realm will be purified from every vice, from every corruption'.[19] John Ponsonby, by contrast, was determined to safeguard his position as the most powerful figure in the Irish House of Commons.[20] His political judgement was not the most assured, however, and like other heads of interests, he may have perceived that the Lord Lieutenant's decision in July 1767 to appoint Theophilus Jones to the chief secretaryship in place of his disaffected brother Augustus was further evidence of the existence of a grand plan to replace him and Hely-Hutchinson with the Beresfords and Henry Flood. Jones was connected by marriage with the earl of Tyrone, and his appointment was seen to corroborate reports emanating from London that Bristol's intention was to administer Ireland with the support of the Beresford interest in the House of Commons.[21]

Flood was informed by Charlemont.in April that the earl of Tyrone met with the earl of Bristol in London, and that because of his marriage into the Beresford fam-

(P 147/3); O'Hara to Burke, 12 Mar.in Hoffman, *Burke*, p. 392; O'Hara to O'Hara, 17 Mar.1767 (N.L.I., O'Hara Papers, Ms 20393); Cummins, 'Opposition and the Irish parliament', p. 144; R.D.C. Collison Black, *A catalogue of pamphlets on economic subjects 1750–1900 in Irish libraries* (Belfast, 1969), p. 37.   18 *A letter to the right honourable J[oh]n P[onsonb]y of the H[ous]e of C[ommon]s of I[relan]d* (3rd edition, London, 1767).   19 Heany to Willes, 17 Feb. (Warwickshire R.O., Willes Papers 7); *A letter to J[ohn] P[onsonby]*, p. 6;Pery to Fitzgerald, Feb.1767 in Hickson, *Old Kerry Records*, 2nd series, p. 281.   20 O'Hara to Burke, 12 Mar. 1767 in Hoffman, *Burke*, p. 403.   21 Bodkin, ed., 'The Irish parliament in 1773', pp 189, 197; Hervey to Grenville, 30 June, 4 July, Hamilton to Temple, 10 July in Smith, ed., *Grenville Papers*, iv, 24, 29–30, 41; Hervey to Bristol and reply, 1 July (Bristol Papers, P.R.O.N.I., T2960/1/7, 8); Bristol to Shelburne, 9 July 1767 in *C.H.O.P.*, ii, 179.

ily, his obscure agreement to support the earl of Tyrone, and the belief that he was in Bristol's confidence, it was widely assumed he was part of the same arrangement. Philip Tisdall even claimed that Flood would be made a revenue commissioner.[22] In fact, Flood's commitment to the earl of Tyrone was less binding than Tisdall suspected, just as the commitment he gave to 'support' the Bristol administration was less total than both the Lord Lieutenant and the earl of Chatham assumed. As a consequence, though Lord Charlemont continued to field queries in England as to Flood's intentions, nothing positive resulted. Charlemont wrote to Flood on 9 April protesting that he had 'been treated ill, and that we have been in some degree both of us deceived', but Flood must shoulder some of the blame for the confusion about his position. Whether because of inexperience (his awe of Chatham may partly account for his awkwardness when the two met in January 1767) or indecision, he failed to spell out clearly that his disposition to match his professions of support with deeds was dependent on his receiving assurances on the four points he presented to Chatham on 2 January, with the result that ministers assumed that he was better inclined than he was in reality. Frustrated by his inability to counter claims that Flood was pledged to support the administration, Charlemont felt obliged to enquire of him if he had been entirely frank with him. Flood's reply, if there was one, has not survived. But he continued to heed Charlemont's counsel that '*reserve* is still absolutely necessary' and that they should both 'keep ... clear of all engagements, and wait for those events by which we must finally be decided' if they were to observe what Charlemont defined as his 'first principle, the desire of serving your country'. As far as Charlemont was concerned, if Lord Bristol came 'to Ireland, armed with those long expected benefits which have ever been the object of our wishes, public and private, an opposition to his measures would most certainly in that case be impossible from those whose first aim is their country's service'. However, he indulged progressively fewer expectations that this would be the case as poor health and an increasingly vigorous parliamentary opposition reduced Chatham's prospects of forming a stable government.[23] This disappointed him, but he was less discommoded by the thought of continued opposition than his 'dearest friend'.

As things turned out, Flood had to reconcile himself to the fact that he would not achieve the political breakthrough he wanted either in England or in Ireland in 1767. He effectively conceded as much when he instructed Charlemont in mid-June to suspend his negotiations to purchase a parliamentary seat for Wareham from John Pitt on the grounds that it was not 'worth while to do anything for the small remainder of this session'. He did express his intention to settle the matter before 'the next' session, but the possibility of his sitting for Wareham had passed forever as Pitt was soon not in a position to deliver on a seat. Indeed, it is improbable

22 Tisdall to Bective, 4 Apr. 1767 (N.L.I., Headfort Papers).   23 Charlemont to Flood, 9 Apr. 1767 in R[odd], ed., *Letters to Flood*, pp 36–41.

that he could have done so in the spring 1767 had Flood sought to purchase the representation of the borough. Flood was alerted to this possibility by Charlemont in June, but since it was accompanied by an assurance that 'there is the highest probability, and I believe almost certainty that, long before the times comes [to hold an election] all difficulties will be totally obviated' he did not give it much thought. In fact, Flood was not to receive another chance. Within a few months, Pitt had disposed of his estate and, with it, his interest in the borough, which left Flood with no option but to look elsewhere if he aspired to become a Westminster MP. He did appeal to Chatham in September for a 'recommendation to a seat in the British House of Commons for the next parliament', but it too fell on stony ground.[24]

Even had he wanted to, Chatham was in no position to advance Flood's request for a parliamentary nomination in the autumn of 1767. He had effectively withdrawn from politics in March, and handed over the task of forming an administration to the duke of Grafton. Bristol's resignation four months later dashed whatever residual hopes Flood may have entertained that he could yet secure the commitments that would allow him to work with a Chathamite administration because it meant that there was now no prospect of either Chatham or Bristol heading a government committed to bringing the politics of 'faction' in Ireland to an end, and to advancing the reforms he cited at his meeting with Chatham in January.[25]

Flood was so distressed by this and by the thought that he had discommoded Chatham that he wrote to him on 12 September informing him that he had 'felt the warmest wishes for the prosperity and honour of a Lieutenancy commenced under your Lordship's auspices', and that he was only 'kept back in the expression of these wishes ... by a punctilio which I imagined to have subsisted between Lord Tyrone and me'.[26] It is not clear precisely what Flood meant by this, since he was not bound by a firm commitment to support his father-in-law, but the fact that he was, as he acknowledged, 'mistaken' on this point is symptomatic of the lack of deftness that characterised his dealings with Bristol and Chatham in 1766–7. It would be wrong at the same time to attribute the outcome to Flood alone. Bristol's utter dependence on Chatham's 'advice ... to guide [him] in this arduous task', and Chatham's 'aloofness and arrogance' makes it plain that he was caught up in a most delicate situation from which even the most dextrous diplomat would have emerged with credit only with difficulty.[27] As it was, Flood could console himself with the fact that the mis-

24 Charlemont to Flood, [11 June] (B.L., Flood Papers, Add. Ms 22930 ff 24–5); Flood to Chatham, 12 Sept. 1767 (P.R.O., Chatham Papers, 30/8/32 ff 255–6); Namier and Brooke, eds, *The House of Commons 1754–90*, i, 272, iii, 284. 25 Bristol to [Grafton], 26 July (Grafton Papers, P.R.O.N.I., T2959/2/7); Hamilton to Temple, [27 July] in Smith, ed., *Grenville Papers*, iv, 109–12; Bristol to Lady Chatham, [30 July] in Taylor and Pringle, eds, *Chatham Corres.*, iii, 279–80; Bartlett, 'Townshend', pp 37–8; *F.L.J.*, 15 Aug. 1767. 26 Flood to Chatham, 12 Sept. 1767 (P.R.O., Chatham Papers, 30/8/32 ff 255–6). 27 Flood to Chatham, 12 Sept. (P.R.O., Chatham Papers, 30/8/32 ff 255–60); Bristol to Lady Chatham, [30 July] in Taylor and Pringle, eds, *Chatham Corres.*, iii, 279–80; Brooke, 'William Pitt' in Brooke and Namier, eds, *The House of Commons*, iii, 298.

takes he had committed had not permanently alienated anybody of political consequence and that had Bristol taken the reins of power in Ireland, his 'premature
attempt ... to break' existing 'connexions', and his readiness to 'heap ... favours' on
'those who had no power to serve him' while refusing 'the first men ... in fortune
and family', would have ended in tears. Needless to say, the Ponsonbys and other
vested interests were delighted when they learned that he would not be coming to
Ireland.[28] They had little real cause for optimism. His successor, George Lord
Townshend, possessed equally reformist (and more emphatically imperialist) views
on the government of Ireland and he was as anxious as Bristol to elicit Flood's support to enable him to proceed with the reorganization of the way in which Ireland
was administered.

FLOOD AND TOWNSHEND 1767–8

Henry Flood had no previous acquaintance with Lord Townshend, who was appointed to the lord lieutenancy of Ireland within three weeks of the earl of Bristol's
resignation. But both Charlemont and he were disposed to regard him favourably
because they held a high opinion of his colourful and talented brother, Charles.

Townshend was a man of 'great abilities' who was enthusiastic about his Irish
posting, having 'bragged' unsuccessfully that the position was his in 1765.[29] As befitted a distinguished soldier, he was at one with George Grenville, Lord Bute and
George III on the need for firm governance of the empire. For this reason, he was
seen as the man to entrust the task of curbing the 'worrying trend of defiance and
opposition' many detected all too readily in Ireland. Specific remedies were less
forthcoming, but like Lord Chancellor Camden, Townshend favoured vesting greater
control and responsibility in the crown and its representatives in Ireland. However,
because Irish affairs were not a priority with the new government, ministers were
slow to provide Townshend with instructions.[30] This did not please the mercurial
Lord Lieutenant whose original intention was to travel to Dublin well in advance of
the meeting of parliament to prepare for the new session. The expectation there was
that he would pursue the same plan as Lord Bristol – that he would become permanently resident and seek to eclipse 'the powerful connexions' by governing on 'popularity'. It was also anticipated that this would involve conceding some or all of the

---

28 Clare to Townshend, 26 Sept. 1767 (B.L.,O.C., Nugent files); Bartlett, 'Townshend', p. 39.   29 Cory
to Townshend, 18 Nov. (B.L.,O.C., Townshend Papers, Box 9); Townshend to Lord Justices, 19 Aug.
1767 (N.A., Irish Correspondence 1697–1798, Ms 2446); Walpole to Holland, 29 May in Lewis et al.,
eds, *Walpole Corres.*, xxx, 88; Burke to O'Hara, July 1765 in Hoffman, *Burke*, p. 318.   30 Camden to
Grafton, 29 Sept. in Sir William Anson, ed., *Autobiography and political correspondence of Augustus
Henry, third Duke of Grafton* (London, 1898), pp 162–3; Bartlett, 'Townshend', pp 49–50; Burke to
Hely-Hutchinson, 3 Aug. 1767 in H.M.C., *Donoughmore*, pp 260–1.

'four favourite bills' Flood had brought to Chatham's notice in January 1766. Because of this, the appointment of Townshend seemed to augur well for Flood's relations with the new administration.[31]

Flood was certainly curious about the political possibilities arising from Townshend's appointment. He wrote to William Markham (his former tutor who had just been appointed dean at his old Oxford college) in the early autumn to enquire about recent events in England. Markham was in no position 'to tell you something certain, as a ground for your own proceedings', but he was on sufficiently familiar terms with Townshend's Chief Secretary, Lord Frederick Campbell, to have 'some discourse ... [with him] on your subject'. It was an intervention that promised to pay handsome dividends because Campbell responded positively, Markham reported:

> He has a great personal regard for you, esteems your talents, and wishes to favour your pretensions. I can venture to assure you that you will find him an honourable, frank man, and that you need have no fear about committing yourself, especially as there is a disposition to accommodate those points for which you have pledged yourself to the public. I advise you, therefore, to be confidential with him. If he thinks your plan practicable, you will have his assistance: if not, you will have a plain answer and secrecy.

This, and Markham's avowal that Lord Townshend's 'plan is, what Lord Bristol had from Lord Chatham, to give way in most of the popular questions' encouraged Flood to believe that he could conclude an agreement to work with the new administration. William Markham certainly believed that the circumstances were right for him to do so 'without any sacrifice of duty or public esteem', but Flood was unwilling to make the first move.[32]

Townshend's arrival in Ireland was delayed until mid-October by the sudden and premature death of his brother, Charles.[33] More consequently, he set out without clear instructions as to how he should respond to 'the popular questions' that would determine Flood's attitude. He had raised these and the pressing matter of appointing a new lord chancellor with the cabinet on 3 October, but though ministers were content to allow him to offer assurances that a bill from Ireland to limit the duration of parliament would be afforded favourable consideration at the Privy Council, 'he could get so little satisfaction on the heads he wished, and particularly

---

31 Camden to Grafton, 29 Sept. in Anson, ed., *Grafton*, p. 163; O'Hara to Burke, 16 Aug. in Hoffman, *Burke*, p. 407; Newscutting, ca 20 Aug. 1767 (B.L.,O.C.,Townshend Papers, Box 10, Alex McAuley file). 32 Markham to Flood, 11 Oct. (Rosse Papers, C/2/1); O'Hara to Burke, 16 Aug. 1767 in Hoffman, *Burke*, p. 407. 33 Bartlett, 'Townshend', pp 49–50; Markham to Flood, 11 Oct. (Rosse Papers, C/2/1); de Grey to Townshend, 9 Sept. (B.L.,O.C., Townshend Papers, Box 12); Townshend to Lords Justices, 1 Oct, Waite to McLeane, 15 Oct. 1767 (N.A., Irish Correspondence 1697–1798, Ms 2446).

the chancellorship, that he burst into a very justifiable rage'.[34] Progress was reported at a follow-up meeting a few days later, but the inexactness of his instructions and the interruption caused by his brother's obsequies gave him little opportunity to explore the possibility of recruiting popular politicians before the meeting of parliament. This worked to the advantage of those who had most to lose if Townshend was able to recruit the likes of Flood, and it is noteworthy that John Ponsonby availed of the good offices of Lord Bessborough to assure Townshend of his readiness to support his administration.[35] Flood, by contrast, made no attempt to make contact, opting instead to devote his energies to local and personal affairs in County Kilkenny. He served on the county grand jury in September, when he and his friends Hercules Langrishe and Gervaise Parker Bushe signed the grand jury address to the knights of the shire urging them to support a septennial bill. Otherwise, he maintained the low profile he had adopted since his return to Ireland in January.[36]

On his arrival in Dublin, Lord Townshend sought to meet 'with the leading and principal persons of this country'.[37] Given the urgency of getting the parliamentary session under way, his most immediate requirement was to secure undertakings of support from the major borough interests and parliamentary managers. These were forthcoming, which freed him from the need to approach potentially sympathetic independents. The price for Flood's public support was a commitment to favour the four points he had raised with Chatham, and while Townshend was personally well-disposed, the fact that they did not have cabinet sanction meant he had little with which to tempt him. Flood did not know this, of course, but he remained hopeful that Townshend would be a reforming lord lieutenant. He was encouraged by elliptical reports (which he, like most people, interpreted as a coded reference to a septennial or militia bill) that the Lord Lieutenant 'had something to propose to our senate', but nothing happened in the run up to the opening of the new session to cause him to make a public declaration of support. There were even rumours that Pery and he had decided not to attend, and while these were groundless, Flood had decided that the administration should be given an opportunity to prove itself and, for this reason, he resolved not to behave as assertively in the House of Commons as he had in 1763–4 and 1765–6.[38]

Despite the optimism engendered by the public speculation as to its content, Flood found Townshend's speech opening the 1767–8 session disappointing. The Lord Lieutenant did signal the administration's support for legislation to amend

34 Whately to Grenville, 5, 8 Oct. in Smith, ed., *Grenville Papers*, iv, 169–73; Townshend to Shelburne, 29 Oct. 1767 (P.R.O., S.P.63/425, *C.H.O.P.*, ii, 219–22).   35 O'Hara to Burke, 20 Oct., in Hoffman, *Burke*, pp 412–13; Rigby to Fitzgerald, Sept. 1767 in Hickson, ed., *Old Kerry records, second series*, pp 282–3.   36 *F.L.J.*, 2, 5, 10, 16 Sept.1767. John Ponsonby also promised to use his 'utmost endeavours' to promote the success of a septennial act.   37 Townshend to de Grey, 20 Oct. 1767 (Norfolk Record Office, Walsingham Papers, P.R.O.N.I., T3428/1/5).   38 *Baratariana: a select collection of fugitive political pieces, published during the administration of Lord Townshend in Ireland* (3rd ed., Dublin, 1777), p. 14; Bartlett, 'Townshend', p. 61.

the tenure of judges from king's pleasure to 'good behaviour', but because it was accompanied by a statement on the necessity of augmenting the Irish army establishment by 3,000 men (which was Townshend's priority measure) and because there was no reference to septennial legislation, Flood was less than impressed. He dismissed it as a 'sop', 'thrown out to us merely for amusement', and he responded by moving and by receiving leave, with Charles Lucas and John Ponsonby, to prepare the heads of a bill to limit the duration of parliaments.[39] Given John Ponsonby's public pronouncements in favour of septennial legislation and the enthusiasm of patriots like Flood, Townshend concluded that the administration's backing for this measure was the key to the ratification of the augmentation. However, he was allowing his enthusiasm for the augmentation cloud his political judgement, and the secretary of state, Lord Shelburne, upbraided him for seeking to go further than the cabinet deemed wise or desirable. The expectation of ministers, Shelburne informed Townshend, was that he should proceed with great circumspection on such matters as the tenure of judges, the duration of parliaments and other popular issues such as a militia and *habeas corpus* legislation desired by Flood. He did reveal that ministers were not opposed in principle either to an Irish militia, a *habeas corpus* act or to legislation to limit the duration of Irish parliaments provided they lasted for eight years, rather than the seven favoured in Ireland, but he was not prepared to authorise Townshend to sponsor any of them.[40]

Ministerial agreement to legislate on these matters would have obliged Flood to reconsider his position. In its absence, he pressed forward circumspectly with his legislative agenda in the House of Commons.[41] His discretion did not pass unnoticed, though he did move successfully for leave on 6 November to prepare the heads of a bill 'for the establishing a national militia' with Sexten Pery, Charles Lucas and four others.[42] This posed the increasingly harassed Lord Lieutenant with a further problem. His instinct was to oppose it because he believed it would obstruct his army augmentation by exciting 'jealousy in the breasts of the advocates of the militia that this measure [the augmentation] is meant to preclude the latter [the militia]', and Castle officials opposed a patriot motion on 6 November averring that 'a militia *was the only effectual security* for the country' for this reason.[43] As this indicates, the fortunes of the augmentation and Flood's militia bill were inextricably linked by early November, and if this did not pose the Lord Lieutenant with

---

39 Townshend to Shelburne, 22, 27 Oct., 5 Nov., in *C.H.O.P.*, ii, 194–6, 198–201, P.R.O., S.P.,63/425; O'Hara to Burke, 20 Oct. 1767 in Hoffman, *Burke*, pp 412–13; *F.L.J.*, 5, 26 Sept.; McAulay to Townshend, 25 Aug. (B.L.,O.C., Townshend Papers, Box 10).   40 Townshend to Shelburne, 27 Oct., Shelburne to Townshend, 27, 29 Oct., 5, 18 Nov. 1767 (P.R.O., S.P., 63/425, *C.H.O.P.*, ii, 195–7, 201–2, 212–15).   41 As note 40; Townshend to Shelburne, 5, 18, 29 Nov. 1767 (P.R.O., S.P., 63/425, *C.H.O.P.*, ii, 198–201, 212–15, 219–22).   42 *Commons Jn. (Irl.)*, viii, 172; Burke to O'Hara, 12 Nov. in Hoffman, *Burke*, p. 417.   43 Townshend to [Granby], 10 Nov., in H.M.C., *Rutland*, ii, 293–4; Townshend to Shelburne, 13 Nov. 1767 (P.R.O., S.P., 63/425, *C.H.O.P.*, ii, 205–6).

problems enough, he also had to ensure that the appointment of a new lord chancellor did not cost him the support of established borough and undertaker interests.

John, Baron Bowes had died in July, and though it was not unusual for major offices to be left vacant for lengthy periods, the uncertainty caused by the unhappiness in England with the undertaker system, the ambition of some of the most powerful Irish politicians to secure the position, and the gathering realisation that ministers planned to continue the practice of appointing an Englishman excited mounting dissatisfaction in Ireland. By early November, patience with government inaction neared exhaustion, and there was talk of a motion of censure being presented to the House of Commons. It was even suggested that MPs would approve a three-month rather than a two-year money bill to demonstrate their displeasure.[44] This was an ideal opportunity for the patriots to adumbrate their message of responsible domestic government, but their effectiveness was much reduced by the reluctance of Henry Flood to stand forward. The redoubtable Lucius O'Brien sought to fill the vacuum, and he moved on 17 November that parliament should address the King on the matter of the vacant seals. This motion, like that for a three-month money bill, was soundly defeated, but one positive side effect of their agitation was that it encouraged Shelburne to look upon Flood's militia scheme with greater sympathy than would otherwise have been the case. 'I will only observe in regard to a militia', he wrote Townshend on 24 November, 'that a well digested and safe plan ... must meet with the approbation of His Majesty's servants, who are too intent on the security of Ireland to see with particular satisfaction every addition which can be made to it'.[45]

This was an issue which Townshend might profitably have discussed with Flood. But the appointment to the woolsack of James Hewitt, a little-known English lawyer and politician, created more pressing problems with John Ponsonby, Lord Shannon, John Hely-Hutchinson and Philip Tisdall.[46] Flood, for his part, had good reason to avoid becoming entangled with the administration on this point as the heads of his bill for limiting the duration of parliament to seven years and for providing for regular general elections from June 1774 came up for debate before the House of Commons towards the end of November. Evidential lacunae mean it is impossible

44 Lords Justice to Bristol, 22 July (N.A., Irish Correspondence 1697–1798, Ms 2446); Lord Townshend's patronage book (N.L.I., Ms 14299, nos 82, 114); Hely-Hutchinson to Fitzgerald, 10 Aug., Rigby to Fitzgerald, Sept., in Hickson, ed., *Old Kerry Records*, pp 290–1, 282–3; Hely-Hutchinson to Bessborough and reply, 20 Aug., 1 Sept. 1767 (T.C.D., Donoughmore Papers, C/2/17); Camden to Grafton, 27 Sept., 20 Oct. in Anson, ed., *Grafton*, pp 158–60, 164–6; Townshend to Shelburne, 27 Oct., 15, 16, Nov., Shelburne to Townshend, 5, 18, 24 Nov., 1767 (P.R.O., S.P.63/425, *C.H.O.P.*, ii, 195–6, 201–2, 205–6, 209–11, 212–15); Memo of Lord Lifford, 11 Apr. 1789 (Pitt (Pretyman) Papers, P.R.O.N.I., T3319/1).   45 Townshend to Shelburne, 15, 16, 17 Nov., Shelburne to Townshend, 24 Nov. 1767 (P.R.O., S.P.,63/425, *C.H.O.P.*, 11, 209–12); Lord Fitzmaurice, *Life of William, Earl of Shelburne* (3 vols, London, 1875–6), ii, 97–100.   46 Bartlett, 'Townshend', pp 62–3; Townshend to de Grey, 26 Nov., 1767 (Walsingham Papers, P.R.O.N.I., T3428/1/6).

to establish Flood's contribution during its various stages, but it is clear that the anxiety of the undertakers not to be seen to oppose a popular measure ensured it an unexpectedly trouble-free passage. The bill met with 'some small but ineffectual opposition' from those resistant to the idea of regular general elections, but neither their suggestion that parliaments should be decennial nor Townshend's that they should be octennial found favour with a majority of MPs. The heads of the bill proceeded through all stages with its septennial provision intact, and it was presented to the Lord Lieutenant by the Speaker, attended by the assembled members, on 26 November. This was, as Townshend put it, 'not usual'. But it accurately attested to the determination of Flood, Charlemont and Lucas that it should not fall, like its predecessors, at the hurdles of the Irish or British Privy Councils. It passed the first easily; with the result by December the hopes and fears of the bill's supporters and critics rested on the response of the British government.[47]

It is not clear if Flood regarded the bill's prospects as good or bad, but Townshend was confident that the good-will the measure's passage through the Irish parliament had bought the administration would enable him to forge a stable Commons' majority that would approve his plans for the augmentation of the Irish army.[48] His priority was to regain the allegiance of the major borough interests and parliamentary managers (Ponsonby, Shannon and Hely-Hutchinson), who had been alienated by the appointment of James Hewitt to the lord chancellorship, rather than to win over individual patriots like Flood, and with this in mind he entertained their exigent requests for preferment and appealed to old allies like the earl of Bessborough to intercede with Irish relations. Several were tempted by the prospect of power and preferment Townshend offered them. But since they were aware of how unpopular the augmentation was likely to be, they insisted that he also brought 'popular' patriots like Flood and coy borough interests like that of the earl of Tyrone onside:

> They could not but think it absolutely necessary to have the D[uke] of Leinster and Lord Tyrone, together with some of the popular speakers in the House of Commons, such as Sir William Osborne and Mr Flood etc persuaded to give their assistance, otherwise they imagined a party would be raised against so expensive and unpopular a measure as might in the end ruin them, and in the meantime prevent this measure from being carried thro' by such a respectable majority as would render such a step advisable to be taken by His Majesty.

There is no evidence to suggest that Flood or Osborne were aware of the undertakers' wish to have them support a measure they disliked, and they were not to

47 Townshend to Shelburne, 29 Nov., 3 Dec. (P.R.O., 63/425, *C.H.O.P.*, ii, 223); H.M.C.,*Charlemont*, i, 24–5; Noble to [Shirley], 3 Dec. 1767 (P.R.O.N.I., Shirley Papers, D3531/A/5 p. 20).   48 Thomas Bartlett, 'The augmentation of the army in Ireland 1767–69' in *E.H.R.*, xcvi (1981), pp 540–44; Bartlett, 'Townshend', pp 54–5.

receive any inkling from Townshend because while he initiated discussions with Lord Tyrone and the duke of Leinster, he made no overtures to Flood or Osborne. He placed his hopes of gaining their support entirely on the early return from London of the bill for limiting the duration of parliaments, but his expectations were dealt a blow by Irish anger at the alteration of the patriot sponsored clause appertaining to an absentee tax on officeholders in the money bill returned in December.[49] The bill passed. But the controversy the matter occasioned; the delay in returning the bill to limit the duration of parliaments; and the amendment to a bill for altering judges's commissions ruled out the possibility of an early fruitful approach to either Flood or Osborne.[50]

Flood's personal assessment of the Lord Lieutenant bears this out. By the end of 1767, he had concluded that Townshend was 'a very incapable man for the situation of lord lieutenant of Ireland'. He believed the Lord Lieutenant displayed a lack of 'wisdom and temper' which compared ill with the forbearance he and others on the opposition benches had shown. He explained to William Markham:

> We flatter ourselves that there are some among us who have prevented private or party heat from taking the lead, as is too common, and have confined opposition to such high objects as are esteemed manly here, and have preserved all decency and temper in the mode.[51]

Flood had certainly conducted himself with discretion throughout the first part of the session. Given the progress of the bill to limit the duration of parliament and the militia bill, there were good political reasons why he should do so. And persistent rumours that he was to be returned to the Westminster parliament may also have had a moderating influence on his public conduct.[52]

Flood found it increasingly difficult to exercise such self-restraint as the political climate disimproved in the winter of 1767–8. The most portentous development was the decision of Shannon, Ponsonby, Hely-Hutchinson, Tisdall and their supporters to withdraw their support for the augmentation because Townshend rejected their patronage demands. They gave the advanced state of the session as their reason but their support, when parliament resumed in late January, for a number of

---

49 Bartlett, 'Augmentation', pp 550–1; Bartlett, 'Townshend', pp 76–7; Bessborough to Townshend, 3 Dec. (N.L.I., Townshend Papers, Ms 394/34); Townshend to Shelburne, 12 (2), 13, 17 Dec., (P.R.O.,S.P.,63/425, *C.H.O.P.*, ii,228–30, 232–3); Townshend to Granby, 13 Dec, Dec., 1767 in H.M.C., *Rutland*, ii, 297–8. 50 Northington to Townshend, 12 Dec. (N.A., Irish Correspondence 1697–1798, Ms 2446); Rigby to Fitzgerald, Dec. in Hickson, ed., *Old Kerry records*, p. 283; Shelburne to Townshend, 19 Dec., Townshend to Shelburne, 28 Dec.1767, 3 Jan. 1768 (P.R.O., S.P.63/425, *C.H.O.P.*, ii, 234–5, 238, 287–9); Cummins, 'Opposition and the Irish parliament', pp 221–2; Townshend to Granby, 25, 26 Dec. 1767, 6 Jan. 1768 in H.M.C., *Rutland*, ii, 297–9; Flood to Markham. 25 Dec. 1767 (Rosse papers, C/2/2). 51 Flood to Markham, 25 Dec.1767 (Rosse Papers, C/2/2). 52 O'Hara to Burke, 5 Dec. [1767] in *Burke's Corres.*, i, 338.

financial motions aimed at discrediting the need to increase the army indicated just how alienated they were from the administration.[53] These motions have been attributed to Charles Lucas and Henry Flood, but none was proposed by leading opposition figures. Indeed, Flood may not have been in the Commons. His movements at this time are elusive, but since there is no reason to doubt his later claim that he 'followed' the septennial bill to England, he may have spent the recess and the early part of the 1768 sitting in London.[54] He was too dissatisfied with the direction of events to let matters pass without comment but, because he was unwilling to oppose the administration openly, he chose the time-honoured device of a *nom de plume*. Styling himself Philadelphus, Flood adopted the popular contemporary conceit of letters to a 'friend in Pennsylvania' as a device to express his dissatisfaction with the current state of Irish politics. First published in consecutive issues of the *Freeman's Journal* between 16 January and 2 February 1768, the six letters in the series constituted the opening salvo in one of the most successful essays in political propaganda produced in eighteenth-century Ireland.[55]

Flood's authorial decision to portray Ireland in his Philadelphus letters in terms of a fictional location he denominated Baratariana suggests that he may have toyed with publishing a sustained satire on Irish political life along the lines of Jonathan Swift's *Gulliver's Travels*. If so, it was wise of him not to try since he did not possess the requisite literary skill. His Philadelphus letters are more impressive for their political jibes than for their satirical style, and the two do not always sit easily together. Yet the image of Lord Townshend as Sancho, 'a plump man, with a merry, round, unstudious-looking countenance; a jovial companion, of great festive mirth, preferring even the latter end of a feast to any part of a fray', is memorable though the satire is inconsistent and gives way too quickly to personalised criticism of the Lord Lieutenant's 'attachment to the Stuart line', his military record, and his capacity to devise and to execute a 'great design'. These and other accusations were part of the arsenal of allegations that became the staple ingredients of patriot propaganda directed at Townshend, and their prominence in Flood's letter indicates that his priority was to score political points rather than to write consistent satire. This is borne out by his inclusion of a dismissive portrait of John Ponsonby (Colonel Promise), and a hostile depiction of John Hely-Hutchinson, whom he labelled Sergeant Rufinus. Flood believed that the parallels between Rufinus and Hely-Hutchinson's rise from obscurity were perfect for his purposes, and he skilfully deployed his intimacy with the classics by citing Claudian's invective against Rufinus as an epigram to his first letter. His depiction of Hely-Hutchinson was more cutting and denigratory than was the case with either Townshend or Ponsonby. Hely-Hutchinson, he pro-

53 Fitzmaurice, *Life of Shelburne*, ii, 105–8; Bartlett, 'Townshend', pp 71–7; Bartlett, 'Augmentation', pp 552–3; Townshend to [Granby], 25 Jan. in H.M.C.,*Rutland*, ii, 300–1; Townshend to Shelburne, 11, 26, 28, 30 Jan., 4 Feb. in *C.H.O.P.*, ii, 291–2, 295–300, 302–3.   54 *H.J.*, 29 Oct. 1773; *Life of Grattan*, i, 195–6.   55 *F.J.*, 16, 19, 23, 26, 29 Jan., 2 Feb. 1768.

nounced, was a 'factious tribune' who had earned the soubriquet 'single session Rufin' because it summed up his career as a patriot; and to be 'stiled a scum in politics' because he lacked 'that liberality of soul, that generosity of sentiment, that noble ardour of principle which dignifies and distinguishes the higher ranks of mankind'.[56]

These offensive sentiments were written to hurt and they did. So, naturally enough, when Hely-Hutchinson learned Flood was their author he countered with a speech in the House of Commons in which he condemned Flood as 'an artificer of attitudes' and a 'petty dealer in seven-fold phraseology'. This elicited a robust reply from Flood, and it seemed that the row was destined to end on the duelling field when Hely-Hutchinson drew back and magnanimously asserted that Flood and he should 'unite' rather than fight, and exert themselves for their country's 'good' against Lord Townshend.[57]

Despite his antipathy towards Hely-Hutchinson, Flood was in no position to dismiss this call for co-operation, because he had called in the first Philadelphus letter on 'the champions of Baratariana' to 'enter ... into a union' to protect the liberties of the people against 'ministerial tyranny' and 'the politics of despotism'. He was certainly of the opinion that the kingdom was being abused by the Crown's representatives: 'We have been treated of late, not as the children, but the bastards of our mother country; ... all our expectations of an equal distribution of inheritance are considered, not as claims of right, but as pretences of contumacy, and presumption'.[58] These were strong sentiments given Flood's own origins, but they were justified, he believed, because, he maintained in letter two, of 'the arbitrary measures, which have for some years past been pursued against this devoted land, by the emissaries sent over here by the rulers of our parent country, with the connivance or concurrence of some of our own parricides associated with them'. As proof of this, he cited the failure to admit to the statute book one of the three bills to limit the duration of parliament approved by Irish MPs since 1761. He also dismissed Townshend's ostensible readiness to favour the alteration of the tenure of judges as a barefaced attempt to buy off Irish opposition, and forecast that the delay in returning his septennial bill meant it would fail once again.[59]

In contrast to the legislation to limit the duration of parliament, which Flood deemed compelling, he could identify no convincing reason why the executive sought to augment the army, since the military need could be served equally well by his proposal for a militia. He addressed this issue in his third and fourth letters, but his case was weakened on both occasions by digressions attacking Hely-Hutchinson. As a result, the defence of the militia bill he presented was less convincing than it might have been. Moreover, his claim that Hely-Hutchinson calculated that 'by

56 *Baratariana*, pp 6–7.   57 *Life of Grattan*, i, 277–8.   58 *Baratariana*, pp 2–3, 8–9.   59 *Baratariana*, pp 10–19 *passim*.

reducing us to become a province only of another kingdom, he hopes to recommend himself to a seat in that senate where he vainly imagines that his parts, but not impossibly his arts, may soon render him considerable' in doubtful taste given his own aspirations in that regard.[60]

Having appeased what was clearly a deeply felt need to flay Hely-Hutchinson, Flood concentrated in his last two Philadelphus letters on major issues such as the threat to Irish 'liberties' he identified in the continued interference of the British Privy Council with Irish legislation; the delay in 'having the highest post in the law here filled in proper time' in which he implicated 'Rufin and his associates'; and the regulations relating to the trade in grain that advantaged England. But it was the assertion by the Irish Privy Council that it possessed the same authority as its British counterpart to respite and amend the legislation of the Irish parliament that he deemed the most intolerable 'invasion upon our liberty', and he devoted his final letter exclusively to this.

According to Flood, the Irish Privy Council was 'a sort of wen or excrescence, that has grown out of the corruption of our constitution'. More consequently, it acted in a manner 'totally destructive of our legislature' because of 'a forced and unwarrantable construction' of Poynings' Law

> which would, if submitted to, render our senates the mere pupils of these high mightinesses [the privy councillors]; to perform those exercises, and discuss those themes, only, that were marked out to them by their preceptors. For, because the reasons for summoning the senate are previously to be certified by them, they pretended to argue that a senate has no manner of right to propose or debate upon any one article which is not within their certificate. This is what they presume to claim. And also because they are to certify the causes for the calling of a senate, they have assumed the sole right of certifying or transmitting, and also of not certifying or transmitting the bills proposed by the senate. And this is what they dare to exercise.

Flood's contention that it was only because of this misinterpretation that members of 'this despotick [Irish] council' were enabled to become 'perpetual dictators', when their British equivalents merely constituted a 'harmless council of deliberation and advice, not an estate of concurrence and co-operation', was problematic given the number of Irish bills that were amended and respited in London. But his contention that the Irish parliament could break free of the constraints the Irish Privy Council placed on its law-making powers if the 'innovations' which sustained it were purged was a potentially important argument if the role of the Irish council moved centre stage. So too was his defence of parliamentary government and his assertion that 'a free senate is the only safe-guard of our liberties'.[61]

60 *Baratariana*, pp 20–34.   61 *Baratariana*, pp 41–4.

Because he wrote under a pseudonym, Flood was not bound in his public actions by the views expressed in the letters of Philadelphus. At the same time, the fact that he entered into print with such opinions indicated that he felt that the prospects of his reaching an agreement with the administration were remote. This is corroborated by the fact that he took a *somewhat* more forward role in the House of Commons in the spring of 1768.[62] He continued to leave the running to others, but he was no longer quite so reserved. So when Sir Charles Bingham proposed on 5 February that a delegation comprising Flood, Lucas and William Ponsonby should travel to England 'to lay before His Majesty the great advantages that must arise to this kingdom by passing the bill for limiting the duration of parliaments', and to do what it could to obviate 'such objections as may have been made', Flood conferred respectability on a suggestion Townshend plainly regarded as ridiculous by supporting it with 'precedents taken from the journals in the times of James I and Charles I'. Bingham's motion was withdrawn without being put to a vote after a debate lasting several hours, but the opposition made it clear they would revive the idea if the septennial bill was not soon returned.[63] They did not need to, as things turned out, because the bill arrived back in Ireland a few days later.

The return of the bill limiting the duration of the Irish parliament placed Flood in a quandary. He badly wanted the measure to become law, but the bill that was returned had been amended. He was, at the same time, acutely aware that many MPs had only voted for the bill in the Irish Commons because they feared the unpopularity that would result from opposing it, and because they anticipated it would either be respited by the British Privy Council or be rejected in Ireland if it was returned in an amended form. The problem for many such MPs, who normally supported British government in Ireland, was that they could not be seen to oppose the measure on these grounds. This was a role the patriots traditionally performed, and the fact that the reference in the preamble of the bill to its being 'the undoubted right of the people of Ireland to a more frequent choice' of representatives was deleted, that the duration of an Irish parliament was extended from seven to eight years, and that the date of the first general election was brought forward from 1774 to 1768, put them under considerable pressure to play this role once more. However, rather than take this course, Flood and Charlemont concluded that their interests would be better served by supporting the measure in its amended state. They were, they calculated, too close to securing a reform they had pursued for nearly a decade to lose it to another of their grievances, particularly, as Flood's sixth Philadelphus letter suggests, they felt less passionately about the interference of the British Council with Irish legislation than they did about the intervention of its Irish counterpart.[64] As a result, the most committed supporters of legislation to limit the duration of

62 *F.J.*, 20 Feb. 1768.   63 Townshend to Shelburne, 4, 6 Feb. 1768 in *C.H.O.P.*, ii, 302–3, B.L., Lansdowne Abstracts, Add. Ms 24137.   64 P.R.O., P.C.2/112 f 25; Shelburne to Townshend, 2 Feb. 1768 in *C.H.O.P.*, ii, 301–2; 'Charlemont's memoirs', in H.M.C., *Charlemont*, i, 26.

parliament determined to do what they could to facilitate the amended bill's ratification. In Dublin city, the decision 'that the public exultation should be made manifest' climaxed on 15 February when the bill embarked on its final Commons' stages with a rally (orchestrated by Charles Lucas) of an estimated 20,000 supporters of the measure at College Green while, in the House, Flood contrived to preempt opposition by moving for an address of thanks to the king for returning it. It was a shrewd piece of parliamentary strategy and it worked like a dream. The bill was approved without difficulty.[65]

Lord Townshend maintained in his report that the bill's ratification caused 'great and universal satisfaction'. This is an exaggeration, but it was a moment of triumph for the small coterie of popular politicians that had pressed for the reform since 1761. The main recipients of public applause in Dublin, where the celebrations were loudest, were Charles Lucas and the earl of Kildare.[66] This was predictable given Lucas's long advocacy of municipal as well as parliamentary reform and the earl of Kildare's transcendant popularity with the Dublin populace. However, it accorded Henry Flood insufficient acknowledgement since he was as prominent as Lucas in advocating the measure from the mid-1760s, and more imposing in the House of Commons. Flood did not appear to mind; he was less interested in public applause than his colleagues, so that while Lucas, the earl of Kildare and, indeed, Lord Townshend revelled in the bouquets that came their way in the weeks and months following the ratification of the Octennial Act, he contented himself with appending his name to addresses from the Grand Jury of County Kilkenny to George III and to Lord Townshend expressing their 'unfeigned thanks' and 'gratitude' for the measure.[67] Besides, his contribution had not passed unnoticed. He was publicly thanked by the influential pressure group, the Aldermen of Skinner's Alley in early March, and a meeting of the Shuttle Club of the Coombe, chaired by the Master of the Weavers Guild, approved an address requesting Lucas and he to stand for the city of Dublin in the forthcoming general election. This suggestion secured the backing of the powerful Guild of Merchants who promised their votes and up to £10,000 towards the cost of campaigning. However, he was not to be Lucas' running mate. Flood continued to receive the applause of the city's middle classes for his oratory and his policies, but he was not to represent them then or at any other time in the House of Commons.[68]

65 'A sketch of facts' (R.I.A., Burrowes Papers, Ms 23K53/10); *Biographical, literary and political anecdotes of several of the most eminent persons of the present age* (3 vols, London, 1797), i, 101–10; H.M.C., *Charlemont*, i, 26–7. 66 Townshend to Shelburne, 16, 18 Feb. in *C.H.O.P.*, ii, 306–7; *F.L.J.*, 24, 27 Feb., 17 Aug. and August passim; Cummins, 'Opposition and the Irish parliament', p. 81; Murphy, 'The Lucas affair', p. 228; H.M.C., *Charlemont*, i, 24. 67 *F.L.J.*, 2 Apr.; Townshend to Shelburne, 13 Apr. in *C.H.O.P.*, ii, 325; Waite to Wilmot, 21 Apr. 1768 (N.A., Index to departmental letters and papers 1760–89, f 322). 68 *F.J.*, 5, 19 Jan., 23 Feb., 8 Mar.; *F.L.J.*, 12 Mar., 27 Apr.; Caldwell to Townshend, [1768] (B.L., Lansdowne Abstracts, Add. Ms 24137); Gardiner to Bedford, 4 Nov., 1760 (Bedford Papers, P.R.O.N.I., T2915/10/47).

As well as indisposition which curtailed his movements, one of the reasons for Flood's relatively low public profile, while the celebrations of the ratification of the Octennial Act were at their height, was his engagement with the militia bill – the heads of which he presented to the House of Commons on 10 February. It was received and given a first reading, but when the committee of the whole house commenced its more detailed consideration seven days later, the conclusion of officials that the ratification of the bill would precipitate the 'defeat [of] the intended augmentation' ensured it made no further progress. In an attempt to salvage something from the episode, one of Flood's friends maintained that though the bill was lost, he successfully 'established the principle [of a national militia] in the minds of the public', but this was wishful thinking.[69]

If Flood's utterances as Philadelphus and his advocacy of militia legislation seemed to suggest that he was reverting to the active patriotism that had brought him fame in the mid-1760s, it did not exclude him from the Lord Lieutenant's calculations, for he was invited to dine at the Castle on 12 February.[70] Townshend needed his support, as Shannon, Ponsonby, Hely-Hutchinson and Tisdall indicated they would oppose the augmentation, and he was not without hope that the ratification of the Octennial Act would cause Flood to consider his position. However, Flood showed no eagerness to move in his direction. With a general election imminent, there was no way an 'independent gentlemen' could allow himself to be identified with the augmentation. Realising he did not have the numbers, the Lord Lieutenant appealed to London to be allowed postpone the augmentation bill until after the general election but permission was not forthcoming. He was refused permission also to become permanently resident, to replace John Ponsonby as speaker of the House of Commons, and to curb his power to bestow patronage in the revenue.[71]

Compelled, against his judgement, to press onwards, Townshend applied himself tirelessly to the task of winning a majority for the augmentation. He did so against a backdrop of mounting public disquiet fomented by Charles Lucas who, Townshend observed angrily, 'has been playing the devil here ... with his harangues and writings'.[72] Flood, by contrast, continued to conduct himself discreetly, though the residual hopes he entertained for his militia bill were finally dashed when notice

---

69 *Commons Jn. (Irl.)*, viii, 225, 245; Militia in Ireland, 10 Feb. in *C.H.O.P.*, ii, 304; O'Hara to Burke, 9 Feb. in Hoffman, *Burke*, pp 423–4; *F.L.J.*, 24 Feb. 1768;'A sketch of facts', (R.I.A., Burrowes Papers, Ms 23K53/10); D.Miller, 'Non-professional soldiery 1600–1800' in T. Bartlett and K. Jeffery, eds., *A military history of Ireland* (Cambridge, 1996), pp 315–34.   **70** A list of the Lords and commoners who have dined with the Lord Lieutenant 1768–69 (N.L.I., Ms 1470).   **71** Bartlett, 'Townshend', pp 82–95; Townshend to de Grey, 18 Feb (Walsingham Papers, P.R.O.N.I.,T3428/1/7); Townshend to Shelburne, 26 Feb., 5 Mar., Shelburne to Townshend, 14 Mar. 1768 in *C.H.O.P.*, ii, 310, 312–13, 315); Fitzmaurice, *Life of Shelburne*, ii, 110–11.   **72** Townshend to de Grey, 2 Apr. (Walsingham Papers, P.R.O.N.I., T3428/1/8); Townshend to Granby, 5, 30 Apr. in H.M.C., *Rutland*, ii, 304; Fitzmaurice, *Life of Shelburne*, ii, 114; Townshend to Shelburne, 6 Apr. in *C.H.O.P.*, ii, 323–4; Cummins, 'Opposition in the Irish parliament', pp 77–83, 148–54; Murphy, 'The Lucas affair', p. 231.

was given on 19 April that the question of the augmentation would be debated on 2 May. And if this was not troubling enough, he also had to accept the loss of the judges' tenure bill, because of the insertion by the British Privy Council of an objectionable amendment giving the Westminster parliament the right to remove Irish judges, and the *habeas corpus* bill, which was respited because Ireland was deemed too riotous and disorderly to have such a law.[73]

In Flood's absence, the patriots' opposition to the augmentation was headed on 2 May by Sexten Pery. He opposed the proposal on the controversial grounds 'that the augmentation was meant to enable Britain to keep more troops in America in order to crush the spirit of her colonies'. Others cited its financial implications; still others the lateness of the session as their reason for voting against the measure, and their combined influence was just enough to ensure its defeat. The Lord Lieutenant's and the government's favourite measure of the session was lost (108 to 104) to an 'odd' coalition of patriots, 'King's servants and people in employment'.[74] Bloody but unbowed, Townshend responded defiantly by bringing the session to a rapid conclusion, by renewing his request to the government to be allowed reside in Ireland for the duration of his appointment and by extending his patronage network. Among those he recommended for 'some mark of His Majesty's favour' was 'the family of the earl of Tyrone and his brother Mr John Beresford' because of their 'fixed resolution to give all the assistance in their power to the augmentation'.[75] No preferment was available for immediate allocation, but the positive opinion the Lord Lieutenant entertained of the Tyrone interest indicated that their decision to work with the Castle had proved more advantageous than Flood's distant and critical stance. Of course, it was not preferment but policy changes that Flood was after, and while he could and did take considerable satisfaction from the ratification of the Octennial Act, the fact that the other bills he urged were lost suggests that this was due less to his role than to a change of heart by ministers. As things stood in the summer of 1768, the likelihood of his working closely with Dublin Castle seemed more remote than it had been in 1766 or 1767. Furthermore, while he apprehended the upcoming general election might diminish his prospects further, Lord Townshend was so confident it would strengthen the Castle connection in the Commons, he did not delay setting matters in train for a poll.[76]

---

73 P.R.O., P.C.2/113 ff 131, 143, 150, 156–7; O'Hara to Burke, 19 Apr. in Hoffman, *Burke*, pp 431–2; Fitzmaurice, *Life of Shelburne*, ii, 109–10; Shelburne to Townshend, 19, 23 Apr. in *C.H.O.P.*, ii, 326–7, 328; Whately to Grenville, 21 May in Smith, ed., *Grenville Papers*, iv, 296–7.   74 Townshend to Granby, 30 Apr., 7 May in H.M.C., *Rutland*, ii, 304–5; E.M. Johnston, *Great Britain and Ireland 1760–1800* (Edinburgh, 1963), pp 379–91; Townshend to Shelburne, 3 May, Shelburne to Townshend, 19 May in *C.H.O.P.*, ii, 330–1, 340; Fitzmaurice, *Life of Shelburne*, ii, 112–16; O'Hara to Burke, 10 May 1768 in Hoffman, *Burke*, pp 432–3.   75 Shelburne to Townshend, 14 May, Townshend to Shelburne, 10 May in *C.H.O.P.*, ii, 337, 333–6.   76 Townshend to Shelburne, 10, 31 May, Shelburne to Townshend, 17 May 1768 (N.A., Irish Correspondence 1697–1798, Ms 2446, *C.H.O.P.*, ii, 344–5).

THE 1768 GENERAL ELECTION AND ITS AFTERMATH

The ratification of the Octennial Act was a mixed blessing for Henry Flood. In Callan where, as we have seen, he was embroiled in a tense battle to retain control, it posed another moment of political danger he could well have done without. But because he had not given up on his ambition to represent County Kilkenny, he was also hopeful that he could capitalise on his much improved political profile and regain the seat in the constituency he had represented between 1759 and 1761.

Flood gave public notice of his intention to stand for County Kilkenny in February 1768, a few days after John Ponsonby and James Agar, and several weeks before Edmund Butler (the son of Lord Mountgarret) announced their candidatures. He offered himself as the 'disinterested and uniform promoter of that great improvement in our constitution' – the Octennial Act – but since Ponsonby and Agar also advertized their support for this measure, it offered him little advantage. His prospects were dented further by 'severe indisposition', which delayed his canvas, and by the decision of Agar and Ponsonby to renew the electoral pact they had concluded so advantageously in 1761.[77] Despite this, Flood refused to withdraw as he had done when faced with a similar alliance seven years earlier. He made a despairing attempt to disrupt his opponents' momentum by appealing to Lord Charlemont to explore with Lord Shannon the possibility of his inviting his brother-in-law, John Ponsonby, to desert Agar but it was futile. This obliged Flood to look elsewhere for allies. He secured the support of Lord Wandesford, and may even have concluded an electoral pact with Edmund Butler.[78] He also provided coaches and accommodation in Kilkenny to enable freeholders resident in Dublin to travel to vote, but it was not enough to give him victory. The poll was conducted under the watchful eye of Gervaise Parker Bushe, the High Sheriff, who was his friend and political ally. He polled well among the 40 shilling freeholders, but Butler and he attracted far fewer votes than Agar and Ponsonby among £10 freeholders with the result that the sitting MPs held their seats by a secure margin. Flood maintained subsequently that he withdrew from the contest before he had polled all his voters, and while this may be true it did not affect the outcome.[79]

Given that his return for Callan was contested, it could be argued that the poll in the county constituency represented a costly electoral rebuff for Flood, but this was only partly true. He had not won a prestigious County Kilkenny seat, but he had polled well and he was guaranteed a parliamentary seat, whatever the outcome of the petition against his return for Callan, by his decision to purchase for Longford. Moreover, the results in Kilkenny and elsewhere strengthened his parliamentary

77 *F.L.J.*, 17, 24 Feb., 9, 12, 19 Mar., 9 Apr. 1768. 78 Flood to Charlemont, 30 May in H.M.C., *Charlemont*, ii, 390; Charlemont to Flood, [1768], Wandesford to Flood, [1768] (B.L., Flood Papers, Add. Ms 22393 ff 8–9). 79 *F.J.*, 5, 19 July; *F.L.J.*, 13, 16, 20, 23 July; *P.O.*, 23 July 1768. The final poll was Ponsonby 494, Agar 438, Butler 331 and Flood 323.

influence. Flood did not possess the personality or the personalty to command a parliamentary interest of any size for any length of time, but he found himself at the helm of a sizeable parliamentary connection in the new parliament because the peculiar circumstances which enabled him to retain his Callan seat also resulted in the election of his cousin John for the same constituency. John Flood was described by one contemporary as 'milder' than many of the Floods, but his temperament was less significant than his readiness to take his lead politically from his more able cousin. Another cousin, Warden Flood, who purchased the return for the borough of Longford when Henry vacated the constituency to take his seat for Callan was prepared to do likewise. The son of Francis Flood of Paulstown, Warden had practised as a lawyer prior to his entry into politics where he quickly made a name for himself as a forthright speaker. As time passed, he moderated his sentiments and he was regarded in Castle circles in 1773 as 'a good kind of man and well behaved, which is extraordinary among the Floods'. This is not entirely sustainable, but it offers an indication of the hostile reaction Henry Flood provoked at this point in official quarters. Others, by contrast, were enthralled by his abilities. One of those who responded most warmly in the late 1760s was Gervaise Parker Bushe. He purchased a seat in the borough of Granard in 1768, when he was described as being 'much connected with Henry Flood' and guided by him in his political actions. For as long as Bushe accepted his lead, Flood led a parliamentary interest of four, though it was never tightly knit; Bushe's interest was preferment, while the Flood cousins' inability to subordinate their personal ambitions and to overcome their personal resentments ensured its fragmentation after a brief existence.[80]

This was in the future; in the meantime, the unexpected emergence of a Flood parliamentary connection increased Henry's appeal to Lord Townshend. The Lord Lieutenant had hoped that the election would result in the weakening of his opponents, but Lord Shannon and Speaker Ponsonby 'carried their men in every town and city and county as they wished'. Charles O'Hara estimated the anti-Castle interest in the Commons possessed a majority of thirty.[81] This meant Townshend faced a formidable task if he was to secure approval for the army augmentation when the new parliament assembled but, having chosen to reside in Ireland, he was determined to construct a Castle connection that would ratify the legislation he and his superiors deemed necessary. Since he was at odds with the major undertaker interests, he was obliged of necessity to turn to those 'independent gentlemen' and borough interests who were motivated by the wish either to bring the mismanagement and jobbery they identified with the undertaker system to a close or to secure positions of influence and power for themselves.[82] The 'independents' he most de-

---

80 List of Irish House of Commons, ca 1770 (N.A., Townshend Papers, Ms 734/1); David Large, 'The Irish House of Commons in 1769', *I.H.S.*, xi (1958), pp 30, 33; William Hunt, ed., *The Irish parliament 1775* (London, 1907), p. 9; Bodkin, ed., 'The Irish parliament in 1773', pp 197, 205; Keane et al., eds, *King's Inns admission papers*, p. 171; *F.J.*, 11 Jan. 1770.   81 Bartlett, 'Townshend', pp 117–20.   82 Bartlett,

sired to win over were Henry Flood and Sir William Osborne, because they were among the most effective performers in the Commons. He approached Osborne in the winter of 1768–9; he did not extract a firm commitment, but Osborne's readiness to accept the Lord Lieutenant's offer of preferment for members of his family suggested that he was amenable.[83]

Townshend was unable to make similar overtures to Flood who spent the early winter of 1768-9 in London, where he witnessed at first hand the political machinations that followed Chatham's belated resignation from office in October. There is no record of his reaction to this or to the manoeuvring that resulted in the duke of Grafton becoming prime minister, but it is hardly likely that it impressed him any more than it did Edmund Burke, who condemned the resultant ministry as 'a set of people of opposition opinions and low principles'.[84] More pertinently, Flood's willingness to assist Gervaise Parker Bushe see his pamphlet, *The case of Great Britain and America*, through the press suggests that his inclination was strongly towards opposition since Bushe was sharply critical of the government's American policy. He urged conciliation rather than confrontation and, while rejecting British assertions that it possessed the 'authority' to 'impose taxes upon the colonies', advocated the inauguration of a 'permanent system' which fixed the 'pretensions' of Britain and the 'claims' of the colonies. Bushe's observation in a letter to Flood that *The case of Great Britain and America* was as much 'your child ... as mine' raises the possibility that Flood may have had a part in writing it, but there is no evidence to support this conclusion. As far as one can tell, his role was confined to the provision of 'encouragement' and advice on matters of style and fact – a service also performed by Hercules Langrishe and Richard Griffith, who were part of the same Kilkenny set.[85]

Flood arrived back in Ireland in early January 1769. He appears not to have tarried in Dublin long enough to meet the Lord Lieutenant, but the appointment of Francis Flood of Huntingbrooke as a justice of the peace suggested that Townshend was anxious to buy his goodwill. Moreover, there was some contact between Flood and Lord Frederick Campbell because he informed the Chief Secretary late in January that he was prepared to pay up to £4,000 for a seat at Westminster. It cannot be established if Flood had explored this option while in England, because this is the only reference to this matter at this time, but his mind, on his return, was not focused on either Westminster or College Green, but on his faltering authority in Callan. He had left matters there delicately poised when he set out for London, and he was obliged on his arrival back in Kilkenny to throw himself into the thick of

---

'Townshend', pp 103–4, 107; Townshend to Shelburne, 14 Oct., 2 Nov., 1768 in *C.H.O.P.*, ii, 378, 381–2.   83 Osborne to Townshend, 28 Dec. 1768 (B.L.,O.C., Townshend Papers, Box 11).   84 Burke to O'Hara, Sept. 1768 in *Burke's Corres.*, i, 114–15.   85 *The case of Great Britain and America addressed to the King and both houses of parliament* (3rd edition, Dublin, 1769), *passim*; B[ushe] to Flood, 31 Nov. 1769 (Rosse Papers, C/1/3).

affairs there. His initial task was to ensure that the Floods' view of events was afforded adequate coverage in the press, but he also had to endeavour to undo the damage caused him and his family by an 'anonymous' letter sent, one must assume by someone close to James Agar, to such notables as the Marquess of Rockingham, the duke of Portland, Lord Clare, Richard Rigby and the earls of Shelburne, Hillsborough, Bristol and Chatham offering a less than sympathetic commentary on the Floods' role in the dispute.[86]

The tension this reflected in the borough of Callan mirrored that in the political nation at large as Lord Townshend intensified his efforts to reinforce the Castle interest in the spring and summer of 1769. Through a combination of patronage, a firm hand (particularly in his dealings with John Ponsonby), and the force of his personality, he was in a position to claim in May 1769 that he had secure commitments from 117 MPs. With 104 MPs definitely against and a further 83, among whom was Henry Flood, 'doubtful', he was not yet in a position to call a parliament. Nonetheless, Townshend was confident he would acquire the necessary numbers.[87] What was necessary, he calculated, was an explicit declaration of support by the government for his policy of creating a Castle party, and authorization to replace unreliable officeholders and borough managers with able men who would manage and lead the Castle interest in the Commons. His targets for this vital responsibility, he informed the duke of Grafton on 21 April, were Henry Flood, Sir William Osborne and John Beresford. He was confident of his ability to secure their support, and of the decisive additional votes they would bring (raising the Castle interest in the Commons to over 160), if he could dismiss the likes of Ponsonby and Shannon, but he took no action while he awaited a response from London to his demands. His ministerial colleagues were unenthusiastic. 'Alarmed, one of his London correspondents informed him, 'in case the administration should be hurt by a failure in Irish government' they instructed him in June to pursue a less confrontational approach, to readmit Ponsonby, Shannon and their allies (who had shown considerable resolution in the face of vice-regal blandishments) into positions of influence, and to reopen discussion with *all* parties to establish if he could, by this means, secure sufficient support for the money bill and the army augmentation.[88] Townshend was aghast. This instruction threatened, he informed the new Secretary of State, Lord Weymouth, to undermine his efforts to bring Flood onside and to forge a dominant

---

86 *P.O.*, 7 Jan., 25 Mar.; Flood to Charlemont, 26 Mar. 1769 in H.M.C.,*Charlemont*, i, 292.   87 Pomeroy to Pomeroy, 9 Jan. (Pomeroy Papers, P.R.O.N.I., T2954/5/4); Townshend to Macartney, 26 Feb., 7 Apr., 14, 18, 20 May in Bartlett, ed., *Macartney*, pp 8–9, 10–12, 14, 16–17; Clements to Townshend, 20, 30 Mar., 14 Aug. (N.A., Townshend Papers, Ms 671–3); Townshend to de Grey, 13 May 1769 (Walsingham Papers, P.R.O.N.I., T3428/1/10); Large, 'The Irish House of Commons in 1769', pp 42–5.   88 Ms list of the Irish parliament, 1769 (H.L. Clements, Celbridge (N.L.I., microfilm p. 4068)); Bartlett, 'Townshend', pp 127–8, 135–40; Townshend to Macartney, 20 May, 3, 6, 7, 12, 14 June in Bartlett, ed., *Macartney*, pp 16–17, 22–3, 26–7; Waite to Macartney, 2 June 1769 (B.L.,O.C., Waite-Macartney letters).

Castle connection because it would encourage John Ponsonby, who claimed in July that he could 'bring 150 men into the field', to persist with his opposition until his terms were met.[89] 'The addition which will follow the taking of Sir W. O[sborne] and Mr Flood', he affirmed on 24 June, 'would secure us against any ill-effects which the clamour of a removal of Mr Ponsonby and those servants of government who follow him might return', whereas an approach to Shannon or Ponsonby would 'shake the confidence of all our friends extremely and probably revolt Sir W[illiam] Osborne and Flood beyond all practicability'. 'Can it be imagined', he repeated some time later, 'that Mr Flood and Sir W[illiam] Osborne will support in hopes of another breach between the Speaker and English government, or that Mr [Thomas] Conolly and such capital characters will drudge on without … cease'.[90]

So far as one can tell, Flood did not have any inkling that he figured so prominently in the dispatches that passed between Dublin and London in the summer of 1769. As a result, one cannot say how he would have responded had he known then that privately Townshend deemed his support vital to the future success of his administration and that he contemplated offering him 'the next vacant seat at that board' with the view to making him 'first commissioner [of the revenue]' in due course.[91] He and his cousin John did have a cordial meeting with Townshend in Kilkenny in August, but the Lord Lieutenant chose to delay broaching the subject of Flood's taking office until his 'way back' from Munster. However, he was not to have the opportunity.[92] While the Lord Lieutenant was in Munster, the simmering dispute between Flood and James Agar boiled over and precipitated the fatal encounter at Dunmore. Townshend's initial reaction was relief that Flood 'stands fair', but the legal complications arising from the incident and the wrong signal a meeting would send the powerful Agar interest caused him to return to Dublin by a different route and the moment passed.[93] More importantly, by the time the legal proceedings arising out of the duel were completed, the political context had changed so dramatically there was no possibility of Flood and he ever working together.[94]

89 Weymouth to Townshend, 9 June (B.L.,O.C., Townshend Papers, Box 14); King to Grafton, 6 June (Grafton Papers, P.R.O.N.I., T2959/2/10); Townshend to Weymouth, 24 June in *C.H.O.P.*, ii, 478–80; Weymouth to Townshend, 21 Oct. (N.A., Irish correspondence 1697–1798, Ms 2446); Waite to Macartney, 7 July 1769 (B.L.,O.C., Waite-Macartney letters). 90 Townshend to Macartney, 24, 28 June, 17 July in Bartlett, ed., *Macartney*, pp 30–2, 34, 37; see also letters of 28(2), 30 June, 28 July 1769 in *idem*, pp 32–4, 35. 91 Waite to Macartney, 17, 28 July (B.L.,O.C., Waite-Macartney letters); Townshend to Weymouth, 17 Aug. in *C.H.O.P.*, ii, 488–93; Townshend to Macartney, 19 Aug.; Note by Townshend re Henry Flood, Aug.1769 in Bartlett, ed., *Macartney*, pp 39, 40–1. Townshend believed he could also 'satisfy' Osborne and Beresford by promising to appoint them to the Revenue Board in place of John Ponsonby and Lord Lanesborough. 92 Macartney to Townshend, 6 Sept., (N.A., Townshend Papers, Ms 733/31); Ward to Macartney, 6 Sept. in *C.H.O.P.*, ii, 495; Townshend to Macartney, 31 Aug. 1769 in Bartlett, ed., *Macartney*, p. 40. 93 [Malcomson, ed.,] *Irish official papers*, i, 103–5; Townshend to Shelburne, 30 Jan. 1768 (B.L.,Lansdowne Abstracts, Add. Ms 24137 f 3); Large, 'Irish House of Commons in 1769', p. 28; *F.L.J.*, 13 June 1770. 94 Above pp 58–9; Townshend to Macartney, 31 Aug., 19

SINDERCOMBE AND MOLYNEUX

Had Lord Townshend's grand design of the summer of 1769 been achieved, Henry
Flood would have acted on behalf of the Castle administration in the brief but dramatic 1769 session. In his absence, the lead for the administration during the opening weeks of the session, when the controversial issue of the army augmentation was
finally settled, was taken by the new Chief Secretary George Macartney with whom
Henry's cousin, Frederick, was on friendly terms. Macartney was described by one
observer as of 'much art and no capacity', but this was no more true of him than it
was of John Beresford, who joined the administration as a revenue commissioner
and who was fully supportive of the augmentation.[95] Had Townshend followed his
instincts and pressed ahead without offering any concessions to Irish feelings, he
would not have been able to carry the measure because the opposition alliance of
'the duke of Leinster, Lord Shannon and Ponsonby stand firm, and their numbers
are certainly a majority'. However, by meeting Irish concerns on the number of
troops that would be garrisoned permanently in Ireland (12,000) and the mode of
proceeding, he ensured the measure was approved with surprisingly little controversy before the end of November.[96] Because the question of his representation
remained unresolved, Flood was not in a position to influence the outcome directly,
though Lord Charlemont's claim that he was swayed 'by the irresistible opinion of
Flood' to vote for the measure suggests that he would have voted with the majority
in the Commons had he been present. Given his previous opposition, Flood's attitude is unexpected, and since he accepted the invitation of the Lord Lieutenant to
dine with him on 3 December it is tempting to concur with Charlemont that it was
not 'real conviction' but ambition that determined his attitude: 'he ... mediated the
future change in his politics, and was therefore more easily convinced' to favour the
proposal.[97] However, he was of little use to Townshend so long as it remained unclear whether he was going to take his seat for Callan or for Longford.

Thomas Mathews' and John Echlin's petition against the return of Henry and
John Flood for the borough of Callan was presented to the House of Commons on
10 November, and ordered to be heard by the committee of privileges and elections

Sept., in Bartlett, ed., *Macartney*, pp 40, 42; Townshend to Weymouth, 16 Sept. 1769 in *C.H.O.P.*, ii,
496–7. **95** Talbot to Flood, 8 Feb. (B.L., Valentia Papers, Add. Ms 19349 f 7); O'Hara to Burke, 22
Nov. in Hoffman, *Burke*, 459; Campbell to Beresford, 30 Nov. 1769 (B.L.,O.C., Townshend Papers, Box
14). **96** Bartlett, 'Augmentation', pp ; Bartlett, 'Townshend', p. 148; O'Hara to Burke, 26 Sept., 4
Nov., in Hoffman, *Burke*, pp 448–9, 456–7; Ponsonby to Bective, 4 Oct. (N.L.I., Headfort Papers, F/5/
84); Weymouth to Townshend, 11, 17, 22 Oct., 1 Nov in *C.H.O.P.*, ii, 507–09, 511–12, 515–16; Townshend
to Weymouth, 15, 21 Nov. in *C.H.O.P.*, ii, 518–22; Hertford to Hely-Hutchinson, 12 Oct. 1769 (T.C.D.,
Donoughmore Papers, C/2/30); Hely-Hutchinson to Lawson, 5 Jan. 1770 in H.M.C.,*Donoughmore*, p.
267; Draft speech of Macartney, ca 16 Nov. 1769 in Bartlett, ed., *Macartney*, pp 334–5. **97** H.M.C.,
Charlemont, i, 31–5 *passim*, especially pp 33–4; Craig, *Volunteer earl*, p. 157; A list of the Lords and
Commons who have dined with the Lord Lieutenant, 1768–9 (N.L.I., Ms 1470).

on 9 December. Suspicious of ministerial intentions, Flood and Charlemont conjectured that the timing, which meant that Flood effectively missed the opening seven weeks of the session, was due to the Castle's wish to keep him out of the house 'till', in Charlemont's words, 'some favourite scheme [the augmentation] be agitated'. There is no evidence to support this, but in an attempt to expedite matters, they appealed to Lord Longford to present a petition on behalf of the voters of his borough deploring the delay. This did not have the desired effect, and Flood was kept busy in the run up to the December meeting the Callan petition committee's requests for poll books and other documents, and with securing permission to present evidence 'of [the] bribery, corruption and undue influence made use of by the petitioners'. The material he supplied cannot be traced, but it was so decisive Mathews and Echlin withdrew their petition claiming an illegal election on 8 December. Six days later, Flood took his place in the House of Commons as MP for Callan.[98]

If Flood's deportment early in the session suggests that he actively contemplated supporting the administration in 1769, the thorny constitutional problems that dominated the political agenda when he took his place precipitated him into decisive opposition. In accordance with precedent, the Irish Privy Council transmitted a money bill to its British counterpart prior to the opening of the 1769 session as cause for calling a new parliament. In Flood's absence, Edmond Pery, Lucius O'Brien, Walter Hussey and other patriots vowed to resist the 'Privy Council money bill' because it challenged what MPs maintained was their 'sole right' to initiate financial legislation and they were able to inflict an embarrassing defeat on the administration when they joined forces with the disaffected Leinster, Shannon and Ponsonby interests to reject it on 21 November. Townshend was furious. He appealed to and secured permission from London to prorogue parliament and to punish those officeholders who had abandoned the administration on this crucial issue, once 'such money bills as are approved are returned'.[99]

This was the signal for the commencement of a no-holds-barred struggle between the administration and its critics, and alarmed by what he regarded as Townshend's insulting and despotic conduct, Flood joined in. The Lord Lieutenant's decision to take an aggressive line following the Commons' rejection of the 'Privy Council money bill' raised fundamental constitutional issues upon which he held strong views. Townshend maintained that the protest he had entered in the journal of the House of Lords was consonant with the action taken by Lord Sydney

---

98 *Commons Jn. (Irl.)*, viii, 303, 315, 320, 343; Charlemont to Flood, 3 Oct., Oct. 1769 in R[odd], ed., *Letters to Flood*, pp 51–2, 94.   99 J.I. McGuire, 'The Irish parliament in 1692' in Bartlett and Hayton, eds, *Penal era and golden age*, pp 1–31; H.M.C., *Charlemont*, i, 28; Townshend to Weymouth, 15, 21, 22, 24 Nov., Weymouth to Townshend, 30 Nov. in *C.H.O.P.*, ii, 518–24, 527; Tisdall to Bective, 17 Nov. (N.L.I., Headfort Papers, F/5/86); O'Hara to Burke, 22, 30 Nov. 1769 in Hoffman, *Burke*, pp 459–60; Thomas Bartlett, 'The Irish House of Commons' rejection of the 'Privy Council' money bill of 1769: a reassessment', *Studia Hibernica*, xxi (1981), pp 74–5.

in similar circumstances in 1692, but this did not register with Flood for whom the constitutional dependency implicit in the practice was offensive and unwelcome.[100] The size of the gulf separating them was demonstrated for all to see when, following the Lord Lieutenant's formal promulgation of his protest and prorogation on 26 December, Flood 'moved that [MPs] might do no business till they should receive a more favourable answer' to a question they posed as to when the prorogation would be put into effect. If Flood's motion had been approved, Townshend would have been unable to get the money bills approved prior to the outbreak of the row on the 'Privy Council money bill' onto the statute book, and it was a matter of great relief to him that it was defeated. However, Flood was not done. The protest signed by Charlemont, Howth, Powerscourt, Mountmorres and Longford in the Lords against the prorogation was drafted with his 'advice and assistance'.[101]

For Flood and the other patriots, eager to assert the constitutional autonomy of the Irish parliament, the prorogation was a galling reminder of the limits of their legislative authority. Their hopes of relief from this situation were raised briefly at the beginning of 1770 by news of the resignation of the duke of Grafton and rumours that Lord Rochford or Harcourt would replace Townshend in Ireland, but these proved unfounded.[102] In fact, Townshend's position was reinforced because he received the backing of both the King and the new prime minister, Lord North, for his policies which, they hoped, would affirm British influence in Ireland.[103]

In sharp contrast to the resolute and united stand taken by the government, the opposition was uncertain and divided. Townshend's critics in the Irish House of Commons were at one in their antipathy towards him and his policies, but not in their vision of the future. Flood, as we know, aspired to put in place a political system which empowered the Irish parliament to govern according to patriot principles, but John Ponsonby and Lord Shannon wanted something closer to the *status quo ante*.[104] It might have been possible to overcome these differences had the principals in the opposition contrived to broker an agreed approach and embarked on a public campaign to raise petitions against the prorogation, but nobody, Flood in-

100 *Life of Grattan*, i, 204–5; Townshend to Weymouth, 8, 11, 13, 15, 17, 18 Dec. in *C.H.O.P.*, ii, 536–40, 543.   101 Walpole,*Memoirs of the reign of George III*, iv, 21–2; H.M.C., *Charlemont*, i, 28–9; Townshend to Weymouth, 31 Dec. in *C.H.O.P.*, ii, 553–4.   102 Grattan to Day, 9 Jan. in *Life of Grattan*, i, 151–2; Townshend to Weymouth, 7 Mar. in *C.H.O.P.*, iii, 17–20; George III to Grafton, 26 Jan. (Grafton Papers, P.R.O.N.I., T2959/2/12); Weymouth to Townshend, 30 Jan. (N.A., Irish correspondence 1697–1798, Ms 2446); Minchin to Townshend, 1 Feb. (N.L.I., Townshend Papers, Ms 21129/2); Bartlett, 'Townshend', pp 241–2; Fraser to Townshend, 13 Feb. 1770 in H.M.C., *Townshend Mss*, p. 407.

103 Bartlett, 'Townshend', pp 166, 173–5, 190–2; Weymouth to Townshend, 22 Feb. in *C.H.O.P.*, iii, 11–12; Allan to Macartney, 29 Mar., Townshend to Weymouth, 7 Mar., Townshend to Macartney, 1, 7 Mar. in Bartlett, ed.,*Macartney*, pp 9–10, 105, 57–8; Fitzgerald to Townshend, 5 Mar. (N.A., Fitzgerald Papers, Ms 2736/7); O'Hara to O'Hara, 29 Apr. 1770 (N.L.I., O'Hara Papers, Ms 20393).   104 Newenham to Macartney, 7 Jan. in Bartlett, ed., *Macartney*, p. 267; T. Bartlett, 'Opposition in late eighteenth-century Ireland: the case of the Townshend viceroyalty', *I.H.S.*, 22 (1981), pp 323–5; Bartlett, 'Townshend', pp 232–6; Grattan to Day, 9 Jan. 1770 in *Life of Grattan*, i, 151–2.

cluded, was prepared to do this. Though described in one confidential Castle document as 'the engineer and mouthpiece of the opposition', he was too much of an old-style political elitist to embrace the populist strategy of rallying support though public agitation. It is indicative that only one member of the Flood family (Henry) was impanelled on the County Kilkenny Grand Jury in August; as John Hasler reported to Townshend, 'was there the least intention of any disagreeable motions more of that family [would] have been impanneled'.[105]

Flood possessed no such reservations about literary propaganda and, as he had done in 1768, he presented his views on the evolving crisis in a series of public letters. He did not work in isolation on this occasion, though it is not possible to establish the precise contribution of each of the patriots that joined in this undertaking. We know Richard Griffith played a part because of his remark in a letter to Charlemont in October 1769 that Flood and he had discussed how best to promulgate their ideas. However, Griffith moved to London shortly afterwards, with the result that his participation was confined to readying copy for Flood and Charlemont for placement in the London press.[106] Griffith's departure left a gap, but as well as his established friends, Hercules Langrishe and Gervaise Bushe, Flood was able to draw on the young Henry Grattan, whose sister was married to Bushe, and his friend Broome.[107] Grattan was less *au fait* than most of Flood's circle with events in Ireland because he was reading law at the Inns of Court in London, but he was a frequent visitor to Kilkenny when he was in Ireland, and he, better than any of the others, reveals the depth of the hostility Flood and his friends bore Townshend and Macartney by the spring of 1770:

> Lord [Townshend] is odious, but so ridiculous, that satire is unedged of her indignation, and dissolves in laughter at the burlesque of his character. He rattles his politics in all companies, gets drunk in all companies, and is uniform to no one political principle, but the publication of his secrets ... Macartney, if possible is more disliked ... An eternal sneer, a nauseating affectation, and a listless lethargy make him (they say) disgusting in general and give him the name of the Macaroni Prime Minister ...[108]

This was the stuff of private correspondence rather than public discourse, but the tone of the 'fugitive pieces' produced in the winter of 1769–70 was only slightly less combative.

Eighteen months after the publication of Flood's Philadelphus letters, the Baratariana series recommenced in the summer of 1769 with a one-off 'answer of

---

105 List of Irish House of Commons, 1770 (N.A., Townshend Papers, Ms 734/1); Hasler to Townshend, 18 Aug. 1770 (B.L.,O.C., Townshend Papers, Box 10). 106 Griffith to Charlemont, 12 Oct. 1769, 8 Jan. 1770 in H.M.C., *Charlemont*, i, 297–8. 107 Grattan to Broome, 8 Feb., 16 Mar. 1770 in *Life of Grattan*, i, 153, 160. 108 Grattan to Day, 30 Mar. 1770 in *Life of Grattan*, i, 162.

the inhabitants of Baratariana to ... Sancho Panca'. It is not clear who wrote this, but it is improbable that it was Flood since he was lionised in its pages as the 'champion of our liberty', a 'man of integrity' and a modern day Demosthenes.[109] Further letters followed at irregular intervals, before Flood re-entered the lists early in 1770, when he presented a series of letters under the penname of Sindercombe – the conspirator and would-be assassin of Oliver Cromwell. This *nom de plume* was more suited to the bad-tempered mood of the country than Philadelphus, and the letters Flood wrote under this soubriquet were among the most successful in the whole Baratariana undertaking. They have been described as 'abounding in spirit, principle and ability' and compared positively with the better-known Junius letters produced at the same time by Philip Francis. This is to exaggerate. They are too 'deficient in ease and burthened with a forced affection of metaphor' to merit sustained aesthetic commendation. However, they were effective political propaganda, as Lord Townshend implicitly acknowledged by authorising and aiding his most talented 'scribbler', the dramatist Henry Jephson, to pen a public reply to Flood.[110]

Flood's first Sindercombe letter was published in the *Freeman's Journal* on 24 February 1770. It thus took its place in the Baratariana series behind three communications by Posthumous (possibly Gervaise Bushe) in which he defended the decision of the Irish House of Commons to reject the money bill in 1769, criticised the Lord Lieutenant for his erratic and dishonest government, and indulged in a display of anti-Townshend invective. These were also themes that attracted Flood, for though he looked backwards in his first letter to Townshend's scheme to augment the army, his main object was to demonstrate that Townshend was duplicitous, despotic and incompetent throughout his term in office. In support of this view, he cited the actions of the British Privy Council for what, he alleged, was the sabotage in 1767 of the judges' bill by the inclusion of a clause unacceptable to Ireland and the unwarranted addition of the provision for the immediate 'dissolution of parliament' to the Octennial Act. This behaviour was all the more disappointing, Flood avowed, because Townshend's ancestors 'were lovers of liberty', but it was the inevitable consequence of his participation in 'an administration which had injured or insulted every part of the British dominions' and which had made 'a barbarous use ... of the military in England and an unconstitutional one in America'. This disposition to attribute malign conspiratorial intent rather than political misjudgment to his opponents is even more manifest towards the end of the letter where Flood engaged in three pages of rather vapid aspersion of Townshend's military career. This sits uneasily with the rest of the letter, and it is hardly surprising that it elicited the sharpest rebuke.[111]

The most effective and skilful reply was provided by Robert Jephson, who wrote under the soundly Protestant pseudonym of Broghill.[112] The bulk of Jephson's ri-

109 *Baratariana*, pp 45-51.   110 *Life of Grattan*, i, 205; *H.J.*, 17 Jan., 2 Nov. 1772.   111 *F.J.*, 24 Feb. 1770.
112 Henry MacDougall, *Sketches of Irish political characters* (Dublin, 1799), pp 217-21.

poste was devoted to an informed rebuttal of Flood's allegations that Townshend was misgoverning Ireland and to the provision of a convincing defence of his career as a soldier and a politician. Like Flood, Jephson possessed a coruscating turn of phrase, but if his dismissal of the first Sindercombe letter as 'the stale refuse of newspaper anecdote and the exploded calumnies of vulgar detraction' was effective, his animadversions on Flood himself were both clever and incisive:

> You are the friend of successful corruption, and an enemy to L[or]d T[ownshen]d, because he does not practise the art of corrupting. You are the admirer and humble imitator of Junius, and a fellow labourer in the great harvest of sedition: the signature you have chosen is perhaps expressive of your disposition, take care that it may not be an omen of your catastrophe, since you would leave behind you, at best, but an ambiguous reputation to be resolved by your friends into an assassin, and by your enemies into a suicide.[113]

Personalised comment of this kind was part and parcel of eighteenth-century public discourse, and Flood could expect no less. Moreover, any hurt he may have he felt was surely mitigated by the fact that the exchange was deemed of sufficient public interest to warrant publication in a pamphlet edition.[114]

By the time this was ready, Flood had completed his second Sindercombe letter – a literary *jeu d'esprit* – which he used to score personal as well as political points off Townshend and his advisors by discussing whom they should impersonate at the Lord Lieutenant's annual fancy dress ball.[115] This was a slight piece, as he was well aware, for on 3 April he followed it with a solemn reply to Broghill that was so long the *Freeman's Journal* was obliged to carry it over three issues.

Flood's third Sindercombe letter, inevitably, possessed little of the vibrancy of the first because it was largely given over to refuting Broghill's defence of his employer with additional material that supported his claims about Townshend's inadequacy as a politician, his deficiencies as a soldier and his unsuitability to high office. This completed, he intensified his attack by claiming that the Lord Lieutenant was corrupt, lacking in commitment to the principles of liberty, and reliant, on both sides of the Irish Sea, on individuals with no political or moral integrity:

> Consider his Lordship's character ... The servile abettor of every unconstitutional measure, the tool of Bute[116] and of everything which wears the livery of Bute; the *practiser* of corruption in every period of his life ... A pretence to prin-

---

113 *F.J.*, 6 Mar. 1770; *Baratariana*, pp 89–98.   114 *A letter from Sindercombe and Broghill's answer* (Dublin, 1770); *Baratariana*, p. 98.   115 *Baratariana*, pp 83–6; *F.J.*, 3 Mar. 1770.   116 Lord Bute, prime minister, 1762–3, was perceived by the Whigs as the *eminence grise* behind George III's supposed attempt to undermine the constitutional monarchy (see K.W.Schweizer, ed., *Lord Bute: essays in reinterpretation* (Leicester, 1988)).

ciple, in such a viceroy, governed by such an administration, instead of being imputable to virtue, or even to the hypocrisy of clumsy vice, can be nothing but the insolent irony of a profligate and audacious venality. And ... to speak of this kingdom, was it the austerity of [Provost] Andrews, the patriotism of Hutchinson, or the consistency and wisdom of the earl of Tyrone that has marked them out to his Excellency's favour? The world will not easily believe, that motives, such as these, induced his Excellency to promise a bishopric to the recommendation of a man, who is fitter to preside over a brothel than a university: or to be conducted by another, whose slippery prostitution has rendered even his infamy ridiculous. Nor will they believe, that the earl of Tyrone, after having violated every engagement, private and public, into which he ever entered, has been selected for his consistency and honour; or that his abilities have recommended him, when they reflect, that the elder Brutus must have been a less dissembler than the earl of Tyrone has been from his earliest years, if his Lordship's incapacity be counterfeit.

Since Flood and he were related by marriage, the earl of Tyrone was entitled to feel that this overstepped the bounds of propriety. But it was at once a measure of the extent of the rift that had emerged between him and the Beresfords, and of his anxiety to expose this 'despotic government's plan of arbitrary power for Britain and its dependencies' that Flood engaged in such personalised remarks. He now believed Townshend's efforts to construct a Castle party posed a greater threat to Irish liberties than the discredited undertaker system because the latter at least guaranteed that some power was devolved to Irishmen within the prevailing dependent relationship that characterised the connection between the two kingdoms:

> Ireland is subordinate, says England, and England is the superior. We allow it. What form can be so proper, or so analogous to this mutual relation, as that the principal rule should belong to Great Britain, and that the subordinate Government should be left to Ireland? And was not this precisely the case, when a chief Governor came from Great Britain, and left deputies behind him when he went, who were natives of this country? This gave all due pre-eminence and authority to England, without stripping this kingdom of all national weight ... I do not contend for the names of Justices, but for the substance; that is, for national weight and dignity. In whatever form, this is maintained, I am content. But by the present system it must be destroyed.[117]

Flood's conviction that Townshend's 'despotic' policies were part of the wider threat being posed to constitutional liberties in the empire at large both reflected and

---

117 *Baratariana*, pp 98–118 *passim*.

derived its ideological impetus from the perception of the Rockingham Whigs that the crown and its ministers were embarked on an orchestrated strategy to undermine parliamentary government. Flood was no simple plagiarist, however. He adopted certain interpretative themes and motifs from the English Whigs, and he gave them a distinctly Irish character.

This was further illustrated in his introduction to the edition of William Molyneux's patriot classic *Case of Ireland ... stated*, published in London in 1770. Flood was an obvious choice for this task because of his high political profile and his deepening interest in Irish history. He had demonstrated his knowledge of recent Irish history by citing Robert, first Viscount Molesworth's allegory *An account of Denmark* and Primate Boulter's *Letters* in support of his position in his third Sindercombe letter. It is not clear when his interest in Molyneux developed. But Peter Burrowes' statement that following the prorogation of the Irish parliament in December 1769, 'Mr Flood's next great point was an examination of the Law of Poynings' indicates that he was particularly agitated at this time by the question of Ireland's political dependency on England, and his introduction to Molyneux provides an excellent insight into his thinking on this and related issues.[118]

Assuming that those who would purchase *The Case of Ireland* needed no guide to the text, Flood focused in his introduction on the context from which it had emerged and on its continuing pertinence to the Ireland of the 1770s. He took the Glorious Revolution as his starting point, though his interest in the event derived less from the welcome fact that the defeat of the forces of confusion, 'which the biggotry of the deluded followers of James had introduced', paved the way for Protestant ascendancy in Ireland and in Britain than for William Molyneux's perception that the Revolution was an opportunity lost to create an equal Anglo-Irish relationship. As Flood saw matters, one of the most salient features of these years was the suffering endured by Irish Protestants in the name of the English connection, and the communal solidarity shown by the Protestant interests in 'the sister kingdoms':

[Irish] Protestant families had been stripped of their properties and forced to seek refuge in this country [England]; they were received with humanity by many particular persons, and money was raised by private subscription for their relief; their lands had been wasted, their houses burned, and the whole island thrown back, as to matter of improvement, at least a century; all this did the *Irish* suffer in the cause of Liberty, for it is beyond a doubt to those who have any knowledge of History of the advantages in number, intelligence and other respects, derived to the English army from the Irish Protestants: that if they had joined their forces with those of the Catholicks, the Kingdom might have been

118 *Baratariana*, pp 113, 115; Patrick Kelly, 'William Molyneux and the spirit of liberty', *Eighteenth-Century Ireland*, iii (1988), pp 139–40; A sketch of facts (R.I.A., Burrowes Papers, Ms 23K53/10).

easily delivered up either to James or to Lewis; they had taken a different resolution; descended from ancestors who brought with them the manners, customs, laws and constitution of England, and communicated them to the wild ferocious natives of Ireland, they were determined to support them.[119]

Given their commitment to the maintenance of the British connection and to the English way of life they had displayed, Flood was utterly persuaded that Irish Protestants were entitled to 'a pure uninterrupted enjoyment of civil liberty'; whereas

> far from receiving assistance from English legislature towards repairing the damages they had sustained, [Irish Protestants] saw their independence as a kingdom unjustly violated, their trade wantonly restrained, and Mr Molineux's modest, dispassionate, irrefragable proof of the rights and liberties of his native country, profanely burned by the hands of the common hangman.[120]

This was shameful, Flood avowed, because, like their English counterparts, Irish Protestants accepted the Protestant succession and the limitation of the monarchy 'under parliamentary establishment'. However, rather than embrace the logic of his argument, which was that the 'English nation' did not believe they were so entitled, Flood contended that the failure to concede the 'blessings of liberty' to Irish Protestants was the handiwork of the 'weak or wicked councils of English ministers' who devised and implemented 'that childish policy which will not permit Ireland to carry on part of a trade, the whole of which, England is confessedly able to maintain'.[121]

This was a conclusion of great contemporary as well as historical significance, and Flood adeptly connected the events of the 1690s, which had prompted Molyneux to write his celebrated tract, with his own experiences as a politician in the 1760s. *Ministerial* refusal to honour the principles of liberty, to apply these principles as equally and impartially to Ireland as to England provided the well-spring for the corrupt and inequitable government that operated with such deleterious consequences in Ireland:

> An English minister would move heaven and earth to corrupt a majority in the House of Commons, and ... he would, in order to secure a single member, the circumstance of whose estate may render it convenient to destroy the entire trade of Ireland, readily sacrifice so respectable a part of the British Empire. To cut off the left arm, in order to save a little finger of the right hand from amputation, would be strange in surgery. Ireland has many unhappy peculiarities in her po-

119 William Molyneux, *The case of Ireland ... stated* (London, 1770), pp v–vi.   120 Ibid., p. vi.   121 Ibid., pp vi–iii.

litical situation, the chief of which seems to be, that she is a kingdom without a king, for the minister with an obsequious British Privy Council, has assumed the power of putting a negative upon the most salutary laws; the man who is not well acquainted with the interest of Ireland must surely be incapable of advising his majesty concerning such interest, as it stands in relation to that of the Commonweal; for it is unjust to say that the interest of England or of Scotland, requires that Ireland shall be treated in this or in that manner; the honest enquiry must be, which is the manner from whence advantage to the inhabitants of that kingdom, in common with those of our own, will arise; none are so likely to be furnished with a knowledge adequate to such enquiry as the Irish ... His Majesty therefore with regard to the true state of Ireland, is totally uninformed, which in effect is not to be king.[122]

This was as stark an analysis of the Anglo-Irish connection within the empire as had yet been advanced by an Irish patriot. It is unlikely, for that reason, that his invocation of the King name was welcomed given the devotion to the Hanoverian succession fostered in eighteenth-century Ireland.[123] Flood was certainly not disinclined to understate his case, as he underlined by his controversial speculation that if William of Orange had lived

> Ireland might have reaped some part of the harvest of his leisure; he probably would have given that kingdom other marks of being a sovereign than quartering upon her a band of lazy, voracious, pensionary sycophants.[124]

Having identified the deficiencies of government that permitted it, and the opportunities that were passed over to extend full constitutional equality to Ireland, Flood turned to the restrictions that confined the Irish legislature. Taking the House of Lords first, he made a powerful plea on behalf of the Irish judiciary for the return to them of the 'dernier power' in law cases on the grounds that they were likely to be better 'acquainted with the matter in dispute' than their English counterparts.[125] His displeasure with the constraints under which the House of Commons operated was more deeply felt. He described at length his concern (previously articulated in the Sindercombe letters) that the special role of the Commons in the constitution was being subverted by an 'aristocratic' reaction being engineered by ministers:

> As to the House of Commons, not one essential of independency of legislature remains to it, except that of raising money ...; in general until very lately the English ministry has carried almost every question in the Irish House of Com-

---

122 Ibid., pp viii-ix.   123 James Kelly, 'The glorious and immortal memory': commemoration and Protestant identity 1660-1800', *R.I.A. proc.*, 94C (1994), pp 25-52.   124 Molyneux, *The case of Ireland*, p. ix.   125 Ibid., pp ix-x.

mons, and why opposition has been more frequent than formerly, may I think be thus accounted for. We plainly see the aristocratic part of our constitution gathering strength every day, the consequence of which has been that the dignity of national representation is sinking apace; the lower house is disgraced by an admission of obscure indigent dependents upon the nobility, who, before their introduction to parliament, owed perhaps the dinner they consumed, and the cloaths they wore to the bounty of their patrons; the scandalous illusory evasions of the qualification laws, we all know; ... the modern friends ... of our grandees ... are fed upon the vitals of the people, and hired to vote away their liberties. Legislature has been further debased by an admission not of merchants, for that respectable character is at present scarce known amongst us, but of a set of illiberal wretches, who by fraud, contracts, stock-jobbing, or a sordid parsimony have wrought themselves into wealth; these purchase seats in the House, under protection of the minister, and are prepared to do his dirty work at half price; before representation had been consigned to such mean hands, the employments in Ireland, except a few very considerable ones, were unworthy the acceptance of an English member of parliament, they were distributed amongst the gentlemen of that kingdom, and scarce anything was refused to administration; but so great the demand for them now at this side the water, such granting of places and of pensions in possession and reversion, that the natives seeing no prospect of being gratified, are easily inclined to oppose our Lord Lieutenants, and points are daily contested; the cause here assigned is no great compliment to Irish Patriotism, but it is something very like human nature ... if a right to be bribed can exist at all, the Irish have a right to be bribed by the materials which their own country furnishes, prior to that of the English; and much more for the real interest of England would it be, that Irish pensions and places were left as before to the members of their own house, their effects were then but of small extent, only to a vote of credit for the crown, or to silence the hue and cry after some petty larcener of the Treasury; but to the dark minister of this day, they are employed to a more dangerous purpose, to support a mercenary majority in the British parliament and under cover of this battery of corruption, to sap the very foundation of our constitution; that this is his scheme is apparent from the cruel treatment of the Americans; careless of the good opinion of the collateral branches of the British Empire, their governments, revenues, offices are all employed to poison the fountain of legislature; this end once attained, how easy it is to vote the Irish, Americans, East India Company etc to be horses, asses, and slaves at his pleasure.[126]

As this elaboration of his perception of the nature of the 'aristocratic' reaction that was taking place attests, Flood shared the view of the British Whigs and many

126 Ibid., pp xi-xiv.

American colonists that ministers were currently engaged in an attempt to restore the corrupt and despotic form of government that had prevailed in the seventeenth century. For this reason, he contended that vigorous opposition by patriots was not just morally defensible, it was politically imperative. Moreover, he maintained that because the decline in 'anti-popery' reduced the dependence of Irish Protestants on 'the powerful protection of an English minister', and commercial opportunities encouraged Catholics and Protestants to cooperate economically, it was possible, if government policy continued unchanged and existing land arrangements were guaranteed, that Ireland might even align with a foreign power and become 'a thorn' in the side of England. There was little prospect of this, of course. But Flood's readiness to posit such an eventuality, when his own preference was for a symbiotic, equal, and harmonious relationship between the two kingdoms and for a political system that exemplified the principles of limited monarchy that had triumphed in 1688–90, reflects the depth of his unease at the direction of events.[127]

Flood's introduction to the 1770 edition of Molyneux's *Case* represented a vigorous restatement of the patriots' core constitutional principles. Despite this, it did not stimulate a concerted opposition campaign to agitate key constitutional points, though it was soon joined on the booksellers' shelves by commentaries by Robert French, Charles Lucas, Gorges Edmond Howard and others on Poynings' Law. The proliferation of such works in 1770 attests to the sharp rise in interest in the subject of the Irish parliament's authority that followed the prorogation of parliament, but this particular 'paper war' was palpably less intense than that sparked off by the Money Bill dispute. It was not passionless, as Flood's writings attest, but the continuing inability of the opposition to concert their efforts, to make Townshend the focus of public and political hostility and to discredit the administration's argument that the crisis was the responsibility of greedy, self-interested aristocrats ensured that the political initiative remained with Dublin Castle.[128]

Conscious that Townshend was destined to prevail if they did not act urgently, Flood and Charlemont persuaded Sir Lucius O'Brien, Edmond Sexten Pery, the duke of Leinster (who had insisted he was removed from the Privy Council when his friend, Sir William Mayne, was dismissed[129]) and a number of other patriots in May of the need to unite all the opponents of Lord Townshend in 'an Association'. However, when Sir Lucius O'Brien raised the idea with John Ponsonby and he, in turn, alerted Lord Shannon, both were paralysed by caution. Despite the acuity of their dissatisfaction with Lord Townshend, and the diminution in status they had experienced since his arrival, they calculated that they stood a better chance of being restored to their former power if they did nothing further to antagonise the British government.[130]

127 Ibid., pp xiv–xxi.   128 Ibid.; O'Hara to Burke, 31 May 1770 in Hoffman, *Burke*, pp 469–70; Murphy, 'The Lucas affair', pp 232–3; Cummins, 'Opposition and the Irish parliament', pp 157–60, 163–5.   129 Leinster to Townshend, 28 May 1770 (N.A., Irish Correspondence 1697–1800, Ms 2446).   130 Bartlett, 'Townshend', pp 237–40; *idem*, 'Opposition in late eighteenth-century Ireland', p. 326.

Following the failure of this attempt to form a 'united' opposition, political life fell into its traditional inter-sessional torpor. The public debate on Poynings' Law simmered on, but the absence of reference to Flood in the public prints or of critical resolutions from grand juries indicates that he and the parliamentary opposition at large were inactive during the summer of 1770.[131] The political quietude was disrupted in the autumn and early winter of 1770–71 by renewed concern about the capacity of Ireland to repulse an invasion force of French or Spanish troops if the dispute with Spain over the Falkland Islands escalated into war, and by the impact of economic recession (exacerbated by the imposition of an embargo on trade) which obliged the Lord Lieutenant to convene a parliament in February 1771 to secure the funding to defray the cost of administering the country.[132]

ACTIVE OPPOSITION

Townshend approached the emergency 1771 session confident that his majority (which he increased from 16 to 36 between October and December 1770) was sufficient to negotiate the strong opposition he anticipated from the likes of Flood.[133] He was encouraged in this belief by the knowledge that it was not to be 'an ordinary session' with regular committees of account, supplies, ways and means. Despite this, nothing was left to chance. Determined 'to convince the public in Ireland that whatever opposition he may meet with arises solely from the vanity and ambition of a few individuals, and by no means from regard for the interests on the country', application was made to every prospective supporter urging their attendance, and propaganda readied to counteract the 'malitious [sic] criticism of our designing, self-interested, mock patriots'.[134]

Townshend's opponents, by contrast, were not nearly so well-organized. Following on the rejection in May of their plan to bring the opposition together in a 'collective body', Flood and Charlemont toyed in December with the idea of sending a 'deputation' from the combined ranks of the opposition to London to meet with ministers. Charlemont did not entertain high hopes of this succeeding, but it was deserving of exploration, he informed Lucius O'Brien, because 'it might ..., if

131 O'Hara to Burke, 31 May in Hoffman, *Burke*, pp 469–70; Carleton to Townshend, 31 Aug. 1770 (B.L.,.O.C., Townshend Papers, Box 8); Bartlett, 'Townshend', p. 194.   132 The pros and cons of convening a parliament can be followed in *C.H.O.P.*, iii, 66–8, 73, 122–4; Smith to Townshend, 2 Oct., Oct., 12 Dec. (B.L.,O.C., Smith Letters, nos 7, 8, 16); Bartlett, 'Townshend', pp 210–20; Allan to Macartney, 27 Nov., 10, 17, 25 Dec. 1770 in Bartlett, ed., *Macartney*, pp 125, 128, 129, 132).   133 Allan to Townshend, 3, 14 Jan 1771 (N.A., Townshend Papers, Ms 730/55, 56).   134 Smith to Rochford, 27 Jan., 4 Feb., Rochford to Townshend, 9, 18 Feb., Townshend to Rochford, 9, 27, 31 Jan., in *C.H.O.P.*, iii, 184–5, 195–6, 198–9, 201, 204–5, 207–8; Smith to Townshend, 31 Jan., 6 Feb. (B.L.,O.C., Smith Letters, nos 30, 35); Fitzgerald to [Townshend], 5 Feb. (N.A., Fitzgerald Papers, Ms 2736/17); Caldwell to Townshend, 25 Feb. (B.L.,O.C., Townshend Papers, Box 8); Cuffe to Townshend, 23 May 1771 (ibid., Box 9).

properly and judiciously executed tend more to extricate us out of our present wretched circumstances than any that could be devised'. With this in mind, he broached Speaker Ponsonby and the duke of Leinster, but, once again, he met with little encouragement. Changes in the composition of the ministry, which saw Lord Rochford take over as secretary of state, also served to dampen his hopes since it distanced the prospect of a friendly coalition comprising Lord Rockingham and the earl of Chatham taking power. Despite this, Charlemont refused to give way to despair. He urged O'Brien and Flood to 'strain every nerve and strive by all possible methods to prevent the foundering of our shattered, weather-beaten, forsaken and unpiloted vessel', but nothing tangible ensued.[135]

If, as this suggests, the patriots were ill-circumstanced to offer strong opposition in the 1771 spring session, their problems were exacerbated by the fact that they could no longer depend on a number of their stalwart voices. Charles Lucas had 'decay'd' perceptibly, while Sir William Osborne was on the verge of concluding his long courtship by the Castle by accepting office. Some like the duke of Leinster and Thomas Conolly remained confident that the administration's majority, variously calculated at between nine and twenty-two, could be overturned, but since John Ponsonby could not be depended upon, Henry Flood's less optimistic mood seemed more appropriate.[136]

Indeed, Flood's expectations were so low he chose this moment to enquire once again of the possibility of his acquiring a seat in the 'better field' of Westminster. William Markham, who had just been made Bishop of Chester and preceptor to the Prince of Wales, promised to do what he could to advance Flood's ambitions, though he cannot have been happy with his former student's stipulation that he would not leave Ireland without 'adequate motive'. In fact, Flood's prospects of securing ministerial support to obtain a seat at Westminster were remote. The duke of Grafton preferred Hely-Hutchinson, while Markham had no influence with Lord North. As a result, Markham could only report back that he could not hold out any 'hopes of assistance'.[137] What impact this had on Flood's demeanour remains unclear; he certainly did not seek to avoid controversy during the short 1771 session which proved so disastrous for the combined anti-Townshend interest in the House of Commons.

The session began badly for the opposition when they failed, after 'a long debate', on 26 February to win approval by 132 votes to 107 for an address in which the

135 Charlemont to O'Brien, 31 Dec. 1770 in H.M.C., *Charlemont*, i, 304.   136 Stratford to Stratford, [1770] (N.L.I., Stratford Papers, Ms 18788/7); Lord Townshend's patronage book (N.L.I., Ms 14299 no 523); Smith to Townshend, 28, 31 Jan., 19 Feb. (B.L.,O.C., Smith Letters, nos 28, 30, 40); Townshend to Rochford, [6 Feb.] in *C.H.O.P.*, iii, 203; Ponsonby to Fownes, 24 Jan. 1771 (N.L.I., Tighe (Woodstock) Papers, Ms 3889/10).   137 Markham to Flood, endorsed 19 Feb., Flood to Markham, 3 Mar. 1771 (Rosse Papers, C/2/3–4); Cunningham, *Lives of eminent and illustrious Englishmen*, viii, 447–50; Grafton to Irwin, 16 Jan. 1770 in H.M.C., *Various collections, viii, Wood papers*, p. 185; Smith to Townshend, [1771] (B.L.,O.C., Smith letters, no 61).

usual compliment to the crown for continuing the Lord Lieutenant in office was purposely omitted.[138] Though Flood voted with the undertakers in this division, he was not party to their deliberations. 'I have no connection with the leaders or heads of interests here that are in opposition', he informed Bishop Markham; 'but Lord T[ownshend]'s conduct to the public has made me hitherto co-operate with them, or rather co-incide.'[139] He certainly demonstrated his independent-mindedness on the following day when the presence of 'riotous mobs' in College Green 'swearing and otherwise insulting the more obnoxious members' caused him to call for the session to be adjourned. This provoked a long and heated debate which ended at 1 a.m. with the defeat of the main motion, for which Flood and Thomas Le Hunte were tellers, by 65 votes to 104.[140] The size of the administration's majority augured poorly for the rest of the session, but Flood remained hopeful that the opposition would be more successful on constitutional points. He was, Townshend reported, 'the mouthpiece of opposition' and, on 28 February, 'he opened his grand question upon Poynings' Law and the right of the House of Commons to grant money'. This was the constitutional issue at the heart of the dispute between the opposition and the Lord Lieutenant on the 'Privy Council money bill', and the Attorney General and Chief Secretary worked together to ensure it was defeated by government amendment by 127 votes to 106. This was a heartening division, and Flood was encouraged by this, by the 'warmth' displayed by Charlemont and his colleagues in the Lords, and by the high level of political 'ferment' in the country to believe that the opposition could yet destabilise the administration.[141] In fact, Townshend had more reason to be confident. He concluded at the beginning of March that the 'grand operations of Mr Ponsonby, Lord Shannon and the duke of Leinster are over', and when the Speaker, John Ponsonby, resigned the chair on 4 March rather than 'suffer the indignity of carrying an address of thanks to Townshend for continuing as Lord Lieutenant', he was provided with a glorious and unexpected opportunity to effect the political 'revolution' he yearned for by putting someone more co-operative in the chair.[142]

Ever since William Conolly's election in 1715, the speakership was one of the keys to the effective management of the House of Commons. For this reason, Flood was as anxious as Lord Townshend about who succeeded Ponsonby. His preferred

138 Townshend to Rochford, 27 Feb. 1771 in C.H.O.P., iii, 210; Bartlett, 'Opposition in late eighteenth-century Ireland', p. 315.   139 Flood to Markham, 3 Mar. 1771 (Rosse Papers, C/2/4). Lord Charlemont took a similar course in the Lords (H.M.C., Charlemont, i, 30).   140 H.M.C., Charlemont, i, 30; Townshend to Rochford, 28 Feb., in C.H.O.P., iii, 211; Cummins, 'Opposition and the Irish parliament', pp 91–2.   141 McCracken, 'The Irish viceroyalty 1760–73', p. 166; 'Notes for a speech, Feb. in Bartlett, ed., Macartney, pp 340–4; Townshend to Rochford, 28 Feb. in C.H.O.P., iii, 212; Flood to Markham, 3 Mar. (Rosse Papers, C/2/4); H.M.C., Charlemont, i, 30–1; Smith to Townshend, 6, 7 Mar. 1771 (B.L., O.C., Smith letters, no. 46, 50).   142 McCracken, 'The Irish viceroyalty 1760–73', p. 166; Bartlett, ed., Macartney, pp xxxvi; Townshend to Rochford, 28 Feb., 2, 6 Mar. in C.H.O.P., iii, 212, 214, 218–19; Flood to Markham, 11 Mar. 1771 (Rosse Papers, C/2/5); Bartlett, 'Opposition in late eighteenth-century Ireland', p. 315; Malcomson, 'Speaker Pery', pp 47–8.

choice, and that of most patriots, was William Brownlow, the respected MP for County Armagh. There was an expectation within the ranks of Castle supporters that his main rival would be Flood's brother-in-law, John Beresford, but since he was leader of the Tyrone interest in the House of Commons as well a commissioner of the revenue, this raised the spectre, if he was successful, of his perpetuating the undertaker tradition, and Townshend was determined this should not happen. So when it emerged that Sexten Pery regarded the position 'as the highest point of my ambition', the Lord Lieutenant threw his weight behind his candidature. Pery, the Townshend camp concluded approvingly, was eminently qualified for the position as 'a man of business, knowledge and the orders of the house' and 'the chief of no party either by connections or property'. Their concern was that he 'came over clearly and explicitly', but once Townshend received assurances that he would 'be a good boy' the Lord Lieutenant was ready to overlook what one of his London correspondents described as his 'perticular trimming trading games ... and flagrant acts of insincerity'. The short delay caused by the need to convince Lord Tyrone and John Beresford 'to relinquish' their hopes gave Flood and other independents time to lobby on Brownlow's behalf. They had some success, but it was not enough to give them victory. Pery was elected speaker by 118 votes to 114 on 8 March.[143]

Flood was deeply disappointed by the outcome. He was convinced that the patriots had a real chance to get their candidate elected, and it depressed him that the Lord Lieutenant was enabled to strengthen his position in the House of Commons because of the impetuosity of John Ponsonby:

In this, as in everything respecting me, Lord Townshend has been governed by a little pique that misbecomes anything [sic] but a girl, and to which he has sacrificed even common justice. By the impatience and misconduct, however, of his principal adversary [John Ponsonby], he is at present victorious, and will a second time reap the laurels which he did not win.[144]

In sharp contrast, opinion in government circles in England was delighted with the outcome, and Townshend was applauded by everyone up to and including the King.[145]

As Flood's chagrined remarks attest, the outcome of the speakership election

---

143 Townshend to Rochford, 6, 8, 11 Mar. in *C.H.O.P.*, iii, 216–19, 221–2; Malcomson, 'Speaker Pery', pp 44–5, 47–8; Bartlett, 'Townshend', pp 246–8; O'Hara to Burke, 11 Mar. in Hoffman, *Burke*, pp 485–6; Smith to Townshend, 13, 16 Mar. (B.L.,O.C., Smith Letters, nos 52, 53); Annaly to Hervey, 12 Mar. 1771 (P.R.O.N.I., Babingdon and Croasdaile Papers, D1514/1/9). 144 Flood to Markham, 11 Mar. 1771 (Rosse Papers, C/2/5). 145 Smith to Townshend, 11, 18 Mar. (B.L.,O.C., Smith Letters, nos 51, 54); Rochford to Townshend, 21 Mar. in *C.H.O.P.*, iii, 226–7; Bradshaw to Lees, 27 Apr. (B.L.,O.C., Townshend Papers, Box 8); Barrington to Gage, 26 Apr. 1771 in H.H. Peckham, *Sources of American Independence* (2 vols, Chicago, 1978), i, 91.

had a demoralising impact on the anti-Townshend interests in the House of Commons. 'Many' members of the 'opposition' who had journeyed to Dublin from England for the session chose to depart. According to a newspaper report, Flood was among those who went to England during the spring recess but, whereas most of those who sailed out of Dublin did not return, he was back by 30 April for the resumption of the session.[146] While he was away, the main focus of the opposition shifted from parliament to debating and political clubs like the Constitutional Free Debating Society, which served as focal points for the increasingly politicised Protestant middle classes of the capital. They were encouraged by the foundation in April 1771 of the *Hibernian Journal*. Espousing the patriot viewpoint articulated by Flood, this newspaper ceaselessly pilloried Townshend as a 'tyrant' and a 'despotic' agent of a government that aspired to return the kingdom to the 'arbitrary' government practised at the time of the Stuarts.[147]

There were also further additions to the Baratariana series at this time, but Flood was not among the contributors.[148] His focus was the House of Commons, and he moved on 14 May that an address 'representing the deplorable situation of this country' be presented to George III. His purpose was to expose the 'malign influence' of Lord Townshend because he cited 'the many difficulties and distresses which this city [Dublin] and all Ireland in general have sustained from the proceedings of the present administration' in justification for his motion. These included the decay in trade, the prorogation of parliament, the alteration of the judges bill in 1767 and the recent revenue bill. His motion was supported by Lucius O'Brien, Barry Barry, William Brownlow, George Ogle, Warden Flood and other stalwart patriots, but the 58 votes he mustered were dwarfed by the 123 who denied an address would serve any useful purpose. Undeterred, Flood urged the rejection on the same day of a revenue bill returned from the British Privy Council because it contained a new clause providing for the collection of the taxes stipulated in the bill 'to the end of the next session of parliament'. Once again, he was on the losing side, this time by 102 votes to 48.[149]

Though his initiative had failed, Flood's efforts to present a statement of the 'real grievances of this unhappy kingdom' to the Crown won him popular applause and a vote of thanks from the Constitutional Free Debating Society.[150] His opposition to the amended revenue bill was also applauded, but despite this, further eulogistic press comment, and the flattering implication of the administration's decision to direct John Scott, MP for Mullingar, to 'stand up' to him, the plain and simple fact was that the anti-Townshend nexus simply did not have the numbers to

---

146 Smith to Townshend, [10, 20 Mar] (B.L.,O.C., Smith letters, nos 48, 49); Townshend to Rochford, 8 Apr. in *C.H.O.P.*, iii, 238–9; *H.J.*, 3 May 1771.   147 Townshend to Rochford, 8 Apr. in *C.H.O.P.*, iii, 238–9; *H.J.*, 1, 3, 8, 10, 13, 15, 17, 20, 24 May 1771.   148 *Baratariana*, pp 119–88; *H.J.*, 26 June, 2 Aug., 25, 27 Sept. 1771.   149 *H.J.*, 13, 15 May; Townshend to Rochford, 18 May 1771 in *C.H.O.P.*, iii, 255–6.

defeat the administration in the House of Commons. Indeed, the Castle interest was so dominant by the early summer it was alleged that George Macartney 'had clearly the better of the famous Flood'. This is doubtful, but there is no question but that by then the Castle interest felt secure. At the close of the session, the Commons ratified what the *Hibernian Journal* deemed a 'scandalous address' to the Lord Lieutenant, in spite of attempts by members of the opposition to amend it.[151] Flood had appealed to his literary, political and oratorical skills to resist Townshend's efforts to remodel Irish politics in a manner that provided for 'a lasting superiority in favour of English government', and he had failed. The struggle was not over, but Flood had little reason to anticipate that the future would prove any more rewarding.

DEFIANT OPPOSITION

Henry Flood spent the summer of 1771 out of the political spotlight. Following the conclusion of the session, he returned to Farmley where he was 'the busiest man in the world all the summer, both as a builder and as an improver of ground'. He so enjoyed the change of activity, it was with reluctance that he returned to Dublin in October for the opening of the regular biannual session.[152]

While Flood occupied himself with estate matters, Lord Townshend concentrated on consolidating his command of the House of Commons. A full session represented a greater challenge than the short spring sitting he had recently negotiated, because it involved securing approval for a *full* programme of financial legislation. Anticipating problems, Townshend was given permission to replace disloyal office holders, to divide the revenue board, to make promotions in the peerage and to win over Lord Shannon. He achieved enough of what he set out to do to maintain confidently in September that he had broken the opposition and 'created a stable ministerial interest', but his failure to secure Lord Shannon's allegiance gave the opposition hope that if they united around an agreed strategy they could pose the administration serious problems.[153]

This was an object that activated Lord Charlemont more than it did Flood. Anxious that the patriots should make an impression during this 'crisis', Charlemont wrote in August 'intreating him, with all the rhetoric of which I was master, to be at the scene of action before the middle of September'. However, his suggestion that they should work on an address 'calculated to make the people of England thoroughly acquainted with our condition and with those real grievances under which

150 *H.J.*, 15 May, 7 June 1771. **151** *H.J.*, 17, 20 May; Thomas Bartlett, 'Chief secretary' in Peter Roebuck, ed., *Macartney of Lisanoure* (Belfast, 1983), p. 80. **152** Flood to Markham, 19 Oct. 1771 (Rosse Papers, C/2/6). **153** Bartlett, 'Townshend', pp 250–65, 269–71; Allan to Townshend, 13 Sept. 1771 (N.A., Townshend Papers, Ms 730/74).

we labour, as well as with the fatal consequences which may be dreaded from a continuance of the measures whereof we are forced to complain' did not appeal to Flood. He no longer shared Charlemont's conviction that once informed 'the ruling people on the other side of the water' would realise the urgency 'of doing something for our immediate relief'. As a result, he did not answer Charlemont's summons to return early to Dublin, though he was back in the capital in time for the opening of what was to prove an exceptionally busy session.[154]

Privately, Flood pronounced himself 'surprized' when he took his place with other MPs and peers in parliament on 9 October that the King's speech was delivered yet again by Lord Townshend:

> I thought he had merited his discharge in every sense, and that English government did not wish to give themselves unnecessary trouble or to embarrass those gentlemen of this country who wish as well to government as any men in the kingdom, but between whom and Lord Townshend there can be no co-operation.[155]

Arising out of this, Flood was determined to resist the administration's plan to relieve the fiscal problems of the Irish exchequer – their legislative priority for the 1771–2 session[156] – by raising taxes and by reducing the amount of money provided for public works, bounties and premiums. He believed that the pension list and civil establishment represented more suitable targets, and with this in mind, he contended that it was 'highly improper to address' the Commons on the budget deficit 'until such time as the accounts were properly brought before' the House, and MPs could determine 'whether this large arrear was more owing to ... grants or to the great number of places and pensions so flagrantly distributed among the members which comprise the party in favour of the court'. These sentiments were endorsed by Charles Lucas, Sir William Mayne, Robert French and Walter Hussey and others, which sent shivers of apprehension through Castle ranks. Acutely conscious of the potential complications should Flood succeed in amending the Commons' reply to the King's speech to reflect his views, 'the servants of the crown strenuously' resisted Flood's move, and both sides were soon enmeshed in a heated debate on all aspects of Castle policy that went on to the exceptionally late hour of 3.30 a.m. when the address was finally approved without Flood's amendment.[157]

Despite the result, Flood took heart from the debate because the Castle connec-

154 Charlemont to O'Brien, 20 Aug., 21 Sept. 1771 in H.M.C., *Charlemont*, i, 305–8 and N.L.I., Inchiquin Papers.   155 Flood to Markham, 19 Oct. 1771 (Rosse Papers, C/2/6).   156 Gordon to Townshend, 4 Jan., 16 Aug. (Yale University, Sterling Library, English Misc Mss 1766–72); Allan to Macartney, 22, 29 Apr., 13 May in Bartlett, ed., *Macartney*, pp 139–42; Memorandum concerning a minimum balance, May 1771 (B.L.,O.C.,Treasury file).   157 Flood to Markham, 19 Oct. (Rosse Papers, C/2/6); *H.J.*, 11, 14 Oct.; Broome to Grattan, 21 Oct. 1771 in *Life of Grattan*, i, 250.

tion was 'deserted by [so] many country gentlemen; ... the whole fabric of their majority gave way'. He had good reason to feel pleased. He had performed so ably in the debate on the address on 9 October that he had 'gained an accession even to his former reputation'. Moreover, he was aware that with the politically compli- cated issues of the division of the revenue board, the setting up of a new board of accounts, and the controversial pension granted to the Englishman Jeremiah Dyson yet to be debated, 'a great deal of business and a great deal of difficulty remains in appearance'.[158]

Flood had no opportunity to take up the cudgels immediately because the House of Commons adjourned until 28 October, but news reports that Townshend was engaged in desperate negotiations to secure the support of Lord Loftus and his parliamentary connection did not cause him to revise his opinion. Certainly, when MPs reconvened, Flood was immediately to the fore. His first action was to support John Fitzgibbon's announcement of his intention of laying 'the wretched state of the nation' before the House.[159] However, he was not prepared to play understudy to Fitzgibbon or anyone else on this or on any other matter, and on Saturday, 2 November, he reasserted his personal ascendancy with an 'eloquent' speech on the 'deplorable state of the nation' in which he analyzed the negative implications of the government's financial policy for the country, and used official figures to good effect to demonstrate that the maintenance of the pension list was more important to the Castle than 'public service' and 'national utility'. 'It was', he pronounced pugna- ciously, 'the intention of government to check all parliamentary grants for public works (except ... the linen manufacture and the Charity schools) since the sums which we are able to grant will scarce pay the ordinary services of the state and the pensions'. This prompted a heated exchange in which the Chief Secretary, the At- torney General and John Scott defended the pension list as 'a mark of honour, a proof of merit'. They also challenged Flood's figures and attributed the exchequer's fiscal difficulties to excessive expenditure on public works. Their influence was suf- ficient to deflect Flood's attempt to secure parliamentary backing for his main mo- tion, which called on the Commons to scrutinise expenditure more closely, as well as a number of subsidiary motions on specific items of expenditure, but he remained defiant. He vowed to raise the issue 'again and again, and never give it up until he had made truth reach the recesses of the Castle'.[160]

It is a measure of the anxiety Flood's assertions caused in Castle ranks that on 4 November the Townshend loyalist and MP for Dundalk, Robert Waller, 'threw some reflections on Mr Flood' which justified the issuing of a challenge, and would have led to one but for Waller's 'submissive retraction'.[161] Unperturbed by the strength of feeling his actions aroused, Flood pressed on, and he raised the 'deplorable state

158 Broome to Grattan, 21 Oct. in *Life of Grattan*, i, 250; Flood to Markham, 19 Oct. 1771 (Rosse Papers, C/2/6); Bartlett, ed., 'Townshend', pp279–80; Bartlett, ed.,*Macartney*, pp xxxix-xl. 159 *H.J.*, 28, 30 Oct. 1771. 160 *H.J.*, 4 Nov. 1771. 161 *H.J.*, 6 Nov. 1771.

of the country' once more on Wednesday 6 November. His purpose on this occasion was to compel the committee of supply to take a global look at government expenditure and revenue, but conscious of the delay this could occasion to the authorization of supplies, the leaders of the Castle connexion were unyielding. Speaker after speaker denied Flood's accusation that the budget deficit of £295,295 for the years 1769–71 was an indictment of their stewardship. They attributed it to a fall in revenue, and this was sufficiently convincing to enable them to repulse opposition efforts to prolong the debate on the issue by the comfortable margin of 135 votes to 97. However, their victory was less complete than these numbers suggest as they deemed it politic to yield to calls for further information on the pension list.[162]

The Castle had to yield to its critics once again two days later when it was obliged to withdraw a 'scandalous amendment', which contended that a motion by Flood that expenditure on public works had fallen by £40,838 in the previous two years was wrong. This was particularly embarrassing for Robert Waller who was responsible for the amendment, but the administration was able, once again, to use its numerical strength to ensure it did not delay its financial legislation. They did likewise on Monday, 11 November, when Flood proposed a motion to the effect that it was 'neither eligible nor practicable' to raise taxes in the 'present ruinous situation of affairs', and on subsequent days in the committee of accounts.[163]

As the newspaper reports, which are the main source of information on the proceedings of the House of Commons in the early 1770s, certify, Flood was the most active and the most assertive of the group of patriot MPs, which included Barry Barry, John Fitzgibbon, Lucius O'Brien, Walter Hussey, William Mayne and George Hamilton, who shared the responsibilities of spearheading opposition in 1771–2.[164] Noticeably absent from their ranks was Charles Lucas who was precluded from playing any part by illness. He died on 4 November with, it was reported, the words 'Propitious Heaven, save Flood' on his lips. This reads more like the invention of a manipulative author than the utterance of a dying man, but it accurately reflected the high esteem in which Flood was currently held in patriot circles. Flood and Lucas were too unlike in background, education and personalities to be friends during their lifetime, but their commitment to the cause of political and constitutional reform brought them together politically, and it was fitting that Flood was 'one of the supporters of the pall' at Lucas' funeral.[165]

Lucas would certainly have approved of Flood's opposition to Townshend's plan to divide the revenue board in order that he could appoint additional commissioners. Flood raised this most sensitive matter in the House of Commons on Saturday 16 November, when he cited the estimated £50,000 it would cost the exchequer to implement in support of his preemptive motion that '*seven* commissioners of the

162 *H.J.*, 8 Nov. 1771.   163 *H.J.*, 11, 13, 15 Nov.; Townshend to Rochford, 11 Dec. 1771 in *C.H.O.P.*, iii, 336–41.   164 *H.J.*, 13 Nov. 1771.   165 *H.J.*, 8 Nov. 1771; Murphy, 'The Lucas affair', p. 233; *Life of Grattan*, i, 91–2.

revenue are sufficient to transact the business of the revenue board'. This was well-calculated to attract maximum opposition support and, ably seconded by William Mayne, who condemned the scheme as 'a regular plan ... laid down for enslaving the nation', it won widespread approval and was carried, to the Castle's dismay, by 129 votes to 83.[166]

Emboldened by this success, William Brownlow proposed on 19 November that 'the whole House, with the Speaker at their head, should go to the Lord Lieutenant and lay the resolution before him, as the joint opinion of the House'. This was a device only resorted to when MPs wanted to impress their attachment to certain bills or resolutions, and it was no surprise that Sir George Macartney and John Hely-Hutchinson strongly resisted the suggestion. They countered by claiming that the motion of the 16th was inconsistent with previous decisions of the Commons, that it was an infringement of the King's prerogative because it acted to 'restrain the crown from improving the revenue', and that the increase in the number of commissioners that would follow the division of the revenue board was merely incidental. Flood was unimpressed. It was, he maintained:

> the opposition's duty ... to inform the King that he had been misinformed; that there was no need to divide the revenue; that it was not desired by the population of Ireland; that it was an expense they could not bear, [and] that English ministers were not sufficiently informed to advise him on this.

A majority of MPs felt likewise, and the House agreed with him, 123 votes to 101, that the motion of 16 November should be carried to the Lord Lieutenant.[167]

This was a further chastening setback for the administration but, determined not to show weakness, Townshend refused to abandon his plan to divide the revenue board. Flood showed no sign of relenting either. He was encouraged by the successes he had already registered 'on five or six material questions' and by the fact that 'the large majority with which Lord Townshend completed the last session is so much diminished that ... where the question is very strong against him he is always in danger'. But it troubled him that the administration refused to amend its erroneous ways:

> The conduct of opposition (I do not say so because I am generally one of that body) has been respectable. Two-thirds of the body are now not under the influence of any of the three great powers of this kingdom, as they have been called;

166 *H.J.*, 18, 22 Nov.; Townshend to Rochford, 20 Nov., 11 Dec. 1771 in *C.H.O.P.*, iii, 327, 336–41.   167 Draft speech, 19 Nov. in Bartlett, ed., *Macartney*, pp 343–7; *H.J.*, 22 Nov; Townshend to Rochford, 20 Nov. 1771 in *C.H.O.P.*, iii, 327; Thomas Bartlett, 'Viscount Townshend and the Irish Revenue 1767–73', *R.I.A. proc.*, 79C (1979), pp 169–70.

nor could all those powers united disturb a sensible and gracious Governor, whose measures were not exceptionable. In the midst of great public distress, we have continued the augmentation of the army voted a few years ago, and have provided for the increased expense of the army in another particular in consequence of a new arrangement of the companies: an instance of no small attention to the sordid interests and wishes of the crown. To accomplish it, we have been obliged, after running considerably in debt the two last years, to empower government now to borrow £200,000 more, and not only this, but to grant for the internal improvements of the country and to our charitable foundations not half what we formerly granted. If the real state of this kingdom were known I am sure it would be better consulted by administration. We are not able to do much and what we can do ought to be reserved for rational and substantial purposes, and not squandered without one solid advantage to the Crown. We are more highly taxed in proportion to our ability, it is thought, than Great Britain herself. Our annual taxes are more than the current cash of the nation, and yet our Revenue is inferior to our expense in a sum of between £200,000 and £300,000 a session.[168]

Because Townshend's plan to divide the revenue board and to add to the pension list exacerbated the kingdom's financial problems, Flood was convinced his stand was justified on budgetary as well as political grounds. He explained to Bishop Markham:

You will not wonder that we should not think this a time for the creation of new offices or for the introduction of new expense. We have therefore applied [to] Lord Townshend in such a manner as to express our disapprobation of such an idea. He has told us that he will refer our resolution to his Majesty. I wished that some of the arguments ag[ain]st this measure might accompany the resolution and therefore proposed an address to the King, a copy of which I enclose to you but which I postponed on the Secretary's declaring that the measure was for the present suspended: wishing that the relief of this kingdom might flow from the spontaneous grace of his Majesty as much as possible.

In Lord Northumberland's government, the House of Commons had an assurance conveyed to them by Mr Tisdall, Attorney General and Secretary of State of this kingdom, that his Majesty had declared it to be his intention not to grant any more pensions for lives or years, except on extraordinary occasions. The first pension granted since, contrary to the idea conveyed to the Commons by this message, was a pension to Mr Dyson for three lives. This being the first and only infraction, the Commons have resolved this session not to provide for it, conceiving the crown to be deceived in its grant.

168 Flood to Markham, 30 Jan. 1772 (Rosse Papers, C/2/7).

With respect to the partition of the Revenue Board, I have only to add that, as the law now stands, the revenue could not possibly be collected if such an arrangement should take place, and that if the law were to be altered in the most advantageous manner for that purpose, the expense would be about £40,000 a session, according to the best estimate we can form, and the advantage nothing, for seven Commissioners can certainly do the business as well as twenty; and as to the business of government, I will venture to affirm that it can be transacted with success and dignity without such an addition of offices.[169]

When this letter was written, the focus of the House of Commons had shifted from the committee of accounts to the committee of supply, and the opposition's attack from the revenue to patronage. Following some early skirmishes, battle was enjoined on 22 November with a debate on an opposition motion (possibly instigated by Flood) calling on parliament 'not to provide for those pensions which seemed most burthensome or unnecessary'. This elicited a rebuke from the committee chairman, Anthony Malone, that they would be sitting for three months if they had to 'investigate the pension list pension by pension', but Flood was not easily dissuaded: 'When the nation was almost ruined and was groaning under an almost unsupportable weight [of debt], it was the duty of every member to try every method to lessen that weight', he observed self-righteously. Indeed, he was unable to mask his impatience at the readiness of the administration to consider every form of cost-cutting except that of the pension list, and it struck him as remarkable that 'those gentlemen [who] were unwilling to bestow their time for the public good ... were ready to do the dirty work for any administration'. This was an offensive remark, and Flood was correctly called to order and instructed to ask Malone's pardon lest his slight provoked an appeal to the laws of honour. No challenge ensued, but it is notable that Flood was less prominent than at any point in the session to date when the opposition failed in their attempt in late November to vote supplies for six months rather than the usual two years. He did not join either in the successful attack on the provision of a pension of £1,000 to Jeremiah Dyson.[170] He was more forthcoming on the controversial matter of the 20 per cent tax on absentee pension holders; and on 27 November, upon the report of the committee of supplies, he presented a motion that all king's letters providing for exemptions from the tax, at an annual cost to the exchequer of £5306, should be revoked. This provoked 'a warm debate' between those who argued that it was both legal and proper to provide adequately for members of the royal family and heroes of the empire, and those who claimed it was an abuse. When the matter was pressed to a vote, the Castle had a modest majority of 12 (118 to 106), but their victory on this point was negated by the ratification of a motion critical of Dyson's pension by the same margin.[171] In a parallel

169 Ibid. **170** *H.J.*, 25, 27 Nov.; Bartlett, 'Townshend', pp 284–6; Townshend to Rochford, 26 Nov. 1771 in *C.H.O.P.*, iii, 329–30. **171** *H.J.*, 22 Nov., 2 Dec.; Townshend to Rochford, 28 Nov. 1771 in

move, Flood recommended on 29 November in the committee of ways and means that the government should borrow £100,000 rather than the £200,000 it requested to secure the national debt, and make up the differential through 'savings and repayments'. The matter was afforded a long discussion, but the debate swung firmly and irrevocably in the administration's direction when Nathanial Clements pointed out that there was only £10,000 in the treasury; Flood's motion was lost by 30 votes.[172]

With this division, parliamentary debate on financial matters approached its conclusion for the session. All that remained was for the money bills to be approved when they returned from England, and this was usually straight-forward. Flood's performance to this point during the session had been exceptional. His was certainly the opposition's most able and most decisive voice. He had 'no equal in the Commons' and the patriot press could not praise him too highly or cite him too often.[173] Much of what was written was in the nature of the hyperbole that usually attached itself to popular politicians at such times, and it was of little consequence in the House of Commons. However, it did confirm Flood's standing as not just the most prominent patriot of the session but the most admired patriot of his generation. Supporters of the opposition were encouraged by his example and by their successes so far to indulge their hopes that they might yet gain control of the Commons; the limits as well as the potential of opposition were amply revealed in December.

The most contentious exchange in the House of Commons in early December arose out of the opposition's attempt, following on their successful motions of 16 and 19 November, to affirm their hostility to the administration's scheme to divide the revenue board. Spurred on by reports that King's letters appointing new commissioners had 'come over', Flood and Lucius O'Brien insisted that the creation of a new Board of Accounts was 'useless and unnecessary', and they were able successfully to repulse the attempt of the Castle to prevent the matter being reopened by securing the agreement of MPs, 96 votes to 86, to consider the issue on 5 December. Because this debate was an important test of their relative strengths, each side sought to muster its full complement of supporters for O'Brien's motion 'that ... an increase of expense in auditing the accounts of the nation would be unreasonable'. The exchanges were keen, but the unease of independents like Thomas Conolly and James Fortescue with what they defined as the patriots' impatience allowed Macartney to have the matter referred to committee by a modest eight votes in a House of two hundred and thirty-six. This was a setback, but encouraged by the fact that their vote had remained strong, Flood and others determined to make one final effort to defeat the measure when the committee made its report. Once again, the vote was preceded by intense lobbying. There is no evidence that Flood participated, but he profited from the kindnesses of others. The duke of Leinster, for example, sent him

C.H.O.P., iii, 331–2.   172 H.J., 2 Dec. 1771.   173 H.J., 29 Nov., 3, 6 Dec. 1771.

'papers relative to ordnance accounts and copies of his late and present majesty's' letters for passing them ... with [his] ... authority to use them'.[174]

The debate which took place on Wednesday, 11 December, was a tense and heated affair. The galleries were packed, and the outcome was so vital to both sides that proceedings commenced with a wrangle over who should occupy the chair. Once this was resolved, Flood was given the floor, and aided by Walter Hussey, Lucius O'Brien, William Mayne, Edward Newenham, George Ogle and George Hamilton, he reiterated his contention that it was counterproductive to create a board of accounts with new commissioners because the exchequer was in no position to bear the increased costs and because it was merely a device 'to increase dependants [sic] on government'. The Castle interest, by contrast, ably directed by Sir George Macartney and John Hely-Hutchinson, defended the plan to create a new board of accounts on the grounds that it would facilitate better financial management and the eradication of fraud. Eventually, after a debate lasting nearly 12 hours, the Castle secured victory, 124 votes to 119, at 3 a.m. on Thursday 12 December.[175]

Flood was deeply disappointed by this outcome. As things stood, the opposition collectively, and he particularly, had made the session so trying and uncomfortable for the administration it was the subject of political comment in England as well as Ireland.[176] However, their real achievements were few. The opposition had scored a number of notable victories, but they had not destabilized the Castle connection or compelled Townshend to alter his policies on any major issue. Henry Grattan insisted, despite this, that their efforts were not in vain:

> The opposition has acted with sport; we have gained in point of constitution, though we have lost our money in the contest. If it were possible to fix in the minds of our countrymen some precise principles of constitution, government would be more reluctant to invade us.[177]

Flood was less sanguine, and his response appears to have been to take a back seat in the second half of December. He was not totally inactive; but he was quieter than he had been at any point in the session so far, and it is noteworthy that he did not participate in the debate on 21 December prompted by the discovery that one of the money bills had been altered by the British Privy Council.[178]

---

174 Townshend to Rochford, 11, 12 Dec. in *C.H.O.P.*, iii, 336–42; *H.J.*, 6, 9, 11 Dec.; Leinster to Flood, 9, 11 Dec. 1771 (Rosse Papers, C/1/4–5).   175 *H.J.*, 13 Dec.; Fraser to Townshend, 30 Nov. (N.A., Townshend Papers, Ms 733/52); Bartlett, 'Townshend and the revenue', pp 169–70.   176 Thomas to R.B. Sheridan, 3 Dec. in Thomas Moore, *Life of Richard Brinsley Sheridan* (2 vols, London, 1828), i, 60; Walpole to Coke, 11 Dec in Lewis et al., eds, *Walpole Corres.* xxv, 165; Burke to O'Hara, 18 Dec. 1771 in Hoffman, *Burke*, p. 407.   177 Grattan to Broome, Jan. 1772 in *Life of Grattan*, i, 256.   178 *H.J.*, 20, 27 Dec.; Townshend to Rochford, 21, 22, 26, 27 Dec., Rochford to Townshend, 28 Dec. in *C.H.O.P.*, iii, 351–5; Longford to Bective, 26 Dec. 1771 (N.L.I., Headfort Papers, F/5/91).

Flood's colleagues accepted his decision to leave the running to others because they trusted his judgement almost as much as they admired his parliamentary skills. Henry Grattan was particularly enraptured:

> Flood's fame is not silent, though he is not speaking. His reputation for wisdom is equal to his reputation for eloquence. I always thought his taste so superior, if it is equal to his deep understanding. He does honour, and I hope he will do service, to his country.

As his tone suggests, Grattan was confident that 'the opposition' would 'probably be victorious' eventually if Flood remained at their head.[179] Flood kept his own counsel, but the fact that he was advised by Bishop Markham to temper his opposition was significant:

> My opinion of Lord T[ownshend], both as a man and a governor, agrees very much with yours. I believe him to be a very reprehensible in both views, nor do I think it likely that he should be continued. But, whatever his character is, it can justify opposition only to a certain point ... [and should not] be aimed at the rights of the crown and the necessary dependence of a subordinate government. I do not pretend to know the limits of powers which never have been defined, but as far as appears to me, though the withholding the supplies was in your power, you exceeded your line in challenging a particular pension.

Markham advised Flood specifically to moderate his opposition to the proposal to grant Jeremiah Dyson a pension on the Irish establishment because of the animus it excited against him in England:[180]

> I am not giving you such a part in that business as the [ministers?] have made you take ... they were pleased to call a part of your speech which appeared to be so much interrelated for the dirty purposes of a contemptible faction on this side, and was every way so unworthy of you that I have ventured to say it was impossible it could be yours, and I find the world disposed to do you that justice.[181]

As Markham put it, if Flood gained a reputation for doing 'outrageous things' and behaving like an 'adventurer', it would fatally injure his hopes of advancement. Flood acknowledged this. But since he believed he was behaving in a highly 'principle[d] manner consistent with a subject's duty', he felt he had nothing to apologise for, and

179 Grattan to Broome, 13 Jan. in *Life of Grattan*, i, 255.   180 See Grafton to Townshend, 7 Jan. 1772 (Lewis Walpole Library, Townshend Papers); Rochford to Townshend, 22 Jan. in *C.H.O.P.*, iii, 421.   181 Markham to Flood, 10 Jan. 1772 (Rosse Papers, C/2/8).

the public's adulation encouraged him in this belief. Nonetheless, Markham's remarks struck home.[182]

The first clear signs that the reserve Flood demonstrated in late December was part of a strategic rethink by him of his political approach were manifested in January 1772 when it emerged that he intended to spend the full Christmas recess at Farmley where, according to Hercules Langrishe, 'he [wa]s the greatest huntsman and the idlest man alive'. Such inactivity troubled both Langrishe and Lord Charlemont because they believed Flood should be preparing the 'great and important work' of an 'exposition of our Parva Charta of Sir Edward Poynings', but though Langrishe 'entreated, accused and abused him', he declined to take up the issue.[183]

Flood's reticence proved short-lived, however, for when it emerged that, the resolutions of the House of Commons notwithstanding, Townshend had determined to proceed with the division of the revenue board, he responded immediately.[184] Supporters of the administration anticipated that Townshend's action would excite some resistance; they did not calculate just how strong that would be. Following Macartney's announcement of the decision on the resumption of parliament on 4 February, John Ponsonby spoke for Flood and other opposition MPs when he described the announcement as 'a new insult on the parliament of Ireland' that could not be allowed to pass unnoticed. Ponsonby's suggestion was essentially moderate; he recommended 'a committee to inform the King that it was an unwelcome development'. Others proposed 'a deputation of twenty-one' MPs to the King. Flood and his supporters took the hardest line; they urged MPs 'to expel the four [new] commissioners' from the House of Commons in order to neutralise the political advantage that would accrue to the Castle from the division of the revenue board, but when he and others of 'that party' sought support for this position, it was less than forthcoming. Lord Shannon, the largest borough manager, declined on the grounds that he had already committed himself to behave 'with the greatest moderation and ... not to join in anything personal against' Townshend,[185] while the duke of Leinster was only prepared to offer his support on condition 'that if they [we]re not able to expel the four commissioners' with his help, 'they will never desire his further concurrence w[it]h them'.[186]

---

182 *H.J.*, 20, 29 Jan. 1772.   183 Langrishe to Charlemont, [early 1772] in H.M.C., *Charlemont*, ii, 400. 184 Bartlett, 'Townshend and the Irish revenue', p. 169; Bartlett, 'Townshend', p. 292; Townshend to Rochford, 9 Jan. and Rochford to Townshend, 22 Jan. in *C.H.O.P.*, iii, 414–15, 420–1; Waite to Macartney, 25, 26, 29 Jan. 1772 (B.L.,O.C., Waite-Macartney letters).   185 Bartlett, 'Townshend and the Irish revenue', pp 169–70; Bartlett, 'Townshend', p. 293; Townshend to Rochford, 5 Feb.and Rochford to Townshend, 12 Feb.in *C.H.O.P.*, iii, 426–7, 429; *H.J.*, 5 Feb.; Paterson to Townshend, 2 Feb. 1772 (N.L.I., Townshend Papers, Ms 8009/2); Grattan to Day, 27 Feb., 1772 in *Life of Grattan*, i, 259–60.   186 Cunningham to Townshend, [10 Feb.] (B.L.,O.C., Townshend Papers, Box 14); Memo by duke of Leinster to Lord Kildare, 10 Feb. (P.R.O.N.I., Leinster Papers, D3078/3/2); Townshend to Rochford, 12 Feb. in *C.H.O.P.*, iii, 429–30; Grattan to Day, 27 Feb. 1772 in *Life of Grattan*, i, 259–60.

Having prepared the ground as well as he could and consented to present a moderately phrased motion which, 'without an alarming violence, would be to the new commission highly embarrassing', Flood formally raised the implementation of the division of the revenue board in the House of Commons on Tuesday 11 February. He had to tread carefully, because of his need to maximise the opposition vote and he did not quite rise to the challenge. Henry Grattan, who was present, maintained that 'Flood did not excel'; he was 'notable rather than eloquent'; 'he was cautious in every assertion, shrewd and guarded in every observation; he watched the varying countenance of the House and hastened to correct every prejudicial impression, in the language of wisdom'.[187] This notwithstanding, Flood offered a powerful argument in favour of the need to

> vindicate the honour of the House, assert the rights, and show a proper resentment for the contumely and insult with which it was loaded. The advice of the House of Commons expressed in a resolution, and laid solemnly before the representatives of His Majesty was that seven commissioners had been found sufficient for the business of the revenue. Was not this an implication, that more than seven would be more than sufficient, and was not this showing the sense of the House to be against this measure, as unnecessary and burdensome? Yet the resolution had been mocked at, their advice slighted, and the measure carried into execution, in express contradiction of the Commons of Ireland. Was it not easy to perceive that the intention of the ministry was not only to throw contempt upon the House, but even to make the people out of love with parliament. The Commons are to give their advice or not; they are to interpose when any ruinous or destructive measure is on foot, or not to interpose. If they are not to advise, not to interpose, they are useless; they are only a mere mockery of parliament. But if they advise, if they interpose, then they are set at naught, what must people think of the dignity and utility of parliaments, when they behold their advice and interposition serves only to bring down upon them, and to confirm the very evils which they deprecate. And people will soon grow out of love with parliament, when they see they are made use of as a sword to wound, not a shield to protect them.[188]

These were sentiments with which many MPs empathised, but Flood's motion to 'disallow any expenses or contingent charges, or salaries which may be incurred by dividing the commissioners of excise from the commissioners of customs and increasing the number of commissioners, contrary to the advice of the house' went further than most believed wise. Realising that he stood a better chance of success if he toned down his proposal, Flood offered, as an alternative, 'that this house will

---

187 Grattan to Day, 27 Feb., Grattan to Broome, 24 Feb. 1772 in *Life of Grattan*, i, 257–60.   188 *H.J.*, 14 Feb. 1772.

refuse their consent to any alterations in the revenue laws of this kingdom, which shall tend to give effect to the dividing the Board of Excise from that of Customs, and the multiplying of Commissioners of the revenue which hath been adopted in contradiction to this house'. This had broader appeal, but it still met with strong resistance from Castle officers. Feelings ran high. There were even some sharp exchanges between Flood and the Chief Secretary, George Macartney, who was widely credited for 'his good temper and firmness in dealing with the opposition'. However, this served as but a temporary distraction from John Monk Mason's more consequential initiative to dilute Flood's motion by adding the clause 'however such alteration might appear to be for the improvement of the revenue'. This was pressed to a vote by its advocates and lost 117 to 107. So too was a proposal to adjourn the debate without putting Flood's motion. This left the way clear for Flood, and when his motion was eventually put after eight hours of debate, he had achieved another notable triumph, 117 votes to one hundred and seven. Buoyed up by this victory, Barry Barry sought to press home the opposition's advantage by urging the House to suspend those members who had accepted commissionerships at the new Board of Excise for as long as 'they sat at that Board'. The debate that followed was bad-tempered, but though Flood supported the suggestion he was unable to bring a majority with him.[189]

The rejection of Barry Barry's motion indicated that the House of Commons had no appetite for a no-holds-barred confrontation with the Lord Lieutenant on the subject of dividing the revenue board. Given Townshend's determination to proceed regardless,[190] this is understandable, but Flood was discontented. His preference was to prohibit the new revenue commissioners from sitting in parliament, and he and others who felt likewise found it frustrating, as Henry Grattan observed, that there was no support for their position:

> you see how little has been done, and how our country disgraces itself by feeble attempts at resentment. The measure was pernicious, the manner was insolent. What has been done? We have declared that we are affronted. We have declared that we will not join with Government to insult Parliament; but we have not expelled, committed, suspended, attacked the advisers of the measure, nor drawn one inference from premises, on whose groundwork men of spirit must advance. The different views of the men who oppose the corruption of the age, and the sordid spirit of the country we live in, disappoint its sanguine advocates, and make their zeal useless and impotent ... The opposition of the winter may have

189 *H.J.*, 14 Feb.; Townshend to Rochford, 12 Feb. in *C.H.O.P.*, iii, 429–30; Bartlett, 'Townshend and the Irish revenue', pp 169–70; H.H. Robbins, *Our first ambassador to China: an account of the life of George, Earl of Macartney* (London, 1908), p. 459; Grattan to Day, 27 Feb. 1772 in *Life of Grattan*, i, 259–60. 190 Townshend to Rochford, 12, 13 Feb. in *C.H.O.P.*, iii, 429–33; Bartlett, 'Townshend', pp 299–300.

shown that our Parliament is not totally prostitute; but it has also shewn that the integrity of parliament can do no service: and the government of Lord Townshend will be an immortal proof that the worst measures may succeed notwithstanding the opposition of the Irish parliament.[191]

Grattan's acknowledgement that the opposition, for all its success[192] and Flood's efforts, was powerless to deflect Townshend was reinforced by reports that 'the leaders of opposition are divided among themselves and disposed to quarrel'. Flood was not involved in or responsible for any quarrels, as far as one can tell, but the disunity among the opposition and the increasing impact of Townshend's overtures to Lord Shannon were probably as important as the outcome of the debates on the revenue board in accounting for the uneventfulness of proceedings in the Commons over the next fortnight.[193] Flood was present, but he played a supportive role and spoke only on those matters about which he felt especially strongly.

One such issue was the debate on the petition presented by the freeholders of County Armagh against Judge Christopher Robinson for fining them £200 for failing to keep a section of road in order. Flood had encountered Robinson when he had delivered 'a judgement of ouster' against his uncle Charles in 1762, and he had little respect for his views. Indeed, it was his suggestion on 24 February that caused MPs to summon the judge to explain his action before the committee established to consider the petition.[194] Four days later, when the whole house assembled in 'Grand Committee' to debate the matter, Flood vigorously supported those MPs, led by William Brownlow of Armagh and his cousin Warden, who urged that the judge be disciplined for behaving 'arbitrarily'. Robinson had a record of 'striv[ing] to sap the very fundamentals of parliamentary authority', Flood charged, and he had acted illegally in levying a fine on County Armagh without due information. A snide reference to the 'confederacy of lawyers' assembled to defend Robinson elicited a sharp rebuke from two of his *quondam* allies, Walter Hussey and John Fitzgibbon, who opposed the attempt to censure Robinson, but the judge's supporters were not numerous enough to prevent the committee approving a motion proposed by Warden and amended by Henry Flood to the effect that Robinson had imposed the fine 'without new or legal evidence'. Two days later, Flood spoke on the matter once again when he helped repel an attempt by the Castle to nullify the vote of 28 February. He was also in the majority on 3–4 March when he spoke in favour of allowing MPs sit on 'petty juries'.[195]

191 Grattan to Broome, 24 Feb. 1772 in *Life of Grattan*, i, 257–8.   192 It should be noted that a motion claiming that the appointment of new commissioners, contrary to the express view of the Commons, represented an attempt to 'extend the prerogative of the Crown beyond its due limits' was approved on the Speaker's casting vote on 19 February (*H.J.*, 21 Feb.; Bartlett, 'Townshend and the Irish revenue', p. 170).   193 Townshend to Rochford, 29 Feb. 1772 in *C.H.O.P.*, iii, 440–1.   194 *H.J.*, 26 Feb. 1772.   195 *H.J.*, 2, 4, 6 Mar. 1772.

Flood enjoyed more success in the division lobbies in February–March 1772 than at any point in his career. However, he also experienced reverses. He was unable, for example, to secure the ratification on 10 March of a bill to legalise quarterage – the controversial customary payment made by Catholics to Protestant guilds. In common with many MPs, Flood was unimpressed by the arguments of those who advocated the abolition of quarterage on commercial and religious grounds. 'If freedom is so desirable, Papists may attain it on conforming without any expence', he pronounced sternly. 'The bill cannot be said to encourage any monopoly – for nothing can be called a monopoly when it is in the hands of everyone who chooses to undertake'.[196] As this confirms, Flood continued to hold the traditional Protestant view that the security of their ascendancy would be endangered by any enhancement of the power of Catholics or diminution of the privileges of Protestants, with the result that he also opposed Thomas Conolly's proposal on 11 March for 'a bill to disarm such Protestants in the north of Ireland as are engaged in the tumults and risings there'. The impetus for this derived from the activities of the Hearts of Steel in Antrim and Down in 1771–2, and Conolly was so anxious that steps were taken immediately to counter their activities that he called on MPs at the same time to request the Lord Lieutenant to issue a proclamation ordering the disarming of 'riotous Protestants' pending the ratification of the bill. This suggestion disturbed Flood because it 'would tend to establish a doctrine that proclamations of government were as valid as statutes', and he, Walter Hussey and others persuaded Conolly to withdraw his motion.[197]

He used a similar argument to justify his opposition, on 9 March, to the clause in the bill 'for improving his majesty's revenue and preventing frauds' which decreed that it should operate for 'two years or to the end of the then next session of parliament'. It was, he alleged, 'of a most dangerous tendency' because it gave the government the freedom to defer indefinitely recalling parliament for 'raising money'. Despite this, the bill progressed to its committee stage where, on Saturday, 14 March, Flood successfully argued that the proposal to increase the fee charged on spirit licenses to remunerate collectors of the excise was a further illustration of the Castle's strategy to render 'the power of administration stronger in the House'. Anxious to avoid further reversals, John Hely-Hutchinson endeavoured to prevent the question of the duration of the bill being discussed, but Flood frustrated him with a powerful speech in which he warned MPs 'that the constitution must be in danger when bills to increase the hereditary revenue [could] be continued no man knows how long' and urged the deletion of the offending words. This provoked a prolonged debate involving the usual stalwarts of government and opposition, and the outcome was again to Flood's liking. At 2 a.m. on Sunday morning, his motion was sanctioned by 84 votes to 77.[198]

---

196 *H.J.*, 13 Mar. 1772.   197 *H.J.*, 16 Mar. 1772.   198 *H.J.*, 11, 16 Mar. 1772.

Unfortunately for Flood, this did not represent the end of the matter. When the bill was reported he was powerless to prevent the Castle reversing the defeat it had experienced in committee on the duration of the bill. He and eighty-six others voted in favour of limiting the bill to four years, but 92 MPs voted to leave the clause as originally drafted. Townshend was delighted, and Flood crestfallen. With this defeat, and the ratification, also against his strong advice, of a measure to raise an additional £50,000 in revenue from the rum trade, Flood was forced to conclude that his repeated efforts to confine the capacity of the Castle to raise revenue had failed, and that his warnings that any legislation which rendered 'government less dependent on parliament would, in proportion', make parliament less relevant had fallen on deaf ears.[199]

With the supply voted on the terms the administration wanted, and negotiations in train to secure funds in England, Townshend had achieved his major financial and political objectives of the session. The fact that the Lord Lieutenant continued to make progress in his negotiations to secure the support of Lord Shannon's extensive connection represented a further setback for the opposition, though reports in the late spring and summer that Shannon had finally 'made his peace with government' were premature.[200] There is no record of Flood's reaction to these developments, but the fact that he is not mentioned in the reports of debates in the Commons after 16 March suggests that he had enough of pyrrhic victories and that he was among the increasing number of MPs who chose to stay away from the House of Commons as the session drew to a conclusion. The absence of reference to him in the end-of-session debate on a complimentary address to the Lord Lieutenant corroborates this. It is hard to imagine, given the controversial events of the preceding months, how Flood could have refrained from comment if he was present.[201] His absence serves to confirm what everybody already knew, that for all his efforts during the 1771–2 session, it was Townshend's vision of the future government of Ireland and not his that had prevailed. Indeed, George Macartney went so far as to claim that Townshend's triumph derived in part from Flood's 'injudicious' management of the House of Commons: 'Never', he maintained, 'was opposition upon such good ground ..., and never opposition was so ill conducted or made so little of it'.[202] This is untenable because it assumes that Flood led a united opposition whereas he was but the most active member of a disunited patriot parliamentary tendency. Moreover, Flood shared Townshend's pleasure at the destruction of the undertaker system; it was the system he put in its place, giving the commanding position in

199 *H.J.*, 16, 18, 20 Mar.; *F.J.*, 19 Mar.; Townshend to Rochford, 18 Mar. 1772 in *C.H.O.P.*, iii, 458.   **200** Bartlett, 'Townshend', pp 306–8; Bartlett, ed., *Macartney*, pp xl–xli, 60–5, 149–50; Gordon to Townshend, 3 Apr. (Sterling Library, English Misc Mss 1766–72); *H.J.*, 24 June; Townshend to Rochford, 10, 13 Apr., Rochford to Townshend, 6 Apr. 1772 in *C.H.O.P.*, iii, 478–9, 484.   **201** *H.J.*, 18, 24 Mar., 6, 8, 11, 27, 29 May, 3 June 1772.   **202** Macartney to Hely-Hutchinson, 21 Jan. 1773 in H.M.C., *Donoughmore*, p. 275.

Irish politics to the lord lieutenant, which was not to Flood's liking. Nonetheless, it was the reality with which he had to come to terms, particularly as he had not forsaken his ambition to shape and influence policy from within – an ambition it had proved impossible for him to fulfil, as long as government was conducted in the arbitrary and despotic fashion he identified with Lord Townshend.

PART THREE
OFFICEHOLDER

Subsequent events suggest that Henry Flood would have found it impossible to reconcile his patriot agenda with London's anxiety to do nothing to vitiate its authority in Ireland if he had undertaken to work with the Irish administration in the late 1760s. Despite this, he did not conclude that office and his brand of patriotism were incompatible. He chose to regard Lord Townshend, as most English whigs did Lord Bute, as an aberration, because to conclude determine otherwise meant accepting that his political grail of an Irish parliament equal in status with that at Westminster was unattainable, and he was unwilling to do this. Moreover, the decision to replace Townshend in the summer of 1772 with Lord Harcourt, who was less assertive and more eager to secure Flood's services, ensured that his relations with Dublin Castle improved. The conclusion of an agreement proved tortuously protracted; but this was less damaging to Flood's political credibility than the consequences of his holding office at the precise moment when the patriots received their finest opportunity in his lifetime of making their vision of Anglo-Irish relations a reality. The example set by the rebellious American colonists and the problems the American war caused the British government and the Irish administration enabled the patriots, energised by powerful new voices and an exigent protestant political nation, to exert a measure of influence they were never allowed while Flood was their leading spokesman in the 1760s and early 1770s. This might not have been a problem if Dublin Castle had responded with a programme of constitutional and commercial reform of its own, but they opted instead for the time-honoured tactic of resisting patriot demands. As a result, Flood found it increasingly difficult to support the Castle interest in the House of Commons in the late 1770s. His estrangement was reinforced by ongoing difficulties arising out of the failure to honour the agreement he concluded with Lord Harcourt when he accepted a vice-treasurership in 1775. As a consequence, the late 1770s were extremely difficult for Flood and he became isolated politically. A lesser figure would not have endured the experience, but Henry Flood was enabled to come through it because he retained an unshakeable belief that he had behaved entirely properly in office and that it was the government and not he which was at fault.

5

Negotiating office, 1772–5

The appointment of Simon, Earl Harcourt as lord lieutenant in 1772 brought about a change in the political atmosphere in Ireland. Harcourt was more disposed to compromise than his predecessor, and though he came to Ireland with the intention of continuing Townshend's policy of maintaining a majority Castle connection in the House of Commons, Henry Flood had no reason to regard him with the same animus and reserve. Indeed, he was sufficiently impressed by his approach and his policies to identify the prospect of co-operating with him in a positive light.

FAMILY FINANCE AND INTELLECTUAL ACTIVITY

Following his decision not to attend the final weeks of the 1771–2 session, Flood returned to Farmley where he resumed improving his estate. Remarkably little evidence survives of his life in Kilkenny, though it was there that he engaged in his favourite rural pursuit – hunting.[1] His estate management practices are also elusive, but legal documents suggest that he was not as involved as his father, and press advertisements that he followed the usual practice in the region of offering land 'for lives or years as may be agreed upon'. Furthermore, unlike some Kilkenny landowners, such as the Agars who 'encourage[d] ... Protestant tenants' and 'Protestant manufacturers', he did not discriminate against Catholics.[2] This is not to suggest that he took little interest in the use to which his estates were put so long as he received an income sufficient to allow him to lead the life of a gentleman-politician. He had as little patience with difficult tenants, as he had with renegades from the Flood interest on the corporation of Callan, and he did not hesitate to intervene decisively whenever his interests were endangered. In 1770, for example, he had 'several persons' in his employ take 'forcible possession' of 'choice meadow grounds

---

1 Flood to Markham, 19 Oct. 1771 (Rosse Papers, C/2/6); Grattan, *Life of Grattan*, i, 199; *F.L.J.*, 14 Apr. 1770, 13 Jan. 1773, 9 Dec. 1778.   2 Warden registered many more leases than Henry (Registry of Deeds, *passim*); *F.L.J.*, 16 Sept. 1767, 10 Feb. 1768, 21 Jan., 16 Sept. 1769, 13 Jan., 19 May 1773; J.S. Donnelly, 'The Whiteboys of 1769–72', *R.I.A.proc.*, 83C (1983), p. 304.

contiguous to the city of Kilkenny' which were in dispute. As this suggests, Flood was determined to secure a good return from his estate, and that the lands he leased were cared for and developed. With this in mind, he let substantial blocks of 80 to 100 acres, encouraged the development of the marble quarries located on lands in his ownership, and was careful to ensure that when he let property in Kilkenny city, he continued his father's practice of registering the leases. [3]

Efficient estate management was a matter of financial importance as well as personal pride for Flood, not least because of the expense of sustaining his family's interest in Callan. The cost of this may have eased in the early 1770s, as his contest with the Agars entered a quieter phase, but it has been suggested that he had already incurred considerable debts. There is no reliable evidence as to their scale, but it would explain why he was so eager, on the death of his uncle Charles in 1770, to receive his bequest of several hundred acres in the barony of Gowran and to reabsorb the Ballymack house and lands Charles had secured on preferential lease from Henry's father. [4]

Flood was of the opinion that because an 'involuntary error' by Charles Flood in the 1760s had exacerbated his family's problems in Callan borough, he had a moral and financial as well as legal entitlement to both the Gowran and Ballymack properties. However, while Charles bequeathed him his Gowran lands directly, his instructions were that another nephew, Francis Flood of Huntingbrooke, should succeed to the 'house and lands of Ballymack' provided he set up home there within six months. It is not apparent how Henry, as the 'sole executor' of his uncle's will, went about implementing his instructions, but the upshot was that he obtained possession of Ballymack and that this contributed to the increase in ill-feeling within the Flood family that hastened the break-up of his political connection in the 1770s. Some of this ill-feeling derived its impetus from family knowledge that Henry's illegitimacy negated his entitlement to any family property, Farmley included, but it was reinforced by the fact that he was not very family-minded. It is salient that he used what he acknowledged was the 'distant mode of communication' of a letter rather than the 'friendship and cordiality' of a face to face encounter to repair some of the damage Charles' will caused with Warden, his cousin who was bequeathed £500 and enjoined by Charles 'to preserve a firm and unalterable attachment to ... Henry ... and his interests as the eldest branch of the family'. [5] Flood was able to repair his damaged relations with Warden, but other family members proved less amenable, and allegations of impropriety in his management of his unmarried sis-

3 *F.L.J.*, 16 Sept. 1767, 20 Aug. 1768, 21, 31 Mar., 14 Apr. 1770, 2 Jan. 1773, 11 Nov. 1778, 26 May 1779; Registry of Deeds, 335/549/226994, 342/556/231502, 363/185/243827, 456/408/293371.   4 Above p 24; Henry to Warden Flood [post 11 Nov.] (R.I.A., Burrowes Papers, Ms 23K/53/10); *F.J.*, 17 Nov. 1771; Will of Charles Flood, 11 Oct. 1770 (Land Commission, Keogh estate Papers, Box 13 (E.C., 2272)).   5 Will of Charles Flood, 11 Oct. 1770 (Land Commission, Keogh estate Papers, Box 13 (E.C.,2272)); Henry to Warden Flood [post 11 Nov.] (R.I.A., Burrowes Papers, Ms 23K/53/10).

ter's interests did nothing to foster confidence in his integrity or to lessen family suspicion of his motives.

As described above, Warden Flood stipulated in his will in 1763 that his daughter, Isabella, should have £4,000 'for her sole and specific use' on his death and that this £4,000 was to be paid from Lady Frances Beresford's marriage portion. Isabella did not seek possession of her inheritance until 1769 when, having used her father's will and the earl of Tyrone's commitment to provide for his children as security, she borrowed £200 to enable her to take up residence with her Candler cousins near York. Shortly afterwards, she received £1,000 from the earl of Tyrone upon whose estates the money due to her was charged, and vested 'power of attorney to conduct all her affairs' in her mother. The main responsibility to which this gave rise was the management of the outstanding £3,000 plus interest that was paid over by the earl of Tyrone before July 1770. In accordance with her daughter's wish that 'a proper security be found for the money', Isabella senior concluded an agreement to lend it to Sir Lucius O'Brien at 6 per cent interest per annum.[6]

It is not clear what prompted the Floods to enter into this arrangement with Lucius O'Brien, since his affairs were in a state of severe embarrassment, and he had 'the reputation of being a slow or bad paymaster'.[7] But it is improbable that Henry played a less than prominent role because of his political connection with O'Brien and his assumption, from his elderly mother, of the responsibility of managing his sister's financial interests. Henry's acquisition of the legal material and deeds of security relating to the O'Brien mortgage was resented by his sister. He maintained subsequently that Isabella senior and junior were very affectionate, and implied that relations between himself and his sister were satisfactory until William Candler insinuated himself into Isabella's affections when her 'reason' began to falter, but this is hardly credible. It would appear, indeed, that relations between brother and sister had been poor for some time, and that this may have been a factor in her decision to settle in England. She was certainly not persuaded by assurances that her mother and he would act for her 'sole benefit as effectually as if she was herself present' because in 1771 she requested the transmission of all documents appertaining to the O'Brien mortgage to her possession. Henry was disinclined to comply. Both he and his mother wanted Isabella to return to Kilkenny, so when William Candler visited Ireland on her behalf, Henry 'expostulated ... upon his [Candler's] unjust conduct and charged him with keeping s[ai]d Isabella and not suffering her to return to Ireland'. Candler denied this, and when he failed to obtain possession of the relevant documents, Isabella authorised the preparation of a bill

6 Above pp 82–3; Memorial of deeds, 28 Jan. 1769, 29 June 1770 (Registry of Deeds, 258/456/174146, 282/113/182208); Copy of public bill: Edward Wallis v Henry Flood and others, 20 Feb. 1778, Consent and mortgage for securing £3,000 (N.L.I., Inchiquin Papers, nos 2951, 2871). 7 Bodkin, ed., 'The Irish parliament in 1773', p. 180; Keogh to Burrowes, 11 June [177?] (R.I.A., Burrowes Papers, Ms 23/K/53/16).

seeking their transfer to her possession. The bill was filed in January 1772, but before it was heard Isabella died. This served merely to intensify the hostility between Henry Flood and William Candler, because Isabella bequeathed all her interest in the £3,000 O'Brien mortgage to her Candler relations and English friends and appointed Candler and Edward Wallis of Accomb, Yorkshire, as her executors. [8]

The absence of reference in her will either to her brother or mother demonstrates that Isabella Flood was alienated from her family at the time of her death. Henry was taken aback by her action. As Isabella's sole surviving brother and guardian of the family standard, he refused to accept the will was genuine. He maintained that he had received a letter (which he never produced) from her shortly before her death in which she stated that she had initiated legal proceedings for the transmission of the O'Brien mortgage papers under pressure from William Candler and that it was her intention to return to Ireland. If this is true, it is hardly surprising that Isabella senior 'caused a caveat to be entered' which obliged Wallis and Candler 'to prove the said will' was not made under duress. This effectively froze the disputed £3,000 until July 1775, when the prerogative court finally determined in favour of the executors and legatees. Flood was appalled by the judgement. He declined to hand over the mortgage deeds and other papers, and 'combin[ed] and confederat[ed]' with Sir Lucius O'Brien (who was in arrears with his interest payments) to prevent Edward Wallis (Candler died shortly after the prerogative court hearing) calling in the debt to obtain the £3,000 at issue, thereby prolonging the dispute by several more years. [9]

Despite the distraction provided by his sister's will and his political undertakings, the easing in the contest for control of Callan borough in the 1770s gave Flood more time to devote to intellectual pursuits. The destruction of his personal papers renders it impossible to applot his reading with any confidence, but if Irish history figured prominently in the late 1760s, the classics, and particularly Greek, regained their previous ascendancy in the 1770s. It is not clear where he purchased books, but Edmond Finn maintained a healthy stock of works – ancient (including Leland's *Demosthenes* and Middleton's *History of the life of Marcius Tullius Cicero*, Pliny, Terence, Aeschylus, Dionysius, Caesar) and modern (including Richardson and Swift) – in his Kilkenny shop. Other texts were readily available by subscription or by purchase from Dublin or London; we know, for example, that Flood subscribed to James Beattie's *Essays on the nature and immutability of truth* in 1776, while his friendship with such noted bibliophiles as Lord Charlemont and Edmond Malone ensured he was kept apprized of notable new publications. [10]

8 Copy of public bill: Edward Wallis v Henry Flood and others, 20 Feb. 1778, Conditional decree in case of Wallis V Flood and others, 16 July 1782 (N.L.I., Inchiquin Papers, no. 2951). 9 Ibid.; below p 287. 10 *F.L.J.*, 11 Feb., 11 Apr. 1767; Daly to Flood, [n.d.] (Rosse Papers, C/110); Richard Ryan, *A biographical dictionary of the worthies of Ireland* (2 vols, London, 1821), ii, 146; Malone to Charlemont, 5 July 1780 in H.M.C.,*Charlemont*, i, 373; James Beattie, *Essays on the nature and immutability of truth in opposition to sophistry and scepticism* (Edinburgh, 1776).

Like his intellectual *confréres*, Flood believed the provision of accurate translations of the classics was a matter of transcendant importance, and he was confident
enough in his own abilities to communicate 'a translation of the opening of the Iliad'
to William Markham in 1772. Bishop Markham detected a disimprovement in Flood's
literary skills since his departure from Oxford and, though he was not unapprecia-
tive, he counselled against publication:

> I wish I cou'd encourage your friend the translator, but it must be malice in me
> to advise him to print. He has lost the simplicity, the spirit and the harmony of
> the original. At the same time I think he has genius, but he is modern all over. [11]

This was good advice, but Flood was not dependent on the encouragement of others to persist with his eclectic intellectual endeavour. According to his family biographer, he 'cultivated' his interest in literature 'with care'; he translated two books
of Homer and the 'finest speeches' of Demosthenes which he read to Walter Hussey,
Henry Grattan and Denis Daly. He also studied sections of Milton's *Paradise Lost*
and transcribed 'the most beautiful passages' of Shakespeare. [12]

As the reference to his reading his translation of Demosthenes to friends attests,
Flood's literary enthusiasm was shared by many of his political colleagues. Indeed,
an interest in the classics and contemporary literature was virtually as important as
political consonance in binding the members of his Kilkenny and Dublin circles in
the early 1770s. It is no coincidence, therefore, that Flood's closest political friend at
this time, Lord Charlemont, translated 'select sonnets of Petrarch', Catullus and
others; that Walter Hussey Burgh wrote poetry and plays; that Sir Hercules Langrishe
was a poet of some ability; that Richard Griffith sent him a translation from French
in 1774; that Henry Grattan's main interest in university was literature, and that
Denis Daly was a bibliophile with an impressive collection of rare and valuable
books. [13] These, in short, were erudite as well as educated men who could discourse
knowledgeably on literature, history and language as well as politics. Edmond Malone,
who was eminently qualified to judge, maintained that Flood was an 'excellent
scholar', and if this flatters him somewhat, the ease and appositeness with which he
could cite Demosthenes and Shakespeare, discuss Montesquieu or critically assess
William Mitford's *History of Greece* in his parliamentary speeches and correspondence attests to the breadth of his reading as well as to the keenness of his mind. [14]

11 Markham to Flood, 15 Sept. 1772 (Rosse Papers, C/2/9); Prior's *Life of Malone*, p. 102.   12 *Life of
Grattan*, i, 198–9; Flood, *Memoirs*, p. 16.   13 Craig, *The Volunteer Earl*, pp ix-x, 29, 219–20; Griffith to
Flood, 30 June 1774 (Rosse Papers, C/1/8); Webb to Flood, 1775 in R[odd], ed., *Letters to Flood*, p. 88;
Griffith to Charlemont, 19 May 1778 in H.M.C.,*Charlemont*, i, 340; Prior, *Malone*, pp 40–1; T.C.D.,
Burgh Papers, Ms 9318/ 4–5, 38–49 and *passim*; *Life of Curran*, ii, 483–511; Kelly, *Grattan*, p. 5; *A
catalogue of the library of the right hon Denis Daly* ... (Dublin, 1792).   14 M. MacDonnell Bodkin,
Grattan's parliament before and after (London, 1912), p. 170; *The Parliamentary Register: or, History of
the proceedings and debates of the House of Commons of Ireland* (17 vols, Dublin, 1782–1801), i, 53; John

Flood was certainly anxious to make an intellectual mark in the early and mid-1770s. His *forte* at Oxford was verse, and following Markham's deflating comments on his translation of Homer, he concentrated on composition in English. He was sufficiently pleased with his efforts to send Markham examples of his work in 1774 but, once again, the bishop was unimpressed. He described the stanzas in one poem as 'careless, as if written *correcte calamo*, the thoughts good but expressed too diffusedly'.[15] Flood was aware of his creative limitations, but he was encouraged by the praise accorded his 'imagination' in his 'Ode on fame', and he worked hard to correct the habitual weakness in phrasing and errors in technique that Markham identified in his compositions. However, no matter how hard he tried, there was no avoiding the fact that he did not possess the ability needed to become a good poet. As he conceded, Markham correctly diagnosed that his composition was 'more formal and technical ... than is consistent with the freedom of the lyrick'.[16]

Everybody was not so stern as Markham. Daniel Webb, the Bath-based, Irish-born author who achieved renown in the 1760s with enquiries into painting, poetry and music, was highly impressed. So too was William Blakeney, and the warmth of their observations encouraged Flood to persist with his poetic efforts.[17] He had his 'Ode to Fame' and his translation of the first Pythian ode of Pindar printed for private circulation in London in 1775, and he had the satisfaction of a largely positive reception as most contemporaries adjudged that the work, in Edmond Malone's words, possessed 'considerable merit'. Flood was too conscious of his problems reconciling rhyme with his desire to be 'graceful', and of the fact that his literary strengths were 'energy, force and argument' rather than 'elaborate structures of words or accurately polished sentences', to be persuaded by the genuine admiration of friends and acquaintances that his literary efforts truly were worthwhile. However, it did have the beneficial effect of widening his circle of acquaintances in England by bringing him into contact with poets like Edward Jerningham.[18] His involvement in amateur theatricals and the Society of Granby Row fulfilled the same social function in Ireland.

Interest in drama and music in Ireland grew so strongly during the mid-eighteenth century that several theatres were opened in towns about the kingdom to

Greig, ed., *The Farington diary* (3 vols, London, 1922–4), i, 202; Prior, *Malone*, pp 40–1, 46, 66, 69–70. 15 Prior,*Malone*, p. 102; Markham to Flood, 30 Jan. 1774 (Rosse Papers, C/2/18).   16 Flood to Markham, 4 June 1774 (Rosse Papers, C/2/19), R[odd] ed., *Letters to Flood*, pp 177–80; A poem [1770s] (Rosse Papers, C/3).   17 Webb to Flood, 14 Apr., W. Blakeney to Flood, 3 July [1774] in R[odd] ed., *Letters to Flood*, pp 64, 90; Kevin Barry, *Language, music and the sign* (Cambridge, 1987), pp 6, 38–42; Daniel Webb, *An enquiry into the beauties of painting ...* (Dublin, 1764); *Remarks on the beauties of poetry* (Dublin, 1764); *Observations on the correspondence between poetry and music* (Dublin, 1769); *D.N.B.*, xx, 1007. 18 [Henry Flood], *An ode to fame: and the first Pythian ode of Pindar* (Dublin, 1775); Prior, *Malone*, pp 454–5; Ridge to Burke, 25 Sept. in Hoffman, *Burke*, p. 600; Flood to Charlemont, 16 Aug. 1775 in Flood, *Memoirs*, pp 345–6; *Gentleman's Magazine*, 61 (1791), p. 1164; Jerningham to Flood, 27 Jan. 1776 in R[odd], ed., *Letters to Flood*, p. 101; Flood to Jerningham, 26 Feb. 1776 (Henry Huntington Library, Jerningham Papers, JE286); Lewis Bettany, ed., *Edward Jerningham and his friends* (London, 1919).

meet public demand.[19] The quality of the performances and the artists on show bore favourable comparison with those elsewhere in Europe. But mounting antipathy in patriot circles to Italian burlettas, which 'almost triumphed over the best productions of our language', caused some to offer alternative fare for their own and their friends' enjoyment. One of the first to do so was William Brownlow of Armagh, and his example was soon followed by the likes of Thomas Conolly, the duke of Leinster, Luke Gardiner, Hussey Burgh, George Ogle, Edmond Sexten Pery and Isaac Corry.[20]

Flood's County Kilkenny circle shared this enthusiasm for amateur theatre, and the early 1770s witnessed stagings by Hercules Langrishe at Knocktopher, Gervaise Bushe at Kilfane, Francis Flood at Floodhall and Flood himself at Farmley. The plays performed ranged from quality Shakespearean drama, through Goldsmith and Gay to ephemeral pieces of little substance. Full length plays were usually abridged and given a contemporary resonance by the addition of an epilogue or prologue which animadverted on current preoccupations. This gave local versifiers an opportunity to display their skills, and while their contributions were generally well-received, this could not be assumed. We know, for example, that on one occasion Flood took severe exception to an epilogue by Hercules Langrishe to Macbeth, in which he had played the lead role, poking fun at his political conduct. Unwilling to accept that the remarks were uttered in jest, Flood composed an *ad hominem* prologue for another play which criticised Langrishe but it was so leaden it embarrassed rather than entertained. Despite his tendency to over-react to personal reflection, Flood's readiness to perform roles as diverse and demanding as Othello, Macbeth, Cassius and Stingo and his ability to extemporise ensured him a welcome place in Kilkenny dramatic circles for as long as he was interested.[21]

Private amateur theatre flourished for a number of decades among members of the Protestant elite. However, Flood appears not to have participated much after the mid-1770s.[22] His was not the personality which submerged itself in any type of collective activity for long. He was happy to lead the attacks by opposition politi-

19 I.M. Hogan, *Anglo-Irish music 1780-1830* (Cork, 1966), pp 16–17; Llanover, ed., *Delany letters*, i, 310–12, 392; W.S. Clark, *The Irish stage in the county towns 1720-1800* (Oxford, 1965); Brian Boydell, *Rotunda music in eighteenth-century Dublin* (Dublin, 1992), *A Dublin musical calendar 1700-60* (Dublin, 1988); *F.L.J.*, 15, 29 Oct. 1768; [W.R.Chetwood], *A tour through Ireland* (London, 1748), pp 89–90. 20 Taylor to Taylor, 8 May. 1743 (N.L.I., Headfort Papers, F/3/17); *The private theatre of Kilkenny with introductory observations on other private theatres in Ireland* ([Dublin], 1825), pp 1–7; Hogan, *Anglo-Irish music*, pp 25–6; Craig, *The Volunteer earl*, p. 108; *Life of Grattan*, i, 145–7; Fitzgerald, ed., *Leinster Corres.*, iii, 112; duke to duchess of Leinster, 29 Dec. 1774 (N.L.I., Fitzgerald Papers, Ms 13022/21). 21 *The private theatre of Kilkenny*, pp 2–3; *Life of Grattan*, i, 135, 146, 199–200; List of actors in a performance of 'She stoops to conquer' at Knocktopher, 27 Sept. 1774 (Rosse Papers, C/1/9); duke to duchess of Leinster, 29 Dec. 1774 (N.L.I., Fitzgerald Papers, Ms 13022/21). 22 P[onsonby] to Ponsonby, [ca 1781] (T.C.D., Barker-Ponsonby Papers, P3/1/14); Printed playbill for Dromana theatre, [1780s] (Villiers-Stuart Papers, T3131/E/9/1–2); N.A., Langrishe Papers, B.R. KK.38/15; *The private theatre of Kilkenny*, p. 3 ff; *Life of Grattan*, i, 147; Stewart, *A deeper silence*, p. 34.

cians on government policy and to join with others in entertainments like amateur theatre and hunting, but he always held something in reserve. This is true also of his involvement with the Society of Granby Row. This grew out of patriot gatherings attended by the likes of Walter Hussey, Denis Daly, Gervaise Parker Bushe, Sir Edward Newenham, Henry Grattan, Lord Charlemont and Flood during the parliamentary sessions of the early 1770s, but it is impossible to assess its role and impact with any confidence.[23] What is indisputable is that Flood was unwilling both to be guided in his political actions by the collective views of this group or to impose his views though he exercised an ascendant influence over Lord Charlemont and was deeply admired by Gervaise Bushe, Hercules Langrishe and the young Henry Grattan, whose political ambitions he encouraged.[24] This can be attributed, in part at least, to the fact that he was less gregarious than most of his fellow patriots. It is significant, for example, that he had little contact with Thomas Leland, though he was a friend of Lord Charlemont, a familiar of Edmund Burke and Bishop Markham, and the author of a renowned translation of Demosthenes orations, a history of Philip of Macedon and a dissertation on the principles of human eloquence. It may be that he found Leland's commitment to confessional toleration uncongenial, given his own pronouncements on the penal laws.[25] But it is also emblematic of his lifelong practice of limiting his personal intimacy and of allowing few people to get close to him.

CHANCELLOR OF THE EXCHEQUER?

Though Henry Flood spent the summer and autumn of 1772 in Kilkenny, the implications of the appointment of Lord Harcourt, of the reports that Lord Shannon had finally agreed terms with the administration and that Sir William Osborne had been dismissed from the board of excise were not lost on him.[26] He recognized that

---

23 David Lammey, 'A study of Anglo-Irish relations between 1772 and 1782 with particular reference to the "free trade" movement' (Ph.D. thesis, Q.U.B., 1984), pp 62–3; Gerard O'Brien, *Anglo-Irish politics in the age of Grattan and Pitt* (Dublin, 1987), p. 26; *Life of Grattan*, i, 251–2.   24 Flood, *Memoirs*, pp 77–8, 87; Charlemont to Flood, [*c.*1771] in R[odd] ed., *Flood letters*, p. 94; *Life of Grattan*, i, 134–7.   25 Joseph Liechty, 'Irish evangelicalism, Trinity College, Dublin, and the mission of the Church of Ireland at the end of the eighteenth century' (Ph.D. thesis, St Patrick's College, Maynooth, 1987), pp 185–7, 189; O'Hara to Burke, 10 May 1770 in Hoffman, *Burke*, p. 463; Walter Love, 'Charles O'Conor of Belanagare and Thomas Leland's philosophical history of Ireland', *I.H.S.*, xiii (1962), pp 2–25; Joseph Liechty, 'Testing the depth of Catholic/Protestant enmity: the case of Thomas Leland's *History of Ireland*, 1773' in A.D. Falconer, ed., *Reconciling memories* (Dublin, 1988), pp 52–87.   26 *H.J.*, June-July, 31 July; Bartlett, 'Townshend' , pp 308–10; *idem*, 'Townshend and the revenue', p. 172; Waller to Macartney, 30 Oct., 21, 23, 25 Nov. in Bartlett, ed., *Macartney*, pp 158–9, 160–2; Waite to Macartney, 18, 22 Nov. 1772, 19 Jan. 1773 (B.L.,O.C., Waite-Macartney Letters); Harcourt to North, 24, 31 Dec. 1772 in W.E. Harcourt, ed., *The Harcourt Papers* (11 vols, privately printed, 1888–96), ix, 60 and D.P.L., Harcourt Papers, Gilbert Ms 93 ff 14–15.

the transfer of responsibility for administering Ireland directly to a new lord lieutenant, without the usual *interregnum* during which power was vested in Irish lords justice, meant that the system of managing the Irish parliament through undertakers was gone forever. It was also apparent, since those whom John Lees tellingly termed the 'unconnected patriots' were currently intent on 'meditating the gratification of their own private views', that there was little point in his taking up the mantle of opposition since the prospects of his making any impression on the Castle 'squadron' in the upcoming session were very slim.[27] For this and other reasons, Flood sought to attract the attention of the new Lord Lieutenant.

As befitted a man who had spent his adult life in the royal household and the diplomatic service, Lord Harcourt was a more urbane and more self-occupied viceregent than his predecessor. He was also more content to delegate responsibility, and he trusted his Chief Secretary, Sir John Blaquiere, who had served as his ambassadorial secretary in Paris and whom George Macartney adjudged 'a very lively, sensible fellow', explicitly. There were occasional problems caused by the Lord Lieutenant's 'unfortunate memory', but the two men had a common interest in protecting and supporting each other, and they proved a capable team during the four years that they served together.[28] Blaquiere's major limitation was his lack of parliamentary experience, and his anxiety on this score was such that following his appointment he actively contemplated entrusting the task of presenting Castle business in the House of Commons to others, and to confining himself to administrative matters.[29] This was information of some pertinence to Henry Flood who perceived possibilities in the 'new scheme' and, as he had done five years previously, he appealed to Bishop Markham for help.

As an 'intimate' of Harcourt, Markham was well-positioned to act as an intermediary between Flood and the Lord Lieutenant, but the demands of his diocese and Harcourt's presence in Paris precluded him raising Flood's situation personally. It did not prevent others speculating. John Hely-Hutchinson, who made use of every avenue to communicate his own cavernous ambitions, reported enviously that Markham was the go-between in 'a negotiation ... between Flood and the ch[ief] g[overnor]' aimed at facilitating the former's path to office.[30] This was inaccurate,

27 Rochford to Townshend, 7 Aug. in *C.H.O.P.*, iii, 531; Lees to Townshend, 13 Aug. (N.L.I., Townshend Papers, Ms 394/13); Acheson to Townshend, 26 Aug. 1772 (N.A., Townshend Papers, Ms 654); Lees' review of Harcourt administration, [1776] in *Harcourt Papers*, x, 249.   28 *Harcourt Papers*, i, 253; Buckinghamshire to Thompson, 9 Apr., 3 Oct. 1779 (B.L., Mackintosh Collection, Add. Ms 34523 ff 198, 203); N.L.I., Harcourt Papers, Ms 5161 passim; Blaquiere to Harcourt, 19 Oct. 1775 (N.L.I., Blaquiere Papers, Ms 877/4); Harcourt to Rochford and replies, 2, 18 June, 2, 3, 5, 12 July 1771 (P.R.O., S.P.78/282 ff 255, vol 283 ff 4–6, 9–10, 26–7, vol 285 ff 239–40, 267–8); Macartney to Clements, 21 Oct. 1772 (T.C.D., Clements Papers, Ms 1743/32).   29 Burke to O'Hara, 30 Sept. in Hoffman, *Burke*, p. 539; Markham to Flood, 15 Sept. 1772 (Rosse Papers, C/2/9).   30 Hely-Hutchinson to Pery, 4 Oct. (Emly (Pery) Papers, T3087/1/48); Hamilton to Hely-Hutchinson, 25 Oct., Hely-Hutchinson to Hamilton, 27 Dec. in H.M.C., *Donoughmore*, pp 270, 273; Hely-Hutchinson to Townshend, 11 Nov. (T.C.D., Donoughmore Papers, C/2/57); Townshend to Rochford, 9 Sept. in *C.H.O.P.*, iii, 542; Burke to O'Hara,

for though Flood appears to have responded to Markham's news 'that the Attorney General [Philip Tisdall] is to take the lead in the House of Commons', with a statement which the Bishop interpreted as authorization to inform Harcourt of his readiness to co-operate with the new administration, no substantive discussions took place. Markham was certainly eager to do what he could to pave the way because, having missed Harcourt on his return from France, he requested Charles Jenkinson, whom he knew intimately from his days in Oxford and who was in Harcourt's 'entire confidence', to brief the new Lord Lieutenant. He was so confident this left only the details to be settled he informed Flood on 12 November that when he presented himself 'at the Castle, his reception will be such as may dispose him to a connexion which may be advantageous to himself as well as to government'. Having, he concluded, done everything 'esteem and friendship could dictate', Markham left the rest to Flood. He should, Markham advised, in the first instance 'take the lead in the H[ouse] of Comm[ons] for the administration', but this was, he reminded him, 'only the first step of the [preferment] ladder'. [31]

Lawrence Parsons maintained subsequently that Markham was acting on his own initiative 'without any previous communication with Mr Flood' when he informed Charles Jenkinson that Flood was disposed to form 'a connection' with the new administration, but this does not accord with the evidence just considered. Flood certainly did not give Markham formal permission to *negotiate* on his behalf, but he did empower him to make overtures to the new administration, presumably in order to pave the way for negotiations he would conduct himself. Flood's destiny, in short, remained in his own control though Markham's contention that matters were 'in as good a train as possible' indicates that as far as he was concerned it made little difference whether Flood or he carried out the negotiations, office was the inevitable next step:

> You must determine whether the negotiation is to be carried on by the party here or whether you will use the means you have of conducting it yourself. From what I know of Lord Harcourt's impression of you, and of your own good judgement, which will not desert you on this critical occasion, I cannot help considering the matter as already concluded. [32]

In accordance with custom and practice, Lord Harcourt's early days in Ireland were 'taken up in levees and receiving addresses'. These assemblies typically were crowded affairs, but what was remarkable about those that took place in 1772 was the exceptional number of opposition figures that attended to greet the new Lord

---

30 Sept. in Hoffman, *Burke*, p. 539; Markham to Flood, 15 Sept. (Rosse Papers, C/2/9); Lill to Macartney, 25 Oct. [1772] in Bartlett, ed., *Macartney*, pp 230–1.   31 Markham to Flood, 15 Sept., 12 Nov. 1772 (Rosse papers, C/2/9–10); Parsons' biography (C/14/1-5); Sutherland, 'Political respectability, 1751–71', pp 156–8.   32 Rosse Papers, C/14/1-5; Markham to Flood, 13 Nov. 1772 (C/2/11).

Lieutenant.[33] Henry Flood was not among their number, but because he travelled from Farmley in December 'on purpose to wait on me', Harcourt concluded that his wish to work with the administration was genuine; and he was disposed to facilitate him. However, the recent unhappy experience with Sir William Osborne caused the Lord Lieutenant to determine not to chase after his support:

> I shall do what I can to improve every favourable circumstance that the times may offer, or that chance may throw in my way. I shall give the greatest attention to everything that passes, but I must endeavour to avoid the appearance of being eager and anxious in closing with those who may seem well-disposed to make their peace with government. I apprehend their terms will be more or less unreasonable, in proportion to their ideas of their own importance.[34]

If this was a defensible strategy given the administration's experience with coy patriots, it caused particular difficulties in Flood's case because he expected the administration to approach him. Indeed, he concluded that because he had let it be known that he was willing to support the administration, provided certain, as yet unspecified, terms were met, it was up to the Castle to make the next move. Harcourt read the situation differently. His decision to receive Flood 'at the Castle with all the civility which [he] could show' (which made John Hely-Hutchinson green with envy) was prompted by Markham's intervention with Jenkinson. His expectation was that Flood would follow it up with a request for a private audience where matters could be taken further, so when Flood made no such request, the Lord Lieutenant concluded that he had returned to 'the country' and got on with other issues.[35]

In fact, Flood had remained in Dublin following his initial encounter with the Lord Lieutenant awaiting an approach from the Castle, but when no contact was made by January, he wrote to Bishop Markham complaining of neglect and querulously challenging the intentions of government towards him. Markham made light of the matter and attributed it simply to 'mismanagement'. He accepted Flood's assurances that he had done all that could be expected of him by attending the levee and by making himself available thereafter, and he moved quickly to soothe his prickly sensitivities. He communicated 'the substance' of Flood's letter to Jenkinson so he could alert Lord Harcourt. Jenkinson, in turn, apprised Markham of Harcourt's positive impression of his brief encounter with Flood and of his hope that Flood

33 Harcourt to Rochford, 2 Dec. in *C.H.O.P.*, iii, 579; Hunt, ed., *Irish parliament in 1775*, p. xxi; *H.J.*, 2 Dec.; Lill to Macartney, 1 Dec., Waller to Macartney, 2, 14 Dec in Bartlett, ed., *Macartney*, pp 233–4, 162–3; O'Brien to O'Brien, [1 Dec. 1772] in Ainsworth, ed., *Inchiquin Mss*, p. 216. **34** Harcourt to Rochford, 8 Dec. in *Harcourt Papers*, ix, 44–6; Harcourt to North, 24 Dec. 1772 (D.P.L., Harcourt Papers, Gilbert Ms 93 ff 14–15); Lees' review of Harcourt administration, pp 248–9. **35** Lees' review of Harcourt administration, pp 248–9; Hely-Hutchinson to Macartney, 23 Dec. 1772 in Bartlett, ed., *Macartney*, pp 235–6.

would seek an audience because the Lord Lieutenant possessed, Markham reassured him on 14 January, 'as high an opinion of your abilities and character as you can wish and is ... in a disposition to favour you as far as prudence will allow him'. This ought to have paved the way finally for an early meeting between Flood and Harcourt, but no meeting took place because Flood had returned to Farmley. It was a critical juncture at which to be absent from Dublin, but Flood's disappointment at the failure of the administration to approach him ran deep. He was also disturbed by the intensifying public speculation as to his intentions and the gossipy relish with which his future was being discussed. It is a measure of Flood's sensitivity on this point that he declined even to confide in Lord Charlemont. [36]

Flood's absence from Dublin both puzzled and discommoded the Harcourt administration. They were still hopeful of his support, if reports of their 'total neglect' of Tisdall, Malone and Hely-Hutchinson, who had taken the lead for the Castle in successive parliaments since the accession of George III, do not deceive. However, like Lord Townshend and Sir George Macartney, who had also sought 'to get him if possible, but not to suffer him to conduct', it remained to be seen if they could agree terms.[37] Their immediate priority was to clear the air and, following Markham's intercession with Jenkinson, Blaquiere sent Flood a short note on 21 February informing him that he had

> very particular reasons for requesting to know how soon you propose coming up to Dublin, and of wishing, if it suits your convenience, that it might be as soon as possible, that I might ask the favour of speaking with you at the Castle. [38]

This was an invitation Flood could hardly refuse, and he travelled to Dublin for a meeting with Harcourt in mid-March. It was an amicable encounter, and Flood was sufficiently impressed by what he heard to conclude that he and the administration were united in their wish to promote 'the welfare and satisfaction of the people, ... the dignity of the Crown and ... the solid interests of Great Britain'. However, to the Lord Lieutenant's surprise, he professed himself unable to enter into a commitment to accept office because of the political problems facing the nation:

> I must say that no period ever required more care or more exertion. Were the same carelessness, profusion and maladministration to continue which we have lately felt, a sum would be wanted next session to be borrowed equal to the whole debt incurred by the last war ... Such a situation of things, the decline of

36 Markham to Flood, 14 Jan. (Rosse Papers, C/2/12); Andrews to Pery, 21 Jan. in H.M.C. *Emly*, 193; Hely-Hutchinson to Hamilton, [1773] in H.M.C. *Donoughmore*, p. 275; Flood to Charlemont, 5 Feb. 1773 in H.M.C. *Charlemont*, i, 314.   37 Hely-Hutchinson to Hamilton, [1773] in H.M.C. *Donoughmore*, p. 275.   38 Harcourt list in *Harcourt Papers*, x, 334–5; Blaquiere to Flood, 21 Feb. 1773 in R[odd], ed., *Letters to Flood*, p. 56.

government securities, a damp on trade and credit universally, a diminishing revenue, distraction and impotence in the collection of it, joined to the remaining fever from the five years' national ferment, form an assemblage of difficulties, to subdue which not only vigilance but address, not only ability but integrity, not only a government [text defective].

The administration that shall succeed in such an arduous attempt will deserve well of their King and country. I sincerely hope Lord Harcourt may. But it must be clear, I think, that, independent of a sense of duty, the common inducements of office would not be sufficient to incline a rational man to embark on such a voyage.[39]

This was not what Castle officials expected. But having opened an avenue of communication with Flood, they ignored the chagrined remarks of borough interests that Harcourt was neglecting 'the late government party' in order to pay 'great court to all the country party', and they were heartened by speculative reports in the summer that Flood 'has stirred'.[40]

Encouraged by this, the administration concluded that Flood could be won over if they offered him a position commensurate with his abilities and gave him a leading role in the Commons. The latter was relatively straightforward because it was within their gift; a suitable office was more problematic. One possibility canvassed in the summer of 1773 was the chancellorship of the exchequer, the appointment of W.G. Hamilton to which Flood had criticised in 1763. Hamilton was notoriously elusive on patronage matters, so Blaquiere sailed to England on 18 June to consult with the Prime Minister, Lord North, and to establish if the Chancellor of the Exchequer would surrender his office on reasonable terms. Hamilton's initial response was not encouraging, which prompted speculation, among those who believed Hamilton would not surrender 'the seals of the exchequer', that Blaquiere and Flood might have to apportion Irish civil and military duties between them. This was improbable. But conjecture that something major was afoot intensified when Flood joined Blaquiere in London in July and chose to live there 'incognito'.[41]

Flood went to England to make himself available prior to a special cabinet meeting on Irish affairs on 18 August at which his situation and the increasingly worrisome finances of the Irish exchequer were the main items on the agenda.[42] The priority of the meeting was to determine a strategy to restore equilibrium to Irish finances and, with this end in mind, Harcourt was instructed to secure a commit-

---

39 Flood to Markham, 20 Mar. 1773 (Rosse Papers, C/2/13).   40 O'Hara to Burke, 3 Apr., 3 June in Hoffman, *Burke*, pp 542, 546–7; Waller to Macartney, 27 July 1773 (P.R.O.N.I., Macartney Papers, D562/5/53).   41 Hamilton to Pery, 18 July (Additional Pery Papers, P.R.O.N.I., T3052/26); *C.H.O.P.*, iv, 59; Lill to Macartney, 29 July, 10 Aug., Waller to Macartney, 14 Aug. in Bartlett, ed., *Macartney*, pp 241, 242, 168; Burke to O'Hara, 20 Aug. 1773 in *Burke Corres.*, ii, 453.   42 Camden to Flood, 12(2), 15 Aug. 1773 in R[odd], ed., *Letters to Flood*, pp 56–8.

ment 'from the Irish parliament' for a complex series of measures aimed at reducing expenditure and raising revenue. These were bound to be unpopular, so ministers authorised the introduction of a ten per cent absentee tax and the reunification of the boards of customs and excise as a concession to Irish opinion. More consequently, as far as Flood was concerned, Blaquiere was authorised 'to treat with Mr Hamilton for the resignation of his office of Chancellor of the Exchequer, and to offer him a pension of equal value for life or a term of years' in order to pave the way for Flood's recruitment.[43]

Having obtained the cabinet's support for his strategy, Blaquiere redoubled his efforts to persuade W.G. Hamilton to stand aside to enable the administration to provide for Flood. The two men met at Worcester on 5 September when the Chief Secretary put 'several proposals to ... [him] for the resignation of [his] employment' but none was acceptable. Hamilton was simply not interested in vacating a lucrative office he deemed 'entirely honourable' for an *equivalent* return from a pension.[44] He was not opposed to the idea of an exchange, but he had no intention of resigning the chancellorship of the Irish exchequer for a pension unless he had a compelling incentive to do so and the offer made to him did not come close.

Flood's decision to return to Ireland in early September suggests that he was deeply disappointed by the inconclusive nature of Blaquiere's discussions with Hamilton. He was aware he was the subject of intense speculation, and while the instinctive alarm of the popular press was moderated by informed reports that 'the ministry ... resolve to introduce an intire new system of politics' to restore the kingdom's finances and improve its trade and manufacture if they secured Flood's active backing, it did not halt conjecture.[45]

Blaquiere, meanwhile, was determined not to let this opportunity of recruiting Flood founder because of W.G. Hamilton's unco-operativeness, and following his return from England he sought urgently to meet him. We do not know what transpired. But it is clear that their inability to offer Flood a suitable office was a source of mounting concern in government circles, and that the optimistic noises of some in the confidence of the Castle that Flood's support in the House of Commons was assured and that all that remained to be settled was 'what Flood is to get' were wide of the mark.[46] Harcourt acknowledged this when he informed Lord North in October that 'the exorbitancy of [Hamilton's] demands ... makes it impossible for me to think of treating any more with him'. This meant that he could not 'expect the assistance of Mr Flood' which would, he averred, cause his administration 'sore

43 Cabinet minute, 18 Aug. 1773 (N.L.I. Blaquiere Papers, Ms 877/1). 44 Hamilton to Pery, 6 Sept.[1773], 18 Jan. 1774 (P.R.O.N.I., Additional Pery Papers, T 3052/28, 34); Hely-Hutchinson to O'Hara, 1 Sept.(N.L.I., O'Hara Papers, Ms 20402); Lill to Macartney, 2 Oct. 1773 in Bartlett, ed., *Macartney*, p. 245. 45 *H.J.*, 30 Aug., 18 Sept., 4 Oct.; *F.L.J.*, 11 Sept. 1773. 46 Hamilton to Pery, 18 Jan. 1774 (P.R.O.N.I., Additional Pery Papers, T 3052/34); Blaquiere to Flood, 13 Sept. in R[odd], ed., *Letters to Flood*, p. 58; Waller to Townshend, 18, 21 Sept. 1773 in Bartlett, ed., *Macartney*, pp 172-3.

distress'. The Lord Lieutenant was not without hope that the clear signal given Flood that the administration wanted to provide him with a suitable position would mean he would not 'be very violent in his opposition', but he had no idea how Flood would react.[47] Flood, for his part, was also in a delicate position. He had compromised his political reputation by entering into an ill-defined relationship with the administration. This ensured that the 1773–4 session would be a severe test of his equipoise as well as of his judgement. He was faced with the choice of supporting the administration in anticipation that it would lead to his early appointment to office, which would antagonize many of his friends and supporters, or of reverting to the assertive patriotism that had brought him praise, fame and recognition, which would antagonize the administration that seemed intent on obliging him. Not surprisingly, he sought to manoeuvre between this Scylla and Charybdis, because he believed that if the administration could soon secure him a suitable office, it was the most appropriate political stance for him to adopt.

NOT 'VERY VIOLENT IN OPPOSITION'

While Blaquiere contrived unsuccessfully to liberate the chancellorship of the exchequer from W.G. Hamilton's grip in order to provide for Flood, Harcourt was busy preparing for his first meeting with the Irish parliament. This was, as Flood had pointed out in March, a task fraught with 'real difficulties' because of the precarious condition of the kingdom's finances and the depressed state of the economy:

> The debt of a million; a sinking revenue; a rising establishment; trade going; credit gone; the annual expense of government near £100,000 above the annual income; how to make the one equal the other and where to find the ways and means; these points require the earliest attention of government and call for the sagacity, ingenuity and expertise of all the King's servants. [48]

The budgetary situation of the kingdom was so critical, John Lees maintained, that 'Ireland was threatened with bankruptcy and disgrace'. [49] This was an exaggeration, but the situation was sufficiently serious to compel the administration to take action to ease the problem. Flood was not actively involved in this. But it is not unreasonable to assume that the proposals for an absentee tax and the reunification of the revenue boards, which were approved at the same cabinet meeting that authorised Blaquiere to secure the chancellorship of the exchequer for Flood, were advanced

47 Harcourt to North, 3 Oct. 1773 in *Harcourt Papers*, ix, 73.   48 Lill to Macartney, 10 Mar. 1773 in Bartlett, ed., *Macartney*, p. 238.   49 Lees' review of Harcourt administration, p. 251; 'A sketch of the public revenue of Ireland' (N.L.I., Joly Ms 29 f 27); Harcourt to North, 31 Jan. 1773 (D.P.L., Harcourt Papers, Gilbert Ms 93 f 25).

with his recruitment at least partially in mind, and in anticipation that they would mitigate his resistance to any attempt to curb parliamentary grants or to increase taxation, which he had resisted when they were proposed by Townshend. [50] The idea of an absentee tax was certainly popular in Ireland, [51] but despite this and the worsening state of the kingdom's finances (which caused mounting arrears in salary and pension payments), the administration was anxious lest its programme of financial legislation was insufficient to win Flood's support and to steer it clear of trouble in the Commons. [52]

In fact, the opening of the session went smoothly. In the absence of an agreement with Flood, the lead on behalf of the Castle interest was taken by John Hely-Hutchinson. He had 'affected age and infirmities and his necessary profitable attention to his profession' when invited to play this role, but once he learned of 'Flood's return [from England] *re infecta*', he grasped at the opportunity to upstage his rival. His relations with Blaquiere were not always tension-free, despite this. He was, for instance,'thrown into a violent huff', which caused him to refuse to talk to the Chief Secretary for a full afternoon, when Blaquiere consented to a minor amendment suggested by Flood to the address to the crown, but the ill-feeling was not permanent. [53] The Castle's continuing courtship of Flood also disturbed the weakened and demoralised opposition though those like Lord Charles Fitzgerald who concluded simplistically that he had 'turned courtier' were quite wrong. He was acting as a well-inclined independent, as he had done previously for a time in the early 1760s and the early part of the 1767-8 session. [54]

50 'Lees' review of Harcourt administration', pp 253-9; H.M.C., *Charlemont*, i, 36-7; Fanning, 'The King's purse', p. 60; *F.L.J.*, 12, 26 Jun.; North to Harcourt, 29 Mar. (N.L.I., Harcourt letterbook, Ms 755 f 10); North to Harcourt, 24 Apr. (D.P.L., Harcourt Papers, Gilbert Ms 93 ff 27-8); Clements to Macartney, 4, 14 Jun. (B.L.,O.C., Clement files); Cabinet minute, 16 Aug.1773 (N.L.I., Blaquiere Papers, Ms 877/1). 51 Clare to O'Brien, 14 Dec. 1771 in Ainsworth, ed., *Inchiquin Mss*, p. 213; Foster to [Holroyd], 21 Oct. (Additional Sheffield Papers, P.R.O.N.I.,T3465/26); H.M.C., *Charlemont*, i, 36; North to Devonshire, 18 Oct. (N.L.I., Harcourt Letterbook, Ms 775 f 19); Diary of a journey through England and Wales to Ireland in 1773 by Rev J. Burrowes (P.R.O.N.I.,T3551); *H.J.*, 27 Jan., 14 June, 9, 11, 13, 18, 25 Aug., 13, 24 Sept. 1773. 52 Clements to Macartney, 4, 14 June, 7, 24 Aug., 28 Oct. (B.L.,O.C., Clements files); Waite to Macartney, 16 June, Hely-Hutchinson to Macartney, 3 July, Waller to Macartney, 31 Aug., 14 Sept., 9 Oct., Lill to Macartney, 2 Oct. in Bartlett, ed., *Macartney*, pp 239-41, 244-5, 170, 172, 175; Harcourt to Rochford, 17 June in *C.H.O.P.*, iv, 59-60; Waite to Macartney, 25 June, 3 July, 31 Aug., 5 Oct. (B.L.,O.C., Waite-Macartney letters); *H.J.*, 20 Aug.; Macartney to Clements, 16 Sept. (T.C.D., Clements Papers, Ms 1743/34); Foster to Holroyd, 12 Sept., 21 Oct. (Add. Sheffield Papers, P.R.O.N.I.,T3465/25, 26); Harcourt to North, 30 Sept. 1773 (D.P.L., Harcourt Papers, Ms 93 ff 28-9). 53 Lill to Macartney, 12 Oct., Waller to Macartney, 12, 16 Oct. in Bartlett, ed., *Macartney*, pp 246, 175-7; *H.J.*, 13, 15, 20 Oct. 1773. 54 Fitzgerald to Leinster, 14 Oct.(N.L.I., Fitzgerald Papers, Ms 13022/130); O'Brien to O'Brien, 19 Oct. in Ainsworth, ed., *Inchiquin Mss*, pp 217-18; Harcourt to Rochford, 21 Oct., Harcourt to North, 21 Oct. (D.P.L., Harcourt Papers, Gilbert Ms 93 ff 32-4); Foster to Holroyd, 21 Oct. (Add. Sheffield Papers, P.R.O.N.I.,T3465/26); Stratford to Stratford, 29 Oct. 1773 (N.L.I., Stratford Papers, Ms 18788/5).

Flood demonstrated this independence on Thursday, 26 October, when he joined with Sir William Mayne, Walter Hussey, Denis Daly, George Ogle, Sir Edward Newenham and other opposition stalwarts in requesting information on a number of financial matters. This prompted some patriots to conclude Flood was ready at last to resume where he had left off in 1772, but they were wrong. His speech displayed so little of the defiance that was his hallmark in recent sessions that others opined, with greater justification, that his object was to pave 'the way for a reconciliation with government':

> Mr Henry Flood declared he never knew a time in which there was so much wanted by government and so much distress in the people; which distress arose from evil counsellors and maladministration. That he had ever, and ever should heartily join the part of administration when it was right, and heartily oppose it when it acted wrong.[55]

This was not enough for Harcourt. He had concluded that since he had committed his administration to secure a major office for Flood, he was among the 'persons from whom I had reason to expect support' and he did not conceal his displeasure with his decision to 'vote against me' on 26 October.[56] Flood, for his part, was in no doubt but that he was behaving honourably. He was not pledged to support the administration in the House of Commons, but his decision to distance himself from his former patriot allies was an eloquent testament to his intentions. The fact that he seemed more eager to speak on personal than on political matters was also significant.

One such occasion occurred on 28 October when Colonel Arthur Browne, MP for Gowran, attributed the ratification of the Octennial Act to Lord Townshend. Flood had refrained from adverting to the controversial Townshend viceroyalty up to this, but he was unwilling to allow anyone ascribe his greatest achievement to date to a man he actively despised, and he rose quickly to assert his claim:

> It was I who first gave the assisting hand to that excellent law; nor am I ashamed to pay myself that compliment; for honest fame is the just reward of an upright heart, and I am not averse to the gift. I followed the bill to the other side, and when it was the doubt of the minister whether it should pass, I told him the arguments that were its foundation. In this I was backed by Lord Chatham, and the minister allowed them unanswerable. I therefore do aver, that from this transaction Lord Townshend cannot expect the shadow of honour. I speak freely, for I am afraid of no man. I seek no favour, but the applause which may flow from

---

55 *H.J.*, 27 Oct.; Harcourt to Rochford, 27 Oct. in *C.H.O.P.*, iv, 94–7; Waller to Macartney, 26 Oct. 1773 in Bartlett, ed., *Macartney*, p. 178. 56 Harcourt to Rochford, 27 Oct. 1773 in *C.H.O.P.*, iv, 94.

performing my duty. I am under (as I said before) no obligation to this or that Viceroy, and I believe I may say I rejected proffered benefits. I shall now only remark, that from every observation I could make – from every observation an honest man could make – Lord Townshend acted as an enemy, a professed enemy to our country, our constitution, and our liberties: for which reason, instead of a panegyric, he should, by every real friend of Ireland, be treated as a PUBLIC MALEFACTOR.[57]

This was, as Henry Grattan junior has observed, a 'remarkable speech' as much for the intensity of the antipathy it displayed towards Townshend as for Flood's determination to claim principal credit for the Octennial Act. It can be assumed that Flood's comments were made *ex tempore* because they were uttered during a finance debate, and that his profession that he was 'under ... no obligation' to Harcourt reflects his determination not to be taken for granted by the administration. Not surprisingly, his intervention was well received by those who yearned for the fiery patriot of previous sessions, but it was not enough to repair the damage already done his reputation, and he did nothing during the debates on the administration's financial legislation in the fortnight that followed to lighten the apprehension of his admirers. He generally sat on the opposition benches and occasionally made a brief statement, but he consciously left the running to William Mayne, Edward Newenham and Lucius O'Brien, and they had neither the rhetorical *gravitas* nor the numerical support to cause the administration any problems. Even the 'irregular' manner Sir John Blaquiere chose to announce the Castle's decision to reunite the revenue boards on 30 October did not prompt him to take up the baton of active opposition. [58]

If Flood's attempts to conduct himself as a well-inclined independent pleased neither his former patriot allies nor his prospective government employers, unsubstantiated rumours that the administration was considering nominating him to the provostship of Trinity College, when its frail incumbent Fr ancis Andrews passed on, also proved personally disadvantageous. There was little sympathy for him on the Castle benches, moreover, despite reports that he had 'grown impatient of opposition and languishes for a great share of administration'. This was an exaggeration, but it was an understandable conclusion given Flood's preparedness to support the administration's fiscal policy as enunciated by the Chief Secretary on Monday 8 November. He was not forward, but while opposition activists contrived to exploit the perception that an absentee tax was the forerunner of a general land tax and a legislative union, Flood highlighted his potential value to the administration when he voted with Blaquiere and the majority on 16 November against his long-

57 *H.J.*, 29 Oct. 1773; *Life of Grattan*, i, 195–6. 58 *H.J.*, 1, 3, 5 Nov.; *F.L.J.*, 2–10 Nov.; Waller to Macartney, 30 Oct., 2 Nov., Lill to Macartney, 4 Nov. in Bartlett, ed., *Macartney*, pp 178–80, 248–9; Harcourt to Rochford, 31 Oct., 3 Nov. in *C.H.O.P.*, iv, 96-8; George III to North, 5 Nov. in Fortescue, *Corres of George III*, iii, 29–30.

time allies Barry Barry, Lucius O'Brien, George Ogle, George Hamilton, Walter Hussey and Sir William Osborne on a resolution presented to the committee of accounts on 'the propriety of local duties'. It was not a critical matter and he did not make a major speech, but these details were secondary in the minds of most contemporaries' to the fact that he supported the proposal. [59]

The administration was delighted by this turn of events. The patriot public, by contrast, was disappointed but unsurprised:

> Mr Flood has been the *silent* spectator of his country's cause during the time elapsed of this session. There can be no virtuous reason on his part assigned for his negligent conduct, for oratorical proofs have convinced the world that his tongue was always at the disposal of his heart, and that *that heart* was once the brightest gem which adorned the House of Commons, and never till now refused the assistance so conspicuous before. [60]

Flood's apparent defection proved all the more galling for his supporters because the skill with which he had advanced patriot aspirations since the mid-1760s had raised the threshold of expectation of those who shared his views. The *Hibernian Journal* captured their disillusionment:

> You have for many years given repose to harassed Liberty. You have soothed it in the moment of despair; you gave it shelter and became the idol of its followers. You have uttered the accents of inspiration, as if possessed with its virtues and have been worshipped with a devotion bordering on idolatry.
>
> In the succession of fleeting Patriots, you presented yourself the champion, and held the shield of public spirit. Independent gentlemen gazed on you as the star of their observation; nor suspected, in their simplicity, that you had yourself the Northern Lights in contemplation. You are now beheld as a great luminary, which has so long commanded wonder, reeling from your sphere, and ready to rush like a meteor into nothing. When the danger of your country grows big, is that the hour of your wane? If ... you have consigned yourself to the abyss which awaits you, recollect ... the loud plaudits of your country will be turned into scornful hisses! The trumpet of fame will sound your downfall to distant regions! The strength of these abilities which have raised you, will oppress you with their weight! And you are become the tool of the Prime Serjeant, and the play-thing of a secretary of yesterday, the pity of your friends will add to your mortification. Dublin, which on the next general election would have opened her arms to receive, will now think her streets polluted by your footsteps. [61]

59 *H.J.*, 10, 12, 15, 17 Nov.; *F.L.J.*, 6, 17 Nov.; Harcourt to Rochford, 9 Nov. in *C.H.O.P.*, iv, 99–103; Waller to Macartney, 9, 17 Nov. in Bartlett, ed., *Macartney*, pp 181–2. **60** *H.J.*, 24 Nov. 1773 **61** *H.J.*, 3, 17, 19, 24 Nov. 1773.

Such commentaries were predicated on the assumption that Flood had finally and irrevocably apostasised and joined the Irish administration, whereas he was not prepared to commit himself wholeheartedly to the administration as long as his relationship with them remained undefined. At the same time, he did not waver in his support for Harcourt's financial programme. So when, on Tuesday, 23 November, the Attorney General advanced proposals for a tax on absentee landowners and an annuity loan of £265,000, Flood spoke decisively and firmly in their favour:

> Government and parliament should mutually aid each other in this present crisis ... The great end was to set the nation clear, and make the income equal to the expence, which could only be done by encreasing the one, and lessening the other 'till they met each other. Government to their honour had made retrenchments and savings to the amount of 50,000£ a year; the rest must be done by new taxes, the overplus of which, and the surplus of the Loan duties would make a saving of 40,000£ a year towards discharging the national debt. Some taxes were necessary, which he would mention: that on absentees he thought proper (under good regulation), that it was once thought popular, but that was whilst it was impracticable; for no sooner was it known to be attainable than the voice both within and without doors was as inveterate against, as the people were before eager to embrace it; that in respect to it, he would only now say, if our apprehensions (as to its evil tendency) were groundless, the tax will then be found useful; that it ought not to be considered as a tax on the people, but as a restitution from those, who by spending the income of the kingdom in another done a real injury to the country. As to the duty on tobacco, that indeed he objected to, as it was oppressing the poor by taxing the only little luxury they enjoyed, that gentlemen ought to concur in abolishing old, and not raising new taxes which were unnecessary; that when people saw that government were not intent upon new loans every year, debentures would consequently rise and that, in justice to the public, we ought to endeavour at this, as there now was 900,000£ under par. ... He added that he thought the present administration good, candid and sincere, and that independent gentlemen should assist all its good intentions, and not waste their time in useless opposition.

Flood was aware that this endorsement of the administration left him 'open to malicious aspersions, and exposed him ... to the censure of those who thought whoever was the opposer of the worst administration must also oppose the best at the expense of popularity', but he vowed not to be guided by such wrong-headed conclusions. He would, he pronounced, 'ever act as he thought best for the good of the nation', but few were convinced by his protestations that he was still a free agent. [62]

62 *H.J.*, 24 Nov.; *F.L.J.*, 27 Nov. 1773.

The Castle loyalist, Robert Waller, maintained that what he described as Flood's 'recantation' was prompted by his calculation that it would secure him the provostship. Others conjectured that his object was the chancellorship of the exchequer. What nobody commented upon was his potential value to the administration, as he emphasised on 24 November when he intervened successfully to negate an attempt by Barry Barry to make an issue of the administration's proposal to introduce a five-shilling tax on writs of *habeas corpus*.[63]

Compared with writs, the absentee tax was a major impost both symbolically and in fact, and Flood was eager to do what he could to advance it. Its progress seemed assured in August when George III and Lord North gave it the green light, but intense lobbying by Irish absentee landowners and their English allies compelled a reconsideration, and both the King and Prime Minster had come to the conclusion by November that it was better for Anglo-Irish relations that it did not proceed.[64] This was so deeply embarrassing for the Prime Minister, who had promised Harcourt privately he would support the proposal when it reached the British Privy Council, that he refused to comment publicly on the matter, lest it upset the administration's whole taxation programme. He wrote instead to the Lord Lieutenant on 20 November to express his 'hope' that the Irish parliament could be induced to 'give some relief to the distress of their country without insisting upon the absentee tax'.[65] This put Harcourt in a quandary. Though there was strong opposition to the proposal from several quarters in Ireland, his judgement was that it would diminish the administration's prospects of securing approval for its other taxes if it alienated potentially valuable supporters like Henry Flood by back-pedalling on this high profile issue. Anxious to avoid this without disobliging his Prime Minister, Harcourt took the only remaining option; he decided to observe 'a strict neutrality ... leaving it entirely to the determination of the gentlemen themselves as a great national point in which the country is most immediately concerned'.[66]

Since these exchanges took place away from the public's gaze, Flood was unaware of the mounting threat to his favourite measure when he pronounced in its favour in the House of Commons on 23 November.[67] The strength of his commit-

63 Waller to Macartney, 23, 25 Nov. in Bartlett, ed., *Macartney*, pp 182–3; *F.L.J.*, 24 Nov.; *H.J.*, 26 Nov. 1773. 64 R.J. Hoffman, *The marquis: a study of Lord Rockingham* (New York, 1973), pp 285–9; R[odd] ed.,*Letters to Flood*, pp 59–62; Taylor and Pringle, eds, *Chatham Corres.*, iv, 296–7; Ellis to Agar, 5, 27 Nov., 14 Dec., Ellis to Rockingham, 5 Nov. (Normanton Papers, P.R.O.N.I., T3719/C/7/5, 8, 9, 10); Fortescue, ed., *Corres of George III*, iii, 14–18, 30–37; Rochford to Harcourt, 22 Oct., North to Harcourt, 29 Oct. (N.L.I.,Harcourt Letterbook, Ms 755 ff 12-4). 65 North to Devonshire, 16 Oct. in R[odd], ed., *Letters to Flood*, pp 59–60; T.F. Moriarty, 'The Irish absentee tax controversy of 1773' in *Proceedings of the American Philosophical Society*, 118 (1974), p. 390; North to Harcourt, 20 Nov. (N.L.I., Harcourt Letterbook, Ms 755 ff 20–1); Harcourt to North, 9 Nov. 1773 (D.P.L., Harcourt Papers, Gilbert Ms 93 ff 37–44). 66 Harcourt to North, 22 Nov. (D.P.L., Harcourt Papers, Gilbert Ms 93 ff 50–51); Moriarty, 'Absentee tax', pp 394–5; *H.J.*, 25 Oct., 1, 8 Nov.; *F.L.J.*, 17 Nov. 1773. 67 Moriarty, 'Absentee tax', p. 393; *Gentleman's Magazine*, xliii (1773), p. 619.

ment was emphasized two days later, when the absentee tax proposal came before the Committee of Ways and Means. At issue on this occasion was whether there should be a tax and, if so, at what level it should be struck. Debate focused on the principal of the tax until Silver Oliver, the MP for County Limerick, proposed that it should be set at two shillings in the pound and levied on the net rental income of those who lived for more than six months of each year outside the kingdom. This was resisted by a combination of independent and government interests who condemned it as 'unjust, impolitick, unnecessary, untimely and unsafe', as a result of which Flood felt compelled to justify the tax as 'the constant wish and object' of Ireland since the time of Swift in a powerful 'forty-two minute speec h'. What was being proposed, he pronounced, was not a stalking horse for a general land tax, as some of its opponents contended, but an attempt to retain a modest percentage of the one million pounds in absentee remittances that was transferred out of the kingdom annually to provide for the administration and defence of the kingdom. Flood's speech was well-received, but it was ably countered by Walter Hussey who 'answered in [so] spirited a manner ... that it was thought many gentlemen gave up to his arguments their former opinions'. Of greater consequence was the admission by John Blaquiere that the tax was 'not a government question', since it freed supporters of the Castle to vote against it, and it was their wholesale defection that consigned it to defeat. An amendment to Silver Oliver's motion providing that the proposed absentee tax should be set at five rather than ten per cent was lost by 119 votes to 107, while Flood's despairing attempt to snatch victory from the jaws of defeat by insisting at 1.23 a.m. on the morning of 26 November that Oliver's original proposal was also put was lost by the slightly larger margin of 120 to 106.[68]

Flood was deeply disappointed by this outcome. Edmund Burke, who was implacably opposed to the tax, maintained that Flood only agitated the issue because Lord Chatham had directed him to, and because he hoped to benefit 'from a ... connexion with the old man of the mountain', but this was inaccurate as well as unworthy.[69] Flood's commitment to an absentee tax was genuine, as he made clear on 25 November when he confessed that 'this tax I confess is an object which has my whole heart; I would entreat you upon my knees to receive it, I would almost die to obtain it'. Puzzled by this, Burke opined that it was 'the measure' on which Flood had concluded his 'treaty' to support Dublin Castle, but he was mistaken here too. Flood and the Irish administration had not yet come even close to concluding an agreement, and his persistent advocacy of the absentee tax in late November did not

68 Moriarty, 'Absentee tax', p. 396; *H.J.*, 26 Nov.; Hunt, ed., *Irish parliament in 1775*, p. xxv; Harcourt to North, 26 Nov. (D.P.L., Harcourt Papers, Gilbert Ms 93 ff 55–8); P.D.G. Thomas, 'Two voting lists for the Irish House of Commons in 1773', *Parliamentary History*, vii (1988), pp 311–20; Flood, *Memoirs*, pp 89–92.   69 C.C. O'Brien, *The Great Melody: a thematic biography of Edmund Burke* (London, 1992), pp 70–1; Burke to O'Hara, 6 Jan. 1774 in Hoffman, *Burke*, pp 560–1; Craig, *The Volunteer Earl*, pp 159–60; Burke to Rockingham, 29 Sept. 1773 in *Burke Corres.*, ii, 466–7.

make it more likely since the Lord Lieutenant and the Chief Secretary were anxious then to put the matter behind them and to get on with the other business of the session.[70]

The instigator of the attempts on 26 and 27 November to persuade MPs to reconsider the absentee tax was John O'Neil, the member for Randalstown, though it was Flood who spoke most luminously in its favour on both occasions. He was clearly deeply upset by recent events, as he alleged incautiously on the twenty-sixth that those who favoured the absentee tax 'were friends to their country; ... [and] those who voted against it ... were its enemies tho' not intentionally'. However, neither this nor his assertion that it was 'inconsiderate ... to agree to tax *two* million of the useful and industrious natives of Ireland rather than five great men who were its bane' had much impact.[71] This ought to have convinced Flood to let the matter rest for the present, but O'Neil and he were reluctant to concede defeat. So, on the following day, when O'Neil proposed a 5 per cent tax on rental remittances sent out of the country to landowners who were absent for nine or more months annually, he was supported by Flood once again. It was of 'the greatest national benefit', Flood argued; but on realising that there was 'no prospect of [his] carrying this once darling measure' he prevailed on O'Neil to withdraw his motion.[72]

Flood was the dominant presence in the Commons' chamber during the absentee tax debates. His performance on 27 November, in particular, was so commanding even hostile Commons' watchers like Godfrey Lill showered him with praise. According to Lord Harcourt, his putdown of John Ponsonby for opposing the reconsideration of the absentee tax was so devastating 'that poor gentleman, I fear, will never recover'. His animadversions on the duke of Leinster were only slightly less 'crushing'.[73] Through all, he remained on good terms with John Blaquiere, though the Chief Secretary's 'neutrality' on the tax and his withdrawal from the debate of 27 November caused Flood to criticise him publicly. Despite this, Flood remained attached 'to the present administration'. The fact that Blaquiere and he frequently sat next to each other in the Commons indicates that this was not just rhetoric, though officeholders as powerful as the Prime Serjeant and the Speaker were deceived by such gestures into exaggerating the intimacy of their relationship. Flood was and remained outside the Castle's inner circle; he was, as Godfrey Lill described it so precisely, 'with government but not in its confidence'.[74]

---

70 Harcourt to Rochford, 27 Nov. in *C.H.O.P.*, iv, 107–8; Burke to O'Hara, 11 Dec., O'Hara to Burke, 18 Dec. 1773 in Hoffman, *Burke*, pp 554–6.   71 *H.J.*, 29 Nov.; *F.L.J.*, 1 Dec.; Harcourt to Rochford, 27 Nov. in *C.H.O.P.*, iv, 107–8; Moriarty, 'Absentee tax' pp 398–9; Lill to Macartney, 27 Nov. 1773 in Bartlett, ed., *Macartney*, pp 250–1.   72 *H.J.*, 1 Dec. 1773; Moriarty, 'Absentee tax', pp 399–400.   73 Harcourt to North, 27 Nov. in *Harcourt Papers*, ix, 116–17; Lill to Macartney, 27 Nov. in Bartlett, ed., *Macartney*, pp 250–1; *H.J.*, 1 Dec. 1773.   74 *H.J.*, 29 Nov.; Lill to Macartney, 27 Nov., 29 Dec., Hely-Hutchinson to Macartney, 3 Dec. 1773 in Bartlett, ed., *Macartney*, pp 250–2; Andrews to Pery, 2 Jan., 1 Feb. 1774 in H.M.C., *Emly*, p. 194.

Flood, characteristically, kept his feelings under a tight rein, but by early December he was growing increasingly impatient with the administration's failure to offer him an appropriate office. His reminder to Bishop Markham that this was 'the third administration I have supported without ever having received a favour from His Majesty' attests to his disquiet.[75] His irritation was heightened by the failure of the absentee tax to reach the statute book because it struck directly at his ambition in office to advance patriot policies. The implications of its loss for his relations with the Castle were not as consequential as some antipathetic contemporaries and recent critics have maintained, but it is no coincidence that Flood's dealings with the Castle in December 1773 were more tense than previously.[76]

The main focus of political attention at the beginning of December was the administration's proposal to increase the stamp duty on newspapers. This was a proposal to which Flood had already signalled his opposition, but he was not prepared to go so far as the newspaper industry and decry it as 'a threat to the liberty of the press'. At the same time, he did not want to erect barriers inimical to the existence of a flourishing press, and with this in mind he recommended that the proposal before the house should be amended to provide for an exemption for pamphlets and a reduction of the planned impost on advertisements. However, when this was put to a vote it was rebuffed by 107 votes to 45.[77]

The grounds on which Flood chose to oppose the stamp duty were narrow, but it did him no harm to be seen to 'support' the 'liberty of the press'. The administration, for its part, took no adverse notice of his independent stand on this and other matters (because their Commons' majority remained secure[78]) and they were rewarded when Flood did not join in the surge of protest against the amended tontine and stamp bill returned from London in late December. This was a situation tailor-made for confrontation, but Flood and the administration both contrived to avoid it. Harcourt consulted widely with his confidential friends and agreed not 'to force the bills' through, while Flood endorsed the administration's approach in the Commons on 27 December.[79]

Flood's readiness to cooperate on the amended tontine and stamp bill did not cause his disgruntlement with the failure of Dublin Castle to offer him an appropriate office to abate. So when the House of Commons adjourned in January 1774 he wrote to Bishop Markham alleging he was being 'deceiv[ed]', and imploring him to use his political contacts to establish if this was the case. 'I hope and confide that we

75 Hely-Hutchinson to Macartney, 3 Dec. in Bartlett, ed., *Macartney*, p. 251; Flood to Markham, 3 Dec. 1773 (Rosse Papers, C/2/14).   76 Moriarty, 'Absentee tax', pp 403–4; Burke to Flood, 11 Dec. in Hoffman, *Burke*, p. 554; Harcourt to North, 15 Dec. 1773 (D.P.L., Harcourt Papers, Gilbert Ms 93 ff 80–1).   77 *H.J.*, 26, 29 Nov., 3 Dec.; *F.L.J.*, 1, 4, 8, 11 Dec. 1773; Thomas, 'Two Irish voting lists', pp 323–6.   78 North to Harcourt, 9 Dec., Rochford to Harcourt, 10 Dec. (N.L.I., Harcourt Letterbook, Ms 755 ff 25–8); *H.J.*, 10, 22 Dec. 1773.   79 Waller to Macartney, 25 (2), 27 Dec., Lill to Macartney, 31 Dec. in Bartlett, ed., *Macartney*, pp 183, 184, 252; Harcourt to Rochford, 25, 27, 30, 31 Dec. 1773 in *C.H.O.P.*, iv, 119–23.

never shall have reason to repent what we have done', he avowed uneasily on 31 January. Uppermost in his mind was the fact that 'Mr Blaquiere has thrown himself in appearance into the hands of Mr [Hely-]Hutchinson' whose 'counsels', he observed testily, 'are not generally thought to be of the wisest or most salutary kind'. [80] Flood's suspicion that Hely-Hutchinson aspired to displace him in the affections of the administration was quite justified. According to Provost Andrews, 'there [wa]s nothing' Hely-Hutchinson 'would not do to prevent Flood's having the conduct of affairs', while Robert Waller went further and claimed that 'Hutchinson hates Flood mortally'. Clearly the animosity and rivalry that had characterised their relationship since the mid-1760s was sharper now than ever. Each professed to possess a low opinion of the other's abilities, and each was convinced that there was only room enough for one of them presenting government business in the Commons – a view endorsed by Philip Tisdall, who had little time for either. [81]

There was nothing Bishop Markham could do to ease these destructive antipathies, but he was as eager as ever to facilitate Flood's elevation to high office, because he approached Charles Jenkinson in an attempt to discover if, as Flood alleged, the government had changed its opinion about recruiting him. What he gleaned was comforting. Jenkinson offered the Bishop 'very full and explicit' assurances, which he communicated directly to Flood, that the government was committed to 'doing justice to the very honourable and effectual part that you [had] taken, and ascribed the success and honour which had attended Lord Harcourt's administration to the frank and disinterested support that you had given, and seemed to have no doubt that your services would be remembered as honourably as they ought'. Indeed, he confided, 'a letter had come [recently from Dublin] as pressing as possible, asking [for] a very high office' for him. This was welcome news and it reinforced Markham's sage counsel that Flood should 'avoid any violent declarations, and treat the professions of service at least with so much respect as to suppose it possible that they have not been treacherous'. Equally saliently, he advised Flood to 'be more particular in explaining to me your wishes and prospects'. His name had been cited, Markham pointed out, with Thomas Leland and John Hely-Hutchinson as a possible successor to Provost Andrews, but when Jenkinson raised the matter he was obliged to revert to 'general[ities]' because he did not know if Flood was interested in the position. [82]

This revealing admonition provides one reason why Flood was displaced by Hely-Hutchinson in the confidence of Dublin Castle in the winter of 1773–4. Compared with the Prime Serjeant, Flood was slow to identify what he wanted and diffident in advancing his own cause. He was also more inclined to perceive slight

---

80 Markham to Flood, 30 Jan., Flood to Markham, 31 Jan. 1774 (Rosse Papers, C/2/14, 16). 81 Flood to Markham, 31 Jan. (Rosse Papers, C/2/16); Andrews to Pery, 2 Jan. in H.M.C., *Emly*, p. 194; Waller to Macartney, 24 Feb. in Bartlett, ed., *Macartney*, pp 186, 254–5. 82 Markham to Flood, 30 Jan., 5 Feb.1774 (Rosse Papers, C/2/15, 17).

and, on taking umbrage, to retreat to Farmley to brood. The fact that in February he requested a private meeting with Lord Harcourt would suggest that, on this occasion at least, he took Markham's advice to press his case with greater urgency. [83] It was important that he did so if he anticipated the early gratification of his hopes, because he was to be allowed few opportunities to display his value to the Castle in the Commons in 1774.

Influenced by the comfortable majorities the administration had enjoyed in 1773, M.P.s returned slowly to Dublin after the recess with the result that the Commons' proceedings in January and early-February were ill-attended and uneventful. Flood kept a low profile during these weeks, though he 'and his friends attend[ed] and vote[d] regularly'. This played into Hely-Hutchinson's hands. The Prime Serjeant contrived to take advantage of Flood's reserve, Blaquiere's limited parliamentary knowledge and problems with respect to the revenue, tontine bills and the corn premium to advance his own cause at the expense of Tisdall and Flood. [84]

One of the matters which caused Flood some unease during these uneventful days, was legislation to enable Catholics to take land on extended lease. There were two measures. That proposed by Thomas Maunsell senior recommended that Catholics should be empowered to take leases for three lives, while that advanced by Hercules Langrishe sought to allow them to lease up to fifty acres in the country and forty perch in urban areas for any term of years on taking an oath of allegiance. Flood 'owned he disliked' Maunsell's bill when it was presented on 8 February because it diluted the security provided the Protestant interest by the Penal Laws; at the same time, he supported its advancement to the committee stage, where it was sidelined. He was more positive about Langrishe's legislation, for though he did not speak in its favour he voted with the minority when the bill was rejected by 123 votes to 69.[85]

Flood's reserved conduct during the debate on Langrishe's bill was further demonstrated during the days and weeks that followed when the Commons' agenda was dominated by the tontine and revenue bills. His coyness did not pass unnoticed, but because it was known that he would not work with John Hely-Hutchinson, who continued to have the Chief Secretary's ear, official criticism was m uted. The administration successfully negotiated the 'very trying questions and very great difficulties' it encountered during the debates on these bills, but they were convinced they would have been able to do so with less 'anxiety' if Flood had been on their

83 Blaquiere to Flood, 14 Feb.1774 in R[odd], ed., *Letters to Flood*, p. 63.   84 *H.J.*, 21, 24, 26 Jan., 14, 27 Feb.; *F.L.J.*, 26 Jan.; Montgomery to Townshend, 2 Feb. (B.L.,O.C., Townshend Papers, Box 11); Andrews to Pery, 23 Feb. in H.M.C.,*Emly*, pp 194–5; Waller to Macartney, 31 Jan., Lill to Macartney, 22 Jan. in Bartlett, ed., *Macartney*, pp 185, 253; Harcourt to North, 3 Feb. (D.P.L., Harcourt Papers, Gilbert Ms 93 f 95); Waite to Macartney, 20 Feb. 1774 (B.L., O.C., Waite-Macartney letters); Webb to Flood, [1775] in R[odd], ed., *Letters to Flood*, p. 88.   85 *F.L.J.*, 13 Feb.; *Life of Grattan*, i, 265-6; *H.J.*, 14 Feb.1774; Day, 'Irish Catholics', pp 97–101, 270. It should be noted that Day's account confuses the two bills.

side. As it was, Hely-Hutchinson's able advocacy served, as he knew it would, to win him special mention in the Lord Lieutenant's dispatches and favourable notice in England in February and March.[86] Flood's reticence, by contrast, caused some to conclude that his flirtation with the administration was over, until his refusal to aid Dublin mercantile interests resist the plans to build a new easterly bridge over the Liffey advanced by John Beresford indicated this was not so.[87] However, if he was to demonstrate to the administration that he was potentially more valuable to them in the House of Commons than Hely-Hutchinson, he had to upstage his rival before the end of the session, and he obtained an opportunity to do precisely that in March when the last major issue of the administration's financial programme – their proposal to cut expenditure on corn bounties – came up for deliberation.

The bounty paid on the land carriage of corn to Dublin was a very popular measure because it was credited with bringing about an increase in grain cultivation in the kingdom and an improvement in the food supply to the capital since its introduction in 1757. However, the nearly £50,000 it cost annually in the early 1770s was more than the exchequer could easily bear and the Castle was determined to reduce it as part of its programme to curb the budget deficit.[88] As the representative of a region which had profited more than most from the corn bounty, Flood was anxious it should be continued, but he was also conscious of the need to curtail the spiralling cost of the scheme. With this dual target in mind, he successfully opposed an attempt by Lucius O'Brien and George Ogle on 8 March to secure the Commons' approval for a bill extending the scheme by providing for a bounty on the coastwise carriage of corn and flour to Dublin, and was given leave to introduce his own proposals to transfer responsibility for paying the excess cost of the corn bounty from the exchequer to parliament. This necessitated two pieces of legislation – a bill amending the 1757 tillage act which authorised the bounties paid on grain carried overland to Dublin, and a resolution committing parliament to provide additional funds to meet the cost of the corn bounty if it exceeded £35,000 annually. He introduced both on Monday 14 March, and since they satisfied those who wanted to expand and those who wanted to curtail the corn bounty by relieving the administration from 'any additional expense', they were warmly greeted. Indeed, it is a measure of their appeal that he was instructed by the house 'to carry' the bill personally to the Lord Lieutenant to ensure its prompt transmission to London and that Harcourt was delighted to receive it.[89] MPs held such firm and contrary opinions on the corn

86 *H.J.*, 11, 18, 21 Feb., 2, 7, 14 Mar.; Rochford to Harcourt, 20 Feb., 6 Mar. in *C.H.O.P.*, iv, 185, 189–93; Waller to Macartney, 24 Feb. in Bartlett, ed., *Macartney*, p. 186; Townshend to Hely-Hutchinson, 25 Feb. in H.M.C., *Donoughmore*, pp 277–8; Malcomson, 'Speaker Pery', pp 56–7 note 65; Harcourt to [ ], 11 Mar. 1774 (N.L.I., Harcourt Papers, Ms 5161/4). 87 *H.J.*, 25 Feb., 7 Mar. 1774; Edward McParland, *James Gandon: vitrivius hibernicus* (London, 1985), pp 41–3. 88 Fanning, 'The king's purse and the absentee's pocket', pp 52–3; Moriarty 'Absentee tax', pp 375–7, 407; *H.J.*, 11 Oct. 1773. 89 *F.L.J.*, 12, 19 Mar.; *H.J.*, 14, 16 Mar. 1774.

bounty that Harcourt knew 'any attempt to repeal the law would have been wild and impracticable, and ... would not have been supported by ten members of the House', whereas Flood's imaginative proposal to curb the cost of the corn bounty to the exchequer worked, he pronounced rapturously, 'in a superlative ... manner'. The Lord Lieutenant's pleasure was all the more deeply felt because he had spent six frustrating weeks consulting 'with almost every gentleman in the House' on the issue. Indeed, not just Harcourt, but the whole Castle machine rang loud in Flood's praise. Even Robert Waller, who believed 'Flood mortally hates me', could not but applaud his strategy and admire the triumph he had scored over Hely-Hutchinson:

> Flood has out-Hutchinsoned Hutchinson. He let him work through the session to the latter end, when he starts up holding in one hand a bill for rendering the act for granting a bounty for exportation of corn effectual, and in the other a resolution promising that the Commons will make good any expense attending that law and also exonerate the hereditary revenue of all the exceedings of £35,000 on the corn bounties. This was battled by opposition but carried by a vast majority. I never saw a man so agitated as Hutchinson was at this lead [gained?] off him by Flood. You have no idea how much they are afraid of and hate each other. I think administration can never keep them both on any terms. [90]

It is not clear what, if anything, Flood expected would flow from this success, but if he anticipated that it heralded the early eclipse of Hely-Hutchinson he was mistaken. Blaquiere remained loyal to the Prime Serjeant in the Commons, and Flood was left to ponder his future. He had, Godfrey Lill observed cruelly, 'sold himself to the devil for nothing, and does not know how to re pent'. This was harsh, but Flood may have entertained similar thoughts when attempts by him in the late spring to remind ministers of his predicament, and to suggest that, if there was nothing else available, English preferment would be acceptable, failed to elicit a positive response. [91]

There certainly was no sympathy forthcoming for Flood from those who had been among his warmest supporters in the past. He was now regarded by in the popular press, which had once lionised him, as 'the most detestable of hypocrites [and] the vilest of apostates' for deserting the opposition. His critics were pleased that what they identified as his naked lunge for power had failed, and they had no hesitation in trumpeting this or in impugning his motives:

> A sordid lust of wealth that you did not want, a rank that could add nothing to the applause of your countrymen [has prompted you to forsake oppositio n]. And what are the wages of your prostitution? Nothing. Not even the place of the

90 Waller to Macartney, 19 Mar. 1774 in Bartlett, ed., *Macartney*, pp 187–8. 91 Lill to Macartney, 9 Apr. in Bartlett, ed., *Macartney*, pp 254–5; Markham to Flood, 13 Apr. 1774 (Rosse Papers, C/2/18).

pension which you expected would be your reward for resigning everything that can be dear to a man of honour. Your enemies beheld, with an inferior spirit of envy, the glory you had obtained, and wanted to deprive you of it. They accordingly represented in the most flattering colours the honours and rewards with which your perfidy should be crowned. Their attempt succeeded, and they now laugh at your folly in giving faith to their promises ... You are now despised as much as you were once beloved and respected. Your fall furnishes fresh occasion to the benevolent mind, to lament the depravity of human nature. It indeed was great. – Pity shall find and half weep over you; but know that contempt, anger and detestation shall be mingled with the tear of compassion. [92]

Flood feigned indifference to criticism, but vitriolic and aspersive comment such as this served to intensify the hurt caused him by the administration's continuing failure to offer him a suitable office and, eager to escape public notice, he took advantage of indisposition to give his excuses to the Speaker of the House of Commons towards the end of April 1774 and to attend rarely thereafter. He was thus not in the House to shepherd his corn export bill, which was returned unaltered from the British Privy Council, into law, but he was present on the final day of the session on 24 May when he gave his *imprimatur* to an address in which the King and Lord Lieutenant were thanked for facilitating the return of the corn bill. It was, he observed archly, a signal personal tribute that the Commons deemed it appropriate to present an address to the King thanking him for the return of the corn bill since they had done the same six years earlier when the Octennial Act, which he had also advanced, was returned. [93]

Encouraged by this, officials believed that all that was necessary now for Flood to cement his relationship with the Castle was a suitable office. The problem for Harcourt, as Thomas Waite observed in May, was that he still did not have an appropriate position at his disposal. However, he was so confident it was only a matter of time, that he authorised Blaquiere to assure Flood in the early summer 'that any object of consideration which falls should be offered him'. [94]

92 *H.J.*, 12 Jan., 25 Mar. 25, 11 Apr., 13 June; *F.L.J.*, 15 Jan. 1774.   93 Pery to Flood, 26 Apr., Langrishe to Flood, 26 Apr. (Rosse Papers, C/1/6,7); Rochford to Harcourt, 20 Apr., Harcourt to Rochford, 25 May 1774 in *C.H.O.P.*, iv. 203, 216; *H.J.*, 29 Apr., 25 May; *F.L.J.*, 28 May; John Almon, *Narrative of proceedings in the parliament of Ireland* (London, 1776), p. 136.   94 *F.L.J.*, 19 Feb.; Waite to Macartney, 21 May (B.L.,O.C., Waite-Macartney Letters); Flood to Markham, 4, 25 June 1774 (Rosse Papers, C/2/19, 22).

SECURING A VICE-TREASURERSHIP

In fact, the 1773–4 session was not long concluded when the elderly Provost, Francis Andrews, was 'taken suddenly on his road to London so ill that there are no hopes of recovery'. Eager to make the most of the opportunity, the Lord Lieutenant calculated that he could use this plum position and the shuffle of a number of existing officeholders to satisfy Hely-Hutchinson and Serjeant Dennis (who was 'the principal friend and first object of Lord Shannon') as well as Flood. And he was so anxious that nothing should discommode his plan that he 'dispatch'd a messenger purposely with it' to Lord North in London on receipt of news of Andrews' demise.[95]

Harcourt was acutely conscious that the most difficult part of the complex arrangement he now sought to accomplish was 'to make a proper provision for Mr Flood'. If he honoured his promise, the Lord Lieutenant knew that he should offer Flood the provostship, but he was reluctant to do this because it was, he explained, inappropriate that someone whose chief duty would be to present government business in the Commons should occupy 'a station of independence' such as the provostship that would 'give ... him the opportunity of becoming really extremely troublesome and formidable to this and all future administrations'. The problem was that he did not rule Hely-Hutchinson out on the same grounds. The Prime Serjeant had let it be known that it was his wish 'to be relieved from his great weight of business at the bar'. But, because his legal practice brought 'him between £4,000 and £5,000 yearly', he could only do so if he secured a lucrative office, and since he hankered, Harcourt reported, after 'an opportunity of cultivating his taste for science and literature which is a distinguished part of his character', the Lord Lieutenant concluded that he, and not Flood, was an appropriate person to succeed Andrews. This was unexpected, but the fact that Hely-Hutchinson got the nomination over Flood was testament to the good use he had made of his access to the Lord Lieutenant in the winter of 1773–4. He had pressed his case so skilfully, indeed, that Harcourt was deceived into concluding that Hutchinson's willingness to accept the provostship attested to his eagerness 'to do everything in his power to remove' the obstacles in the way of providing for Flood.[96]

Hely-Hutchinson was formally offered the provostship and a lucrative revenue position by John Blaquiere in June. In return, he was invited to vacate the prime serjeancy and the alnage office, but since he expressed his 'greatest readiness to fall in with [this] arrangement', the Lord Lieutenant concluded that the way was now clear for him to appease Lord Shannon and, finally, to offer Flood the major office he had long been promised:

95 Harcourt to Rochford, 16 June 1774 (D.P.L., Harcourt Papers, Gilbert Ms 93 f 136).   96 Harcourt to North, 8 July, Harcourt to Rochford, 19 July 1774 in *Harcourt Papers*, x, 220–6.

Your Lordship will observe that by these arrangements the great and ancient office of Alnager, which is now granted for a period of years, will be brought back to the crown; and that government will obtain the assistance of a gentleman of powerful abilities by the acquisition of Mr Flood. Lord Shannon will be gratified in his first and highest wishes, and the place of Provost will be worthily and ably filled by a gentleman whose talents and experience will be of great use to government in every situation. The attainment of all these points at the charge of £1,000 a year will, I flatter myself, be thought very good economy. [97]

Lord North was happy to approve this ambitious and complex scheme. He conceded that 'Flood has good pretensions to as considerable an office as a vice-treasurer in Ireland or indeed a better', but he rejected this suggestion on the grounds that it would set a bad precedent if an office that has 'been so long and so uniformly bestowed on members of the British parliament' went elsewhere, and he concurred with the Lord Lieutenant that the provostship was simply inappropriate because of Flood's voting record:

That office [provostship] is much better than the other [vice-treasurership, and] I do by no means think it above Mr Flood's merit, but I submit to your excellency whether Mr Flood, whose early principles, prejudices and practices have led him to oppose British government can be with safety and propriety be trusted with such a place for life, which besides rendering him totally independent gives him in a manner the disposal of a borough, and the means of forming the principles of the young nobility and gentry of Ireland. Perhaps this office may enable your excellency to make arrangements which may satisfy Mr Flood. But we cannot be too careful of the hands into which the Provostship is put. It seems very dangerous to put it into the hands of any man who has long followed popular courses and as may be disposed to continue in them either from inclination or to establish a reputation of consistency. [98]

These were important considerations for ministers on both sides of the Irish Sea; the problem was that they assumed that Flood would be happy to accept Hely-Hutchinson's leavings, which anyone familiar with the man would have known was not the case. So when, on 20 June, a messenger from the Lord Lieutenant presented him with a note offering him 'the alnager's place in the room of the Prime Serjeant, whom he [Harcourt] recommends to be Provost', he 'refused it in civil terms to his messenger, but with no small contempt of mind'. [99] He felt 'grossly abused' that he

97 Harcourt to Rochford, 19 July 1774 in *Harcourt Papers*, x, 220–6; Lees' review of Harcourt administration, pp 259–60. 98 North to Harcourt, 23 June 1774 (N.L.I., Harcourt Letterbook, Ms 775 f 37). 99 Flood to Markham, 20 June [1774] (Rosse papers, C/2/20); Hunt, *The Irish parliament in 1775*, pp 20–1; Lees' review of the Harcourt administration, p. 261.

had been made such an 'inferior' offer, though the alnager's salary had been more than doubled by the addition of £1,000 (bringing it to £1,800), when he had been given to expect by John Blaquiere that he would be offered what he described as 'the first great employment which should become vacant'. He explained to Bishop Markham:

> The last time your friend [Flood] was in town Mr Blaquiere without solicitation and of his own accord did say to your friend that ... [he would be offered 'the first great employment which should become vacant']. Without therefore entering into the merits of the Provostship one way or the other, what could be more unexpected by your friend than to have not that which had fallen, but a thing inferior, offered to him? He can consider this in no other light than that of offence and violation ... Many things have happened contrary to just expectation before, all against him ... Moderation is trespassed upon, generosity ill-used and confidence broken. This is unwise.

In Flood's mind, he was the victim of 'a breach ... of good faith' and he accused Blaquiere of lacking both 'firmness and candour'.[100]

As the injured tone of these comments emphasizes, Flood was grievously offended by the suggestion that he should be happy with the alnagership, and he felt the hurt all the more deeply because it collided with the idealized image he held of the relationship of Crown and subject:

> Nothing can be more erroneous in my poor sense of things than to make the crown and the subject treat with each other like two hostile powers where there is no duty or attachment taking place, but each is to take every advantage it can over the other. It can never be really wise in governors to destroy all sense of honourable confidence in those they employ. It is the thing of all others they ought to encourage. At least I am sure no man of sense and competency will have any connection with such governors beyond that of being a loyal subject. No man ever taught perfidy by word or example who did not suffer by it. I have never said anything to you that events did not verify, and will venture to assert that justice and honour will be found the best foundations for ease and dignity. At least as far as I can this shall be so.[101]

Flood's predisposition to draw sweeping moral and political conclusions from his own experiences tested the patience of Blaquiere and Harcourt, whose priority was to construct a strong Castle phalanx in the House of Commons. They certainly

---

100 Flood to Markham, 21, 25 June (Rosse Papers, C/2/21, 22); Lill to Macartney, 21 Oct. 1774 in Bartlett, ed., *Macartney*, p. 255; Lees' review of Harcourt administration, p. 259; Hunt, ed., *Irish parliament in 1775*, p. xxvii.   101 Flood to Markham, 21, 25 June [1774] (Rosse Papers, C/2/21, 22).

found Flood's scruples more tiresome than John Hely-Hutchinson's sinuous efforts to grasp preferment, and the fact that Flood refused to say whether or not he would have accepted the provostship if it had been offered to him merely intensified their irritation with his behaviour. [102] Things would have been worse had the press got hold of the full story. As it was, there was intense speculation towards the end of June and beginning of July that 'a once great patriot, who deserted his country this last session ... and openly avowed the maxims of a courtier' would be made provost. News in mid-July of Hely-Hutchinson's appointment to an 'independent employment for life' took the spotlight off Flood, but the relief was only temporary. Flood, it was claimed, would 'yet [be] provided for' and his name was confidently linked with both the chancellorship of the exchequer and the prerogative court. [103]

Dublin Castle, inevitably, was less sure that a suitable position could be found for Flood. Harcourt was annoyed that his plan to 'gratify' him with the alnagership had come unstuck, but he was determined it should not create a permanent rift. Flood, for his part, did not attribute any culpability to the Lord Lieutenant, but his anger was slow to dilute, for when the two men met on 7 July Harcourt was left in no doubt as to the strength of his feelings:

> He complained most bitterly of the treatment he had received from government, laying the greatest stress on the promise Mr Blaquiere had made him that he should have the first great office that became vacant, [and] ... took occasion to set forth his important services which he thought very justly entitled him to the preferment which had been given to Mr [Hely-]Hutchinson ... He laid great stress on the difficulties and obstructions which he could have thrown in our way had he been disposed to be adverse and to put himself at the head of the opposition; which, insignificant as it was latterly, would have been very formidable in the earlier part of the session under the guidance and direction of an experienced leader.

Harcourt sought to deflect Flood's anger by pointing out that Hely-Hutchinson had made a major sacrifice by resigning two offices, but Flood was unrelenting:

> He observed that he had made as great, if not a greater, sacrifice, meaning his popularity and reputation which he had risked in support of government. He said that he was now treated with a degree of contempt that determined him never more to have any concerns with the Castle that paid so little regard to

102 Lees' review of Harcourt administration, p. 259; Harcourt to North, 8 July 1774 in *Harcourt Papers*, ix, 220–6. 103 *F.L.J.*, 29 June, 13 July; *H.J.*, 6, 11, 15 July; Stratford to Stratford, 7 July (N.L.I., Stratford Papers, Ms 18788/6); *Two translations from the Greek addressed to H[enr]y F[loo]d Esq* (Dublin, 1774), p. iii; Flood, *Memoirs*, pp 92–3; Charlemont to Beauclerk, [July], Charlemont to Lord Bruce, 17 July 1774 in H.M.C., *Charlemont*, i, 320, 324–5.

engagements. He conceived he had been treated extremely ill by Lord Frederick Campbell, in Lord Townshend's time, but much worse by Mr Blaquiere in my administration.

He added that it would be a lesson for everybody to be very cautious for the future in their dealings with ministers. He said he could make it appear that he had saved the Crown more than five times the value of the favor he asked; that I could not but be very sensible of the very different behaviour that might have been expected from many gentlemen if things had taken a different turn in parliament.[104]

Harcourt cannot have enjoyed this experience, but he was also conscious that Flood's position was not as strong as his anger. So was Flood, because he conceded that he was

now reduced to a most humiliating and perplexed state, either to become a humble suppliant for favour, or to give up all hopes of it, and to submit tamely to every species of ridicule and contempt.

This was a condition Flood's pride demanded he escape at all costs, and anxious to grasp the opportunity it provided, Harcourt assured him that matters would yet be resolved to everyone's satisfaction because 'the faith of government was pledged to make an ample provision for him'. He knew that any such 'provision' would have to appeal strongly to Flood if it was to assuage the disappointment he experienced when he was passed over for the provostship, but he was convinced the vice-treasurership would meet this criterion since Flood had mentioned it in conversation, and since it was infinitely preferable to 'some employment for a term of years, or for life'.[105]

Harcourt had not encouraged Flood's hopes when the vice-treasurership was first mentioned because of the opposition of the King and Prime Minister and the problem of persuading one of the current incumbents – Lord Clare, Welbore Ellis and Charles Jenkinson – to vacate the position. However, following his rejection of the alnagership, the urgency of providing adequately for Flood caused him to reconsider, and he made an exceptionally strong appeal to Lord North on 8 July to support its implementation:

There are times when everything is to be risked rather than involve government in certain difficulties. This must be considered as one of those critical moments on which a great deal hereafter may depend. How far it may concern me is a matter of very little importance, in comparison of the effect it may hereafter

104 Harcourt to North, 8 July 1774 in *Harcourt papers*, ix, 220–6. 105 Ibid.

have on the affairs of the kingdom. It is submitted to your Lordship whether it may not be advisable to secure Mr Flood almost at any expense, rather than to risk an opposition, which, conducted by a man of his abilities, may render the success of administration more precarious the next session, a state of things which might endanger, perhaps defeat, some of the capital arrangements that have lately taken place, and which now stand in need of all the support that government can give them to make them complete and desirable ... Should it however, unfortunately appear that I am unable to make good such engagements as the circumstances of this government may have required, I fear it may be out of my power to do his Majesty any further service in this Kingdom.

This was clear and unambiguous. The problem was that many obstacles remained to be negotiated. These included the King who, when he was alerted to Harcourt's request by Lord North in August, conceded that Flood merited an employment worth £2,000 per annum, but opposed 'appointing him a vice-treasurer ... as it would be giving an additional employment to Ireland at the expense of providing for a man of talents in the English House of Commons'. [106] This was not what Lord Harcourt wanted to hear because he knew that Flood *wanted* to return the vice-treasurership (just as he had wanted to return the chancellorship of the exchequer) to Ireland. Indeed, it was an article of his political *credo* that it was inimical to Irish interests that Irish offices should become reserved sinecures for English politicians whose interest in them rested on what one commentator euphemistically termed their 'pence'. In the case of the vice-treasurership, which had been held by Englishmen since the reign of George I, these were considerable. [107] Until the 1750s, the three vice-treasurers were entitled to an equal share of the 2.5 per cent levied on the hereditary revenue paid into the Irish exchequer. Administrative changes introduced in the late 1750s reduced the return to the region of £2,300 per annum, but plans were afoot to restore it to its former level. [108]

106 Ibid.; Harcourt to North, 20 July in *Harcourt Papers*, ix, 232; George III to North, 24 Aug. 1774 in Fortescue, ed., *Corres of George III*, iii, 124-5. 107 Barrington to Townshend, 8 July 1723 (P.R.O., S.P. Domestic, 35/44/29); H.M.C.,*Egmont diary*, ii, 331; Devonshire to Lords justice, 17 July 1742 (N.A., Calendar of departmental correspondence 1741–59 f 29); Walpole to Mann, 15 Apr. 1746, 3 July 1757 in Lewis et al., eds, *Walpole Corres.*, xix, 241, xxi, 109–10; Chatham to Bowe, 20 Sept. 1766 in Taylor and Pringle, eds, *Chatham Corres.*, iii, 72; *F.L.J.*, 13, 16, 20 July 1768; Wilmot to Waite, 19, 21 Apr. 1763, 18 Jul. 1768 (N.A., Index of departmental letters and papers 1760–89, ff 304, 324); Sackville to Irwin, 23 Dec. 1765 in H.M.C., *Stopford-Sackville*, i, 21; Grafton to Townshend and replies(10), 2, 3 Nov. 1768 (B.L.,O.C., Grafton files); Memo on vice-treasurership, [1770] (P.R.O., Chatham Papers, 30/8/84 ff 93–6); *Parl. Reg.(Irl).*, v, 143-6; Morres to Rutland, 11 Dec. 1785 in H.M.C., *Rutland*, ii, 207. 108 Lindsay to Huntingdon, 10 Oct. 1755 in H.M.C.,*Hastings*, iii, 105; Caldwell's *Debates*, ii, 464–5; Rigby to Fitzgerald, 28 Jan. 1768 in Hickson, *Old Kerry records*, 2nd series, p. 284; N.L.I., Joly Ms 29 f 73; Lees' review, [1776] (D.P.L., Harcourt Papers, Gilbert Ms 94 ff 135–6); North to Harcourt, 19 Feb., 23 June (N.L.I., Harcourt Letterbook, Ms 755 ff 32, 37–8); Harcourt to North, 15 July 1774 in *Harcourt Papers*, ix, 229.

Dissatisfaction with the remuneration accruing to the existing vice-treasurers was a complication Harcourt could have done without as he sought to overcome the opposition of the King and Prime Minister to Flood's appointment. Blaquiere and he even contemplated reviving the office of President of Munster to provide for one of the incumbents, but this was rejected on the grounds that 'Mr Flood would not take the office of vice-treasurer if vacated by the revival of another great office in Ireland'. With this option denied them, the Irish administration directed its energies to persuading London to sanction a pension with which to compensate the vice-treasurer who surrendered his position to pave the way for Flood. Harcourt also sought to soothe his superiors' anxiety by explaining that there was 'no danger of lessening the patronage of England by lending an office for a short time and for a very particular purpose to support H.M.s government in Ireland'. What was at stake was of such consequence to the Crown as well as to the Irish administration, it was worth paying any price to secure Flood's services:

> Allow me ... to say that the question with regard to Mr Flood seems not a very difficult one merely upon the point of publick oeconomy, putting the considerations of the confidence in government, justice for past services, and good faith totally out of the case. Is it worth while to hazard the stamp and other duties, the writ of assistants, and the many other essential points so lately effected, and out an able and most active man at the head of a numerous opposition the last session of an octennial parliament, to save one thousand pounds a year for one life, and that perhaps not a very good one, besides the other mischiefs which a desperate and disappointed man may devise ...
>
> Indeed my Lord, it is so very material to the future ease and tranquillity of this country and to the well being of His Majesty's government, that I may presume to say that the acquisition of Mr Flood circumstanced as things are cannot be purchased at too dear a rate, and when it is considered that the expence will not really exceed what was last year deem'd not an unreasonable sum, I should hope that the mode of doing it by the means of a pension will not be objected to if all other methods of doing it should be deem'd inexpedient. [109]

As this suggests, Harcourt was determined that Flood would be a vice-treasurer by the beginning of September 1774. He even set matters in train to admit Flood to the Irish Privy Council and sent John Blaquiere to London to talk to ministers and to help with any other arrangements that needed to be made. Shortly afterwards, Flood and his wife also left for England. [110] This gave rise to reports in Ireland that Flood would not secure a vice-treasurership, but these were groundless, as the Castle's

109 Harcourt to North, 3 Sept. 1774 (D.P.L., Harcourt Papers, Gilbert Ms 93 ff 153–6).   **110** Lill to Macartney, 21 Oct. in Bartlett, ed., *Macartney*, p. 255; *F.L.J.*, 12 Nov.; Rochford to Harcourt, 18 Nov. 1774 (P.R.O., S.P.67/14 ff 150–51)..

persistence finally overcame royal resistance towards the end of November. With a breakthrough achieved, the administration believed the way was finally clear for Flood's appointment. The problem was that they had not kept Flood apprized of developments, and when he was informed by John Blaquiere on 15 December that his 'appointment should instantly take place', his response was unexpectedly cool. What troubled him was the suggestion that his appointment as a vice-treasurer would necessitate movements in the Irish patronage chain that would add to the pension list, and thereby increase the cost to the Irish exchequer of providing for officeholders.[111] Flood was entirely within his rights to do this, since he was not 'pledged to accept that office'. At the same time, he did not close the door completely. He 'declined the office', he informed Lord Harcourt some time later, 'as it came originally to me with the burden upon it; but said that, if it should come eased as to that incumbrance, I should not object to it.[112]

Flood's unwillingness to accept the vice-treasurership, if it added in anyway to the burden of patronage already borne by the Irish exchequer, was predictable given his stand on this matter to date, but for reasons that elude discovery he seems not to have conveyed this response promptly to either the Lord Lieutenant or Chief Secretary. As a result, matters soon became confused. Flood maintained later that he informed Lord Harcourt of his decision by letter from England in December. However, it either went astray or he did not express himself with sufficient clarity, because when reports appeared in a London newspaper early in 1775 that Charles James Fox had agreed to exchange the Office of Clerk of the Pells for a £1,700 pension on the Irish establishment to facilitate Flood's appointment as vice-treasurer, he felt obligated to ask Bishop Markham to communicate, via Charles Jenkinson, to ministers that he 'would not accept that office' as it was offered. Markham did as requested, following which Jenkinson wrote to Flood to inform him that his concern for the Irish pension list was exaggerated because Ireland would suffer little financial loss by his appointment. Indeed, he claimed, speciously, that since there was now no need for the £1,000 which had been earmarked to provide an additional salary for the alnagership, this and the absentee tax meant 'the nett burden of the whole pension' to be given to Charles James Fox would be a modest £350 which was a small price to pay for 'the restoration to the kingdom [of Ireland] of a great office with a considerable salary'. Flood considered this carefully, but it did not induce him to change his mind. He explained to Harcourt:

I confessed that this state altered the matter: it brought it so near in effect to the idea I had originally stated as one upon which I was capable of accepting the

111 Robinson to O'Hara, 6 Dec. (N.L.I., O'Hara Papers, Ms 20392); Scott to Agar, 10 Dec. (Normanton Papers, P.R.O.N.I., T3719/C/8/7); *H.J.*, 16 Dec.; Blaquiere to Flood, 15 Dec. 1774 in R[odd], ed., *Letters to Flood*, p. 64; Burgh to Foster, 5 Jan. 1775 (P.R.O.N.I., Foster Papers, D562/719); *F.L.J.*, 16 Nov.; *H.J.*, 18 Nov. 1774.   112 Flood to Harcourt [Feb./Mar.] 1775 in R[odd], ed., *Letters to Flood*, p. 69.

Office, that I thought it but candour to say, that upon that ground I could concur on the subject, and possibly disembarrass your Excellency. Your Lordship, seeming to doubt that Lord North might have been disposed of the Office in the interim, asked me whether I desired you should write to stop him from doing so; I said not, my motive being to disembarrass your Lordship and to serve the public, whereas that would have the appearance of asking the Office for my personal emolument.[113]

Flood's rejection of the vice-treasurership because it did not meet his demanding terms was regarded as 'extremely vexatious' by politicians and officials on both sides of the Irish Sea.[114] The fact that his decision was so long in coming, that he chose to spend the winter of 1774–5 in England rather than in Ireland and to stay in Bath, rather than London where he could be contacted more readily, contributed to the feeling of irritation. It is not at all clear what Flood was at; he may, unconsciously, have been imitating Lord Chatham who had done likewise in 1766; whatever his precise thinking, his errant behaviour added considerably to the administration's difficulties.

In the absence of a definitive response from Flood, but convinced that only the details of his admission to office remained to be settled, John Blaquiere sought out Lord North in late January 1775 for some 'hurried conversation' in order to 'urge ... upon him, with all my might, the absolute necessity there was to bring Mr Flood's business to a conclusion'. North concurred, but he was 'so *accablé* ... with American affairs ... he had less time than ever to think of anything else'. Blaquiere's plan was that Viscount Clare, who had expressed himself ready 'to resign' his vice-treasurership in the mid-1760s, should exchange his position for the chief chamberlain's office (salary £2,600) for life and he requested North to impress upon him the importance of his agreeing to the exchange.[115] Unfortunately for Blaquiere, Clare now perceived that any exchange involving his office would 'make so much clamour he could not bring himself to encounter it ... at his age'. Welbore Ellis, too, was uncooperative (perhaps because of his Agar connection) which left only Charles Jenkinson, whom Lord North sought to exclude on the grounds that since he was already possessed of 'the reversion of a very great office ... it was not in the King's interest to reinforce his independence with further preferment of this kind'. Blaquiere countered that he did not think, from Jenkinson's 'principle, education and practice', there could be any worries on this score, but North was reluctant to change his mind. Instead, he 'threw out the idea of giving Mr Flood th[e] ... chamberlain's

113 Ibid.   114 Hamilton to Pery, 13 Jan. [1775] (Additional Pery Papers, P.R.O.N.I., T 3052/41); Lees' Review of Harcourt Administration, p. 261.   115 For Nugent see Namier and Brooke, eds, *The House of Commons*, iii, 218–22; Wilmot to Waite, 19 Apr. 1763 (N.A., Index of departmental letters and papers 1760–89 f 304); Hamilton to O'Hara, [1766] (N.L.I., O'Hara Papers, Ms 15368/1); Charlemont to Flood, 13 Apr. 1775 in R[odd], ed., *Letters to Flood*, p. 71.

office for life', which was simply impracticable. Desperate for some breakthrough, Blaquiere made a further approach to William Gerard Hamilton, but this foundered once more on the 'inadmissible conditions' he continued 'to demand ... for quitting' the exchequer.[116]

Having failed to secure a vacant vice-treasurership by this means, Blaquiere adopted another tack. He approached the financially embarrassed Clerk of the Pells, Charles James Fox, with the suggestion that he should exchange his office for a pension to enable the pells to be offered to Welbore Ellis.[117] Both Fox and George III were agreeable, and the Chief Secretary was soon confident that when matters were settled with Fox's trustees and creditors, Flood would find no grounds for not accepting the vice-treasurership since 'it will come to him unencumbered with the odious consideration of having been the means of inducing any permanent expense upon the [Irish] establishment'. However, he was sufficiently anxious to keep Bishop Markham at hand to iron out any last minute difficulties that might be raised by Flood. As this indicates, Flood and the Chief Secretary were not in direct contact at this delicate moment, and Flood clearly wanted to keep it that way for when he visited London from Bath early in 1775, he declined to meet with Blaquiere.[118]

If this did not cause enough problems, matters were further complicated by the fact that what was defined in Bath in 1775 as Flood's 'outrageous' conduct also isolated him from his two most loyal friends – Bishop Markham and Lord Charlemont. The precise cause of the rift with Markham is not clear, but feelings ran high because in March/April 1775 Flood accused the Bishop of not being 'warm enough in [his] interests' and requested the return of his letters. Given the repeated efforts he had made on Flood's behalf, Markham was understandably irked by this, but he complied on the grounds that, as a 'friend', it was his 'duty to bear' Flood's 'ill-humour'. He also calculated that this was the best way to ensure that the breach was 'transient'. However, Flood was less inclined than Markham to put the difference behind him, and relations between the two men remained cool until the end of the year.[119]

If Flood's breach with Markham cannot easily be explained, it was inevitable that his friendship with his oldest political ally, the earl of Charlemont, should become strained as the prospect of his finally accepting government office drew closer. Following some 'conversation' they had 'immediately before' Flood left for England in the autumn of 1774, in which he gave the anxious peer to believe that he had 'seen and felt [his] mistake with regard to our present ministry' and that his 'con-

---

116 Ellis to Agar, 31 Oct. 1773 (Normanton Papers, P.R.O.N.I., T3719/C/7/4); Blaquiere to Harcourt, 25 Jan., 2 Feb. 1775 in *Harcourt Papers*, ix, 296–300.   117 Markham to George III and reply, 27 Mar. in Fortescue, ed., *Corres. of George III*, iii, 189–90; Blaquiere to Harcourt, 14 Apr. in *Harcourt Papers*, ix, 322–3; Markham to Flood, 6 Apr. 1775 (Rosse Papers, C/2/23).   118 Blaquiere to Harcourt, 25 Jan., 2 Feb., 14 Apr. 1775 in *Harcourt Papers*, ix, 297–300, 322–3.   119 Markham to Flood, 6 Apr., 30 Oct. 1775 (Rosse Papers, C/2/23, 24).

duct for the future would be such as I [Charlemont] wished it', Flood did not keep
his titled friend informed of either his movements or his dealings with the administration. Perturbed by this, and by reports of Flood's imminent defection, Charlemont
wrote him on 9 January 1775 to inquire where and how he was and, more pointedly,
to establish 'whether I am now writing to a lessened man or to a great legislator'. [120]
It was an affectionate letter otherwise, and Flood was warm in his affirmations of
his 'ardent and unalterable attachment' in his tardy reply. He was palpably less forthcoming on his reasons for going to Bath and on his dealings with government, though
this is what Charlemont most wanted to hear. Indeed, Charlemont can only have
been puzzled by the elliptical references Flood made to his encounters with John
Blaquiere in which, he maintained, they did 'not converse upon any kind of business'.[121] Charlemont believed he deserved better because, in his reply of 18 March,
he pleaded with Flood 'to account for [his] long and unprecedent[ed] silence'.
Charlemont knew that Flood was negotiating to take office, and he had no hesitation
in letting him know that he believed it was contrary to his personal and political
interests because, contrary to what Flood had concluded, government had not
changed:

> [My] visionary hopes that there might be a possibility of seeing such an admin-
> istration in this country as might induce me to alter my mode of conduct are
> now absolutely at an end; and I firmly believe that, however ineffectually, I shall
> remain an opponent even to my dying day. [122]

Flood's response to this friendly admonishment has not survived, but it was,
Charlemont purred happily in turn, 'just and friendly', 'the letter of a true friend ...
disburthening his heart, and pouring forth his complaints into the bosom of his
friend'. Charlemont was especially pleased by Flood's assurance that he would ' *leave
nothing uncommunicated that did not belong* to others, and which had not come ...
under confidence and secrecy', because this would allow him to contradict the 'vexatious slanders' and 'disgustful' reports of Flood's defection that were on everyone's
lips in Ireland. It was and remained Charlemont's fondest wish that Flood would
avoid 'the impropriety of ... taking office'. And deceived by their exchanges into
believing that Flood had decided to remain an independent patriot, Charlemont
offered him a full, frank and friendly assessment of the reality of Irish politics which,
he maintained, invalidated Flood's conviction that he would be able to use official
position to advance patriot policies:

---

120 Charlemont to Flood, 9 Jan.1775 in R[odd], ed., *Letters to Flood*, p. 65.   121 Flood to [Charlemont],
[pre 18 Mar.] 1775 in H.M.C., *Charlemont*, ii, 390–1.   122 Charlemont to Flood, 18 Mar. in R[odd],
ed., *Letters to Flood*, pp 66–7; see also Charlemont to Flood, 13 Apr. 1775, p. 76.

In the first place, I must suppose, that in taking office, as in every other circumstances of your public life, your first and principal aim and object would be to do your country service; and this being taken for granted, as by me at least it ever must be, I declare it as my firm and fixed opinion, that, whatever may be the case in England, it is utterly impossible that office in Ireland can confer the power of doing good; no office with us being in any degree ministerial. This has long been my opinion, though never so fixed and rooted in my mind as it has been since I have seen how little you, my friend, were able to do when in a situation far more powerful than actual office. A man in office may do mischief – witness H[utchinso]n; but that he can do no good we have a recent example in a person undoubtedly well inclined [Pery], and whose station, if in this country any could be ministerial, ought certainly to be considered as such ... It may be said that, though political power be not absolutely conferred by office, yet, as a confidential approach to the minister is naturally obtained by it, there will be an opportunity for the salutary operation of good advice; and noxious measures may by this means be so tempered as to be rendered less hurtful, ... but I am sorry to say the facts and experience uniformly declare against it. No good man will ever be the favoured agent of an Irish viceroy. His giving wholesome and patriotic counsel will be alone sufficient to exclude him from favour ...; in the Irish cabinet a H[utchinso]n will ever take the place of a Flood. I have hitherto supposed that the patriot, even under the baleful shade of court influence, will yet remain a patriot, and that the wholesome herb, though transplanted into a poisonous soil, will still retain, unimpaired, its salutary qualities. But are we sure of this? A man may no doubt accept of office with the best and purest intentions; and that this would be your case I am more than confident. But what preservative can secure us against political contagion? What strength and soundness of constitution could justify a man for venturing into a climate poisoned by the plague? Let us, for a moment, suppose a Sidney, a Hampden, a Flood in office. Their intentions will no doubt still continue unaltered; but will their judgement remain unwarped? Unknown to themselves, their sentiments, their opinions will change; they will view objects through a different medium, and instead of looking at all court measures with suspicion, as every patriot ought to do, they will see them in their most advantageous light; instead of searching for latent mischief; they will labour to discover some barely possible good; and should the evil be too conspicuous to be concealed even from their clouded sight, still they will endeavour to palliate it, and will frame to themselves excuses which their unbiased judgement would spurn at ... Narcotics applied to the conscience will have the natural effect of all opiates; they will stupefy while they lull, and by degrees all feeling will be lost. An honest man may say to himself, I will accept of office, but I will retain it no longer than is consistent with my duty to my country; and by a timely resignation I shall gain more credit than I should do if I remain unplaced, which might be attributed to inability of procuring office. This, too, is specious; but, alas! sad experience has taught us, that, of all duties, that of timely resignation is the most difficult ...

This was, as time was to show, a most percipient assessment of the state of Irish and Anglo-Irish politics at this time. Moreover, Flood cannot but have been impressed by Charlemont's genuine solicitude or struck by the sincerity of his conviction

that in office it is utterly impossible you ever could be happy. Certain as I am of this truth, friendship alone, unbiased even by patriotism, warns you against it; and what the patriot would recommend, the sincere and tender friend from the bottom of his heart advises. [123]

However, Flood had no intention of turning his back on the administration at this late stage, with the result that relations between the two men remained strained. They met during Flood's brief stay in Dublin on his return, still officeless, from England in late May/early June. Charlemont 'flattered' himself following this that they had 'cleared the important point', but it was not long before he was once again 'completely miserable' and complaining about 'this impenetrable gloom of mystery which still hangs over you'. [124]

Harcourt and Blaquiere also found Flood's continuing aloofness very trying. They did not let it show publicly, but the Chief Secretary's confession in June 1775 that securing an office for Henry Flood was the 'hard[est] and tough[est]' negotiation he had ever pursued tells its own story. [125] This was not exclusively Flood's fault. Virtually, none of the officeholders Blaquiere approached with a view to vacating their position was prepared to co-operate. Indeed, having finally concluded in the summer that Welbore Ellis would not provide him with the vacant vice-treasurership he so earnestly desired, the Chief Secretary was obliged to revert to Charles Jenkinson. He had hoped he would not have to do this, but he was left with no alternative by Harcourt's strengthening conviction that his administration needed Flood in the Commons for the 1775–6 session whatever the cost:

The great abilities of this gentleman, and all the powers he is possessed of, have made him formidable to former administrations, and give him the capacity of being much more so hereafter...His terms, however great and exorbitant they may appear, are little in comparison of the trouble he may give, or even of the

123 Charlemont to Flood, 13 Apr. 1775 in R[odd] ed., *Letters to Flood*, pp 72–5.   124 There were further communications which, though courteous, did not manifest the friendship they had previously enjoyed. *F.L.J.*, 3 June.; Charlemont to Flood, 5, 15 June 1775 in R[odd] ed., *Letters to Flood*, pp 79, 81–4; Flood to Charlemont, 8 June in H.M.C., *Charlemont*, i, 331.   125 Hunt, ed., *Irish parliament in 1775*, pp 20–1; Blaquiere to Harcourt, 3 June 1775 in *Harcourt Papers*, ix, 330.

expense that may be incurred on his account, if no method can be devised to engage his services.[126]

Lord North was not pleased when it was explained to him that Charles Jenkinson alone possessed the solution to the problem of providing for Flood. However, once Jenkinson indicated his readiness to exchange his vice-treasurership for the pells' office for life if it was to the advantage of government, Blaquiere persuaded North that this is what must happen when they met on 3 June.[127] North remained sufficiently doubtful about the merits of what was being proposed to restate his reservations about putting Jenkinson in such 'an independent situation' as the pells, about returning a vice-treasurership to Ireland and appointing Flood, and about compensating Charles James Fox so generously at a subsequent meeting on 9 June, but he made no effort to reverse his decision of 3 June. And when he was finally convinced in July 'that the bargain will not be so unreasonably advantageous to Mr Fox', he agreed to seek George III's approval for a complex arrangement that involved Fox exchanging the pells for a thirty-one year pension worth £1,700 p.a, Jenkinson succeeding him at the pells, 'and Mr Flood [accepting] the vacant vice-treasurership [during pleasure] upon condition that the Lord Lieutenant exert[ed] himself to restore the vice-treasurers places to their ancient value ..'. These changes were acceptable to the King, and since John Blaquiere wasted no time putting them into effect, they were soon the subject of informed political gossip.[128]

Everything seemed set fair for Henry Flood finally to accept the vice-treasurership.[129] Harcourt arranged a meeting with him in mid-August to relay the good news, but instead of welcoming the offer, Flood harped on the breach of trust he had endured when the provostship was offered elsewhere in June 1774. He had no difficulty acknowledging Harcourt's personal 'kindness', but he expressed concern that his vice-regal successors 'might treat him with less regard and attention and dismiss him from an employment of a very precarious tenure without ceremony'. Harcourt contended this would not happen. He pleaded his *bona fides*, and having delineated the difficulties he had overcome to provide Flood with a suitably eminent office, he requested 'a decisive answer'. To his dismay, Flood protested his inability to accept the offer as made though 'he was willing to waive his just claim to a more desirable situation and to accept the vice-treasurership, provided it was not to induce any additional burthen on the kingdom'. This was progress of sorts, but it did not satisfy the Lord Lieutenant. He was unsure whether Flood's 'very extra-

126 Harcourt to Blaquiere, 17 June 1775 (D.P.L., Harcourt Papers, Gilbert Ms 93 f 240). 127 Blaquiere to Harcourt, 3 June 1775 in *Harcourt Papers*, ix, 330. 128 North to George III, 1 July, George III to North, 3 July in Fortescue, ed., *Corres of George III*, iii, 229, 231; Rockingham to Burke, 11 July in *Burke Corres.*, iii, 176; Blaquiere to Harcourt, 11 July in *Harcourt Papers*, ix, 339–40; Sackville to Irwin, 26 July in H.M.C., *Stopford-Sackville*, i, 31; Rochford to Harcourt, 29 July 1775 (N.A., Index to departmental letters and papers 1760–89 f 211). 129 *F.L.J.*, 9 Aug.; Townshend to Pery, 23 Sept. 1775 (Emly (Pery) Papers, P.R.O.N.I., T3087/1/61).

ordinary determination' derived from a belief that he could wring more from the administration or from personal awkwardness. He remained hopeful that Flood would accept the vice-treasurership, but he doubted 'he will take so prudent a part'. As this suggests, Harcourt's patience with Flood was now close to breaking point, but he was prepared to give Flood time to consider his position. He had nothing to lose by waiting, as he made clear when he advised Lord North to keep the office 'open', since 'nothing is so likely to operate powerfully on some of the leading interests in this kingdom', and 'his majesty's government may derive no less advantage from Mr Flood's refusal, than from his acceptance of the vice-treasurership'. [130]

Harcourt's strategy seemed well-judged when Flood travelled from Farmley for 'further talk' with the Lord Lieutenant towards the end of August. However, no decision was forthcoming. Flood's punctiliousness bothered Harcourt, who did not pretend to understand his resistance to adding to the Irish civil establishment since 'the additional burthen upon Ireland is the unavoidable consequence of his promotion'. [131] There were many in Ireland, 'friends' of Flood included, who were of the same opinion and this encouraged Blaquiere to conclude that his 'virgin modesty will soon give way'. Flood's remoteness (he based himself at Farmley throughout the summer of 1775) was a complicating factor. But confident that he had sufficient votes to repel John Ponsonby's decision to challenge Pery for the speakership and to forward financial legislation in the upcoming session, Harcourt believed it was best to leave Flood to his own devices on the grounds that he could not 'be in earnest to refuse'. [132] Events *seemed* to prove him correct. On 9 October Harcourt informed Lord North that Flood had accepted the vice-treasurership on the terms on which it had been offered in August, i.e. 'during pleasure', which reserved to the crown the right to dismiss him should that prove necessary.

There is no detailed surviving account of the final exchanges (verbal or written) which resulted in Flood accepting the vice-treasurership or of the terms of the agreement that they reached. But later events, and a tantalising outline of its content provided by the earl of Buckinghamshire in 1779 suggests that Harcourt's reports on his dealings with Flood were less than complete and that, in return for his agreeing to accept the vice-treasurership early in October, Flood obliged the Lord Lieutenant to agree to advance him to another major office for life, to promote his interest in Kilkenny by granting him the 'exclusive patronage' of the county 'including the nomination of sheriffs', and to 'influence the Agar family to give up the borough of *Callan*'. [133] If, and there is no reason to believe it is not, this is an accurate

130 Harcourt to North, 13 Aug. 1775 (D.P.L., Harcourt Papers, Gilbert Ms 93 ff 242–3, partly printed in *Harcourt Papers*, ix, 343–5.   131 *F.L.J.*, 26 Aug.; Harcourt to North, 27 Aug., North to Harcourt, 19 Sept in *Harcourt Papers*, ix, 348–9, 352–3; North to Blaquiere, 19 Sept. 1775 (N.L.I., Harcourt Letterbook, Ms 755 ff 50–1).   132 Ridge to Burke, 25 Sept. in Hoffman, *Burke*, p. 600; Harcourt to North, 20 Sept., Blaquiere to North, 27 Sept. 1775 (D.P.L., Harcourt Papers, Gilbert Ms 93 ff 251–3).   133 Buckinghamshire to North, 25 Oct. 1779 (B.L., Mackintosh Collection, Add. Ms 34523 f 266).

abstract summary of the deal Flood struck with Harcourt, he had made the administration pay a very high price for his support. Moreover, it was also more than Harcourt had permission to agree, which may explain the absence of any documentation relating to it in Harcourt's papers and his apparent failure to inform his ministerial colleagues of its terms.

If Harcourt did exceed his authority to secure Flood's allegiance, he was almost certainly influenced by his wish to ensure that what he anticipated would be his last session in Ireland was trouble free. The acquisition of Flood certainly improved the prospects of this, and if the Lord Lieutenant was disappointed that he was not in a position to take 'any part in the business of the House' of Commons when MPs gathered in early October, he did not mind waiting a little. He knew it would take time to prepare a formal letter of appointment. Besides, his overwhelming feeling was one of relief that the prolonged discussions to bring Flood over had concluded favourably:

> Since I was born, I never had to deal with so difficult a man, owing principally to his high-strained ideas of his own great importance and popularity; but the acquisition of such a man, however desirable at other times, may prove more than ordinarily valuable in the difficult times we may live to see, and which may afford him a very ample field to display his great abilities; and if he exerts them, as he ought to do, in the services of the Crown, I shall think myself amply rewarded for all the pains I have taken to bring this long-depending affair to a happy issue.[134]

Flood's decision to accept office without an assurance that the Irish exchequer would incur no additional cost provoked criticism from disgruntled patriots. However, since he had reduced the additional cost to Ireland to a modest sum and exacted several other promises of favour, he accepted friendly advice that it need serve no longer as a barrier to his taking office.[135] Flood always insisted that he was not induced to take office by financial greed, and his protestations on this point deserve to be taken seriously. At the same time, the hard bargain he struck with Harcourt indicates that he was well aware of the financial as well as political advantages that could accrue to him as a result. How could he not be? In most cases, the motive for taking office was fiscal, and the rewards on offer were oftentimes considerable. John Hely-Hutchinson, for example, was in receipt of £5,800 *per annum* from crown appointments in the 1780s. Others, like Gervaise Parker Bushe, Sir Lucius O'Brien, Godfrey Lill, Isaac Corry, Denis Daly, John Forbes, George Ogle and Barry Yelverton who also took office during Flood's lifetime did not enjoy returns that were quite so

---

134 Harcourt to North, 9 Oct. in *Beresford Corres.*, i, 4–6; Jenkinson to Flood, 10 Oct. 1775 (B.L., Liverpool Papers, Add. Ms 38306 f 2). 135 *H.J.*, 4 Oct.; R.I.A., Burrowes Papers, Ms 23K/53/10; Ridge to Burke, 25 Sept. 1775 in Hoffman, *Burke*, p. 600.

handsome, but their gains were substantial nonetheless. [136] Moreover, since it was an acknowledged reality of Irish politics that 'abilities ... are at market and must be purchased for the use of government', Flood had not breached any political or legal convention. [137] Indeed, he too may have needed the money.

Flood's financial circumstances remain obscure. The widely accepted view is that his 'private fortune amounted to £4,000 or £5,000 a year' in the 1770s and that there was no fiscal reason therefore for his taking office. There is another possibility. One not altogether reliable Irish 'patriot' maintained in the 1820s that Flood was induced to take office by his wish 'to disencumber his estate' of a £20,000 debt. Francis Hardy, Lord Charlemont's biographer, likewise maintained that Flood was induced to take office by financial need. There is no firm contemporary evidence to support this, but it may be that the cost of the campaign to retain control of Callan, the dispute over his sister's will and his own lifestyle snowballed to cause him financial problems in the mid-1770s. Flood certainly was not in the same financial league as grandees like Thomas Conolly, who were able to follow their political star wherever it took them because of their expansive rent rolls. [138] Money, in short, was not something Flood could overlook or a biographer can ignore in explaining his actions in 1774-5, though his personal testimony suggests strongly that political ambition rather than financial need was his primary reason for accepting office.

He was certainly encouraged to take this step, Charlemont's advice to the contrary notwithstanding, by the example of his father and a significant number of prominent patriots since the late 1760s. The cases of Pery, Osborne, and Bushe have already been encountered, but William Brownlow and William Mayne also chose this option in the early 1770s. [139] Lord Charlemont greatly oversimplifies, therefore, when he alleges that 'the rapid decline of opposition ... in earl Harcourt's time' can 'principally be attributed to the unhappy defection of my friend Flood', and claims that he was duped by 'an artful, a corrupt and a cunning minister' into betraying his principles are equally ill-informed. Moreover, the approving citation of assertions that 'patriots were ... void of principle' or were merely government spokesmen waiting to be bought offers an unduly unflattering and reductionist perspective on how most patriot MPs perceived themselves and behaved. [140] It assumes that one accepts

136 E.M.Johnston, 'Members of the Irish parliament 1784-7', *R.I.A.proc.*, 71C (1971), pp 211, 194-5; Bodkin, ed., 'Irish parliament in 1773', p. 180; Ms list of the Irish parliament in 1783 (N.L.I., Ms 2098); Hunt, ed., *Irish parliament in 1775*, p. 39; Lill to Townshend, 9, 10 July, 18 June 1771 (N.L.I., Townshend Papers, Ms 394/39–44); Hillsborough to Corry, 10 Sept. 1781 (B.L., Auckland Papers, Add, Ms 34418 ff 95–6).   137 Pelham to Portland, 24 Oct. 1783 (B.L., Pelham Papers, Add. Ms 33100 ff 372–5).   138 *Blackwood's Magazine*, xix (1826), p. 268; Grattan, *Life of Grattan*, i, 207; Flood, *Memoirs*, pp 114–15; Camden to Londonderry, 22 Apr. 1790 (K.A.O., Camden Papers, U840/C173/105); P.R.O.N.I., Conolly Papers, T2825.   139 Harcourt to Rochford, 14 Jan 1775 in *C.H.O.P.*, iv, 315-6; *F.L.J.*, 22 Oct. 1774; Namier and Brooke, eds, *History of parliament*, iii, 125–6. Mayne purchased the English borough of Gatton in 1774.   140 *Life of Grattan*, i, 206–7; Craig, *The Volunteer earl*, p. 160; Conway to Hartington, 7 Aug. 1755 (Chatsworth Papers, P.R.O.N.I., T3158/807); Erskine to Townshend, 30 May 1771 (Lewis Walpole Library, Townshend Papers); Skelton to Knox, 30 Jan. 1772 in H.M.C., *Knox Mss*, p. 443.

the definition of patriotism advanced by its political critics or by patriots like Lord Charlemont for whom opposition alone was legitimate. This may have a certain descriptive allure, but it is wrong to assume that opposition and patriotism were synonymous. The fact is that Flood did not change his views on accepting office. Indeed, according to Lawrence Parsons, he informed the earl of Buckinghamshire in 1779 that 'he came into office not to relinquish his opinions, but to enforce them with greater effect'. At the same time, there is no corroboration for the claim by an obituarist that, before accepting the vice-treasurership, Flood made 'a precise and explicit stipulation with government in favour of all the great principles which he had before maintained in parliament' or for the assertion by Parsons that 'it was not that he bent to the government, but the government which bent to him'. [141] Flood certainly did not abnegate his patriot principles on taking office because he genuinely aspired to use his position to make laws that would benefit Ireland. Parsons is not an impartial witness on this issue, but he comes closer than anyone else to offering a convincing insight into his thinking at this time:

> He had grounds for believing that ... holding the first office, he would be the first in weight; and that his influence would extend to the general administration of Ireland, directing every measure of importance in the manner most consonant to its welfare and its liberties. However, therefore, Mr Flood disapproved of the English administration, yet, as Ireland was a distinct kingdom, having a legislature of its own, he thought, with the assurances he had received and the measures which were promised, that he might secure good government for that part of the Empire which was naturally the peculiar object of his regard and solitude ... There was no incompatibility between good government in Ireland and bad in England ... In uniting with that government [the Irish], he separated from no party, for he had never been connected with any party in England or in Ireland. The opposition in Ireland was not like that of England, formed on a party system. It was composed of a number of independent gentlemen, who had no tie to each other, who always disclaimed the idea of party, who acted on every occasion each according to his own judgement, sometimes supporting, sometimes opposing, the administration, as the measures seemed to them laudable or censurable. [142]

Though ministers knew from experience that Flood's conception of Anglo-Irish politics was different than theirs, they were still hopeful his acquisition would 'prove more than ordinarily valuable in the difficult times we may live to see, and which may afford him a very ample field for the display of his great abilities'. They knew

---

141 Rosse Papers, C/14/1–5; *Gentleman's Magazine*, 61 (1791), p. 1225; see also Ryan, *Worthies of Ireland*, ii, 147. 142 Rosse Papers, C/14/1–5.

also there was no guarantee he would 'exert them ... in the service of the crown'. [143] It may have seemed that their sustained efforts to secure him office were only justifiable if he did perform as expected, but this could not be assumed.

Flood's decision to embrace office was, for all the previous speculation as to imminence, a serious blow to the patriot interest in the Commons because he, more than anybody, gave hope to its aims and aspirations. Despite this, there were few expressions of anger. Indeed, sorrow was the dominant emotion, and it is best exemplified by Lord Charlemont's well-known jeremiad:

> Flood, the champion of his country, the bulwark of her liberties, her strong tower of defence against all assailants, – Flood, my friend Flood, – the dear partner of my heart and of all its councils, – anchor of my hope, and pillar of my trust, – Flood gave way, and deserted the glorious cause in which he had been for fourteen years triumphantly engaged ... he accepted a vice-treasurer's place, and was lost to his country, to his friend, to himself. [144]

Charlemont's emotional outpouring was prompted by his conviction that he had lost a dear friend (someone to whom he was prepared to entrust the education of his children) as well as a valuable political ally, and that Flood had fundamentally misjudged the nature of Irish politics and the Anglo-Irish connection. More recent commentators incline to the view that Flood had an 'exaggerated notion of his ability to influence government'. [145] Both assessments are compatible; what is undeniable is that officeholding for him proved a most trying and unrewarding experience.

---

143 Harcourt to North, 9 Oct. 1775 in *Harcourt Papers*, ix, 361–2.   144 H.M.C., *Charlemont*, i, 38, ii 388.   145 R. Dunlop, 'Ireland in the eighteenth century', *Cambridge Modern History*, vi (Cambridge 1934), p. 494.

6

In office, 1775–81

A number of reasons are adduced to explain why Henry Flood's tenure as an officeholder proved unfulfilling. One is that he was temperamentally unsuited to the discipline of government. Flood was, and remained, essentially a political loner who was accustomed to doing as he pleased. This was feasible as long as he remained an independent patriot; officeholders were expected to follow the Castle line. Moreover, since there was no automatic equation between office and political power in eighteenth-century Ireland, the political influence Flood aspired to did not come to him *ex officio*. Influence had to be earned, and many possessors of high office carried little weight either because they did not seek to or because they were unable to gain the confidence and trust of Dublin Castle through the time-honoured devices of personal contact and the advancement of government business in parliament. In so far as one can tell, Flood did not appreciate how important these were. It may be that he anticipated he would have power and influence presented to him since, according to Lawrence Parsons, he was given to understand 'that he would have ... the lead in the House of Commons', but this hardly accounts for six years in the political wilderness.[1] Flood could be, as Lord Harcourt observed, an infuriatingly difficult person. However, since he was also an experienced politician and a highly intelligent man, it is difficult to accept that he allowed his *amour propre* get so completely in the way of political common sense.

Perhaps, for this reason, most modern explanations of Flood's failure to prosper in office focus less on his temperamental unsuitability to high office than on his misjudgment of the political mood and public opinion. It is commonly advanced that throughout his time as an officeholder his heart was in opposition, and that only his highly developed sense of self prevented him acknowledging that he had made a mistake when he accepted the vice-treasurership. There is plenty of evidence to sustain this view. It is undeniable that the ineffectiveness of the patriots in parliament following Townshend's retirement, and the *ostensible* readiness of his successor to advance patriot policies (such as the absentee tax) encouraged Flood to

1 Rosse Papers, C/14/1–5.

contemplate office in anticipation that it would prove legislatively advantageous. However, he soon discovered that the priority of Dublin Castle and their ministers in London was not a reformist legislative programme, but the traditional object of perpetuating Ireland's dependency. Realisation of this was masked for a time. But as Britain's crisis in America intensified, it became unmistakeably clear that Flood's espousal of a patriot agenda was not shared by government and, ironically, that his erstwhile patriot allies (rather than his new colleagues) were better placed to achieve these goals.

The fact that he continued to adhere to patriot principles was an important factor in Flood's estrangement from Dublin Castle. However, the tension that developed between them during these years was not caused primarily by political differences or by personal remoteness, but by Flood's insistence that the implementation in full of the deal he had concluded with Lord Harcourt in 1775 was a precondition of his for supporting the administration. Since Harcourt had promised Flood more than he should and Flood expected the administration to prove its *bona fides*, and since neither was entirely frank with the other, it is frequently difficult to unravel what is going on in the late 1770s. However, it is the key to understanding why, from the outset, his relationship with Dublin Castle proved so troubled.

A BASHFUL 'NEW FRIEND'

The intensification of political activity among the kingdom's literate and educated classes was one of the most important developments in the early 1770s. It drew inspiration, in the main, from the stimulus provided by the efforts of the redoubtable John Wilkes to negate the attempts of his establishment opponents to nullify his election to represent Middlesex, and the resistance of the American colonists to what they identified as the oppressive policies of the crown. Much of what was written in the Irish press on these matters was consonant with what Flood and Gervaise Bushe had been arguing since the mid-1760s. But of greater consequence for the future and for Henry Flood was the readiness now to attribute malign intent to the King and his ministers, and to conclude that if they imposed their will on America they would extend their 'tyranny' to Ireland.[2]

The most visible manifestation of this heightened politicisation is to be found in Dublin in the pronouncements of bodies like the Society of Free Citizens in support of the colonists, in the resolutions entered into by 'freemen and freeholders' against electoral entertainment, and in the publication in the liberal press of essays

2 James Kelly, 'Parliamentary reform, pp 75–6; Giblin, ed., 'Nunziatura di Fiandra, pt 7', p. 58; *H.J.*, 11 Mar., 13 Apr., 4 May, 3, 17, 27 June, 6 July, 3, 12. Aug. 1774, 27 Feb., 3, 17 May, 12, 21, 28 June, 16 Aug. 1775; *F.L.J.*, 12 Oct. 1774, 29 Apr., 6 May 1775.

and articles urging 'the voice of the people' to exertion to 'save the constitution'.[3] Its main achievement in the early 1770s was to formulate oaths by which electoral candidates could register their support for popular policies. But the vigour of the pronouncements in support of Ireland's 'freedom of trade', 'the liberty of the people', the 'Protestant interest' in Ireland and the 'just rights' of the American colonists against Britain's 'tyrannic sway' indicate that if Flood was encouraged to take office by the demoralised state of the patriots in the Commons he underestimated the burgeoning strength of popular patriotism outside the House.[4] He was not alone in this. There was a pervasive air of pessimism in patriot political circles in the early mid-1770s (reinforced by rumours of Flood's intentions) that their political spokesmen were powerless to put 'a stop to the current of destruction that ... will be adopted ... to enable administration to conquer the spirit of independence and dragoon us into a servile compliance with their demands'. However, the outbreak of the American War of Independence in the summer of 1775 provided them with an issue around which they could unite.[5]

The absence of any public pronouncement by Flood on the gathering enthusiasm for patriot and reformist causes outside parliament does not mean that he was disinterested in the debate that was taking place. In an unpublished reply he wrote in 1775 to Samuel Johnson's controversial pamphlet *Taxation no tyranny*, Flood dismissed virtual representation as impractical as well as illogical and, lamenting what he identified as the narrowing of representation since the feudal era, urged that 'declining and decayed boroughs' should be revitalised. These were not the views of a typical officeholder, and Flood's non-conformity was compounded by his continuing unhappiness with British policy in America. He maintained that Britain's attempts to assert its right to tax the colonists was indefensible because it could not be justified by 'the fundamental principles of the British constitution, by the established practice of it' or 'by the dictates of sound sense, of natural justice or of public convenience'. At the heart of the Anglo-American dispute, Flood contended, was the relationship of the British parliament with all its 'provincial legislature[s]', and it was his considered opinion that the former should be supreme only 'as to ... those things which are essential to Great Britain'. He conceded that it should have the authority to raise such taxes 'as are necessary to the public safety and public prosperity', but he deemed it legitimate to resist if it 'exceed[ed] its powers'. This was contrary to Johnson, but for all his affection for the 'great lexicographer', Flood could not accept his conservative views on this subject, on virtual representation or on the operation of the Westminster electoral system because his conception of the

3 Kelly, 'Parliamentary reform', pp 76–7; *H.J.*, 9 Feb., 2, 14 Mar. 1774.   4 Kelly, 'Parliamentary reform', p. 77; *H.J.*, 4, 25 Mar., 6, 22 July, 10 Aug., 8, 12, 14 Oct. 1774; *F.L.J.*, 6 May, 2 Sept. 1775; J. Hill, 'Religious toleration and the relaxation of the Penal Laws: an imperial perspective', *Archivium Hibernicum*, 44(1989), pp 98–109.   5 R.E. Burns, 'Ireland and British military preparations for war in America in 1775', *Cithara*, ii, 48–9; Revenue of Ireland, Mar. 1775 in *C.H.O.P.*, iv, 513–4; *F.L.J.*, 29 Oct. 1774, 16 Aug., 23 Sept.; *H.J.*, 5 May, 22 Sept.; Ridge to Burke, 25 Sept. 1775 in Hoffman, *Burke*, p. 600.

relationship between England and its dependencies was egalitarian rather than dependent. Whereas Johnson urged continued subordination, Flood cautioned that any attempt to enforce dependency in a 'litigious' or oppressive way by 'straining the prerogative of this country' would 'encrease your difficulties without end'. He drew attention to the fact that no attempt had ever been made to tax Ireland in the same objectionable way that was being pursued in America, and he urged that the Irish practice was followed elsewhere because the American colonists were not responsible for the controversial debts they were being taxed to pay and because any attempt to oblige them to do so would only hasten 'universal contention':

> Instead of exasperating them by system, you should bind them to you by every demonstration of liberal attachment; ...you should have them to conduct themselves to prosperity without the alarming interposition of imperial authority, except where it is *bona fide* essential to preserve Great Britain at the head of an united empire? And as taxing the colonies in the British parliament or making them tax themselves by compulsory requisition from hence is inconsistent with all the rights of British prosperity; and as it is evident from your own past experience that such a power is not necessary to the union of your empire, but probably inconsistent with it, have they not reason to hope that you will renounce the idea with a manly decision, and not hold over their heads, *in terrorem*, a claim which even arbitrary countries do not exercise over their colonies, the establishments of which are maintained at the expense of the parent state, without raising in them any conception that their colonies are therefore useless, or that their empire is in danger of being dissolved?[6]

This plea for a more 'permissive' empire reflected Flood's conception of how the British empire should be structured. He believed, indeed, that it was the only way to safeguard the Anglo-American connection, but since these were not sentiments likely to be well-received from someone in his position, it is hardly surprising that his reply to Johnson's pamphlet was not published.

It is also not surprising that he was less than eager to stand forward on the opening day of the 1775–6 session, on 10 October, to back Lord Harcourt's request that the Irish parliament should manifest its 'unavoidable attachment' to the crown by supporting George III's 'just rights and ... legal authority in America'. He had a ready made excuse in the fact that the bureaucratic details of his appointment were still incomplete, for though he gave 'indisposition' as the reason, it is difficult not to conclude that Flood wanted to avoid disagreeing with Thomas Conolly, Barry Yelverton, Denis Daly, Sir Edward Newenham, George Ogle and Hussey Burgh, who opposed Harcourt's request on the grounds that, in Ogle's words, 'if you assist

6 'An answer to *Taxation no tyranny*', 1775 (Rosse Papers, C/3).

England, you vote away your own liberties'. The Lord Lieutenant got his way by a comfortable forty votes, but Flood's private reservations with government policy on this matter and the patriots' expressions of support for 'our suffering fellow subjects in America' indicated that this was an issue on which he was well-advised to tread carefully. Furthermore, the fact that John Hely-Hutchinson had refused 'to support' the Castle because (some of his 'enemies' claimed) of his displeasure at Flood's recruitment, and that Philip Tisdall was also intent on taking a back seat indicated that he could expect little support or goodwill from other officeholders.[7]

Flood was allowed a temporary respite from the pressure of public and political expectation when the Commons' adjourned for ten days following the ratification of the address to the King. During the recess, 'the warrant for ... [his] appointment' as vice-treasurer was transmitted by Lord North with the hopeful message 'that government will be greatly benefited by his assistance and abilities'. Flood received the warrant on 23 October. Five days later, the authorization secured eleven months earlier to make him an Irish privy councillor was put into effect, and conscious that he was expected to show gratitude for these honours, Flood made his first Commons' speech as an officeholder on 31 October.[8]

Because Blaquiere was an inexperienced parliamentary performer and there were few other combative voices available, circumstances were tailor-made for Flood to move to the head of the Castle interest in the Commons, but he was disinclined to do so. He did join with the Chief Secretary on 1 November in opposing a motion by Yelverton which alleged that the revenue was inadequate to meet the expenses of the establishments', but the impact of his contribution was vitiated by an exchange with the Solicitor General, John Scott, which highlighted the hostility with which established Castle advisers regarded him. This was precipitated by a remark by Scott which Flood 'imagined to be a reflection on his conduct, and marking an inconsistency in supporting this administration and being so violent against the last'. Unwilling to allow any critical reflection pass unanswered, Flood responded with 'a very sharp reprimand', which excited unease in some quarters that it might lead to a duel until the intervention of the House defused the dispute.[9]

Neither Harcourt nor Blaquiere was perturbed by this incident. The Chief Secretary's observation in his report on the debate that 'Mr Flood supported and I

7 Ridge to Butler, 11 Oct. in Hoffman, *Burke*, p. 605; John Almon, *Narrative of proceedings of the parliament of Ireland* (London, 1777), pp 1–11; Harcourt to Rochford, 11 Oct. in *C.H.O.P.*, iv, 426; Blaquiere to North, 11 Oct. (D.P.L., Harcourt Papers, Gilbert Ms 93 ff 449–50); Conolly to Leinster, 11 Oct. in Fitzgerald, ed., *Leinster Corres.*, iii, 157; *H.J.*, 16, 18, 20 Oct. 1775. 8 Almon, *Narrative*, pp 15–16; North to Harcourt, 15 Oct., North to Blaquiere, 25 Oct.(N.L.I., Harcourt Letterbook, Ms 755 ff 52–4); Harcourt to Flood, 23 Oct. 1775 in R[odd], ed., *Letters to Flood*, p. 86; N.A., Index to Irish Privy Councillors 1711–1910; Rochford to Harcourt, 18 Nov. 1774 (P.R.O., S.P. 67/14 ff 150–1). Flood's speech of 31 October was a short statement in support of a suggestion that the committee of accounts should adjourn to enable the Chief Secretary to secure material information (Almon, *Narrative*, pp 56–7; *H.J.*, 1 Nov.; *F.L.J.*, 4 Nov. 1775). 9 Almon, *Narrative*, p. 66; *H.J.*, 14 Feb. 1774, 3 Nov. 1775.

think cordially' suggests that they were conscious that they had little choice but to allow him considerable latitude until they honoured the other commitments they had made him. With this in mind, Blaquiere applied to Lord North in early November to deliver on the 'promise' that 'Flood should have a seat at the Council board in Great Britain, as every vice treasurer constantly has had'.[10] This should have eased Flood's anxieties and encouraged him to make little of the strident and, frequently, ill-informed criticism to which he was subject in the press, but it appears not to have done so. In an attempt to defend his reputation, Flood placed stories in the British and Irish press claiming that the 'nett charge' to Ireland of his appointment was a mere £360 a year and that, 'if the restoration of an office of considerable salary be included, the public is at no loss at all on the transaction', but it only bought him temporary respite. Indeed, hot on the heels of his criticism of the Townshend administration on 1 November, one commentator alleged that the total cost of Flood's recruitment was £100,000 and that, on his own, he exceeded the total cost of the additions to the civil establishment sanctioned by Lord Townshend.[11] This was wildly inaccurate, but personalised attacks of this kind encouraged Flood to keep a low political profile to the dismay of the Lord Lieutenant who complained to Lord North on 12 November that 'the timidity or bashfulness of new friends' obliged Blaquiere 'almost singly, to sustain the weight of argument and acrimonious altercation of debate' in the Commons.[12] This was not what was intended, and it was a matter of increasing import as the patriot interest in the House was emboldened by mounting popular support in Dublin and Belfast for the cause of the American colonists to intensify their opposition to the provision of troops on the Irish army establishment for deployment abroad.[13]

Flood clearly realised he could not avoid supporting the administration on this contentious issue, and he made his first significant contribution of the session on 12 November when he helped John Blaquiere to repel opposition allegations that the kingdom's defences had been grievously weakened by the decision to make soldier's available to fight in America. Flood's defence of the administration's management of the military establishment was vigorous, but it was his observations on the 'commotions' in America and his contention that Thomas Conolly's motions, which urged the maintenance permanently in the kingdom of 12,000 troops, 'were slanderous on the honour of our sovereign' that attracted most attention. These were not sentiments expected from a patriot, in office or out, as Charlemont's protest against the deployment in the Lords attests, but Flood's 'eloquent' and 'able' speech

10 Blaquiere to North, 2 Nov., Blaquiere to Rochford, 2 Nov. (D.P.L., Harcourt Papers, Gilbert Ms 93 ff 279–80); Harcourt to Rochford, 2 Nov. 1775 in *C.H.O.P.*, iv, 458.   11 *F.L.J.*, 28 Oct.; *H.J.*, 25 Oct., 8 Nov.; Webb to Flood, 14 Nov. 1775 in R[odd], ed., *Letters to Flood*, pp 86–7.   12 *F.L.J.*, 11 Nov.; Almon, *Narrative*, pp 66–8; Harcourt to North, 12 Nov. 1775 in *Harcourt Papers*, x, 27.   13 Almon, *Narrative*, pp 70–2; *H.J.*, 6, 27 Nov. 1775.

delighted Harcourt who concluded optimistically in his report on the debate that 'his majesty will derive from his assistance an able supporter to his government'.[14]

In fact, Harcourt was allowing his understandable eagerness to prove that the high price he had paid for Flood's services was well spent cloud his judgement for, on the very next day when the controversial matter of Jeremiah Dyson's pension was raised by the opposition, Flood 'absconded as soon as the debate began'. Since he was not the only member of the Castle connection to do this, and the administration had a comfortable majority in the division (as in most divisions that mattered), Harcourt declined to make an issue of his conduct. It was becoming apparent that Flood had concluded that his elevation to the vice-treasurership did not oblige him to support the administration unconditionally, as he further demonstrated on Tuesday, 21 November, when he introduced a bill to rectify a defect in the Corn Act he had piloted through the Commons in 1773.[15]

Flood would have greatly eased the administration's mounting doubts about his commitment if he had wholeheartedly supported them on the conduct of the war in America. This took centre stage once more on Saturday, 25 November, when the Irish parliament was formally requested to authorize making 4,000 troops available for deployment in America. Flood did not play a dominant part in the debate because of his antipathy to the suggestion emanating from government circles that the troops transferred out of Ireland would be replaced by 'foreign [Hessian] Protestants'. However, he did contribute to the formulation of the resolutions which were the focus of the discussion, and he did vote for the provision of troops. Moreover, since the Castle administration did not regard the acceptance of 4,000 Hessians as a vital matter he was at liberty to

> expatiate ... strongly on the impropriety and danger of admitting foreign troops as there was no immediate danger of an invasion, and our internal commotions might be suppressed by ourselves, since if gentlemen would exert themselves, the Whiteboys might be quelled without the aid of a single soldier.

Flood was convinced it was both politically more appropriate and constitutionally safer to entrust the domestic security of Ireland to a civilian militia rather than to foreign troops. He did not personally advocate the founding of such a body at this time (though he had done so in the 1760s), but it is possible he was active behind the scenes. According to Warden Flood, he was the instigator of George Ogle's call in

14 Almon, *Narrative*, pp 70–7; *H.J.*, 15 Nov.; Harcourt to North, 15 Nov. in *Harcourt Papers*, x, 29–31; Harcourt to Rochford, 15 Nov. 1775 in *C.H.O.P.*, iv, 467–8. It was on this occasion that Flood reputedly uttered his infamous remark on sending 'four thousand armed negotiators' to the colonies. It was a vivid image, but an incautious phrase (Thomas Mac Nevin, *The history of the Volunteers of 1782* (Dublin, 1846), pp 69–70). 15 *H.J.*, 15, 17, 20, 22 Nov.; *F.L.J.*, 25 Nov.; Almon, *Narrative*, pp 77–80, 84; Harcourt to North, 15 Nov. (D.P.L., Harcourt Papers, Gilbert Ms 93 ff 285–6); Shannon to Dennis, 17 Nov. 1775 (P.R.O.N.I., Shannon Papers, D2707/A2/3/36).

late November for leave to bring in the heads of a bill to establish a militia. He
certainly could take pleasure in the fact that John Beresford's motion of 25 November declaring that the admission of foreign troops was 'unnecessary at present' was
supported by a majority of MPs, and that his conduct was applauded by Lord
Harcourt who reported approvingly to Lord North that Flood 'spoke with great
ability and showed the utmost zeal on this day's debate'.[16]

Though the record shows that Flood's support for the administration during
the opening weeks of the 1775–6 session was fitful, officials in England as well as
Ireland were loathe to conclude that he was less than fully committed. This was
certainly Charles Jenkinson's view. He wrote to Flood on 27 November to congratulate him for 'the very eloquent and spirited manner in which you supported
the measures of administration and the honour of the crown' and to inform him
'that the English ministry as well as Lord Harcourt have great obligation to you for
your services'. It is improbable that Jenkinson would have been so complimentary if
the administration had been under pressure in the Commons, but Flood's defection
had, Robert French conceded, contributed to the identifiable lack of 'spirit' in opposition ranks following their failure to prevent the deployment of troops in
America.[17] For his part, Flood was content to continue to leave the political running
to others as the session moved towards Christmas. He attended meetings of the
Privy Council, but he remained reserved in the Commons.[18] It was appropriate (he
was complimented by Barry Barry for doing so) at the same time that he did not
participate in the discussion on 15 and 16 December of the petition of his fellow
vice-treasurers, Welbore Ellis and Lord Clare, that their salary be restored to the
level from which it had fallen by the withdrawal of some additional and loan duties
from their collective entitlement to 2.5 per cent of the exchequer receipts for which
they were responsible. There was broad agreement that something should be done,
and the departure in protest from the Commons of 35 patriots, of whom Henry
Grattan who made his maiden speech on the issue was one, ensured that the proposal of Sir Lucius O'Brien to set the vice-treasurers' total annual remuneration at
£10,500 plus £2,500 in expenses was ratified without a division.[19]

Since the restoration of 'the vice-treasurers' places to their ancient value' was
one of the promises made Flood when he was offered that office, the administration

16 *H.J.*, 29 Nov.; Harcourt to North, 28 Nov. (D.P.L., Harcourt Papers, Gilbert Ms 93 ff 295–301);
Fitzgerald to Leinster, 2 Dec. 1775 (N.L.I., Fitzgerald Papers, Ms 13022/145).   17 Jenkinson to Flood,
27 Nov. (B.L., Liverpool Papers, Add. Ms 38306 f 7); *H.J.*, 1, 4, 6, 8, 15 Dec.; Almon, *Narrative*, pp 97–
111; French to O'Brien, 12 Dec. in Ainsworth, ed., *Inchiquin Mss*, p. 219; Harcourt to North, 9 Dec.
1775 (D.P.L., Harcourt Papers, Gilbert Ms 93 f 304).   18 *F.L.J.*, 9 Dec. 1775.   19 *F.L.J.*, 20 Dec.; *Life
of Grattan*, i, 281–3; North to Harcourt, 19 Sept., 24 Oct. 1775, 22 Jan. 1776 (N.L.I., Harcourt letterbook,
Ms 755 ff 58–9, 82–3, 110–11); Almon, *Narrative*, pp 111–17; Harcourt to Weymouth, 17 Dec. 1775 in
C.H.O.P., iv, 502. This represented a significant improvement on the current return of £2,331 from a
gross return of £11,500. Provision was also made for a salary of £3,500 plus £350 expenses for Charles
Jenkinson as Clerk of the Pells.

could reasonably have anticipated that he would be more forthcoming in his advocacy of and support for government policies in the Commons thereafter. But this was not to be. He was no more active in late December 1775 or early January 1776 than he had been earlier in the session, though the subjects debated included militia and corn export bills, on which he had a proven political record. However, he was also silent during 'the most violent heats' prompted on 21 December by the identification of amendments by the Commons' committee of comparison in two money bills returned from the British Privy Council.[20] Dublin Castle managed to have revised heads, minus the clause stating that parliamentary sanction was needed to send troops abroad, approved but it is clear from Harcourt's reports of the opposition's criticism of the 'constant practice' of amending Irish bills that he would have warmly welcomed his vice-treasurer's support.[21] The adjournment of the House of Commons between 6 and 31 January gave both an opportunity to assess their position.

Though their different legislative priorities were obviously important, Flood's reserve in the House of Commons in 1775 was also influenced by the administration's tardiness in implementing in full the terms of the agreement he had reached with Lord Harcourt in October. It is very difficult to establish what his strategy was at this time because of the shortage of personal testimony, but his request to Bishop Markham to investigate the possibility of his securing a seat at Westminster, and to intercede on his behalf with the prime minister on this matter and on his aspiration to become a British privy councillor indicates that he had concluded that a direct approach, by-passing the Irish administration, might be more productive. Markham, dutifully, did as requested. But following discussions he had with one minister 'about your pretensions to a place in the [British] Privy Council', he reported back to Flood on 5 January that it was likely to meet with strong resistance:

> I found it had been taken up strongly as a thing new and unprecedented that a man who had no seat in the English parliament and even no property in England should be brought to that board, that it was a new thing to consider the place [of vice-treasurer] as giving pretensions.

This was pretty categorical, but Markham continued to press Flood's case. He maintained that because Flood had been promised the position by Harcourt, his

case should be attended to as being particular; that they were misinformed if

20 *H.J.*, 18, 20, 22, 27 Dec. 1775, 5 Jan., 1776; Almon, *Narrative*, pp 118–23; Harcourt to Weymouth, 22 Dec. in *C.H.O.P.*, iv, 506; *F.L.J.*, 27 Dec. 1775.   21 McDowell, *Ireland in the age of imperialism*, p. 246; Harcourt to North, 22, 24 Dec. in *Harcourt Papers*, x, 61–2, 66; Harcourt to Weymouth, 28 Dec. (P.R.O., S.P., 63/451 ff 7–10); see also Blaquiere to Germain, 30 Dec. 1775 (D.P.L., Harcourt Papers, Gilbert Ms 93 ff 332–6).

they believed it had been asked by you, that it had been offered among other inducements before you had accepted the office, that the Lord Lieutenant might have been inadvised in offering it, but that as matters stood, it was a serious question whether they would refuse maintaining the faith of his engagement. The truth is that no one, I believe, aims at you, but there are some who are not his [*sic*] friends.[22]

Markham's persistence won him further audiences, one with Lord North on 19 January and another a few days later with North and John Robinson, following which he expressed confidence that the objections in the way of Flood's appointment to the British Privy Council could be surmounted. He was distinctly less hopeful about Flood's wish to obtain a seat at Westminster. The Prime Minister, Markham reported after their second meeting, was 'well acquainted with your abilities, and with such talents he did not wonder at your desire to get a seat in the English House and aiming at any honours or emoluments that this country could afford'. However, he was in no position to help him because of 'engagements to several who had spent large sums and lost their election'.[23] This suggested that the obstacles in the way of Flood's securing a Westminster seat with government support were also surmountable and, encouraged by Markham, Flood sought to advance his case through established channels. At his request, Harcourt raised the matter with the Prime Minister, but the response was the same. North maintained he 'should be very happy to have the assistance of Mr Flood's abilities in the House of Commons', but he was

really so embarrassed by a variety of applications for seats in the House of Commons to which I am obliged to give attention, that I cannot at present venture to promise to bring Mr Flood or any other person into parliament. Several of my friends were unsuccessful candidates at the general election – others have been since displaced by the decisions of the committees of election, so that many persons are to be served, and few very few opportunities offer of serving them.[24]

There is no record of Flood's reaction to this, but his continued reserve in the Commons is testimony to his displeasure. Puzzled by his inactivity, some concluded simply that he had 'been silenced with the vice-treasurership'. Others were angry:

Don't use the word Patriot, it makes me quite sick,
I give them all up, for they'll never do good,
O G[o]d, what I'd give for the hanging of Flood.[25]

22 Markham to Flood, 5 Jan. 1776 (Rosse Papers, C/2/25).   23 Markham to Flood, 19, post 19 Jan. 1776 (Rosse Papers, C/2/27, 26).   24 Markham to Flood, post 19 Jan. (Rosse Papers, C/2/26); Harcourt to Flood, 2 Feb. in R[odd], ed., *Letters to Flood*, p. 91; North to Harcourt, 25 Mar. 1776 (N.L.I., Harcourt letterbook, Ms 755 ff 90–1).   25 Arthur Young, *Tour of Ireland* (2 vols, London, 1780), i, 20; *H.J.*, 8 Jan. 1776.

His conduct on the resumption of the House of Commons on 1 February gave his critics further fuel with which to feed their ire.

Much of the time of the House of Commons in the second part of the 1775–6 session was taken up with legislation to make eight regiments on the Irish army available for deployment abroad, and the implementation of the embargo on provision exports to the American colonies.[26] Flood supported both measures, though the brevity of his contributions suggest that his commitment was not whole-hearted. Despite this, he had to endure stern public criticism, as patriot MPs like Robert French, Barry Barry, George Ogle, Lucius O'Brien, Edward Newenham, Barry Yelverton and Walter Hussey contrived successfully to whip up a storm of controversy. Dublin Castle stood firm. The administration was under pressure from London to advance both measures *sine die*, and they were pleased simply to have Flood's support during the key debate on the army on 14 February though he confined himself to exposing the invalidity of an amendment proposed by Walter Hussey which challenged the thrust of the Castle motion.[27]

The embargo excited deep emotions because it struck at the long-held patriot conviction that the kingdom of Ireland should be allowed conduct its commerce free of restriction, and because it exacerbated the already troubled financial and commercial state of the country.[28] It was an ideal issue for the patriots for this reason, and they were not coy in condemning it as both unconstitutional and economically deleterious. The main debate on the measure took place on 22 February when Walter Hussey moved that a proclamation issued on 3 February prohibiting the export of provisions (with the exception of corn which was exempted on 19 February) be declared illegal. Flood was unmoved. There is no evidence linking him directly with the promulgation of the supplemental proclamation of 19 February, but his knowledge of the corn legislation and his readiness to oppose Burgh's motion suggests that he was consulted. It would, he pronounced with uncharacteristic understatement, 'be very indiscreet to enter into any resolution founded on the corn bounty, at a time we were in hopes of having a bill to perpetuate that bounty returned from England'. This registered with MPs, though Flood vitiated its impact somewhat by defending 'the prerogative of the crown to issue proclamations in time of war, quoted many precedents, and said that if a power is given to the crown by law, by law only that power could be taken away ... yet necessity would often justify what it could not legalize'. This elicited a sharp rebuke from Henry Grattan who

26 Harcourt to Weymouth, 13 Jan., 3 Feb., Weymouth to Harcourt, 26 Jan. 1776 (P.R.O., S.P.,63/451 ff 104–6, 116–18, 226). 27 Almon, *Narrative*, pp 128–32; *H.J.*, 7, 9, 14, 16 Feb.; Cunningham to Huntington, 9 Feb. in H.M.C.*Hastings*, iii, 170; Conolly to Leinster, 15 Feb. 1776 in Fitzgerald, ed., *Leinster Corres.*, iii, 184. 28 See, *inter alia*, duke to duchess of Leinster, 17 Dec. 1775 (N.L.I., Fitzgerald Papers, Ms 13022 no 38); Knox to Style, 28 Mar. 1776 (N.A., Style Papers, Ms 600 (a)/2); *Life of Grattan*, i, 283–4; T.M. O'Connor, 'The embargo on the export of Irish provisions 1776–9', *I.H.S.*, ii (1940), pp 4–11.

observed acidly that 'necessity was the tyrant's plea' and provoked an altercation with Sir William Osborne. However, in the end, Flood had the greater reason to feel content since Burgh's motion was lost by 89 votes to 66.[29]

This was a satisfactory outcome for Dublin Castle, though both the embargo and the deployment of troops abroad remained topical issues.[30] Flood, for his part, was more interested in advancing militia legislation. He now deemed this an urgent matter because of the moves afoot among Protestants in Birr, Roscrea, Limerick and elsewhere to found 'independent companies' of volunteers 'in defence of their lives and properties, and for the preservation of the peace of the country against ... Whiteboys and all other disturbers of the peace and tranquillity of the Protestant inhabitants'. Flood empathised with the impulse though he believed it should have the explicit sanction of the law. However, he kept his own counsel as the session wound down and adjournments became more frequent and lengthy.[31]

Flood's reluctance to participate in the end of session debates was prompted by the realisation that, with a general election imminent, it was not in his interest to be seen to defend or to support the Castle. Besides, the fact that Harcourt wanted to leave his Irish posting (his request in the late spring to do so was rejected by Lord North), that the British Privy Council had 'postponed' his act for the further encouragement of tillage because it would 'sink too deep into the hereditary revenue', and that important aspects of his agreement with Harcourt had not been implemented gave him no incentive to pit his wits against the *saeve indignatio* of eager patriots like Grattan.[32] His immediate priority at this moment was to rehabilitate his public reputation, and with this in mind he sought, once more, to use the press.

The publication by the popular *Hibernian Journal* in April of a lengthy justification of Flood's legislative record and, in particular, of an affirmation of his role in securing the Octennial Act is a testament to his concern at his diminishing public reputation. This appeared under a pseudonym, but the inclusion of a strong defence of his record *in office* suggests that Flood (or someone close to him) was the author, and that their primary motive was electoral:

29 Harcourt to Weymouth, 5 Feb. (P.R.O., S.P.,63/451 f 260); O'Connor, 'Embargo', pp 5–9; Almon's *Narrative*, pp 133–9; *F.L.J.*, 28 Feb. 1776. 30 Weymouth to Harcourt, 28 Feb., Harcourt to Weymouth, 18 Feb., 4 Mar. (P.R.O., S.P.,63/452 ff 101–4, 146–8, 182–3); *H.J.*, 28 Feb., 1 Mar.; *F.L.J.*, 2, 6 Mar. 1776. 31 Harcourt to Weymouth, 28 Feb.(D.P.L., Harcourt Papers, Gilbert Ms 93 ff 355–6); *F.L.J.*, 2, 6 Mar.; *H.J.*, 5, 26 Feb., 1 Mar. 1776; Almon, *Narrative*, pp 140–4. 32 Weymouth to Harcourt, and Privy Council minute, 18 Mar. (P.R.O., S.P., 63/452 ff 247–9); Privy Council Register, 1776 (P.R.O., P.C.2/119 f 445); Harcourt to Weymouth, 20 Mar.(2), 17 Apr., 1 May (P.R.O., S.P.63/452 ff 296, 453 ff 149–53, 222–3, 298–300); Harcourt to Weymouth, 5 Apr. (N.A., Index to departmental letters and papers 1760–89 f 215); North to Harcourt, 27 Mar. (N.L.I., Harcourt Papers, Ms 755 ff 92–3); Harcourt to North, 29 Mar. in *Harcourt Papers*, x, 133–4; Harcourt to North, 6 Apr. (D.P.L., Harcourt Papers, Gilbert Ms 93 ff 373–4); Almon, *Narrative*, pp 144–51; Hamilton to Pery, 13 Mar. (Add. Pery Papers, P.R.O.N.I., T3052/43); Lees to Robinson, 7 Apr. 1776 in *Beresford Corres.*, i, 6–9.

He has added a security to the bounty on the inland carriage of corn. He has obtained a bounty on the exportation of corn; and a duty on corn imported. He has supported a militia bill, withstood the introduction of foreign troops and promoted an absentee tax, which was till lately esteemed one of the best things that could happen to us, and too good to be expected. In fine, he has shown a liberality of action, and an attention to the public good in the service of the crown. I do not mean to make an encomium on him; but surely he is not a person to degrade, for whom all the rules of common justice and of common charity ought to be violated; neither is the printing a malicious election ballad a necessary exercise of the liberality of the press.[33]

ELECTORAL PROBLEMS

Given his unhappy experience in County Kilkenny in 1768 and his inability to turn the tide in his favour in Callan, Henry Flood had good reason to regard the 1776 general election with apprehension. At the same time, the fact that he had secured a commitment from the Lord Lieutenant in 1775 to advance his interest in both the county and the borough constituencies must have provided some encouragement. The patronage to which he gained access arising out of his relationship with the Castle certainly enhanced his local profile. He was, for example, appointed one of the commissioners to oversee the navigation of the river Nore by the Board of Inland Navigation in May 1775. More pertinently, he was in a position the following May to solicit a small pension for William Phillips, a minor revenue officer, who had supported him electorally. In addition, he obtained two hearth money collectorships, two ensigncies, the distributorship of stamps for County Kilkenny, a hearth money supervisorship and three gaugerships for friends and supporters. Most importantly of all, he secured the appointment of his cousin Francis to the shrievalty of County Kilkenny. This was an impressive haul for such a short time, and it indicates that, in respect of the patronage of County Kilkenny, Harcourt sought to keep his promise to favour Flood.[34]

Even with the county sheriff on his side, Flood knew that the electoral challenges he faced were forbidding. The problem in Callan was that he no longer held the legal or political initiative in the borough. He placed great store on the commitment he had extracted from Lord Harcourt 'that the government should influence the Agar family to give up the borough', but this was not a promise any lord lieutenant could fulfil. In the county, his task was to overcome the Ponsonby, Agar or Butler/Mountgarret interests which were larger and more powerful than he.[35] In this

33 *H.J.*, 12 Apr. 1776. 34 *F.L.J.*, 27 May 1775; Harcourt to North, 4 May 1776 (D.P.L., Harcourt Papers, Gilbert Ms 93 ff 397–8); Harcourt list [Jan 1777] (Gilbert Ms 94 f 255). 35 Buckinghamshire

respect, patronage was useful in solidifying a political interest, but it was not able on its own to create a voter majority, particularly, when rival interests were also in receipt of government patronage. In County Kilkenny, for example, members of the Wemys, Butlers, Desarts and Wandesfords also served as commissioners of the Nore navigation, while the Agars secured more minor revenue appointments than Flood. It is true that the Ponsonbys did not reap similar rewards in the 1770s, but Flood was in no position to challenge their command of freehold votes.[36]

Election fever was already at a high pitch in County Kilkenny when the proclamation announcing the poll was promulgated on 30 April 1776.[37] Unlike 1768, when Flood had enhanced his chances by joining forces with Edmund Butler, it was clear early on that this would not be repeated in 1776, and that the best he could hope for would be the second seat in a three-cornered contest. However, it soon emerged that Flood would be hard-pressed to poll even second, for following the announcement of his candidature *in absentia* on 21 March 1775, similar announcements were made by the sitting members – John Ponsonby and James Agar.[38] Flood and his rivals offered periodic reminders to freeholders of their candidature while they awaited the dissolution of parliament, but Flood was visibly less adept than they at massaging local opinion. It is salient, for example, that his presence in Dublin prevented him 'from paying his personal respects' to gentlemen and freeholder voters at the assizes in August 1775, that he was not among the contributors to the collection for the establishment of a house of industry in Kilkenny (John Ponsonby, James Agar and John Butler each made substantial donations), and that he did not emulate Ponsonby in contributing to the relief of poor families in the county. Compared with this, appeals in the press to the 'gentlemen, clergy and freeholders' to 'keep themselves disengaged until he has an opportunity of waiting upon them' were lame and ineffectual.[39]

On his return to Farmley in September 1775, Flood sought to animate his campaign with an address 'to the gentlemen, clergy and freeholders of the county' in which he appealed that his 'past services to you will not be forgotten', but he continued to trail John Ponsonby in fostering local support.[40] His hopes were boosted momentarily by the announcement by the soon to be ennobled James Agar in November that he was withdrawing from the election in favour of his 'near relation' George Agar, whose father Flood had killed in 1769. This might have worked to Flood's advantage had Edmund Butler, 'many' of whose 'friends' were committed to support James but not George Agar, not taken advantage of James Agar's enno-

to North, 25 Oct 1779 (B.L., Mackintosh Collection, Add. Ms 34523 f 266); Power, 'Parliamentary representation', pp 308–9.   36 Harcourt to Weymouth, 4 May (P.R.O., S.P., 63/453 ff 253–68); Hunt, ed., *The Irish parliament in 1775*, p. 1; Harcourt to North, 21 Apr. 1776 in *Harcourt Papers*, x, 138–9; *H.J.*, 21 Apr. 1775; *F.L.J.*, 1 May 1776.   37 *F.L.J.*, 4 Jan. 1775, 4 May 1776.   38 *H.J.*, 18 Mar.; *F.L.J.*, 22 Mar. 1, 26 Apr. 1775.   39 *F.L.J.*, 7 June, 9, 23, 26 Aug.; *H.J.*, 4 Aug. 1775, 10 July 1776.   40 *F.L.J.*, 6, 16, 27 Sept. 9 Dec. 1775, 13 Jan., 3, 10 Feb. 1776; Almon's *Narrative*, p. 98.

blement to announce his candidacy. As the eldest son of Lord Mountgarret and brother-in-law of Lord Carrick (who was one of the wealthiest landowners in County Kilkenny) Butler was well-connected, and his entry into the race seems to have destroyed George Agar's hopes as he did not sustain his candidature. The contest now was between three men but, before Flood could take advantage of this, John Ponsonby moved to eliminate the possibility of a voting pact disadvantageous to him by concluding an agreement with Butler that he would not enter into any such arrangement.[41] To compound Flood's difficulties, he had also to combat the mounting suspicion that attached itself to him as an officeholder,[42] and family problems which reduced the Floods' electoral effectiveness.

The full history of Henry Flood's relations with his family is beyond recovery. What is incontrovertible is that the unity of purpose that bound his father and uncles and that contributed to their electoral success was not replicated by his own, and that the death of several members of his parental generation in the late 1760s and early 1770s exposed deepening cleavages that contributed to the enfeeblement of the Floods' political influence in County Kilkenny. The death of John Flood of Floodhall in September 1774 certainly contributed to the emergence of differences between Henry and his irascible cousin John, who had represented the borough of Callan with him since 1768. The precise cause of their estrangement is not immediately identifiable. It may have been financial since John Flood seems to have had money worries, but the propriety of Flood's possession of the Farmley estate also lurked beneath the surface.[43] What is certain is that existing differences were heightened by Henry's anger that John did not support him in 1776, and that this led to bitter recrimination as one of Henry's few surviving letters to his cousin attests:

> You say I talk as if the last opportunity in the county for exertion was not attended to; I do say it was not by you. My interest on that occasion was undone by you. I wrote to you from England to lay aside those foolish family animosities with which you abound, and to have family meetings for the purpose of arranging and canvassing the county. You did not do so. You took my advertisement for the county out of the papers just at the time of the assizes ... During the poll, you attended the Carlow election more than the Kilkenny one as a lawyer, nor did you canvas nor consult, nor scarce dine with me or my friends during that season, and the returns of your agent, which you mention, were so incorrect that they were at best useless.

41 *F.L.J.*, 13 Sept., 8, 22 Nov. 1775; Cromie list 1776–82 (B.L., Pelham Papers, Add. Ms 33118); Harcourt list, Jan. 1777 (D.P.L., Harcourt Papers, Gilbert Ms 94 f 235); Power, 'Parliamentary representation', p. 309; Day, 'Irish Catholics', pp 115, 118; Henry to John Flood, [post 1776] (R.I.A., Burrowes Papers, Ms 23K53/10). 42 *H.J.*, 6, 8 May 1776. 43 *F.L.J.*, 14 Sept. 1774, 8 Feb. 1775; Hunt, ed., *Irish parliament*, p. 21; Keane et al., eds, *King's Inns admission papers*, p. 171; John to Frederick Flood, 17 Nov. 1776 (B.L., Valentia Papers, Add. Ms 19349 ff 15–16).

Worse than that, Henry alleged that John discouraged his brother Francis, the High Sheriff, from advancing his cause at the poll for County Kilkenny:

> He [Francis] made a return ag[ain]st me and did nothing that any sheriff not inimical wou'd not do except giving me the jury rooms. He was in an office in which I wou'd not ask him to be partial and he knows I never did. He was told at the time indeed that you reproached him with partiality and abused him for counterfeiting sickness. If he had been partial to me, it wou'd not be to you I should have referred it, for you were upon bad terms with him at the time, as you have been at dif[feren]t periods with your mother, sister and almost all your nearest relations.

Henry was not in a strong position to lecture his cousin on correct familial behaviour. But citing the electoral support he received from another (unnamed) cousin, he appealed for family harmony while absolving himself of any culpability for the unsatisfactory state of his relations with his cousins:

> There is not one of my name whom I have not always wished to prosper. I think relationship should increase not diminish friendship – people have rivals and enemies enough elsewhere not to seek for them at home. The family have sometimes mistaken a spirit of discord for a spirit of independence. They have weakened themselves by it. As to me, I was in a situation to suffer the least by it, having as little interest or temptation as any man alive to give myself the trouble I have done on that subject. I thank God I have nothing to ask or fear, though I have sense enough not to think more of a man being my relative if he does not behave as my friend.[44]

These fine sentiments would have rang more true if Flood had patched up his differences with his cousin. Instead, the ill-feeling between the two men endured because of this and differences arising out a number of obscure financial transactions well into the next decade.[45]

As his row with John Flood attests, the contest for County Kilkenny in 1776 proved another unhappy electoral experience for Henry Flood. He performed creditably in the poll which commenced on 20 May, but he always trailed his rivals. In a desperate attempt to boost his stuttering cause he published a notice in *Finn's Leinster Journal* on 25 May entreating 'the attendance and support of his friends, who have

---

44 Henry to John Flood, [post 1776] (R.I.A., Burrowes Papers, Ms 23K 53/10).   45 Ibid; John to Henry Flood, 29 Apr. 1780 (T.C.D., MUN/P/1/1383/9); G.O. Sayles, ed., 'The Irish parliament in 1782', *R.I.A. proc.*, 56C (1954), p. 252; Manuscript account of Irish parliament in 1782, p. 135 (Henry Huntingdon Library); Flood to Carlisle, 12 Sept. [1783] in H.M.C., *Carlisle*, p. 637.

not yet poll'd'.[46] At that point he had 199 votes, Butler 230 and John Ponsonby 240, but as the margin between Butler and he grew daily, he had little option but to withdraw, which he did on Tuesday the 28th. He had registered 248 votes, but Edmund Butler had 285 and John Ponsonby 300. All three candidates maintained they had a substantial number of freeholders still to poll (Butler claimed he had 270, Ponsonby 100 and Flood 86). But it is clear that the result which, significantly, Flood did not invite the sheriff to scrutinise, accurately reflected the relative weight if not, necessarily, the full voting strength of the contending parties.[47]

Having failed in County Kilkenny, Flood turned his attention to Callan, but he was in a weak position there too. He supported his claim that his was the only legitimate authority in the borough by overseeing the appointment annually in the mid-1770s of Ambrose Smith as sovereign of a Flood-controlled borough authority, but his only real chance of success rested on the Agars responding to the elevation of James Agar to the peerage by withdrawing from Callan and they had absolutely no intention of doing this.[48] Determined, nonetheless, to do what was possible to improve his electoral chances and those of his friend, Hercules Langrishe, Flood enjoined the High Sheriff to give the election precept to Smith rather than to Arthur Webb, who led the Agar-controlled corporation. Francis Flood complied, but when Smith, attended by burgesses and freeman in the Flood family interest, attempted to hold an election on 8 May, Webb demanded the precept was given to him and publicly swore the requisite oaths to oversee the election of Pierce Butler, the youngest son of the earl of Carrick, and George Agar, the eldest son of James Agar. Smith refused to give way, and a confused poll ensued in which he, allegedly, 'improperly rejected' several votes cast for Butler and Agar and pronounced Flood and Langrishe elected. Unwilling to accede to this, Webb declared Butler and Agar elected, which meant that the representation for Callan would be decided once again by an election petition committee in the House of Commons.[49]

As the invalidation of his election for Callan would leave him without a parliamentary seat, Flood was greatly disappointed by the outcome of the 1776 general election. Things would not, he concluded, have come to this sorry pass if the Harcourt administration had seen its way to aid him as it did John Scott and Charles O'Hara. This was a rather ungrateful conclusion since Harcourt had clearly sought to advantage him in both Callan and County Kilkenny. The problem for Flood, as the result in both constituencies attested, was that ministerial influence alone could not

46 *F.L.J.*, 11, 18, 22, 25 May 1776.   47 These figures differ slightly from those provided by Power ('Parliamentary representation', p. 308); see *F.L.J.*, 29 May, 1 June; *H.J.*, 31 May 1776.   48 Above p 60; *Commons Jn. (Irl.)*, ix, 312; N.L.I., Heron Papers, Ms 3532; Burtchaell, *Kilkenny members*, pp 148–9; Manuscript account of the Irish parliament in 1782 (Henry Huntington Library).   49 Henry to John Flood, [post 1776] (R.I.A., Burrowes Papers, Ms 23K 53/10); *Commons Jn. (Irl.)*, ix, 312; *F.L.J.*, 15 May; *H.J.*, 17 May 1776; Burtchaell, *Kilkenny members*, pp 148–9; Manuscript account of the Irish parliament in 1782 (Henry Huntington Library); Cromie list 1776–82 (B.L., Pelham Papers, Add. Ms 33118).

achieve what he desired. This left purchase or petition as his only options and, since Flood was disinclined to spend the estimated £2,000 to £2,500 it cost to purchase a seat,[50] he moved to have the election of Edmund Butler for County Kilkenny over-turned on the grounds that he had resorted to 'threats, undue influence, entertain-ments and every other species of bribery and corruption'. Given that he faced a petition against his return for Callan, Flood may have felt this improved his chances of securing a seat for one the two constituencies for which he had sat throughout his parliamentary career to date. The two petitions were presented to the House of Commons on 19 and 20 June 1776, when the newly elected MPs gathered to chose a Speaker (Pery was re-elected) and to ratify the 'Privy Council' money bills trans-mitted in accordance with the provisions of Poynings' law. This was achieved with-out controversy,[51] and in Flood's absence as he was indisposed. Anyhow, since it was not clear what, if any, constituency he would represent in the new parliament, he was in something of a limbo situation. Things were to remain thus for some time as neither his nor any other petitions were scheduled to be heard until the parliament reassembled in October 1777.

FLOOD AND BUCKINGHAMSHIRE – TROUBLED BEGINNINGS

Flood's problematic parliamentary position following the 1776 general election was not animadverted upon by Lord Harcourt whose priority was to resign a 'station' he 'no longer' felt 'able to sustain'. Lord North agreed to his request to leave Ireland with great reluctance, because the only willing replacement he could find was the ambitious, ineffectual, punctilious and peevish earl of Buckinghamshire who had served without distinction as ambassador to St Petersburg.[52] Unlike when Townshend and Harcourt were appointed, Flood made no attempt to establish an avenue of communication with the new Lord Lieutenant via Bishop Markham. It maybe that Markham's recent dismissal as tutor to the Prince of Wales and his controversial sermon to the Society for the Propagation of the Gospel meant there was little point, but it seems also that Flood expected the new Lord Lieutenant to approach him. Certainly, one is struck by the fact that whereas Edmond Sexten Pery and John Hely-Hutchinson promptly fired off letters of congratulation and offers of support

50 A.R. Black, ed., *An edition of the Cavendish Irish parliamentary diary 1776–8* (3 vols, Delavan, 1985), i, 18; *H.J.*, 23 Oct. 1775.   51 Black, ed., *Cavendish's parl. diary*, ii, 2–13; *H.J.*, 21 June; *F.L.J.*, 26 June; *Commons Jn. (Irl.)*, ix, 298, 315; Harcourt to Weymouth, 18, 19, 20 June (P.R.O., S.P.63/454 ff 180, 203, 205); Harcourt to North, 18, 19 June 1776 (D.P.L., Harcourt Papers, Gilbert Ms 93 ff 424–5).   52 [Harcourt] to North, 21 June (D.P.L., Harcourt Papers, Gilbert Ms 93 ff 426–7); North to Harcourt, 29 June 1776 (N.L.I., Harcourt letterbook Ms 755 f 109); Buckinghamshire to Hotham Thompson, 4 July (Hotham Papers, P.R.O.N.I., T3429/1/1); *The royal register with annotations* (9 vols, London, 1779–84), iv, 106–10; *Last Journals of Horace Walpole* ed., A.F. Steuart (2 vols, London, 1910), i, 589–90.

to Buckinghamshire, and others, who 'long viewed every lord lieutenant with a suspicious eye', travelled to the Castle to greet him on his arrival in January 1777, Flood did neither. He gave people to understand that his absence was due to illness, but the fact that he was well enough to seek answers to queries appertaining to the payment of his salary as vice-treasurer suggests that this was just an excuse.[53]

The payment of Flood's salary was not an inconsequential issue because the teller of the exchequer, Sir Henry Cavendish (who died in 1776), had allowed the affairs of the office fall into such disorder that a sum of £135,999 (£1,500 of which was owed to Flood) was outstanding at the end of that year. To complicate matters further, there were problems implementing the decision of the Irish parliament providing for enhanced salaries for the vice-treasurers and the clerk of the pells, and appointing William Burton Conyngham as Cavendish's successor and Henry Theophilus Clements as deputy vice-treasurer.[54] Flood wisely kept these matters at a distance. Nonetheless, he was pleased that the 'superintendence' of the office of vice-treasurer was entrusted to Clements, whom he regarded highly, and he was unfailingly courteous in his dealings with him and correct in his attention to his own modest duties.[55]

Flood's was equally correct in his expressions of sympathy with Bishop Markham following his embarrassing dismissal from the Royal Household in 1776. He was gracious also in his somewhat belated reply to Lord Charlemont's communication that he had become a father. Charlemont accepted Flood's excuse that illness was the reason for his tardiness in characteristically generous fashion. But Flood's refusal 'to tell me how you are, what you are doing, and how the world goes', and his failure to respond to further communications in which Charlemont openly avowed how greatly he valued Flood's friendship indicates that Flood's acceptance of office had created a gulf between the two men. It also illustrates well how cavalier and neglectful Flood could be of others when it did not suit his immediate needs.[56]

---

53 Markham to Flood, 25 June 1776, 10 Aug. 1777 (Rosse Papers, C/2/28, 29); Rockingham to Markham, 21 Feb. 1777 (S.C.L., Wentworth-Woodhouse Mss, Rockingham Papers, R1-1713); Pery to Buckinghamshire, 30 Nov., Hely Hutchinson to Buckinghamshire, 5 Dec. in H.M.C.*Lothian*, p. 297; Buckinghamshire to Hotham Thompson, 11 Mar. 1777 (Hotham Papers, P.R.O.N.I., T3429/1/8); Charlemont to Flood, 30 Sept. in R[odd], ed., *Letters to Flood*, pp 92–3; Flood to Clements, 10 Aug. 1776 (T.C.D., Clements Papers, Ms 1743/40). 54 Clerk of the Pells report in regard to Sir Henry Cavendish's affairs, 31 Dec.(T.C.D., Clements Papers, Ms 7302/ 11); North to Harcourt, 24 Nov. (N.L.I., Harcourt letterbook, Ms 755 f 113); Jenkinson to Ellis, 8 Oct., Jenkinson to Harcourt, 20 Nov., Jenkinson to Scott, 7 Dec. 1776, 9 Jan. 1777, Jenkinson to Harcourt, 13 Dec. 1776, Jenkinson to Waite, 14 Feb. 1777 (B.L., Liverpool Papers, Add. Ms 38306 ff 39, 44, 47–9, 51, 55, 58); Harcourt to North, 5 Dec. in *Harcourt Papers*, x, 220; Blaquiere to Clements, 21 Jan. 1776, 3, 8,12 Jan. 1777 (T.C.D., Clements Papers, Mss 1742/85, 86, 1743/43, 45); Entry book for fees on patents (B.L., Add. Ms 23711 f 121). 55 Flood to Clements, 11 Jan., 24 July, Burton to Clements, 7 Apr.(T.C.D., Clements Papers, Ms 1743/44, 56, 49); Townshend to Flood, 29 June 1777 in R[odd], ed., *Letters to Flood*, pp 97–8. 56 Markham to Flood, 25 June 1776 (Rosse Papers, C/2/28); Charlemont to Flood, 13 Aug., 30 Sept. 1776, 22 Jan. 1777 in R[odd], ed., *Letters to Flood*, pp 92–3, 95–6, Rosse Papers, C/1/11.

Flood's unwillingness to discuss his situation with Lord Charlemont and his reticence with the earl of Buckinghamshire inevitably prompted speculation as to his intentions. According to one report, which reached the ears of George III, his ambition was to bind himself more closely to the government and to support Lord North by taking a seat at Westminster. Others conjectured that he was so disillusioned by the experience of having 'his treachery to his country ... constantly rung in his ears' that he 'solicited for and obtained the promise of a peerage, by the title of *Lord Baron Gowran*'. Neither claim was accurate, though the fact that he was appointed to the British Privy Council in the autumn encouraged thinking along these lines. Ironically, given the comment to the contrary, Flood's prospects of satisfying his ambition to become a Westminster MP at this time had been damaged by his disappointing electoral performance in Ireland because it excited concern in ministerial circles at his retaining the vice-treasurership while 'out of parliament'. Indeed, John Robinson advised George III in October that it would neither be 'prudent' nor advantageous to further his ambition to secure Westminster representation 'since it might not make him more dependent than being only in the Irish parliament' and the King concurred.[57] In the circumstances, Flood could be forgiven for wishing after the less complicated world of opposition, but the fact that he continued to be demonised in the popular press as treacherous, corrupt and 'an apostate' indicated that this was hardly a feasible option.[58]

Such vehement comment was fuelled by the disimproving domestic economy, though the prime foci of public and political resentment remained the embargo on trade (which was reinforced by additional restrictions in October 1776) and the war in America.[59] Behind the scenes, Sir Lucius O'Brien, and Lord North's Irish-born adviser, William Knox assayed how the restrictions on Ireland's freedom to trade within the empire might be eased, but Flood's acceptance of the vice-treasurership deprived him of O'Brien's political confidence, and he was not privy to these discussions.[60] The issue of most pressing concern for him at this moment was the shape the new administration would take.

On his arrival in Ireland in January 1777, the earl of Buckinghamshire was encouraged by Thomas Conolly, to whom he was related by marriage, and the duke of Leinster, whom he won over by restoring him to the Irish Privy Council, to 'discard ... everything that belongs to Lord Harcourt'.[61] He did not go quite so far, but he

57 Robinson to George III and reply, 7 Oct. 1776 (B.L. Robinson Papers, Add. Ms 37833 ff 79–80, 216).
58 *H.J.*, 27 Sept. 1775, 16 Aug., 14 Oct., 1 Nov., 4 Dec. 1776, 12, 22 Jan. 1777; *F.L.J.*, 2 Oct. 1776; Buckinghamshire to Germain, 27 June 1777 (N.L.I., Heron Papers, Ms 13035/7).   59 *F.L.J.*, 29 June., 23 Nov.; *H.J.*, 13, 15 Nov. 1776; Weymouth to Harcourt, 26 Oct., Text of Proclamation, 26 Oct., Harcourt to Weymouth, 2, 7, 15 Nov. 1776 (P.R.O., S.P., 63/455 ff 115–18, 140, 156, 170, 180–2).   60 William Knox, 'Proceedings in relation to the American colonies' 1774–5, O'Brien to Knox, 7 July, 30 Sept. 1776 in H.M.C., *Knox Papers*, pp 258, 232–3   61 Conolly to Buckinghamshire, 27 Nov. (N.L.I., Heron Papers, Ms 13034/2); duke to duchess of Leinster, 15 Dec. 1776 (N.L.I., Fitzgerald Papers, Ms 13022/45); Jenkinson to Heron, 12, 20 Feb. (N.A., Index of departmental letters and papers 1760–89 f 359);

spent the nine months between his arrival and the opening of the 1777–8 session constructing a 'broad-bottomed' administration in which Philip Tisdall, the aged Attorney General, assisted by Walter Hussey Burgh, the new Prime Serjeant, John Scott, the Solicitor General, and John Foster, who was promised 'some office of business' when there was a suitable vacancy, would direct the Castle connection in the House of Commons.[62] This was a potentially effective combination, though the neglect of John Hely-Hutchinson and Henry Flood was risky. Hely-Hutchinson's omission is attributable to his ongoing feud with Tisdall, while the main reason for Flood's exclusion was his failure to establish contact with the Lord Lieutenant which caused the administration to conclude that he intended opposing in the Commons.[63] Buckinghamshire certainly had no intention of pursuing him. He had, he pronounced in March, secured offers of support from 'all the great leaders of parties' which rendered it 'unnecessary for me to court little men and to attend to their little interests'.[64] As a result, when Flood belatedly communicated his 'joy' on Buckinghamshire's arrival in Ireland on 3 February, in a letter whose primary purpose was to secure the appointment of his nominee to the shrievalty of County Kilkenny, he suffered the indignity of having the request denied. Buckinghamshire adjudged that this would demonstrate to Flood that vice-regal goodwill could not be assumed; in fact, it served merely to antagonize. By the terms of his agreement with Harcourt, Flood believed he was entitled to nominate to the shrievalty, and Buckinghamshire's refusal to honour his request caused him to conclude that the new administration was not prepared to abide by its terms. Indeed, following this exchange, Flood made no further early attempt to contact Dublin Castle. Buckinghamshire did assure an anxious Lord George Germain, the secretary of state for the colonies, in June that 'care' would 'be taken to press' Flood to acquire a seat in parliament if he failed to prevail in one of the two election petitions in which he was involved, but no meeting took place.[65] Quite the contrary; the absence even of reference to him in official correspondence during the summer indicates that he figured little, if at all, in Buckinghamshire's calculations.

The exclusion of Flood and Hely-Hutchinson, two of the Irish House of Commons ablest parliamentary performers, from the ranks of the Castle interest ought to have emboldened the patriots, but they could perceive little reason for optimism. The defection of Hussey Burgh, and the realisation that they were unlikely to mus-

---

Harcourt to Weymouth, 25 Jan. 1777 (P.R.O., S.P. 63/456 f 55). **62** Buckinghamshire's vindication (Lothian Papers, P.R.O.N.I., T3502/1 part 1); Germain to Buckinghamshire, 12 Feb. (N.L.I., Heron Papers, Ms 13052/1); Heron to Robinson [1777] (Ms 13035/5); Buckinghamshire to Weymouth, 3, 8 July 1777 (P.R.O., S.P., 63/457 ff 181, 183–4). **63** Buckinghamshire's vindication, f 6; Robinson to Buckinghamshire, 18, 27 June, 15 July (N.L.I., Heron Papers, Ms 13035/7); Kelly, *That damn'd thing called honour*, pp 167–8; Buckinghamshire to Germain, 14 June (Ms 13035/6); State of the House of Commons of Ireland in Jan 1777 (D.P.L., Harcourt Papers, Gilbert Ms 94 f 316). **64** Buckinghamshire to Hotham Thompson, 11 Mar. 1777 (Hotham Papers, P.R.O.N.I., T3429/1/8). **65** Buckinghamshire to Germain, 27 June 1777 (N.L.I., Heron papers, Ms 13035/7).

ter more than eighty votes in any division when MPs assembled suggested to them that the Castle would prevail comfortably, though the intensifying economic crisis caused by decreased commercial activity, bad weather and rising rent arrears offered the opposition a series of ready targets.[66] Buckinghamshire, by contrast, was quietly optimistic. He was hopeful that 'some further expedient indulgence to the commerce of Ireland', which he authorised 'two or three well-informed, judicious men' to consider, would enable him to overcome any difficulties he might encounter in the Commons. And he was confident that the steps he was taking to bolster the kingdom's defences and to combat the activities of American privateers would win him goodwill, as reports in July suggested that 'the French are not inclined to quarrel with us this year'. At the same time, given his awareness of the need to be ever ready for 'a equinoctial gale though no quarter is foreseen from whence it may come', his failure even to seek a meeting with Flood to clear the air prior to the opening of parliament was an act of political folly that set the tone for the troubled relationship they shared throughout the late 1770s.[67]

This was not immediately apparent as there was no 'gale' in the short term, but the crew Buckinghamshire had assembled to negotiate the reefs and rapids of the parliamentary session lost its first mate even before the session commenced when Philip Tisdall succumbed to illness in September. This seriously disrupted Buckinghamshire's plans, and forced him to look for someone new to undertake the onerous task of presenting Castle business in the Commons. This represented a further opportunity for Flood, but he gave no indication that he was willing and the Lord Lieutenant made no overtures to him about his services. Indeed, prospects of Flood joining the administration were disimproved by Buckinghamshire's decision to entrust the responsibility of leading the Castle connection to the new Attorney General, John Scott, because Flood and he were long time Commons' antagonists.[68]

The fact that Flood, who was an abler orator than both Tisdall and Scott, was passed over twice within such a short space of time is a measure of the depth of the chasm that emerged between him and Dublin Castle in the year following Harcourt's departure. This point is reinforced by the fact that the administration even considered the inexperienced Barry Yelverton as a more likely spokesman in the House of

66 *F.L.J.*, 6, 13 July; duke to duchess of Leinster, 26 June (N.L.I., Fitzgerald Papers, Ms 13033/49); Baker to Harrison, 30 June (N.L.I., Baker Papers, Ms 21004/1); Buckingham to Weymouth, 20 June, 12 July 1777, enclosing petition of Cork and Dublin merchants (P.R.O., S.P.63/457 ff 147, 217–19). 67 Buckinghamshire to Hotham Thompson, [7] Apr., 18 July (Hotham Papers, P.R.O.N.I., T3429/1/9, 12); Statement on trade by Sackville Hamilton, Apr., Memorandum on exports, Apr. in H.M.C., *Lothian*, pp 301–4, 306–10; O'Brien to Knox, 5 Aug. in H.M.C., *Knox Papers*, p. 233. Buckinghamshire to Weymouth, 29 Apr., May, 25, 29, 30 June, 2, 8 July (P.R.O., S.P., 63/457 ff 17, 36–69, 143–6, 149–51, 161–3, 171–7, 194–202); *H.J.*, 7 July 1777. 68 *H.J.*, 26 Sept.; Buckinghamshire to Germain, 20 Sept., 2 Oct. (N.L.I., Heron Papers, Ms 13035/11, 12); Buckinghamshire to Weymouth, 27 Sept. 1777 (P.R.O., S.P., 63/458 f 85–8).

Commons.[69] Of course, Flood's value to the administration was diminished as long as there was uncertainty about his parliamentary status, but this was not an insuperable obstacle to a determined administration and it does not explain their lack of contact.

Flood was understandably anxious that his electoral fate was determined as soon as possible. He believed it would be to his advantage if his petition against the return of Edmund Butler for County Kilkenny was heard before the petition against his return for Callan. However, when his cousin Frederick, who now represented the borough of Enniscorthy, presented his petition against the return for County Kilkenny on 15 October, neither Warden Flood nor he were able to secure agreement that it should be heard on 30 October, as they requested. It was scheduled instead for 17 November – ten days after the hearing of the Callan petition.[70] There was nothing sinister about this, but Flood was upset that his wishes had not been heeded. He kept a low profile, though the administration could have done with his support as they struggled, during the opening weeks of the session, to come to terms with the combined oratorical power of Barry Yelverton, Barry Barry, Denis Daly, Sir William Osborne, George Ogle and the precocious Henry Grattan. To make matters worse, the Castle interest's equilibrium, and hence their effectiveness, was disturbed by the presence in their midst of patriots like Hussey Burgh, though this lack of solidity did not undermine their majority, and they suffered no embarrassing defeats during the opening weeks of the session.[71]

As the elected MP for Callan until the Commons adjudged otherwise, Flood was free to attend the House throughout November. His time was largely occupied with 'petition business' but, as ever, he was not prepared to allow any untoward reflections on his character or reputation pass unnoticed. Arising out of this, his first recorded contribution of the session, on 8 November, was an attempt to defend the Harcourt administration and himself against the imputation of corruption. However, his comments in this respect were less important than the distance he sought to put between himself and the Castle:

> I do not rise up as the profess'd panegyrist of that administration. I do not make myself responsible for that administration. I never was the minister. I never had the ostentation of a minister about me. I suffer'd the oracle of the administration to make its own responses.[72]

These sentiments did not come as a surprise to the Buckinghamshire administra-

---

69 Heron to Robinson, 13 Oct. 1777 (N.L.I., Heron Papers, Ms 13035/12). 70 Black, ed., *Cavendish's parl. diary*, ii, 17–20. 71 Black, ed., *Cavendish's parl. diary*, ii, 20ff; Buckinghamshire to Heron, 13 Oct.(N.L.I., Heron Papers, Ms 13035/12); Buckinghamshire's vindication, P.R.O.N.I.,T3502/1 part 1); Beresford to Allan, 14 Oct. in *Beresford Corres*, i, 16–20; Buckinghamshire to Weymouth, 1 Nov. (P.R.O., S.P., 63/458 f 164); *H.J.*, 15, 25 Aug. 1777. 72 Black, ed., *Cavendish's parl. diary*, ii, 79–80.

tion, which had already concluded that Flood was 'little inclined to the service of government'. They were simply relieved that he was disposed to be 'moderate' and was 'very much occupied' by the Kilkenny election petitions.[73]

The determination of Flood's electoral fate began in earnest on 7 November when a committee was appointed to decide the return for Callan. It was normal practice, once an election committee was chosen, for it to get down to business quickly. But since Flood believed he was entitled to have the return for County Kilkenny adjudged first, he requested MPs to respect his wishes by claiming, on 8 November, that it was not the practice either at Westminster or at College Green that petitions delivered together were heard in the sequence in which they were 'read', and that the House of Commons had erred on 15 October when it decided that the County Kilkenny petition should be heard after, rather than before, that concerning Callan. The House agreed, but since the adjudication of the Callan petition was already underway it did not prove personally advantageous.[74]

As with most contested election petition hearings, the deliberations of the Callan election committee do not survive. However its report has, and its determination (announced on 25 November) that Pierce Butler and George Agar were duly elected was a decision Flood found difficult to accept. He was offered a glimmer of hope that the result might be overturned when, on 26 November, Sir Hercules Langrishe and Sir Richard Annesley challenged the report on the grounds that the committee chairman, Sydenham Singleton, did not vote when the final decision was taken, but they were ruled out of order.[75] With this went any realistic hope Flood entertained of bringing the corporation of Callan under family control once again, and the celebrations that followed in the borough suggests that it was the preference of the residents. This setback was compounded by the decision a few days later to deny Flood's petition against the return of Edmund Butler for County Kilkenny.

A month before the commencement of the 1777–8 session, the *Hibernian Journal* reported that Henry Flood had been killed in duel with Edmund Butler. The report was wrong, as the newspaper later acknowledged, but the implication that relations between Flood and Butler were badly strained was correct, and following the tabling of Flood's petition, in which he maintained that Butler had obtained his election by 'evil and corrupt practices', they deteriorated further.[76] Butler objected so strongly to Flood's charges that he took the unusual step of inviting him to withdraw it. Flood was taken aback by what he deemed a 'very improper' request and, anticipating a challenge, he appealed to the Commons for protection on 3 November. This was forthcoming when he assured the Speaker that he would not fight 'another gentleman', but recognizing that he had been given a gilt-edged opportu-

73 Tighe to Eden, 12 Aug. 1781 in H.M.C., *Carlisle*, pp 514–16.   74 *Commons. Jn. (Irl.)*, ix, 337; Black, ed., *Cavendish's parl. diary*, ii, 90–1.   75 *Commons. Jn. (Irl.)*, ix, 342, 375; Black, ed., *Cavendish's parl. diary*, iii, 341–4; Burtchaell, *Kilkenny members*, p. 148; Cavendish's parl diary, v, 1–3 (Library of Congress).   76 *H.J.*, 8, 15 Sept. 1775; *Commons Jn. (Irl.)*, ix, 315.

nity to embarrass his rival and, perhaps, to advantage his petition, he made a full statement to the Commons on his role in what was, he maintained nine days later, 'a dispute of right':

> I petitioned the house with regard to the County of Kilkenny ... The hon. member, against who I petition'd, applied to me upon this subject in a manner I thought very improper. He sent to me to withdraw that petition. Had I ever made any promise, or engagement of honour to do it, I should have done it instantly. I desir'd to know if I had made any promise. But in my apprehension, sir, the idea of any gentleman sending to another to say, you have a dispute of right with me, that you shall not dispute it by right, but by force is a thing so intolerable in a civilis'd country that it can't too soon meet with a rebuke. In justice to the Hon. Gent., I must say, he never sent any message to me to meet him in arms; he never sent any insulting letter. A message was sent to me, if I did not withdraw that petition, I should be insulted. When the House were occupied upon this subject the other night, I had not the honour of having taken my seat, otherwise I should have risen to say that I apprehended it was unnecessary for the House to interfere. It was my original, and unalterable determination, *that no man alive sho'd take a dispute of right and alter it to a dispute of force*; no man has a right to do that. The man that attempts to do it does not act under the laws of honour. Were a man just enter'd the world, it is a sentiment I should avoid in the face of the world. I think it becomes every man to do so; it is nothing but a pusillanimity in every man to do otherwise. I have not the smallest apprehension that any man would think I am influenc'd by personal apprehension; there is not a man of whom I am afraid. But there is a tyranny in this, that any man should be subjected to say you have a good cause and therefore the goodness of your cause shall be an injury. I do not mean to say anything disrespectful of the Hon Gent. I don't wish to think anything personally hard. I wish to have this subject stated, that the mind of gentlemen may be taken and satisfied upon it, and that it may not rest upon my private judgement.[77]

Flood's account of his dealings with Butler won him considerable applause. However, it did not influence the outcome of his election petition. The committee established under the chairmanship of William Brownlow on 17 November determined that Butler was duly elected, and it reported to that effect on 27 November.[78]

This judgement meant that Flood was in the market for a parliamentary seat, and he availed of the opportunity afforded by the elevation to the Lords of Sir Archibald Acheson, who had been returned to represent the borough of Enniskillen

---

77 Black, ed., *Cavendish's parl diary*, ii, 48, 94–5.   78 *Commons Jn. (Irl.)*, ix, 357, 360, 377; Black, ed., *Cavendish's parl. diary*, ii, 115, iii, 341.

in 1776, to purchase the vacant seat from Lord Mountflorence.[79] There is no information on how much he paid, but since the current market price was £2,000 or more, it is unlikely he received it for less. It was a chastening experience for a man whose pride was so strong and ambition so great, but, having failed to secure his return in Kilkenny, it was the price he had to pay if he wished to remain a participant in the political world in which he had vested so much.

Despite the heavy demand on his time caused by his engagement with two election petition hearings, Flood did participate in a number of Commons' debates before he took his seat for Enniskillen. As in 1775–6, he did not propose motions or initiate debates. His practice was to make brief statements on matters of current debate (as instanced by his opposition to an attempt by Barry Barry on 12 November 1777 to secure information on the Privy Council oath[80]), and to reserve his longer contributions for matters appertaining to his own reputation. Criticism of the Harcourt administration fitted the latter category, for nine days after his first record comment of the session, which was on this subject, he advanced a stout defence of Harcourt's government and of his own *bona fides*, while distancing himself further from Sir John Blaquiere, who was the main focus of opposition criticism:

> When I first entered into the support of that administration, I entered into it upon every prospect a man could have of publick advantage. I entered into it upon grounds which I remember in this House I was ready to lay upon the floor of the House of Commons. Would to God I had. I would then have stated what I shall never state now. This however, I will say for that administration that they proposed an idea to you at one time which for a century this country had languish'd after. We saw a phenomenon in this country, the resident gentlemen in this country contending they should have no advantage. (Here Mr Flood mentioned the proposed tax upon absentees, for which he said gentlemen had been speaking and writing for near a century, and when the time came that they had it in their power to grasp it, they considered it as a shadow, and let it go, never to recover it.) Give me leave to say that administration did what is not often to be expected; it made a reduction of not only of parliamentary expenses. I remember it sarcastically said, that the fan of economy had brushed off the pens and paper from the table. It made not only a reduction of parliamentary expenses, it made a more manly step in the retrenchment. It struck even at your establishments. It reduced twelve commissioners, and by that means put an end to a system, that could not have been completed at a less expense than £20,000. It promised economy and performed. I speak with pleasure, because the prom-

79 *Commons Jn. (Irl.)*, ix, 378; Bodkin, ed., 'Notes on the Irish parliament of 1773', p. 192; Falkland, *Parliamentary representation being a political and critical review of all the counties* (Dublin, 1790), p. 36; Sayles, ed., 'The Irish parliament in 1782', p. 282; earl of Belmore, *Parliamentary memoirs of Fermanagh and Tyrone from 1613 to 1885* (Dublin, 1887), pp 67–8.   80 Black, ed., *Cavendish's parl diary*, ii, 98–101.

ise of one administration performed in part may be an omen of another's performance. I say it made a retrenchment in the military expence, lessening the number of regiments – a saving of not much less than £26,000 a year. I have been always cautious in stating the measures of that administration, I find I ought to make it a larger sum. If they laid taxes to the amount of £188,000 they have not yet produced as much as they promised, they have come so near it, are in so rising a state, it is evident the persons who laid these taxes can't be charged with an ignorance of the country, as they are not attended with any particular hardship, it seems they have been laid with ability, and effect.[81]

Exhausted by illness and by the effort involved in making this speech, Flood broke off at this point, uttered as few words of apology and resumed his seat. It was a theatrical conclusion to an effective performance. But because he did something similar on 22 November, officials in the Irish administration became increasingly puzzled by his behaviour. The earl of Buckinghamshire was perplexed. It was, he avowed on 25 November, the conduct of 'one [who] seems inclined to be hostile'.[82]

The Lord Lieutenant's impatience with Flood and, indeed, Hely-Hutchinson, 'for the purchase of whose abilities former administrations have paid the highest price', increased in December as news of France's treaty with the American colonists filtered through, and the opposition successfully exploited the impact of the embargo on domestic economic activity.[83] On 17 December, for instance, during a 'disagreeable' debate on the latter subject, Flood left the House before a vote was taken in protest against the fact that he 'had not been sufficiently consulted'. If this suggests that his alienation arose primarily from the absence of communication, the reality was that he was irritated by the administration's refusal to back his 'demands of support in his election'. The precise nature of what he sought from the administration remains elusive,[84] but Buckinghamshire's failure to support his attempt to appeal the decision of the Callan election committee caused him to continue to criticise the embargo throughout December, though he did promise his support when 'the question ... comes on again'.[85] This was a promise Flood may have intended fully to keep, but it is a measure of his dissatisfaction with his position that

---

81 Black, ed., *Cavendish's parl diary*, ii, 142–3.   82 Black, ed., *Cavendish's parl. diary*, ii, 152–244, iii, 251–79; Buckinghamshire to Hotham Thompson, 25 Nov. 1777 (Hotham Papers, P.R.O.N.I., T3429/ 1/15).   83 Buckinghamshire to Hotham Thompson, 25 Nov., 7 Dec. (Hotham Papers, P.R.O.N.I., T3429/1/15–16); Buckinghamshire to Weymouth, 10 Dec. 1777 (P.R.O., S.P., 63/458 ff 263–4); Black, ed., *Cavendish's parl. diary*, iii, 369–425; Cavendish's parl. diary, v, ff 65–77 (Library of Congress).   84 It is not clear whether he had one or both petitions in mind. Callan is the most likely because of the controversy arising out of the final vote on its report, but the *Hibernian Journal* of 3 December suggests it might have been County Kilkenny because there was a delay in producing the finished report.   85 Black, ed., *Cavendish's parl. diary*, iii, 470ff; Heron to Robinson, 17 Dec. (N.L.I., Heron Papers, Ms 13035/15); Lammey, 'Free trade', p. 181; Buckinghamshire to Weymouth, 17 Dec. 1777 (P.R.O., S.P., 63/458 ff 274–5); Jenkinson to Flood, 24 Jan. 1778 (B.L., Liverpool Papers, Add. Ms 38206 ff 81–2).

he appealed once again to William Markham, who had been elevated to the Arch-bishopric of York at the beginning of the year, to establish the government's attitude. His letter has not survived, but from Markham's reply it is clear that Flood felt he was being deliberately excluded from the confidence of an administration he had little respect for, and the victim of jealousy as less-talented men, like John Scott, with whom he could not cooperate, were taken into the administration's confidence. Markham sympathised with Flood's situation. But while he undertook to enquire from Jenkinson and others if there was anything happening behind the scenes to account for 'the strange behaviour' of which Flood complained, he also made it clear that Flood could help himself by supporting the 'King's business' in a more forthright fashion:

> I am exceedingly mortified at the uneasiness you suffer and at the causes of it. I can easily conceive that little men should be jealous of your abilities, and that such a man as Hutchinson should find favour and trust with a jobbing adminis-tration. But I do not see so easily why you ought to be mortified, because I con-sider you as advanced to a higher line, and that though an attention to the public service may reasonably be expected from you, yet no men can expect more from you than belongs to the part which is assigned to you, and that it is of little consequence to you what part they assign. The rank which belongs to your office is a new thing in their system, and they possibly may themselves be cautious of seeming to expect more than you choose to give, especially if they think that you have not been explicit and hearty in offering it. They know very well that they are not your principles and that the administration which you look to must be that of this country, and this alone may beget a jealousy in that temper of mind which delights in cherishing its own creatures, and places its trust in those sor-did motives by which itself is governed.[86]

Markham did not uncover anything to justify Flood's suspicions because there was nothing to be uncovered, but anxious to reconcile him to the Irish administration, he requested Charles Thompson, Buckinghamshire's brother-in-law, to write to the Lord Lieutenant about the matter. It is not clear if Thompson complied, but Flood's refusal to cooperate with John Foster in amending the legislation 'relative to the trial of [controverted] elections' on 17 December suggests that if he did, it made little difference.[87]

Flood held very strong opinions about this legislation because of his recent ex-periences, and on 23 and 25 December he wrote to Charles Jenkinson, having pre-viously sought the advice of John Hatsell, the author of the standard guide to parlia-

86 Markham to Flood, 9, 12 Dec. 1777 (Rosse Papers, C/2/30-1).   87 Cavendish's parl. diary, v, 98-9 (Library of Congress).

mentary procedure, on the wisdom of his appealing the decision of the election committee. Jenkinson offered him no encouragement. 'I conceive ... committees for the trial of elections are courts of supreme judicature from which there is no appeal' he pronounced categorically. The role of the House of Commons was simply to record decisions; it has 'no power ... to question or [to] alter their judgements. They are final, as the judgements of all supreme courts must always be; any injustice they may commit is without remedy; any defect in their form of their proceedings can be judged of only by themselves'. In any event, it was Jenkinson's assessment that it was too late for an appeal: 'if any relief could be given by the House, it could only have been given at the time when the report was made or before when the report was entered and the member who claims under it had taken his seat; I conceive that the House if they had any right to exercise their judgement have thereby given it and that the business is closed'.[88]

This was not what Flood wanted to hear but it did at least help him to overcome the disappointment of the 1776 general election. The problem he had was that little else seemed to go in his favour at this time, as his attempts to advance his request for a seat at Westminster and a 'life office' *in lieu* of the vice-treasurership were both repulsed. Markham, as ever, was eager to facilitate Flood to make the imperial parliament his primary 'theatre'; but neither he nor Jenkinson could offer him more than moral support.[89] Indeed, Markham reiterated his advice that Flood would better enhance his hopes of advancement by co-operating with the administration (which needed firm voices in the Commons) rather than by making unrealistic demands that the current administration should 'fulfil some engagement' made by Lord Harcourt:

> You will forgive me if, with the freedom of a friend, I question the wisdom of such an application at this time. As the matter stood before, whoever hears the story will allow that you had good reason to be dissatisfied with their want of civility and attention, and that degree of respect which your rank and abilities entitle you to. But I am afraid you have now given a colour at least to lay it to ill-humour on your part for not being gratified in demands which, in common opinion, the present Governor will not be thought bound to answer, for it is certainly true that, if he gave a life office in lieu of your present, he would have nothing to [do] with the disposal of it; and you cannot suppose that the plea of your services can have the same weight with the present, as they had with the late, who was benefited by them and had bound himself to reward them. I did not tell you that in the judgement of many people, and those who had no ill-will towards you, the reward which you have got is thought, not only unusual, but for any services in your line of politics excessive. I believe it is right in prudential

88 Jenkinson to Flood, 24 Jan. 1778 (B.L., Liverpool Papers, Add. Ms 38206 ff 81–2). 89 Ibid.; Markham to Flood, 9 Dec. 1777 (Rosse Papers, C/2/30).

decisions to estimate the things by the standard at which the world takes them
...; and nothing in my opinion disgraces a public man more than ... fickleness of
mind ... I should be sorry, too, that in such a moment as this, when this country
is beset with embarrassments, a war with France expected, and everything around
us so critical as to call for union and exertion, not only among the King's servants, but among all honest men, any conduct of yours should put it in the power
of your enemies to say there is a spot on that character which I am confident
before had none.[90]

Flood was not used to such straight-talking and, rather than be guided by it, he
placed his hopes in reports that there would soon be a change of government. This
was clutching at straws. The government may not have been dynamic, but it was
stable. More consequently for his future, both the Lord Lieutenant and Chief Secretary were already tired of his 'dissatisfaction and unreasonable demands'. Richard
Heron even queried in an *aide memoire*, penned on 26 December 1777, 'how far (if
Mr Flood should quarrel with government) we might have a chance of recommending
a successor to his employment'.[91] There is no indication that this was yet being
considered seriously, but its very existence illustrates just how poor relations were
between Flood and Dublin Castle by the end of 1777. Moreover, there was little
support for improvement in 1778 as the focus of political discourse moved onto the
economy and the liberalisation of Ireland's right to trade with Britain and the empire.

CONTINUING DIFFICULTIES

When parliament reassembled in late January 1778, the patriots resumed their attack on the administration where they had left off in December. Henry Grattan,
who was now one of their most active voices, set the tone for the remainder of the
session by giving notice of his intention to ask the Commons to address the King on
the subject of 'the increase of the publick expense and the national ability to bear it'.
Grattan's anxiety on the subject of the kingdom's finances was widely shared. Shortly
before the Commons had gone into recess in December, Speaker Pery had taken the
unusual liberty of addressing the House to inform MPs that 'limiting the expence,
or of extending the trade of this kingdom' were the choices that faced them. The
former was the focus of parliamentary debate in January and early February, and it
put office-holding patriots like Flood and Hussey Burgh in a serious dilemma since
they agreed with many of the opposition's criticisms. Burgh, for example, felt he

90 Markham to Flood, 10 Jan. 1778 (Rosse Papers, C/2/32).   91 Memoranda of Mr Heron, 26 Dec. 1777
(N.L.I., Heron Papers, Ms 13035/16).

could not, in conscience, vote on 2 February against Robert Stewart's motion that 'the expense of the nation had exceeded its income since 1763', though it meant breaking ranks with the Castle which deemed the motion 'an unjust censure upon government'. Flood, by contrast, sought to steer a path between the Castle and the patriots. His declared preference was for 'some method ... of attuning and reconciling ... discordant sentiments', but since there was no prospect of this he determined to oppose the motion. In defence of this action, he offered a detailed analysis of the state of the country's finances, applauded the efforts made in the past by Lord Harcourt and, currently, by Sir Richard Heron to equalise revenue and expenditure and offered the House a motion which simply noted that the exchequer's position would be more 'promising' once the duties recently granted came into effect. However, both his and Robert Stewart's motion were denied.[92]

Though Flood had not acted in concert with the Castle in the House of Commons on 2 February, his conduct suggested that he had not closed his mind to the possibility. However, Buckinghamshire continued to ignore him. Flood was simply too selective and careful with his contributions to attract positive notice from that quarter. He did not, for example, oppose Henry Grattan's motion for an address to George III on the state of the nation on 6 February, though the occasion was tailor-made for him.[93] Given this context, Burgh's return to the fold came as a great relief to the Lord Lieutenant, who had been badly shaken by his defection on 2 February, but it did not solve his problems in the Commons where the Castle connection was regularly 'out-talk[ed]' by the opposition. This served to make Flood's silence, 'except', Denis Daly observed not wholly accurately, 'to convey an oblique censure upon the present administration by praising the last', all the more testing. Indeed, Buckinghamshire's observation on 20 February 1778 that 'Mr Flood is exceedingly out of humour, and indeed from my first knowledge of him, has never been otherwise' suggests that by this date the Lord Lieutenant despaired of securing his support.[94] This was unfortunate because though Flood continued to hope in a change of government setting everything right, he was convinced that he had behaved entirely honourably, and that his continuing commitment 'to have the country governed according to those principles [of "frugal government and constitutional liberty"] which he had previously maintained' offered a solid basis for a long and productive relationship with Dublin Castle.[95]

92 Cavendish's parl. diary, v, 166–238 (Library of Congress).   93 Buckinghamshire to Germain, 2 Feb. (B.L., Mackintosh Colln., Add. Ms 34523 ff 204–5); Buckinghamshire to Thompson, 7 Feb. (Hotham Papers, P.R.O.N.I.,T3429/1/22); Cavendish's parl. diary, vi, 3–141 (Library of Congress); Buckinghamshire to Weymouth, 7 Feb. 1778 (P.R.O., S.P.,63/459 f 57).   94 Daly to Malone, 22 Feb. in Prior, *Life of Malone*, pp 62–3; Germain to Buckinghamshire, 17 Feb. (N.L.I., Heron Papers, Ms 13052/2); Buckinghamshire to Germain, 20 Feb. (B.L., Mackintosh Collection, Add. Ms 34523 f 205).   95 Political reflections of the second earl of Rosse (Rosse Papers, F/13); Markham to Flood, 26 Mar. 1778 (ibid., C/2/33); Rosse Papers, C/14/1–5.

In view of this, it is not surprising that Flood did not participate in the Commons' debates prompted in the spring of 1778 by the renewed attack of the patriots on the administration's management of the embargo and the pension list. The final illness and death of his mother kept him out of the House during the heady days of March, when the alarm generated by the announcement of a treaty between France and the American colonies caused politicians of all political hues to forget their differences momentarily. The most visible manifestation of this was the support of MPs for the proposal of Denis Daly for an address to George III affirming their inviolable attachment to his person and to the British constitution, parliament and people against France, but practical support was also forthcoming in the shape of legislation to raise an additional £300,000 for the defence of the kingdom.[96]

Flood supported these initiatives on his return to the House of Commons. Members had, he pronounced approvingly, responded properly when they agreed the address to the King, and he advised that they should not hesitate to approve the measures proposed to secure the promised revenue:

> there does not seem to be any difference of sentiment which sh[oul]d induce me to delay the H[ouse]. The vagueness of the estimate has b[een] mentioned. I hope this is no objection. I do not consider it as an estimate that sh[oul]d either bind or justify the grant of this sum of money. Everybody knows this country must be put into a state of defence, and can't be put into a state of defence but by granting the vote of credit. We grant this money in o[rde]r to put the c[ountr]y into a state of defence as to the generality of that estimate when no precise estimate can be made the more general the better, than you oblige gov[ernmen]t to lay it out to the best advantage.[97]

This was what the administration wanted to hear. They were understandably less content with Flood's observations on the proposed national militia and Luke Gardiner's Catholic relief bill – the other major current issues which he had been prevented from animadverting on by his recent bereavement.

Flood was particularly anxious that the current enthusiasm for Volunteering did not pre-empt a Protestant militia because, like Catholic relief, it had major long-term implications for the continued security of the Protestant interest in Ireland, and he was convinced that, for this reason alone, MPs should approve one and reject the other:

96 Cavendish's parl. diary, vii, 29–136, ix, 43–78, 111–78, 184–211 (Library of Congress); Weymouth to Buckinghamshire, 13, 27 Mar. (N.A., Index to departmental letters and papers 1760–89 f 221); Buckinghamshire to Weymouth, 12 Mar., 2 Apr., Weymouth to Buckinghamshire, 15, 18 (2) Mar., Heron to Porten, 23 Mar. (P.R.O., S.P., 63/459 ff 139–41, 143, 145, 147–8, 183–7, 250); Buckinghamshire to Hotham Thompson, 21 Mar.(Hotham Papers, P.R.O.N.I.,T3429/ 1/27); Beresford to Allan, 21 Mar. 1778 in *Beresford Corres.*, i, 21–2.   97 Cavendish's parl. diary, ix, 178–211.

It [the establishment of a Protestant militia] is a very great and important subject. It is a subject upon which I h[ave] always taken a decisive part; the *indecision
of no men, or any body of men shall prevent it*. In the last A[dministration] the
m[inister] of that day did not take a decisive part; that did not prevent me f[rom]
doing so ... Neither, sir, *now shall I be prevented from doing so*. W[ith] regard to all
great institutions in the world, sir, there h[ave] b[een] always some plausible
objections. W[ith] regard to this there are many. They h[ave] appeared in a thousand forms. I h[ave] endeavoured to hunt this proteus thro' all its different shapes,
but in vain; some unexpected objections h[ave] always arisen; and the independent g[entlemen] of this c[ountry] h[ave] not taken it by the hand as it deserved. If
the bill had passed last session of p[arliament] you would h[ave] this moment six
thousand men, accoutered and in some degree disciplined, spread thro' every
part [of the] c[ountry] and all at this moment to keep down all domestic insur-
gents. I shall ever be a friend to tollerating all differences in religious opinions,
yet as the unfortunate situation of the c[ountry] is such as that we can't unite as
we ought to do, so that one part [of the] community must lie at the mercy [of the]
other. I say the Protestants must lie at the mercy [of the] Catholicks, or the
Catholicks must lie at the mercy [of the] Protestants. I do say the Protestants
ought to use the power w[ith] lenity. This country, however, ought to h[ave] a
power of protecting itself. In numbers which are the natural strength of men,
the Papists are superior. What h[ave] we to do as wise statesmen? To give artifi-
cial strength upon that idea [by] supporting a militia not opposing it to the standing army is a necessary defence. I mean it is an auxiliary adequate to certain
purposes. Ireland must have a great extent of coast to defend; it is impossible
w[ith] the standing army to line our coasts, w[ith] a militia you can do it.[98]

As these observations highlight, Flood possessed a strong sense of the vulnerability
of the 'Protestant interest' in Ireland, and of the need to secure it against Catholic
revanchism. Despite this, he was not in the country when the matter of Catholic
relief was considered by the Commons in early April.

It is not clear why Flood chose to forsake the House of Commons for England at
this moment, but it aroused considerable curiosity. Because Speaker Pery, who had
been discussing relaxing the restrictions on Ireland's freedom to trade with the
administration, went to London on a private visit about the same time, John Beresford
suspected Flood's departure was somehow connected and he was anxious than neither man should be seen to gain credit from any relaxation of these laws.[99] Beresford's
suspicion was not unwarranted, as William Knox's efforts to clear the way for such

---

98 Cavendish's parl diary, ix, 211–13 (Library of Congress).   99 *F.L.J.*, 8 Apr.; Beresford to Allan, 4
Apr. in *Beresford Corres.*, i, 27–8; Absentee members of the House of Commons upon the Catholic bill
[1778] (N.L.I., Heron Papers, Ms 13060/1).

an initiative seemed about to bear fruit. This is not the place to analyse Knox's attempt to frame a proposal to grant Ireland what Richard Heron termed 'a free commerce', or the value of his contacts with Lord Nugent, Sir Lucius O'Brien, Edmond Pery, Sir John Blaquiere and Edmund Burke. But they are pertinent in so far as they offer no evidence to sustain Beresford's conjecture that Flood was involved, though his familiarity with O'Brien, Pery and, to a lesser extent, Edmund Burke possibly gave him access to some inside information.[100] It is certainly true that the relaxation of the restrictions on Irish trade was the sort of initiative Flood had hoped to advance when he contemplated office, but if he anticipated prior to his departure that he could perform some useful function in London, it did not prove to be the case and he spent most of his time avoiding the company of politicians and old friends. He did not, for instance, contact Richard Griffith. He was less coy with Lord North, but it is salient that his decision in late May to inform the Prime Minister of his readiness 'to go over immediately' to Dublin 'to give [his] assistance in parliament if wanted' was greeted sceptically. North was convinced Flood would appeal to his familiar excuse of ill-health if he was requested to return to Dublin, and so no invitation was extended.[101] As a result, Flood missed the debates on the mounting security, fiscal and economic problems that further eroded the credibility of the Buckinghamshire administration in the late spring and summer of 1778.

The cumulative impact of the various wartime embargoes, the increased threat posed shipping by French and American privateers, a banking crisis, reduced economic activity and poor revenue returns had so reduced the liquidity of the Irish exchequer by April 1778 that the administration was obliged to appeal to London for a subvention.[102] One consequence of this was the suspension of the payment of all salaries and pensions, which may have inconvenienced Flood, but he expressed no disquiet.[103] The decision of the British government to make £50,000 available eased the crisis temporarily, while the administration bought itself more time by overcoming strong political resistance in early June to its proposal to raise £300,000 through a tontine offering an exceptional 7.5 per cent return. It was also encouraged by the British parliament's decision to open the colonial trade to Irish ship-

100 R.I.A., Knox letters, Ms G.5.1; H.M.C., *Knox Mss*, p. 234; Additional Pery Papers, P.R.O.N.I.,T3052/ 50, 51, 58, 59; N.L.I., Heron Papers, Mss 4135, 13036/7; Ainsworth, ed., *Inchiquin Mss*, pp 221–2; Normanton Papers, P.R.O.N.I.,T3719/C/12/4, 5, 6, 7.   101 North to Buckinghamshire, 1 June (N.L.I., Heron Papers, Ms 13036/11); Griffith to Charlemont, 19 May 1778 in H.M.C., *Charlemont*,i, 340.   102 See, *inter alia*, Barnes and Owen, eds, *Sandwich papers*, ii, 65–6, 83, 85, 129; *F.L.J.*, 29 July; N.L.I., O'Hara Papers, Ms 20395; Fitzgerald Papers, Ms 13022, nos 55, 58, 206, Buckinghamshire to North, 26, 29, 30 Apr., 16 May in *Life of Grattan*, i, 317–23, 325; *Beresford Corres.*, i, 28–30; Heron to Porten, 10 Apr., Buckinghamshire to Weymouth, 30 Apr., 28 May (P.R.O., S.P., 63/459 ff 306–7, 460 ff 23, 174–5); Heron to Brown and Collison, 30 Apr. (N.A., Irish Correspondence 1697–1782, Ms 2447 f 307); Buckinghamshire to Thompson, 10, 30 May (Hotham Papers, P.R.O.N.I., T3429/1/30, 32); Buckinghamshire to Germain, 5, 7, 12, 27 May. 1778 (N.L.I., Heron Papers, Ms 13036/8, 10).   103 Buckinghamshire to North, 16 May 1778 (N.L.I., Heron Papers, Ms 13036/9).

ping and to relax embargo restrictions.[104] However, it was not to be allowed rest for long as the Protestant public manifested its disappointment at the narrowness of the commercial concessions yielded the kingdom by entering into non-importation agreements targeted at British goods. And, if this did not cause them sufficient unease, the acceleration in Volunteer recruitment, caused by an invasion scare, and divisions within the Castle interest over Catholic relief, were further sources of anxiety.[105]

Despite these storm clouds, Buckinghamshire was upbeat as the session, which had lasted ten challenging months, drew to a conclusion. His optimism is belied by his own reports which indicate that both 'the immediate friends of the late government', of whom Henry Flood was the most eminent, and those 'whose expectations of emolument have been disappointed' were discontented.[106] Ministers were certainly troubled by Buckinghamshire's ineffectual stewardship because he was instructed in September to form 'an administration which may be depended upon'. His difficulty was that he did not have a large pool of talent from which to draw. He ruled out Flood and Hely-Hutchinson on the grounds that 'they are equally unpopular and impracticable', but whereas the wily Hely-Hutchinson availed of the opportunity to mend his fences with the administration by agreeing to support them in the Commons, Flood kept his distance. Indeed, he did not even attempt to make contact on his return from England.[107]

Given his reserve, it is hardly surprising that Buckinghamshire chose to conclude that Flood was hostile, but this was not so. The promise he gave to North in May that he would return to Ireland to support the administration if requested to do so indicated that he could still be won over. He certainly had no thoughts of joining with the patriots. When Lord Charlemont approached him in late December with the suggestion of Lucius O'Brien that the parliamentary opposition should

---

104 Buckinghamshire to Weymouth, 3, 6 June (P.R.O., S.P., 63/460 ff 180, 205–8); Heron to Clements, 3 June (T.C.D., Clements Papers, Ms 1743/60); Cavendish's parl. diary, x, 76–247, 261–5, xi, 1ff (Library of Congress);Weymouth to Buckinghamshire, 18, 20, 22 June, 2, 20 July 1778 (P.R.O., S.P., 63/460 ff 251, 253, 261, 293, 350).   105 Buckinghamshire to Thompson, 19 July (Hotham Papers, T3429/2/33); *F.L.J.*, 18, 22, 25 July, 5, 26 Aug.; Hamilton to Abercorn, 19 July in J.H.Gebbie, ed., *An introduction to the Abercorn letters* (Omagh, 1972), p. 119; N.A., Calendar of miscellaneous letters and papers 1760–89, ff 23–4; Buckinghamshire to Bacon, 25 June, Buckinghamshire to Thompson, 16 July, Buckinghamshire to Germain, 14 Aug. (B.L., Mackintosh Colln., Add. Ms 34523 ff 210, 212, 217); Mac Nevin, *History of the Volunteers*, pp 96–8; Cavendish's parl. diary, xiii, 25–138 (Library of Congress); Knox to Heron, 28 May, June (R.I.A.,Knox Letters, Ms G.5.1); Thomas Bartlett, *Fall and rise of the Irish nation* (Dublin, 1991), pp 88–90; Buckinghamshire to Weymouth, 24 May, 20 June, Weymouth to Buckinghamshire, 31 May 1778 (P.R.O., S.P., 63/460 ff 143, 160, 263–7).   106 Fitzgerald to Leinster, 16 Aug. (N.L.I., Fitzgerald Papers, Ms 13022/218); Buckinghamshire to Thompson, 15 Aug., Buckinghamshire to Germain, 7 Sept. (B.L., Mackintosh Colln, Add. Ms 34523 ff 220, 223–7); Buckinghamshire to Germain, 23 Aug. in H.M.C., *Stopford-Sackville*, p. 60.   107 Buckinghamshire to Germain, Sept., 7 Sept. (B.L., Mackintosh Colln., Add. Ms 34523 ff 222–7); Hely-Hutchinson to Agar, 24 Nov. (Normanton Papers, P.R.O.N.I., T3719/C/12/21); Hely-Hutchinson to Buckinghamshire, 29 Nov. 1778 in H.M.C., *Lothian*, p. 340.

by-pass the Irish executive and present an address outlining 'the state of this country' directly to George III, Flood did not even reply.[108] He believed it was the administration's rather than his responsibility to make the first move. Indeed, he was now so convinced his 'honour' was being impugned by the failure of the administration to treat with him that he even contemplated resigning in January 1779 and, perhaps, might have had Archbishop Markham not advised him against such a course for personal as well as political reasons.

As this suggests, Markham remained as determined as ever to bring Flood and the Irish administration together. Upon hearing that Flood was contemplating resignation he contacted Richard Heron who was in London, and he was sufficiently assured by what he heard to inform Flood on 9 February 1779 that his belief that the Irish administration was hostile to him was unfounded:

> I have had some conversations with Sir R. Heron upon this subject, and he assured me with solemn protestation that both Lord B[uckinghamshire] and himself had never upon any occasion the least idea of doing anything which could be offensive to you, that they knew and valued your consequence, and should deserve to be esteemed idiots if they had used a disobliging carriage towards you; that however they might fail in their power to gratify you in all your wishes, yet that they never had a thought which was adverse to your interests. I will own to you that, when I find declarations to be founded in commonsense, it goes a great way towards making me believe then to be true.[109]

Flood was too adamantine to act on such information and, in the absence of a contrary signal from him, the administration continued to assume he was hostile, and to ignore him as they canvassed a long list of potential leaders in the House of Commons. As a result, Flood played no part in the intense 'behind the scenes' discussions on the issues of Ireland's right to trade, finance and parliamentary management that occupied the administration's time in the spring and early summer of 1779. It is a measure of how marginalised he had become that the Lord Lieutenant deemed it more appropriate to appeal to Sir Lucius O'Brien, Thomas Conolly, William Burton, the duke of Leinster and Theophilus Clements for advice on these subjects than to his only Irish vice-treasurer.[110]

In theory, the administration could afford to ignore Flood since it obtained promises of support in the course of 1779 from a substantial majority of MPs. However,

---

108 Charlemont to Flood, 22 Dec. 1778 in R[odd], ed., *Letters to Flood*, pp 102–3.   109 Markham to Flood, 9 Feb. 1779 (Rosse Papers, C/2/34).   110 Buckinghamshire to Clinton, 28 Mar. (B.L., Mackintosh Colln., Add. Ms 34523 f 245); Heron to Buckinghamshire, 4, 23, 29 Mar., Tighe to Heron, 3 Mar., Buckinghamshire to North, 6 Mar., Buckinghamshire to Heron, 6, 27, 28 Mar., 19 Apr., 28 May, Beresford to Buckinghamshire, 30 Mar., 1 Apr., Lifford to Heron, 31 Mar. (N.L.I., Heron Papers, Mss 13037/1, 2, 5, 6, 9, 15, 13046); Buckinghamshire to Weymouth, 20 May (2) 1779 (P.R.O., S.P. 63/464 ff 349, 351).

these promises could not all be relied upon, and experienced observers and officials were convinced it was essential 'that effectual means be immediately adopted to calm the minds of the people' if they were to sustain a working majority in the Commons.[111] The urgency of concessions was underlined by the gathering pace of the public campaigns against the importation and consumption of British goods. This attracted little official notice until it was taken up in Dublin in late April and early May. But the public's resolve, hardened by continuing economic difficulties,[112] convinced Buckinghamshire that he had to persuade the Prime Minister to agree to the further liberalisation of Ireland's right to trade, and he sought to do this by demonstrating the widespread support for such a strategy among Irish politicians, Henry Flood included.

Following the ratification at Westminster on 11 May of Lord Rockingham's address calling on ministers to pursue 'effectual methods for promoting the common strength and commerce of His Majesty's subjects in both kingdoms', Buckinghamshire invited the Lord Chancellor, the Primate, the Speaker, the Prime Serjeant, the Attorney General and a number of others to provide him with 'their sentiments'. On 7 June, he extended this invitation to Flood.[113] It is not immediately apparent what the Lord Lieutenant hoped to achieve by this, but it can plausibly be seen as an attempt to open an avenue of communication. If so, the answer he received was discouraging. In common with most respondents, Flood was of the opinion that the liberation of Irish trade from the mercantilist regulations that continued to bind it was the only appropriate solution to the kingdom's economic problems, but he declined to justify his recommendation because he did not possess the relevant information and because he correctly concluded that it was a political decision for the British government:

> I have ... had the honor to give it [the Westminster Lords' address] a very serious consideration, and the more I have considered it, the more I have felt the peculiarity of my situation. Official information has at least not been extended to me,

---

111 Tighe to Heron, 3 Mar., Waite to Heron, 9 Apr., Buckinghamshire to Germain, 13 May (N.L.I., Heron Papers, Ms 13037/1, 8, 12); Scott to Robinson, 13 Apr. in *Beresford Corres.*, i, 39–40; Bruce to Townshend, 3 May 1779 (N.A., Townshend Letterbook, Ms 5040 ff 2–4).   112 *F.L.J.*, 14, 28 Apr., 5, 12, 23 June *H.J.*, 28 Apr.; Buckinghamshire to Weymouth, 29 Apr., 13 May (P.R.O., S.P., 63/464 ff 315–8, 345); *Life of Grattan*, i, 461–2; Barron to Villiers, 17 Mar. (Villiers-Stuart Papers, P.R.O.N.I., T3131/E/6/1); duke to duchess of Leinster, 10 Apr., 13 May (N.L.I., Fitzgerald Papers, Ms 13022/59, 60); Denham to Rockingham, 17 May (S.C.L., Wentworth-Woodhouse Manuscripts, Rockingham Papers, R1-1829); Buckinghamshire to Weymouth, 28, 29 May 1779 (P.R.O., S.P.63/465 ff 21–2, 32–3).   113 Weymouth to Buckinghamshire and reply, 18, 23, 27 May (P.R.O., S.P. 63/464 ff 343, 371, 465 ff 1–5); Hoffman, *Lord Rockingham*, pp 353–4; Flood to Waite, 7 June 1779 (N.A., Calendar of miscellaneous letters and papers 1760–89 f 41). Flood's and the other responses are in P.R.O., S.P. 63/465 *passim*. Most are printed in George O'Brien, 'The Irish free trade agitation of 1779', *E.H.R.*, 38 (1923) pp 564–81, 39(1924), pp 96–109.

for some weeks I have not seen even a Treasury Abstract,[114] and mercantile detail is not here within my reach. I should not trouble your excellency with the mention of this but to account for my being less circumstantial than I wish. There is reason, however, to believe that at this time materials are not wanting. The difficulty is to depart from an established system however wrong, as the restrictions upon the trade, commerce and manufactures of Ireland are, which diminish the wealth of these kingdoms and the strength consequent on wealth. Objections do not rise in Ireland to a departure from that system. The objections arise in England and must be so much better known to the ministers and parliament of that country than they can be here, that it might seem presumption in us to point them out and how to obviate them by anticipation I confess I know not.[115]

However accurate his analysis, Buckinghamshire can hardly have been impressed by the terseness of Flood's reply, but he made a further attempt to break down the barriers of silence and suspicion that separated Flood from the administration by initiating a further exchange of letters in which the two men discussed the capacity of the country to defend itself in the event of a French offensive – a matter on everyone's lips following the 'sham invasion' of Munster on 4 June.[116]

Flood had no fears for his own 'safety' in 1779, but he was acutely conscious of the 'distress' that would be caused by enemy activity in Ireland, and he was more than a little troubled by the disposition he detected 'in the countenances of many of the lower order' to 'join ... to a man' with any invading French force.[117] His unease did not cause him to subscribe to the fever for 'volunteering' that gripped the Protestant 'nation' in the weeks and months that followed, that brought about the transformation of the Volunteers from a small, scattered auxiliary body, estimated at 6–10,000 in the spring of 1779, into a formidable para-military organization numbering 30–45,000 by September.[118] Flood's reluctance was entirely consistent with his

---

114 Following this, Flood wrote H.T. Clements requesting abstracts (Flood to Clements, 24 June (T.C.D., Clements Papers, Ms 1743/61)). 115 B.L., Liverpool Papers, Add Ms 38211 f 119. See also Buckinghamshire to Heron, 13, 23 June 1779 (N.L.I., Heron Papers, Ms 13038/2, 4). 116 Buckinghamshire to Flood, 12 June in R[odd], ed., *Letters to Flood*, pp 105–6; Flood to Buckinghamshire, 14 June (N.L.I., Heron Papers, Ms 13038/3); P.R.O., S.P., 63/464 ff 49–51, 53–70, 157 and *passim*; Shackleton to Leadbeater, 18 May (B.L.,O.C., Ballitore Papers); Buckinghamshire's vindication (N.L.S., Lothian Papers, P.R.O.N.I., T3502/1 part 1); Buckinghamshire to Eardley–Wilmot, 15 Feb. 1779 (B.L.,O.C., Buckinghamshire files). 117 Flood to Buckinghamshire, 14 June (N.L.I., Heron Papers, Ms 13038/3); Bruce to Townshend, 3 May 1779 (N.A., Townshend letterbook, Ms 5040 ff 2–4). 118 Mary to Chum Ponsonby, 10 Apr. (T.C.D., Barker Ponsonby Papers, Ms P3/1/29); James Kelly, 'A secret return of the Volunteers in 1784', *I.H.S.*, 26 (1989), pp 268–9; *Life of Grattan*, i, 351–4, 356–7; P.R.O., S.P.63/465 ff 64–97; Weymouth to Buckinghamshire, 24 June, Buckinghamshire to Weymouth, 23 May, 3, 23 July, Weymouth to Irvine, 27 July (ibid., 464 ff 361–2, /465 ff 141, 249, 437, 455); North to George III, 30 July in Fortescue, ed., *The corres. of George III*, iv, 401–2; Pery to Heron, 27 Aug. (N.L.I., Heron Papers, Ms 13038/12); Buckinghamshire to Eardley-Wilmot, 15 Feb.(B.L.,O.C., Buckinghamshire files); *F.L.J.*, 18 Aug., 25 Sept. 1779.

long-stated preference for a militia and his known reservations with the very idea of 'independent' Volunteer corps. So, when he was nominated to canvas the barony of Shillelogher at a meeting of noblemen and gentlemen held in County Kilkenny on 2 September, which agreed 'that two or three gentlemen of each barony in this county be nominated and appointed ... to enroll the names of such gentlemen and other as shall offer themselves volunteers to serve for the defence of their country', he declined the invitation. As a result, Shillelogher was conspicuously missing when a return was made two months later of 475 men who had enrolled in the county. Ten Volunteer corps were founded in County Kilkenny in 1779; and Flood was not involved in any of them.[119]

He was not a member either of the convivial and political gathering of patriot MPs, peers and barristers known as the Monks of the Order of St Patrick (more commonly known as 'the Monks of the Screw') which assembled for the first time in Dublin on 3 September. Many claims have been made for this body though none have been convincingly demonstrated. Nonetheless, the fact that Flood was not a founding member and was not elected to honourary membership emphasises just how isolated he was at this time. It need not have been so. Both Walter Hussey Burgh and Lord Townshend were 'monks', and it is certain that Lord Charlemont would have welcomed his participation. This was true also of the administration as the limitations of Sir Richard Heron as a parliamentarian and a manager became increasingly obvious as the commencement of the 1779–80 session drew near.[120]

Given the scale of the political problems he faced, the earl of Buckinghamshire would have preferred to have avoided meeting the Irish parliament in October 1779, but the refusal of the British government to bail out the straitened Irish exchequer ruled this out. More consequently, in the light of the government's unwillingness to make concessions on 'commercial points', the administration was ill-placed to assemble a team strong enough to present government business and to sustain a Commons' interest that would enable them both to implement their legislative agenda and to repulse the determined attempts the patriots were bound to make to secure further commercial concessions. Fearful that any change would critically weaken their control of Ireland, ministers longed to recall Buckinghamshire and to press ahead with a legislative union but the moment was not opportune. Indeed their fears of separation were exaggerated, for as Speaker Pery correctly noted 'the body of this [Protestant] nation, [wa]s sincerely attached to the British nation'.[121] Despite

---

119 Flood to Buckinghamshire, 14 June (N.L.I., Heron Papers, Ms 13038/3); above pp 104–5, 127, 225–6, 230; *F.L.J.*, 25 Sept., 9, 30 Oct., 20 Nov. 1779; The Volunteers of Ireland 1715–93 (N.L.I., Dudley Westropp Papers, Ms 24937); Mac Nevin, *The Volunteers*, pp 223–36; Kelly, 'A secret return', pp 286–7. 120 Achmet to Townshend, 18 Oct. (N.A., Townshend letterbook, Ms 5040 ff 81–2); W.H.Curran, *The life of John Philpot Curran* (2 vols, Edinburgh, 1822), i, 121–5; Lammey, 'Free trade', pp 65–6; Ellis to Hely-Hutchinson, 16 Dec. 1779 in H.M.C., *Donoughmore*, p. 294. 121 Buckinghamshire to Weymouth, 12 July. (P.R.O., S.P. 63/465 f 367); Buckinghamshire to North, 29/30, 30 July in *Life of Grattan*, i, 374–7; P.R.O., S.P.63/466 *passim*; North to Buckinghamshire, 30 July (N.L.I., Heron

this, ministers were understandably ill-at-ease as it emerged in August and September that Hussey Burgh 'declared he can no longer stand forth in parliament as the leader of the public business'; that Attorney General Scott, John Foster and John Beresford would support but not take the lead; that the duke of Leinster could no longer be relied upon; and that Flood's continued residence 'in the country' indicated that he too would not stand forward.[122]

In fact, Flood had determined to revert to the independent stance he had last taken in the House of Commons in the early 1770s. He shared the disappointment of the population with the free trade act of 1778, and he was sufficiently perturbed by rumours that a legislative union was in the offing to feel compelled to exhort the public to persist with its campaign in support of free trade. The means he chose to convey this message was by pamphlet, but in contrast to his Philadelphus and Sindercombe pseudonyms, he preserved his anonymity on this occasion.[123]

As the inclusion in the title of reference to 'the expediency and necessity of the present associations in favour of our own manufactures' bears out, the primary focus of Flood's 'letter to the people of Ireland' was the advancement of the campaign for free trade. There was, of course, no reason for him to conceal his support for free trade, but the non-importation and non-consumption campaigns were a more delicate matter. However, he was sufficiently confident that the pamphlet would not be traced to him to endorse both without hesitation on the grounds that history amply demonstrated the universal truth that countries that did not stand up for their rights would find them 'plundered' by others, and that 'Ireland is an instance of a country losing her trade, impairing her liberty and reducing her people to want by an unparalleled propensity to surrender everything to Great Britain'. Flood reserved sharp words too for what he maintained was the exploitative and ill-informed disposition of English mercantile and political interests to Ireland, but he did not excuse Irish opinion which, he alleged, acquiesced too readily in its exploitation. This accounts for his endorsement of 'the associations in favour of our own manufactures', and the lengths he went to throughout the tract to applaud the associative spirit they manifested. Indeed, he maintained that because 'the constitution is now reduced to a

Papers, Ms 13038/10); Callen, ed., 'Cavendish's parl. diary', ii, 80–2; Memo, July in H.M.C., *Knox Mss*, 261; Kelly, 'Origins of the Act of Union', pp 251–3; Beresford to Robinson, 31 July in *Beresford corres.*, i, 40–3; North to Pery, 3 Aug. in H.M.C., *Emly*, p. 201; Phipps to -, 10 Oct.in P.W. Phipps, *Life of Colonel Pownoll Phipps* (London, 1894), pp 7–9; Pery to North, 13 Aug. 1779 in H.M.C., *Emly*, p. 202. **122** Burgh to Heron, [2] Aug. (N.L.I., Heron Papers, Ms 13038/11); Beresford to Robinson, 2 Aug., Heron to Robinson, 20 Aug. in *Beresford Corres.*, i, 43–52; Buckinghamshire to Germain, 20 Aug. in H.M.C., *Stopford-Sackville*, p. 61; Leinster to Buckinghamshire, 14 Sept. 1779 (Norfolk Record Office, Hobart Papers, P.R.O.N.I., T3110/1/95). **123** He did this so effectively that the pamphlet, *A letter to the people of Ireland*, is also attributed to Henry Grattan (R.B. McDowell, *Irish public opinion 1750–1800* (London, 1944), p. 270). However, since a contemporary manuscript note in Grattan's copy (in private possession, but see Emerald Isle Books, catalogue 93) maintains that Flood was the author and this is the attribution favoured by the National Library of Ireland, it is reasonable to accept that Flood's claim is stronger.

state in which no public benefit can be obtained but by the collective body of the people', the people could also hasten its restoration as much by voting for those parliamentary candidates who favoured free trade as by 'agreeing' not to patronise those drapers, mercers and others who imported foreign goods. This was a more unconditional endorsement of street agitation than Flood had previously enunciated, but it reflected his acute dissatisfaction with current government policy towards Ireland. His disquiet was reinforced by the rumours that a legislative union was under contemplation, because he was convinced a union held no advantages for Ireland. Indeed, he urged the population to be on the *qui vive* to repulse any such 'treacherous offer'. 'The times have made England and Ireland one people', he maintained, 'without abolishing the parliament of either' and any attempt to set aside the Irish legislature would only compound that kingdom's financial problems at a moment when it was incumbent on Britain to 'court our affection by giving us an interest in her success, and some safety in her return to power instead of leaving us to experience relief from contumely in nothing but her humiliation'.[124]

Because the British government had no intention of following Flood's advice and courting Irish affections, there appeared to be no basis for a working arrangement between Flood and the administration in the autumn of 1779. Indeed, Lord North's instruction to Buckinghamshire to resist 'steadily and uniformly every offensive and violent measure which may tend to embarrass the ordinary course of business, or to create jealousy and ill-humour between Great Britain and Ireland' and, specifically, to overcome any attempt the patriots might make to push the issue of free trade by amending the address to the king or by voting a six-months money bill ran directly counter to what he urged. It is hardly surprising, therefore, that he (along with the duke of Leinster and Hussey Burgh) did not attend the 'usual meeting' of Castle advisers and officeholders on the eve of the session.[125] At the same time, he was still not prepared to acknowledge that his term in office had been a failure by allying with the patriots in the House of Commons. He approached the 1779/80 session in much the same way as he had that of 1777/8 – aligned neither with the Castle nor with the patriots. The fact that, unlike Hussey Burgh, who was about to break decisively with the administration, he chose not to declare his intentions meant that there was a degree of mystery about his position. But he was clear in his own mind about where he stood. He was determined to conduct himself as an independent, because he believed it was the only honourable course open to him,

---

124 [Henry Flood], *A letter to the people of Ireland on the expediency and necessity of the present associations in Ireland in favour of our own manufactures with some cursory observations on the effects of a union* (Dublin, 1779), *passim.* 125 Buckinghamshire to Hillsborough, 26 Sept., Buckinghamshire to Germain, 10 Oct., Buckinghamshire to Thompson, 12 Oct. (B.L., Mackintosh Colln., Add. Ms 34523 ff 260, 262–4); *F.L.J.*, 9 Oct.; Heron to Leinster and reply, 7, 9 Oct., North to Buckinghamshire, 5 Oct., Burgh to Heron, 13 Oct. (N.L.I., Heron Papers, Mss 13054/3 13038/14); Buckinghamshire's vindication (Lothian Papers, P.R.O.N.I., T3502/1 part 1); Buckinghamshire to Weymouth, 13 Oct. 1779 (2) (P.R.O., S.P.63/467 ff 17–25).

and because he hoped, even yet, to secure a resolution of his own unhappy position as an officeholder.

INDEPENDENT PATRIOT ONCE MORE

Dublin Castle sought to ensure the debate on the Commons reply to the address from the throne, which provided the first opportunity during the 1779/80 session for rival interests to test their strength, was low-keyed and non-controversial by presenting a carefully modulated and non-committal statement. The patriots were not appeased, and Henry Grattan countered with a long and complex amendment which stated that Ireland sought the right to export its produce freely and without restriction. This was precisely what the Castle was instructed to prevent, but the attempt by its spokesmen to deflect the amendment without being seen to oppose the liberalisation of Ireland's right to trade was unconvincing. Flood observed all this keenly. He favoured calling for commercial concession, and when Prime Serjeant Burgh suggested that instead of Grattan's proposition the address to the King should simply state 'that [it is] not by temporary expedients that this nation is to be saved, but by the universal opening of the ports of this kingdom' he rose to endorse this idea. 'The only thing in common sense you can ask is a free trade', he observed decisively.

Flood's support for Burgh's amendment was widely welcomed. However, there was visibly less endorsement of his assertion that the position he took on free trade was entirely honourable because he was not bound by any commitment to the administration and because it was consistent with his previous conduct:

> *I have never retracted one publick sentiment*; if I have, I challenge any man to produce the subject. *I have no obligations, I have no engagements, I have no expectation from the present ministry.* Whether I ever maligned one man in the nation, whether I ever disparaged, whether I ever discouraged the promotion of one man; I know it has been insinuated no man ever preserved a more equal conduct with respect to others, a more honourable demeanour with regard [to himself]. As to the office, it came to me from the spontaneous condescension of my sovereign, unsolicited. When it was vacated without my knowledge, I would not accept it, 'till I was told in writing that another office would be let fall in order to counterbalance the pension given at the time. If any man can hold an office upon more honourable grounds, maintaining sentiments [instead of] swerving from them ...[126]

126 Callen, ed., 'Cavendish's parl. diary', i, 16–17. The text breaks off at this point, but the meaning is clear.

Given his obsession with being seen to behave honourably and his wish to counter public speculation as to his intentions, it was predictable that Flood would make such a statement at some point in the session. However, his call for unity among those who favoured 'free trade' was of potentially greater political consequence. Indeed, when Burgh agreed to reword his motion to employ Flood's phrase 'free trade' in place of his own infelicitous 'universal opening of the ports of this kingdom', Flood strongly supported its incorporation into the address and it was acceded to by the House.[127]

This outcome was a triumph for Flood as well as for Burgh and the patriots generally. Some observers were so nonplussed by the conduct of the two officeholders that there was even speculation they were working together on behalf of the Castle.[128] The truth was more prosaic. Flood was operating without reference to anyone; it just so happened that his and Burgh's approach to the address coincided. The two men did not get along, and a few days later, when Flood referred to the events of 12 October in a manner that caused Burgh and Grattan, who were sitting together, to conclude that he sought to appropriate 'more credit for the part he took in the business' than he deserved, Burgh disputed the point with him.[129]

If this evidence of dissension within the ranks of the victors of 12 October consoled the administration, there was no concealing how bad a start they had made to the session. Buckinghamshire described the events of 12 October as a 'catastrophe', and following a further rebuff on 13 October when the Commons approved a resolution of thanks to the Volunteers, he consulted with his most trusted advisers on how he might reinforce his frail administration.[130] They undertook to identify individuals, who might realistically be approached but, more pertinently for Flood, advised against disturbing

> opposers in office ... to prevent the tumult that must arise from turning men out for supporting popular measures and the mischief that those men might make at this moment, if considered by the country as victims to the prosperity of Ireland.

127 This and the previous paragraph are based on Callen, ed., 'Cavendish's parl. diary', i, 1–30; Lammey 'Free trade', pp 97–8; *Life of Grattan*, i, 383–8; Buckinghamshire to Weymouth, 13 Oct. (P.R.O., S.P.63/ 467 ff 22–5); Beresford to Robinson, 13 Oct. 1779 in *Beresford Corres.*, i, 53–60). This invalidates the legend that the introduction of the phrase 'free trade' into the political lexicon resulted from Flood's throwing out the words 'why not a free trade' while Burgh was speaking (Recollections of Lawrence, earl of Rosse (Rosse Paper, F/13)). Flood has no claims to be either the author or populariser of the term 'free trade'. It was already in common currency. 128 Caldwell to Townshend, 25 Oct. 1779 (N.A., Townshend letterbook, Ms 5040 ff 107–8). 129 *Life of Grattan*, i, 387–8; Callen, ed, 'Cavendish's parl. diary', ii, 91–2. 130 Buckinghamshire to North, 13 Oct., Buckinghamshire to Germain, 13, 15 Oct. (B.L., Mackintosh Colln., Add. Ms 34523 ff 192, 265); Buckinghamshire to Thompson, 12 Oct. (Hotham Papers, P.R.O.N.I., T3429/1/49); Callen, ed., 'Cavendish's parl. diary', i, 24–6, ii, 93; Heron to Robinson, 13 Oct. in *Beresford Corres.*, i, 60–1; Buckinghamshire to Weymouth, 14 Oct. 1779 (P.R.O., S.P.63/467 ff 28–32).

This meant that Flood was secure in his possession of the vice-treasurership for the present. But the recommendation that the government should target 'such men as were foremost in opposition upon a solemn assurance of their stepping into the shoes of those persons now abusing their stations, on the last day of the session, by which the present possessors might be muzzled a little, and the assistance of others rendered less suspect' suggested that he was unlikely to remain so for very long.[131]

Flood, meanwhile, held fast to his belief in his integrity as an officeholder despite his refusal to support the administration in any practical way. His decision to go to England, without informing Buckinghamshire, during the customary adjournment that followed the ratification of the address to the King bears this out. It is not clear once again what Flood's purpose was in travelling at this time, but it is likely that it had something to do with his agreement with Harcourt, because it was at this moment that Buckinghamshire outlined its 'terms' to Lord North.[132] Buckinghamshire's avowal, for the first time, that the 1775 agreement lay at the heart of Flood's alienation from the administration cut little ice with the hard-pressed Prime Minister or, indeed, with Archbishop Markham who appealed once more to Flood to 'forget' his 'discontents' and to cooperate with the Castle to ensure that the 'epidemic madness' currently gripping Ireland was stemmed. Markham was appalled by the reports doing the rounds in Britain that 'the Protestants of Ireland threaten rebellion', and it was his deeply felt wish that Flood should strive to 'take the business out of the hands of the madmen and put it into a sober and temperate train'.[133] This was not what Flood had in mind. He had invested too much in the 1775 agreement to back down, and following his return from England (in time for the resumption of parliament on 1 November), he took up with Richard Heron the case of a Mr Walters whom, he alleged, had been removed from the office of distributor of stamps at Kilkenny 'without sufficient cause'. In fact, Walters had been removed for 'neglect', but when Heron pointed this out, Flood insisted that Walters 'should have some other office' and authorised Sir Frederick Flood to represent him on the matter.[134]

Flood cited the treatment accorded Walters as further evidence that he was being 'treated with mark'd indignity', and it encouraged him to attempt to press his 1775 agreement to a resolution. With this in mind, he requested Sir Henry Cavendish a short time later to state formally on his behalf to the Chief Secretary

that the preceding administration had not fulfill'd their engagements to him,

131 Note re Provost, 15 Oct.; Scott to Buckinghamshire, 18 Oct., Buckinghamshire to Heron, 23 Oct. (N.L.I., Heron Papers, Ms 13038/15); Scott to Robinson, 15, 20 Oct., Beresford to Robinson, 24 Oct. in *Beresford Corres.*, i, 61–70; Buckinghamshire to North, 18 Oct. 1779 in Bartlett, ed., *Macartney*, pp 316–17.   132 Buckinghamshire to Weymouth, 18 Oct. (P.R.O., S.P.63/467 ff 44–6); Buckinghamshire to North, 25 Oct. 1779 (B.L., Mackintosh Colln., Add. Ms 34523 f 266).   133 Markham to Flood, 30 Oct., 16 Nov. 1779 (Rosse Papers, C/2/35, 36).   134 Memorandum re Mr Flood, Nov. 1779 (N.L.I., Heron Papers, Ms 13038/16).

that he had receiv'd no favors from me [Buckinghamshire], that his seat in parliament was his own [and] that he had declin'd communicating with you [Heron] because you had not given him the support you had promised him.

This rather stark communication might, if the timing had been different, have precipitated a show-down, but the Lord Lieutenant was so desperate not to give Flood cause to go into formal opposition that he responded with an offer of 'an equal share of the patronage of County Kilkenny'. However, he did not conceal his 'dissatisfaction at these repeated messages', and he expressed his unwillingness to enter into further discussions with Flood until he was more forthcoming in his support for 'His Majesty's measures'.[135] It was not sufficient to win Flood over. Indeed, given his public support for 'free trade' on 12 October, it is unlikely that anything less than a commitment to concede on this and an undertaking to honour in full the 1775 agreement would have induced him to become the advocate the Lord Lieutenant so badly needed. The fact that Flood even spoke warmly of the critique John Hely-Hutchinson published in 1779 of the commercial restraints still on the statute book reinforces this conclusion.[136]

The Irish parliament resumed its proceedings on 1 November with a rather inconsequential debate on a financial motion by Benjamin Chapman remarkable mainly for an altercation between Flood and Barry Yelverton. This was prompted by a slighting aside by Yelverton to 'vice-treasurers that labour in our vineyard, that is fruitful to those only who labour in it'. Since this was the sort of remark Flood refused to allow pass unchallenged, he demanded that Yelverton justify his 'personal censure' on the grounds that he was not an absentee officeholder. This was an open invitation to Yelverton to turn the full weight of his oratorical ordnance on Flood, but he judiciously chose moderation over invective:

I complained that he, and such as he, has not the management of the Treasury. I complained that it is open to the rapacity of the English ministry over whom we have no control. When he was set up at the head of the Treasury, we rejoiced at it. He has given eminent and distinguished proof as well of the most consummate abilities, as the strictest attention to the interest and, let me add, the constitution of this country. Before long I had a seat in this House, I heard with rapture his struggles to restore that constitution which has suffered so may wounds from the usurped authority of a foreign parliament. I do not desire to labour with him in that vineyard. I shall endeavour to do something for my country in

---

135 Ibid.; Markham to Flood, 16 Nov. (Rosse Papers, C/2/36); Memorandum by [Buckinghamshire] to [Heron], Nov. 1779 (N.L.I., Heron Papers, Ms 13038/16). **136** Memorandum by [Buckinghamshire] to [Heron], Nov. 1779 (N.L.I., Heron Papers, Ms 13038/16); Mac Nevin, *History of the Volunteers*, p. 60 note.

that only in which he has laboured so effectually, that [wine] press has produced a liquor like to overflow this country with ruin.

Realising that he would only intensify the ill-will MPs on all sides bore him by prolonging the exchange, Flood made a graceful, complimentary reply and the attention of the House moved on.[137]

Perhaps chastened by this experience, Flood did not participate in the heated debates that took place during the following days on the national debt and the opposition's attempts to ratify a six-month rather than the usual two-year money bill. He broadly supported the tactics the patriot leadership sought to employ to elicit the additional commercial concessions they and he believed necessary to lift the kingdom's economy out of depression. However, he was not prepared to play a supporting role to the likes of Yelverton and Grattan, which won him no bouquets with a public insistent on the concession of 'free trade', or with Dublin Castle, which did not have the numbers to resist the short money bill. Conscious now that concession was essential if they were to retain any political influence in the Commons and to stave off the 'rebellion' and 'independence' many in Britain apprehended, the Lord Lieutenant and Chief Secretary sought desperately to impress upon London the importance of immediate commercial concession.[138]

Lord North was unresponsive, with the result that the Castle had nothing with which to rally potential supporters during the key debate on the opposition's proposal for a six-month money bill on Tuesday and Wednesday, 23 and 24 November. Flood did not speak on the 23rd. But on the 24th he unexpectedly aided Henry Grattan to resist the administration's request for new taxes for the usual term of two years on the grounds that if the House concurred it would fatally undermine the opposition's strategy to compel the government to concede 'free trade'. At the same time, he made clear his wish that the patriots did not provoke a 'rupture' with Britain. The result was a triumph for the proponents of free trade; they won the critical division for approving a six-month money bill by 170 votes to 47. Flood was on the winning side on the following day also when, after a long and emotional debate, the committee of supply voted the loan duties for six months by the narrower margin of 38 votes. He did not speak on this occasion, possibly because of continuing problems in his relations with the patriots. Indeed, he was rebuked by Edward Newenham for asserting 'the establishment was the King's' rather than the people who paid for it.[139]

137 Callen, ed., 'Cavendish's parl. diary', pp 27–34.   138 Callen, ed., 'Cavendish's parl diary', i, 41–63; Buckinghamshire to Hillsborough, 8 Nov. (P.R.O., S.P.63/467 ff 101–2); *F.L.J.*, 10, 13 Nov.; Buckinghamshire to Thompson, 13 Nov. (Hotham Papers, P.R.O.N.I., T3429/1/50); North to Buckinghamshire, 14 Nov. 1779 in H.M.C., *Emly*, p. 204; Price to van der Capellan, 26 Oct. in Thomas, ed., *Correspondence of Richard Price*, ii, 55; Lennox to Leinster, 5 Nov. in Fitzgerald, ed., *Leinster corres.*, ii, 297; Blaquiere to Townshend, 8 Nov. 1779 (N.A., Townshend Letterbook, Ms 5040 ff 116–18).   139 Callen, ed., 'Cavendish's parl diary', i, 78–136; *F.L.J.*, 1 Dec. 1779.

To committed patriots like Newenham, Flood's refusal to resign the vice-treas-urership was unfathomable, and it was set in stark relief by the decision of Hussey Burgh to resign the prime serjeancy following his celebrated 'smothered war' speech which he delivered during the debate on the six-month money bill on 25 Novem-ber. Flood would almost certainly have joined him out of office but for the fact that the administration still clung to its 'no dismissal' policy.[140] However, dismissal now seemed only a matter of time because when Buckinghamshire took stock of his po-sition in December, he singled out 'the unbecoming conduct of some particular gentlemen who have receiv'd the most distinguished marks of His Majesty's fa-vour', and requested Lord North to authorise him 'at the close of the sessions of making examples in the instance of the Provost and Mr Flood'. The Prime Minis-ter's tardiness in replying irritated the Lord Lieutenant who deplored the reluc-tance of 'ministers ... to dismiss those [Flood and Hely-Hutchinson] who, tho' loaded with accumulated favours, had strenuously opposed me'. But the instinctively cau-tious North could hardly be faulted for not agreeing to Buckinghamshire's sugges-tion given the current state of Ireland and his refusal to accept Richard Heron's offer of resignation.[141]

Flood was not pleased when he became aware that his dismissal was being con-sidered. He still clung to the hope that his agreement with Lord Harcourt would be honoured and, eager for accurate information, he followed up a rather tactless re-quest to William Markham in early December to arrange an audience with the King with a further request to him to enquire if his 'place' was 'being offered'. Markham could not 'learn anything', but he did advise Flood, who now claimed that his legiti-mate expectation of an office for life and a seat at Westminster had been denied because of the malign intent of his 'enemies', that he had no 'enemies' that he (Markham) could detect, but that if he (Flood) had 'you have given them strong advantages'. This was plain speaking, but it reflected Markham's conclusion that Flood had pursued the wrong political strategy for some time. Indeed, he reiterated his contention that Flood was 'much better with [the] administration than with the leaders of opposition', and advised that because the present crisis provided a 'glori-ous opportunity for men of virtue to make a stand', he could yet redeem his fallen reputation by defending the existing trading arrangements and the policies of the British government.[142]

The window of opportunity, identified by Markham, proved short-lived, be-cause with Castle loyalists like Beresford, Scott and Blaquiere urging Buckingham-

140 *F.L.J.*, 8, 11 Dec.; Callen, ed., 'Cavendish's parl. diary.', i, 137–232; Buckingham's vindication (Lothian Papers, P.R.O.N.I., T3502/1 part 1). 141 Buckinghamshire to North, Dec. 1779 (B.L., Mackintosh Colln, Add. Ms 34523 ff 274–5); Buckinghamshire to Clinton, 19 Aug. 1781 in H.M.C., *Lothian*, pp 391–2; Buckinghamshire's vindication (Lothian Papers, P.R.O.N.I., T3502/1 part 1). 142 North to Buckinghamshire, 13 Mar.1780 (N.L.I., Heron Papers, Ms 13038/17); Markham to Flood, 10, 13 Dec. 1779 (Rosse Papers, C/2/37, 38).

shire's recall,[143] Lord North finally determined to ease his Irish crisis by agreeing that Ireland should be ceded the right to trade freely with Britain and the rest of the empire. This would, he hoped, 'satisfy' Irish opinion, and the response was encouraging.[144] Indeed, Buckinghamshire was so eager to spread the good news, when he was informed of the Prime Minister's decision on 12 December, that he 'summon[ed] a number of the principal lords and gentlemen in the evening to the Castle'. Surprisingly, Henry Flood was among their number. Buckinghamshire was anxious not to let the opportunity pass to induce all officeholders to commit themselves to the administration, and the overwhelming majority of those present responded, as he anticipated, with 'the strongest language of gratitude and satisfaction at the fullness of the propositions' reported to them. However, Flood and three others (Speaker Pery, John Hely-Hutchinson and William Brownlow) declined to join in the euphoria of the moment. Their 'gloomy silence' irked the bulk of the peers, councillors and officeholders present, especially as none of the four explained their position. However, within a few days each came out in support of what was being proposed. Pery maintained he had approved of the resolutions from the outset, but that he had felt obliged to behave as he did on 12 December because of his position in the House of Commons. Flood could not shelter behind his office, so when he met with Buckinghamshire on 13 or 14 December, he expressed his readiness 'to support measures consequential to the liberal proceedings of Great Britain', albeit 'with some little degree of reserve'.[145]

Despite his tactless initial response, Flood warmly welcomed the resolutions encapsulating 'free trade' when they were presented to the House of Commons by John Foster on 20 January 1780. Indeed, he even commented approvingly upon the contribution of the Volunteers to their achievement and congratulated those MPs, on both sides of the Irish Sea, who paved the way for the removal of 'the fetters of our commerce', because it represented the embrace by government of the 'great and noble principle ... that Ireland had *a right* to an unlimited trade with all foreign countries'. He was fulsome too in his praise of Lord North and other ministers, and, characteristically, drew attention to his own role in popularising the term 'free trade'. Nobody took umbrage. MPs were happy to accept his statement that the reticence he had shown when 'free trade' was first announced was inappropriate, and that this was a moment for the country as a whole to exult:

143 Scott to Robinson, 2 Dec., Beresford to Robinson, 2 Dec. in *Beresford Corres.*, i, 100–5; Beresford to Townshend, 3 Dec., Blaquiere to Townshend, ca 3 Dec., Scott to Townshend, 3 Dec., Paterson to Townshend, 3, 7 Dec., Montgomery to Townshend, 3 Dec. 1779 (N.A., Townshend Letterbook, Ms 5040 ff 126–30, 184–92, 195–8).   144 Lammey 'Free trade', pp 227–8; North to Buckinghamshire, 4, 9 Dec. (N.L.I., Heron Papers, Ms 13038/17); Fortescue, ed., *Corres. of George III*, iv, 509–13; North to Scott, 9 Dec. in *Beresford Corres.*, i, 109; Ellis to Hely-Hutchinson, 16 Dec. 1779 in H.M.C., *Donoughmore Mss*, p. 294.   145 Beresford to Robinson, 13 Dec. in *Beresford Corres.*, i, 112–18; Beresford to Townshend, 16 Dec. (N.A., Townshend Letterbook, Ms 5040 ff 243–5); Pery to North, 13 Dec. in H.M.C., *Emly*, p. 206; Buckinghamshire to North, 14 Dec. 1779 in Bartlett, ed., *Macartney*, pp 321–2.

The ungenerous, and mistaken reception that seemed to have circulated for twenty-four hours about this metropolis... required to be corrected, and it stands now corrected. It is the business of this House to favour the rights, and to correct the prejudices of the people. This House has stood a monument of mighty virtue. No assembly of men that I have ever read of, have ever appeared with more majesty, because none with more rectitude. The voice of this House has been truly the voice of the nation; not of this man, or that man, however respectable; there was not one man, or one set of men in this country, that could have made, or unmade that which you have done it was the voice of the nation, it was the voice of the people. You have been treated as that conduct deserved, not as mercenary individuals, but the nation of Great Britain has spoken to the nation of Ireland, and it has spoken satisfactorily. Thank God it has! My heart is full of the subject, and if I was not sensible how much too much I have trespassed upon you already, I should endeavour to say something more; I should, amidst all the calamities that impend over this nation; I should congratulate you, that you have a king who has effectually interposed in favour of this country, that you have a minister that has dared to state a truth as bold as any minister has spoken to the people of England.[146]

Flood's generous and well-judged welcome for 'free trade' in the Commons secured a deserved mention in Buckinghamshire's report of proceedings. The endorsement free trade received at meetings of grand jurors and freeholders throughout the country (including County Kilkenny) in the weeks and months that followed indicated that he had judged the national mood correctly.[147] The earl of Buckinghamshire, for his part, interpreted the outcome as a personal triumph. He was confident that he would be able to build on the good will engendered by the concession as he busied himself in late December and early-January with plans to restructure his government in Ireland.[148] Since Flood did not figure in the Lord Lieutenant's calculations, he concluded that his situation could only be resolved by his bypassing the Irish administration and going straight to the font of power; with this in mind, he made another mid-session trip to England.

146 *Some authentic minutes of the proceedings of a very respectable assembly on the 20th of December, 1779* (Dublin, 1780), pp 49–50.   **147** Buckinghamshire to Germain, 21 Dec. 1779 in H.M.C., *Stopford Sackville*, p. 63; copies of addresses of thanks in P.R.O., 63/468–9 *passim*.   **148** Buckinghamshire to Thompson, 3, 9 Jan. 1780 (Hotham Papers, P.R.O.N.I.,T3429/1/52, 53); Buckinghamshire to Hillsborough, 28 Dec. 1779, 1, 2, 5 Jan. 1780 (P.R.O., S.P.63/467 ff 297, 468 ff 5, 9–12, 14); North to Buckinghamshire, 26 Dec. (N.L.I., Heron Papers, Ms 13038/19); Buckinghamshire to North, 31 Dec. 1779 in *Beresford Corres.*, i, 122–5.

LAST CHANCE

The date of Flood's departure for England is not known, but he was in London by 5 January because Edmund Burke wrote him at his London hotel on that day to thank him for defending his reputation during the Commons' debate of 20 December.[149] His strategy is not entirely clear but, like Burke, he was concerned to vindicate his reputation because he informed Markham that he could 'challenge any man in the nation to say that I had ever broken an engagement public or private or swerved from the honour and consistency of a man'.[150] From Flood's perspective, the most important facts were that the agreement made with him by Lord Harcourt had not been implemented and that, as a result, he was blameless of any wrong doing. For this reason, the question of his following the example of Hussey Burgh and resigning his position did not arise. Indeed, he maintained to Archbishop Markham, to whom he once again appealed to plead his case, that the vice-treasurership was 'as fairly mine for life as if it were by patent' because he had not been given the 'permanent office' he was promised. This was untenable, but as far as Flood was concerned he had vested his 'unlimited confidence ... in the honour of government' and had been let down:

> a confidence which no man in his sense would have reposed who did not himself mean fairly and who did not act fairly to others. Why so capital and wanton a breach ... was then committed? Why in two years after another flagrant violation was added? Why Sir [Richard Heron] added a third two years ago together with all that has happened since. Why my office has been rendered less useful to others and less distinct to me I know not and have often entreated. I see it as determined that I shall not serve here with honour.[151]

Officials in both Dublin and London saw things differently, of course, as they made clear in January. The chronology of events is obscure, but it appears that once he became aware of the full extent of ministerial displeasure with his behaviour, Flood requested Markham to inform George III that he had been prompted to take office in 1775 by 'zeal for his majesty's service', and that because his conduct was deemed 'unacceptable', he was willing to tender his resignation:

> I neither have had, nor have the smallest connexion with any man or set of men in opposition to his government in England or Ireland, but that my services having been rendered unacceptable to his majesty in an honourable form I beg leave ... to resign my office into his royal hands ... It would give me pain to have

---

149 Burke to Flood, 5 Jan. 1780 in *Burke Corres.*, iv, 181–2.   150 Tattered draft of Flood to [Markham] [ca Dec.-Jan. 1779–80] (Rosse Papers, C/2/42).   151 Ibid.

kept it a moment contrary to that sense of fairness which my own mind acknowl-
edges and to which I think the minds of influential men will accede. In any other
respect the permanent tenure of an office is not an object of prime significance
to me, and I mention this lest casual and general words of mine might at any
time have led your Grace to think otherwise. Neither is an exchange [of] my
office for any in this kingdom in my pursuit for [if I was?] driven from my present
situation, I know [it is something?] I would never think of.

There was more than a hint of special pleading about Flood's talk of resignation, as
his reference to being 'driven' from office attests. He certainly perceived himself as
the injured party, because he had 'never received a single favour' from the earl of
Buckinghamshire and, armed with this information, he requested Charles Jenkinson
to facilitate him present his case directly to ministers. It is not clear what ensued,
but it is surely significant that Lord North informed Buckinghamshire on 16 January that he would 'not have the least objection' if 'at the close of the session' he
removed Flood from the vice-treasurership and gave the office to Lord Shannon.[152]
Flood was not made aware of the prime minister's recommendation, though the
designation of him as 'doubtful' in a Castle list prepared in February suggests that
the administration had still not given up on him entirely. Indeed, considering his
unpredictability, they were probably relieved that he elected to stay in England rather
than return for the resumption of the session, as it released them from the responsibility of 'tak[ing] strong notice' of his 'misconduct' should he misbehave.[153]

Flood's failure to return from England disappointed those patriots who hoped
that he would rejoin the patriot fold to guide the fast-emerging demand for constitutional reform. The most eminent of his advocates was John Forbes, the MP for
Drogheda, who wrote Flood on the subject on 20 January. Forbes' object was to
advance constitutional reform without attenuating the primacy of parliament, without alienating the Volunteers and 'without producing any jealousy in Great Britain',
and he believed Flood was the man most capable of striking this delicate balance.[154]
William Jephson concurred, but for a somewhat different reason. Worried by the
level of public support for the repeal of Poyning's Law, he concluded it was best for
Anglo-Irish relations and moderate patriots like himself if Flood's contention that
the interference of the Irish Privy Council with Irish legislation was predicated on
'a vicious and corrupt misconstruction'[155] was agitated:

---

152 Tattered draft of Flood to –, 1779/80 (Rosse Papers, C/2/43); Jenkinson to Flood, 6 Jan. (Rosse
Papers, C/1/12); North to Buckinghamshire, 16 Jan. 1780 (N.L.I., Heron Papers, Ms 13039/1). North
also agreed to the removal of Hely-Hutchinson as comptroller of Strangford. 153 Buckinghamshire
list (P.R.O., S.P.63/468 ff 210–20); Instructions for Sir Richard Heron, 5 Mar. 1780 (N.L.I., Heron
Papers, Ms 13039/4). 154 Forbes to Flood, 20 Jan. 1780 (Rosse Papers, C/1/13). 155 A sketch of
facts [1780s] (R.I.A., Burrowes Papers, Ms 23K53/10).

The most that can be done by the moderate party (my party) is to retain that part of it which gives the King and Council of England a power of altering etc.; but the other part, which relates to the interference of the Council of Ireland, will and ought to be destroyed. This, as I remember, was your plan in the days of Lord Chatham. Now, what I want is that you should be the man to procure the repeal of this latter part with the good will of England. You will, if I [am] not much deceived, do much good and get much honour. Both are objects. I wish also that it should be known that you have been the man to procure this improvement of the Irish constitution. Depend on it, *the thing* must be done, and sure the Ministers can better do it at once, and with good grace.[156]

If Flood was tempted by the prospect of a quick return to the forefront of patriot politics, he gave no hint of it, and his non-committal reply to Jephson indicates that he did not perceive it to be quite as logical as his correspondents that he should take up the issue of constitutional reform. Dublin Castle was certainly anxious that he did not, as it prepared to resist calls for constitutional change in the early months of 1780.[157]

Following the announcement of 'free trade', a host of press commentators and Volunteer assemblies in Dublin and Belfast identified the legislative constraints in force on the Irish parliament as the next issue the patriots should agitate. This demand took shape while Flood was in London and it was already sufficiently advanced by the time Forbes wrote him in January 1780 for the former Chief Secretary, George Macartney, to inform the Prime Minister that the 'points' that would be pressed were Poynings' Law, the Declaratory Act, annual parliaments, the tenure of judges, a land tax and an Irish mutiny bill. Lord North was profoundly concerned that this might precipitate a 'fatal quarrel' between Britain and Ireland, but his alarm was unwarranted. A number of these issues were raised in the weeks following the reassembly of parliament on 25 January, but the Castle was able to defeat every attempt by the patriots to cause the House of Commons to endorse constitutional reform.[158]

If the administration was able successfully to frustrate the attempts to advance constitutional reform without Flood's help, his return to Ireland, ostensibly, the Chief Secretary reported from London, 'to oppose all constitutional questions',

156 Jephson to Flood, 12 Feb. 1780 (Rosse Papers, C/1/14).   157 Flood to Jephson, (damaged), post 12 Feb. (Rosse Papers, C/1/14); Buckinghamshire to Heron, 5 Mar. 1780 (N.L.I., Heron Papers, Ms 13039/5).   158 M.G. O'Brien, 'The exercise of legislative power in Ireland, 1782–1800' (Ph.D. thesis, Cambridge University, 1983), pp 8–10, 19; *F.L.J.*, 22, 29 Dec. 1779; *H.J.*, 14, 17 Jan., 21 , 23 Feb., 1 Mar.; Macartney to North, 8 Jan. in Bartlett, ed., *Macartney*, pp 324–5; North to Buckinghamshire, 16 Jan. (N.L.I., Bolton Papers, Ms 16039/1); Hillsborough to Buckinghamshire, 22, 24 Jan.(N.L.I., Heron Papers, Ms 13039/2); Buckinghamshire to Hillsborough, 12, 26, 29 Jan., 9, 10, 12, 17, 25 Feb., 1, 2, 8 Mar. 1780 (P.R.O., S.P.,63/468 ff 43–4, 110–11, 122–5, 205–8, 221–4, 251–3, 296–7, 330–5, 375); Callen, ed., 'Cavendish's parl. diary', i, 263–9, 314–24.

suggested that they would find it even easier to repel the efforts of the leading patriots, headed by Henry Grattan, Barry Yelverton and Gervaise Bushe, who were determined to press for constitutional reform when parliament reconvened on 11 April.
Heron speculated that Flood's resolution to resist the agitation of constitutional
points derived from his realisation that the government intended to remove him
from office, but there is no corroboration for this.[159] He had an opportunity to make
a more considered judgement beginning on Tuesday, 18 April when Gervaise Bushe
inaugurated a series of debates on constitutional matters with a request for permission to introduce an Irish mutiny bill transferring legal responsibility for the army
from the British to the Irish parliament. Significantly, Flood supported Bushe's
motion with his vote rather than his voice but, despite this, it was denied when the
administration moved successfully for an adjournment.[160]

If Flood's stance on the mutiny bill suggested that Heron's information that he
was opposed to constitutional reform was wrong, its patriot proponents had little
reason to feel happy with him either. Indeed, on the following day, Wednesday 19
April, during the marathon debate on Grattan's controversial proposition that 'the
Lords and Commons of Ireland are the only power competent to enact laws to bind
Ireland', Flood offered a long justification of his reasons for disagreeing with the
motion while supporting the sentiment. In the course of this, he drew on his extensive researches into the application of English law in Ireland to demonstrate that
historically 'the parliament of England enacted laws respecting Ireland and Ireland
enacts laws to bind herself'. It was 'extraordinary', he opined, that this was so, and
because Grattan's motion would not undo this, and because its ratification would be
construed in England as a threat to the Anglo-Irish connection, he deemed it appropriate at this moment not to press it:

> When it is considered the many instances of all these British parliaments enact-
> ing laws to bind Ireland, our resolutions on this subject will not appear as the
> voice of faction, but as the determination of a wise and judicious parliament;
> and having said this much, I beseech Gentlemen to consider the tendency at this
> time of such a resolution being passed, as a resolution of the House of Com-
> mons; and that we should consider that the resolution of one House of Parlia-
> ment, or the resolution of both Houses are not equal to one statute. I leave it to
> my hon. friend that a resolution cannot be conclusive, it [is] only opening a field
> for dissention, let us refer the consideration to some future day. I have been 21
> years among you, a member of this parliament; I must reflect upon the situation
> of my native country. If it was necessary for the welfare of Ireland that this ques-
> tion should be supported, I would support it; England has no intention to en-

159 *H.J.*, 12 Apr.; Heron to Buckinghamshire, 3 Apr. 1780 (N.L.I., Heron Papers, Ms 15039/8). 160
Callen, ed., 'Cavendish's parl. diary', ii, 140–6; Buckinghamshire to Hillsborough, 14, 17 Apr. (P.R.O.,
S.P.63/468 ff 65, 77); O'Brien, 'Exercise of legislative power', pp 11–16.

force the act of 6 Geo[rge] I as we have received lately a grant of a free-trade
from England, they have evinced their intentions to secure Ireland, let us not
then exasperate them by groundless jealousies. I do not want to get rid of the
subject. I only want to have it duly, impartially and maturely considered, and let
us give it due weight before it is finally decided.

A majority of MPs thought likewise, for when a motion to adjourn was proposed by
Hussey Burgh on Flood's suggestion, it was carried by 136 votes to 97.[161]

Flood's refusal to support Grattan's attempt to pave the way for a declaration of
rights won him honourable mention in the official report of the debate, but it has
been accorded a distinctly less positive reaction by historians. It has been claimed
that he was prompted by jealousy of Grattan. He has also been criticised for failing
to take full advantage of England's embarrassment abroad to advance Irish rights.[162]
This is to misunderstand Flood's position. He was not opposed, as his speech made
clear, to the motion *per se*; he simply considered the timing inappropriate. By the
same token, it is misleading to claim, as Lawrence Parsons has, that Flood 'spoke
strongly in favour of the principle of the resolution'. According to Parsons, Flood
indicated to Buckinghamshire before the debate that he would support the motion,
and that when the Lord Lieutenant 'remonstrated with him', he replied 'he came
into office, not to relinquish his opinions, but to enforce them with greater effect'.[163]
This cannot be corroborated. What is indisputable is that Flood was better disposed
towards constitutional reform than his statement of 19 April indicated, because a
week later he endorsed Barry Yelverton's motion calling for the modification of
Poynings' Law to deprive the Irish Privy Council of the power to suppress bills.
Ironically, he was in a minority on this occasion; the motion was defeated by a modest twenty-five votes in a packed house.[164]

Dublin Castle was understandably greatly relieved it had prevailed in all three
divisions. Flood's state of mind is more difficult to establish. He was clearly not
committed to opposing 'all constitutional points', as Heron had reported, but he
was not prepared to join with the patriots either. His continuing caution, when his
political instincts favoured constitutional reform, can be attributed, at least partly,
to the influence of William Markham, who described those who 'move [constitu-
tional] questions' as 'wicked citizens'. At the same time, his observation that 'the
people in general do think that their law ought to be made by the Irish parliament

161 *Debates in the House of Commons of Ireland on a motion whether the King's most excellent majesty and
the Lords and Commons of Ireland are the only power competent to bind or enact laws in this kingdom* (Dublin, 1780), pp 21–2; Buckinghamshire to Germain, 22 Apr. 1780 in H.M.C., *Lothian*, p. 363; *Grattan's
speeches*, i, 54–5.   162 Buckinghamshire to Hillsborough, 20, 21 Apr. 1780 (P.R.O., S.P.63/469 ff 95–6,
104–6); Mac Nevin, *History of the Volunteers*, pp 132–6, 150–1.   163 Political recollections of Parsons
(Rosse Papers, F/13); Notes on Flood by Lawrence Parsons (ibid., C/14).   164 Callen, ed., 'Cavendish's
parl. diary', ii, 155–67; *H.J.*, 8 May; Buckinghamshire to Hillsborough, 27 Apr. 1780 (P.R.O., S.P.63/
469 ff 134–5).

only' and that the refusal of some magistrates to enforce the British Mutiny Act demanded that 'something must be done' suggests that he had concluded that some reform was unavoidable.[165] However, the main influence on his behaviour remained the 1775 agreement, as he had not given up hope that he might, even yet, secure its implementation in full. This is surprising, given that only a few months earlier he had considered tendering his resignation. One can only assume that he was not entirely serious when he raised this possibility.

When Flood left England in April, he entrusted the representation of his cause, while reserving the right 'to negotiate', to Archbishop Markham. Despite his previous lack of success, Markham used a highly placed intermediary[166] to re-raise the question of Flood acquiring a seat at Westminster with Lord North, but the Prime Minister was unwilling to advance the matter. He was, Markham reported, on 28 April:

> sorry for the ill-treatment that was complained of, when it was impossible it could be intended by him, and that he should have been happy to prevent it; that he was perfectly informed of your abilities and consequence, and would gladly have availed himself of them, particularly by a seat here; he remembered it had been agitated, but that by his accounts he understood that it would make a difference in your expenses of at least £1,000 a year, and you would expect it should be made up to you; but as he did not know when that might be in his power it made a difficulty, especially as you had never explained yourself upon the subject.

This was a polite but firm no, and Markham was clearly not best-pleased to learn that Flood had discussed the matter in such detail with the Prime Minister. He let Flood know that he believed he had been less than 'fair and explicit' with him, though he continued to make his services available.[167]

Flood for his part seemed quite desperate to extract some commitment from the administration because, having failed with Westminster, he switched his attention to Callan. This was unheralded, but the fact that he requested Markham to press it with the Prime Minister at this moment emphasizes how hurt he was by the Castle's failure to support his electoral aspirations in 1776–7, and how important Callan and County Kilkenny continued to be to him:

> My elections are a point which a certain person [Buckinghamshire?] ought surely to decide in my favour without delay. To a man that knows the world, difficulties

---

165 Markham to Flood, 28 Apr., 21 May, Flood to Markham (damaged draft), 4 May 1780 (Rosse Papers, C/2/39, 40, 41).   **166** This was either Charles Jenkinson or Lord Mansfield (Heron to Buckinghamshire, 3 Apr. 1780 (N.L.I., Heron Papers, Ms 13039/8)).   **167** Markham to Flood, 28 Apr. 1780 (Rosse Papers, C/2/39).

in such points prove nothing unless indisposition. A peerage to Mr George Agar would free me from him in Callan, and the county [of Kilkenny] could be settled for me with Lord Clifden and the Archbishop of Cashel.[168]

Flood evidently regarded this suggestion as reasonable; but it made no sense at all to ministers. Indeed, given Flood's voting record and the fragmentation of his parliamentary connection, no government could contemplate antagonizing such a well-committed interest as the Agars and, possibly, every other major interest in County Kilkenny simply to satisfy an errant officeholder.

Despite the inherent improbability that the request could be met, Markham sought and secured a meeting with Lord North in May to plead Flood's case. The Prime Minister reiterated that he bore Flood no ill-will. He had, he pronounced, been well-inclined towards him, and he avowed with more than a hint of dissimulation that if Flood's original request for a government nomination for a seat at Westminster had 'been followed it might probably have made him [North] more industrious in trying to find an opportunity' as there were 'many occasions on which he could have helped him'. He expressed regret that Flood had allowed himself to become 'alienated ... from the public service', but his conclusion that Flood's 'credit and consequence had in general gone into the opposite scale' indicates that as far as he was concerned, Flood deserved no more preferment.[169]

North's response was almost certainly informed by events in the Irish House of Commons in May when Flood failed to support the Castle on the key constitutional and commercial points that dominated that month's proceedings. The first was Gervaise Bushe's request for permission to introduce the heads of an Irish mutiny bill. In the absence of an instruction from London as to how he should respond on this point, Buckinghamshire convened a meeting 'of the principal servants of the Crown'. Flood was among those present, and he was one of the minority (which also included John Foster and John Hely-Hutchinson) which 'strongly' favoured an Irish mutiny act. However, Buckinghamshire was not prepared to take such a step without authorization from London. Flood had no difficulty accepting this. Indeed, when the issue came up for discussion in the House of Commons on Monday, 8 May, he supported Heron's successful motion, against fierce criticism from the patriots, to delay consideration of the matter for another fortnight. However, when Buckinghamshire convened a further meeting of 'principal servants' to inform them that the government was firmly opposed to conceding the point, Flood and several others present deemed this impractical, and Bushe's motion was approved by a large majority on 22 May.[170]

168 Flood to Markham (draft fragment), 4 May 1780 (Rosse Papers, C/2/40).   169 Markham to Flood, 21 May 1780 (Rosse Papers, C/2/41).   170 Callen, ed., 'Cavendish's parl diary', ii, 174–6, 178–85, 201–5; Heron to Porten, 2, 13 May, Hillsborough to Buckinghamshire, 7 May, Buckinghamshire to Hillsborough, 13, 21, 22 May 1780 (P.R.O., S.P.63/469 ff 159, 165–6, 195–8, 211, 264–6); Buckinghamshire to Pery, 22 May 1780 in H.M.C., *Emly*, ii, 158.

Perhaps influenced by his inability to shape government policy, Flood did not contribute to any of the Commons' discussions on the mutiny bill or the other controversial matters, such as the duty on refined sugars imported from England, that excited MPs in May and early June. He did make a short speech on 11 May against the establishment of a national bank, which he deemed unnecessary, but otherwise he maintained his own counsel.[171] His reserve was also influenced by his preoccupation with the administration of the corn bounties, which prompted him to apply to the House on 6 May for leave to prepare the heads of a bill for the further encouragement and regulation of the corn trade. The bill which resulted was presented to the House of Commons on 1 June.[172] The purpose of the measure was to encourage domestic grain production by increasing the bounties on corn and flour sent for export to the level currently applied in England and to impose an impost on imports of these commodities when their price was below a designated level. The administration was less than happy with these proposals, because of their perceived anti-English thrust, but policy as well as personality differences deterred them from seeking their modification,[173] or the modification of those reducing the bounties on the inland carriage of corn, flour and malt to provide revenue to fund the proposed new bounties. The main points of controversy in the Commons were the level at which the export bounty was set, and whether farmers or millers should be the main beneficiary. Surviving accounts of the debates are incomplete, but it is clear that Flood dominated proceedings. It was he, for instance, who led the resistance to the objections of the spokesmen for the corn industry. Flood's priority was Irish agriculture and the enhancement of the lot of farmers, which brought him into conflict with William Colville, the MP for Limavady, who maintained on Monday, 12 June, that the bill would disadvantage farmers by restricting their access to the Dublin market and by increasing their dependence on millers. The exchanges that followed between Flood and he became so heated that some apprehended a duel. This did not come to pass, but Colville's opposition did ensure that the proposed bounty on flour and wheat was reduced from Flood's preferred level. However, the bill itself was not endangered, and Flood was honoured when he was instructed to present it to the Lord Lieutenant with the request of the House that it should be conveyed to 'Great Britain in due form', which was done on 21 June.[174]

This was a satisfying conclusion to this sitting, and to the prolonged 1779–80 session for Flood. In June, he left Dublin and the political world of parliament and

171 Callen, ed., 'Cavendish's parl diary', ii, 170–245 *passim*; Buckinghamshire to Hillsborough, 28 May 1780 (P.R.O., S.P., 63/469 ff 284–6).   172 Callen, ed., 'Cavendish's parl diary', ii, 177–8; *Commons Jn.(Irl.)*, x, 122, 124, 151.   173 Scott to Robinson, 4 June in *Beresford Corres.*, i, 137; Buckinghamshire to Germain, 25 May (B.L., Mackintosh Colln., Add Ms 34523 f 287); Buckinghamshire to Hillsborough, 21 June 1780 (P.R.O., S.P., 63/469 ff 383–90).   174 Callen, ed., 'Cavendish's parl. diary', ii, 230–8; *Commons Jn.(Irl.)*, x, 151, 153, 160–1, 163, 165–6; Buckinghamshire to Hillsborough, 21 June 1780 (P.R.O., S.P.63/469 ff 383–6).

Volunteer reviews for Farmley. Indeed, the only public mention of him in the months that followed arose from his apprehension and committal of a local malefactor.[175] He was not far from the Lord Lieutenant's mind, however. Buckinghamshire felt deeply angry that Flood, Hely-Hutchinson and others in receipt of government favour now voted 'almost uniformly' with its opponents. His intention was to have them dismissed once he negotiated the final weeks of the session. Flood's absence helped him do this, but the support he secured from members of 'distinction and property' was of greater importance because it enabled the administration to negate the attempts of the patriots to undo the changes made to the mutiny and sugar bills by the British Privy Council. It was not enough to save Buckinghamshire's career, however, as steps were already underway behind the scenes to replace him and Heron.[176]

If Flood thought that his absence from the Commons in July–August might stave off disciplinary action, Buckinghamshire did not weaken in his resolve to have him dismissed. On 4 September, he wrote formally to Lord North requesting permission to remove him and Hely-Hutchinson 'from their situations'. In view of the Prime Minister's agreement in January that it should be done once the session was over, Buckinghamshire anticipated that approval was just a formality, and this presumably accounts for the reports in the Dublin press a few days later that Flood was to be replaced as vice-treasurer by Lord Shannon. It was essential from the Lord Lieutenant's perspective that Flood and Hely-Hutchinson were not allowed 'remain undisturb'd in their present employments' if (as he believed) he was to remain in Ireland because otherwise 'it would obviously be infer'd that the opposing Lord Buckingham[shire]'s administration was but a venial sin'.[177] Flood and Hely-Hutchinson obviously had a different perspective on the matter. The Provost, once he realised the danger, embarked with characteristic brio on a vigorous campaign to protect his position by explaining at length to friends and officials in Britain and Ireland the qualitative difference between his occasional defections and Flood's frequent absences.[178] Flood for his part did nothing as usual, and it proved just as successful. Lord North declined to approve Buckinghamshire's request to dismiss both men on the grounds 'that it would now only create opposition to Lord Carlisle'

175 *H.J.*, 28 July 1780.   176 Buckinghamshire to Thompson, 3, 30 June, Buckinghamshire to Hillsborough, 6 June (B.L., Mackintosh Colln., Add. Ms 34523 ff 287–9, 292); *Life of Grattan*, ii, 103–4, 118–9, 122, 186–8, 447–55; Explanatory minute, 1780 (B.L., Auckland Papers, Add. Ms 34417 f 98); Gower to Carlisle, 24 July, Carlisle to Hillsborough [July] in H.M.C., *Carlisle*, pp 436–8; Callen, ed., 'Cavendish's parl. diary', ii, 247–301 *passim*; *H.J.*, 11, 18, 23 Aug.; Heron to Porten, 14 Aug. 1780 (P.R.O., S.P.63/470 f 275).   177 Buckinghamshire to North, 4 Sept. (B.L., Mackintosh Colln., Add. Ms 34523 f 295); above, p. 269; *H.J.*, 6 Sept.; Buckinghamshire to Germain, 13, 20 Sept. 1780 in H.M.C., *Stopford Sackville*, p. 65.   178 Hely-Hutchinson to North, 5 Sept, Hely-Hutchinson to Ellis, 6, 7 Sept., Hely-Hutchinson to Jenkinson, 6/7 Sept., Hely-Hutchinson to Hillsborough, Sept., 17 Oct., Hely-Hutchinson to Hertford, 5 Sept., 4 Nov. in H.M.C., *Donoughmore*, pp 298–300; Conolly to Buckinghamshire, 16 Oct. (N.L.I., Heron Papers, Ms 13050/2); Buckinghamshire to Hillsborough, 28 Oct. 1780 (B.L., Mackintosh Colln., Add. Ms 34523 f 299).

whom he had decided should take over the reins of power in Ireland.[179] This was a humiliating rebuff for Buckinghamshire, as he recognized, and it was compounded by the fact that Flood took this moment to advance a number of claims for preferment. It is ironic that among the final matters with which Buckinghamshire had to deal as Lord Lieutenant was a request by Henry Flood that he should have a say in the disposal of a minor military office in County Kilkenny as well as the more prestigious office of counsel to the commissioners of the revenue in which both Frederick Flood and Henry Cavendish were interested.[180] Flood had outlasted Lord Buckinghamshire in office, but it was due more to good fortune than to good judgement. Lord Carlisle was to prove a sterner test.

DISMISSAL

Lord Carlisle and William Eden, his Chief Secretary, arrived in Dublin in late December 1780. Some questioned Carlisle's capacity for the onerous task of governing Ireland, but his experience on the 1778 peace commission to America and his reserved, indeed taciturn, disposition proved advantageous, not least because it complemented Eden's more gregarious temperament. They also took office at a good time as, following the conclusion of the eventful 1779–80 session, Irish politics briefly presented 'a face of tranquillity'.[181] This was encouraging because the new executive was instructed to continue the policy of its predecessor and to repulse any attempt by the patriots to assert Ireland's claim to greater legislative and constitutional authority. With this in mind, they were heartened by the promise of support forthcoming from moderate patriots (like the duke of Leinster and Thomas Conolly) who were uneasy with the attempts by hardliners to agitate constitutional points. As well as this, Eden successfully won over disaffected Castle loyalists like John Beresford and John Scott; and he and Carlisle were sufficiently confident by the middle of 1781 to conclude that 'order and good government will be restored ... in Ireland'. In order to ensure this, the Lord Lieutenant and Chief Secretary determined that all

---

179 Lucan to Pery, 3 Oct. in H.M.C. *Emly*, p. 159; Buckinghamshire to Germain, 20 Oct. in H.M.C., *Stopford-Sackville*, pp 65–6; North to Eden, 21 Oct. (B.L., Auckland Papers, Add. Ms 34417 f 229); Hillsborough to Buckinghamshire, 27 Oct. (Hobart Papers, P.R.O.N.I., T3110/1/126); Robinson to George III, 5 Nov. in Fortescue, ed., *Corres.of George III*, iii, 147–8; Buckinghamshire to Hillsborough, 8 Nov.1780 (P.R.O., S.P.63/471 f 200).   180 Minute of what passed between Sir Henry Cavendish and Sir Richard Heron, 8 Nov., Buckinghamshire to Hillsborough, 20 Nov. (P.R.O., S.P.63/471 ff 308–10, 294–5); Heron to Eden, 22 Dec.(B.L.,Auckland Papers, Add. Ms 34417 f 270); Buckinghamshire to Foster, 28 Oct., Buckinghamshire to Thompson, 10 Dec. 1780 (B.L., Mackintosh Colln., Add. Ms 34523 ff 299, 302).   181 A.I.M.Duncan, 'A study of the life and public career of Frederick Howard, fifth earl of Carlisle 1748–1825' (Ph.D. thesis, Oxford University, 1981), pp 104–6, 109; Moira to Hastings, 17 Mar. 1782 in H.M.C., *Hastings*, iii, 197; Buckinghamshire to Hillsborough, 23 Dec. 1780, Carlisle to Hillsborough, 9 Jan. 1781 (P.R.O., S.P.63/471 f 465, 474 ff 20–1); Buckinghamshire's vindication (Lothian Papers, P.R.O.N.I., T3502/1 part 1).

officeholders should be brought into line, and they demonstrated their intentions in this regard in May 1781 when they recommended the dismissal of Judge Richard Power 'for continued absence from duty' and, in August, when they elicited 'fresh assurances' from John Hely-Hutchinson that his support would be forthcoming.[182]

Hely-Hutchinson's success in overcoming the distrust with which he was regarded in official circles demonstrates well how a canny politician could use a change in Castle personnel to personal advantage. Flood, as usual, was less adept. Shortly after Carlisle's arrival, he travelled to Dublin to meet the new Lord Lieutenant who informed him 'that in consideration of the very high and lucrative employments [he] held under the crown' Carlisle 'expect[ed] a decisive conduct'.[183] Flood expressed no outward displeasure with this instruction, but in the absence of any indication that the new administration was prepared to honour in full the terms of the 1775 agreement, he did not see any reason why he should alter his behaviour. So when Eden requested a meeting to discuss political matters in late January 1781 he excused himself on the grounds that he had urgent business to attend to in Kilkenny.[184] This was not acceptable to an administration which was determined

> to show a marked disapprobation of that double conduct which leads men here to endeavour to retain good offices and at the same time to sacrifice all the interests and character of government to the popular nonsenses of the day.[185]

It was not possible, obviously, to dismiss Flood or any other recalcitrant officeholder for declining an invitation to a meeting, but his decision to stay in County Kilkenny throughout the summer of 1781 suggests that he realised his days as an officeholder were numbered. This would also explain the renewal of his relationship with Lord Charlemont and his suddenly acquired interest in Volunteering. He planned, but was unable because it clashed with the poll to elect a new sovereign to the corporation of Callan, to meet Charlemont at the Carlow review, and subsequently undertook to accompany him on part of his northern tour.[186] This was cancelled when Flood was struck down by gout, but despite this Carlisle was already convinced by the end of June that Flood was resolved to be 'determinedly hostile' and that all that remained to be resolved was

182 Duncan, op. cit., p. 108; Carlisle to Hillsborough, 7 Jan. (2) (P.R.O., S.P.63/474 ff 18–19, 22); Beresford to Robinson, 8 Jan., 27 June, Scott to Robinson, 12 June in *Beresford Corres.*, i, 150–1, 163–4; Eden to Knox, 11 Mar. in H.M.C., *Knox papers*, p. 339; Eden to Pery [spring] (2) (Additional Pery Papers, P.R.O.N.I., T3052/129, 130); Carlisle to Hillsborough, 12 May (N.A., Index of departmental letters and papers 1760–89 f 245); Hillsborough to Carlisle, 10, 29 Aug. (B.L., Auckland Papers, Add. Ms 34418 ff 10–11, 73–4); Conolly to Buckinghamshire, 19 Mar., Tighe to Buckinghamshire, 17 July 1781 in H.M.C., *Lothian*, pp 386, 390.   183 Carlisle to Gower, 30 June 1781 in H.M.C.*Carlisle*, p. 510.   184 Flood to Eden, 23 Jan. (B.L.,Auckland Papers, Add. Ms 34417 f 298).   185 Eden to Jenkinson, 29 Jan. (ibid., ff 306–8); Tighe to Buckinghamshire, 31 July 1781 in H.M.C., *Lothian*, pp 390–1.   186 Flood to Charlemont, 12 May in H.M.C., *Charlemont*, i, 381; Charlemont to Flood, 12 July 1781 in R[odd], ed., *Letters to Flood*, pp 106–7.

whether he will fling the v[ice] treasurership at my head, or force me to strip him of it (which I think I shall be necessitated to do).

There was, of course, a possibility that Flood would 'behave as he ought', but few in the administration anticipated this. In its absence, they were determined not to repeat what they believed was Buckinghamshire's crucial mistake of not punishing him when he was 'hostile', and Flood's request to Charlemont in August to provide him with 'the digested sentiments of the north on the sugar duties and mutiny bill' suggested that he also accepted that he would be dismissed.[187]

The enthusiastic endorsement by Volunteer Corps throughout the country of resolutions urging the agitation of constitutional points can only have encouraged Flood to conclude that it was time for him finally to turn his back on the arrangement he had made with Harcourt in 1775, but Eden gave him another opportunity to change his mind. In August, when preparations for the 1781–2 session were still at an early stage, he invited Flood to come to Dublin so the administration could avail of his 'abilities and judgement' in preparing 'the system of business for the approaching session'. Both Eden and Carlisle were disposed to adopt an understanding attitude to MPs who could not attend in person, but they were unwilling to allow those like Flood, who avoided contact throughout the summer, evade making a declaration of their opinions, as Eden made clear:

> If your private business should necessarily detain you from Dublin for some time, it would give the highest satisfaction to obtain the favour and advantage of your sentiments, which should receive in return every acknowledgement of the friendliest cordiality – indeed, I should be most happy to submit to you without reserve every information that I have been able to collect respecting either the public accounts or the other expected business of the session.[188]

This reduced Flood's room for manoeuvre, but he made no reference to written advice in his prompt reply of 24 August when he cited an attack of gout as his reason why he could not accept the Chief Secretary's invitation to meet him in Dublin. Two weeks later, he cited 'a hurt' he received to his 'eyes' as the reason for his failure to respond to a further communication. Eden accepted that Flood's poor 'health and spirit' made it difficult for him to stand forward, which is why neither Carlisle nor he instructed him (as they instructed Brabazon Ponsonby) that 'it was his duty ... to be present'.[189] However, they were not disposed to offer him any indulgence when he displayed the same reserve on the commencement of the 1781–2 session.

187 Carlisle to Gower, 30 June in H.M.C., *Carlisle*, p. 510; Tighe to Buckinghamshire, 31 July in H.M.C., *Lothian*, p. 391; Flood to Charlemont, 7 Aug. 1781 in H.M.C., *Charlemont*, i, 388.   188 Eden to Flood, 21 Aug. 1781 (B.L., Auckland Papers, Add. Ms 34418 ff 42–3).   189 Flood to Eden, 24 Aug., 8 Sept., Eden to Hillsborough, 21 Sept., Eden to [North], [13 Oct.] (B.L., Auckland Papers, Add. Ms 34418 ff

Flood was present on 9 October for the opening day of the session to hear statements by Yelverton and Grattan which suggested that proceedings would be dominated by the patriots' attempts to secure a *habeas corpus* bill, a judges bill, a mutiny bill, the reform of Poynings' Law and the resolution of the Portuguese trade dispute, but he 'stood' so aloof, Eden was uncertain how to interpret his 'cold civility'.[190] His uncertainty did not last long, for when the Commons reconvened after the customary recess that followed the approval of an address to the King, Flood availed of a debate on 1 November on Portugal's refusal to allow Irish goods enter its ports on the same terms as English goods to recommend decisive action and to express unease that the representation of Ireland's case was entrusted to 'the King's ministers'. There are a number of versions of what he said, but the most vivid was provided by Lord Carlisle:

When it was proposed to delay the consideration of the subject, [Flood] urged immediate proceeding, asserting that the loss of free trade lately granted to Ireland would be the consequence of procrastination; that he had no objection to the appointment of the Committee, except that it would tend to delay; that the House of Commons was in possession of sufficient information; and he recommended to them instantly to address His Majesty the King of Great Britain and Ireland, to use his influence effectually with the Court of Portugal, that Irish exports should be admitted as British; that a decision should take place before the sitting of the Committee of Supply; that though it might not be prudent to increase the Revenue by a duty on Portugal wines, the purpose with respect to Portugal might equally be answered by a diminution of the duties on French wines, which would be a preferable mode of pressing the Ministers to a spirited conduct, as a loss of Revenue is not generally agreeable to them. To the observation that the business was in negotiation by the King's ministers – that he would not have it taken out of the hands of parliament to put it into the hands of men who had destroyed the freedom of this country by a perpetual Mutiny Bill; that every word of that law was written with the blood of the Constitution, and that he would move for a Bill to explain, amend, and limit the duration of that Act. Through the whole of his speech his abilities were exerted to excite a jealous distrust of British Administration, and to connect the subject before the House with every other popular ground of apprehension. Recommending firmness to the Members, he said that if they failed they would be punished for their audacity, and that their spirit only could protect them; and sanctifying his opinion by the most solemn appeals, he asserted that the Kingdom was in a worse condition

57, 88, 119, 244); Pomeroy to Pomeroy, 13 Oct [1781] (Pomeroy Papers, P.R.O.N.I., T2954/4/7).   **190** Leinster to Spencer, 16 Oct. (Pomeroy Papers, P.R.O.N.I., T2954/4/7/2); *Parl. Reg. (Irl.)*,i, 1–2; Carlisle to Hillsborough, 10 Oct. (P.R.O., S.P.63/476 ff 227–9); Eden to North, 13 Oct. 1781 in *Beresford Corres.*,i, 176.

than it was two years ago; and that upon the determination of that night hung the fate of the nation; concluding with announcing the blessing that would accompany their concurrence with the motion, and denouncing the execrations that would attend a contrary conduct.[191]

As Carlisle's account makes clear, Flood's call for a vigorous response cut right across the administration's efforts to prevent the question of access to the Portuguese market being elevated into a *cause célèbre* with the opposition. He used, Edward Tighe alleged, 'every means to persuade and to inflame', and the administration concluded that they could not allow it to pass unnoticed. Flood's speech, Carlisle reported to the Secretary of State, Lord Hillsborough, was 'too marked and decided to escape observation'. Indeed, since he was convinced that Flood was 'fully aware of his situation, which he said was not to be flung away for a trifle', Carlisle concluded that Flood was inviting the administration to dismiss him, and he was determined to oblige. He informed Hillsborough on 2 November that Flood should be dismissed and his position offered to Lord Shannon.[192]

Once the decision was made, no time was lost conveying the news to Flood. He was informed of his fate within twenty-four hours. A few days later, matters were set in train to deprive him of his place at the British Privy Council. The suggestion that he should be dismissed from the Council came from Lord Hillsborough rather than from Dublin Castle, and while it smacked of vengeance, the need to 'cleans[e]' the Council was deemed too compelling.[193]

Dublin Castle's conclusion that Henry Flood courted dismissal on 2 November 1781 is almost certainly correct. His relations with the Carlisle administration had been strained from the moment the Lord Lieutenant made clear that as an office holder he would have to follow the Castle line or suffer the consequences. Lord Carlisle was puzzled that Flood should throw away an office worth £3,500 per annum so easily, but that is to miss the point. The money was of secondary consideration. The key was Flood's realisation that Carlisle had no intention of implementing the 1775 agreement. From Flood's point of view, it was not he but the administration who were in breach of their agreement. He had, he maintained, done nothing wrong so there was no question of his resigning.[194] Dismissal was an honourable outcome; resignation was not though he did keep this option under consideration. For this reason, those who write of Flood's 'resignation' or 'desertion' from 'the ministerial

191 Carlisle to Hillsborough, 2 Nov. 1781 (P.R.O.,S.P.63/477 ff 37–9).   192 Tighe to Buckinghamshire, 2 Nov. in H.M.C., *Lothian*, pp 400–1; Carlisle to Hillsborough, 2 Nov. 1781 (P.R.O., S.P., 63/477 ff 37–9).   193 Eden to North, 3 Nov., Robinson to Eden, 9 Nov. in *Beresford Corres.*, i, 179–82, 185; Eden to [Hillsborough], 4 Nov., Hillsborough to Eden, 13 Nov. (B.L., Auckland Papers, Add. Ms 34418 ff 156, 169); North to George III and reply, 10 Nov. 1781 in Fortescue, ed., *Corres of George III*, v, 298–9; Buckinghamshire to Tighe, 11 Mar. 1777 (Lothian Papers, P.R.O.N.I., T3502/2 part 2 f 60); Privy Council Register, P.R.O., P.C.2/126.   194 Carlisle to Selwyn, 20 Nov. in H.M.C., *Carlisle*, pp 532–3; Carlisle to Eden, 10 Nov. 1781 (B.L., Auckland Papers, Add. Ms 34418 f 163).

benches' miss the point.[195] Flood believed that for him to resign would be to acknowledge that he had made a mistake by taking office or misbehaved while in occupancy, and he simply did not accept that this was so. Indeed, he was so emphatic on this point that when Denis Daly subsequently attributed his behaviour to 'disappointed ambition', Flood insisted he withdrew the remark.[196]

For many on both sides of the Irish sea, Flood's dismissal from office was welcome news. Carlisle's supporters were convinced the Lord Lieutenant had done the right thing.[197] Many patriots too were happy; none more than Lord Charlemont who, virtually uniquely of Flood's old friends and political associates, had remained well-disposed to him through the late 1770s. Flood was frequently trying of his patience as well as of his goodwill, but Charlemont's delight on hearing of his dismissal demonstrates that he, at least, was prepared to forget the past. 'With Flood on our side it is impossible to despair; our sun has broke out from the cloud with redoubled lustre', he gushed.[198] Flood was less euphoric. His priority was not the advancement of constitutional reform (which dominated Charlemont's concerns) but the rehabilitation of his reputation. What both could agree upon was that his dismissal signalled the start of a new phase in his political life.

195 Flood, *Memoirs*, pp 129–30; Craig, *The Volunteer earl*, p. 107; Parsons' biography of Flood (Rosse Papers, F/13); *Life of Grattan*, ii, 185.   196 Rosse Papers, F/13; *Parl. Reg. (Irl.)*, i, 47–9.   197 Starr to Carlisle, 26 Nov. in H.M.C.*Carlisle*, p. 436; Townshend to Shannon, 2 Dec. 1781 (N.L.I.,Shannon Papers, Ms 13032/1/150).   198 Charlemont to Malone [1781/2] in Prior's *Life of Malone*, pp 103–4.

PART FOUR
INDEPENDENT RADICAL

Flood's dismissal from office in November 1781 restored to him the political freedom he had last possessed in the early 1770s. It was a potentially critical moment in his career, but his celebrated parliamentary skills were undiminished, and he moved easily onto the opposition benches where he sought to reassume the prominent role he had forsaken in 1775. It is not clear how he anticipated he would be received, but few of those patriots who had achieved eminence in the six years that he had been an officeholder felt inclined to share the limelight with a man who had allowed his 'virtue' to be impugned in so egregious a fashion. Many were also ill-at-ease with his assertive approach and unco-operative attitude, and this combined with his inability to subordinate his ego as well as his agenda to the collective will of the patriot connection to ensure he regained the trust and confidence of few of his old colleagues. Flood manifested no obvious anxiety with the reserve with which he was regarded. He was intent on going his own way and in taking a firm stand in favour of radical constitutional and parliamentary reform, and if this did not win him back the esteem he had been accorded by his colleagues prior to his taking office, he had the consolation of popular applause. This was sufficient, following on the controversial tack he took on legislative independence in the spring and summer of 1782, to permit him to spearhead a successful campaign in 1782–3 to compel the government to renounce its claim to legislate for Ireland, and to eclipse Grattan as the most popular patriot of the day. He appeared to consolidate this reputation when he was more forward than Grattan, Charlemont and most other patriots in advocating parliamentary reform in 1783–5. However, instead of carving out a new role as a popular politician, Flood gravitated away from College Green and devoted most of his energies thereafter to the political stage at Westminster. It proved a disappointing experience. Unwilling to align himself with either of the main British party interests and dogged by electoral problems, he failed to overcome the suspicion and disfavour with which he was regarded because of his radical patriotism and never fully came to terms with the more formal Westminster arena. He made a number of set-piece orations on major issues, but it was only with his final speech – on parliamentary reform in 1790 – that he can be said to have achieved the applause if not the legislative impact he sought.

7

Radical patriot, 1781–3

The early 1780s were the most eventful years in Flood's political life. Relieved of the restrictions of office, he was at liberty once more to articulate his opinions on all the major issues of the day and he revelled in the freedom this brought him. He did not, as far as one can detect, possess a specific legislative agenda; he responded to events and to the opportunities they offered. But his object remained what it had been in the 1760s – to enhance the status of the kingdom and parliament of Ireland *vis à vis* Great Britain – and he was guided in his response to the major issues of the day by that principle.

FAMILY DISPUTES

Flood had few political friends, when he had the vice-treasurership removed from him in 1781. This was a consequence, not of his dismissal, but of his withdrawal from active personal and political engagement while an officeholder, as a result of which he retained few of the friendships he had forged in the 1760s and early 1770s. Part of the reason for this was his practice of spending long stretches in London or in Farmley; but his personal aloofness and carelessness in sustaining relationships was equally consequential. Flood did, it is true, retain the devoted friendship of Ambrose Smith, but Smith was not politically active. He also maintained a relationship with his academic mentor, William Markham, over a long period. But it is significant that, a few literary exchanges excepted, their correspondence related primarily to Markham's efforts to plead Flood's case with ministers and they had little contact after 1781.[1]

To compound his isolation, the Flood borough interest had also fragmented. Gervaise Parker Bushe had gone his own way, and while there was no confrontation in the 1780s as dramatic as that which permanently soured his relationship with his cousin John, his relationship with his other cousins, Warden and Frederick, also

---

1 Rosse Papers, C/2 *passim*; R.Pares, *George III and the politicians* (Oxford, 1953), p. 24.

became progressively more distant. Both men supported him during the controversial Commons' investigation into the election returns for Callan and County Kilkenny in 1777, but their decision to seek government office thereafter drew them apart. This was unanticipated because the three cousins were perceived by outsiders in the mid-1770s to be at one politically. Indeed, Warden was described dismissively in one Castle list as 'a follower' of Henry. However, Warden's introduction by Lord Harcourt to Lord Carysfort, from whom he purchased a seat for the eponymous borough in 1776, reduced his dependence on his cousin in the late 1770s, and he proved more attentive to government interests thereafter. [2] This was so though his request for a judgeship in 1779 was denied. Despite this, Warden's natural 'self possession ... and modest assurance' ensured he ended the decade on good terms with the administration and with Henry though they acted entirely separately in the House of Commons. They subsequently drifted apart till, by the time Warden was appointed as judge of the admiralty court in 1785, they were on opposite sides in the House. [3]

Henry's relationship with his cousin Frederick was more complex. Frederick was politically independent of Henry following his election for the borough of Enniscorthy in 1776. Having purchased his seat, Frederick sought remunerative office, but his judicial 'incapacity' proved a formidable obstacle to his wish for legal preferment. He was considered for appointment as counsel to the revenue board in 1778 and 1780, and canvassed to be made third serjeant in 1779, but the Lord Chancellor's opposition precluded his appointment and he had to be content with a baronetcy, following the intervention of his father-in-law, Lord Valentia, in the spring of 1780 and the commissionership of stamps some time later. [4] Like Warden, Frederick was only 'tolerably satisfied' with the middle-ranking office he obtained, but he declined to cause the administration 'any degree of embarrassment' by pressing his aspirations for an eminent law office with unreasonable vigour. At the same time his

---

2 Hunt, ed., *Irish parliament in 1775*, p. 21; Heron's lists, 1776, 1777 (N.L.I., Heron Papers, Mss 3532, 5168); Account of the Irish parliament in 1782 (Henry Huntingdon Library); List of Commons of Ireland, Dec. 1778 (Oireachtais Library, Ms 7:H:37); Warden died a wealthy man, see his will, 1793 (Land Commission, Flood-Hanford estate Papers, Box 13 (E.C.2272)).   3 Cromie list, 1776–82 (B.L., Pelham Papers, Add. Ms 33118); Flood to Buckinghamshire, 5 Apr. 1779 (N.A., Calendar of Misc letters and papers, 1760–89, f 36); Flood, *Memoirs*, pp 7–9; Johnston, ed., 'Members of the Irish parliament', pp 162, 181, 231; McDougall, *Sketches of Irish political characters*, pp 284–5; Scott, *Principal characters of the Irish Commons*, pp 177–81; Civil establishment list for 1789 (N.L.I., Ms 4109).   4 Harcourt List, 1777 (D.P.L., Harcourt papers, Gilbert Ms 95 f 256); Cromie List, 1776–82 (B.L., Pelham Papers, Add. Ms 33118); Heron lists, 1776, 1777 (N.L.I., Ms 3532, 5168); Beresford to Allan, 27 Apr. 1778 in *Beresford Corres.*, i, 30; Buckinghamshire to Heron, 20 Apr., 11, 19 May 1779, 8 Apr., 1 May 1780, Heron to Buckinghamshire, 14 Apr., 5 May, 1779, 18 Jan., 3, 7, 19 Apr, 1780, Flood to Buckinghamshire, 7 Mar. 1780 (N.L.I., Heron Papers, Mss 13037/7,9,11–13, 13039/1,4,8); Buckinghamshire to Heron, 8 Apr., 1 May 1779 (B.L., Mackintosh Collection, Add. Ms 34523 ff 248–9, 252); Buckinghamshire to Hillsborough, 29 Apr. and reply 6 May 1780 (P.R.O., S.P.63/469 ff 145, 163). The commissionership of stamps was worth £500 p.a.

vote could never be assumed as he deemed 'the prosperity and improvement of my own country a chief object of my exertions'.[5] He was equally reasonable in his private life, though his relations with Henry were complicated by a difference over 'Mr Flood's fortune'. It is not clear what this was about, but it was a source of tension that Frederick's readiness to join with Henry at times in the House of Commons and in Callan could not fully allay and they gradually drifted apart in the 1780s.[6]

Frederick's disenchantment with what one contemporary elliptically termed Henry Flood's 'private principles' was more deeply felt by John Flood, and it was reinforced in the late 1770s by the ongoing dispute over his sister's will. Flood's refusal to accept the judgment of the prerogative court in 1775 that Isabella's will was genuine and that he and Sir Lucius O'Brien should surrender all documents appertaining to the £3,000 in dispute led, inevitably, to further court proceedings. These commenced on 4 March 1776 when Edward Wallis filed a bill with the Court of Exchequer in which he cited Flood and O'Brien, and the latter's trustees who had been party to the mortgage agreed in 1770. Cases such as these were frequently prolonged, but the delay was extended in this instance by the need for all parties to respond and by changes in legal personnel. The upshot was that Wallis's bill had to be resubmitted on 20 February 1778 and, again, on 1 February 1781. As far as one can discern, these delays caused Flood little anxiety, though Lucius O'Brien and not he was the main beneficiary. Edward Wallis was visibly less relaxed, but he could console himself with the fact that his request for the repayment of the loan and £1,710 in outstanding interest payments was making progress.[7] Flood, for his part, did not withdraw his claim that the disputed will was fraudulent; it was, he insisted, 'fabricated', and 'dictated' to Isabella when 'the disorder with which she was affected' towards the end of her life 'deprive[d her] ... of the use of her reason'. However, since the legality of the will had already been established this was not *ad rem*, and when the case was submitted to the chief remembrancer by the barons of the Court of Exchequer on 16 July 1782 with the instruction that he examine 'all witnesses', it was his conclusion that the 'plaintiff be awarded his costs' unless 'the defendants shall show cause'. As this attests, legal opinion favoured Wallis, though one cannot say for sure that he received the disputed money as the documentary trail dries up at this point.[8]

5 Flood to [ ], 22 Dec. 1783 (N.A., Calendar of misc. letters and papers 1760–89 f 84); Flood, *Memoirs*, pp 5–7; Flood to Buckinghamshire, 7 Mar. 1780 (N.L.I., Heron Papers, Ms 13039/4); *Parl. Reg. (Irl.)*, iii, 24; Flood to Peel, 27 Oct. 1812 (B.L., Peel Papers, Add. Ms 40218 f 5).   6 Anglesey to Flood, 22 Aug. 1765, Oct. 1771 (B.L., Valentia Papers, Add. Ms 19349 f 1); Day to Glandore, 11, 22 Nov. 1783 (N.L.I., Talbot-Crosbie Papers, Ms 2054/ 1, 2); Sayles, ed., 'Irish parliament in 1782', *R.I.A. proc.*, 56C (1954), pp 270–1.   7 Above pp 173–4; Wallis v Flood and others, 20 Feb. 1778, Mortgage for securing £3000, 12 July 1770, Consent, 7 Feb. 1781, Plaintiff's demands on O'Brien's mortgage, 12 July 1781 (N.L.I., Inchiquin Papers, nos. 2951, 2871).   8 Conditional decree in the case of Wallis v Flood etc., 16 July 1782, Consent, 7 Feb. 1781 (N.L.I., Inchiquin Papers, No 2951).

THE EMERGENCE OF A RADICAL PATRIOT

Flood was not prepared to allow family disputes inhibit him politically, and he threw himself into the thick of Commons' business within days of his dismissal. He made his first parliamentary contribution as an ex-office holder on 6 November when a petition from Dublin merchants criticising the level of import duty on sugar was debated. He had avoided commenting when this matter was considered in 1780, but he now warmly supported John Forbes' suggestion that the petition should be referred to a 'special committee' rather than to the committee of ways and means. He justified this on the grounds of efficacy: a 'special committee' would 'methodize and arrange the information necessary for the committee of ways and means', he contended. He also felt it was more likely to secure 'free trade' against dilution. This was not a matter of minor consequence. There was widespread suspicion, which Flood shared, that the Castle was predisposed 'to pilfer from the nation that free trade which had been granted'. He offered no hard evidence in support of his contention, and he struck another poor note when he responded too 'vehement[ly]' to hissing from the Commons' gallery. He redeemed himself subsequently with a formidable display of 'ingenuity and parliamentary knowledge' on 'the business of managing the question', though it did not produce the result he wanted. The administration prevailed easily, and the petition was referred to the committee of supply rather than to a 'special committee', by 111 votes to 43.[9]

Encouraged by his first taste of opposition politics, Flood engaged in a further procedural exchange on 7 November, in the course of which he alleged that if the administration proposed to raise 'extraordinary supplies' it would destroy the nation.[10] This was rather alarmist, but given Flood's longstanding commitment to financial rectitude and his current anxiety at 'the state of the nation', it was appropriate that he should make his first major statement of the session on this issue on Thursday, 8 November. It was not an unqualified success. Flood's preparation was inadequate, but the most striking feature of the occasion was the hostility directed towards him from all quarters of the house. Flood facilitated his many critics by turning up an hour after the Commons had convened and by not offering a specific proposal. Moreover, his controversial analysis of the kingdom's finances and his comments on the impolicy of continued borrowing invited a strong reaction. As a result, he was subject to a personalised attack by the Attorney General, John Scott, and others who were determined he should not seize the moral highground on this or any other issue. George Ponsonby was most *ad hominem*, though Flood responded to his snide reference to his 'seven year eclipse' with a brief, but effective, defence of his conduct:

9 *Parl. Reg.(Irl.)*, i, 35–8.   10 *Parl. Reg.(Irl.)*, i, 38; Eden to [ ], 6 Nov. 1781 (B.L., Auckland Papers, Add. Ms 34418 f 161).

It is true I supported Lord Harcourt's administration – but was I eclipsed when, on several occasions, I went not with them, and gave my reasons for so doing? I also supported the last administration; but on that great day when a Free Trade was demanded, was I eclipsed? When a Declaration of Rights was the subject of debate in this House, did I shrink from the question?

However, neither these remarks, nor a more lengthy statement, in response to Denis Daly, on 'his future conduct', was sufficient to persuade MPs to support Flood's suggestion that MPs should consider whether it was appropriate to vote new taxes prior to convening a committee of supply. It was comprehensively defea ted, 155 votes to 49.[11]

Flood's assertive conduct in the Commons in November 1781 contributed to the confrontational mood of MPs at this time, but it was not the only destabilising influence. Of equal importance was the success of William Eden and Lord Carlisle in detaching Denis Daly and Barry Yelverton from the opposition.[12] This ought, one might suggest, to have facilitated Flood's absorbtion into the patriot fold, but this would be to underestimate the sharp resentment with which he continued to be regarded by his erstwhile colleagues.[13] It is significant, for example, that both Hussey Burgh and Henry Grattan were distinctly unexcited by his motion on 8 November.

The administration, for its part, observed the disunity within patriot ranks caused by Flood's presence with glee. Eden averred that it vindicated the decision to dismiss him. It was an 'absolute necessity', he observed on 10 November, if the Castle connection in the Commons was to avoid 'eternal scrapes'; and he was so encouraged by their success in neutralising Flood's attempt to make an issue of the 'state of the nation' on 8 November that he wondered why he had been recruited in the first place:

Mr Flood ... has disappointed me beyond description; he sometimes uses a strong sentence or two, and points a parcel of antithesis in a declamation; but as a debater or leader of an opposition he makes a wretched figure, and the wonder is how it can come into contemplation to purchase him at such a price.[14]

---

11 *Parl. Reg.(Irl.)*, i, 38–45; Carlisle to Hillsborough, 9 Nov. 1781 (P.R.O., S.P., 63/477 ff 65–7); Mr Flood, 8 Nov. 1781 in H.M.C., *Carlisle*, p. 527. 12 Carlisle to Hillsborough, 5 Nov. in H.M.C., *Carlisle*, p. 525; Carlisle to Hillsborough, 9 Nov. (P.R.O., S.P.63/477 ff 65–7); Carlisle to Hillsborough, 10 Nov. (B.L., Auckland Papers, Add. Ms 34418 f 163). For Daly see Carlisle to Hillsborough, 10, 18 Nov. (P.R.O., S.P., 63/477 ff 76, 93); Eden to Hillsborough, 10 Nov. (B.L., Auckland Papers, Add. Ms 34418 f 163); Eden to Loughborough, 19 Nov. in Bishop of Bath and Wells, ed., *The journal and correspondence of William, Lord Auckland* (4 vols, London, 1861–2), i, 318–20. For Yelverton see O'Brien, *Anglo-Irish politics*, pp 50–1. 13 *Parl.Reg.(Irl.)*, i, 47–9. 14 Carlisle to Selwyn, 5 Nov., Carlisle to Gower, 23 Nov in H.M.C., *Carlisle*, pp 525, 533–4; Eden to Hillsborough, 10 Nov. (B.L., Auckland Papers, Add. Ms 34418 ff 165–6); Eden to North, 10 Nov. in *Beresford Corres.*, i, 187–9; Eden to Loughborough, 19 Nov. 1781 in *Auckland Corres*, i, 319. The quotation is from the latter.

Precisely the opposite sentiment was expressed by Lord Charlemont. His expectation was that when Flood and Grattan joined forces, the Castle would be powerless to withstand their combined efforts to advance the patriot demand for constitutional concessions. [15] The problem was that they showed no eagerness to do so in November 1781. Flood did, it is true, second Grattan's failed attempt to move for an annual mutiny bill on 13 November with a wide-ranging speech in support of his contention that standing armies represented a threat to civil liberties. [16] However, relations between the two remained strained. Flood did not seek actively to discommode his former friend, but his superior attitude and instinctive tendency to conduct himself as if he was the foremost patriot in the Commons was poorly received.

If Flood was conscious of his disruptive impact on the equilibrium of the opposition, he did not manifest it or let it restrict his Commons' performance. So on 15 November, he endorsed David La Touche's call that mercantile experts should be invited to provide testimony on the sugar trade, on the grounds that the Irish parliament had as much right to regulate this commodity as its Westminster equivalent, and supported Lucius O'Brien's unsuccessful attempts to draw attention to the escalating trade dispute with Portugal by requesting the Commons to approve duties on French and Portuguese wines for six months rather than two years. His contributions in both instances were too brief to allow him to display his abilities to full advantage, but the fact that he supported such assertive propositions illustrates that his intention was to reestablish himself as a radical as well as a leading patriot in the Commons. [17]

This was underlined on Thursday, 22 November, when he contrived to elevate a debate in the committee of ways and means above the particular of the level at which sugar duties should be pitched (the administration's preference) and the appropriateness or otherwise of receiving testimony from refiners (the opposition's object) to the 'general' and more politically charged issue of 'our rights, as an independent nation, and our rights as connected with Great Britain'. Flood's four-hour speech was a *tour de force*, but of greater consequence than his performance was his reminder to MPs how much remained to be done if Ireland was to attain its grail of constitutional equality with England:

> Ireland is an independent kingdom; she has a completely free and supreme legislature of her own, and has accordingly a full right to enter into commerce, and conclude treaties with every nation upon the globe ... Having a right, as an

15 Charlemont to Malone [2 Jan 1782], in Prior, *Life of Malone*, pp 103–4.   16 *Parl. Reg. (Irl.)*, i, 53–4; Carlisle to Hillsborough, 14 Nov. 1781 (P.R.O., S.P., 63/477 ff 80–2). The two men also co-operated during a finance debate on 7 December (*Parl. Reg.(Irl.)*, i, 130–9; S.P.,63/477 f 175).   17 *Parl. Reg.(Irl.)*, i, 71–5; Carlisle to Hillsborough, 17 Nov. (P.R.O.,S.P., 63/477 ff 91–2); Eden to Loughborough, 19 Nov. 1781 in *Auckland Corres.*, i, 319.

independent kingdom, to trade and treat with all the world, let us examine the deductions from this principle. Nations who have separate estates and separate kings, if in amity with one another, are entitled by the law of nations to reciprocal favours from each other, or according to the terms of foederal language, to the *Jura amicissima gentis*. If their kingdoms, who have separate kings and separate interests, are intitled to the *Jura amicissima*, to what are we entitled from England, with whom we are united by joint interest, and under the same king. Further, nations who are intitled to the *Jura amicissima*, have those rights upon the truest footing, when the reciprocal advantages gained by the mutual intercourse, exactly balance. When such intercourse inclines in favour of one nation, and the intercommercial exchange nevertheless continues, that kingdom, in whose favour the scale preponderates, is under an *obligation* to the other, who suffers a trade to exist to its disadvantage.

These positions being general and incontrovertible, let us see whether we have applied them in managing our trade. Our conduct is the reverse of these maxims. We have not secured our independency; we have not demanded the *Jura amicissima*; and having established our commerce on principles the most favourable to Great Britain, *we* have in addition submitted *ourselves* to the disgrace of *obligation*. Had we attended to our independence in this question, we should not have granted 100,000£ a year in tax, without stipulating for the repeal of that law, which confines our trade to the very article on which the tax is imposed. Does not the 6th of George III stand unrepealed, in which we are forbidden to trade with the colonies of other kingdoms; a law which was framed to tax America and to continue Irish slavery; a law which has torn, ruined, dismembered, dissipated and destroyed the noblest empire that ever flourished in the world; yet this law was offered to be repealed in favour of America. We have regulated our commerce so as to give all the profit of it to Great Britain, and exclude it from ourselves; we have shut ourselves out of the trade of the world in favour of her colonies; and then excluded ourselves from ever trading *with them* in favour of *her refiners*; and what is more absurd, still we profess ourselves to be *obliged*, and gentlemen talk of our *obligations* to Great Britain for the colony trade. Sir, it is no obligation; it is commutation, it is purchase; we have given up for it the trade of the world, to which we have the amplest right; and we have purchased it by the revenue we have granted; by the assistance we have afforded and by the relaxation of the non-importation agreement.

Given this context, Flood avowed that it was entirely proper that Ireland should impose high duties on imported sugars in order to aid 'our infant and trembling manufacture' compete with its 'rich and powerful competitor' on its doorstep.[18] A

18 *Parl. Reg. (Irl.)*, i, 85–7.

considerable number of patriot MPs concurred, but the Castle connection was un-impressed. Flood's brother-in-law, John Beresford, argued persuasively that Ire-land was not disadvantaged by British competition, while Gervaise Parker Bushe maintained that it was inappropriate for the Irish parliament to do anything to dis-rupt the Anglo-Irish nexus so soon after the kingdom had benefited from the 'gen-erosity' of the concession of 'free trade'. This registered forcibly with most of those present, for when a division was called on the proposal to increase the import duty on refined sugars it was defeated by 144 votes to 63.[19]

The outcome of this and other debates suggested that the Castle was well-posi-tioned to repel any attempt by Flood, or by anybody else, to advance commercial or constitutional grievances, but the Lord Lieutenant and Chief Secretary knew oth-erwise. They concluded that some concessions had to be made to calm Irish opinion if they were to maintain their authority in the House of Commons. Indeed, Eden signalled to Lord North prior to Flood's speech of 22 November that a *habeas corpus* bill 'must be passed'. Three days later, Carlisle transmitted a list of points – the establishment of a national bank and an Irish post office, the assembly of a small fleet of frigates to protect shipping, the augmentation of judicial salaries, eight or ten baronetcies, the speedy return of bills from England, and the reduction of the drawback on hops – he hoped would be received favourably.[20] The necessity of some at least of these matters being conceded was certainly reinforced by Flood's ener-getic actions. He even attempted to reopen the debate on sugar duties, when the report of the committee of ways and means was presented to the House of Com-mons on 24 November, on the grounds that it was 'teaming with consequences and grounded upon principles utterly subversive of our free trade', but he was rebuffed once more.[21] Unabashed, Flood gave notice of his intention of bringing forward a motion on the Mutiny Act. This cut across Charles O'Hara of Sligo who had similar ideas, but on 29 November he yielded to Flood's pointed proposition 'that a law of indefinite duration [the Mutiny Act] ... was repugnant to the principles of the Brit-ish constitution'.[22]

O'Hara's co-operativeness contrasted sharply with the impatience of the ad-ministration. Having defeated Henry Grattan's attempt to agitate the question of an Irish mutiny act sixteen days earlier, and anxious to keep the focus of political de-bate away from constitutional points, they determined to teach Flood a lesson in the hope that it would deter him from raising other sensitive constitutional issues and force him to adopt a lower political profile. Flood opened the debate with an indif-

19 *Parl. Reg.(Irl.)*, i, 81–99; Carlisle to Hillsborough, 23 Nov. (P.R.O., S.P.63/477 ff 119–20); Eden to North, 23 Nov. (B.L., Auckland Papers, Add. Ms 34418 ff 182–3); Burgh to Buckinghamshire, 28 Nov. 1781 (N.L.I., Heron Papers, Ms 13048).   20 Tighe to Buckinghamshire, 23 Nov. in H.M.C., *Lothian*, p. 403; Eden to Loughborough, 19 Nov. in *Auckland Corres.*, i, 320; Carlisle to Hillsborough, 22 Nov. (P.R.O., S.P., 63/477 ff 107–10); Eden to Hillsborough, 23 Nov. 1781 (B.L., Auckland Papers, Add. Ms 34418 f 184).   21 *Parl. Reg.(Irl.)*, i, 100–2, 104–5.   22 *Parl. Reg.(Irl)*, i, 79–80; *H.J.*, 28 Nov., 1781; *Life of Grattan*, ii, 192–3.

ferent speech in which, following a rebuttal of press criticism of his stand on the sugar duties, he repeated the familiar arguments that the application of a perpetual mutiny act was an insult to Irish 'liberties' and that an unregulated standing army represented a threat to the constitution. Few were convinced by this or by the belligerent tone of his motion. Realising that it stood no chance, Flood withdrew it, and moved instead for the heads of a bill to repeal the perpetual mutiny act. This was the signal for the administration's heavy guns to launch a concerted attack. Eden set the tone, but the most devastating contribution came from the Attorney General, John Scott. The tactic he adopted was to relate the story of Flood's political life in the form of an allegorical fable in which he gave Flood the persona of Harry Plantaganet, the huntsman. It was a clever trope, and it worked beyond Scott's fondest expectations because 'it was fully suited to the taste and disposition of the audience':

I perceive, Mr Speaker, that we are all growing warm, and if the House will permit me, I'll tell you a story, which may help to bring us into a better temper. [A great cry of hear him, hear him.] When I was at the Temple, there was a parish clerk that used to raise the psalm, and who went by the name of *Harry Plantaganet*; I had taken it into my head that the family of the *Plantaganets* was quite extinct, and was induced by curiosity to ask this man how he came to be called by that name; accordingly I went to him one day, and mentioned my wish to know his story: I was once a King, Sir, said he, and reigned with uncontrouled dominion over hounds and greyhounds, beagles and tarriers, by which I have acquired this name; but if you please I will relate my story at large: *Go on, Harry, said I.* I lived in the neighbourhood of Windsor Forest when a boy, and used frequently divert myself with hunting the King's deer; for I always loved to hunt the *King's* deer. *Go on, Harry, said I.* I hallooed and I shouted so loud and so often, that there was not a dog of the pack but what obeyed my voice; not a lad in the forest but attended my call: *Go on Harry, said I.* At last, Sir, the chief huntsman perceiving what command I had over the dogs, and the sportsmen, resolved to take me into his pay: *Go on Harry, said I.* I accepted of his offer, but I now found myself so much at my ease, that I grew indolent, and insisted upon riding out to hunt in *furniture*, for I always loved to hunt in *furniture: – Go on, Harry, said I.* I was indulged with furniture, but I soon perceived that the younger fellows who could now outride me, became greater favourites with the chief huntsman. *Go on, Harry, said I.* This stung me to the quick, and I determined to pick a quarrel about some of the fringe of my furniture which was torn, and which I would have repaired at the chief huntsman's expense. *Go on, Harry. I immediately began to hunt in opposition*; but not a dog obeyed me, not a sportsman attended my call: *Go on, Harry.* I hallooed, and I roared, and I shouted until I was weary, but still without any effect. I had the mortification to find out that I had totally lost my influence in the forest; and I retired to this parish to devote the rest of my days to the making of my soul, and I now raise the psalm and join in the thanksgiving. This, sir, is the story of *Harry Plantaganet*, and his story I would apply to every man who cannot be quiet without expense, or angry without rebellion.

The convulsions of laughter the Attorney General's remarks elicited placed Flood in a most invidious position. His instinct was to let the matter pass unnoticed, but he was persuaded by colleagues that this would not be appropriate. He, instead, offered a short but sharp critique of the Attorney General which, Lawrence Parsons concluded loyally, 'completely turned the laugh' against his critics, but this is not sustained by contemporary reports. More saliently, it did not influence the outcome; Flood's motion was soundly defeated by 146 votes to 66.[23]

Because of the destructive thrust of Scott's witty speech, some apprehended that a challenge must inevitably follow. However, Flood judiciously concluded that what had been said was not a matter of honour and a few private words between the two protagonists before the conclusion of the debate ensured that the matter went no further. This was a relief to Dublin Castle. Otherwise, Eden was unable to contain his pleasure that Scott had made so successful an 'attack upon the whole life and character of ... [Flood] with more acrimony where he was serious, and with more wit when he chose to laugh than I have ever seen blended together in a philippic against one man'. The Chief Secretary conceded that Flood 'hardly merited the treatment ... he received', but he was delighted that it was Flood's turn to

pass ... the night in all the tortures of the damned. The character painted in great detail and mixed with many humorous, but coarse and awkward allusions, was that of a malevolent outcast from all social intercourse of life, driven to madness by spleen and vanity, forlorn in reputation, and sunk in abilities.[24]

If the events of 29 November well illustrated that Flood's return to active opposition had been less smooth and triumphant than he might have hoped, he could take consolation from the fact that the extensive (if not always entirely accurate) coverage accorded his deeds in the popular press was fast regaining him the favour of the politicised middle classes.[25] This is highlighted by the fact that on 30 November, the Liberty Volunteers in Dublin compared his dismissal to that of the earl of Chatham in 1761. Flood was flattered by the comparison, and he gave a commitment in his response to continue 'to promote to the utmost of my power the glory of my sovereign and the prosperity of his people', as he had done, he maintained,

23 *Parl. Reg.(Irl.)*, i, 106–19; Eden to Loughborough, 30 Nov., Eden to [ ], 31 Nov. 1781 (B.L., Auckland Papers, Add. Ms 34418 ff 197–8, 249); Parsons' memoirs (Rosse Papers, F/13).   24 Eden to Loughborough, 30 Nov. in *Auckland Corres.*, i, 322–3.   25 *H.J.*, 26, 28 Nov., 5, 7, 12 Dec.; *F.J.*, Nov.-Dec. 1781.

throughout his political life. More saliently, he urged the Volunteers to 'exertion' on the grounds that 'nothing but the most manly and most upright counsels can save us'. He was encouraged to do this by the fact that the Volunteers were better disposed towards his brand of patriotism than his erstwhile parliamentary colleagues, and the fact that he was made an honourary member of three Dundalk-based corps in December 1782 served to strengthen his appreciation of their importance to the cause of constitutional reform and to his own political rehabilitation. [26]

Stimulated by this, Flood took his most controversial stand to date in early December when he objected to Barry Yelverton's decision, following news of the humiliation of Lord Cornwallis at Yorktown, to postpone the motion for the repeal of Poynings' Law he had undertaken to present on 4 December to make way for a loyal address to the crown. Yelverton's decision reflected the traditional disposition of MPs during moments of imperial crisis, but radically-minded patriots like Flood resented the loss of any opportunity to press for constitutional reform. Flood also shared the doubts about Yelverton's motives because of his intimacy with Eden, but his unease derived primarily from his perception that because Yelverton's understanding of constitutional law left something to be desired, he would advance a defective solution to the problem of Ireland's constitutional dependence. Flood's uneasiness would have been greater had he known that in return for presenting a loyal address on 4 December, Yelverton had secured a commitment from the Chief Secretary that the administration would remain neutral when he moved for leave to introduce legislation to amend Poynings' Law. The administration reserved the right to oppose the bill at a later stage, but the promise made Yelverton ensured his plan to reform the Anglo-Irish constitutional nexus a definite advantage over all others. However, Flood had no intention of allowing him a free run. [27]

Despite his conviction that a loyal address was inappropriate and badly timed, Flood left the running on behalf of the opposition to Brownlow, Grattan and Forbes on 4 December, and he had the satisfaction of watching them argue a case he could endorse. It would, Grattan maintained, 'be madness in Irishmen to support' the war in America when Britain continued to assert its 'claim to control this country' by modifying Irish legislation (as happened on four occasions during the 1779–80 session). Yelverton was taken aback by this, but his counter-argument that it was not in Ireland's 'interest' to 'sit sullen down with folded arms and see the empire destroyed' made little impression on the patriots whose support he desired. Indeed, when John Forbes contended that this was their moment to press home their advantage to secure a resolution of Ireland's grievance on Poynings' Law, Flood was quick to express his agreement. He pointed to the number of occasions in the past when Britain had 'laid hold of times of distress and difficulty to establish claims favour-

26 *H.J.*, 3, 5 Dec. 1781; P. Ó Snodaigh, 'Notes on the Volunteers ... of County Louth', *County Louth Archaeological Journal*, 18 (1976), p. 285.   27 Carlisle to Hillsborough, 5 Dec. 1781 (P.R.O., S.P.63/477 ff 165–6); O'Brien, *Anglo-Irish politics*, pp 49–51.

able to her constitution'. And he presented the House with a delicately worded amendment for insertion in the address which, a worried Lord Carlisle explained, effectively embraced 'a demand of recognition from Great Britain of the legislative independence of Ireland'. It was a bold move, but only a small minority of MPs believed it was proper to proceed in this way. When it was put to the House it was rejected without a division, and Yelverton's original proposal carried by a crushing 130 votes.[28]

This outcome did not surprise Flood, but having stolen a march on Yelverton by asserting his right to raise the subject of legislative independence, he was determined to consolidate his advantage and, as soon as the division was declared, he gave notice of his intention to 'make a motion relative to the law of Poynings in the Commons on 11 December'. His declaration so troubled Yelverton that he felt obliged to inform the House three days later that 'he had not deserted' the issue. This prompted a poorly recorded exchange between the two men, in the course of which it emerged that they 'differ[ed] as to the mode' of proceedings they intended to adopt, which temporarily eased Yelverton's concerns.[29]

As was his normal practice when he planned to make a major speech, Flood prepared thoroughly for the debate on Poynings' Law. This involved him making a detailed analysis of the history and operation of the act, which so impressed Lord Charlemont and Edmond Malone that they encouraged him when he contemplated publishing his conclusions. No statement by him saw print at this time, though surviving manuscript notes suggest he may have made some preparations.[30] From these and his three and a half-hour speech on 11 December, it is clear that Flood saw no reason to alter the conclusion he had first arrived at in the 1760s that the practice of the Irish Privy Council amending and respiting legislation emanating from one or both houses of the Irish legislature was founded on a misconception of the constitution as well as of the law. The constitution, Flood explained, possessed 'executive' and 'deliberative' arms each with 'its separate and distinct province':

> The *deliberative* authority of the state resting with the Houses of LORDS AND COMMONS, the *executive* with the KING. ... The constitution had invested the two Houses with the deliberate authority of propounding and framing laws, by which the people were to be governed, because they themselves were the people's representatives, and had given the king only a negative on the laws when proposed, because he was the executive officer, and had no occasion for any right of interference in the business of legislation; but just so much as was necessary to defend his own prerogative from the incroachments of other estates, which he was

---

28 *Parl. Reg.(Irl.)*, i, 119–29; Carlisle to Hillsborough, 5 Dec. 1781 (2) and addresses (P.R.O.,S.P.,63/ 477 ff 156–9, 163–4).   29 *Parl. Reg.(Irl.)*, i, 129, 149.   30 Malone to Charlemont, [ca Dec. 1781] in H.M.C., *Charlemont*, ii, 401; Rosse Papers, C/4.

sufficiently enabled to do from a power of negativing any law which he thought might be injurious to that prerogative.

This was both an effective and apposite arrangement, Flood conceded; it encapsulated 'the beauty and the strength of the British constitution', and 'the people of Ireland were fully entitled to' enjoy the same. The problem, as he saw it, was that the right of 'participating in that constitution had been wrested from the people' in the seventeenth century by the 'corrupt and vicious construction and interpretation' of both Poynings' Law and the explanatory act ratified in 1558. As a result, the act had been transformed from 'prevent[ing] the governors of Ireland from giving the royal assent to laws that might be injurious to the king' to restraining the freedom of parliament.

Flood supported his argument that the prevailing 'false and vicious interpretation of Poynings' Law' demanded to be overturned with an extensive range of examples from British and Irish parliamentary history in an attempt to convince MPs that 'the Privy Council here had no authority to alter any heads of bills before their transmission into Great Britain, and that the spirit of [Poynings' Law] required no more than that the bill should be certified under the great seal'. He was well aware that it would be difficult to have this affirmed in law, but he was convinced that the Commons should proceed by a declaratory act rather than by amending Poynings' Law:

because he said that if the declaratory bill should pass the House of Commons, tho' it should not receive the Royal assent, yet the sense of the Commons being declared by the bill would operate in effect to his design of amending the practice in the constitution – whereas if a bill for altering the law should pass the House [of Commons], tho' it should not receive the Royal assent, it would nevertheless contain an acknowledgment that the law is agreeable to the present practice of the Privy Council, and would leave the evil acknowledged to exist in the law without succeeding in obtaining the remedy. [31]

However, because MPs were not ready to approve such a proposal, he simply requested that they should examine his argument and moved for the establishment of a Commons' committee to examine 'the precedents and records' in order to identify 'what the law ... and what the constitution of this country actually was'. [32]

Given their eagerness to prevent the discussion of constitutional points, the administration inevitably sought to deny Flood his request, and his old adversary John Hely-Hutchinson took the lead in presenting their case. The provost was in sprightly form and he made an 'elegant and learned' speech in the course of which he acknowledged the value of Flood's researches as well as some of his conclusions. At

31 Carlisle to Hillsborough, 12 Dec. 1781 (P.R.O., S.P., 63/477 ff 185–6).   32 *Parl. Reg. (Irl.)*, i, 149–53.

the same time, he ably defended the role of the Irish Privy Council and found fault with Flood's approach. Flood had the backing of his cousin Frederick, who seconded his motion, David Walshe (who urged that Poynings' Law be repealed), Hussey Burgh, Benjamin Chapman and George Ogle, but it is significant that Henry Grattan and Barry Yelverton remained silent, and that Ogle appealed to Flood near the end of the debate to withdraw his motion in the name of patriot unity:

> he lamented the unfortunate difference of opinion between the two great supporters of the nation's rights against the law of Poynings, or the misconstruction of that law and most pathetically intreated Mr Flood to accommodate himself to the wishes of his friends, and unite with Mr Yelverton in his mode of bringing forward heads of a bill.[33]

This was an impractical, if well-intended, suggestion. Flood could not accommodate himself to Yelverton's plan because they disagreed strongly on how the abuses they identified with Poynings' Law might be eradicated. He insisted his motion was put to a vote and, as expected, it was soundly rejected, 139 votes to 67.[34]

This was a more decisive rebuff than Flood may have anticipated, but he did not dwell on the outcome. On the following day, 12 December, he sought and was given leave with Sir Lucius O'Brien to prepare the heads of a bill to continue an act for better regulating the corn trade. A day later, following his failure to advance an enquiry into the size and cost of the army, he was given leave (once again with O'Brien) to prepare a bill to regulate 'marine forces while on shore' – an issue he took up to ensure that the legislation on this subject currently being debated at Westminster did not extend to Ireland.[35]

Flood's industry greatly pleased admirers like Lord Charlemont,[36] but it bothered most moderate patriots, who were content to trust Grattan and Yelverton. Their irritation was ill-concealed on Tuesday, 18 December, when Barry Yelverton finally gave notice of his intention to present legislation which would 'take from the Privy Council those rights which had unconstitutionally been wrested from parliament; to prohibit totally their power of altering bills, and instead of the words "we pray it may be enacted" to introduce these words "be it enacted"'. Yelverton's proposal was as brief as his statement of intent,[37] and encouraged by the Chief Secretary's acknowledgement that whatever he proposed 'commanded his particular attention',

---

33 *Parl. Reg. (Irl.)*, i, 173.   34 *Op. cit.*, pp 153–74.   35 *Commons Jn.(Irl.)*, x, 275; Carlisle to Hillsborough, 14 Dec., Hillsborough to Carlisle, 24 Dec. (P.R.O., S.P.,63/477 ff 189, 199); *Parl. Reg.(Irl.)*, i, 175–6; Eden to [ ], [14 Dec] (B.L., Auckland Papers, Add. Ms 34418 f 227); Carlisle to Hillsborough, 29 Dec. 1781 (N.A., Irish Correspondence 1697–1798, Ms 2446).   36 Charlemont asserted that Flood's 'incomparable conduct stands unrivalled through all the annals of parliamentary history' (Charlemont to Malone, 17 Dec. 1781, Malone to Charlemont, 8 Jan. 1782 in H.M.C., *Charlemont*, i, 391, 394).   37 There is a copy of the bill in P.R.O., S.P.63/480 f 16.

he did not seek to offer an extended justification of what he proposed to recommend. Flood was not satisfied with this, and his provocative observation that the measure was likely to prove 'not only insufficient, but detrimental and pernicious' obliged Yelverton to offer some remarks by way of a justification for his proposal. His bill was founded, Yelverton pronounced, on the acknowledgement of 'every lawyer', that 'by the act of the 3rd and 4th of Philip and Mary, the Privy Council have a *right* to *stop*, and if they please *to alter* our bills'. Flood queried this. He accused Yelverton of misciting the 3rd and 4th of Philip and Mary and rejected his literal and restrictive interpretation of Poynings' Law. These were fundamental differences, but Yelverton was not interested in debating them. He left it to John Fitzgibbon and the Recorder to take up the baton on his behalf, and it was their intervention which shifted the focus from him onto Flood, who rose to the test supremely well. He offered a masterly digest of his extended statement of 11 December in support of his strategy, and a stirring appeal to the people as well as to MPs to join with him to prevent Yelverton making things worse:

> He [Flood] said that by a Declaratory Law we should fix our constitution on a solid basis; by a law to regulate the manner of certifying bills, we confessed our rights were taken away, but there was no power on earth could take them away; for if some god or some devil should inspire the House to pass an act destructive of the constitution, yet it would be but a dead letter, and the representatives of the people might think themselves happy, if the people did not *tear them piecemeal*; for neither God nor man had given them authority to destroy the people's rights. But as parliament had been the protectors of the people's rights, (he wished he could speak in the present tense) he hoped they would be so again. They had power, he said, to redress every grievance; they needed but to pass a short Money-bill, and then demand their rights; this was the effectual way to have them restored. Formerly even Money-bills were altered; but the moment parliament asserted their rights, the enormity was removed.
>
> He said that he could not perceive any disposition in the councils of England to assist us in asserting the rights of our constitution: that the Mutiny bill was an incontestable proof of this: that as our laws at present stood, the constitution was safer than it might be made by the way in which the bill moved for might be permitted to pass. If that should be the case, he declared he would lift up his voice to Heaven, and Earth should resound with his cries against it. He therefore begged that if gentlemen had not some assurance of making the constitution better, they would not run the risk of making it worse. [38]

This combative statement amounted to a challenge to those MPs who favoured constitutional change to side with him or to demonstrate the flaws in his argument.

38 *Parl. Reg. (Irl.)*, i, 184.

He can hardly have been pleased that more chose to do the latter than the former. Some were encouraging; a number who dismissed his conclusions as 'inapplicable' applauded him on the quality of his research; however, a majority rejected his argument and alleged that he was damaging the prospects of progressing the question. Emotions ran so high that 'some expressions that ... passed' between Flood and David Walshe were drawn to the Speaker's attention by Henry Grattan (who did not speak on the motion) in order to ensure it did not lead to a breach of the peace. [39]

This was unnecessary, but the strength of ill-feeling towards Flood and the dissension his stand on Poynings' Law generated within patriot ranks was even more starkly revealed on the following day when Flood re-stated his controversial contention that Poynings' and allied acts of parliament did not contain

> a tittle in them that deprived parliament of the power to originate bills or that gave the council of either kingdom power to alter bills after the meeting of parliament and ... called upon gentlemen to point out the sentences by which they maintained doctrines hostile to the constitution.

This was as direct a challenge as Flood could offer but, rather than respond with argument, both John Fitzgibbon and Barry Yelverton had recourse to abuse. Fitzgibbon's observations on Flood's 'wild and extravagant ideas' were severe, but Yelverton was harsher, for he 'took notice in the most pointed terms of the impropriety of Mr Flood's conduct'. His most severe remark was prompted by Flood's attempt to justify his stand as the product 'of twenty years in the study of ... [the] question', for he alleged that Flood had no right to press an issue he had shamefully abandoned '*for seven years*'. At this distance, this may appear discreditably *ad hominem*, but it epitomises the suspicion with which Flood continued to be regarded by MPs who might, in other circumstances, have been classed among his foremost allies. [40] He was clearly somewhat troubled by the strength of the reaction he generated because he absented himself from the Commons during the week before the winter recess.

Flood earned the extended break he gave himself at the end of 1781. He had, in the course of six weeks, reestablished himself as one of the dominant patriot voices in the House of Commons and pushed the matter of Poynings' Law to the top of the political agenda. However, it won him little goodwill on either side in the House of Commons and did not enhance the likelihood of his achieving constitutional reform since the administration had a majority in every division that mattered between October and December. Indeed, ironically, his very assertiveness on Poynings' Law had the effect of increasing the appeal of Yelverton's less aggressive suggestion that the Irish parliament should pass a short act stating that in future it would simply 'certify' and transmit Irish bills.

39 *Parl. Reg.(Irl.)*, i, 176–83. No duel ensued.   40 *Parl. Reg.(Irl.)*, i, 184–6; *Life of Grattan*, ii, 197–8.

ASSERTING THE RIGHTS OF IRELAND

It is not clear how Flood assessed his return to active opposition, but Lord Charlemont certainly gave him to believe that his presence improved the opposition's prospects of achieving constitutional reform. Charlemont was the only prominent patriot who responded so encouragingly, and it is significant that he wrote to Flood on New Year's Day with his concerns about Luke Gardiner's Catholic relief bill. Flood had not participated in the early stage debates on this measure in December but, as in 1778, he was not entirely happy with the concessions being proposed. So, when Charlemont 'express[ed] his hope Gentlemen would, in this delicate point, let the country alone; suffer things to remain as they are, and not hazard the ruin of that growing coalescence which, to my certain knowledge, was beginning to take place between men of all persuasions',[41] Flood concurred unreservedly:

> I agree with your lordship that we are too apt to run mad in all subjects, and as to that of liberality, I hate the name of it above all others. I wish we could borrow some of the public virtues from our sister England, and I think we could send her some of the liberal ones. I am frightened about the Popery business. It ought to be touched only by a master hand. It is a chord of such wondrous potency that I dread the sound of it, and believe with you that the harmony would be better, if, like that of the spheres, it were at least for a time inaudible.

This was not to be, but Catholic relief was forced into the background in early 1782 by the rising enthusiasm Flood, among others, detected for legislative independence. He was particularly pleased to observe that the spirit of 'patriotism' and 'liberty' he now identified with the Volunteers was making an impression in the erstwhile stony soil of County Kilkenny.[42]

Lord Carlisle and William Eden were understandably less content. Eden was confident that the administration would successfully negotiate the second sitting of the session which, he calculated, would close 'in the course of April'. But 'the temper' MPs showed in late December, when a number of bills were returned in an amended form from London, strengthened his conviction that some concessions to Irish feelings were essential if the administration was to isolate Flood and put 'a permanent system of administration in place'. With this object in mind, Carlisle transmitted two requests to Hillsborough on 29 December seeking authorization to address 'the chief subjects of popular ferment, as may either allay men's spirits by shewing them their errors or draw their gratitude by complying with their reasonable wishes'.[43] The issues he cited included an annual Irish mutiny act, a *habeas*

41 *Parl. Reg.(Irl.)*, i, 171–2, 190–1, 193–4; Charlemont to Flood, 1 Jan. 1782 in R[odd], ed., *Letters to Flood*, pp 107–8. 42 Flood to Charlemont, 7 Jan. 1782 in H.M.C., *Charlemont*, i, 392. 43 Eden to Loughborough, 27 Dec. 1781, 12 Jan. 1782 in B.L., Auckland Papers, Add. Ms 34418 f 221, *Auckland Corres.*, i, 326; Carlisle to Hillsborough, 29 Dec. 1781 (2) (P.R.O., S.P., 63/480 ff 3–7, 10–13).

corpus act, the termination of the practice of including Ireland in English acts of parliament (specifically the current marine bill), Catholic relief, the Portuguese trade dispute and Poynings' Law. The inclusion of the marine bill on this list was prompted by Carlisle's wish to neutralise Flood's 'invidious insinuation' that Ireland's inclusion under the jurisdiction of the act threatened to 'disturb ... the confidence subsisting between the two kingdoms'. He was grateful, therefore, when Hillsborough assured him, on the eve of the resumption of parliament, that the offending clause would be dropped.[44]

The secretary-of-state had nothing positive to report on the other matters, however. He directed that every attempt to modify Poynings's Law should be resisted, despite the favourable contrast Carlisle drew betw een Yelverton's moderate proposal and 'the wild and extravagant ideas of Mr Flood'. Indeed, the Lord Lieutenant was confident that Yelverton's proposal could be 'amended and specifically worded so as to amount to a recognition of the whole present usage as practised under Poynings' Act, and merely to provide that the heads of all bills sent to the Lord Lieutenant and Council shall be transmitted to England'. Carlisle knew full well that an attempt to do this would be strongly opposed by Flood, but he was optimistic he could outmanoeuvre him if he was authorized to ease the concerns of those of 'moderate minds', and he went so far as to observe that the royal prerogative would be more effectively upheld, and that the Irish Privy Council would excite less controversy if its role was confined to the transmission of bills 'accompanied with the recommendation of such amendments or ejections as they would otherwise adopt' for consideration by its British counterpart. This was more than ministers were prepared to countenance, but the fact that it was being discussed indicates how essential Carlisle believed it was to isolate Flood if he was 'to quieten ... these great questions'.[45] Ironically, his task was exacerbated rather than eased by news that Flood had been removed from the British Privy Council on 9 January. Flood was 'vexed extremely', Eden reported, by what Lord Buckinghamshire deemed 'a violent measure', but Eden was persuaded it would 'have [a] permanent effect'.[46]

Eden anticipated a 'rancour[ous]' display from Flood on the recommencement of the session because of his removal from the Privy Council. However, Flood was not present for the debates on Catholic relief, the alteration of the tenure of judges or the delay in returning the *habeas corpus* bill which dominated parliamentary time on the Commons' resumption.[47] He was back in place by Wednesday, 6 February,

44 Carlisle to Hillsborough, 29 Dec. 1781 (2), Hillsborough to Carlisle, 24 Jan. 1782 (P.R.O., S.P.63/480 ff 10–15, 84–5).   45 Carlisle to Hillsborough, 29 Dec. 1781 (P.R.O., S.P.63/480 ff 14–15).   46 P.R.O., Privy Council Papers, P.C.2/126; Hillsborough to Carlisle, 14 Jan., Carlisle to Hillsborough, 22 Jan. (P.R.O.,S.P. 63/480 ff 64, 95); Eden to Loughborough, 22 Jan. 1782 in *Auckland Corres.*, i, 329; Buckinghamshire to Thompson, 11 Mar., 1777 (Lothian Papers, P.R.O.N.I., T3502/1 part 2 f 60).   47 Carlisle to Hillsborough, 29 Jan. (N.A., Irish Corres., 1697–1798 Ms 2446); Eden to Hillsborough, 29 Jan. (B.L., Auckland Papers, Add. Ms 34418 f 309); Carlisle to Hillsborough, 4 Feb. 1782 (P.R.O., S.P.63/480 f 150); *Parl. Reg.(Irl.)*, i, 195–6, 202–4.

but the only matter that elicited more than a brief comment from him was the bill he and Lucius O'Brien had prepared 'for regulating the corn trade'. Consideration of this legislation, scheduled for early February, was delayed to allow the Commons' committee established to investigate export bounties to make its report. Flood attributed this to the wish of the Castle interest to discredit the provision of bounties on corn exports because of faults in the administration of the current scheme, and when the report had not been presented by 12 February he sought leave to introduce his bill. This precipitated a heated exchange with John Foster, who shared some of the concerns of coastal merchants who deemed the bounties unfair and inequitable, and John Beresford whose priority was the elimination of fraud. Flood conceded that the existing arrangements were defective in this respect, but he defended the provision of bounties on the transportation of corn to Dublin and on exportation as 'essential' to the country's prosperity, and he secured the leave he sought. However, he was left in no doubt that the bill's passage was not assured. [48]

Progress on the question of legislative independence seemed even more problematic, though the decision of the Ulster Volunteers to hold a convention of delegates on the matter at Dungannon on 15 February gave this cause a much needed boost. As Flood was not a member of an Ulster corps, there was no question of his attending the convention in an official capacity, but his mounting enthusiasm for Volunteering, symbolised by his acceptance of a lieutenant colonelcy in the Dublin Independent Volunteers, prompted him to accept Lord Charlemont's invitation to join with him, Grattan, the pamphleteer Francis Dobbs, and the MP James Stewart of Killymoon in preparing resolutions for presentation to the Convention. [49] Flood and Grattan drafted the resolutions appertaining to Poynings' Law and the Declaratory Act. Grattan's asserted it was 'unconstitutional, illegal and a grievance' for 'any body of men other than the King, Lords and Commons of Ireland to make laws to bind this kingdom', while Flood's simply affirmed 'that the powers exercised by the Privy Council of both kingdoms under, or under colour or pretence of the Law of Poyning are unconstitutional and a grievance'. In addition, without Flood's or Charlemont's knowledge, Grattan prepared a further resolution supporting Catholic relief. All three were carried to Dungannon by Dobbs where they were afforded a warm reception. Grattan's first resolution was approved unanimously; Flood's resolution with one dissentient, and Grattan's second with two. [50]

48 J. Kelly, 'The Irish trade dispute with Portugal 1780–87' in *Studia Hibernica*, 25 (1989–90), pp 19–20; *Parl. Reg.(Irl.)*, i, 211–33; Carlisle to Hillsborough, 31 Jan., 7 Feb., Eden to Hillsborough, 7 Feb. (P.R.O., S.P.,63/480 ff 125–6, 162–6, 189); Hardman to Foster, 17 Feb. 1782 (P.R.O.N.I., Foster Papers, D562/1396); *Commons Jn. (Irl.)*, x, 275. 49 List of Volunteer companies and officers, Feb. 1782 (N.L.I., Military memorandum, Ms 743). Grattan was colonel to this corps. 50 Bristow to Ross, 17 Feb. 1782 (P.R.O., S.P., 63/480 ff 228–30); *Life of Grattan*, ii, 204–6; Stewart, *A deeper silence*, pp 36–7; Mac Nevin, *History of the Volunteers*, pp 154–61; P. Ó Snodaigh, 'The Volunteers of '82: a citizen army or armed citizens', *Irish Sword*, xv (1983), pp 183–4.

It is not clear what Flood anticipated would ensue from the Ulster Volunteer convention, but he was pleased that the public meetings of Volunteer corps convened to endorse the Dungannon resolutions generated unprecedented public enthusiasm for the cause of legislative independence. Flood also profited personally from his identification with the cause. The invitation to him to second Travers Hartley's candidature in the bye-election that took place in the Dublin city constituency in late February, which he did 'with great force of reasoning and elegance of diction', attested to his rising profile. [51]

The increasing goodwill with which Flood was regarded out of doors was not replicated in the House of Commons. Indeed, the serjeant-at-arms was instructed to take him into custody on 14 February for non-attendance. [52] This was a relatively trivial matter. The question of Catholic relief was not, and following the Dungannon delegates' pronouncement in favour of 'the relaxation of the Penal Laws', Flood felt compelled to break ranks with them on the issue. He did so during the committee stage debate on Gardiner's relief bill on 20 February when the point at issue was the right of Catholics to purchase land in fee, which they had been refused in 1778. Like many patriots, Flood's opposition to easing the disabilities imposed on Catholics moderated appreciably in the early months of 1782. He now expressed himself well-disposed in principle towards Gardiner's bill, which proposed to allow Catholics buy and sell land without restriction, to practice their religion freely, to establish schools and to marry whom they pleased, because of his wish 'to enbosom' that 'estimable body of men'. However, he remained resolute in his antipathy to allowing Catholics access to the political process, which is why he supported the amendment proposed by John Fitzgibbon and Barry Yelverton aimed at prohibiting Catholics from purchasing 'advowsons and lands to which a right of making seneschals is annexed, or any burgage or borough-right, by which members might be returned to serve in parliament'. [53]

Flood justified his stand on the grounds that MPs were too ready to highlight the negative features of the Penal Laws when it was their duty as members of 'a Protestant parliament' 'to explain and declare the whole scope of their intentions'. He did not do this himself. But he was convinced that the experience and circumstance of Irish Protestants justified the retention of the prohibition on Catholics purchasing property since it was essential to the maintenance of a 'Protestant constitution':

In the former laws, leases for years were granted to them [Catholics] upon the avowed principle of restraining them from any influence in elections. This law

51 C.H. Wilson, *A compleat collection of the resolutions of the Volunteers ... of Ireland ...* (Dublin, 1782), *passim*; Mac Nevin, *History of the Volunteers*, pp 160–1; *H.J.*, 20 Feb., 11 Mar.1782. 52 *Commons Jn.(Irl.)*, x, 297. 53 Day, 'Irish Catholics', pp 164–7; Eamon O'Flaherty, 'The Catholic question 1774–93', (M.A. thesis, U.C.D., 1981), pp 60–4; *Parl. Reg.(Irl.)*, i, 247, 252.

then goes beyond toleration, it gives them a power, and tends to make a change in the state. I have a great respect for the Roman Catholics, and though I will not condemn, yet I will not wholly approve their conduct. Ninety years ago the question was whether Popery and arbitrary power should be established in the person of King James, or freedom and the Protestant religion in the person of King William – four-fifth of the inhabitants of Ireland adhered to the cause of King James; they were defeated, and I rejoice in their defeat. The laws that followed this event were not laws of persecution, but of political necessity, and are you now prepared for a new government? Can you possibly suppose, though the Roman Catholics prefer you to every other people, that they will prefer you to themselves? What then is the consequence, if you give them equal power with the Protestants? Can a Protestant constitution survive? Yet should the majority of this motion attempt to alter the constitution, I firmly believe they would be repelled by the minority, and then a total convulsion must follow.

It is necessary when you are granting Roman Catholics indulgence, that you should distinguish between the rights of property and the rights of power; while a man is engaged in acquiring property he is in a habit of industry, and when acquired, it ties him to the state ... Though we wish to extend toleration to Roman Catholics, we do not wish to shake the government; we should allow them to purchase lands, but we should carefully guard against their possessing any power in the state. Therefore, for the benefit of all, and that we may not destroy the balance of the state (for I am sure no sensible Roman Catholic wishes to unhinge the state) let us grant them full security in matters of property, but prevent their interference in matters of state. [54]

This was a lucid articulation of a perception widely shared within the Protestant interest in Ireland. But it is a measure of how far Flood's outlook had changed since 1778, as well as how unrelenting were the die-hard critics of Catholic relief, that he was put in the same pro-relief category as Henry Grattan by Richard Woodward, the Bishop of Cloyne. [55] This is unduly reductionist, for though Flood pronounced himself 'a friend to the principle of the bill' and to the proposition that Catholics should be permitted to own 'property, permanent property' once more on 26 February, he continued to argue that the security of the Protestant interest in Ireland was dependant on the maintenance intact of a Protestant constitution. For this reason, he deemed the suggestion that Catholics should be allowed bear arms (which was mooted by Denis Daly) as inadmissible as the suggestion that they should be allowed exercise political power. However, as on previous occasions, Flood's oratory was insufficient to cause the measure to be amended to meet his anxieties, and the relief bill was ratified without the conditions he desired. [56]

54 *Parl. Reg.(Irl.)*, i, 252–3.   55 Cloyne to Buckinghamshire, 20 Feb. 1782 in H.M.C., *Lothian*, pp 410–11.   56 *Parl. Reg.(Irl.)*, i, 281–3; Day, 'Irish Catholics', pp 168–70; Carlisle to Hillsborough, 3

The proceedings of the House of Commons in late February were dominated by the question of Catholic relief. The patriots refused to allow this distract them from the larger issue of legislative independence, however, and on 22 February Grattan had the support of both Flood and Forbes when he sought approval for an address to the King denying the right of the British parliament to legislate for Ireland because it asserted

> that the people of Ireland are a *free people*; that the crown of Ireland is a distinct kingdom with a parliament of her own, the sole legislature thereof ... [and] the subjects of this kingdom cannot be bound, affected or obliged, by any legislature, save only the King, Lords and Commons, of this his Majesty's realm of Ireland; nor is there any other body of men who have power or authority to make laws for the same.

This was the most direct attack on the Declaratory Act that the patriots had made to date. It was ameliorated a little by the inclusion of an assurance 'that next to our liberties, we value our connection with Great Britain', but this attracted less notice than their explicit demand for 'a renunciation of the claim of the British parliament to make law for Ireland, a claim useless to England, cruel to Ireland, and without any foundation in law'. The Castle interest, inevitably, opposed it. The Attorney General, John Scott, dismissed the address as 'improper and impracticable' because the empire was in 'peril' and the sixth of George I, was of 'little use'. More pointedly, he queried the security of possession of those landowners who held lands under English law if the patriots' rejection of the right of Britain to legislate for Ireland was upheld. This was a quite deliberate tactic to deter MPs from pursuing sensitive constitutional issues like the Declaratory Act, and it is significant that neither Forbes nor Flood challenged him on the point. John Forbes simply urged MPs, who supported the country's rights, to seize the moment and vote for the address. Flood maintained it was 'necessary to make a declaration of the liberties and constitutional rights of Ireland', though he was not entirely at one with Grattan and Forbes because he devoted the bulk of his contribution to arguing that the Attorney General sought to uphold English not Irish rights. It was a modest contribution, and it did not impress the House which decided by 137 votes to 68 to deny the request for an address. This bode ill for the patriots hopes of advancing their constitutional grievances in the short term but, determined to press on, Flood chose to interpret the result as a rejection of Grattan's strategy rather than a rejection of the policy and he immediately announced his intention of moving a motion 'to assert the rights of Ireland' on Monday, 25 February.[57]

Mar. 1782 (P.R.O.,S.P.63/480 f 288).   **57** *Parl. Reg.(Irl.)*, i, 263–76; Carlisle to Hillsborough, 23 Feb. 1782 (2) (P.R.O., S.P.63/480 ff 247–50).

Flood's 'short but eloquent speech' introducing his motion on 25 February lasted a mere fifteen minutes and provided a precise justification of his motion which simply 'affirmed that the members of this House are the only representatives of the people of Ireland'. This encapsulated the essence of the Grattan authored resolution agreed at Dungannon, so it was appropriate that he should endorse it and that Forbes, Ogle, Brownlow and other patriots should do likewise. Barry Yelverton was less happy, but eager to upstage his most persistent critic, he made a more assertive statement in support of Ireland's 'right' to legislative autonomy. It made little difference to the outcome. Flood's motion was defeated by only a handful of votes fewer than Grattan's address a few days earlier.[58]

Despite these decisive defeats, the patriots did not succumb to defeatism. So when, on 27 February, Grattan gave notice of 'his intention to move immediately upon the meeting [of parliament] after the recess [for] a full and explicit declaration of the rights of Ireland to an independent legislature', Flood announced his intention, 'should Mr Grattan's proposition fail of success, to repeat the motion' he had made on the 25th.[59] Indeed, Flood was so determined to continue to press this issue he let his other legislative concerns slide. Thus he made no attempt to sustain the opposition he articulated on 27 February to the bill to establish a national bank.[60] He also handed over the management of the corn bill to his cousin, Frederick, secure in the knowledge that the bounty on corn transported to Dublin was to be retained even if the export bounty from Dublin was denied.[61]

Liberated from these distractions, Flood was free to focus on the need to eliminate uncertainty about the security of the property title of Irish landowners and other potential obstacles that might be adduced to engender opposition to constitutional reform. With this in mind, Carlisle reported on 23 February that Yelverton had determined to introduce a 'bill for quieting possessions held under British acts of parliament'.[62] Flood was in agreement with him on the political advisability of such legislation though he did not believe it necessary. However, w hen Yelverton took the Commons' floor on 1 March, he chose to focus on the fact that the Irish courts were being brought into disrepute by the refusal 'to pay any respect to such British statutes as affect to bind Ireland' rather than the security of land titles. He cited a smuggling case which had collapsed in justification, and indicated that he would seek permission to introduce the heads of a bill 'to give force to such British

58 *Parl. Reg.(Irl.)*, i, 277–80; Carlisle to Hillsborough, 3 Mar. 1782 (P.R.O., S.P.63/480 ff 290–5). 59 Carlisle to Hillsborough, 3 Mar. 1782 (P.R.O., S.P.63/480 ff 290–5). 60 He maintained it was under capitalised and that it would encourage the importation of a greater volume of luxury goods thus weakening domestic manufacture. *Parl.Reg. (Irl.)*, i, 292–301; Carlisle to Hillsborough, 28 Feb., 7 Mar. 1782 (P.R.O.,S.P.63/480 ff 280, 329). 61 *Commons Jn.(Irl.)*, x, 306, 308, 309–10, 314, 317, 323; Carlisle to Hillsborough, 16 Mar. 1782 (P.R.O., S.P.63/480 ff 369–70); *Parl. Reg.(Irl.)*, i, 245. 62 Carlisle to Hillsborough, 23 Feb. 1782 (P.R.O.,S.P.63 /480 ff 249–50); see also O'Brien, 'The exercise of legislative power', pp 28–30.

statutes as have been enacted for regulating the commerce of this kingdom' by extending the provisions of the Henrician act for confirming all statutes made in England.[63] Flood did not speak during the debate, but he clearly disagreed with Yelverton's decision not to pursue his promise to secure land titles because, later in the day, he requested leave 'to bring in heads of a bill to quiet possessions held in this kingdom'. This was resisted by several 'friends of government' (including John Beresford and Hussey Burgh) because of the lateness of the hour, and when the House resumed on the following day, Flood found that his opponents had the numbers to deny his request. Lord Carlisle could see no merit in it at all. It was, he alleged, 'selfish in its purport, coarse in its intent and unqualified with any civil expression whatever towards' Britain. More significantly, he maintained that 'to admit the necessity of an I[ris]h Act for giving permanent security to the landed property of the country, is to confess that some additional aid is required to disperse doubt and uncertainty upon this important subject'. The Lord Lieutenant believed, indeed, that if the bill was accepted it would lead, inevitably,

> to other measures, violent in their nature, tending to destroy all amity and confidence between the two kingdoms, but which they w[ould] be obliged to have recourse to as remedies to still those waters they had so intemperately moved. These remedies were to be looked for in parliamentary declarations, Volunteer resolutions, and solemn compacts not to avail themselves in any suits touching their property of any provisions of an Eng[lish] Act of parliament. [64]

This was speculation, but when the Commons came to debate Flood's proposition on 3 March, the Castle interest was in the enviable position of being able to take a back seat while moderate patriots led the opposition to the request. Barry Yelverton, inevitably, was to the fore. He deemed it 'not commensurate to the evil which we wish to redress' since Irish property held under acts of forfeiture or 'regulated' by private acts was as secure as if it had been determined to be so in the courts. Gervaise Parker Bushe was even more dismissive; he characterised Flood's bill as 'a complicated private act of parliament', and while this was partly countered by sympathetic comment from Sir Lucius O'Brien and Henry Grattan (both of whom expressed a wish to support the proposals of both Flood and Yelverton), the predominant view of MPs was that the motion was ill-advised because it would excite unnecessary 'alarm'. It was rejected decisively by 94 votes to 29, and Flood's isolation on this issue was further highlighted when his was the sole voice against appointing a committee to prepare legislation to give effect to Yelverton's proposal of the previous day.[65]

63 *Parl. Reg.(Irl.)*, i, 303; Carlisle to Hillsborough, 3 Mar. 1782 (P.R.O., S.P.63/480 ff 290–5). 64 Note by Carlisle, [Mar. 1782] in H.M.C., *Carlisle*, p. 556. 65 *Parl. Reg.(Irl.)*, i, 309–11; Carlisle to Hillsborough, 3 Mar. 1782 (P.R.O., S.P.63/480 ff 290–5).

Though this outcome might seem to suggest that Flood was as unpopular as ever, it would be wrong to portray him simply as a loner. He participated briefly in the patriots' campaign to engender public support to improve the prospect of their forging a Commons' majority which would support constitutional reform. Details are scarce, but it was confidently reported that Flood and Grattan sought 'not only by their conversation but by letters to the country ... to obtain addresses from the Volunteer Corps and from the Grand Juries at the ensuing assizes, as well as instructions from the counties to their representatives strongly insisting upon the exclusive right of the parliament of Ireland to enact laws binding upon this kingdom'.[66] Grattan and he may longer have been friends but, as their involvement in the preparation of resolutions for the Dungannon Convention attests, they were prepared, when their interests coincided in the spring of 1782, to co-operate in support of the cause of constitutional reform.

Such co-operation troubled the Irish administration. Both Carlisle and Eden were in agreement that it was in Britain's interest, if it aspired to 'permanent good government in this kingdom', to favour 'moderate men of principle and sense' like Yelverton over hardliners like Flood. The problem was that the implementation of such a policy necessitated meeting some of the patriots' demands for constitutional reform. The situation was 'serious', Carlisle pronounced in a 'most secret' dispatch in early March in which he sought authorization to support Yelverton's proposal to give force to British statutes. In contrast to Flood's proposal, Yelverton's bill was 'perfectly inoffensive in expression, exclusive of the safety which it will give to the hazarded estates of individuals and the beneficial laws of English commerce', and it was the administration's view that it should be allowed progress.[67]

As this makes clear, by early March Dublin Castle deemed the neutralisation of Flood as one of its priorities. To this end, they agreed to support Yelverton's bill on 1 and 3 March on condition that it committed them to confirm only commercial legislation. They calculated that by doing so they could win over Burgh, Fitzgibbon and, possibly, Grattan, and that this would result in the marginalisation of Flood, whom they saw as the *deus ex machina* of assertive patriotism.[68] If this accounts for Eden's readiness to defend Yelverton, and for his claim that 'it would have been the extreme both of folly and wickedness' to have 'resisted' his legislative intentions since it would have 'for ever destroyed the weight and credit of our friends' and led to 'rancour and ill blood of the most dangerous kind', it also created its own difficulties. One occurred on 5 March when Barry Yelverton reported from the committee established to draft legislation to confirm statutes made in England that the bill

---

66 Carlisle to Hillsborough, 3, 7 Mar. 1782 (P.R.O., S.P.63/480 ff 290–5, 323–5); Killaloe to Buckinghamshire, 5 Apr. 1782 (N.L.I., Heron Papers, Ms 13047/2). 67 Carlisle to Hillsborough, 3 Mar., Hillsborough to Carlisle, 12 Mar. (P.R.O., S.P.63/480 ff 296–80, 335–6); Note by Carlisle on Irish bills, [Mar. 1782] in H.M.C., *Carlisle*, pp 556–7. 68 Carlisle to Hillsborough, 19 Mar. 1782 (P.R.O., S.P.63/480 ff 397–400).

would appertain to property as well as to commerce. [69] This contradicted the arguments advanced to reject Flood's proposal on this very subject two days earlier, but the administration manifested no embarrassment. As far as they were co ncerned, Flood's priority was 'private property, professedly for the purpose of excluding all other English laws', whereas the proposition advanced by Yelverton, Grattan, Burgh and Fitzgibbon

> took a middle course, was respectful towards the M[other] country, re-enacted almost even law of G[reat] B[ritain] that reached the sister kingdom, as well as these that touched the landed property, and in short gave validity and force to a variety of legal regulations of reciprocal advantage, which before had no operation whatever, and were regularly resisted in [e]very part of the Island without adverting to their properties or uses, merely because they did [not] originate in the [Irish] parliament.

It was, in short, the handiwork of 'moderate men of principle and sense', compared to whom Flood was a troublemaker, 'ill-inclined to peaceable government and the public tranquillity'. [70]

Given the Castle's determination to frustrate his every move, it is no surprise that the efforts Flood made in late February-early March to forward his case for constitutional reform were rebuffed. Thus his attempt on 28 February to resist Yelverton's heads of a bill to modify Poynings' Law attracted no support. His solo effort, five days later, to defeat Yelverton's 'pernicious' proposal for enacting ' *in gross*, and without examination, a great number of English laws, many of them perhaps ill-suited to the circumstances of Ireland', was repulsed, as was his recommendation that its property and commercial provisions should be separated on the grounds that the former was an 'impediment to a declaration of the independence of the legislature of Ireland'. In a desperate last attempt to register some progress, Flood called for the establishment of a Commons' committee 'to investigate the subject fully before any bill was framed', but this too fell on deaf ears and the bill was ordered to make progress. [71]

Discouraged by these repeated rebuffs, Flood absented himself from all further stages of the debate on the bill for confirming English statutes. This paved the way for its proponents to broaden its scope till it became, in Grattan's eyes at least, 'a measure of conciliation' which, by demonstrating Irish resolve to keep its legislation uniform with that of Britain, cleared the way for the removal 'forever [of] all

---

69 Eden to Loughborough, 30 Mar. 1782 (B.L.,Auckland Papers, Add. Ms 34418 ff 387–8); *Parl. Reg.(Irl.)*, i, 314; Rosse Papers, C/14/1–5.   70 Eden to Loughborough, 30 Mar. (B.L.,Auckland Papers, Add. Ms 34418 ff 387–8); Note by Lord Carlisle on Irish bills, [Mar. 1782] in H.M.C.,*Carlisle*, pp 556–7.   71 Carlisle to Hillsborough, 7 Mar. 1782 (P.R.O., S.P.63/480 ff 327–8); *Parl. Reg.(Irl.)*, i, 302–3, 314–7.

rankling jealousies between the two countries, and [the] prevent[ion of] any suspicion on either side from interrupting their mutual confidence and harmony'. [72] This was precisely what Carlisle and Eden wanted to hear, and they were sufficiently confident they had an opportunity to forge the harmonious Anglo-Irish connection they identified as the way out of this crisis, they lobbied London to return the bill unaltered and to undertake to repeal the Declaratory Act. Flood, meanwhile, returned to Farmley for the duration of the parliamentary recess which commenced on 14 March. He had no inkling that Carlisle, who congratulated himself that he had so effectively out-manoeuvred Flood 'he retired to the country', was pressing the cabinet to sanction such fundamental constitutional change, but he had no intention of giving up his struggle to ensure that what was agreed did not accord with Yelverton's flawed proposals. [73] Moreover, the fact that Carlisle's stay in Ireland was to be brought to a precipitous close provided him with a powerful incentive to persist.

LEGISLATIVE INDEPENDENCE

Six days after the Irish parliament adjourned for a spring recess on 14 March, the government of Lord North collapsed. His successor, Lord Rockingham, was a Whig, and while there was an assumption in some quarters that Carlisle and Eden might be invited to retain their Irish postings, the Whigs preferred their own nominees, and the duke of Portland and the talented, but untried *roué*, Richard Fitzpatrick were appointed to take their place at the head of the Irish executive. [74] The change of government complicated the efforts of the under-secretary, Edward Cooke (who was in England), to secure Privy Council sanction for Yelverton's bill to confirm British statutes, but the expectation of patriots like Charlemont, Grattan and Forbes was that the accession of Rockingham enhanced rather than diminished the prospect of constitutional concession. Flood's reticence suggests that he was less convinced of the benignity of the Whigs' intentions, but the change in personnel at the top of the Irish administration and the burgeoning groundswell of Volunteer support for legislative independence did increase the likelihood that constitutional reforms would be forthcoming and his prospects of influencing the outcome. [75]

72 Carlisle to Hillsborough, 12 Mar. 1782 (P.R.O., S.P.63/480 ff 352–6); *Parl. Reg.(Irl.)*, i, 324–6.   73 Carlisle to Hillsborough, 16, 19, 27 Mar. (P.R.O., S.P.63/480 ff 367, 397–400, 426); Eden to [North], 18 Mar., Eden to Loughborough, 24 Mar. (B.L., Auckland Papers, Add. Ms 34418 ff 367, 378); Carlisle to Gower, 23 Mar. (P.R.O., Grenville Papers, 30/29/1/15); Webb to Flood, 27 Mar. 1782 in R[odd], ed., *Letters to Flood*, p. 89.   74 Duncan, 'Carlisle', pp 129–30; *The Royal Register with annotations*, viii, 30–7; Carlisle to Gower, 17 Apr. (P.R.O., Grenville Papers, 30/29/1/15); Fitzgerald to Leinster, 25 May 1782 (N.L.I.,Fitzgerald Papers, Ms 13022/176).   75 Eden to Gower, [Apr.] (P.R.O., Grenville Papers, 30/29/1/15); Cooke to Eden, 2 Apr., Hely-Hutchinson to Eden, 4 Apr. (B.L.,Auckland Papers, Add,

There was a widespread expectation in Ireland following the change of government that, in the words of Charles Francis Sheridan, 'a declaration of the independency of our parliament upon yours will certainly pass our House of Commons immediately after the recess'. The question remained as to how this was to be achieved. Lord Charlemont wanted Flood and Grattan to share the responsibility. He was confident that matters were 'in as good a train as possible', as he informed Flood on 13 April. However, he was troubled by news that Grattan was indisposed and by communications from Lord Rockingham and Charles James Fox which made it clear that their priority was not the unconditional satisfaction of Irish demands, but the negotiation of 'a compact' – 'a new system and new arrangement of connection between the two kingdoms'.[76] Charlemont was disinclined to take up the offer and, desperate for guidance at this critical moment, he pleaded with Flood to 'come immediately to town' so he could avail of his 'wisdom and advice', but it is not clear that he even responded. Indeed, Henry Grattan junior, who was well-placed to know, maintained that he did not, and while his return to Dublin in time for the recommencement of the session means he may have responded orally, the fact that he did not join with Charlemont and Grattan suggests that he remained as determined as ever to provide himself with maximum room to pursue his own agenda. This was entirely in character; he had behaved in a like fashion on previous occasions, though none was so consequential. By declining Charlemont's invitation he effectively put a gap between himself and those patriot leaders who had direct access to the new government, and since both Charlemont and Grattan were instinctively less confrontational, it was no surprise that they opted for the way applotted by Yelverton rather than by him.

This was not immediately apparent. Indeed, whereas Flood agreed with Daly, Yelverton and Burgh that Portland's request for an extension to the parliamentary adjournment to give him more time to familiarise himself with Irish affairs should be granted, Grattan and Charlemont vetoed the suggestion.[77] The House of Commons reconvened on 16 April as planned, and Grattan ensured it was a red-letter day in the annals of Irish patriotism by overcoming indisposition to counter the moderate address proposed by the administration, which enjoined MPs only to 'take into their most serious consideration the discontents and jealousies which have arisen in this kingdom', with an amendment affirming Ireland's entitlement to legislative autonomy. Flood was in the House of Commons to hear Grattan's oratorical *tour de force*, but he remained silent. It is not clear what he thought of the day's proceedings. But since he supported Grattan's unsuccessful attempt to resist a vote of thanks

Ms 34418 ff 401, 405–6); James Kelly, *Prelude to Union: Anglo-Irish politics in the 1780s* (Cork, 1992), pp 35–6; Killaloe to Buckinghamshire, 10 Apr. (N.L.I., Heron Papers, Ms 13047/2); Jebb to Forbes, 13 Apr.(N.L.I., Forbes Papers, Ms 10715); *H.J.*, 1, 8, 15 Apr. and *passim*; Leinster to [Spencer], 26 Mar. 1782 (Pomeroy Papers, P.R.O.N.I., T2954/7/3); *Life of Grattan*, ii, 226–7.   **76** Sheridan to Sheridan, 27 Mar. 1782 in *Life of Grattan*, ii, 214–5; Kelly, *Prelude to Union*, pp 35–6; Charlemont to Flood, 13 Apr. 1782 in R[odd], ed., *Letters to Flood*, p. 109.   **77** O'Brien, 'The exercise of legislative power', p. 48.

to Lord Carlisle later in the day and chaired the meeting of the delegates of 139 Leinster Volunteer Corps in Dublin on the 17 April which approved a resolution expressing 'satisfaction' with 'the unanimous sense of the House of Commons' and congratulating Henry Grattan 'for his extraordinary exertion and perseverance in asserting the rights of Ireland' it can be assumed that whatever reservations he possessed were tactical rather than material.[78]

As his presence at the Leinster meeting attests, Flood's enthusiasm for Volunteering continued to appreciate. This is underlined by his acceptance of a nomination to the standing committee of thirteen Volunteer colonels appointed 'to correspond and commune with all the other provincial committees or delegates of Ireland', and his invitation to Lord Charlemont to act as reviewing general at the Volunteer field days to be held at Dublin, Bellewstown and Carlow during the summer.[79] In taking this step, Flood appeared to affirm Richard Fitzpatrick's contention that 'the parliament no longer met in College Green but at Dungannon'. This was hyperbole, but there was no doubt but that Flood's involvement with the Volunteers in the late spring and early summer of 1782 contributed to the continuing enhancement of his public profile, though he still trailed a long way behind Grattan in the popularity stakes.[80]

The unity of purpose demonstrated by the Volunteers and patriot MPs in April 1782 placed the Lord Lieutenant under intense pressure to yield to Irish demands on Poynings' Law and the Declaratory Act. Rather than concede unconditionally, the duke of Portland sought to explore the possibility of a formal settlement which would satisfy the demand of Irish patriots for greater legislative autonomy and London's wish for what Charles James Fox, on 24 April, described as a 'clear understanding with respect to what we are to expect from Ireland'. He also contrived to win over Grattan, Charlemont and Forbes whom, he hoped, would constitute the nucleus of an Irish Whig party.[81] To this end, he controversially replaced John Scott and others he found politically uncongenial with amenable moderate patriots (Yelverton became Attorney General and Hussey Burgh Prime Serjeant in May), and he took heart from the declaration by Grattan on 18 April that he was 'willing to take any part in the administration provided it is not emolumentary'.[82]

Predictably, Flood was less forthcoming. Portland requested the 'discretionary

78 *Parl. Reg.(Irl.)*, i, 340–1; *Life of Grattan*, ii, 232–3, 246–5, 269; *H.J.*, 19 Apr. 1782; Wilson, *Resolutions of the Volunteers*, pp 227–9.   79 *H.J.*, 19 Apr. 1782; Charlemont to Flood, 5 May 1782 in R[odd] ed., *Letters to Flood*, pp 110–11.   80 Fitzpatrick to Shelburne, 24 Apr. (B.L.,Lansdowne Abstracts, Add. Ms 24137); *H.J.*, 22, 24 Apr.; Shannon to Heron, 30 Apr. 1782 (N.L.I., Heron Papers, Ms 13040/2).   81 Portland to Shelburne, 24 Apr. (P.R.O.,H.O.100/1 ff 133–9); Portland to Shelburne, 27 Apr. (B.L.,Lansdowne Abstracts, Add. Ms 24138); Fox to Fitzpatrick, 20 Apr. 1782 (B.L., Fox Papers, Add. Ms 45580 f 94); Kelly, *Prelude to Union*, p. 39.   82 Grattan to Fox, 18 Apr. in *Life of Grattan*, ii, 248; Conolly to Bunbury, 26 Apr. (W.S.R.O., Bunbury Papers, P.R.O.N.I., Mic 238); McDowell, *Ireland in the age of imperialism*, pp 285–6; Scott to Robinson, 26 Apr., Beresford to Townshend, 25 May, Beresford to Eden, 27 May. 1782 in *Beresford Corres.*, i, 196–7, 202–6.

power' to restore him to the Privy Council if he 'was persuaded he would feel a just
and proper sense of the King's condescension and goodness towards him',[83] but
when it was put to Flood that he might

> repossess his seat at the council board, ... he looked upon the offer as an insult
> and rejected it with disdain – a privy councillor's place both in England and in
> Ireland having been a trifling appendage of his late office.

This episode refutes Charlemont's contention that Portland came to Ireland 'pre-
possessed against Flood'. However, he was not long in the country before he was
persuaded by his 'private friends in Ireland [who] were by no means partial to the
late vice-treasurer ... that his aid was unnecessary, and his enmity not to be feared.
His impracticability ... [was] insisted on and magnified; and he ... [was] described
as a man in whom government ought not to confide.[84] Flood's remoteness encouraged such negative perceptions; even Lord Charlemont was hard-pressed to remain
well-disposed when Flood ignored further invitations to meet him in Dublin (he
returned to Farmley in late April) to discuss political developments.[85]
    Flood's snubbing of Charlemont ensured that he played no part in the behind
the scenes exchanges that caused ministers to yield to Irish demands for concessions on the Declaratory act, Poynings' Law and the Mutiny Act. Resolutions acknowledging this were approved at Westminster on 17 May, with the result that
when the Irish House of Commons reassembled after a further recess on 27 May,
MPs were presented with an address from the Lord Lieutenant in which it was
announced that the King had agreed

> to give his royal assent to acts to prevent the suppression of bills in the Privy
> Council of this kingdom, and the alteration of them anywhere; and to limit the
> duration of the act for the better regulation and accommodation of his Majesty's
> forces in this kingdom to the term of two years.

This was music to Grattan's ears, and since he had also been informed that the
Declaratory Act would be repealed, he appealed to MPs to approve a reply assuring
the King of 'our unfeigned affection to his royal person and government'.[86]
    Flood did not share Grattan's elation. He was instinctively more suspicious of
governmental intentions, and he was so disturbed by what he read of the debates on

83 *Cork Evening Post*, 8 Apr.; [Portland] to [Shelburne], 27 Apr. (B.L., Pelham Papers, Add. Ms 33100
f 108, Lansdowne Abstracts, Add. Ms 24137).   84 H.M.C., *Charlemont*, i, 64, 400; see also Jenkinson to
Weston, 23 May 1782 (N.A., Calendar of departmental letters and official papers 1760–89, i, f 392);
Rosse Papers, C/14/ 1–5. The *London Gazette* reported in error that Flood was restored to the Council
(Fortescue, ed., *Corres of George III*, vi, 48).   85 Charlemont to Flood, 5 May 1782 in R[odd], ed.,
Letters to Flood, pp 110–11.   86 Kelly, *Prelude to Union*, pp 38–42; Beresford to Barré, 3 May in *Beresford
Corres.*, i, 197–9; Pery to Shelburne, 6 May 1782 in H.M.C., *Emly*, ii, 166–7; *Parl. Reg. (Irl.)*, i, 347, 356.

Irish affairs at Westminster that he concluded that the government's strategy was to concede the minimum necessary to deflate Irish demands. Anticipating his opposition, Grattan sought to leave him with little room to manoeuvre on 17 May by pronouncing that once the concessions announced were implemented 'that no constitutional question between the two nations will any longer exist, which can disrupt their harmony', because 'Great Britain gives up *in toto* every claim to authority over Ireland.' And addressing Flood's contention that Westminster must acknowledge it had acted illegally by interfering with Irish legislation, he contended reasonably that it was impolitic to press the point:

> I have not the least idea that in repealing the 6th of George I, Great Britain should be bound to make any declaration that she had formerly usurped a power. No, this would be a foolish caution – a dishonourable condition. The nation that insists upon the humiliation of another is a foolish nation – Ireland is not a foolish nation.[87]

This was also the opinion of the bulk of the two hundred plus MPs present, but Flood and a small number of others were convinced the issue was too important to be let go. He countered by claiming that the inclusion of a statement in the address that 'no constitutional question' could now be deemed to exist between the two countries was 'inappropriate and dangerous' because it did not reflect the reality of English intentions. He acknowledged that

> nothing appeared to him, at present, which could disturb the general harmony, but there were many English acts still existing, which operated in this kingdom, and notwithstanding the laudable acquiescence which appeared in the renunciation of English claims, who could engage, that the present administration, might not, at some future period, change its mind? He begged the gentlemen to consider the language held out in the English House of Commons. They asserted a right to external legislation; and he that seconded the motion on the Irish business did not give up that right, but as matter of convenience and compact. Even the Secretary [Charles James Fox] asserted this right to external legislation, though he gave up that of internal. It may therefore be imagined in England (continued he) that you imply what they asserted, and that they had a right to bind you.[88]

Because of this, it was important, Flood argued, that the offending passage was dropped from the address but, with the exception of David Walshe, the radical MP for the County Tipperary borough of Fethard, and Sir Samuel Bradstreet, the recorder of Dublin, he was without support. Walshe maintained combatively that Fox's

---

87 *Parl. Reg.(Irl.)*, i, 355–6.   88 *Parl. Reg.(Irl.)*, i, 356.

claim that Britain 'had not given up the power of external legislation' demonstrated conclusively that 'the repeal of the 6th of George the 1st … is inadequate to the emancipation of Ireland' because it 'does not deny the power hereafter to make laws to bind Ireland, whenever England shall think herself in sufficient force for the purpose' and because it left 'untouched and unrelinquished' the 'assumed and usurped power of England to make laws to bind Ireland'. Until this was 'expressly declare[d]' Ireland could not, he averred, be said 'to be completely emancipated'.[89] Surprisingly, Flood chose not to endorse this interpretation. He 'retire[d]' from the chamber before a vote was taken to avoid having to choose between supporting an address he disliked or experiencing a humiliating rebuff.[90]

The assertion by David Walshe that the repeal of the Declaratory Act did not represent an explicit disavowal by Westminster of its the right to legislate for Ireland was not new. The influential pamphleteer Charles Francis Sheridan had pointed out in 1779 that because the Declaratory Act acknowledged 'rights presumed to be antecedently existing', its repeal would not amount to the legal abnegation of those 'rights'.[91] This raises a question over Flood's silence on the point on 27 May. It may be that the sense of gratitude in Ireland for what had been conceded was so overwhelming that Flood sought to put some space between himself and Walshe and the rest of what was perceived as a faintly disreputable group of malcontents. Even so, he did not escape criticism; his conduct was described by his opponents as 'outrageous', while even sympathetic acquaintances like Edmond Malone expressed themselves 'quite at a loss to account for [his] not having stood more forward in this business'.[92]

Flood's decision to avoid the limelight in late May was understandable. Grattan was the man of the moment as the House of Commons emphasised when it awarded him £50,000 as an expression of gratitude for his role in securing the recently announced constitutional liberties. The majority in favour of the award was large, but a small number of Flood loyalists did not accept that Grattan deserved the entire credit for what had been secured, and Alexander Montgomery of Donegal (who was instrumental in ensuring that Grattan received £50,000 rather than the £100,000 originally suggested) recommended that Flood too should receive a mark of favour but that this should take a form other than 'alms from his country' which, he observed pointedly, he 'was above receiving'. Henry Flood, Montgomery contended, was 'the best, the most able, the most indefatigable, the most sincere [gentleman]

89 Ms account of the Irish parliament in 1782, p. 242 (Henry Huntington Library); *Parl. Reg.(Irl.)*, i, 357–8.   90 *Parl. Reg.(Irl.)*, i, 351–71; Foster to Buckinghamshire, 27 May in H.M.C.,*Lothian*, pp 414–5; Fitzgibbon to [Carlisle], 27 May in H.M.C.,*Carlisle*, pp 629–30; [Portland] to Shelburne, 29 May 1782 (B.L., LansdowneAbstracts,Add. Ms 24138). Grattan's address was approved by 211 votes to two. 91 C.F.Sheridan, *A review of the three great national questions relative to a declaration of right, Poynings' Law and the mutiny bill* (Dublin, 1781), p. 37; O'Brien, 'The exercise of legislative power', p. 25.   92 Fitzgibbon to [Carlisle], 27 May 1782 in H.M.C., *Carlisle*, pp 629–30; Malone to Charlemont, 8 June 1782 in H.M.C., *Charlemont*, i, 407.

that had ever sacrificed private interest to the advantage of his country'. He had 'relinquished the most lucrative office of the state rather than desert the constitution of Ireland' and it was appropriate for that reason that he was restored 'to the office he lately held'. This extraordinary proposition, which it was not in the Commons' power to bestow, was supported by David Walshe and Frederick Flood, but not by Flood himself. He had no prior knowledge that Montgomery intended to make such a suggestion, as he revealed on 1 June, and he was more than faintly embarrassed by the suggestion. [93]

There was no possibility of Flood being appointed to any major office of state because it was widely believed in official circles that he was responsible for what the percipient under-secretary Edward Cooke described on 2 June as the 'ill blood' that 'is everywhere brewing'. This threatened, he observed gloomily , to culminate 'if not in formidable opposition, certainly in dangerous animosity' because of mounting public unease with what was seen as the limitations of legislative independence. The prospect of unrest certainly increased when, following his withdrawal of his 'former bill' on 1 June, the Attorney General, Barry Yelverton, was given leave to introduce a new and 'more perfect' measure 'for regulating the passing of bills and preventing delays in the summoning of parliaments'. [94] Flood did not speak during the debate, but he was clearly unimpressed because he joined with David Walshe in opposing the bill when it commenced its committee stage on Thursday, 6 June.

Flood's central objection to Yelverton's redrafted bill was that it was neither 'adequate to the idea held out and entertained by the nation' nor sufficient 'to do justice to the constitution'. It was not, he maintained haughtily, to the kingdom's advantage to pursue what he defined as expedient and deficient solutions which did not preclude the reaffirmation of the offending power, since

> the privy council might recall this power under a corrupt ministry ... It was not to be supposed that the breed of the Strafford's in political principles were yet extinct; and an arbitrary government might at some future period take advantage of the negligence of the present hour. [95]

Ireland, Flood insisted, was entitled to possess 'a similar constitution with England' and Yelverton's bill did, he conceded, move in this direction. However, 'since there was no provision by this bill which could prevent the smothering of bills or explain the reasons of a silent negative', more was necessary, and he recommended that instead of Yelverton's current proposal the House should press instead for the 'express repeal of the law...with a saving clause of such and such things as should be

93 *Parl. Reg. (Irl.)*, i, 375–83; Cooke to Eden, 2 June (B.L., Auckland Papers, Add. Ms 34418 ff 466–9).
94 Shelburne to George III, 29 May 1782 in Fortescue, ed., *Corres. of George III*, vi, 48; Cooke to Eden, 2 June 1782 (B.L., Auckland Papers, Add. Ms 34418 ff 466–9); *Parl. Reg. (Irl.)*, i, 380.   95 *Parl. Reg. (Irl.)*, i, 388–9.

found necessary to retain'. This was a constructive suggestion, and it f orcedYelverton
into the telling admission that his bill 'did not entirely restore what the constitution
of England enjoyed, but circumstanced as Ireland was now, it was the best calculated that could be devised'. Encouraged by this, Flood pressed home his advantage
by pointing out that the way Poynings' Law had been applied supported his contention that the only sure way permanently to extend the liberties of Ireland was by
repealing, rather than by amending, Poynings' Law, since it:

> had expressly provided that their bills should not be altered, and yet the English
> privy council had the effrontery to continue such alterations. No ambiguous
> words were sufficient to protect the rights of the weak against the strong, nor
> were the provisions of the present bill as explicit as the original law of Poynings.
> Lawyers might create doubts hereafter, and they should prefer certainty to doubt,
> by a repeal.[96]

The full effect of Flood's speech is not conveyed by the imperfect version recorded
in the *Parliamentary Register*, but it is a fair measure of its impact that Gervaise
Bushe and John Fitzgibbon were impressed by the argument. However, their support was offset by the support afforded Yelverton's bill by Lucius O'Brien, Hussey
Burgh and John Forbes with the result that the measure completed its committee
stage without a division being called.[97]

Despite their modest number, Flood and his allies were emboldened by the fact
that they had (as John Beresford conceded) 'much the better of the argument' on 6
June to renew their attack when Yelverton's bill was repor ted on the following day.[98]
Walshe took the lead on this occasion. Taking up the argument Flood had advanced
on Thursday, he roundly condemned the measure on the grounds that it provided
for the transfer of 'the power of altering [Irish bills] from the Irish to the English
Privy Council and the English attorney general'. This was denied by Yelverton, but
Walshe's statement set the tone for an ill-tempered debate in which, among other
incidents, Flood took exception to remarks by George Ogle which questioned his
truthfulness. More materially, he offered a substantial amendment aimed at precluding the British Privy Council from amending Irish bills and defining precisely
how the royal assent should be given:

> Whereas ... doubts have arisen on the construction of the law commonly called
> Poynings', and of the third and fourth of Philip and Mary, explanatory thereof:
> Be it enacted by the King's most excellent Majesty, by and with the advice and
> consent of the Lords Spiritual and Temporal, and Commons, in this present

96 *Parl. Reg.(Irl.)*, i, 386.   97 Ibid., pp 383–7; Sayles, ed., 'The Irish parliament in 1782', p.
243.   98 Beresford to Eden, 7 June (B.L.,Auckland Papers,Add. Ms 34418 ff 470–1); see also Fitzpatrick
to Dobbs, 1 June 1782 (N.L.I., Dobbs Papers, Ms 2251 f 95).

parliament assembled, and by the authority of the same, that the said law of Poynings, and the said third and fourth of Philip and Mary, be and stand repealed, save only as follows: that is to say, be it enacted that no parliament shall be holden in this kingdom until a licence for that purpose be had and obtained from his Majesty, his heirs and successors, under the great seal of Great Britain: And that all bills, considerations, causes, ordinances, tenors and provisions, of either or both Houses of parliament, shall be of right certified to his Majesty, his heirs and successors, unaltered, under the great seal of Ireland, by the Lord Lieutenant, or other chief governor or governors, and the council of this kingdom, for the time being; and that such bills, and no others, being returned unaltered, under the great seal of Great Britain, shall be capable of receiving the royal assent or dissent in parliament, according to his Majesty's commission, either for giving his assent or dissent to the same respectively.

It was unusual for an MP to seek to introduce an amendment as substantial as Flood sought to do in this instance. But he felt compelled to do so because

I have a feeling in the inmost pulse in my heart, it is that which tells me, that this is a great and awful day; it is that which tells me, that if, after twenty years service, I should pass this question by neglectingly, I should be a base betrayer of my country; it is that which tells me that the whole earth does not contain a bribe sufficient to make me trifle with the liberties of this land. I do, therefore, wish to subscribe my name to what I now propose, to have them handed down together to posterity, that posterity may know there was at least *one man* who disapproved of the temporising bill now before the House; a bill that future parliaments, if they have power, will REFORM, if they have not, with tears will DEPLORE.

This was an exceptionally candid avowal, but few MPs regarded it any more positively than previous personal statements Flood had made. Indeed, the Prime Serjeant, Hussey Burgh, maintained that because Flood's motion amounted to nothing less than 'a new bill in the room of that which had received the sanction of the House in committee ... it would be breaking through the rules of that House to receive' it. In his reply, Flood reiterated that Yelverton's bill 'did not expressly prevent [the British] privy council from altering' Irish legislation, but this did not impress Burgh, who maintained that the ratification of Flood's amendment would endanger the Anglo-Irish connection. Yelverton was more accommodating. He was willing to receive an amendment prohibiting the practice of certifying bills in Britain 'as a cause or consideration for holding a parliament' in Ireland but, while this went some of the way to meet Flood's concerns, he was less forthcoming on the bigger issue of the power of the British Privy Council. On being allowed the floor once more, Flood stressed how important it was that MPs spoke 'out in fair and open language' to 'defend the rights of the people against arbitrary power'. His object, he pronounced soothingly, was '*renovation*' (not innovation) to ensure Ireland 'a constitution similar to that of England', but he was unable to overcome the suspicions of his critics that he was being unnecessarily confrontatio nal. The loss of his amendment was assured when Henry Grattan, who was inhibited by illness from playing an active part in the Commons' proceedings at this time, signalled his support for the bill and it was ratified, with Yelverton's rather than Flood's amendment, without a division being called.[99]

The persistence and conviction with which Flood and the small nucleus of radical patriots – David Walshe, Alexander Montgomery and Samuel Bradstreet – who looked to him for leadership as well as ideas,[100] challenged the constitutional settlement being implemented was regarded with such concern in official circles that they contrived to discredit them by placing negative stories in the press. Each, it was alleged, was motivated by disappointed ambition rather than by principle. There was more than a germ of truth in this in a number of cases, but more specific allegations were directed at Flood. For instance, one exceptionally well-briefed commentator remarked that he had reverted to opposition in the late 1770s when he held the lucrative vice-treasurership, because he 'was refused the patronage of County Kilkenny as well as a peerage for Mr Agar in order to secure to himself the borough of Callan'. There was just enough truth in the allegation to embarrass Flood. Indeed, he drew the attention of the House of Commons on 10 June to the 'low illiberal sarcasms' resorted to in the press to depict him 'as a leader of sedition' and cited his record to justify his contention that he had behaved in a wholly legal and constitutional manner.[101]

The fact that Flood felt compelled to raise the matter indicated that he found these personal attacks trying. At the same time, it is significant that they did not cause him to moderate his opposition to the constitutional changes being made. Having failed to remodel Yelverton's bill to accommodate his objections, he promptly shifted his focus to the ostensibly less complex and contentious subject of the Declaratory Act. The galleries of the House of Commons were full on Monday, 10 June to hear him present his promised motion on the subject of the repeal of the Declaratory Act, but an attack of 'influenza' caused this to be postponed for twenty-four hours.[102] He had recovered sufficiently by the following day to attend, and he set proceedings in train by enquiring from the Chief Secretary, Richard Fitzpatrick, 'whether' the bill for repealing the Declaratory Act 'was only a simple repeal, or whether it contained any declaration for giving up the declaratory right assumed by England'. Fitzpatrick replied, as Flood anticipated, by stating that it was the former.

99 *Parl. Reg.(Irl.)*, i, 387–97; Haliday to Charlemont, 7 June 1782 in H.M.C., *Charlemont*, i, 406–7.   100 *Parl. Reg.(Irl.)*, i, *passim*; Sayles, ed., 'The Irish parliament in 1782', pp 266, 271 etc; McDougall, *Sketches of Irish political characters*, p. 171.   101 *H.J.*, 10 June 1782; *Parl. Reg.(Irl.)*, i, 398.   102 Barnard to Buckinghamshire, 10 June (N.L.I., Heron Papers, Ms 13047/2); Allan to Macartney, 12 June–3 July 1782 (P.R.O.N.I., Macartney Papers, D572/19/87 ff 365–6).

However, instead of accepting this as his cue to attack 'simple repeal' as inadequate, he offered what John Beresford described as a 'silly resolution' aimed at pre-empting the 'ideas of final adjustment and negociation' currently in the air. [103] This was unanticipated, and Flood did nothing to enhance the appeal of his motion, which took the form of a counter-resolution to that approved at Westminster urging a 'final settlement', by informing the Chief Secretary he 'would withdraw' it if he was given an assurance that a 'final adjustment' was not government policy. Fitzpatrick could not do this, which prompted Flood to assert that if Ireland acquiesced in the 'simple repeal' of the Declaratory Act it was failing to avail of a glorious opportunity to oblige Britain to agree unconditionally that it had no right to legislate for Ireland:

> Britain on this occasion ... was so embarrassed abroad, and you were so strong at home, that she could not deny the repeal of the Declaratory-law. Yet it must ever be her wish to retain the principle of it, because it is the principle of power, which no nation has ever relinquished while it could maintain it. What then has she done? By seeming to yield unconditionally to you, she seized on the generous credulity of your nature, and took full advantage of a change in her own administration. Her first step was bold, in order to strike your imaginations with something that seemed to be decisive. She resolved that the Declaratory-law ought to be repealed: she did not say, however, that it ought to be repealed as having been a false and erroneous declaration of law; far from it; not a man in the British parliament held such an idea: the very mover and seconder of the resolution said the contrary ... They declared the constitutional right of the British parliament to make laws for every part of the empire; one of them said externally; and the other both externally and internally. One said the repeal must be accompanied by a final adjustment, and the other that the law could only be repealed on a principle of compact.

There was little in this statement that had not been said by others. What was different was the conviction with which Flood pronounced that Britain must explicitly 'renounce' its claim. A 'simple repeal', he enunciated,

> is so far from a renunciation, that it is the very contrary;... a repeal without a renunciation leaves you in effect only where you were. It is a first principle of law, that a declaratory act only declares the law to be what it was before; that is to say, that it only declares, and that it does not alter the law. What follows? That as making a Declaratory-act does not alter law, so neither can the mere unmaking of such an act alter law ... The repeal of a Declaratory-law (unless it contains a

103 *Parl. Reg. (Irl.)*, i, 402–3; Beresford to Eden, 13 June 1782 in *Beresford Corres.*, i, 207–9. The Westminster resolution read 'that the interests of the two kingdoms are inseparable, and that their connexion ought to be founded on a solid and permanent basis'.

renunciation of the principle) is only a repeal of the declaration, and not of the legal principle. The principle remains behind in full force, unless it be renounced. This is universally true, and it is strengthened in this case by this circumstance. Many acts have been made by the British parliament binding Ireland, some of them before the Declaratory-law of George the 1st. Now whilst one of these remains, there is an exercise and a proof of the right, stronger by much than the Declaratory-law. A simple repeal, therefore, of the Declaratory-law is no vindication of your legislature. But it is argued, that because in your first address you declare that the British parliament has no such right, therefore the repeal joined to this will be equal to a renunciation by England. But what man in his senses can believe that our renunciation of the British claim can be equal to her own renunciation of it? Or that in any controversy, an assertion of a party in his own favour is equal to the admission of his antagonist? If Britain renounces it, no other power on earth can pretend to maintain it. But if all the rest of the world were to deny her pretension, yet as long as she maintains it, our rights are vindicated, and our constitution is in danger ... But to put the argument to a decisive proof, let us suppose that after such a simple repeal, that at future day the British parliament should revive the principle, and make a law for us. Suppose that Ireland should remonstrate on this – Suppose she should read that paragraph of her address, and quote the British repeal of the Declaratory-law, and should argue from both, that England had forever renounced her claim, do you think that England would listen to such an interference, or that any reasoner in Europe would allow the force of her argument? [104]

Flood conceded that he could not be certain that England would ever seek to 'revive the claim' to legislate for Ireland, but he was determined 'she' should not be given the opportunity to do so. If 'she does not renounce the claim, she certainly may revive it', he pronounced logically. He acknowledged Grattan's point that it would be a 'blow' to the 'pride' of England if it was obliged to do this, but he could see no alternative if the 'security' of the legislative autonomy of the Irish parliament was not to be left vulnerable and incomplete:

we must chuse one of two things, either to hurt her pride, in order to obtain our security, or to relinquish our security in order not to hurt her pride; but if there be a pride on one side, there is a pride also on the other; if there be a pride of England, there is a pride of Ireland too. Now I ask which ought to give way, for one must, and I answer impartially, that which has the worst foundation. Now which is that? The pride of England in this case, is the pride of wrong, and the pride of usurpation. The pride of Ireland is the pride of right, the pride of jus-

104 *Parl. Reg.(Irl.)*, i, 403–5.

tice, the pride of constitution. I will not ask you, after that, which ought to give way: but it is wrong to put this question principally upon pride. England it is true, has a pride in the matter, but she has what she values more, a principle of power. Ireland too, has a pride in the matter, but she has what she ought to value much more, a principle of permanent security. Now that a nation will be the wisest in this transaction, that sacrifices her least object to preserve her greatest, and England will do this precisely, if she can prevail on you to accept of a simple repeal without a renunciation; for in that case she will sacrifice a little pride to preserve all her power; whereas you will, for a petty sacrifice to your pride, forfeit all your security.[105]

Flood reinforced this conclusion by reminding MPs not to repeat the mistake they had made in 1779/80 when their failure to insist on the repeal of all laws 'restrictive of our foreign commerce' had (as the ongoing trade dispute with Portugal testified) deprived the kingdom of the freedom to shape its external commercial relations. It also, he noted ruefully, left 'both your trade and your money at the mercy of the ministry and parliament of England' because they retained the authority to set duties on such key commodities as sugar.[106]

Flood's clinical assessment on 11 June of what 'free trade' and legislative independence meant for Ireland contrasted vividly with the woolly effusions produced by moderate patriots who displayed little capacity or inclination to assess the reality of the legislative concessions they had secured. Most concluded simply that they had gained everything they desired and that their priority now should be to set Anglo-Irish relations on a new and harmonious footing. This was Flood's wish also. The difference was that whereas he believed that legislative independence was incomplete without Britain's renunciation of the principle of the right to legislate enshrined in the Declaratory Act, moderates concluded that no further action was necessary. Indeed, as far as a majority of MPs were concerned, Flood's insistence on the radical amendment of Poynings' Law (if its repeal could not be secured) and the renunciation of the right to legislate were the most imposing obstacles in the way of an early Anglo-Irish accommodation. They were encouraged to reach this conclusion by their disapproval of Flood's confrontational demeanour as well as by their belief that the constitutional changes that had been implemented were sufficient, with the result that his frequently perceptive assessments of the limitations of 'legislative independence' were not even accorded the courtesy of extended parliamentary discussion. Quite the contrary; following a dismissive claim by George Ogle on 11 June that 'the repealing [was] a sufficient relinquishment of any right' the order of the day was called. This was to treat Flood's provocative analysis of the legislative changes that were being implemented with contempt, but since only David

105 *Parl. Reg.(Irl.)*, i, 406–7. **106** *Parl. Reg.(Irl.)*, i, 402–3.

Walshe and James Browne (MP for Tuam) supported him, there was nothing he could do. Nor was Flood's anxiety about the nature of the new legislative and constitutional arrangements eased by Henry Grattan's promise that if the 'simple repeal' of the Declaratory Act did not amount to a 'renunciation', he would sponsor a declaration of 'rights', because Grattan was reprimanded by Yelverton who had no doubts that 'repeal was sufficient' and that there was no need for any further parliamentary pronouncement on the matter.[107]

RENUNCIATION

If Grattan's reference to a declaration of rights suggested that there was some grounds for cooperation between Flood and he on what was fast becoming known as the 'renunciation' question, this was misleading. Indeed, following the debate of 11 June, an attempt was made 'through Lord Charlemont and others' to get moderate patriots to close ranks, arising out of which Grattan 'was prevailed [upon] not to adhere to his first intention of moving a declaration of rights as a preamble to a bill'. Grattan was not altogether pleased with this, since Flood's assertive stand impressed the patriot public and, eager to restore his sliding popularity, he drew the attention of the House of Commons on 14 June to the fact that a West Indies sugar importation act recently approved at Westminster 'comprehended' Ireland. This was a perfect opening for Flood to reiterate his contention that 'nothing but a final renouncing of the principle of this law [the Declaratory Act] is adequate to our security' and he did not pass it up. This was not what Grattan wanted to hear and eager to discredit his rival, he contended that it was politically and diplomatically inappropriate for the kingdom of Ireland to be beholden to a British statute other than for the repeal of the Declaratory Act. This was rather tendentious, and it prompted a prolonged exchange with Flood in which the latter displayed his more profound understanding of the constitution and the workings of parliament and the empire, and his greater capacity as an *ex tempore* debater to rebut the case of his younger opponent. Why, he asked pointedly, was Grattan now satisfied with the simple repeal of the Declaratory Act when in 1780 he had promised to 'bring in a declaratory Irish law in order to have the great seals of both kingdoms affixed to the recognition of our constitution'. Equally tellingly, he appealed to the spirit of William Molyneux to support his assertion that moderate patriots were showing a lack of resolution, though this was vitiated by his emphasis on how prescient and correct his conduct had been in the 1770s. Grattan, for example, countered tellingly that he seemed to believe he was 'the only man who could be found to stand up for the constitution'. It is hardly surprising given this context that Flood's request to the house to refer the question of whether the repeal of the Declaratory Act amounted 'in legal construction to a

107 *Parl. Reg.(Irl.)*, i, 413–15; Beresford to Eden, 13 June 1782 in *Beresford Corres.*, i, 207–9.

repeal or a renunciation of the legal principle on which the Declaratory Act grounded itself' was lost.[108]

As the debate of 14 June emphasized, it was widely believed in political circles that Flood's 'doctrine of renunciation' did not derive from firmly held political convictions. Lord Mornington, for example, ascribed his behaviour to disappointment at not being 'restored to office'. This was an old canard, which gave way in the summer of 1782 to the equally unsustainable allegation that his object was 'to arrogate to himself the whole merit of the late transactions'. Even Lord Charlemont, who ought to have known better, joined in the criticism. He maintained that Flood was driven by 'envy and disappointed ambition':

> Enraged at his neglect, conscious of his proud abilities, and wishing to depreciate his rival [Grattan], whose merits were, he well knew, indissolubly linked with the security of our late acquisitions, he first broached the doctrine of renunciation, disseminated on all sides doubts and jealousies, harangued in parliament, and inflamed the people.[109]

This was also Grattan's view. He attributed Flood's actions to his wish 'to crown' himself with 'laurels ... torn from his [Grattan's] own brow', and many commentators, from the eighteenth century to the present have agreed.[110] That this impression has survived unchallenged for so long is largely attributable to over-reliance upon the testimonies of people who had a vested interest in ascribing Flood's actions to base motives. Grattan is certainly not to be depended upon at this point. According to Charlemont, he became so 'obstinate in support of our original measure' following the debate of 11 June he 'could hardly be induced to quit the ground ... He looked upon the parliamentary promise of contentment as binding upon the nation, and peculiarly so upon him as mover of the address'. Grattan, in short, was less able than Flood to prevent his private feelings shaping his public conduct, and a 'personal dislike ... concurred the more to irritate him, and private spleen ... inasperated [*sic*] and exalted the venom of party animosity'.[111]

As this implies, differences in temperament as well as policy contributed to the rift that developed between Flood and Grattan at this time. Flood's 'temper, which in politics was suspicious, intractable, and too fond of preeminence, [did not] tend much to conciliate', as Charlemont noted, whereas Grattan was 'admired and loved for his conciliatory manners'.[112] MPs were not guided in their actions solely by their

---

108 *Parl. Reg. (Irl.)*, i, 415–31; Beresford to Eden, 17 June 1782 in *Beresford Corres.*, i, 209–11.   109 H.M.C., *Charlemont*, i, 65, 79; see also Ogilvie to Leinster, 31 July 1782 (N.L.I., Fitzgerald Papers, Ms 624 f 112); Stewart, *A deeper silence*, p. 41.   110 H.M.C., *Charlemont*, i, 65; Pembroke to Carmarthen, 2–11 Aug. 1782 in Lord Herbert, ed., *Pembroke Papers 1734–94* (2 vols, London, 1939–54), ii, 203; McDougall, *Irish political characters*, p. 239; O'Brien, 'The exercise of legislative power', p. 101; Fitzmaurice, *Life of Shelburne*, iii, 328; Craig, *The Volunteer earl*, p. 182; Mac Nevin, *History of the Volunteers*, pp 175–8.   111 H.M.C., *Charlemont*, i, 80, 65 note 2.   112 H.M.C., *Charlemont*, i, 65 and note 2.

response to personality, of course, but the combination of Flood's assertiveness on constitutional points and his personal remoteness obscured the fact that he was better informed on constitutional matters, with the result that a large majority of MPs found it easier to accept that he was impelled by the wish to supplant Grattan in the public's affections than by political principle. Flood may well have resented Grattan's popularity, but it would have been so out of character for him to have indulged a solipsistic wish for personal popularity that it can be discounted as his dominant motive. He was activated first and foremostly by conviction. Most patriots found this difficult to accept because of the negative impressions they had built up of him based upon his behaviour in the late-1770s, and their resentment at his refusal to join in the euphoria of the moment in 1782. However, a steadily growing number of people were sufficiently impressed by the logic of his arguments to question the merit and meaning of the constitutional changes being implemented to provide him with reason to persist. They were encouraged to do this by rising doubts about Grattan's 'virtue' arising out of his acceptance of the Commons' *donum* of £50,000 because, Charlemont observed shrewdly, 'nothing is more certain than that ... the man who wishes to retain his influence with the people must cautiously abstain from every species of emolument'.[113] Flood knew this from personal experience, but he made no attempt to use it to his advantage. Indeed, in contrast to Grattan, he did not regard the difference that had arisen between them on constitutional points as personal, or harbour the virulence of feeling that his opponent (Grattan deemed him his 'hated rival') reserved for him.[114]

Disturbed by the impact of Flood's criticism, the popular press, which was still overwhelmingly pro-Grattan joined its Castle equivalents in targeting Flood and the small number of MPs which constituted his 'party', for sharp and personalised criticism in the summer of 1782.[115] Flood did not command a party, of course. Rather, he was the most eminent and talented of a loose connection headed by what was known pejoratively as the 'quadruple alliance', which comprised David Walshe, Alexander Montgomery, Samuel Bradstreet and himself. In addition, he could usually rely on the support of William English (MP for Taghmon), Eland Mossom (MP for Kilkenny city), Richard Martin (MP for Jamestown), all political lightweights, and the more consequential Lawrence Parsons (who was elected to represent Trinity College in July), Sir Edward Newenham, James Browne and Travers Hartley. In addition, there was a small nucleus of sympathetic peers, including the erratic earl of Bellamont, the disaffected earl of Altamont and Barry Barry, Viscount Farnham who shared his views on 'simple repeal'.[116]

113 H.M.C., *Charlemont*, i, 66. It is noteworthy that it was also caricatured (M.D. George, *Catalogue of political and personal satires preserved in the Department of prints and drawings in the British Museum* (12 vols, London, 1935–54), no. 6003). 114 H.M.C., *Charlemont*, i, 80. 115 Sayles, ed., 'The Irish parliament in 1782', pp 248, 271; *H.J.*, 12, 14, 19, 24, 26 June; see also Cleaver to O'Hara, 25 June 1782 (N.L.I., O'Hara Papers, Ms 20396). 116 Allen to Montgomery, 12 June–13 July (P.R.O.N.I., Macartney

Despite the increasing appeal of their views, the adjournment of the House of Commons for a month from 15 June deprived Flood and his allies of their main platform. He did fight off illness to appeal to MPs on the final day of the sitting to insert a clause in the Irish marine forces bill stating that the Irish parliament was 'the only possible power on earth competent to make statutes of force in this king-dom', but he was obliged to withdraw it when it was pointed out to him that the parallel British act did not, as he had contended, mention Ireland. [117] This was not an encouraging note on which to end the sitting, but it was of little consequence as the tide of opinion and, most significantly and visibly, Volunteer opinion, outside parliament shifted in Flood's direction. Throughout the country, but particularly in Ulster, Volunteer activists had closely monitored events at Westminster and College Green in April and May. It was even proposed that a Volunteer 'military congress' should convene in Dublin to 'watch with a scrutinizing eye ... and be ready to act ... as the moment may occur'. [118] The need for this diminished with the announcement that the Declaratory Act was to be repealed and Poynings' Law modified, but con-cern mounted in Volunteer circles from early June as Flood's arguments in support of the renunciation by London of its right to legislate for Ireland struck a cord. In an attempt to counter this, moderate patriots and Volunteers connected with Lord Charlemont rallied to the support of 'simple repeal'. This was signalled by the Vol-unteer National Committee which met in Dublin on 18 June and, somewhat more ambivalently, by a delegate meeting of Ulster Volunteers at Dungannon three days later. Some corps were easily persuaded to follow the lead provided by these bodies, but others demurred. They were confined initially to those with links to the parlia-mentary advocates of 'renunciation', but the decisions of the Belfast First Volunteer company on 27 June, the Belfast review three days later, and the Goldsmith Corps of Dublin to make similar pronouncements emboldened others. Flood did not so-licit these expressions of support, but his gracious and fulsome reply to the Belfast First Volunteer Company was well-received, not least because it contrasted sharply with Grattan's curt and grudging response. [119]

It is easy, of course, to respond warmly to compliments. But Grattan and Charlemont had genuine grounds for disquiet as hitherto moderate corps, like the

Papers, D572/19/87 ff 365-6); Ms account of Irish parliament in 1782, p. 242 (Henry Huntington Library); McDougall, *Irish political characters*, pp 169-71; *H.J.*, 12, 14 June 1782; Ms list of Irish parlia-ment in 1783 (N.L.I., Ms 2098); Sayles, ed.,'Members of parliament in 1782', *passim*; Carlisle to Hillsborough, 24 Jan. 1782 (N.A.,Index of departmental letters and papers 1760-89 f 255); Cooke to Eden, 27 July 1782 in *Auckland Corres.*, i, 335-6. 117 *Parl. Reg. (Irl.)*, i, 415, 431-2. 118 Thompson to Dobbs, [*c*.16 Apr. 1782] (N.L.I., Dobbs Papers, Ms 2251 ff 3-6). 119 *Life of Grattan*, ii, 305-8; *H.J.*, 15 July, 30 Aug.; Charlemont to Flood, 28 June 1782 in R[odd] ed., *Letters to Flood*, p. 111; W.R. Hutchinson, *Tyrone precinct*, pp 99-100; P. Ó Snodaigh, 'Notaí ar Óglaigh...Chontae na Gaillimhe', *Galvia*, xi (1979), pp 21-3; J.Mitchell, 'Colonel William Persee', *Journal of the Galway Archaeological and Historical Society*, xxx (1963), pp 62-4. Resolutions of the inhabitants of Clonmel, 25/6 June (T.C.D., Donoughmore Papers); H.M.C., *Charlemont*, i, 95 note 3.

Goldsmiths which had elected Flood as its Lieutenant Colonel on Charlemont's personal recommendation, denied 'that the repeal of the sixth of George the first ... is, in faith and in *law*, a compleat surrender by the parliament of Great Britain of all its claims to bind this kingdom'. In an attempt to tip the balance, Charlemont encouraged loyal supporters like Francis Dobbs to greater efforts. [120] He also appealed personally to Flood to desist:

O, my dear Flood, what are you about? You never have taken a part so disagreeable to my feelings, because you never, till now, have done any thing which I could not somehow justify to myself and consequently to others. The cry is against you; I do not join in it: friendship forbids me. But, alas! why must I be silent? why cannot I defend you, as hitherto I have ever done? [121]

There was little Flood could say in response to such an emotional entreaty and, since no reply survives, it is unlikely that he did. Charlemont's wish was that Flood would use his influence with radicals to end the agitation of a 'renunciation' but, as his positive answer to addresses from Volunteer corps indicates, he had no intention of doing so. Besides, he could not have stopped it even if he had wanted to.

At the same time, the fact that he did not directly encourage the Volunteers' actions suggests that he was not totally at ease with the direction of events or with being the centre of political attention. Yet this is where he stood at the end of June, as members of the Protestant polity defined themselves politically in accordance with how they perceived 'simple repeal'. One beneficial consequence of this for Flood was his personal rehabilitation in the eyes of many erstwhile critics. On the negative side, both his Castle and moderate patriot opponents became even more sharply antagonistic. Thus the columns of the *Hibernian Journal* in July echoed to the sound of criticism of Flood's stand on 'simple repeal' on the grounds that it was 'poison[ing] the source of our happiness, peace and freedom' by exciting unwelcome jealousies and tensions between Britain and Ireland. There was also a further spate of negative personal profiles by commentators who believed character assassination was the most expeditious means to discredit his arguments. One correspondent even compared him to Milton's Satan:

A jealous unsociable ambition, an indignant uncontroulable pride, a sullen gloomy majesty, a baneful and faded splendour, a mind relieving its own pangs by disquieting others, an insatiable thirst for revenge, an unamiable malignant courage ... In your mind, to reign were worth ambition, tho' in Hell, better in Hell than serve in Heaven.

120 Charlemont to Dobbs, [June 1782] (N.L.I., Dobbs Papers, Ms 2551 ff 57–9); H.M.C., *Charlemont*, i, 95 note 3.   121 Charlemont to Flood, 28 June 1782 in R[odd], ed., *Letters to Flood*, pp 111–12.

As in this instance, most such commentaries were ill-informed essays in the politics of prejudice.[122] The publication in July of Flood's speeches of 11 and 14 June on the repeal of the Declaratory Act in a pamphlet edition and its distribution throughout the country provided his opponents with an opportunity to offer a better informed critique of his arguments, but though some experienced controversialists took up the cudgels, their basic contention that Irish patriots could trust London did little to diminish the appeal of Flood's argument.[123]

Some in the corridors of power contrived to convince themselves otherwise. The under-secretary, Edward Cooke, maintained on the eve of the reassembly of the House of Commons in mid-July that Flood's opposition to 'simple repeal' had 'done no harm' to the cause of moderate patriotism, but this was wishful thinking.[124] For instance, the young Newry doctor, William Drennan, overcame his initial suspicion of Flood's intentions (he maintained he was 'discontented' as well as 'desperate'), because 'commonsense' persuaded him that 'renunciation' was preferable to 're-peal'. Despite this, he did not believe that the supporters of renunciation in Belfast would muster more than 'an inconsiderable minority' at the annual Volunteer review, which was scheduled to take place in early July. Lord Charlemont was less sure. Like Drennan, he realised that Belfast had to be 'the very focus of Flood' if he genuinely aspired to secure the 'renunciation' he urged so persuasively – not least because of the support he received from the influential local magnate, Lord Beauchamp. In any event, unlike Drennan, Charlemont was 'offended' that Flood accepted the invitation of the First Volunteer Company of Belfast to attend the re-view, and he was determined to ensure that he did not use the occasion to popular-ise his views.[125]

Given his disinclination to participate in events such as this, it is improbable that Flood would have attended the Belfast review but for the fact that his party there 'must soon give way and perhaps never recover unless it was cherished by his sanction and animated by his voice'. His presence certainly had an influence on the outcome. The atmosphere at the review was tense as 'papers of all sorts and sizes', some penned by Flood others by his opponents, 'were every hour distributed thro' the camp'. There was even speculation that Flood would make 'a personal appeal to the people' to 'strengthen his cause in this place', but he wisely declined to sully 'the august dignity of his character' in this way. The key to the outcome was the meeting of officers to draft an address to their commander-in-chief, Lord Charlemont, that took place after military manoeuvres, and though Flood was not a

122 *H.J.*, 1, 3, 5, 8, 10, 12, 15, 17, 22 July 1782. 123 *H.J.*, 10, 15, 17 July; Henry Flood, *Two celebrated speeches on the repeal of the Declaratory Act of the sixth of George I as delivered in the House of Commons of Ireland on 11 and 14 June 1782* (Dublin, 1782); Beresford to Eden, 18 July 1782 (B.L., Auckland Papers, Add.Ms 34418 f 508). 124 Cooke to Eden, 14 July 1782 (B.L.,Auckland Papers, Add. Ms 34418 ff 493–4). 125 Drennan to Bruce, [late June], 6 July (P.R.O.N.I., Drennan-Bruce letters, D 553/3,2); H.M.C.,*Charlemont*, i, 95 note 3; *Life of Grattan*, ii, 347–8; Beauchamp to Dobbs, 2 July 1782 (N.L.I., Dobbs Papers, Ms 2251 ff 7–10).

participant he encouraged his supporters and secured a moral victory when the-Charlemont interest was obliged to remove 'political paragraphs' which described the repeal of the Declaratory Act as 'full, final [and] irrevocable renunciation'. The address that was presented did not affirm his position, but it was a measure of its increasing popularity that it did not affirm Charlemont's either. [126]

The 'renunciation' cause was given a further fillip a few days later by the earl of Abingdon at Westminster. As virtually everybody who knew him concurred, Abingdon was personally eccentric and politically maverick, but, if his manners and deportment were singular, he was not the only British politician who was disturbed by the implication of the repeal of the Declaratory Act. Like many, he had vested considerable hope in the allusion by Charles James Fox to a 'final adjustment' and by Lord Shelburne to a 'national compact' that would firmly bind Britain and Ireland, and when he saw no evidence of progress in this direction, not least because of Flood's demand for renunciation, he moved on 5 July 'that the parliament of Great Britain hath ever had, and of sole and exclusive right ought always to have, power to enact laws and statutes to regulate and controul the external commerce of ... all such kingdoms ... as now are ... connected with ... the imperial crown'. [127] This was denied on procedural grounds, but it made little difference in Ireland. There, the fact that the issue had been raised at all was seized upon by the proponents of 'renunciation' as evidence that British political opinion did not accept that the Irish parliament was legislatively independent. Eager to take maximum advantage from the opportunity, they produced a pamphlet with the text of Abingdon's bill and accompanying speech with Flood's speeches of 11 and 14 June. It was a clever ploy, and it dismayed Castle loyalists who were only too aware of its 'mischief' making potential. [128] In the words of the bishop of Killaloe, Abingdon's intervention gave

> weight to all the suspicions that Flood before vainly endeavour'd to suggest that Great Britain has by no means resigned her claims to legislation, but only wishes us to think so till a convenient time for reasserting her antient claims shall come. [129]

In a vain attempt to prevent the 'misrepresentation so generally articulated' from disturbing 'that harmony which is ... fully and finally established between the kingdoms', the Chief Secretary, Richard Fitzpatrick, briefed well-inclined MPs. [130] Henry

---

126 H.M.C., *Charlemont*, i, 95; Drennan to Bruce, 6 July, [July] (P.R.O.N.I., Drennan-Bruce letters, D553/2, 4); Charlemont to Stewart, 2 Aug. (P.R.O.N.I., Stewart Papers, D3167/1/3); Pembroke to Carmarthen, 2–11 Aug. 1782 in Herbert, ed., *The Pembroke Papers*, p. 204.   127 Malone to Charlemont, 11 July 1782 in H.M.C., *Charlemont*, i, 412–13; *Parliamentary History*, xxiii, 148–51; *Parl. Reg. (Irl.)*, i, 441.   128 Beresford to Eden, 18 July (B.L., Auckland Papers, Add. Ms 34418 f 508; Flood, *Two celebrated speeches on the repeal of the Declaratory Act*; Burton to Stafford, 16 July 1782 (N.A., Burton Papers, Ms 3249).   129 Killaloe to Buckinghamshire, 10 Sept. 1782 (N.L.I., Heron Papers, Ms 13047/2).   130 Fitzpatrick to Hutchinson, 22 July 1780 [recte 1782] in *Life of Grattan*, ii, 351–2.

Grattan engaged in similar activities, while the moderate patriot and Castle press concurred that Abingdon's bill was of no consequence. Indeed, in an ironic twist, Flood and Abingdon were both portrayed as 'individuals' possessing 'singular opinions', who threatened 'the reciprocal endeavours of both kingdoms ... to establish an unanimity founded in policy and wisdom and the implicit confidence of sister nations'.[131]

The capacity of the government and moderate patriots to resist the growing support for renunciation in Ireland was further diminished when, following the death of Lord Rockingham, the new government, headed by the earl of Shelburne, recalled the duke of Portland with whom Charlemont and Grattan had established a good working arrangement.[132] John Beresford, for example, was convinced by mid-July that Grattan and Charlemont would be unable to resist 'Flood's doctrine' on renunciation; others remained hopeful that the combined weight of the Castle and moderate patriot interests would prevail unless the Volunteers rallied the population to Flood's side. Much depended upon Grattan's ability to counter Flood in the Commons. Illness had obliged him to maintain a low profile during the recess, but his prompt response to Lord Charlemont's summons to reengage indicated that he was confident he could rise to the task during the final sitting of this much interrupted session which began on Monday, 15 July. It was a formidable challenge, and some experienced observers believed he had so badly misjudged the mood of the country on the issue that Flood would 'strip him of his popularity':

> Had [Grattan] been contented with saying that England had granted all that she could give and all that we had a right to desire, he might have defied his opponent. But when he attempted to prove that the repeal of 6th of George 1st was an absolute renunciation of the principle of legislating internally or externally for Ireland, he gave Mr Flood an advantage of which he will make his own use.[133]

Flood was certainly at his assertive best on the Commons' resumption. On 16 July, when David Walshe sought unsuccessfully to force a debate on Yelverton's bill for the better transmission of bills to England, Flood condemned the measure as 'a desperate wound to the constitution' on the grounds that it did not specifically preclude the Irish Privy Council originating bills.[134] Later the same day, when the

131 *H.J.*, 15 July; Grattan to Charlemont, 16 Jan. [recte 16 July] 1782 in H.M.C., *Charlemont*, i, 395. 132 Charlemont to Forbes, 10 July (N.L.I., Forbes Papers, Ms 10713); Mornington to Grenville, 12 July in H.M.C.,*Fortescue*, i, 162–3; Temple to Grenville, 12 July in duke of Buckingham and Chandos, eds, *Courts and cabinets of George III* (4 vols, London, 1853–5), i, 61–3; Beresford to Eden, 13 July 1782 in *Beresford Corres.*, i, 216–9. 133 Beresford to Barré, 13 July in *Beresford Corres.*, i, 220; Beresford to Eden, 18 July (B.L., Auckland Papers, Add. Ms 34418 f 508); Killaloe to Buckinghamshire, 15 July (N.L.I., Heron Papers, Ms 13047/2); Charlemont to Forbes, 10 July (N.L.I., Forbes Papers, Ms 10713); Agar to Eden, 16 July 1782 (B.L., Auckland Papers, Add. Ms 34418 f 504). 134 *Parl.Reg.(Irl.)*, i, 437–8.

Chief Secretary, Richard Fitzpatrick, sought to make it clear that Lord Abingdon's bill posed no threat, Flood chose to lay 'no blame to the ambition of the English'; what Abingdon had done was simply to offer 'the opinion of a great part of England'. His purpose, Flood pronounced, was to demonstrate 'the folly of the Irish' for assuming that 'England has renounced the legislation of Ireland' when they had done no such thing:

> A total silence, on the contrary, tacitly admitted that external legislation was not given up. Had they renounced that claim, would Lord *Abingdon* rise to make his motion; or would any lord listen him if such a renunciation was allowed? Nothing but a renunciation, continued he, can be valid. Can any man be content with the less security, if the greater is in his power? An act of renunciation would be an act that they never had any right to bind you. You cannot take away the rights of posterity, but you can prevent posterity from those rights they ought to enjoy. Had an act of renunciation been passed, could any man in the House of Lords hear, with honour, the claim of Lord *Abingdon*? But did one man in the House of Lords oppose Lord *Abingdon*, or utter a syllable in behalf of Ireland?[135]

Having made clear his position on Abingdon's bill, Flood shifted his focus to what he termed the 'milk and water assertion of constitution' of Barry Yelverton's bill for confirming English statutes. Encouraged by the support he received from Sir William Osborne, he appealed directly to the advocates of constitutional reform to show courage, and to replace this dangerous and defective measure with one 'fully expressive of our rights':

> there could be nothing so dangerous, at some times, as fear. After the whole kingdom had come forward and offered its support, every idea of fear became criminal. Did they think, when they stammered at their rights, that England would come to their bar and articulate them? Such a conduct was womanish. It was the first time, he said, he ever knew a national body legislate by the lump, in the adoption of the laws of a rival nation, who was wrestling with her for her liberties. He asked who was to be the judge of those equal benefits and restraints they adopted? The Admiralty of England. In case of an appeal to that court, by what laws can it be guided by those at present existing? Had England passed an act of renunciation, and afterwards attempted to coerce the shipping of Ireland on the seas, the judge of that admiralty would have a statute law to treat as pirates the force that would molest her commerce. Situated as the kingdoms stood now, should they bring their complaint before that court, the Englishman demands, "where is your act for bringing such complaint?" The Irishman says, you

repealed the 6th of George the Ist, and the delegates acknowledged that the repeal was sufficient. I shall go to the rolls, replies the judge, to examine by what law I can proceed, for I cannot find your claim founded upon any law that I know. An *influenza* seized your senses, when your sovereign offered the grant of all you wanted, that you neglected to obtain unequivocal freedom. [136]

As he surely anticipated, Flood's exhortation fell on deaf ears. Undeterred, he gave notice on the following day that he would move to obtain 'a legal security of our independence'. This was too overt a challenge for Grattan to ignore and he signalled his opposition to whatever proposition Flood presented in an hour-long exchange in which Flood and he each challenged the other's opinion on the merits of 'simple repeal'. This exchange 'was conducted with coolness and good temper' by both parties. Moreover, neither had the better of the argument. Despite this, there was widespread agreement that Flood's was the dominant presence in the Commons. Indeed, he so intimidated Barry Yelverton with the force and authority of his rhetoric that the Attorney General chose to remain 'silent' rather than to engage in debate.[137]

Yelverton's reticence encouraged Flood's hopes for his bill to 'obtain the best possible legal security for her liberties', which he recommended to the House with a short speech on Friday, 19 July. As expected, the bill amounted to a declaration of rights because it affirmed that

> the Irish parliament hath ever had and always ought to have the sole and exclusive right and power to make laws for Ireland in all cases whatsoever, internal or external, and that no other body of men on earth hath ever had or ever ought to have any such right or power.

At the same time, it was not a declaration of independence. Quite the contrary; it explicitly affirmed Ireland's commitment to maintain a permanent constitutional link with Britain:

> And we pray it may be enacted that this law declaratory of the rights of the Irish parliament and the provisions aforesaid, whereas the crown of Ireland is annexed to the Crown of Great Britain, and whereby the consent of the common sovereign under the great seal of Great Britain must be had to any bill before it can receive the royal assent in the parliament of Ireland, may be, and that they be deemed and taken to be laws, reciprocally and equally fundamental and irrevocable, in such sort as to form a national and inviolable convention by express law for the reciprocal permanency and operating effect of both, thereby constituting

---

136 Ibid., i, 444–5.   137 *Parl. Reg. (Irl.)*, i, 448–9; Beresford to Eden, 18 July 1782 in *Beresford Corres.*, i, 224.

an everlasting bond of concord and an unalterable connexion of constitution and of common interest between the respective kingdoms of Great Britain and Ireland.[138]

This was a significant proposition, but even its dexterous phrasing did not win Flood the support he needed to have the bill become law. A succession of speakers, many of them well-known patriots, maintained that they were 'perfectly satisfied' with the concessions they had been yielded, and that they were, in the words of William Brownlow, content to rely on 'the good will of Great Britain and the mutual interest of both nations'. This did not satisfy Flood's requirement for 'legal security', but even though he was supported by no more than a handful of MPs (Alexander English, James Browne and David Walshe) and did not bring Richard Martin and Travers Hartley with him, he did not ease up on his opposition to Yelverton's bill. Indeed, he chided his critics, though a large majority were persuaded by the strident critique offered by Grattan. In truth, Grattan was not entirely convincing. His speech did serve to blur the distinction Flood drew between repeal and renunciation, but his specific objections were less persuasive. However, since he articulated views widely held among MPs that Flood's persistent opposition to the constitutional changes agreed in May had 'tarnished the faith of the British nation' and disrupted the 'harmony existing between both nations', he had no reason to conduct himself temperately. This explains his transmogrification of Flood's expression of support in 1775 for the dispatch to America of 4,000 'armed negotiators' into the provision of troops 'to cut the throats of our American brethren'. This was plainly disreputable, but Grattan was less concerned with being fair than with discrediting his opponent. With this in mind, as soon as Flood's motion was defeated he offered one of his own personally critical of his antagonist. This provoked a heated debate in which Flood was both 'most severe' and 'eloquent'. As a result, Grattan was obliged to re-word his motion, but he still secured approval for a resolution stating that

> leave was refused to bring in [Flood's] bill, because the sole and exclusive right to legislate for Ireland in all cases whatsoever, internally and externally, has been asserted by the parliament of Ireland, and has been fully, finally and irrevocably acknowledged by the British parliament.[139]

This was as unambiguous a rejection of his stand on 'simple repeal' as Flood could have experienced.[140] However, it did not make a huge impression because 'the

138 Heads of a bill for declaring the sole and exclusive right of the Irish parliament to make laws in all cases whatsoever internal or external for the kingdom of Ireland, 19 July 1782 (P.R.O.N.I., Foster Papers, D562/9321).   139 *Parl. Reg. (Irl.)*, i, 452–65; Flood, *Memoirs*, pp 167–72; Mac Nevin, *History of the Volunteers*, pp 178–9.   140 He could rely on no more than 'five or six' MPs on 19 July (Alexander Montgomery, David Walshe, Alex English, James Browne and John James Barry Maxwell (Pery to Shelburne, 20 July in H.M.C., *Emly*, ii, 170; Cooke to Eden, 25 July 1782 in *Auckland Corres.*, i, 332–3)).

country ... [wa]s not so near unanimity as the parliament', as Lord Mornington observed:

> the poison of Flood's insinuations has diffused itself through the country with more rapidity than even despondency could imagine. The people began to think the repeal of the 6th of George 1st an inadequate concession; they begin to lose their confidence in Grattan, the most upright and temperate *demagogue* that ever appeared in any country. Flood rises upon the ruins of Grattan's popularity.

It disturbed Mornington (and those of like mind) that support for Flood's position was increasing among moderate Volunteers. This is why Flood's presence at the Belfast review, characterised by Lord Pembroke as 'a perfect Boston' where 'treason ... was ... freely spoken', excited such concern. [141]

Following his rebuff by Grattan on 19 July, Flood kept a low profile as the administration and moderate patriots contrived to bring the session to a conclusion. [142] He did make one final defiant gesture by offering an amendment to the anodyne address to the departing duke of Portland proposed by Grattan, in which he criticised Yelverton's bill to amend Poynings' Law and the 'simple repeal' of the Declaratory Act in familiar terms. The amendment was rejected, but it was appropriate that Flood should end the session during which he had redeemed his reputation as an exceptional parliamentarian with a contribution along these lines. He had not, however, forged an effective working relationship with the mainstream patriot leadership in the House of Commons with the result that he exerted little real influence on the shape of the constitutional settlement that has been ratified. Indeed, because of his heated disagreement with Yelverton and Grattan as to what constituted legislative independence, he was only slightly less-isolated politically in the summer of 1782 than he had been prior to his dismissal in 1781. He was, it is true, revered by a small number of radical MPs such as Richard Martin, who were in awe of his 'transcendant abilities', but the majority continued to regard him with suspicion and distrust. [143] His support outside parliament was tangibly greater, and since there was a growing popular constituency which shared his opinions on 'simple repeal', the way was clear for him to develop as a radical popular representative and to redefine what it meant to be a popular politician if he could make the political and intellectual leap.

---

141 Mornington to Grenville, 23 July in H.M.C., *Fortescue*, i, 163; Cooke to Eden, 25 July (B.L., Auckland Papers, Add. Ms 34418 ff 519–20); Ogilvie to Leinster, 31 July (N.L.I., Fitzgerald Papers, Ms 624 f 112); Pembroke to Carmarthen, 2–11 Aug. 1782, Pembroke to Coxe, 8 Aug. 1782 in Herbert, ed., *Pembroke Papers*, pp 203–8. 142 Cooke to Eden, 27 July in *Auckland Papers*, i, 334; *Parl. Reg. (Irl.)*, i, 466–8. 143 *Parl. Reg. (Irl.).*, i, 469–72, 475.

VINDICATION

As a consequence of his radical stand on 'simple repeal', Flood eclipsed Grattan as the most popular Irish politician of the day in the summer of 1782. It was not a situation with which he was entirely comfortable, but once parliament went into recess, public opinion was the only means available to him to advance his views on 'simple repeal'.

Flood's persistent advocacy of 'renunciation' exacerbated the split between moderate and radical patriots. He was, the *Hibernian Journal* pronounced on 26 July, 'the great ... *mischief maker*', and reports that he planned to travel to Ulster 'for the purpose of beating up General Lord Charlemont's quarters and explaining to the northern army the true nature of legal security' prompted a torrent of aspersive comment about his 'corrupt character' and '*quondam*' patriotism. 'Little Harry', 'nimble Harry', 'King Harry', the 'Grim Patriot' and the 'mock patriot' were favourite terms of disparagement, and they figured prominently in the campaign that was conducted throughout the late summer and autumn to persuade the public that 'renunciation' was unnecessary and to caricature its proponents as 'incendiaries' who sought to stimulate the 'fears and jealousies' of the ill-informed'. [144]

Such criticism ought to have forced Flood into a close alliance with the Volunteers. He acknowledged to the Liberty Volunteers of Dublin that 'it is men such as you' upon whom the hopes of 'an unconditional legislative independence' rested, but though he made a further controversial visit to Belfast in early August, he did not seek to engender a strong campaign on the subject of 'simple repeal'. [145] This was a great relief to Grattan, Charlemont and Mornington who were anxious there should not be 'another [delegate] meeting at Dungannon'. Indeed, Charlemont used his position as commander-in-chief of the Volunteers to emphasise the moderates' conviction that 'our rights ... have been vindicated; our constitution has been restored'. But Charlemont's influence only carried so far, and the decision of Grattan to leave Ireland on 29 July to drink the waters at Spa was a serious setback to the moderates' cause. [146]

It is not possible to say how Flood interpreted these events, because he too spent part of the summer outside the country and away from Irish politics. His precise purpose in travelling abroad remains opaque, but his wish to acquire a Westminster seat was prominent in his mind. This, at least, has a history. His presence, according to a spy report dating from late August, 'in Paris ... to watch the negociation for

144 *H.J.*, 26, 31 July, 2, 5, 7, 12, 14, 16, 21 Aug., 11, 25 Sept. 2, 4 Oct 1782.   145 *H.J.*, 2, 7, 9, 12, 14 Aug., 9 Sept. 1782.   146 Mornington to Charlemont, 7 Aug., Charlemont to Haliday, 11 Aug. in H.M.C., *Charlemont*, i, 414, 416–17; Charlemont to Stewart, 17 Aug.(P.R.O.N.I., Stewart Papers, D3167/1/3); H.M.C., *Charlemont*, i, 160–4; Grattan to Forbes, 4 Aug. 1782 (N.L.I., Forbes Papers, Ms 10713); *Life of Grattan*, ii, 363–4; Grattan to Barrington, 2 Mar. 1818, Charlemont to [ ], 29 July 1782 in ibid., pp 361–3, 335–6; *H.J.*, 2 Aug.; Mornington to Grenville, 1 Aug. 1782 in H.M.C., *Fortescue*, i, 164

peace with a view to their effects on Ireland' is less easily accounted for. [147] But assuming it is correct, it can be suggested that he believed that the negotiations currently taking place between Britain and America held important implications for Ireland.

In his absence, reports and rumours of Flood's intentions abounded in Ireland. It was even suggested that he had gone to England to hold discussions with the disgruntled former foreign secretary, Charles James Fox. Reports that he was to be reappointed a vice-treasurer were accorded greater credence because of a chance encounter he had with Lady Temple, the wife of the new Lord Lieutenant, at Holyhead on his way back to Ireland in October, but it was of no political significance whatsoever. Indeed, it is striking that he made no attempt to pay 'his respects to her or his Excellency at the Castle' prior to his departure for Kilkenny a few days after he arrived in Dublin. [148]

Flood's decision to return so promptly to Farmley disappointed many rank and file Volunteers who had anticipated that he would join with them to resist Dublin Castle's scheme to replace them with provincial regiments of fencibles. His name was cited at Volunteer meetings held in Galway, Dublin and Belfast to galvanize opposition to this plan and to win support for his stand on 'renunciation', but he ignored all pleas to become personally involved. [149] Perhaps, he was dissuaded by the continuing hostility of the press, and the antipathy of a majority of his parliamentary patriot colleagues. The latter certainly displayed no inclination to alter their views on 'simple repeal'. Indeed, on arriving in England on his way back from Spa in October, Henry Grattan actively lobbied against the modification of the constitutional settlement that had been implemented earlier in the year. [150]

Grattan's intervention was prompted by the realisation that earl Temple, who was taken aback on his arrival in Ireland by the level of support for 'renunciation', was of the opinion that concession of the point was the only way to quieten the country. With this in mind, he dispatched his brother, the Chief Secretary William Grenville, to London in mid-November to press the matter, and the protests of outrage that greeted the pronouncement by Lord Mansfield, the lord chief justice of England, on an Irish case appealed to the English Court of King's Bench *prior* to the restoration of the appellate jurisdiction to Ireland, seemed to vindicate his deci-

147 French spy to Mme Ex, 23 Août 1782 in H.M.C., *Lansdowne Papers*, p. 256 (5th Report, Appendix). 148 *H.J.*, 26 Aug., 9, 11 Sept., 9 Oct.; Drennan to McTier, Sept. (P.R.O.N.I., Drennan Papers, D765/ 1/44); Temple to Shelburne, 19 Sept., Oct. (B.L., Lansdowne Abstracts, Add. Ms 24137); Cooke to Eden, 16 Oct. in *Auckland Corres.*, i, 336–7. 149 Cooke to Eden, 16 Oct. in *Auckland Corres.*, i, 336–7; *Annual Register*, xxv (1782), p. 221; Mac Nevin, *History of the Volunteers*, p. 183 n; McCreagh to Flood, 11 Oct. (Rosse Papers, C/1/15); *H.J.*, 28 Oct., 20 Nov.; Cuffe to Grenville, 25 Oct. (Grenville Papers, P.R.O.N.I., T3122); *Life of Grattan*, ii, 354, 364–6; [ ] to [ ], 27 Oct. 1782 in R[odd], ed., *Letters to Flood*, p. 113. 150 *H.J.*, 28 Oct., 15, 18, 29 Nov., 11 Dec.; Conolly to Buckinghamshire, 23 Nov. (N.L.I., Heron Papers, Ms 13050/2); Pery to Grattan, 3, 17 Oct., Grattan to Pery, 10, 20 Oct. 1782 in *Life of Grattan*, ii, 373–6, Additional Pery Papers, T3052/151–2.

sion.[151] It has been claimed that Flood contrived to use the Mansfield incident to inflame passions on the subject of 'simple repeal', but this is not so. Like Lord Charlemont, who advised Temple that 'renunciation on the part of England was now become absolutely necessary' because 'the country would never be quiet without it', Flood conducted himself responsibly. [152] He did, it is true, assure the Londonderry Independent Volunteers on 18 December that he would 'steadily co-operate with my countrymen to obtain for the rights of the nation that solid security which has been so unfortunately omitted', and that he would raise the subject of renunciation again when the Irish parliament reconvened in 1783, but this was much less than what many hoped for. It was, at the same time, more apt, and effective, than Grattan's attempt to deny that Mansfield's decision was relevant, since it reinforced the efforts of the Castle executive and its allies, like Lord Mornington, to convince the Prime Minister to renounce the Westminster parliament's claim to legislate for Ireland. If this was done, they avowed it would restore political stability in Ireland and deprive Flood of the credit of putting the coping stone to the arch of constitutional changes that comprised legislative independence. [153] Moreover it proved decisive, for on 20 December William Grenville announced at Westminster that 'England had fully and completely renounced all legislative and judicial jurisdiction' over Ireland and that he would introduce legislation to 'remove the grounds of jealousy' in January. Legislation proved difficult to draft, but a bill *recognizing* the legislative authority of the Irish parliament as defined in 1782 was made law in the spring of 1783.[154]

This news was warmly welcomed in Ireland where it was interpreted as a vindication of Flood's stand. In truth, the legislation did not meet his specific demands because it did not renounce 'past rights'. Indeed, Thomas Mac Nevin is essentially correct when he maintains that the legislation 'did not afford any additional security to [Irish] liberty'.[155] Perhaps this is the reason Flood declined to comment on the bill. When he was invited by Henry Joy, the Belfast liberal, in March 1783 to offer his views he maintained that he had not seen the measure. This is improbable, but Flood clearly wished to distance himself from the ill-feelings renunciation had en-

151 P.J. Jupp, 'Earl Temple's viceroyalty and the renunciation question 1782–3', *I.H.S.*, 17 (1971) pp 511–12; Temple to Grenville, 1, 4, 12 Dec. in H.M.C., *Fortescue*, i, 167–70; Portland to Ponsonby, 5 Dec. 1782 (Grey/Ponsonby Papers, P.R.O.N.I.,T3393/3). 152 *Courts and cabinets of George III*, i, 111; H.M.C., *Charlemont*, i, 80. 153 *H.J.*, 4, 9, 11, 16 Dec. 1782, 11 Jan. 1783; Grattan to Pery, 21 Dec. in H.M.C., *Emly*, ii, 175; Mornington to Grattan, 9, 11 Dec. 1782, 24 Jan. (B.L., Wellesley Papers, Add. Ms 37308 ff 5–8, Ms 38103 ff 8–9); Grenville to Temple, 20 Jan. 1783 (B.L., Dropmore Papers, Add. Ms 59407A ff 77–8); Temple to Shelburne, 12 Dec. 1782 (B.L., Lansdowne Abstracts, Add. Ms 24138 ff 106–8); Jupp, 'Renunciation', p. 512. 154 *Parl. Hist.*, xxiii, 324–5; Jupp, 'Renunciation', pp 514–16: *Courts and cabinets of George III*, i, 123–238; H.M.C., *Fortescue*, i, 182–97; *Parl. Hist.*, xxiii, 325–42, 730–57; Peter Jupp, *Lord Grenville 1759–1834* (Oxford, 1985), pp 26–7. 155 Temple to Grenville, 29 Dec. [1782] in H.M.C., *Fortescue*, i, 175; Mac Nevin, *History of the Volunteers*, p. 182.

gendered and to move on to other matters, because he informed Joy that he had 'nothing to gain by promoting dissatisfaction; but I am a friend to precision'. [156]

It is not clear what Flood anticipated his next political move would be once the question of 'renunciation' was resolved. It was reported in late January that he was 'very angry' with the failure to create a separate admiralty court in Ireland and that he had directed his cousin, Warden, to research the background to the matter so he could raise it when the Irish parliament reconvened. [157] He did not take up this issue, but the fact that he was activated by it indicates that he was not tempted to shift the centre of his political activity from parliament to the streets. Flood must have been gratified, nonetheless, by the warm welcome accorded the 'renunciation act', and by the fact that it caused some elements of the patriot press – hostile up to this – to assess his political career in a new and positive light. His contributions to the enactment of the Octennial Act and the Corn Laws were recalled; his political 'cunning' celebrated, and his 'distinguished' record as a 'defender' of the rights of Ireland emphasised. [158] He can also hardly have been unhappy that his increased popularity was at Henry Grattan's expense. The mainstream liberal paper, the *Hibernian Journal* continued to side with Grattan, but the weight of opinion went the other way. The respective reputation of the two men is neatly encapsulated in their popular sobriquets 'Great Harry' [Flood] and 'little Harry' [Grattan]. More abusive commentators simply termed Grattan 'the Spa Patriot' and accused him of being more concerned with his own 'gasping popularity' than with the rights of Ireland. Inevitably, there were renewed calls that Flood should be returned to represent a popular constituency in the general election that was expected before parliament was recalled in the autumn, and Dublin city and county were frequently cited as constituencies becoming a man of his abilities and reputation. [159]

Flood's public rehabilitation was not matched by any diminution in suspicion with which he was regarded in the corridors of power in Dublin and London. Few may have felt quite so strongly as the duke of Portland, who described him as 'the arch-enemy of Ireland', but there was broad agreement at this time on the desirability of reducing his public stature in order to limit his capacity to create difficulties in the House of Commons. [160] In this context, ministers were heartened by positive signals from Grattan and Charlemont that they were well-inclined. E arl Temple read too much into Charlemont's acceptance of his invitation to become a member of the Order of St Patrick in early 1783, but Grattan was more forthcoming. He indicated his willingness to co-operate with the administration if they fought 'his battle [with Flood over renunciation] more avowedly'. [161]

156 Flood to Joy, 5 Mar. 1783 (Linenhall Library, Joy Papers, Ms 11/3).   157 Temple to Grenville, 22 Jan. 1783 in H.M.C., *Fortescue*, i, 184.   158 *D.E.P.*, 2, 4, 9, 16, 18, 28, 30 Jan.; 6, 8, 15, 18, 24 Feb. 1783; Flood, *Memoirs*, pp 201–2.   159 *D.E.P.*, 2, 7, 14, 21, 23, 28. 30 Jan., 6 Mar., 15, 24 May, 2 Aug.; *H.J.*, Jan.Feb. 1783.   160 Temple to Grenville, 2 Jan. in H.M.C., *Fortescue*, i, 177; Grenville to Temple, 7 Jan, Portland to Temple, 22 Feb. 1783 in *Courts and cabinets of George III*, i, 116–7, 164.   161 Temple to

The British parliament's recognition of the legislative independence of the Irish parliament and the collapse of Lord Shelburne's government rendered Grattan's offer redundant. However, the Whig element in the coalition headed by Lord North and Charles James Fox which succeeded was anxious that Grattan should work with them, and there were elements too which sought to bring Flood onside. Flood was contacted by Edmond Malone, the Shakespearean scholar, with whom he had been friendly for a number of years. Malone first referred to the possibility of Flood's supporting the Fox-North coalition in a rather off-hand manner, but following the appointment of Lord Northington, as Lord Lieutenant, he enquired off Flood on 24 April if he had 'any wish or intention to form any part in the new administration in the next session in Ireland'. Malone seems to have been acting on instructions because he informed Flood 'that the new government is thoroughly impressed with the sense of your importance' and suggested that he could anticipate a style of government that would be agreeable to him, as the new Chief Secretary, William Windham, was 'a man of strict honour [who] ... does not go to Ireland with any view to emolument'. Most significantly, he dangled the offer of the chancellorship of the exchequer before him.[162]

The fact that a government which contained so many figures who resented Flood's stand on 'simple repeal' should make such a suggestion is a measure of their determination to bring to an end the demands for constitutional and political change in Ireland. The offer of the exchequer was certainly calculated to arouse his interest. Flood had been attracted by the prospect of returning the office to Ireland in 1774–5, and, though he was understandably wary in 1783, his response to Malone suggests that he was reluctant to rule out the idea out of hand. He was at the same time rightly chary of the motive for the offer. He responded to Malone that he believed it had been made to him under the impression that his stand on 'simple repeal' was impelled by a wish 'to recover office' which was not so. He had vowed when he was dismissed from the vice-treasurership 'never' to 'resume it'. However, since he made no reference to the chancellorship of the exchequer, and he did profess his goodwill to English government, he clearly did not seek to close off this option completely:

I am sincerely disposed to English government. This you will readily believe, who knows my principles and my situation, neither of which I will abandon. They are above vulgar faction and above vulgar ambition. I was suggested into office on higher motives. I embraced administration with an unsuspecting cre-

Grenville, 15, 20 Jan. in H.M.C., *Fortescue*, i, 182–3, 197; Charlemont to Temple, 27 Jan.(N.L.I., Buckingham Papers, Joly Ms 39 f 30); Grenville to Temple, 15 Feb. 1783 in *Courts and cabinets of George III*, i, 150; Peter Galloway, *The most illustrious order of St Patrick* (Chichester, 1983). 162 Chandos to Flood, 22 Apr. in R[odd] ed., *Letters to Flood*, p. 115; Hely-Hutchinson to Hely-Hutchinson, 27 May in H.M.C., *Donoughmore*, pp 306–7; Flood to Malone, 5 May (Rosse Papers, C/1/6); Malone to Flood, 24 Apr. in Prior, *Life of Malone*, pp 108–9;

dulity. I felt it was their interest to act as they spoke. But I found myself deceived. I do not know the author or the motive to [*sic*] this. You know the consequence.[163]

This encouraging, but essentially non-committal, response was welcomed by Lord
Northington. Though Flood was scrupulously careful to avoid entering into any
commitment, Lord Northington was hopeful. He believed the acquisition of Flood
would prove such a valuable addition to his and Portland's plan to constitute a
Whig-patriot administration in Ireland that he met with William Markham to discuss the point. Flood and Markham had not corresponded since 1781, but the
bishop's wish to see his former student in government employment had not diminished in the interval, and following his encounter with Northington he wrote Flood
on 3 May offering himself as an intermediary, and explaining that there was nothing Flood could not aspire to:

> He [Northington] said he knew your value, and esteemed your character, and
> wished for nothing so much as to have the assistance of your abilities; that it
> should depend upon yourself what share in the public business you might choose
> to engage in; that you should be as confidential to him as you pleased, and should
> never have reason to complain of his conduct.[164]

Edmond Malone affirmed this message two weeks later when he informed Flood
he did not see any reason why he should not be reappointed vice-treasurer if that
was his wish. Malone personally believed the chancellorship of the exchequer for
life was more appropriate, though he knew that William Gerard Hamilton was
'rather disinclined' to vacate the position. Fearing, it is to be assumed, a repeat of
what had happened in 1774–5, Flood determined not to take the matter any further. The absence of any further reference to it indicates that, having reflected on
the matter, he knew that office was not right for him; he decided to retain his political independence and to put up with the brickbats as well as plaudits that it would
bring him.[165]

One of the matters for which he was criticised in the summer of 1783 was the
corn law he had helped to pilot through the House of Commons in 1782. A central
provision of this measure was the prohibition of the importation of foreign grain
when the domestic price was less that 53s.4d a quarter. This was an extremely high
price, but since the domestic harvest had been buoyant for a number of years, Flood
had calculated that this would ensure that the bill's main object – the encourage-

---

163 Flood to Malone, 5 May (Boston Public Library, Autograph Mss, CH, G.7.1a (p.1)). The letter is
published in Prior, *Life of Malone*, pp 110–11. Flood's draft is in Rosse Papers, C/1/16. 164 Markham
to Flood, 3 May 1783 in R[odd], ed., *Letters to Flood*, pp 117–18. 165 Malone to Flood, 18 May
(R.I.A., Burrowes Papers, Ms 23/K/53/18); *D.E.P.*, 12, 24 June 1783.

ment of grain exports – was attained. However, the harvest was deficient in 1782, and the resultant shortages combined with the prohibition on imports to inflate prices and to reduce parts of the country to extreme distress in the summer of 1783. It also provided Flood's critics with welcome ammunition and, as 'the parent of the bill', he was soon being described, even by sympathetic sources, as 'a ... blundering senator'.[166] Flood did not seek to refute these criticisms or to comment on the fact that ships 'freighted with corn' were unable to discharge their cargo because of his bill. He made no public comment either when, in one of the first acts of his viceroyalty, Lord Northington authorised the suspension of the 1782 corn act and the provision of £100,000 for bounties on oats and wheat imports, though rumour had it that he was less than pleased.[167]

If this was the case, it would explain why Flood did not contact Lord Northington on his arrival in Ireland, or in the months that followed as the country eased itself out of a potential food crisis. It may also partly explain why Flood did not figure in the Lord Lieutenant's plans as he set about forming his whig-patriot administration. This could only succeed if Northington attracted the cream of the patriot leadership and, with this in mind, he approached Charlemont and Grattan (both of whom were made privy councillors early in July) and Hussey Burgh (whose price was a peerage). No further approaches were made to Flood, whom it was now anticipated, would remain in opposition. This, certainly, is the implication of William Windham's intriguing denial, on his resigning the chief secretaryship in mid-July, that 'the idea of Flood's oratory' held any 'terror' for him.[168] His successor, Thomas Pelham, who took up office on 20 August, had no other expectation. 'Nothing', Edward Cooke reported, 'shall induce him [Flood] to accept office'; he believes himself 'an abused and ill-treated man'. This worried George Macartney, who apprehended that 'Flood will do all the mischief a bad heart and working brain can invent'; 'he is worth a temporary purchase', he advised.[169]

As Macartney's caution attests, the approaches made to Flood in 1783 were prompted first and foremostly by the wish to neutralise him as a potential opponent in the Commons. They also reflect the antipathy with which he continued to be regarded in the corridors of power. This contrasted vividly with his continuing popularity with the Volunteers and protestant middle-class activists,[170] and it was their

---

166 McTier to Drennan, June (P.R.O.N.I., Drennan Papers, D765/1/96); James Kelly, 'Scarcity and poor relief in eighteenth-century Ireland: the subsistence crisis of 1782–4', *I.H.S.*, 28 (1992), p. 48; *D.E.P.*, 3, 10, 21 June 1783.   167 Kelly, 'Scarcity and poor relief', pp 48–9; *D.E.P.*, 3, 21 June 1783.
168 Kelly, *Prelude to Union*, pp 59–62; Northington to North, and reply, 26 June, 2 July (P.R.O., H.O., 100/9 ff 181–4, 193); Burgh to Leinster, mid-1783 (T.C.D., Burgh Papers, Ms 9318/110); Burke to Charlemont, 5 Aug. in *Burke Corres.*, v, 103; Windham to Northington, 16 July in L.S. Benjamin, ed., *The Windham Papers* (2 vols, London, 1913), ii, 34–8; Northington to North, 20 Aug. 1783 (B.L.,O.C., Northington letterbook, f 19).   169 Northington to Postmaster general, 20 Aug. (B.L.,O.C., Northington letterbook f 20); Cooke to Grenville, 18 Aug. (P.R.O.N.I., T3122/19); Macartney to [Northington], 30 Aug. 1783 (B.L., Pelham Papers, Add. Ms 33100 f 294).   170 He was, for example, warmly received at

enthusiasm to reform the representative system that provided Flood with his next major political challenge.

PARLIAMENTARY REFORMER

The subject of parliamentary reform, which was one of the primary concerns of patriots in the 1760s and early 1770s, was pushed down the political agenda in the late 1770s and early 1780s when the reform of the kingdom's commercial and constitutional relationship with Britain dominated political discourse. It was never entirely eclipsed, however, and encouraged by the example of the Association movement in Britain and by the empathy of English reformers like John Cartwright and John Jebb, patriots like Francis Dobbs and Edward Newenham were more convinced than ever by 1782 that the Irish representative system needed to be recast to embrace the protestant politicised population. This conclusion was reinforced by the perception, widely articulated in 1782, that it was essential to consolidate as well as to complement the reform of the Anglo-Irish nexus with the internal reformation of the Irish representative system and, following the introduction of the 'renunciation' bill, Volunteers in Ulster took up the matter.[171] A wide range of issues, including a 'bill of rights', the appointment of 'natives alone' to the 'chief offices' of Ireland, annual parliaments, an absentee tax and sundry commercial and constitutional issues (including an Irish admiralty court jurisdiction) arising out of 'free trade' and legislative independence were identified as meriting advancement.[172] But the matter which emerged from this confection of ideas and grievances as most pressing was the reform of the representative system because the arguments advanced in its support were most compelling and because, as R.L.Edgeworth, John Jebb and others pronounced, it was the logical next step.[173]

The cause of parliamentary reform was propelled from the realm of discourse to agitation by the decision, on 1 July 1783, of delegates representing 45 corps of Ulster Volunteers who gathered at Lisburn to authorise 'a general meeting of the Volunteer delegates at Ulster on the subject of a more equal representation of the people in parliament'. It was anticipated that the meeting which, it was agreed, should take place at Dungannon, would have as galvanic an impact as that of 15 February

---

the Galway Volunteer review in July, and there were continuing suggestions as to the constituency he should represent in the new parliament. *D.E.P.*, 17 July; *Belfast Mercury*, 5, 15, 19 Aug. 1783.   171 James Kelly, 'The Irish parliamentary reform movement: the administration and popular politics 1783–5' (M.A. thesis, U.C.D., 1981), pp 4–5; Cartwright to [Dobbs], 12 Jan, 13 Oct. 1780 (N.L.I., Dobbs Papers, Ms 2251 ff 27–34, 127–54); Jebb to Forbes, 20 Apr. 1782, 15 Aug. 1783, Jebb to Dobbs, 1782–3 (N.L.I., Forbes Papers, Ms 10713).   172 Haliday to Charlemont, 1 Feb., 17 Apr. in H.M.C., *Charlemont*, i, 424–6; *D.E.P.*, 23 Jan., 15, 18 Feb., 15 Mar., 1 Apr., 24, 29 May, 22 July, 19 Aug. 1782.   173 Kelly, 'Parliamentary reform', pp 18–30; Address of R.L. Edgeworth, 31 May 1782 (P.R.O.N.I., Babington and Croasdaile Papers, D1514/1/16).

1782 had on the campaign for legislative independence, and in order to present delegates with a clear statement of their options, a committee of correspondence was authorised to collate 'the best authorities and information on the subject'. [174] Because of his stand on 'simple repeal', Flood was an obvious Irish authority. So too were David Walshe and Sir Samuel Bradstreet and, despite their faltering popularity, Henry Grattan and Lord Charlemont. In contrast to Grattan and Charlemont, who maintained that parliamentary reform was not an issue with which the Volunteers should concern themselves (they advised that it was 'best ... left entirely to the mature deliberation of ... parliament'), Flood was supportive. [175] 'The principle has my warmest good wishes', he avowed, 'and as so respectable a body have taken it up, I will give my utmost and immediate attention to the subject'. He had, he went on, long advocated the reform of the representative system, and highlighting once more his role in advancing the Octennial Act, he pronounced himself disappointed that the electorate had not made fuller use of regular general elections to return more 'honest constitutional representatives':

> From that time whenever there was a trace of popular election remaining, it was in the power of the people to do themselves justice and particularly in counties. I cannot say that they have availed themselves of that opportunity as much as they ought to have done. This part of the evil the people must reform themselves. Nobody else can do it. Honest and constitutional electors will soon find or make honest constitutional representatives. Nothing else ever will. A few representatives indeed may rise above the corruption of their times. But the majority will submit to and avail themselves of it.

Flood was unwilling, for all that, to address the specific queries put to him but, unlike the committee of correspondence's other Irish respondents, he did this in a manner that gave it to conclude that he would be guided by them:

> As to the ... queries, I shall with your leave, say only at present that there are bodies which it becomes one to assist or obey, rather than advise. The rule I have generally prescribed to myself are these. To finish what I have begun. To undertake nothing that is not truly important as well as salutary and clear in its nature as that it should be unlikely to be retracted and not to engage in a multiplicity of objects at one time. [176]

174 *Proceedings relative to the Ulster assembly of Volunteer delegates* (Belfast, 1783), pp 1–4.   175 Walshe to Sharman, 4 Sept., Grattan to Sharman, 31 July, 14 Aug., Charlemont to Sharman, 5 Aug. (Linenhall Library, Joy Papers, Ms 11/34, 21, 24); McTier to Drennan, Aug/Sept. in D.A. Chart, ed., *Drennan Letters* (Belfast, 1931), no. 96; Grattan to Charlemont, [Aug.] 1783 in H.M.C., *Charlemont*, i, 114–5.   176 Flood to Sharman, 2 Aug. 1783 (Joy Papers, Ms 11/22).

Flood's disgruntlement with the failure of the electorate to return suitably, 'honest' candidates was all the more strongly felt since he once again experienced electoral difficulties in 1783. His name, we have seen, was speculatively linked with such constituencies as Dublin city and county and Antrim county in 1782–3, but when the general election was called, no attempt was made to launch a campaign on his behalf.[177] To compound his problems, his electoral support among the 1,050 freeholders in County Kilkenny had so diminished since 1776 he did not even deem it worthwhile to join in the early canvassing. The Flood family was still *one* of the main political interests in the county, but internal disagreements and Flood's querulousness inhibited its effective mobilisation.[178] He did appeal to his one-time ally, Lord Wandesford, and to John Butler (the heir to the Ormonde interest who was married to Wandesford's only daughter and who was for a time under his 'guidance') for their support but it was not forthcoming. Desperate for allies, Flood sought to win Butler over by offering to assist his attempts to be 'restored to his family honours', but it was in vain. Opposition to the Ponsonby-Agar coalition in County Kilkenny came from Pierce Butler, the son of the earl of Carrick, and not Flood, and it was not strong enough to secure victory. William Brabazon Ponsonby and Henry Welbore Agar were elected by a comprehensive margin.[179]

Failure in County Kilkenny increased the appeal of Callan to Flood, though his prospects there were only slightly more hopeful. He had 'obstinately' maintained his claim to the borough in spite of all the setbacks he had experienced by maintaining a rival corporation. However, the corporation controlled by the Agars was commonly regarded as the legal borough authority, and Flood's prospects of eclipsing this diminished rather than improved in the late 1770s and early 1780s as George Agar tightened his grip by reducing the number of 'legal votes' to five and then to two. As a result, he and not Flood was invariably described as the borough 'proprietor' by 1783, though some speculated that a new charter might be necessary to settle the matter once and for all.[180]

The likelihood of this happening was remote. In any event, a new charter was unlikely to advantage Flood because of the suspicion with which he was regarded by government, and because of his inability even to unite his family behind his candi-

177 *D.E.P.*, 15 May, 8, 10 July, 2 Aug. 1783.   178 *D.E.P.*, 1 Mar. 1783; Falkland (pseud. for J.R. Scott), *Parliamentary representation, being a political and critical review of all the counties...* (Dublin, 1790), pp 46–7; *History of the proceedings and debates of the Volunteer delegates* (Dublin, 1783), p. 149; Irish parliament, Oct. 1785 (P.R.O., Chatham Papers, 30/8/320 f 70).   179 Address of High Sheriff, nobility and gentry..., 23 Apr. 1778 (P.R.O., S.P.63/462 ff 2–3); Ms list of the Irish parliament, 1783 (N.L.I., Ms 2098); Harcourt list, [Jan. 1777] (D.P.L., Harcourt Papers, Gilbert Ms 94 ff 237–8); E.M. Johnston, ed., 'Members of the Irish parliament 1784–7', *R.I.A. proc.* 71(1971), pp 162, 173; Power, 'Parliamentary representation', p. 308.   180 Scott, 'Parliamentary representation', p. 47; *Proceedings of the Volunteer delegates*, p. 149; Ms list of the Irish parliament, 1785/6 (Rutland Papers, Belvoir Castle); Sir John Newport, *The state of the borough representation of Ireland in 1783 and 1800* (London, 1832), p. 13; Ms list of the Irish parliament in 1783 (N.L.I., Ms 2098); Burtchaell, *Kilkenny members*, pp 149–50.

dacy. He did persuade Frederick, the cousin with whom he remained on friendliest terms, to stand with him for Callan in 1783, but when the election precept was delivered to Arthur Webb, George Agar's sovereign, it was inevitable they would not be elected. Webb returned Agar and, his distant relative, John Bourke O'Flaherty. Flood determined to appeal the outcome, but since his experience in 1776 indicated that his prospects of success were slim, Frederick and he were obliged to look elsewhere if they intended to continue to sit in parliament. [181] Frederick bought a seat from Lord Glandore; while Henry joined with John Philpot Curran in purchasing the representation for the borough of Kilbeggan (County Westmeath) from Charles Lambert. [182] Kilbeggan was anything but a prestigious constituency, but the fact that Flood had a seat at least meant that he would be in the Commons to advance the cause of parliamentary reform.

Flood gave his clearest hint to date in September that he would actively support parliamentary reform when he accepted the invitation of the Belfast First Company of Volunteers, of which he was an honourary member, to represent them at the reform convention at Dungannon. The fact that he set out from Dublin in plenty of time to arrive at the meeting suggests that he was anxious not just to make an appearance, but to influence proceedings which were scheduled to be held on Monday, 8 September. However, he never arrived. The explanation he gave was that he was compelled to turn back by an attack of gout, but many doubted his sincerity and his actions were widely interpreted as evidence of his dissatisfaction with the way the reform issue was being managed. It was noted that Flood did not abort his journey until he reached Moy, which was only a few miles from Dungannon, and that he subsequently travelled onwards to Armagh. It was also reported that he did not attend the meeting of delegates of the Leinster Volunteer corps on 9 October, though he was nominated to represent the Goldsmith Corps at that gathering. This was harsh criticism, given that Flood was prone to gout and that he was in England when the Leinster meeting took place, but his numerous critics showed no scruple in proffering a less than charitable explanation of his every action. [183] It was even alleged that his trip to London was prompted by his wish to 'smoke the pipe of peace with Charles Fox'. [184] This was baseless. However, one cannot be so categorical about his failure to attend the Ulster Convention, and it may be well be that it did reflect his wish to reserve to himself the freedom to reject aspects of the plan of reform approved by the Dungannon delegates.

181 Burtchaell, *Kilkenny members*, pp 177, 149–50; *Commons Jn.(Irl.)*, xi, 31–2.   182 Johnston, ed., 'Members of the Irish parliament', pp 216, 229, 281; *D.E.P.*, 16 Aug.; *Proceedings of the Volunteer delegates*, p. 154. Subsequently, Frederick and Henry grew apart. Frederick accepted government office and the two men were described as 'not united' in the late 1780s (Buckinghamshire Record Office, Hobart Papers, P.R.O.N.I., T2627/1/1).   183 Pelham to [Portland], 10 Sept. (B.L., Pelham Papers, Add. Ms 33100 f 308); *D.E.P.*, 13, 23 Sept., 7, 9 Oct.; Hutchinson, *Tyrone precinct*, p. 101; Mornington to Grenville, 8 Oct. in H.M.C., *Fortescue*, i, 222; Drennan to Bruce, 23 Sept. 1783 (P.R.O.N.I., Drennan-Bruce letters, D553 no 15).   184 It may be pertinent that Speaker Pery reported to Pelham in mid-September that Fox spoke approvingly of Flood (B.L., Pelham Papers, Add. Ms 33117).

The resolutions ratified at Dungannon were devised with the express purpose of setting a process in train that would bring about significant change to the political system in which Flood and all other MPs operated. To this end, they recommended the introduction of annual parliaments, a secret ballot, the abolition of decayed and depopulated boroughs, the distribution of representation according to demography, the extension of the franchise to all Protestant males possessed of £20 in property or 40 shilling freeholds, the eradication of electoral abuses, the synchronisation of polls, and a prohibition on placemen and pensioners sitting in parliament. These changes could all be accommodated within the existing confessional political system, and it is likely for this reason that Flood would have given them his broad support had he been present. However, like a number of delegates, several of whom were 'friends' of Lord Charlemont, he did not believe it appropriate to widen the franchise to embrace Catholics, which was also approved, so that his absence from the convention gave him the freedom to oppose it at the Grand National Convention which was scheduled to gather in Dublin in November to determine the specific plan to be agitated. Flood's reluctance to commit himself on this matter at this point was matched by his reserve on the continuing efforts of Lord Northington to persuade Grattan, John Forbes and Lord Charlemont to join with him in forging a strong whig-patriot Castle connection. However, he remained very much on the mind of officials on both sides of the Irish sea, because his was the voice they most feared.[185]

If Flood had decided for understandable tactical reasons to reserve his opinions on the most exciting political developments of the moment, this worried the patriot public which anticipated that he would present their demand for parliamentary reform in the Commons. Their greatest fear was that he would be tempted once again by the fruits of office, and the premature death of Hussey Burgh in September prompted a flurry of speculation that he was about to be raised to the provostship in return for presenting Castle business in the Commons. This was without foundation, but the rumour mill went into overdrive when he left for England on 29 September.[186] It was inevitable that his departure so close to the opening of a new parliament should attract attention, but conjecture that it proved that his commitment to reform was a matter of expediency was wide of the mark; it was prompted by the prospect of his achieving his long time ambition of a parliamentary seat at Westminster arising out of a promise made him by the duke of Chandos in 1782.

185 *Proceedings relative to the Ulster Assembly*, pp 7–14; H.M.C., *Charlemont*, i, 117–18; Pelham to Windham, 14 Sept., (B.L., Windham Papers, Add. Ms 37873 f 65); Portland to Northington, 18 Sept. (B.L., Northington letterbook, Add. Ms 38716 ff 154–73); Northington to Charlemont, 23 Sept. in H.M.C.,*Charlemont*, i, 428; Mornington to Grenville, 8 Oct. 1783 in H.M.C., *Fortescue*, i, 222.   186 *A letter to Henry Flood on the present state of representation in Ireland* (Belfast, 1783); Mitchell, 'Colonel William Persee', p. 65; *D.E.P.*, 4, 9 Oct.; Mornington to Grenville, 8 Oct. 1783 in H.M.C., *Fortescue*, i, 222.

The origins of Flood's acquaintance with Chandos is obscure, but by the early winter of 1782 the two men were sufficiently close to provide each other with detailed accounts of politics in their respective kingdoms. [187] Sometime later, Chandos offered to return Flood for the borough of Winchester, which he jointly controlled with Henry Penton, whenever a vacancy arose. This occurred unexpectedly in September 1783, when Lovell Stanhope died and, pursuant to his promise, the duke moved to ensure Flood succeeded him. Matters were sufficiently far advanced by 10 October for Chandos to inform Flood (who had yet to arrive in the borough) that everything was in train, for though his nomination was not universally welcome, there was no concerted opposition. As a result, Flood was returned by the small electorate to represent the constituency on 17 October. [188]

Flood's visit to Winchester meant he missed the opening fortnight of the new parliament. In his absence, Isaac Corry, the MP for Newry, took the lead on behalf of the opposition, but he possessed little of Flood's oratorical menace and the opposition soon floundered. The Castle executive, by contrast, echoed to the sounds of contentment. They so revelled in their secure majority (according to one list they had promises of support from 183 MPs as against 99 for the combined opposition [189]) that they took little notice of experienced (and disillusioned) officeholders like John Beresford who warned that an administration which depended on popular politicians, and which did not have 'ministers' in place to steer business through the Commons was unlikely to prosper for long. [190] Flood was expected to be more formidable, but though he was back in the country by the time the house resumed (after the traditional recess) on 27 October, he made no attempt to fulfil these predictions. Indeed, he surprised everyone by announcing on 28 October that he would vote according to issue:

> I am no partizan here or in England, I can gain nothing by it; I am ready in either place, like a man, to support ministers while they are right and whenever they are wrong to oppose them, and resist their measures. [191]

This was a much more explicit avowal by Flood than he had given for some time of his continuing commitment to the independent stand he had determined upon following his dismissal in 1781, and his statement indicated that he was prompted to make it by his recent electoral success at Westminster. It disappointed those who

---

187 Chandos to Flood, 10 Nov. 1782 in R[odd], ed., *Letters to Flood*, pp 112–3.   188 Graham to Chandos, 8 Oct., Chandos to Flood, 10 Oct. in R[odd], ed., *Letters to Flood*, pp 118–20; Newspaper cutting, Nov. 1783 (Normanton Papers, T3719/A19/2); Namier and Brooke, eds, *House of Commons*, i, 302, iii, 463–4; T.H.B. Oldfield, *The representative history of Great Britain and Ireland* (6 vols, London, 1816), iii, 495–9.   189 Memorandum as to the state of the House of Commons, 1783 (N.L.I., Melville Papers, Ms 54 ff 18–20).   190 Beresford to Eden, 17 Oct. (B.L., Auckland Papers, Add. Ms 34419 ff 286–8); Kelly, *Prelude to Union*, pp 61–4; *Parl. Reg.*, ii, 1, 20; P.R.O., H.O., 100/10 f 179ff; Northington to North, 14, 15 Oct. 1783 (B.L.,O.C., Northington letterbook ff 19–24).   191 *Parl. Reg.(Irl.)*, ii, 36.

hoped that his outspoken stand on renunciation signalled his formal re-embrace of outright opposition, and it contributed to the hostility with which he continued to be regarded by most of his parliamentary colleagues. This was highlighted by two events. The first was the presentation, on 28 October, of his and Frederick Flood's petition against the election of John Burke O'Flaherty and George Agar to represent the constituency of Callan. 'The lawful and acting sovereign', Flood maintained, was Ambrose Smith because he was the lineal successor to Charles Flood, whose position had been upheld by 'the High Court of parliament' in the early 1760s. This was a weak case as Flood was aware, and when it became clear that the committee of MPs appointed to adjudicate the matter was not prepared to back him, he withdrew his petition on 3 December, the day before it was scheduled to be heard.[192] With it went his lingering hopes of retaining control of the borough in which three generations of the Floods had vested so much emotional, physical and financial effort.

The second, and better-known, illustration of the hostility borne Flood is provided by his infamous altercation with Henry Grattan. In many accounts, this is attributed to Flood's personality. He is portrayed as a 'brooding and saturnine figure' with few friends compared with Grattan who is described as 'an honest, warm enthusiastic character' with 'many attachments'.[193] There is much to sustain this analysis of their characters, but the implication that Flood was responsible for their row runs contrary to the weight of evidence which indicates that the antipathy and jealousy that characterised their mutual attitude arising out of Flood's public criticism of 'simple repeal' was more strongly felt by Grattan. More importantly, Grattan bitterly resented the fact that Flood was now widely perceived to possess the stronger claim to be seen as the more principled patriot. This was an invidious distinction, but the perception engendered during the renunciation dispute that Grattan was too willing to meet British fears was reinforced by the ongoing public criticism of his acceptance of the Commons' grant of £50,000 and by his cooperation with the Temple and Northington administrations. In his defence, Grattan could point out that he had not accepted office, but this impressed few.[194] Grattan certainly bitterly resented the partisan and ill-informed criticism to which he was subject and, as his closest friends acknowledged, 'hated' Flood for ruining his moment of triumph. He had, it is true, given little indication publicly of the hurt he felt up to this, but he determined to expose the 'Great Henry' in the House of Commons and, Edward Cooke observed, 'to justify his conduct' against the constant flow of criticism which had cost him the accolade of the country's leading patriot.[195]

192 *Parl. Reg. (Irl.)*, ii, 30; Burtchaell, *Kilkenny members*, pp 149–50; *Commons Jn. (Irl.)*, xi, 31–2, 133, 150. **193** Sayles, ed., 'The Irish parliament in 1782', p. 235; C[ooke] to Eden, 4 Sept. (Auckland Papers, Add. Ms 34419 ff 261–3); Lord Teignmouth, *Reminiscences of many years* (2 vols, Edinburgh, 1878), i, 202; Kelly, *Grattan*, pp 19–22. **194** Above p. 334; *D.E.P.*, 20, 24, May, 25 Sept.; Portland to Northington, 18 Sept. 1783 (B.L., Northington letterbook, Add. Ms 38716 ff 154–73). **195** Above pp 338–9; Flood, *Memoirs*, pp 230–1; Cooke to Eden, 29 Oct. 1783 in *Auckland Corres.*, i, 338–40.

The opportunity he awaited was provided on 28 October (Flood's second day in the Commons) during a largely routine debate on financial retrenchment initiated by Sir Henry Cavendish. Flood had not intended to speak in the debate but, anxious to support his friend, he fought off indisposition to urge the merits of 'greater oeconomy' and to express amazement at the opposition to the motion emanating from the government benches where Grattan sat. It was not an aggressive speech, though a tetchy exchange with George Ponsonby did elicit a warning from the Speaker. However, there was no question of it escalating above a run-of-the-mill Commons' disagreement until Grattan was given the floor.

Grattan rose with the ostensible object of defending the Northington administration against Flood's criticisms. This was entirely appropriate given his involvement with the administration and his commitment to economical reform, but it quickly became clear that his primary purpose was to attack Flood because he commenced with the hostile observation that, unlike Flood, he would not

> take up the time of the House, by apologizing for bodily infirmity, or the affectation of infirmity. I shall not speak of myself, or enter into a defence of my character, having never apostatized.

Neither the Speaker nor any member present made any attempt to call Grattan to order for this abusive remark and, having justified his commitment to financial retrenchment, he went on to query Flood's *bona fides* in this respect. It was a fine example of *ad hominem* advocacy, and he did not trespass the boundaries of propriety until he introduced the subject of Flood's endorsement of the deployment of '... four thousand men to butcher our brethren in America'. When Grattan had made this allegation previously, on 19 July 1782, Flood had not responded, but he was unwilling to let it go on this occasion and he countered with an 'able, playful, sarcastic and vehement' reply,[196] that was both personally critical and politically pointed:

> I am not afraid of the Right Honourable Member, I will meet him any where, or upon any ground, by night or by day. I would stand poorly in my own estimation, and in my country's opinion, if I did not stand far above him. I did not come here dressed in a rich wardrobe of words to delude the people. I am not one who has promised repeatedly to bring in a bill of rights, yet does not bring in that bill or permit any other person to do it. I am not one who threatened to impeach the Chief Justice of the King's Bench for acting under an English law, and afterwards shrunk from the business. I am not the author of the simple repeal. I am not one who, after saying the parliament was a parliament of prostitutes, endeavoured to make their voices subservient to my interest. I am not one who would

196 Above p. 334; Cooke to Eden, 29 Oct. 1783 in *Auckland Corres.*, i, 339.

come at midnight, and attempt by a vote of this little House to stifle the voice of the people, which my egregious folly had raised against me. I am not the gentleman who subsists upon your accounts. I am not the mendicant patriot who was bought by my country for a sum of money, and then sold my country for prompt payment. I am not the man who in this House loudly complained of an infringement made by England, in including Ireland in a bill, and then sent a certificate to Dungannon that Ireland was not included. I never was bought by the people, nor ever sold them; the gentleman says, he never apostatized, but I say I never changed my principles; let every man say the same, and let the people believe them if they can. But if it be so bad a thing to take an office in the state, how comes the gentleman [is] connected with persons in office? They, I hope, are men of virtue, or how came the gentleman so closely connected with Colonel Fitzpatrick: I object to no man for being in office; a patriot in office is the more a patriot for being there. There was a time when the glories of the great duke of Marlborough shrunk and withered before those of the Right Honourable Gentleman; when palaces superior to Blenheim were to be built for his reception, when pyramids and pillars were to be raised, and adorned with emblems and inscriptions sacred to his virtue; but the pillars and pyramids are now sunk, though then the great earl of Chatham was held inferior to him; however, he is still so great, that the queen of France, I dare say, will have a song made on the name of Grattan.

Most contentiously, he cited the recent debate over legislative independence in support of his contention that there were stronger reasons for questioning Grattan's political record than there were for imputing his:

If this country is now satisfied, it is owing to that gentleman? No, the simple repeal, disapproved and scouted by all the lawyers in England and in Ireland, shews the contrary; and the only apology he can make is that he is no lawyer at all. A man of warm imagination and brilliant fancy will sometimes be dazzled with his own ideas, and may for a moment fall into error; but a man of sound head could not make so egregious a mistake, and a man of an honest heart would not persist in it after it was discovered. I have now done – and give me leave to say, if the gentleman enters often into this kind of colloquy with me, he will not have much to boast of at the end of the session. [197]

Grattan could not let such accusations pass unanswered if he was not to be seen to have been bested in the exchange. So having corrected Flood's misrepresentations, he embarked upon an unrestrained attack on Flood as a politician and as a person. In respect of the former, he maintained that Flood's political career to date could be

[197] *Parl. Reg. (Irl.)*, ii, 39–41.

divided into three phases – each of which was a disimprovement on that which preceded it:

> At the outset ... [he] pursued an intemperate course on the opposition benches. Subsequently, he embarked on his 'corrupt' phase, which coincided with his acceptance of government office; currently his behaviour was 'seditious' because of his partisan advocacy of 'renunciation' and reform.

This was a profoundly unflattering summary of Flood's career to date, but it was positively tame compared with what was to follow when he addressed himself to assessing Flood as a person as well as a politician:

> Sir, your talents are not so great as your life is infamous; you were silent for years, and you were silent for money; when affairs of consequence to the nation were debating, you might be seen passing by these doors like a guilty spirit, just waiting for the moment of putting the question, that you might hop in and give your venal vote; or, at times, with a vulgar brogue, aping the manner, and affecting the infirmities of Lord Chatham; or like a kettle-drummer, lather yourself into popularity to catch the vulgar, or you might be seen hovering over the dome like an ill-omen'd bird of night with sepulchral notes, a cadaverous aspect, and broken beak, ready to stoop and pounce upon your prey – you can be trusted by no man – the people cannot trust you – the ministers cannot trust you – you deal out the most impartial treachery to both – you tell the nation it is ruined by other men, while it is sold by you – you fled from the embargo, you fled from the mutiny bill – you fled from the sugar bill – I therefore tell you in the face of your country, before all the world – you are not an honest man. [198]

Flood retained sufficient composure in the face of one of the most malicious speeches uttered in the Irish House of Commons to dismiss it as 'the venom that ingenuity and disappointed vanity ... has produced'. However, he was not prepared to leave it at that because honour demanded that insult was expiated and not endured, and he reiterated his readiness to meet Grattan 'anywhere, or upon any ground, by night or by day'. In accordance with normal practice, MPs ought to have intervened to prevent challenges being issued, but they were so enthraled by the gladiatorial nature of the confrontation and by their predisposition to favour Grattan to interpose as long as he was having the best of the exchanges. Flood had the support of the packed galleries, but the public was powerless to help him when the Speaker finally brought the exchange to a close as Flood was 'cooly defending himself'. [199]

198 *Parl. Reg.(Irl.)*, ii, 41–2. The version of the speech published by D.O. Madden (*The speeches of Henry Grattan* (Dublin, 1847), pp 91–5) differs in several respects.   199 *Parl. Reg.(Irl.)*, ii, 42; Cooke

Following the Speaker's intervention, Flood immediately departed the Commons' chamber, and he was not to be found when John Foster belatedly secured approval for an order authorizing the serjeant-at-arms or the sheriff of Dublin to take both Grattan and he into custody. Flood was visited subsequently at his Dominick Street residence by Alderman Exshaw, whom he successfully dissuaded from enforcing the Commons' order by giving him to understand that he would keep the peace. In fact, Flood was determined to press the matter to its logical outcome, and he wasted no time conveying a challenge to Grattan, who had gone into hiding to avoid being bound over. This 'was instantly accepted', and it was agreed by their seconds that the principals should meet on 30 October at Blackrock, County Dublin. The authorities were determined no duel would take place. Because of the enormous publicity accorded their dispute, Sheriff Kirkpatrick and Alderman Exshaw were authorised by Lord Chief Justice Annaly 'to bring these gentlemen before me [Annaly] to give security to keep the peace etc. towards each other'. Kirkpatrick stationed vedettes on all the main roads leading from the city, and when one of these spotted the duelling party heading towards their agreed destination the authorities intervened before they could proceed to an exchange of shots. Flood and Grattan were brought before Annaly who bound them to official recognizances of £20,000 each to keep the peace.[200]

To everybody's surprise, the two principals made no attempt to evade the court's jurisdiction by taking their dispute abroad. Flood, in particular, had no incentive to do so, because there was broad agreement that he had emerged best from the whole unsavoury episode. Alexander Knox spoke for many neutral observers when he opined many years later that Grattan had gone too far on 28 October: 'if ever [a] man was possessed of the devil it was his friend Grattan on that occasion'.[201] Few of Grattan's supporters were capable of such detachment at the time. Indeed, the primary concern of partisans on both sides was to defend the reputation of their favourite. Compared with Flood, who was not regarded with particular favour in many quarters, Grattan had the support of polite and respectable political society in Britain as well as Ireland.[202]

to Eden, 29 Oct. in *Auckland Corres.*, i, 338–40; Northington to North, 29 Oct. (B.L.,O.C., Northington letterbook, ff 29–32); Burgoyne to Fox, 31 Oct. 1783 (B.L., Fox Papers, Add. Ms 47568 ff 199–203); Kelly, *'That damn'd thing called honour'*, pp 135–6. **200** *Parl. Reg.(Irl).*, ii, 43–4; Flood, *Memoirs*, pp 208–9; Conolly to Leinster, 29 Oct. in Fitzgerald, ed., *Leinster Corres.*, iii, 372–3; Ogilvie to Leinster, 30 Oct. (N.L.I., Fitzgerald Papers, Ms 624 f 119b); Cooke to Eden, 29 Oct. in *Auckland Corres.*, i, 338–40; Annaly to Pery, 29 Oct. in H.M.C., *Emly*, ii, 181; *V.E.P.*, 16 Dec.; *D.E.P.*, 30 Oct. 1783. **201** *D.E.P.*, 30 Oct.; Carlow to Carlow, 31 Oct. in Mrs Godfrey Clark, *Gleanings from an old portfolio* (3 vols, Edinburgh, 1895–8), i, 233–4; Fox to Ossory, 5 Nov. in Lord John Russell, ed., *Memorials and correspondence of Charles James Fox* (4 vols, London, 1853), ii, 210; Hotham to Buckinghamshire, 7 Nov. 1783 in H.M.C., *Lothian*, p. 423; Teignmouth, *Reminiscences of many years*, i, 187. **202** Conolly to Leinster, 29 Oct., 2 Nov. in Fitzgerald, ed., *Leinster Papers*, iii, 372–3, 376; Conolly to Napier, 31 Oct. (W.S.R.O., Bunbury letterbooks, xviii, ff 10–20 (P.R.O.N.I., Mic 238 reel 2)); Fox to Northington, 7 Nov. (B.L., Fox Papers, Add. Ms 47567 f 42); Chandos to Flood, 9, 12 Nov. in R[odd], ed., *Letters to Flood*, pp 123–6; Herbert,

The lack of sympathy for Flood in Britain ought to have given him some cause for pause considering his recent election for Winchester, but he appears to have taken little notice of how his conduct in Ireland would register there. His priority was 'to vindicate' his reputation in the Irish House of Commons, and he received the opportunity he awaited on Saturday 1 November when he offered a comprehensive and convincing justification of both his political career and his stand on 'simple repeal'.[203] Grattan sought the right of reply, but he was prevented by the House, many of whose members now conceded that his attack on Flood a few days earlier was pre-meditated. Flood was content that the dispute should end this way because he had the satisfaction of knowing 'that an attack that was meant to do me the utmost mischief will redound as much to my honour and advantage as it was intended to do the contrary'. This, indeed, was what transpired. Flood was congratulated by the patriot press and by various Volunteer corps, while his opponent's reputation fell further in the esteem of these key interests.[204]

This outcome encouraged Flood to participate in Commons' debates in the days that followed. His involvement was curtailed by illness, but when he was present, he was the *eminence grise* behind the small corps of opposition figures – Lawrence Parsons, Denis Browne, Capel Molyneux, John Philpot Curran, Isaac Corry and Luke Gardiner – that sought to persuade MPs to curb the accumulating national debt by reducing expenditure. Thus, on 3 November, he made a characteristically vigorous speech in which he contrived to demonstrate that the rise in the country's 'debt' coincided with the augmentation of the army. However, the Castle's contention that any reduction in the military would be detrimental to 'the safety of the empire' and Ireland's capacity 'to assist in alleviating the burthen of Great Britain' proved more persuasive.[205] Despite this, Flood persisted, and on 10 November he presented a motion aimed at reducing public expenditure by £250,000 annually by undoing the augmentation agreed in 1769. This prompted a wide-ranging debate in which the value of the army to the kingdom, the Anglo-Irish connection and the empire were repeatedly cited. As a result, Flood's motion was soundly defeated. Thereafter, he absented himself from the House of Commons, and the administration was able easily to secure the implementation of its financial legislation.[206]

Though the poor state of his health was a factor, the main reason for Flood's

ed., *Pembroke papers*, ii, 245; Walpole to Ossory, 8 Nov., Walpole to Strafford, 10 Nov., Walpole to Mann, 12 Nov. 1783 in Lewis et al., eds, *Walpole corres.*, xxxiii, 428–9, xxv, 379–80, 437–8.   **203** *Parl. Reg. (Irl.)*, ii, 61–70.   **204** Flood to Chandos, 1 Nov. (Henry Huntington Library, Chandos Papers, STB, Box 10 no 46); Flood, *Memoirs*, pp 219–20; *D.E.P.*, 1, 4, 8, 13, 18, 25 Nov.; *V.J. (D.)*, 5 Nov., 2 Dec; Drennan to McTier, [1 Nov. 1783] in Chart, ed., *Drennan letters*, no 17.   **205** O'Regan, *Curran*, pp 221–3; Northington to North, 4 Nov. (B.L.,O.C., Northington letterbook ff 82–5); *Parl. Reg. (Irl.)*, ii, 71–85; *D.E.P.*, 6, 8 Nov. 1783; *Commons.Jn. (Irl.)*, xi, 64, 85, 94; *Parl. Reg. (Irl.)*, ii, 94.   **206** Northington to North, 12 Nov. (B.L.,O.C., Northington letterbook ff 45–52); Ogilvie to Leinster, 13 Nov. (N.L.I., Fitzgerald Papers, Ms 624 f 121b); *V.J. (D).*, 14 Nov. 1783; *Parl. Reg. (Irl.)*, ii, 94–107, 126 ff. He was present on 24 November to contribute to the debate on the petition of the Dublin Chamber of Commerce, during which he spoke in favour of allowing the public attend Commons debates (ibid., pp 209–10).

absence from the House of Commons in November was his involvement with the Grand National Convention of Volunteer delegates. His membership of the Convention derived from his nomination to represent the Volunteers of Galway city. Flood welcomed their endorsement, but he also contrived to reserve some freedom to manoeuvre by offering only a general commitment to support 'every salutary measure that shall be proposed'.[207] This was predictable given his known antipathy to the suggestion that the franchise should be extended to Catholics. But whereas George Ogle, who shared Flood's reservations on this point, was prepared to bring the Convention into disrepute by announcing that he had received assurances from the leaders of Catholic opinion that they did not request the right of franchise, when no such decision had been taken by the Catholic Committee, Flood hoped that he could use the Convention to engender support for a practical Protestant plan of reform.[208] He attended the opening of the Convention on Monday, 10 November, but because he had to be ferried around in a chair he was unable to participate in the ceremonial 'march with the other delegates' from the Royal Exchange to the Rotunda, and he was absent again on 11 November when Ogle made his fateful intervention.[209] His indisposition also ensured he was not one of the forty delegates nominated to the Convention's subcommittee 'to digest and prepare a plan of reform'. It is not clear how Flood felt about this, but given the eagerness with which he accepted the invitation of the earl-bishop of Derry to join the sub-committee as an 'assessor' when it became dead-locked on the practicalities of devising a plan of reform, it can be assumed that things worked out well as far as he was concerned. He was certainly given a perfect opportunity to shape the Convention's plan according to his own radical Protestant principles.[210]

As anticipated by those who had invited him to come 'to their rescue', the 'moderation' Flood brought to the sub-committee's deliberations significantly enhanced the prospects of the Convention producing a plan of reform that stood a realistic chance of acceptance.[211] Subject to his direction, the plethora of competing plans

207 *Proceedings of the Volunteer delegates,* pp 137–41. *D.E.P.* 11 Oct., 13, 27 Nov., 4 Dec.; Ogilvie to Leinster, 22 Oct. 1783 (N.L.I., Fitzgerald Papers, Ms 624 f 118a).   208 Ogilvie to Leinster, 7 Nov. 1783 (N.L.I., Fitzgerald Papers, Ms 624 f 120e); J. Kelly, 'The parliamentary reform movement and the Catholic question', *Archivium Hibernicum,* 43 (1988), pp 95–117.   209 *D.E.P.,* 11 Nov.; *Proceedings of the Volunteer delegates,* p. 27.   210 *Proceedings of the Volunteer delegates,* pp 40–2; *D.E.P.,* 13, 20 Nov.; Day to Glandore, 11 Nov. (N.L.I., Talbot-Crosbie Papers, Ms 2054/1); Drennan to McTier, Nov. (P.R.O.N.I., Drennan Papers, D765/1/117); Mornington to Grenville, 23 Nov. in H.M.C.,*Fortescue,* i, 224–5; B[eresford] to Eden, 23 Nov. (B.L., Auckland Papers, Add. Ms 34419 ff 298–300); Hervey to Foster, 17 Apr. 1782 (R.I.A., J.L. Foster Papers).   211 Day to Glandore, 22, 25 Nov. (N.L.I., Talbot-Crosbie Papers, Ms 2054/2, 3); Burgoyne to Fox, Northington to Fox, 17 Nov. in *Mems and Corres. of Fox,* ii, 192–7, 204–16; Northington to North, 19, 22 Nov. (B.L.,O.C., Northington letterbook, ff 52, 57–60); Pelham to Chichester, 19 Nov., Pelham to Pelham, [Nov.], Pelham to Portland, [late Nov.] (B.L., Pelham Papers, Add. Ms 33128 ff 229, 260, Ms 33100 ff 431–5); *Proceedings of the Volunteer delegates, passim; D.E.P.,* 18, 20 Nov.; Ogilvie to Leinster, 25 Nov. 1783 (N.L.I., Fitzgerald Papers, Ms 624 f 123q).

with which the sub-committee had become enmeshed prior to his co-option were swept away, and a more coherent set of proposals was presented for discussion. No formal record of the sub-committee's deliberations was maintained, but there is agreement that the plan of reform commended was primarily Flood's wo rk. The absence of any mention of Catholic enfranchisement certainly reflected his resistance to any 'transfer of the power of the Protestants, and [any] transfer of the constitution into [Catholic] hands'.[212] Otherwise, the resolutions that constituted the plan presented by the sub-committee to the full Convention on Friday, 21 November, was a practical scheme to eradicate the ills and inequities the reformers perceived in the parliamentary system. Thus, to ensure voter residency and to counter the effects of the infamous Newtown Act, new registration provisions were advocated which would oblige electors to reside for at least six months annually in the constituency in which they voted unless they were possessed of property worth more than £20 (resolutions 1–3). In order to combat electoral corruption in county constituencies, it was urged that polls were held on one day at multiple venues (resolution 4); while in borough constituencies it was recommended that electorates were increased by extending their geographical boundaries to include neighbouring baronies and parishes after the manner of the Shoreham and Cricklade reform in England (resolution 6). On the face of it, this ought to have been a straightforward process but because both the protestant population and borough constituencies were unevenly distributed, it was perceived necessary to lay down a gradated minimum of electors ranging from 200 for boroughs in Ulster, 100 in Munster and Connaught and 70 in Leinster to ensure 'as large a number of electors as could be obtained in order to emancipate every borough'.[213] As this suggests, the priority of Flood and the sub-committee was to improve the existing rather than to design a new representative system, and the intrinsic moderacy of their approach to the reform of the constituencies was also identifiable in their suggestions for franchise reform because they recommended the extension of the vote to all Protestant freeholders (resolutions 7, 8 and 11) and leaseholders worth £5 per annum in 'decayed boroughs' and £10 elsewhere provided they held 31 year leases with ten years unexpired (resolutions 9 and 10). In conformity to this approach, they also rejected the secret ballot ('viva voce' voting was to be retained) because, Flood contended, it was impractical and had failed whenever it had been tried, and annual parliaments (triennial elections were favoured (resolutions 12 and 13)). This was acceptable to all but the most radical reformers,[214] as was the provision for a comprehensive oath to combat electoral bribery (resolution 17) and the proposal to ban those found guilty of electoral perjury from sitting in parliament (resolution 18).

---

212 Above pp 304–5; H.M.C., *Charlemont*, i, 124; *V.J. (D.)*, 22 July 1784; *Proceedings of the Volunteer delegates*, pp 48–52; Flood, *Memoirs*, pp 243–5.   213 *Proceedings of the Volunteer delegates*, p. 71; John Cannon, *Parliamentary reform 1640–1832* (Cambridge, 1973), pp 70–1.

As this suggests, and as the absence for a provision for universal Protestant male suffrage[215] highlights, the plan of reform offered to the Convention reflected Flood's conclusion that it was necessary to advance a programme that stood a reasonable chance of acceptance. Its first hurdle was the Convention's 'general committee', and eager that it should not be delayed there, Flood persuaded the delegates to commence their consideration on Saturday, 22 November by raising the spectre of 'a depopulated assembly' if delegates acceded to the requests advanced in some quarters for a recess.[216] This took longer than calculated (he originally hoped they would have completed their passage by 24 November), but while debate on a number of resolutions was extended and, in a number of instances, prolonged, no amendments were accepted unless Flood agreed and he was disinclined to do so. This prompted allegations that Flood was behaving in a 'dictatorial' manner, but he made no attempt to prevent debate.[217] Indeed, Lord Farnham, who maintained that the proposals 'comprehended too wide a circle', and George Ogle and Charles O'Hara, who offered more specific objections on a number of points, were given plenty of opportunity to speak their mind and to offer amendments. However, it is a measure of Flood's ascendancy that even George Ogle was obliged, by Flood's resistance, to withdraw a proposal to provide for the compensation of borough owners. In the main, Flood relied on his tactical good sense, and occasional displays of charm and magnanimity to ensure that even complex resolutions like the sixth, which provided for a differing minimum numbers of electors in different provincial constituencies, and the ninth, which recommended the enfranchisement of leaseholders, were approved with a minimum of dissent. He was helped by his affirmation on Monday, 24 November, that he would 'ABOLISH HIS OWN INTEREST' in Callan borough. This was a palpably less generous offer in reality than it sounded, but it was well-received by delegates, and dovetailed with his profession that his object 'was ... to avoid unnecessary obstacles' to ensure he prevailed on all issues of consequence.[218] Of the five divisions called on the sub-committee's report, Flood's critics won none and obtained a minority of 26 votes or more on only two occasions. The most hotly debated matter was the oath to combat electoral bribery; once it was negotiated the rest was plain sailing. The resolutions were reported and forwarded from the general committee to the full Convention where they were subject to further discussion on Friday and Saturday, 28 and 29 November.[219]

With an agreed plan of reform imminent, the proponents of reform contemplated their next step. It was assumed by moderate delegates that the intention was

214 *Proceedings of the Volunteer delegates*, p. 95. 215 It was argued that this was a response to the refusal to extend the franchise to Catholics (Cloyne to Buckinghamshire, 22 Nov. 1783 in H.M.C., *Lothian*, p. 424). 216 *Proceedings of the Volunteer delegates*, pp 52–60. 217 Flood, *Memoirs*, p. 243; C.F. Sheridan, *Letters of a Dungannon and Munster delegate* (Dublin, 1784), p. 17; *Proceedings of the Volunteer delegates*, p. 91; H.M.C., *Charlemont*, i, 124. 218 *Proceedings of the Volunteer delegates*, pp 68, 70–90; *D.E.P.*, 25 Nov.; Day to Glandore, 25 Nov. (N.L.I., Talbot-Crosbie Papers, Ms 2054/2). 219 *Proceedings of the Volunteer delegates*, pp 96–124. The votes on the five divisions were 26:112; 2:119; 15:108; 5:122; 57:62.

to send 'the resolutions ... into the country ... in expectation that they will be taken up by county meetings of ... freeholders, and by them appointed to parliament in the form of petitions'. Others, Flood included, were eager to offer the plan to parliament as soon as possible, and it was they who seized the initiative. The decisive moment came at the end of the general committee's debate on the resolutions on Thursday, 27 November, when Sir Edward Newenham, who had already given the House of Commons notice of his 'intentions to bring ... forward' a reform bill, moved 'that Colonel Henry Flood be requested to introduce into parliament a bill for the more equal representation of the people'. Newenham's motion was accorded general support, and it was decided, on James Stewart's recommendation, that William Brownlow should join with Flood in presenting the bill. A majority of the delegates present were hopeful that the combination of Flood oratory and the support of the Volunteers would enable them to advance their plan of reform without having to return it to the country for endorsement. [220]

Flood's failure to comment on Newenham's intervention at the Convention on 27 November suggests that he had prior knowledge and approved of the move. This conclusion receives some corroboration from the fact that Francis Hardy maintains that he had offered the Volunteer-earl 'a hint' that this was his preference. Hervey, the earl-Bishop of Derry and other hardliners certainly wanted to present the Convention's plan to parliament at the earliest opportunity, which explains why some concluded that Flood and he were working in tandem at this point. [221] There is no evidence to support such a conclusion, and it is more likely that their interests simply converged. Flood was anxious to get to Westminster to take his seat there, while Hervey felt that the reformers would not receive a better opportunity to put parliament and the administration under pressure to agree to reform the representative system. Indeed, in an attempt to guarantee a positive outcome, Hervey suggested at a dinner attended by some of 'the most active members' of the Convention that the delegates should escort their plan of reform to the House of Commons attired in their Volunteer uniforms, but this was rejected as too overtly confrontational. [222]

The realisation that Flood planned to seek parliamentary approval immediately for the plan of reform approved by the Grand National Convention on 29 November sent a ripple of excitement through the political nation. [223] Dublin Castle had been instructed by London to resist the measure at all costs, and once Pelham gleaned what was intended, he sent 'immediately for a few friends, with whom I determined

---

220 Northington to North, 22 Nov. (B.L., O.C., Northington letterbook ff 52–5); Day to Glandore, 22 Nov. (N.L.I., Talbot-Crosbie Papers, Ms 2054/2); Burgh to Buckinghamshire, 9 Dec. (N.L.I., Heron Papers, Ms 13048); *Proceedings of the Volunteer delegates*, p. 106; *D.E.P.*, 29 Nov. 1783.   221 Hardy, *Charlemont*, i, 269;Jonah Barrington, *Historic memoirs of Ireland* (2 vols, London, 1835), ii, 189.   222 H.M.C., *Charlemont*, i, 125–7; *V.J. (D.)*, 24 Nov. 1783. Edgeworth, *Edgeworth memoirs*, ii, 63–4; Craig, *The Volunteer earl*, pp 186–7.   223 *D.E.P.*, *V.J. (D)*, *V.E.P.*, 27–9 Nov.; Carlow to Carlow [28 Nov.] 1783 in *Gleanings from an old portfolio*, i, 238.

to refuse the leave [to introduce a bill of reform] openly declaring our pleasure to be that we would not receive any proposition coming from an armed association'. [224] This was a strategy well-calculated to win support because of the unease of MPs with what was perceived as a blatant attempt by the Volunteers to dictate to parliament. The Castle certainly left little to chance. The Lord Lieutenant and Chief Secretary lobbied 'all the friends of government' to attend the debate on the bill and convened a meeting of forty to fifty supporters from the Lords as well as the Commons 'for the purpose of fixing how [Flood's] motion should be trea ted'. These endorsed the stand already determined upon. Encouraged by this, the Castle was confident that they would be successful on the day though the evident unhappiness of Henry Grattan, John Forbes and George Ogle, who supported reform in principle and who favoured a less confrontational approach, caused them some disquiet. [225]

In contrast to the Castle, there is no evidence to suggest that Flood or any of the other advocates of parliamentary reform gave any attention to lobbying MPs. The fact that the administration's vote had collapsed on a number of occasions during the previous fortnight may have encouraged Flood to believe that MPs could be persuaded to support an appropriate bill, [226] but there was no avoiding the conclusion that his support derived primarily from the Volunteers and reform-minded MPs, or that the outcome would be as much a judgement on their involvement in politics as on the merits of Flood's plan.

The proceeding of the House of Commons on 29 November began in a deceptively low-keyed manner with a discussion of the merits of appointing a committee to assess what reductions could be made 'with propriety' in the military establishment. Ever ready to air his views on this subject, Flood reaffirmed his contention that the augmentation of 1769 should be 'discontinu[ed]' which prompted a sharp exchange with the Attorney General. This completed, the House moved onto the main item of business, and Sir Edward Newenham set proceedings in train by formally inviting Flood to move for leave to present a bill for parliamentary reform.

Despite the expectation that he would make a major speech, Flood chose to delay making his case in favour of reform until the bill 'comes under discussion'. He had done so before to advantage, but it was a mistake in this instance because it handed the initiative in the debate to his opponents and they eagerly grasped the opportunity. The Attorney General, Barry Yelverton, set the tone with an appeal to MPs to deny Flood's request because it was 'inconsistent with the freedom of debate for the legislature to receive a bill originating with an armed assembly'. 'We sit not here to register the edicts of another assembly or to receive propositions at the point of a bayonet', he pronounced, prior to warning MPs that

---

224 Pelham to [Chichester], 30 Nov. 1783 (B.L., Pelham Papers, Add. Ms 33128 ff 336–7). 225 *D.E.P.*, 29 Nov.; Mornington to Grenville, 30 Nov. in H.M.C., *Fortescue*, i, 225; Northington to Fox, 30 Nov. 1783 in *Mems and Corres. of Fox*, ii, 184–9. 226 Kelly, *Prelude to Union*, pp 69–70.

our self-preservation, as a parliament, depends on the vote we shall now give – this is the spot to make our stand, here we must draw our line – for we have retired step by step as they have advanced, we are now on a precipice and to recede one step more plunges us into inevitable ruin.

As Yelverton portrayed matters, the Volunteers were seeking to dictate to the legislature what laws it should make and, determined that such a dangerous precedent should not be set, he called upon the Volunteers to

beat your swords into ploughshares, return to your different occupations, leave the business of legislation in the hands where the laws have placed it and where you have ample proof it will be used for the advantage of your country. [227]

This was a persuasive enunciation of the administration's position, and it was well-received by the exceptionally full house. In his response, Flood sought to deny the bill had its origins in the Grand National Convention. He claimed that William Brownlow and himself were its authors. However, the fact that both Brownlow and he were arrayed in Volunteer uniform and that he maintained 'the Volunteers and the people are the same' vitiated his argument. It certainly did not impress the assembled House, as speaker after speaker endorsed the line taken by the Attorney-General. Indeed, most of the forty-eight MPs who participated in the marathon debate that ensued spoke against receiving the bill on the grounds that it originated with an armed assembly. This ensured that the occasion was a disaster for the proponents of reform who performed in a lacklustre and timid way throughout. The result, when it came at 3 a.m., was conclusive. Flood's move for leave to introduce a reform bill was defeated by a majority variously computed at between 80 and 85. The supporters of the bill mustered ten votes more than the Lord Lieutenant had anticipated, and they had the backing of two-thirds of the county MPs, but this was little consolation. Indeed, Flood and thirty or so others left the House immediately after the division to avoid being implicated in an address to the King sanctioned by the House assuring him of their 'perfect satisfaction [with] ... our present happy constitution'. [228]

This decisive reversal left Flood and the Grand National Convention with no option but to reconsider their tactics. Many shared Lord Charlemont's anger at the aspersions cast upon the Volunteers, but when they reconvened on Monday, 1 December, the prevailing mood was against confrontation. Nobody, not least Flood

---

227 *Parl. Reg.(Irl.)*, ii, 226–7.   228 *Parl. Reg.(Irl.)*, ii, 226–64; Northington to North, 30 Nov. (B.L.,O.C., Northington letterbook, ff 62–7); Johnston, *Great Britain and Ireland*, pp 391–401; Northington to North, 30 Nov. (P.R.O., H.O., 100/10 ff 314–17); Cannon, *Parliamentary reform*, p. 106; Woodward to Buckinghamshire, 30 Nov.1783 in H.M.C., *Lothian*, p. 426. The vote is variously given as 157:77 (*Commons Jn.(Irl)*) and 163:78 (*Belfast Newsletter*).

and Brownlow, could see any merit in forcing a showdown with parliament. A number of delegates did urge defiance, but Flood's sober outline of events ensured this would not happen, and he contributed further to the calming of emotions by supporting a suggestion for an investigation into the state of the borough representation. Further resolutions calling on the people to manifest their commitment to reform and on delegates to address the crown affirming their readiness 'to sacrifice their lives and fortunes to preserve the principles of the constitution inviolate from the gross abuses of election and representation' excited a more ambivalent response, and Flood's suggestion that they should not be put to a vote was accepted. Flood was not opposed to an address to the King *per se*. Indeed, on the next day, the last day's sitting of the Convention, he recommended that the delegates asserted 'the purity of their intentions' by preparing an address to the King in which they affirmed their 'inviolable attachment to the perpetual connection of His Majesty's crown of this kingdom with that of Great Britain' and their 'wish to have certain manifest perversions of the parliamentary representatives of this kingdom remedied'. This encapsulated Flood's personal commitment to reform as well as to the Anglo-Irish connection, and it provided him with a perfect reason for travelling to London since he was invited to present the address to the King. [229]

The discipline displayed during the final two days of the Convention mitigated the humiliation Flood and other reform delegates had experienced in the House of Commons on 29/30 November. Lord Northington was so alarmed by this that he instructed Henry Lawes Luttrell, the MP for the Westminster constituency of Bossiney who served in a military capacity in Ireland, 'to accompany [Flood] in order to prevent any false state[ment] in the English House of Commons of what has passed here'. [230] Flood had no intention of raising the matter at Westminster. His sole object was to present the Convention's address to the King. However, George III was persuaded by the intervention of Dublin Castle to decline Flood an audience when he requested one on 12 December, with the result that Flood was left with no alternative but to submit the address to Lord North for presentation to the King. This too proved unsuccessful till Flood finally overcame George III's antipathy by handing it directly to him at a levee on 19 December. [231]

The obstacles raised to Flood's presenting the Convention's address to George III bear ample witness to the determination of the authorities on both sides of the Irish Sea to do everything in their power to frustrate reform and to obstruct Flood.

229 *Proceedings of the Volunteer delegates*, pp 124–35; *V.E.P.*, 4 Dec.; Northington to North, 4 Dec., Pelham to Nepean, 1 Dec. 1783 (B.L.,O.C., Northington letterbook, ff 67–8, 70–2). **230** Joy to Wyvill, *c.*2 Dec. (North Riding Record Office, Wyvill Papers, Ms ZFW/ 7/2/39/29); Northington to Fox, 30 Nov. (B.L., Fox Papers, Add. Ms 47567 f 71); Pelham to North, 4 Dec. 1783 (B.L., Pelham Papers, Add. Ms 33100 f 445). **231** Pelham to Northington, 4 Dec., Eden to Pelham, 12 Dec., North to Northington, 13 Dec. (B.L., Pelham Papers, Add. Ms 33100 ff 445, 456, 458); Northington to North, 4 Dec. (P.R.O., H.O., 100/10 f 351); George III to North, 9 Dec., North to George III and reply, 18 Dec. in Fortescue, ed., *Corres. of George III*, vi, 472–3, 476; *V.E.P.*, 20, 24 Dec. 1783, 27 Jan. 1784.

Opinion in Ireland was distinctly more supportive. The *Dublin Evening Post*, for example, applauded Flood's efforts and urged freeholders to approve resolutions in support of reform on the grounds that this was the way forward recommended by 'that great man'.[232] However, there were dissentients who attributed the defeat of the reform bill on 29/30 November to his 'precipitancy' to get to Westminster. Others alleged that it reflected his private disinclination towards reform, while still others asserted that he was motivated simply by the desire for personal aggrandizement.[233] It was inevitable that Flood should be the target of some criticism given the outcome and, in particular, that the supporters of Catholic enfranchisement and the plan of reform approved at Dungannon should be displeased.[234] However, much of what was said was claimed was unsubstantiable because, as William Drennan accurately observed, 'the Roman Catholic question was our ruin'. Drennan did not entirely exonerate Flood; he was critical of his failure to 'give that *previous* advice' which would have ensured that the question of Catholic enfranchisement did not clog up the Convention. More perceptively, he concluded that Flood was not the right man to lead the reform movement:

> Times of *reformation* require *impetuosity* of spirit. Our religious reformation required such a man as Luther. Flood is too wise, too cool, *perhaps* too selfish to be a Luther in civil reform ... Your assembly would have been less *wise* by adopting the passion as well as the reason that characterize every popular assembly, but perhaps more successful than it has been as Mr Flood's convention...It is the people which government fear, the wide, illiterate views of the people, not Mr Flood.[235]

But this was to blame Flood for being something he was not and could never be. He was not an agitator, a hustings orator or even an effective conspirator. He was simply a parliamentarian who was guided by the combination of his own conscience, his interests and his honour. Having done what he believed was best for reform in Ireland, his focus shifted to the imperial stage at Westminster where he was hopeful he might yet emulate his hero – Lord Chatham – and attain the recognition and make the legislative mark that would bring him fulfilment.

232 *D.E.P.*, 4, 9, 27 Dec. 1783 and *passim*.   233 *V.E.P.*, 4, 6, 13 Dec. 1783, 5 Feb. 1784; Woodward to Buckinghamshire, [2]9 Nov. 1783 in H.M.C., *Lothian*, pp 425–6; [Sheridan], *Letters of a Dungannon and Munster delegates ...*, pp 17, 20–1; Flood, *Memoirs*, pp 256–8.   234 *V.J. (D)*, 12, 24 Dec.; *V.E.P.*, 18 Dec. 1783.   235 Drennan to Bruce, 17 Dec. (P.R.O.N.I., Drennan-Bruce letters, D553/17); Drennan to McTier, Dec. 1783 (P.R.O.N.I., Drennan Papers, D765/1/113).

8

Anglo-Irish politician, 1783–91

Though many of his Irish supporters concluded that he was turning his back on them and on Ireland, Henry Flood perceived his election to the Westminster parliament in 1783 as a logical step, and a tangible expression of his commitment to the maintenance of a secure and equal Anglo-Irish connection. He had no intention at the time of forsaking Irish politics; his object was to play an active role in both legislatures. Indeed, he saw no reason at all why he might not register an impact at Westminster at least equal to that which he had made at College Green. He was, as he was fully aware, an exceptionally talented orator, and he anticipated that the rhetorical skills that had served him so well at College Green would prove just as useful at Westminster. However, he overlooked the fact that his style was ill-suited to the 'mother of parliaments' and that most Englishmen regarded him with particular reserve because of his record as an assertive advocate of Irish rights. More consequently, he discovered that the evolving two-party system in the House of Commons provided few opportunities for independents to shape policy or legislation. His problems were compounded by his age (according to Henry Grattan he 'was a tree of the forest, too old, and too great to be transplanted at fifty'[1]); by his inability to secure a safe Commons' seat, which kept him out of British politics for most of the years 1784–86; and by his increasing disenchantment with the Irish parliament. Despite this, he remained a figure of consequence capable, on occasion, of turning in a commanding parliamentary performance. However, his failure to register an indelible impression in either kingdom in the 1780s is testament both to the increasing powerlessness of the individual voice and to the firmness of the command exercised by the government and administration at Westminster and College Green respectively.

1 *Grattan's miscellaneous works* (London, 1822), p. 118.

DIFFICULT TIMES

In taking his seat in the British House of Commons in December 1783, Henry Flood was following in a long line of Irish gentlemen. According to the typology devised by Namier and Brooke, Flood fits most easily into the category they define as landed upper-class with estates in both kingdoms but, unlike most Irish MPs at Westminster, he did not possess an English patrimony, and he made no attempt to acquire an English estate or, even, a permanent London home.[2] Despite this, he felt at ease in England which may partly explain why he underestimated the obstacles – personal as well as political – he had to surmount to prove himself on the Westminster stage.

In contrast to most of his co-nationals, Flood came to the House of Commons with a reputation. This was a source of confidence for partisans like Daniel Webb and the duke and duchess of Chandos, who were confident that he would shine because of his famed oratorical ability and his avowed commitment to put principle above party and the security of the Anglo-Irish connection above personal interest.[3] However, it excited unease in virtually every other quarter. This derived its impetus from antipathy to Flood's character as well as his politics. It was widely acknowledged that he was an 'able' politician, but his 'saturnine' demeanour and his disinclination to compromise alienated many. He was perceived, Horace Walpole observed, as the 'principal engine of confusion' and, following his controversial stand on 'simple repeal' and his row with Grattan, accounts from Ireland describing him as 'the phlogiston' that energized the demand for parliamentary reform reinforced such perceptions.[4] Compared with Grattan, Flood was perceived to be personally difficult and politically irresponsible, and willing to put the security of the Anglo-Irish connection at risk in pursuit of personal political glory. This was inaccurate; no less than Grattan, Flood was convinced 'that Ireland cannot exist as a nation independent of England'.[5] However, because most Englishmen typified every manifestation of assertiveness in Ireland as a challenge to Britain's authority, it was inevitable, that Flood would be regarded with hostility. The fact that weeks before he made his maiden speech at Westminster, 'literary assassins' were at work 'misrepresent[ing] and mangl[ing]' his reputation highlights how eager his English critics were to ensure he did not prosper on the imperial stage.[6]

Flood's journey to London took two days. He arrived at his destination on Wednesday, 3 December exhausted, but eager to signal his arrival, he attended the

2 Namier and Brooke, eds, *The House of Commons*, i, 163–4.   3 Webb to Flood, 7 Nov., Chandos to Flood. 18, 22, 21, 26 Nov. 1783 in R[odd], ed., *Letters to Flood*, pp 121–2, 127–30, 132–5.   4 *Short history of opposition to the present time in a letter to a member of parliament* (Dublin, 1796), p. 59; Walpole to Mann, *c*.6 Dec. 1783, 24 June 1785 in Lewis, et. al., eds *Walpole Corres.*, xxv, 453–4, 589; Hamilton to Buckinghamshire, 27 Nov. 1783 in H.M.C., *Lothian*, pp 424–5.   5 Chandos to Flood, 29 Nov. 1783 in R[odd], ed., *Letters to Flood*, p. 135.   6 George III to North, 29 Nov., Portland to George III, 11 Nov. 1783 in Fortescue, ed., *Corres. of George III*, vi, 470, 464; *V.E.P.*, 22 Nov. 1783.

House of Commons that evening to hear Charles James Fox defend his controversial East India bill. According to Lawrence Parsons, Flood went to the Commons with the intention of 'speak[ing only] a few sentences, but the House expected from him an oration', and he was so awed by the 'calm' and 'curiosity' accorded his request to speak, with members returning from nearby coffee houses to hear him, that he chose at the last minute to make a lengthy statement.[7] It was a serious error of judgement. He was neither sufficiently rested nor sufficiently informed on the legislation being debated to make a useful contribution. To compound matters, he was not attuned to the mood or expectation of the House, as Nathaniel Wraxall (who was more generous in his response than most) observed:

> His sentiments were strongly inimical to the East India Bill. Though possessing *little local, or accurate information* on the immediate subject of debate, he spoke with great *ability and good sense*; but, the slow, measured and sententious style of enunciation which characterized his eloquence, however calculated to excite admiration it might be in the senate of the sister kingdom, appeared to English ears, cold, still and deficient in some of the best recommendations to attention.[8]

Flood certainly commenced his speech badly, with a plea for indulgence more becoming a maiden speaker than a seasoned veteran:

> Mr Flood began with apologizing for venturing, totally unacquainted as he was with the subject of Indian concerns, not having read the Reports on the table, and knowing no more of their contents than he had heard at a distance, to deliver any opinion upon a Bill so important as that under consideration. He thought it, however, an indispensable act of parliamentary duty to say something upon the occasion, and when he did so ... he begged the House to given him credit for speaking his sentiments impartially. He was connected with no party, and equally unacquainted with administration or opposition, though he entertained the most profound respect and veneration for many gentlemen on both sides of the House, whose characters were justly entitled to his esteem, as they had long since obtained the esteem of the public. He declared he had anxiously desired to be present before a measure of such magnitude had entirely passed that House; and when he assured the Speaker that he had been in the Irish House of Commons in Dublin on Wednesday last, he trusted that it would be admitted, that he had been as expeditious as possible, in order by that time to reach the House in which he had the honour to stand.[9]

---

7 Rosse Papers, C/14/1–5; Flood, *Memoirs of Flood*, pp 275–6; Ryan, *Worthies of Ireland*, ii, 148–9.   8 Nathaniel Wraxall, *Historical memoirs of my own time* (3 vols, London, 1818), iii, 587.   9 *Parl. Hist.*, xxiv, 56–7; Flood, *Memoirs*, pp 278–83.

Preliminaries completed, Flood proceeded to offer 'a series of general remarks on the bill'. These were not without insight, but they were more suited to a first stage debate, when people were still unfamiliar with the issues, than at a late-night sitting to determine whether the bill should proceed to its third reading stage.[10] Moreover, by criticising the bill and by defending the East India Company as 'the best' means of administering India, he reinforced the suspicion on the government benches (arising out of Chandos' support for William Pitt) that 'he had been introduced into the British senate for the secret purpose of opposing the thunder of [Charles James] Fox'. Certainly, the hostile response of John Courtenay, the Foxite Irish-born MP for Tamworth, who had propagandized for Lord Townshend, suggests that it had previously been determined to give him a rough reception.[11]

Courtenay was a clever speaker who excelled at using the words of his chosen target to ridicule and, thereby, to discredit his argument. In Flood's case, he began very effectively by citing Flood's acknowledgement that 'he knew nothing of the important subject of debate' to invalidate his criticisms of the India bill and to deride his call that more time should be provided to assess the measure. His deconstruction of Flood's claim that he owed allegiance to no individual or party at Westminster was even more devastating:

> Mr Courtenay observed he was not acquainted with ... [Flood's] political connexions: he gave his own definition to the word 'independent'. For instance, whenever he heard a member of that House speak without any knowledge of the subject, without any previous information of facts, and without any sound or solid argument, he denominated such a gentleman an independent member of parliament, as he certainly spoke independent of points and circumstances, which shackle and confine other members of a more abject and less enterprising spirit.

Flood was not used to being treated so dismissively, but Courtenay, in flow, was a formidable opponent. Indeed, he even corrected a number of Flood's classical allusions. This added insult to the considerable injury he had already inflicted, and it is a fair measure of the impact of the 'battery of ridicule and wit, seasoned with allusions or reflections of the most personal and powerful kind', Courtenay deployed that Flood did not seek to respond.[12]

10 Eden to Northington, [9 Dec. 1783] (B.L., Pelham Papers, Add. Ms 33100 f 437). 11 *Parl. Hist.*, xxiv, 56–9; MacDougall, *Sketches of Irish political characters*, p. 285; Macartney to Burke, 8 Mar. 1784 in C.Collon Davies, ed., 'The private correspondence of Lord Macartney', *Camden*, 3rd series, 77 (1950), p. 226; Namier and Brooke, eds, *The House of Commons*, ii, 261–2; Flood, *Memoirs*, p. 286. 12 *Parl. Hist.*, xxiv, 60–1; Wraxall, *Historical memoirs*, iii, 587; Stanford, *Ireland and the classical tradition*, p. 213. 13 McDougall, *Sketches of Irish political characters*, p. 285; Wraxall, *Historical memoirs*, iii, 587; Burgoyne to Northington, 9 Dec.(B.L., Pelham Papers, Add. Ms 33100 f 448); Walpole to Strafford, 11 Dec. in Lewis et al., eds, *Walpole Corres.*, xxxv, 381–2; Carlow to Carlow [late Dec. 1783] in *Gleanings from an old portfolio*, i, 243.

Both Warden Flood and Sir Lawrence Parsons have minimised the scale of Flood's failure on 3 December, but to many contemporaries 'never was defeat more perfect, certainly never more satisfyingly conspicuous'. Horace Walpole concluded that Flood's performance was so 'wretched' it posed a very real 'question [as to] whether [he] will ever recover'.[13] Few were as categorical, but it was essential if he was to have any political credibility at Westminster that he redeemed himself with a sterling performance at an early date. Flood was conscious of this but, despite having given himself a week to recover, his contribution to the debate on the army estimates on 11 December was equally ill-judged.

The size of the army establishment was an issue on which Flood had spoken on many occasions in Ireland and on which he held firm, if controversial, views. However, instead of articulating these in a formal fashion he cited a slighting reference to the loyalty of the Irish Volunteers uttered the previous day (when he was not in the House) to justify the Crown's sending English troops to Ireland as his pretext for seeking the floor. On this specific point, Flood denied that the existence of the Volunteers warranted the deployment of English troops in Ireland; but his main purpose was to present a motion urging the reduction of the Irish army.[14] This was precisely the sort of opportunity Flood's opponents awaited, for no sooner had he made his statement than Henry Lawes Luttrell rose to express his 'astonishment' at Flood's remarks. Flood refused to allow Luttrell's aggressive tone disturb him, but he was clearly ill-at-ease, and his discomfort was compounded by the invocation by the Speaker of the standing order that no member should speak more than once in a single debate because it prevented him from fully explaining his position. He was enabled, subsequently, to communicate his wish to withdraw his motion, but this too was ruled out of order. His motion was put and negatived decisively, and his humiliation emphasised by Charles James Fox's claim that it was essential for the smooth conduct of parliamentary affairs that MPs checked 'frivolous conversation [and] frivolous amendments'.[15]

In the light of this and his previous experience on 3 December, it is not surprising that Flood decided not to make any further parliamentary speeches for a time. It was a good moment to take stock because the political landscape was dramatically changed a week later with the fall of the Fox-North coalition, and the appointment of William Pitt the Younger as prime minister. Anticipating that Flood would be hostile to the new administration, one of Lawrence Parsons' correspondents opined that Flood's 'stationary vigour' would 'easily scourge' Pitt's 'protean' rhetoric, but this was not Flood's intention. In fact, he held Pitt in higher esteem than he did Fox:

14 *Parl. Hist.*, xxiv, 113.   15 *Parl. Hist.*, xxiv, 111–17; Eden to Northington, 10 [recte 11] Dec. 1783 (B.L.,Pelham Papers, Add. Ms 33100 f 452).

The predilection of his mind ... were all on the side of Mr Pitt. He venerated the abilities and the character of his father. He disapproved of many passages in the public and private conduct of Mr Fox.[16]

Arising out of the change in government, there was speculation in Ireland in late December 1784 that Flood might be elevated to a ministry, but if he indulged any such hopes they were dashed by the fact that 'one party was too strong in numbers, ... the other too strong in abilities to court his aid'. Some hostile observers interpreted this as evidence that Flood 'stood isolated, without any person feeling an interest in his exertions or success', whereas it is more correct to say that he was free to determine his own position.[17] It was assumed in political circles that he was well-inclined towards Pitt, but since he voted with the coalition on a number of occasions in the early months of 1784, his allegiance was soon described as 'doubtful'. This troubled the duke of Chandos, who was rewarded for his support of Pitt with the office of Lord Steward and who was anxious that MPs in his interest should follow his lead.[18]

Events in Ireland, too, worked to Flood's disadvantage, as the Lord Lieutenant, Lord Northington, pressed ahead with his policy of replacing undependable patriots like Grattan, Forbes and Ogle with 'men of business' like John Foster, John Fitzgibbon and John Scott who could be depended upon to put the security of the Anglo-Irish connection above personal popularity. Flood was not entirely at ease with Northington's actions, though he was sufficiently realistic to acknowledge that an administration 'with a narrow basis that can be depended upon is better than a broader [one] that cannot'.[19] The reconstituted administration, for its part, did not conceal its pleasure that Flood's lack of impact at Westminster mirrored the ineffectiveness of the parliamentary opposition in Ireland. Isaac Corry continued to be its most active voice, but personal resentments as well as principled differences reduced it to a rump of little more than fifty by the spring of 1784.[20] This caused the administration (from February 1784 guided by the duke of Rutland and Thomas Orde) to conclude that they would have little difficulty repulsing an attempt by

16 [ ] to Parsons [Jan. 1784] (R.I.A., Burrowes Papers, Ms 23K53/10); Rosse Papers, C/14/1–5; see also, Prior, *Life of Malone*, p. 361.   17 *V.E.P.*, 24 Dec.; Flood's obituary, *Gentleman's Magazine*, 61 (1791), p. 1227; Flood, *Memoirs*, pp 231–2.   18 John Cannon, *The Fox-North coalition: crisis of the constitution* (Cambridge, 1969), pp 218 note 2; Paul Kelly, 'The establishment of Pitt's administration 1783–86' (D.Phil., Oxford, 1971), pp 18, 59, 116, 118; Macartney to Burke, 8 Mar. 1784 in Davies, ed., 'The private correspondence of Macartney', p. 226.   19 Kelly, *Prelude to Union*, pp 69–73; *D.E.P.*, 20 Nov. 1783; Flood to Parsons, 16 Jan. [1784] (Rosse Papers, C/8/1).   20 *V.E.P.*, 8, 15, 24, 27, 29 Jan., 14 Feb.; Drennan to McTier, 1784 (P.R.O.N.I., Drennan Papers, D765/1/137); Johnston, ed., 'Members of the Irish parliament', pp 206, 181; *Commons Jn.(Irl.)*, xi, 149, 152, 188, 194, 195; Northington to Sydney, 9 Feb. (B.L.,O.C., Northington letterbook, ff 80–2, 86–7); Charlemont to Corry, Feb. 1784 in *Life of Grattan*, ii, 193.

Flood or by anybody else to reanimate the issue of parliamentary reform though it was supported by petitions from twenty-two counties and eleven towns.[21]

Flood's absence in London meant he played no part in the preparation or presentation of the petitions of the freeholders of County Kilkenny or elsewhere. Because of this, it was anticipated that the task of presenting the case for reform in the Irish House of Commons would be assumed by William Brownlow. Some were convinced that Flood would be more effective, and an approach was made to him. Flood was delighted to be, as he put it, 'summoned' to return, though he did not arrive in time to attend the meeting of forty or so reformers at Lord Charlemont's Dublin house on 7 March at which it was agreed that the reform bill to be presented should be 'framed on the plan of the National Convention ... [but that] all allusion to that assembly should be studiously avoided'. His arrival three days later did not affect this decision but it did oblige Brownlow and Sir Edward Newenham, who was chosen in his absence to second the bill, to give way to him. It was a compliment Flood hardly deserved. But he was entrusted with the responsibility of presenting the bill because it was believed he was more likely than Brownlow or Newenham to convince wavering and undecided members by the power of his rhetoric of the necessity of parliamentary reform.[22]

Flood's first political action on his return was to attend the committee stage debate in the House of Commons on John Foster's corn bill on 10 March. One of the main purposes of this measure was to prevent a recurrence of the shortages that had contributed to the scarcity of grain in 1783, and with this in view it provided for a more flexible duty regimen than Flood had recommended in 1782 in order to facilitate importation at times of distress. At the same time, it maintained export bounties. The bill, in short, represented a more balanced attempt than Flood's legislation to encourage exportation when grain supplies were good, while facilitating importation during times of distress, and as a result it was warmly received by MPs and by mercantile bodies such as the Belfast Chamber of Commerce, who were acutely aware that events in 1783 had vindicated those who had warned that the price at which grain could be imported unencumbered by duty had been set too high in 1782.[23] Flood was not entirely happy with the proposed changes, but though he claimed he 'had something to offer on that subject', he made no attempt to do so because he did not anticipate he would be accorded a sympathetic hearing and because he feared it would distract attention from the more compelling issue of parliamentary reform.

21 *Parl. Reg.(Irl.)*, ii, 332–3, 344, 363, 381, 389–90, 402; Kelly, 'The parliamentary reform movement', pp 124–6; *Commons. Jn. (Irl.)*, xi, 204. 22 Flood to Chandos, 23 April in R[odd], ed., *Letters to Flood*, p. 153; Rutland to Sydney, 10, 14 Mar. in H.M.C., *Rutland*, iii, 79–80, H.O., 100/12 f 187; *V.E.P.*, 11 Mar.; *V.J.(D)*, 15, 17 Mar.; *D.E.P.*, 11 Mar. 1784. 23 Kelly, 'Scarcity and poor relief', pp 54–5; *Parl. Reg. (Irl.)*, ii, 289–91, iii, 1; Swift, *Dublin bakers*, pp 182–4; Petition of Belfast Chamber of Commerce, 14 Nov. 1783 (P.R.O.N.I., Belfast Chamber of Commerce Papers, D 1857/1/AB/1 ff 13–6).

Pursuant to notice, Flood moved for leave to bring in a bill for the 'more equal representation of the people in parliament' on 13 March. In accordance with the decision taken at Lord Charlemont's on 7 March, he justified the measure on the grounds that the public at large wanted the representative system reformed and that the purpose of the bill was to restore the constitution to pristine purity. As this suggests, Flood's speech was studiously moderate. He did not, at the same time, seek to conceal the fact that borough owners and others who benefitted from the existing abuses would be penalised if his bill was approved. But neither this, a heated exchange on Volunteering, nor Flood's pointed response to some of his critics injected any real passion into proceedings. The Castle interest was so secure numerically that MPs knew that Flood's bill stood no chance – a point underlined by John Scott when he indicated that the administration was prepared to allow the bill progress to its next stage, but no further:

> I believe every man who hears me, must concur in this, that the bill now permitted to be brought in, more from motives of civility to the decorous manner in which it is at present offered, and of respect due to the many petitions of those at whose desire it is introduced, than from any possible idea of the propriety of the requisitions which those petitions contain; it is permitted to be introduced with an hope of convincing the petitioners that they are wrong, rather than from any the least intentions to yield to their ill-timed opportunity.[24]

This effectively sealed the fate of the reform bill. What was more perturbing for Flood personally was the fact that an attempt by him to take the floor late in the debate 'was cried down by the clamour of the whole house' and ruled out of order by the Speaker. Flood was not used to being bound by the convention that MPs should speak once and no more during a debate. But encouraged by the successful application of this rule at Westminster, the Castle interest in Ireland vowed to curb his influence by limiting his freedom to speak at will, and there was optimism in official circles following the 13 March debate that the 'wretched figure' he had cut on that occasion would 'repress his insolence'.[25]

Realising there was nothing to be gained by challenging the numerically preponderant Castle interest at every opportunity, Flood enquired from officials during the first reading of the reform bill on 18 March when they intended opposing the measure. Informed that it would 'not be suffered to enter into ... committee', he determined to make a stand during the second stage debate.[26] This was postponed for 24 hours to 20 March to facilitate him, but when he took his place on that day he simply prefaced his motion that the reform bill should be committed with a request

---

24 *Parl. Reg. (Irl.)*, iii, 13–23; *Commons Jn. (Irl.)*, xi, 227.   25 *Parl. Reg. (Irl.)*, iii, 22–3; Mornington to Grenville, 16 Mar. 1784 in H.M.C., *Fortescue*, i, 226.   26 *Parl. Reg. (Irl.)*, iii, 37, 40; *Commons Jn. (Irl.)*, xi, 234; *V.E.P.*, 20 Mar. 1784.

that all petitions in favour of such a measure should be laid on the Commons' table. This was unusual, but Flood calculated that he would make a greater impression if he reserved the one major speech he anticipated he would be allowed to make until after he had heard the Castle spokesmen. Meanwhile, he was obliged to endure a host of homiletic appeals to use his influence to calm 'the people whom he had agitated, and [to inform] them that they lived under a constitution which approached nearer to perfection than any the annals of the world could suggest'. More perturbingly, when Brownlow and he claimed that the reform bill was 'brought in at the general desire of the whole nation', they were greeted with a chorus of 'no no' from the Castle benches. When Flood took the floor, he cited the large number of counties that had petitioned in favour of the bill in support of his contention, pointed out deficiencies in the arguments of his opponents and rehearsed the well-known arguments in favour of parliamentary reform, but it registered little impact. According to one hostile observer, his speech 'was as dull as a tired horse', and while this is unfair, he was doubtlessly inhibited by the fact that he did not possess the freedom to speak at will he traditionally enjoyed. He did seek, towards the end of the debate, to respond separately to a particularly vehement censure of his bill by Denis Daly, but he was prevented from doing so by the orchestrated opposition of the Castle interest guided by John Foster. It was no surprise that his motion was rejected, 159 votes to 85.[27]

This was a significant setback given that Flood had returned to Dublin specifically to advance the reform bill. This was emphasised by the ruthless way in which the Castle phalanx, guided by John Foster and John Fitzgibbon, used the rules of the House to thwart him. It would be wrong, at the same time, to interpret this reversal, following so soon after his failures at Westminster in December 1783, as bringing the curtain down on the career on one of the finest orators the Irish parliament produced in the eighteenth century. However, it did signal the end of the period of dominance he had enjoyed since his dismissal from office in 1781, though the decisive factor was less the restrictions on his freedom to speak his mind than the lack of impact of his speeches when he did. One commentator claimed that the 'fire, which used to animate his former philippics' was visibly absent in the House of Commons debate on 20 March; another noted that he was no longer 'as formidable as he thinks himself'. Flood's speech was certainly not his finest, but the negative perception was due more to the altered political mood in both kingdoms than to any decline in his faculties. What was irrefutable was that his plan to combine a political career at Westminster and at College Green had begun badly, and that his public reputation suffered proportionately.[28] The fact that he had to hurry back to

27 *Parl. Reg.(Irl.)*, iii, 43–85 (Flood's speech is on pages 78 to 82); Orde to Nepean, 21 Mar., Rutland to Sydney, 22 Mar. (P.R.O.,H.O.,100/12 ff 201–8); *Commons Jn.(Irl.)*, xi, 238; Cooke to Eden, 21 Mar. 1783 (B.L., Auckland Papers, Add. Ms 34419 ff 367–9). 28 *V.E.P.*, 23 Mar., 15, 27 Apr., 11 May; Barnard to Buckinghamshire, 25 Mar. 1784 (N.L.I., Heron Papers, Ms 13047/3).

England shortly after the reform bill was rejected at College Green emphasises just how demanding it was to sustain an active political career in both legislatures.

ELECTORAL PROBLEMS AT WESTMINSTER

Flood's precipitate, and publicly criticised,[29] departure from Ireland was prompted by the dissolution of the Westminster parliament. Ever since the controversial eclipse of the Fox-North coalition in late December, William Pitt had been entrusted with the responsibility of government, but he did not have a majority in the Commons. Because of this and the manner of his appointment, the general election was fought with exceptional passion in open constituencies, while borough proprietors everywhere went to great lengths to ensure that their nominees reflected their own political attitudes.[30] This spelled problems for Flood, whose determination to remain independent of all parties and factions put him on a collision course with the duke of Chandos.

As an officeholder in Pitt's government, Chandos did not conceal his displeasure at Flood's decision to switch from voting with William Pitt in December 1783 to Charles James Fox in February 1784.[31] Though it can be assumed that Flood's decision was prompted by his unease with the behaviour of Pitt and George III, it angered the people of Winchester and caused Chandos who had, Flood later maintained, previously informed him that his seat was safe, to review his commitment. The duke was eager to return 'a steady friend' to the new Prime Minister for his share of the borough of Winchester.[32] This was incompatible with Flood's insistence on maintaining his independence of action, but because Chandos said nothing to him prior to his departure for Ireland, he assumed the assurance he had received stood and he was taken aback when, following the dissolution of parliament, he received a letter from Chandos, dated 24 March, informing him that he would not be returned for Winchester. Determined to ensure that the duke honoured his commitment to him, Flood set out for England without delay, but when he arrived in London on 5 April, he was already too late to influence the outcome. Three days earlier, Chandos had overseen the election of his brother-in-law, Richard Gamon, who had been his choice to represent the borough before he had been tempted by Flood. This was as conclusive a *fait accompli* as it was possible to face, and anyone less resolute than Flood would have acknowledged defeat. He requested Edmond Malone to inform the duke that he had made a binding verbal agreement with him

29 *V.E.P.*, 27 Apr., 11 May 1784. 30 Kelly, 'The establishment of Pitt's administration', part 2. 31 Kelly, 'The establishment of Pitt's administration', p. 118. 32 W.T. Laprade, ed, 'The parliamentary papers of John Robinson', *Camden*, third series, xxxiii (1922), p. 88; Flood, *Memoirs*, p. 292; Chandos to Flood, 13 Apr. in R[odd], ed., *Letters to Flood*, p. 140; The draft of this letter is in Henry Huntington Library, Chandos Papers, STB, Box 10, no. 60).

in 1783 that he would continue to represent Winchester. Malone did as instructed on the morning of 6 April. Following this, Chandos, who was anxious to facilitate Flood in whatever way he could, called on him at his Cleveland Row apartments. No account of the meeting exists, but from a letter he sent Chandos four days later in which he put on record his demands and expectations, it is clear that Flood was unyielding; the duke had breached their understanding, he alleged, and he was honour bound to set this right.[33]

According to Flood, Chandos' promise to him of 'the first vacancy to which he could recommend' (made in the summer of 1782) was realised in September 1783 when the duke offered to nominate him to represent the borough of Winchester. It was then, 'for the first time', that he learned of Chandos' long term 'engagement to the Duchess for her brother, Mr Gamon', but he had concluded that it was no more as 'the Duchess was pleased readily to relinquish that engagement and repeatedly to declare that she wished Mr Flood to represent Winchester for life'. It was at this point also, Flood reminded the duke, that he had stipulated that 'he could not enter parliament but as a free representative' and that he had agreed to vacate the seat at Winchester if requested to do so provided an *alternative* 'could be found by his Grace'. The fall of the Coalition had, he acknowledged, complicated matters but 'not a hint ever fell that his Grace had any intention to have Mr Gamon returned for Winchester' or that it was incumbent upon him to 'look for a seat elsewhere'. As far as Flood was concerned, he had a binding agreement with Chandos, and he cited the fact that prior to his departure for Ireland he had set matters in train, 'by his Grace's desire', to secure his electoral representation for the constituency in the event of an election, in support of his interpretation of events.[34]

This ostensibly complete account of what had passed between the two men seemed to leave Chandos with little room for manoeuvre. His options were reduced further by Flood's invocation of 'his honour' and by his insistence that Chandos returned him for Winchester within fourteen days of the opening of the new parliament 'unless or until another return can be obtained, Mr Flood bearing the expence'.[35] Chandos took a few days to compose a reply. He consulted with his law agent, who was party to his discussions with Flood in 1783, to establish if his recollection of events coincided with his own and, happy that this was so and that he had behaved entirely properly, he 'endeavour[ed] to put his position as clearly as possible' in his reply of 13 April. In this, he explicitly affirmed that while he was of the view in 1783 that 'he was equally serving Mr Flood and the public' by recommending him as a proper representative for Winchester, his intention was that Flood

---

33 Malone to Flood, 15 Apr. in R[odd], ed., *Letters to Flood*, p. 146; Flood to Chandos, 10 Apr. (Henry Huntington Library, Chandos Papers, STB, Box 10 no. 47); the letter is printed in R[odd], op. cit., pp 136–7. **34** Flood to Chandos, 10 Apr. (Henry Huntington Library, Chandos Papers, STB, Box 10 no. 47). **35** Notes from Flood to Chandos, copy of notes of Flood re Winchester [Apr. 1784] (Rosse Papers, C/8/2, 3).

should not sit for the constituency 'for a longer period than the then session of parliament' because of his promise to Richard Gamon. Moreover, it was his understanding that they had agreed 'that whenever the conduct of Mr Flood did not meet with approbation, he would instantly accept of the Chiltern Hundreds and vacate his seat, without any condition whatever, or without ever mentioning that it should be on the duke's finding another seat'. This conflicted with Flood's account, but encouraged by the recollection of his agent, which supported his own memory, Chandos reiterated that while he was eager 'to serve' Flood, 'consistent with his claims of his own family' and was happy he should behave as 'a free representative', he had 'never stipulated, or promised to secure [him] a seat in another parliament'.[36]

If this account of what had passed between Flood and Chandos prior to the former's election in 1783 indicated that the duke was within his rights not to return Flood for Winchester in March 1784, the picture was muddied by his account of his meetings with Flood late in 1783 and early in 1784 for he conceded that it had been his intention then 'to recommend' Flood to represent Winchester for another term. However, he insisted this did not supersede their agreement that Flood 'would vacate his seat when his conduct was not approved'. He did not go so far as to state explicitly that Flood's voting record in early 1784 demanded that he should do so, but his allusion to 'Mr Flood's conduct having displeased his constituents' indicates that if this was not his own view it was the conclusion of the voters of Winchester. This interpretation is reinforced by Chandos' affirmation that if Flood had been in England when the election was called he 'would have desired the duke not to recommend him again', because to do so would cause Chandos to 'risk ... losing his own interest and disobliging his friends' in the constituency. This was wishful thinking on Chandos' part. But the duke was clearly anxious to resolve the dispute without further ill-feeling because he reiterated his pledge 'to assist Mr Flood in his present wish for a seat in parliament as far as possible', though the fact that it was accompanied by a protestation that it was not in his power to obtain an alternative seat diminished its impact.[37]

Flood was not appeased by such assurances. Like Chandos, he sought not to offer gratuitous offence, but he remained utterly convinced that he was in the right. In his response, dated 15 April, he rejected the duke's claim that the voters of Winchester did not want him as their MP and dismissed the evidence of his law agent as irrelevant because it related to a period 'antecedent by a year to those expressions and events which governs the present occasion'. Maintaining this assertive tone, he contended that he sat for Winchester as a 'free representative', and that he could not be expected to vacate the constituency without having 'another seat'. And, he af-

36 Chandos to Flood, 11, 13 Apr. in R[odd], ed., *Letters to Flood*, p. 138, Henry Huntington Library, Chandos Papers, STB, Box 10 no. 60.   37 Chandos to Flood, 13 Apr. 1784 (Henry Huntington Library, Chandos Papers, STB, Box 10 no. 60).

firmed that as a man of honour it behoved Chandos to 'adher[e] to his own explicit declarations' made during the winter of 1783–4 and return him for Winchester:

> The duke, in his letter, admits that both *before* and *after* Christmas last his Grace intended to bring Flood in for Winchester; it is clear, therefore, that then his Grace was *not engaged* to Mr Gamon. On the 10th of March last, about a fortnight before the dissolution, the duke wrote a friendly letter to Mr Flood to Ireland, but made no mention of this change of sentiment. Is it just, that, at so late a period, engagements should be taken regardless of Mr Flood, without communication with him, and without any notice to look elsewhere; or any care on the part of the duke and of his agent to provide a substitute for the seat so to be taken away from Mr Flood, contrary to his confessedly just and grounded expectations? If such declarations are of no weight in matter of honourable engagement, what can constitute claim, or establish security?[38]

As this attests, Flood and Chandos were now locked into an increasingly intractable dispute. Flood acknowledged this when he conceded on 15 April 'that there cannot be two sentiments finally with respect' to Winchester. It certainly seemed unlikely that the difference could be settled amicably, and it may have been this that caused Edmond Malone to withdraw as Flood's representative at this point.[39] His place was taken by the irascible earl of Bellamont, who had fought a celebrated duel with Lord Townshend in 1773. He was anxious not to become embroiled in another controversial affair. For this reason, he sought prior assurances from Flood 'that no word, sentence, or implication was contained in your letter liable to give umbrage' and, when this was not immediately forthcoming, he delayed delivering Flood's letter of 15 April for four days. As this attests, Bellamont's priority was not to advance Flood's cause but to defuse his simmering dispute with Chandos, and he believed he had made progress because he reported back from his meeting with the duke on 19 April that the way was now clear for the two principals to meet 'upon a more conciliatory footing'.[40] Flood was not pleased. He had directed Bellamont to inform Chandos that he required a 'precise answer', and when he gleaned that Bellamont had not done as requested, he reiterated his instruction. Bellamont was disinclined to oblige. He was, he affirmed, determined not to become implicated in 'your ultimatum' and, realising that he could only do so if he withdrew completely, he informed both principals of his decision on 21 April. This produced an exchange of correspondence between Flood and Bellamont in which Flood sought to per-

---

38 Chandos to Flood, 15 Apr. 1784 (Henry Huntington Library, Chandos Papers, STB, Box 10 no. 48). Flood's copy is in R[odd], ed., *Letters to Flood*, pp 141–5. 39 Ibid.; Malone to Flood, 15, 16 Apr. 1784 in R[odd], ed., *Letters to Flood*, p. 146, B.L.,O.C., Malone files. 40 Kelly, *That damn'd thing called honour*, pp 106–11; Bellamont to Flood, 19, 27 Apr. 1784 in R[odd], ed., *Letters to Flood*, pp 147, 157–8.

suade the peer, if he was determined to withdraw, to do so 'in the manner least injurious to my cause' but Bellamont was immovable.[41]

Flood's exchanges with Bellamont stuttered on for a week or so,[42] but it had no further bearing on his row with Chandos which intensified on 22 April when he received his most curt communication to date from that quarter. In this, Chandos avowed that 'he never intended to pledge or bind himself to ... assist Mr Flood at Winchester for a longer period than that session', and pronounced that he 'had it never in his idea to promise ... Flood [another] seat on ... [his] vacating' the borough; his departure was expected to be 'unconditional'. He was also more explicit in his commitment to Richard Gamon. He would not, he pronounced pointedly, 'sacrifice his own family and connections' and endanger 'his interest in Winchester' by nominating Flood whom 'most of his friends [in the borough] were determined not to re-elect'.[43]

This, inevitably, produced a further exchange of letters in which Flood accused Chandos of a lack of candour and the duke admitted that he had been prompted to suggest in December 1783 that Flood could continue to represent Winchester by the erroneous expectation that 'he might probably come into office'.[44] With an amicable solution to the dispute receding, Flood was faced with the choice of escalating it into a public affair of honour or backing down. His instincts propelled him in the former direction, and in his response to Chandos' communication of 26 April he dismissed the reference to his accepting office as irrelevant and accused him of a breach of faith:

> Mr Flood is free to say that intentions repeatedly declared in serious matters, and between serious men, embarking persons of a certain description in concerns of depth and moment, affecting their whole situation, held on to the last moment, and until opportunities are lost that cannot be retrieved; he is free to say, that in his mind, and as he conceives in that of all mankind, such circumstances do constitute a serious ground of obligation to all the feelings of honor. To those feelings in his Grace's breast Mr Flood has confidently appealed, and to those feelings he wishes to give the freest scope.[45]

The way was now clear for the duke of Chandos to challenge Flood to a duel but, as he had been careful to do throughout the dispute, Chandos contrived not to take

---

41 Bellamont to Flood, 21, 27 Apr., Flood to Bellamont, 21, 22 Apr.in R[odd], ed., *Letters to Flood*, pp 147–51, 157–9; Chandos to Bellamont, 21 Apr. 1784 (N.L.I., Buckingham Papers, Joly Ms 39 f 50). 42 Bellamont to Flood, 23, 29 Apr., Flood to Bellamont, 23, 29 Apr. 1784 in R[odd], ed., *Letters to Flood*, pp 154–5, 161–2. 43 Chandos to Flood (draft), [19–22] Apr., 22 Apr. (Henry Huntington Library, Chandos Papers, STB, Box 10 nos 64, 61). The latter is printed in R[odd], ed., *Letters to Flood*, pp 151–2. 44 Flood to Chandos, 23 Apr., Chandos to Flood, 26 Apr. in R[odd] ed., *Letters to Flood*, pp 153, 155–5 and draft in Chandos Papers, STD, Box 10 no. 62. 45 Flood to Chandos, 27 Apr. 1784 in R[odd], ed., *Letters to Flood*, p. 160, Chandos Papers, STB, Box 10 no. 50.

offence. Quite the opposite; he concluded his reply of 1 May with further expressions of his 'wish to accommodate Mr Flood to the utmost of his power from principles of friendship and regard'. Flood was unimpressed. He believed that a duel was the only honourable solution and he invited Lawrence Parsons to act on his behalf.[46]

Parsons' first step was to invite Chandos' law agent to deliver on the promise that Flood should be given a parliamentary seat. He replied that Flood's expectation of 'a free seat' was unrealisable without a personal recommendation from William Pitt, but that he believed a seat was to be had for between £3,500 and £4,000. This was clearly inadequate, so Flood prepared an ostensible letter to Parsons on 19 May in which he contended that it was 'not the value of a seat but superior feelings that actuate me'. He did not, he pronounced ominously, want to fight Chandos, but if his injured 'feelings' were not vindicated, he would have no option but to defend his honour in the traditional manner.[47] This was not a formal challenge (though it did contain the implication that in the absence of a satisfactory solution a challenge would follow) and Chandos responded, as he had done throughout, by reaffirming his commitment 'to assist Flood as far as lay in his power'. With this in mind, he requested that Flood should wait until the opening of the new session to see if a suitable parliamentary vacancy arose. Since it was important that he was seen to behave properly in a dispute that had already attracted the attention of caricaturists Flood did as requested, but when no progress was made he instructed Parsons on 12 June to re-present his letter of 19 May with a 'postscript' in which he alleged 'that the duke of Chandos had acted dishonourably by him'. This was the ultimatum Flood had been putting off for some time, and he was so sure that it would provoke the challenge he sought to provoke the duke into delivering, he instructed Parsons that 'on the duke's desiring personal *satisfaction*, to appoint the *shortest* day, as Mr Flood was obliged to return to Ireland the week following'. However, Chandos remained as determined as ever to avoid a trial by arms. He 'repeat[ed] what he had already said before on several occasions – that he was ready to give Mr Flood every assistance in his power to procure him a seat in parliament'. Anticipating that this would not satisfy Flood, Parsons indicated that 'he might have something *further to add*', but Chandos' determination to avoid duelling meant there was no point.[48] Flood left London in the middle of June without any hope of representing Winchester. He did not accept this was the end of his Westminster career, however,

46 Chandos to Flood, 1 May, Flood to Chandos, 1 May 1784 in R[odd], ed., *Letters to Flood*, pp 163–4 (The original of the latter is in Chandos Papers, STB, Box 10 no. 51.); Ms list of the Irish parliament, 1783 (N.L.I., Ms 2098); Johnston, ed., 'Members of the Irish parliament 1784–7', p. 197; Marianne Elliott, *Wolfe Tone: prophet of Irish independence* (Yale, 1989), p. 81.   47 Memorandum by Parsons, post 4 May, Flood to Parsons, 19 May 1784 (Rosse Papers, C/8/4, 5).   48 George, ed., *Catalogue of political and personal satires*, vi, 6607; A memorandum of Sir Lawrence Parsons, 12 June 1784 in R[odd], ed., *Letters to Flood*, pp 164–5, Rosse Papers, C/8/8.

because, prior to his departure, he requested Parsons to explore the possibility of his securing the representation for the vacant cinque port of Seaford.[49]

FURTHER DISAPPOINTMENTS

Flood sought to press his dispute with the duke of Chandos to a conclusion in May/ June 1784 because he had agreed to act as reviewing general to the Connacht Volunteers in July. Pursuant to this promise, he attended the south Connacht review at Galway on the fifth and the north Connacht review at Boyle seventeen days later, but the organization he encountered was already a pale shadow of that which had played so decisive a part in Irish politics between 1779 and 1783. Membership had fallen dramatically, while the question of parliamentary reform had caused such controversy that Lord Charlemont, their commander-in-chief, instructed all corps to confine themselves to less contentious matters.[50]

Despite this, middle-class reformers in Dublin and Ulster refused to forsake the issue, and they came together in early June to launch a new campaign. They were more radically-minded than their predecessors because they included Catholic enfranchisement on their agenda, but their major initiative was to call upon reformers throughout the country to nominate delegates for a reform 'congress' which was calendared to meet in October.[51] Flood was not involved at this stage. The fact that his antipathy to Catholic enfranchisement was highlighted (at his request, one hostile newspaper maintained) in the press suggests that he was not happy with this aspect of their programme. However if this was so, it did not prevent him from supporting the campaign; he signed the requisition requesting the sheriff of County Kilkenny to convene a meeting of freeholders to endorse parliamentary reform and to choose five delegates to represent the county. Subsequently, when the county aristocratic interest, led by John Ponsonby and Lord Clifden, persuaded the High Sheriff to decline the request, he participated in the meetings held in Kilkenny in August which chose four delegates (of whom he was one) to represent the city and five to represent the county. Flood's critics countered by claiming that his involvement with the reform movement in County Kilkenny was selfishly motivated. Lord Clifden avowed that his object was to ensure the nomination of delegates with views similar to his own 'in order to shew government what power he has among the gentry and ... sell them at the best market he can'.[52] This was patently untrue, but

49 Parsons to Chandos, 1 June, Flood to Parsons, 18 June (Rosse Papers, C/8/7, 9).   50 P. O'Snoddy, 'Notes on the Volunteers ... of County Roscommon', *Irish Sword*, xii (1975–6), pp 27–8; *V.E.P.*, 29 Jun.; *D.E.P.*, 28 Jun. 1784. Mitchell, 'Colonel William Persee', *J.G.H.A.S.*, xxx (1963), p. 74; and for the Volunteers generally, Kelly, 'The Volunteers in 1784', pp 272–82.   51 Kelly, 'Parliamentary reform', pp 205–9.   52 Clifden to Orde, 15 Aug., Ponsonby to Orde, 19 Aug. (N.L.I., Bolton Papers, Ms 16350/5,

the fact that Flood had not changed his views on the subject of Catholic enfranchisement and that he still conceived of himself as the leader of reform in parliament encouraged such perceptions.

One of the main reasons why Flood was singled out for aspersion by those opposed to parliamentary reform was because his involvement gave this overwhelmingly middle class campaign respectability.[53] It was insufficient to give the movement the momentum necessary to triumph over the concerted opposition of the Castle authorities and established borough interests, however, and a mere forty delegates turned up at the Exchange rooms in South William Street for the reform Congress on 25 October. Flood was among their number, and his appearance 'was received by the populace who had assembled ... with three cheers'. The crowd was too excitable and the critics of the Congress too numerous for the delegates to conduct their business in public view, and since no formal record of its proceedings was maintained, it is not possible to analyze what transpired with any confidence. It may be significant that William Sharman, the MP for Lisburn, and not Flood was chosen to chair the meeting. However, since James Napper Tandy, the leading Dublin activist, reported to his brother that 'Flood [is] strongly with us', it can be assumed that he did not seek to subordinate the Congress' agenda to his own.[54]

Flood possessed firm ideas as to what the Congress should accomplish, nonetheless. As a priority, he wanted it to change its name to 'the assembly of delegates for promoting a parliamentary reform' in order to obviate unfavourable comparisons with its American predecessor.[55] More significantly, he urged the assembled delegates to concentrate on 'vindicat[ing]' themselves and not 'entering into new matter'. Both recommendations were acceded to following which the assembly endorsed the programme of reform he had piloted through the Grand National Convention in 1783. It is at this point that the accounts of proceedings conflict. The Castle press maintained that Flood spoke against the embrace of Catholic enfranchisement, but Flood's own account suggests it was not discussed, and that debate centred on a number of resolutions, possibly drafted by him, the most significant of which was that the assembly should adjourn until 28 January 1785 to allow those counties and cities which had not elected delegates to do so.[56] This was a logical

6); Report on meeting ... Kilkenny (Oireachtas Library, Ms 8 H 10, pp 42–5); Methodized abridgement ... Kilkenny (Bolton Papers, Ms 15958/1); Kelly, 'Parliamentary reform', p. 243; *V.E.P.*, 22 July, 24 Aug.; Orde to Pitt, 16 Aug. 1784 (Ms 16355 ff 1–4). **53** *D.E.P.*, 4 Sept.; *V.E.P.*, 16 Sept., 7 Oct. and *passim* 1784 **54** *V.E.P.*, 26 Oct.; *D.E.P.*, 26 Oct.; James to George Tandy [25 Oct] (P.R.O., Chatham Papers, 30/8/330 f 270); Joy to [ ], 26 Oct.(30/8/328 ff 221–2); Rutland to Sydney, 25 Oct. (P.R.O., H.O.,100/14 ff 195–7); Orde to Putt, 24 Oct. 1784 (N.L.I., Bolton Papers, Ms 16358 ff 151–5). **55** *V.E.P.*, 12 Oct.; Flood to Parsons, 30 Oct. 1784 (Rosse Papers, C/8/15). **56** Flood to Parsons, 26, 30 Oct.(Rosse Papers, C/8/ 14, 15); *A candid review of the most important occurrences that took place in Ireland during the last three years* (Dublin, 1787), p. 8; *V.E.P.*, 2 Nov.; Mac Nevin, *History of the Volunteers*, p. 211; Extract of a letter from Dublin, 29 Oct. (P.R.O., H.O., 100/14 ff 211–12); Kelly, 'Parliamentary reform', pp 287–9; Orde to Pitt, 24 Oct. 1784 (N.L.I., Bolton Papers, Ms 16358 ff 147–55).

course of action, but it did not please all. The Presbyterian radical, William Drennan was deeply disappointed that the resolutions of the meeting were so tame. They should, he pronounced, 'have sounded throughout the nation like the last trumpet' in order to ignite 'the people in the largest sense of the word', though he was fully aware this was not Flood's style.[57] Moreover, for all his limitations as a popular politician, it was Flood's presence which conferred on the Congress the modicum of respectability it garnered and who was most harshly criticised as a consequence. The Chief Secretary, Thomas Orde, described him in November as 'the most stupid blockhead that ever existed' simply because he attended the Congress, while the Castle press grasped at every opportunity to abuse him and his fellow delegates.[58]

Their most telling accusation was that Flood withdrew from the assembly in a huff before it had completed its deliberations because he disagreed with the pro-Catholic wishes of a majority of delegates. This was untrue. Flood returned to Farmley once the assembly adjourned, as he had always intended. Enthusiasts like William Drennan understandably wanted him to take a more active role in promulgating the reform message, but he had other priorities. He did accept membership of the Constitutional Society established in Dublin in November 'to support the constitution in its original form' but he appears not to have attended any of its meetings.[59] Moreover, Flood's withdrawal was counterproductive given his decision to remain in Ireland for the first annual meeting of the Irish parliament which was scheduled to commence in January 1785. This was not a prospect that excited Flood. Indeed, it brought home to him just how much he had lost as a result of the duke of Chandos' treachery with the result that he instructed Parsons in December to 'see the duke ... and tell him I shall publish our correspondence with observations, but before I do so, will give him the satisfaction of arms whenever he pleases'. As he had done before, Chandos ignored the invitation to fight, with the result that Flood was reduced to belittling and ridiculing the recalcitrant peer.[60]

As this belated attempt to animate his dispute with Chandos highlights, Flood remained eager to secure Westminster representation, and the Sussex port of Seaford, which had been brought to his notice shortly before he set out for Ireland in June, offered the most hopeful prospect of success. Historically, control of Seaford had oscillated between Whig grandees and the Treasury. The duke of Newcastle's command of the borough in the mid-eighteenth century rested on his ability to restrict the number of voters, while the ascendancy of the treasury interest, which became the pre-eminent force in the constituency in the early 1760s, was based upon the

57 Drennan to Bruce, Nov. 1784 (P.R.O.N.I., Drennan-Bruce letters, D 553 no 34).   58 Extract of a letter from Dublin, 29 Oct. (P.R.O., H.O., 100/14 ff 211–12); Orde to Pitt, 24 Oct., 6 Nov. (N.L.I., Bolton Papers, Ms 16358 ff 147–55, 61–7); *V.E.P.*, 26, 30 Oct., 4, 6 Nov.; *D.E.P.*, 27 Nov. 1784.   59 *V.J.(D)*, 24 Nov., 3 Dec.; *V.E.P.*, 4, 6 Nov.; *D.E.P.*, 30 Oct. 1784.   60 Flood to Parsons, 25 Nov. 8, 30 Dec. 1784 (Rosse Papers, C/8/18, 19, 20).

substantial number of customs and excise officers among the small electorate. There was, also, an active independent interest which contrived, unsuccessfully, to make the borough more responsive to the interests of the town's residents, though it was not sufficiently well-placed to figure prominently in the contest between the Pelham and treasury candidates in 1784. Only one vote separated the four candidates when the poll closed with the result that the return was appealed to the House of Commons. They did not get round to deciding that the election should be voided and a new contest scheduled until March 1785, which was some time after the withdrawal of one candidate ensured that there was likely to be one vacant seat whatever the Commons' decision and, anticipating this, the various interested parties set about jockeying for position.[61]

Given its unusual electoral profile and history, Seaford did not seem the kind of constituency in which Henry Flood would prosper. However, Thomas Oldfield, the reform activist and author, was sufficiently impressed by his support for reform in Ireland to conclude that he was the person to lead a drive to deprive vested interests of control of the borough. This was a burning issue with Oldfield, who was appalled that the borough franchise, which the House of Commons in 1670 had vested 'in the populacy' (defined in 1761 to mean the 'inhabitant housekeepers paying scot and lot'), had been so attenuated by privileged self-interest that the number of voters in 1784 was a modest twenty-four. Oldfield's goal was to ensure that 'the inhabitant housekeepers', whose disfranchisement had been achieved by the simple device of omitting their 'names... from the poor rate', were restored and he anticipated that Flood's involvement would facilitate this.[62]

Flood, for his part, had few expectations that Seaford would provide him with the parliamentary seat he so desired. However, since he calculated that his candidature would cost him a modest £50, when the going rate for a borough seat (which he was prepared to pay) was £5,000, he had little to lose. So prior to his return to Ireland in June, he instructed Lawrence Parsons to enquire from the duke of Chandos if he would help him secure the eight votes promised to Thomas Alves, one of the Pelham candidates.[63] It is not clear how Chandos respond, but Flood's hopes rose once an agreement was reached with the Pelhams that 'he [Pelham] would vote for me against [Lord] Mountmorres [the new ministerial nominee] and in preference to any but his own candidate'.[64] The key to success, Oldfield insisted, was to broaden

61 Namier and Brooke, eds, *The House of Commons*, i, 454–6; T.H.B. Oldfield, *The representative history of Great Britain and Ireland* (6 vols, London, 1816), v, 349 ff, 441–53; Laprade, ed., 'Papers of John Robinson', p. 80; *Parl.Hist.*, xxiv, 795.   62 Oldfield, *Representative history*, v, 438–9, 441–53; Flood to Parsons, 24 July 1787 (Rosse Papers, C/8/38); E.C.Black, *The association: British extra-parliamentary political organization 1769–93* (London, 1963), pp 283–4; Haliday to Charlemont, 25 Oct.1792 in H.M.C., *Charlemont*, ii, 201.   63 Namier and Brooke, *The House of Commons*, i, 448; Oldfield, *Representative history*, v, 454; Mornington to Rutland, 31 May in H.M.C., *Rutland*, iii, 100; Parsons to Chandos, 1 June, 1784, Flood to Parsons, 24 July 1787 (Rosse Papers, C/8/7).   64 Orde to Rutland, 9 June in H.M.C., *Rutland*, iii, 105; Flood to Parsons, 18 June, 27 July 1784 (Rosse Papers, C/8/9, 10).

the electorate by ensuring the enfranchisement of 'as many of our club as possible'; with this in view he initiated legal proceedings to overturn the exclusion of non-rated inhabitants at the October quarter sessions on the grounds that it was enforced 'to answer election purposes'. This was rejected on procedural grounds, but Flood did not withdraw his candidacy. He was kept apprised of developments by Parsons, to whom he regularly sent instructions. This was hardly an ideal arrangement, but since the House of Commons was in no hurry to determine the outcome to the 1784 election and he did not entertain high hopes of success, Flood was happy to let matter develop. Meanwhile, he occupied himself with Irish politics.[65]

THE COMMERCIAL PROPOSITIONS

In sharp contrast to Flood and others on the opposition benches, Dublin Castle approached the 1785 session in a positive frame of mind. They retained the allegiance of a large majority of MPs, and they were confident that this would enable them to withstand any attempt Flood might make to forward parliamentary reform and to overcome his anticipated opposition to their plan to replace the Volunteers with a Protestant militia under government control. In fact, the main obstacle the administration had to negotiate on this was not provided by Flood but by the Prime Minister. Pitt was uneasy lest the proposed abolition of the Volunteers endangered his main objective of the session – the implementation of a commercial union which would bind Britain and Ireland in mutual economic interest and, thereby, dilute the impact and implications of the constitutional changes agreed in 1782–3. Flood's opposition to any attempt to weaken the constitutional settlement agreed in 1782–3 was assured. But he was not without hopes of Pitt because of his known support for parliamentary reform, and rumours that Pitt favoured the implementation in Ireland of a modest plan of 'Protestant' reform in order to bolster the confidence of the protestant middle classes in parliamentary government encouraged him to believe that the first annual session of the Irish parliament might be an important event in his as well as Irish political life.[66]

If Pitt's legislative agenda promised to provide Flood with plenty of opportunity to demonstrate that reports of his decline were exaggerated, the fact that neither the administration nor the few dejected figures who attempted, without success, to in-

65 Flood to Parsons, 30, 31 Oct., 5, 25 Nov., 8, 21, 30 Dec. 1784, early 1785, 25 [Jan./Feb.], 26 Feb. 1785 (Rosse Papers, C/8/15–24). O'Brien is wrong therefore to suggest that Flood was 'handicapped by his not infrequent absences in London during the [1785] session' (O'Brien, *Anglo-Irish politics*, p. 101).   66 Pitt to Orde, 12 Jan. in Lord Mahon, ed., *The correspondence between William Pitt and Charles, Duke of Rutland* (London, 1890), pp 86–7; Cabinet minute, 13 Jan. in A. Aspinall, ed., *The later correspondence of George III* (5 vols, Cambridge, 1962–70), i, 127; Cabinet minute of 10 Jan. (N.L.I., Sydney Papers, Ms 52/P/4); Sydney to Rutland, 11 Jan., Rutland to Sydney, 13 Jan. 1785 (P.R.O., H.O.,100/16 ff 43); Kelly, *Prelude to Union*, p. 105.

stil some coherence and commitment into the patriots' disjointed ranks invited his support indicated that he had much to prove.[67] The opening weeks of the session certainly produced little to lift his spirits or those of other opposition figures as the administration easily prevailed in every debate. Flood observed this with such dismay that it caused him, 'the obstinate independent', to conclude that more co-ordinated opposition was necessary if parliament was to exercise any control over the executive and to maintain public liberties:

> Mr Flood said ... he knew of no opposition. There were some independent, incoherent gentlemen, who sometimes when they thought administration wrong, opposed them; and when they thought them right agreed with them. In England, there was an opposition; because there were men who agreed to do every thing to turn out the ministers, and to get into their places; but that was not the case here. He believed it would be better if there was an opposition; for a great writer had said that the liberty of England had been preserved by great and able men going with a faction.[68]

Despite the obvious weakness of the opposition, Flood was determined to do what he could to advance parliamentary reform. However, before he was to receive an opportunity to do this, he was to find himself embarked on a rearguard action to resist the attempts of the administration to advance measures aimed at further weakening popular patriotism and implementing Pitt's plan to mitigate the implications of the commercial and constitutional reforms implemented since 1778.

Flood was absent on the opening day of the session because of the ill-health that limited his actions in the early months of 1785. But he shared the reservations expressed by Isaac Corry and Lord Edward Fitzgerald with the reference to the Rutland administration's 'moderation' in the debate on the Commons' address to the King, because he condemned its conduct on the following day as 'highly improper and unconstitutional'. He cited the unwillingness of ministers to treat Irish commercial and political interests as equal to those of Britain, and the failure to resolve the Portuguese trade dispute, among other matters, as justification of his charge. He also disapproved strongly of the inclusion in the address of a reference to the desirability of a commercial settlement with Britain. It was 'absurd', he contended, to suggest that the Irish legislature should 'consolidate itself with that of Great Britain and take into consideration the interests of every part of the British dominions'. MPs did not possess the information to make such a decision and it was not in Ireland's interest that they should do so:

---

67 Yelverton to Forbes, 15 Jan. (N.L.I., Forbes Papers, Ms 10713); Mornington to Grenville, 1 Apr. 1785 in H.M.C., *Fortescue*, i, 249. It is misleading for this reason to avow that Flood's 'behaviour suggested a fresh attempt on his part to seize control of events' (O'Brien, *Anglo-Irish politics*, p. 101).   68 *Parl. Reg. (Irl.)*, v, 41; see also *D.E.P.*, 28 Apr. 1785.

where are the documents to enable us to judge and determine on the interests of the remote parts of the British empire? We have nothing to do with England – we have only to protect our own trade – let us grant protecting duties to it – and leave the trade of England to its own legislature, which is much better able to judge what could advantage it.[69]

Such sentiments flowed logically from Flood's conception of Ireland as an independent kingdom. However, he was equally forceful in his observations on the reference in the Lord Lieutenant's address to 'lawless outrages and unconstitutional risings', since these terms could, he alleged, be applied with greater justification to the administration's unrelenting and, on occasions, illegal resistance to parliamentary reform which was not even accorded a mention:

> You have seen politics enter the Four-Courts, and almost sit on the bench – you have seen acts performed which have brought princes from their thrones. You are called upon to thank administration for acts you condemn ... But you are not called on to make a provision for a reform in parliament. That is not even glanced at. No notice is made of it; not a hint to gratify the public, that such a step will be taken, patronized or encouraged; though the Prime Minister of England hath publicly pledged himself to bring in, and to support both as a man and as a minister, such a reform.

Perturbed by well-informed reports that the Irish administration was determined to resist parliamentary reform even if the Prime Minister succeeded in advancing such a measure at Westminster, Flood proposed an amendment to the address committing the Irish parliament to 'comply with the wishes' of the people of Ireland and the King's ministers.[70] This was an unusual suggestion for someone of his outlook, and such was his isolation that his motion was opposed by patriots like Isaac Corry as well as by Castle officials and lost without a division. His isolation was highlighted further in the debate that followed, for when the issue of reform was raised, he was opposed by Denis Daly, John Fitzgibbon and Henry Grattan, who were at one in deeming the Congress unconstitutional.[71]

The lack of support Flood received on these occasions prompted further claims that he was in irrevocable decline and that he would soon have to cede his place at the head of the Commons' opposition to Isaac Corry, Lawrence Parsons and Capel Molyneux.[72] In fact, Flood's persistent criticism of the style of Castle government, and the administration's position on parliamentary and commercial reform demonstrated that he had still plenty to offer. However, the fact that the delegates that

69 *Parl. Reg. (Irl.)*, iv, 3–19; Cooke to Grenville, 20 Jan. 1785 (P.R.O.N.I., T 3122/20).   70 *Parl. Reg. (Irl.)*, iv, 19–22.   71 *Parl. Reg. (Irl.)*, iv, 22–43; Orde to Nepean, 26 Jan. 1785 (P.R.O., H.O., 100/16 ff 86–9).   72 *V.E.P.*, 27 Jan. 1785.

gathered in Dublin on 20 January for another reform convention were unable to revitalise the cause of reform bode ill for his chances of advancing this matter and dashed the expectation of its supporters that the galvanizing effect of William Drennan's *Letters of Orellana* combined with the decision to drop Catholic enfranchisement would enable them finally to make a breakthrough. Delegates were expected from twenty-three counties and twelve urban centres, but most, including the nineteen MPs among their number, stayed away. Flood was among them.[73] If this reflected his wish to distance himself from a body that was now a public laughing stock rather than ill-health, it failed memorably. His absence on the opening day won him no applause with the increasingly antagonistic Castle press or with the advocates of reform who were casting around for a saviour. Flood was certainly neither physically nor temperamentally inclined to play this role, for when he visited the assembly on 25 January, he simply advised the delegates to endorse the resolutions agreed at the Grand National Convention as 'the plan of the freeholders of Ireland' and warned that any attempt to alter them must run 'the danger of changing the ground and destroying all unity in the designs of the people'. It was for this reason too that he urged that no mention should be made of Catholic enfranchisement. According to the Ulster activist, Archibald Hamilton Rowan, Flood's advice was repudiated. This cannot be corroborated, but the weight of evidence suggests that it was Rowan's proposals for the addition of a provision for a secret ballot and the disfranchisement of 'rotten' boroughs that was rejected. Whatever the precise course of events, it made little difference as Flood was well aware. He withdrew from the assembly after one day, and left the delegates to their deliberations.[74]

Flood's withdrawal from the assembly of delegates neither reflected his disenchantment with parliamentary reform or, as was alleged, a wish 'to seize control of events' in the Commons. Indeed, he did not participate in any parliamentary debate between 21 January and 7 February when Thomas Orde presented Pitt's plan for a commercial union between Britain and Ireland. This comprised ten propositions which provided for the neutralisation of the Navigation Act of 1662, the equalisation of existing duties, bounties and prohibitions on goods traded between the two kingdoms, a ban on new duties and prohibitions, and the payment by the Irish exchequer to the crown of income accruing to the hereditary revenue over and above a designated figure.[75] Flood and most patriots believed this was going too far. William

73 Cooke to Grenville, 20 Jan. (P.R.O.N.I., T 3122/20); *V.E.P.*, 22 Jan. 1785; Proceedings of delegates, newscuttings (Oireachtas Library, Ms 8 H 10, p. 93). 74 *A short account of the affairs of Ireland during the years 1783, 1784 and part of 1785 in a letter from a clergyman in Ireland* (Dublin, 1792), p. 57; Joy's notes for a history of Belfast, Jan 1785 (P.R.O.N.I., Joy Papers, Ms 4, p. 277); W.H. Drummond, ed., *Autobiography of Archibald Hamilton Rowan* (Dublin, 1840), pp 122–3; *V.E.P.*, 3 Feb.; Proceedings of the assembly, ca 25 Jan. (Oireachtas Library, Ms 8 H 10, p. 93); *Belfast Mercury*, 28 Jan.; *V.J. (D)*, 2 Feb. 1785; R.B.McDowell, *Irish public opinion*, p. 108; Kelly, 'Parliamentary reform', pp 315–6. 75 O'Brien, *Anglo-Irish politics*, p. 101; *Parl. Reg. (Irl.)*, iv, 44–111; Kelly, *Prelude to Union*, pp 92–105.

Brownlow, for instance, condemned the proposal on the grounds that it would reduce Ireland to the status of a 'tributary nation'. John Forbes, who was more tactically alert, simply requested an adjournment to give MPs and others 'time to consider the propositions'. Flood supported the call, and after a number of short contributions and a rather sharp exchange with John Foster on the status of the Irish
hereditary revenue, MPs agreed.[76]

Flood's opposition to the proposed commercial arrangement was more broadly
based than his initial expressions of opposition to what he deemed an attempt to
qualify the fiscal autonomy of the Irish parliament by curtailing its freedom to allocate the hereditary revenue. Indeed, whereas Grattan and other patriots were won
over once a proposition providing for a balanced budget, thereby reducing the sum
of money from the hereditary revenue that could be made available, was added Flood
actually broadened the grounds of his opposition; he also now argued that the Irish
economy would be better served by a regime of protective tariffs rather than by the
inauguration of an equal trade arrangement with England:

> will any man say that Ireland, a poor country, is a match for England, a rich and
> powerful country? No, every man knows that Ireland is no match for England.
> Ireland, therefore, was wise in desiring protecting duties; and no man can say
> that the same duties which for a long time existed in England ought not now to
> be granted in Ireland. I say that such a country as Ireland cannot protect its
> home market without laying duties against the importation of the manufactures
> of its rich and powerful neighbour. And it is a very great question, whether this
> be beneficial to the general interests of Great Britain, to deprive Ireland of her
> home market, though Great Britain hereafter has the supply of it? In every country
> the home market is infinitely more profitable, and a much greater object than the
> foreign. In England, which has the trade of all the world, her foreign trade is but
> one two-and-thirtieth part of her home consumption; therefore I say the home
> trade of Ireland should be our first object: for it is the greatest absurdity to say
> that any country shall pretend to manufacture for others which is unable to sup-
> ply itself; and it would be equally absurd to give up the greatest object for the
> letter, or to take the first in point of time which ought to be a secondary consid-
> eration. Besides, I say whatever is best for Ireland is best for England, for by
> each taking care of itself, and of the other, both will flourish together.[77]

Guided by this traditionalist mercantilist outlook, Flood's first action on 11 February when the propositions were debated was to request more time to assay mercantile opinion. This was denied, following which Flood embarked on his exposition of
how mercantilism offered more to Ireland than free trade. Because of his ill-health,

---

76 *Parl. Reg.(Irl.)*, iv, 116–31; Rutland to Pitt, 6 Feb. 1785 in H.M.C., *Rutland*, iii, 175.   77 *Parl.
Reg.(Irl.)*, iv, 177–8.

his manner of 'running from one [proposition] to the other' in the course of his ninety minute speech was not best-suited to the occasion and it elicited a sharp response from both John Beresford and John Foster who were better disposed than he towards free trade economics. Others simply disliked what they interpreted as Flood's monopolising of the debate, but he was not dissuaded by the unreceptive atmosphere from making it clear that he was also strongly opposed to the amended proposition providing for a contribution from the Irish hereditary revenue. It must, he pronounced, 'excite the indignation of every member who has too much sense to be easily deceived'; Ireland should not in justice pay a 'tribute' for commercial concessions. This was precisely the sort of emotional patriotism the administration was anxious should not fuel an Irish campaign against the propositions, and they were relieved therefore, when, having registered his opposition, Flood returned to the subject of protecting duties and presented an amendment to the first proposition according domestic produce 'preference in the home market'. This was not welcomed by those members whose priority was the linen industry. However, it was less this than the fact that it ran counter to the spirit of the scheme being proposed that obliged Flood to withdraw it.[78]

Disappointed at the lack of support for his stand in favour of protecting duties and inhibited by poor-health, Flood did not make any further contribution to the debate on the propositions, and the administration used its strong majority to secure approval for all eleven in one prolonged sitting. It was a ruthlessly effective display of Commons' management, and it left the opposition, which could muster no more than a token thirty-three votes in the one division they pressed, reeling. Ill, and 'abashed' by the experience, Flood was not in the Commons to witness the propositions complete the report stage on 12 February, though he made it clear two days later that he would have opposed if he had been present.[79]

With the commercial propositions approved, the Castle sought to shift the focus of Commons' attention onto its financial legislation and to its plans to replace the Volunteers with a militia. Flood held strong views on both matters, but he was also not prepared to let the subject of the propositions go. He was determined to ensure that if the commercial settlement was implemented, that money was not made available from the Irish exchequer for imperial purposes as long as the kingdom continued to sustain a hefty budget deficit. With this in mind, he took advantage of a finance debate on 14 February to criticise the propositions prior to proposing a motion for 'an immediate and effectual retrenchment of our expenses'. It was not a suggestion to which John Foster, with whom Flood debated the matter, was hostile *a priori*. However, he was irked by Flood's brusque manner, and ill-at-ease with his contention that the kingdom should allocate the hereditary revenue surplus to the

78 *Parl. Reg. (Irl.)*, iv, 172–83; Morres' report on Commons (2), 11 Feb. 1785 (Additional Rutland Papers). 79 *Parl. Reg. (Irl.)*, iv, 184–201, 212, 224; Morres' report on Commons, 11 Feb. 1785 (Additional Rutland Papers).

maintenance of an Irish rather than an imperial navy. The kingdom's finances, Flood avowed, had disimproved sharply following the augmentation of the army in 1769; and this would reoccur if, parallel with its payment of an 'annual tribute' to Britain, the Irish parliament did not sanction an absentee tax and embark on a policy of financial retrenchment. Flood's analysis was supported by Lawrence Parsons, Charles O'Hara, John Philpot Curran and William Brownlow, but his motion was rejected by 131 votes to forty-three.[80] Despite this, Flood pressed on with his efforts to persuade MPs of the need for financial retrenchment. This resulted in further sharp exchanges with John Foster, whom Flood showed singularly little respect, but the administration refused to be provoked by his aggressive behaviour.

Emotions ran high once more, on 18 February, when Flood objected to the proposal to vote £20,000 for the upkeep of a militia on the grounds that it was 'intended as a check to a Volunteer army'. This represented, he acknowledged, a reversal of the position he had adopted in the 1760s and 1770s when he had advocated the establishment of a militia, but he now had no hesitation in supporting William Brownlow's motion that the Volunteers had 'been eminently useful to their country'. It was not a view that found much favour with the rest of the House. Most MPs believed that those still engaged in Volunteering were 'giddy, turbulent and ... desperate men' amenable 'to every factious demagogue' and that they had little in common with the respectable and upright citizenry who had arrayed during the American War of Independence. Flood rejected this distinction. He defended the Volunteers in fulsome terms as 'the constitutional army of the people' and, citing previous praiseworthy Commons' motions in support of his position, he targeted the 'unconstitutional ... mercenary army' sustained by the state for criticism. This was a profoundly unpopular tack, but Flood insisted the current heavy deployment of soldiers in Dublin, the attempt to undermine the freedom of the press and to dispense with trial by jury in 1784 were part of the same despotic impulse that now sought 'to annihilate the Volunteers'. This was unjustifiable, he pronounced angrily, because the Volunteers had made such an invaluable contribution to the kingdom: 'they fixed our constitution; they avoided the very shadow of offence, they defended their country; they served the arm of the civil power, [and] they honoured this House.' Desperate to defeat the administration's attempt to negate Brownlow's motion, Flood affirmed their right as freemen 'to the possession and use of arms' and proposed a motion to this effect, but it only stimulated the Castle interest, led by the Attorney General, John Fitzgibbon, to offer a robust defence of the administration's conduct. He argued that the existence of the Volunteers was incompatible with the supremacy of parliament, and cited the prospect of further recruitment of Catholics by radical corps and the reservations Flood expressed on this very point in the late 1770s, as reasons why they should be disbanded. Flood responded with a further combative defence of his position and of the principle of Volunteering, and sought, at the last minute, to meet Protestant fears on the subject of Catholic enrolment by agreeing to include the word 'Protestant' in his motion but it made no difference. Once again, he found that numbers were firmly on the side of his political opponents.[81]

Though the issues considered included the Portuguese trade dispute, the administration's tax measures and the right to trial by jury, Flood did not participate in the Commons' proceedings in the week following his failure to rally support for the defence of the Volunteers. He was encouraged to keep a low profile by a barrage of criticism in the Castle press. This was part of an orchestrated initiative to discredit him – the 'Giant Harry' – in the eyes of the public since he was systematically and repeatedly described as 'the contemptible *pygmy* of a contemptible faction'. Flood was sufficiently troubled by this to draw it to the notice of the House of Commons, but he did not seek or secure any redress and, determined not to allow it curb his activities for long, he resumed his attack on the administration by raising the controversial issue of attachments on 24 February.[82]

The use made by the Attorney General in 1784 of attachments to compel sheriffs and other officials not to co-operate with the reform movement had already been cited by Flood as one of the most blatant illustrations of the abuse of power by the Castle administration. However, such criticism made no impression on Fitzgibbon, who steadfastly maintained that he had behaved in an entirely proper manner in defence of public liberties. This line of argument did not appease Flood, and he and others were encouraged to pursue the matter by the London Society for Constitutional Information, which provided pamphlets on the rights of juries for distribution in Ireland, and by legal opinion which held that it was illegal to try an office holder at the Court of King's Bench without a jury.[83] Flood believed the procedure should be outlawed. With this in mind, he gave notice on, Thursday, 24 February of his intention of moving a 'general resolution' on the matter. More pointedly, he moved on the following day to have the Commons' committee on courts convened and 'the rule books of the crown side of the King's Bench in the years 1761, 1762 and 1763' laid before the House but officials were not prepared to give Flood the freedom to investigate their conduct, and both his requests were denied.[84]

Obliged, as a result, to concentrate on his 'general resolution', Flood was influenced by the fact that proceeding by attachment were applied more restrictively in England to present a motion on 26 February calling on MPs to agree 'that the practice of attachment for contempt of court' should stand 'on the same ground of law

81 *Parl. Reg.(Irl.)*, iv, 265–97; Morres' report of Commons, 18 Feb. 1785 (Additional Rutland Papers). The vote on the division on his motion was 175 votes to 64.   82 *Parl. Reg.(Irl.)*, iv, 303–410; *V.E.P.*, 19, 22 Feb.; Rutland to Sydney, 20, 22 Feb. 1784 in H.M.C., *Rutland*, iii, 182, N.L.I., Sydney Papers, Ms 51/C/2.

in both kingdoms and ought not to be extended further in Ireland than in England'.[85] This was a shrewd motion because it gave weight to Flood's contention that the powers of attachment vested in the courts by parliament was 'limited' to cases of necessity and that this criterion had been infringed in the way in which it had been applied against Sheriff Reilly of Dublin in 1784. He supported this assertion with an erudite survey of the history of the law and a stout defence of the county meetings held to select delegates for the reform congress. It was an impressive speech, as Charles O'Conor observed, but the Crown's law officers were quick to defend both the recourse to attachment and the Attorney-General's actions.[86] John Hely-Hutchinson was their most constructive spokesman. He justified the prosecution of Sheriff Reilly on the grounds that officials could not allow 'any representatives for national purposes except members of parliament' and presented an amendment to Flood's motion directly negating its intent. Flood, in response, condemned Hely-Hutchinson's proposal as a blatant attempt to deny (what the courts had already acknowledged) that the power of attachment was applied more extensively in Ireland than in England and he appealed to the House to affirm the primacy of the common law. It was a vintage performance, but the Castle was uncompromising. His counter-motion to Hely-Hutchinson was lost, 48 votes to 120, and the amended motion carried without a division.[87]

Having failed to register any progress on attachments, Flood resumed his attack on the commercial propositions two days later with an assertion that it would be to Ireland's advantage if they were rejected at Westminster as it would relieve Ireland of an inappropriate 'system' and 'a very heavy burthen of [additional] taxation'. He was prompted to make this observation by reports that the claims Chief Secretary Orde had made for the propositions in Ireland had been denied by Pitt at Westminster, but he also determined to avail of every opportunity to make it clear that Irish opinion shared his view that protecting duties were more appropriate to Irish needs than free trade.[88] Orde was so perturbed by Flood's persistence and by his ability to use Pitt's difficulties at Westminster to his own advantage that he sought to regain the initiative on 2 March by presenting the House with the text of the first proposition as it had been amended at Westminster. This was a mistake. It provided Flood with an unexpected opening, which he eagerly grasped, to attack the whole scheme by challenging the manner in which it was being advanced as well as to reiterate his conviction that the proposal was not to Ireland's advantage:

83 *Parl. Reg.(Irl.)*, iv, 12; Jebb to [ ], post 29 Oct. (P.R.O., Chatham Papers, 30/8/329 f 69); *Letters of William Russel on the doctrine of constructive contempt with … an report of the judgement of the King's Bench* (Dublin, 1786); Vindex, *A treatise on the origin of attachments and information* (Dublin, 1785); G.R. Fitzgerald, *The law of attachments* [Dublin, 1785]. 84 *Parl. Reg. (Irl.)*, v, 1–4. 85 Flood to Parsons, 26 Feb. 1785 (Rosse Papers, C/8/24). 86 *Parl. Reg. (Irl.)*, v, 15–23; O'Conor to Walker, 23 Mar. 1785 in C.C. Ward and R.E. Ward, eds, *The letters of Charles O'Conor of Belanagare* (2 vols, Ann Arbor, 1980), ii, 221. 87 *Parl. Reg. (Irl.)*, v, 23–32. 88 *Parl. Reg. (Irl.)*, v, 34–43; Kelly, *Prelude to Union*, pp 150–3.

The negociation began with England, and ought therefore to have began with the English parliament; but, on the contrary, you are made to commence the negociation, and you agree to a price, before you know what you are to purchase. This is unlike the dealing between man and man; for who ever went to a fair or market, and said, here, I'll give you, Sir, so much money, and now tell me what I am to get in return?

Sir, the people of this country wanted protection for her trade, and I am inclined to think that protection would be an advantage, and that the community of market will be a disadvantage. If by a non-importation agreement Great Britain suffered, and Ireland received benefits, then it is clear that community of market will be of service to Great Britain, and a disadvantage to Ireland; and yet, Sir, Ireland is called upon to pay for that disadvantage.[89]

Flood was supported on this occasion by Isaac Corry. It would have been mutually advantageous if they had joined forces more frequently, but they did not see eye to eye personally or politically. It is notable, for example, that Flood helped scupper Corry's attempt on 18 April to advance a motion calling for the application of the Navigation Act equally to Britain and Ireland.[90] Such behaviour explains why Flood had few friends in the Irish Commons in 1785. It is, at the same time, a fair measure of his continuing influence that his persistent queries about the commercial arrangement raised such unease in government circles that it was deemed necessary to continue the abusive criticisms of him in the Castle press. He was now routinely described by the *Volunteer Evening Post* as 'the knight of the broken beak' and 'the itinerant orator'.[91]

Castle officials received a brief respite from Flood's attentions in the late spring when he opted to leave to others the task of opposing the legislation raising £140,000 in new taxes, arising out of the commitment given Henry Grattan in February that there would be no Irish contribution forthcoming from the hereditary revenue while the country ran a budget deficit. While this dominated the political agenda, Flood's time was occupied with the reform of the representative system which was his priority issue of the session. Despite the Irish administration's known antipathy to reform he remained hopeful that he could capitalise on William Pitt's plan to reform the Westminster parliament to achieve a breakthrough in Ireland. He had requested and been given leave to prepare a bill for the more equal representation of the people on 2 March, but he had indicated then that its content and timing would depend on what Pitt proposed at Westminster and how it was received.[92] Since the assembly of reform delegates was scheduled to reconvene in Dublin on 20 April, his announcement displeased reform activists. There is some evidence to suggest that

89 *Parl. Reg.(Irl.)*, v, 49–51.   90 *Parl. Reg. (Irl.)*, v, 122–8.   91 *V.E.P.*, 16, 21 Apr., 7, 10, 19 May 1785. 92 *Parl. Reg.(Irl.)*, v, 48, 60–146; *Commons Jn.(Irl.)*, xi, 379; Report of Morres [15 Apr. 1785] (Additional Rutland Papers).

Flood may have consulted with some of their number as to the content of his legislation but, if so, it did not satisfy William Drennan who accused Flood (and Pitt) of
treating them 'very cavalierly'. Drennan, in particular, was angry that Flood proceeded with his plan of reform 'without waiting for the assistance of the convention'
and that he viewed the fate of Pitt's reform legislation at Westminster as more ger-
mane to the fate of his own measure than the feelings of reform activists in Ireland.
In fact, Flood was just being realistic; the public campaign for parliamentary reform had all but ground to a halt for when delegates gathered for the reform meeting in April they were too few to accomplish anything worthwhile.[93]

Flood's calculation that the ratification of Pitt's reform bill would facilitate the
ratification of his own measure was seriously setback by news from London that the
Prime Minister's proposal was unexpectedly defeated on 18 April.[94] Having given
himself a number of days to consider how he might best rescue what seemed a
hopeless position, he moved on 28 April

> that the house do resolve itself into a committee of the whole House, for the
> following purpose: to prepare a clause or clauses to be inserted in the bill to be
> brought in by the committee appointed to bring in a bill for the more equal
> representation of the people in parliament, the better to promote due popula-
> tion in small contracted or decayed cities, towns corporate, and boroughs, whereby
> it shall be provided that any city, town corporate or borough returning members
> to serve in parliament, which shall not, twelve months before the next general
> election, contain, duly registered, a number of resident protestant leasehold
> house-keepers, not less in Leinster, Munster or Connaught than seventy, nor
> less in Ulster than one hundred and forty, in each city, town corporate or bor-
> ough respectively, shall return to parliament one representative only on the next
> general election; and shall continue on every subsequent election to return one
> representative, and no more, until such number shall be compleated, then the
> said city, town corporate or borough, shall again return two representatives to
> parliament, and shall continue so to do as long as, and no longer than, it shall
> retain the aforesaid number compleat.[95]

This was an exceptionally long motion, but since it encompassed the feature of the
plan of reform sanctioned by the Grand National Convention that most closely
resembled the central feature of Pitt's legislation, Flood clearly calculated that he
might yet benefit from the presence of a reformer in Downing Street. This explains
why his speech possessed a distinctly British dimension. For example, he attributed

93 Bruce to Joy, 26 Mar. (Joy papers, Ms 14/20A); Drennan to Bruce, post dated 13 Apr. (P.R.O.N.I.,
Drennan-Bruce letters, D553/40); Orde to Nepean, 30 Apr. 1785 (P.R.O., H.O., 100/16 ff 355–6); Kelly,
'Parliamentary reform', pp 325–6.   94 *Parl. Hist.*, xxv, 475–8; Black, *The association*, pp 117–22.   95 *Parl.
Reg. (Irl.)*, v, 152.

Britain's current budgetary problems and the reversal it had experienced in America to the unreformed state of the Westminster legislature and justified the need to reform the Irish representative system, which was even more replete with abuses, by reference to it:

There is scarce a corporate body in the kingdom, but has been deprived of their rights of election; to remedy which, it seems necessary, first to take away by act of parliament every bye-law or usage that hath crept into places to deprive electors of their original right of voting; secondly, that every leasehold housekeeper in every borough or town corporate should vote; thirdly, to register all freeholds whatever. We have seen elections carried on from day to day for a very long period, where it was well known that not one freeholder was polled, and these mockeries of electors were polled as ten pound freeholders. To remedy this, let every freeholder be registered at least as a 40s. freeholder, or not have a vote at all. It is well known that gentlemen in different counties agree to make freeholders on this condition: I will make forty or fifty freeholders in your county, if you will make the same in mine. And they shall go to you on condition that yours come to me. Thus they travel about, and a band of itinerant freeholders dispose of the representation of the country, while mock electors are brought from the North to the South, and from the South to the North; an army of fictitious freeholders produced as true. In towns, too, what is the practice? A parcel of friends are made honorary members, who deprive the electors of their franchise, and bestow the name of representative on one who has really no relation to them. My idea, therefore, is that no man shall be admitted to have a vote in any town, unless he has one hundred pounds a year freehold; or resides within the precincts of the place. I should also wish to enforce a residence personally and actually for six months before the test of the writ of election; that every man should be acquainted with them upon the tender of their votes. I wish too that the sheriff should be deprived of all discretional power, and rendered merely ministerial, as to the act of election, that he should be enabled to appoint persons who might hold the election in every barony on one and the same day. This I think, would prevent corruption, and accelerate the election. Besides the prosecution now allowed by law for false registry, my intention is to give a penalty to be recovered by any kind of action before any judge of assize. It is also my wish that every man shall be registered in the barony where he resides, and poll there and no where else. The precedent of the disfranchisement of the borough of Shoreham was a good one. It had its right of election restored by annexing certain parishes annexed to it. To restore and keep up a chain of populous towns in the kingdom will be one of the great means of improving the representation.[96]

96 *Parl. Reg. (Irl.)*, v, 151–2.

This was a strong case in support of moderate reform, but such was the antipathy of the generality of MPs that the details of what Flood proposed were quickly lost sight of. In an attempt to deflect opposition, Flood signalled his readiness to accept an instruction authorising the bill committee charged with preparing a bill of reform 'to take into consideration the state of decayed boroughs in general', but it made no difference. Indeed, towards the end of the debate, the Attorney General threatened to preclude any further discussion of reform by indicating that he would apply to the House to discharge the order granted on 2 March on the grounds that those charged with the responsibility ought by now to have completed their task. Flood was taken aback by this. But he successfully resisted an attempt to compel him to present a reform bill within seven days at the price of losing his current motion.[97]

Compelled by the events of 28 April to accelerate the preparation of his reform bill, Flood had it ready for discussion on Thursday, 12 May. As he had done when the reform bill was given a first reading in 1784, Flood chose not to speak to the measure at the outset, and it was received and given its first reading. As a result of *ennui* with the subject and the distraction offered by a balloonist on Leinster lawn the House was thin and debate did not begin in earnest until the question was put that the bill should be read a second time. Flood made a short speech denying the accusations that the bill was the handiwork of 'a parcel of factious agitators' and 'incendiaries', and that there was no demand for reform but, though he had the support of hardcore patriots and county members, the bill was lost by 112 votes to sixty.[98]

This defeat effectively signalled the end of parliamentary reform as a live political issue in Ireland during Flood's lifetime. He was unwilling to let the matter drop, however, and he requested Lawrence Parsons, who was in England, to elicit the response of English reformers 'to Pitt's idea', and conveyed 'a short outline of his bill' for transmission to John Jebb, one of the busiest English reformers. Flood was eager to establish 'a confidence and communication' with Jebb, because he subsequently communicated printed copies of his bill to Parsons with a request to seek Jebb's 'free thoughts' on its '*deficiencies*' so that 'I shall be able to meet his idea with an amendment, or to show that the defect is owing to something irremediable in the state of *this* country, of which there is no pretence in England'.[99]

Flood's attempt to make contact with some of the leading advocates of parlia-

---

97 Conolly to Napier, 29 Apr. (W.S.R.O., Bunbury Papers, letterbook xx, f 8); Fitzpatrick to [Foster], Apr. (P.R.O.N.I., Foster Papers, D 562/8673); *Parl. Reg,(Irl.)*, v, 151–68; Orde to Nepean, 30 Apr. 1785 (P.R.O., 100/16 ff 354–6).   98 *Parl. Reg.(Irl.)*, v, 188–96; Rutland to Sydney, 14 May (P.R.O., H.O., 100/16 ff 362–3); *Commons Jn.(Irl.)*, xi, 437; Report of Morres, 9 May (Additional Rutland Papers); Flood to Parsons, 13 May 1785 (B.L.,O.C., Flood file).   99 Flood to Parsons, 30 Apr., 5 Jun. (Rosse Papers, C/8/26, 28); Flood to Parsons, 13 May (B.L.,O.C., Flood file). Jebb maintained contact with John Forbes with whom Flood was friendly (Jebb to Forbes, 18 May 1785 (N.L.I., Forbes Papers, Ms 10713)).

mentary reform in England was the only positive outcome of an otherwise disappointing time for him politically as the Castle interest continued to dominate the Commons. 'We are required, unchewed, to swallow and digest whatever comes from the other side of the House', he observed despondently on 7 May.[100] He chose the issues upon which he spoke carefully, but his most significant contributions were made on the commercial arrangement on which he continued to be the principal dissenting voice.[101] He kept himself *au courant* with developments on this issue at Westminster through pamphlets, reports and speeches sent to him by Parsons. He did not read everything this controversial measure spawned, but he encouraged Parsons to send him copies of 'everything of any note' on this and allied matters.[102] This reinforced his conviction that more information should be made available to the Irish public, and on 14 May he requested that the Lord Lieutenant 'use[d] his influence' to ensure that 'authentic copies of all the accounts and returns, and also of the evidence heard at the bar of the British House of Commons' were laid before the Irish House. It was a clever tactic to refocus attention on the perfunctory consideration afforded the arrangement in Ireland and on the public's preference for protecting duties, and it perplexed the Chief Secretary, whose preference remained to say as little as possible on the subject.[103]

Despite his eagerness to debate the commercial arrangement, Flood was glad when the House adjourned for a fortnight at the end of May and he could make his escape to Kilkenny. Farmley was now his preferred Irish place of residence, but his decision to leave Dublin at this time meant, effectively, that he surrendered his strong claim to lead the slowly burgeoning opposition in Ireland to the commercial arrangement to the moderate patriots, who finally, and somewhat belatedly, took up the issue in the summer. They included John Forbes, Isaac Corry, Thomas Conolly and John Philpot Curran, but the single most welcome intervention for most opponents of the arrangement (though not for Flood) was provided by Henry Grattan's pronouncement on 13 June that the amended and extended resolutions being debated at Westminster were so 'subversive of the rights of the parliament of Ireland' he would 'oppose them with the last nerve of my strength and with the last breadth of my lungs'.[104] Grattan's typically bombastic statement was prompted by the growing perception that the commercial arrangement now represented a threat to the legislative independence of the Irish parliament, because of the introduction at Westminster of a new fourth resolution which provided that the Irish parliament should

---

100 *Parl. Reg.(Irl.)*, v, 178.   101 In May, they included smuggling and commercial legislation and John Foster's proposal to cap the funds of the Inland Navigation Board, which Flood opposed because it threatened his hope that the rivers Barrow and the Shannon might be linked (*Parl. Reg.(Irl.)*, v, 196–9, 206, 225, 231–8).   102 Flood to Parsons, 18 Apr., 25 May 1785 (Rosse Papers, C/8/25, 27).   103 *Parl. Reg.(Irl.)*, v, 200–4, 241; Flood to Parsons, 5 Jun. (Rosse Papers, C/8/28); Rutland to Sydney, 14 May 1785 (P.R.O., H.O., 100/16 ff 362–3).   104 Kelly, *Prelude to Union*, pp 158–62; *Parl. Reg.(Irl.)*, v, 246–7, 255–65; Report of Morres, [13 Jun.] (Additional Rutland Papers); the House of Commons met on two occasions – 13 and 27 June – between 19 May and 19 July.

implement the same trade laws as Britain to ensure both kingdoms possessed uniform commercial regulations. Surprisingly, Flood did not conclude that this demanded his early return to Dublin, and it is a measure of his isolation that nobody expressed any regret at his absence. Indeed, he kept such a low profile during the adjournment that he did not even contribute to the formulation of the County Kilkenny petition against the arrangement.[105] This notwithstanding, there were some in the patriots' ranks, who concluded that their prospects of defeating the commercial arrangement would be significantly enhanced by his co-operation and it fell to John Forbes to bring this about.

John Forbes was the key figure in orchestrating resistance to the commercial arrangement in Ireland in the late summer of 1785. He was one of the opposition's main points of contact with the English Whigs, and the *eminence grise* who did most to bring unity, albeit temporarily, to their fragmented ranks. His most significant achievement was to reconcile Henry Grattan and Lord Charlemont, who had fallen out in 1784, but his and Charlemont's invitation to Flood and Grattan to co-operate in defending the 1782 settlement was no less consequential.[106] There is little information on how this came about, but it appears that it arose out of the debate in the House of Commons on 2 August when they both spoke against the commercial arrangement. Flood was the first to rise on this occasion to respond to the announcement by the Chief Secretary, who was reputedly 'terrified' by the prospect of facing the two most formidable popular orators, that he would introduce a bill giving effect to the commercial arrangement as modified and extended at Westminster within a few days. There was little question but that Flood would oppose no matter what form the commercial arrangement took, and he underlined this by pronouncing that 'the business had taken such a turn that he thought no man would venture to bring it forward in the Irish parliament' because:

he considered it as the most infamous attack upon Ireland, an independent nation, to demand of her to abdicate that independence; yet that demand was made in the fourth resolution of the British parliament. He had been reproached with having been in a minority of one. He gloried in it; for he now believed every member of the House wished it had not been a minority ... Indeed, he said, there was a radical absurdity in the whole business; it was absurd for Ireland to attempt a negociation with Great Britain. This he told the house in 1782, and repeated in 1785. How could Ireland negociate with England upon equal terms? With England! who names her ministers, her negociators. With England! who influences her cabinet, her privy council, and who has influenced every parliament of Ireland except the present. But besides the nonsense of negociating at

105 Kelly, *Prelude to Union*, p. 162; *Parl. Reg. (Irl.)*, v, 266–304.   106 Kelly, *Prelude to Union*, pp 163–4, 167; Beresford to Rose, 25 Aug. 1785 in H.M.C., *P. V. Smith Ms.*, p. 348.

all, it is of all absurdities the greatest to negotiate for your constitution and your commerce by parts. In negociating for your commerce you destroy your interests, but in negociating for your constitution you abdicate your legislative supremacy.[107]

This was a prospect Flood deemed quite intolerable, and he called on the House of Commons to affirm its commitment to

maintain in full and undiminished force, the legislative supremacy of the parliament of Ireland to legislate for Ireland in all cases, internally, commercially, and externally.

As in 1782, this was too assertive for the bulk of the Irish opposition, and Flood was unable to secure backing either for it or for a less assertive alternative. However, the sight of Flood, Grattan and Forbes on the one side (if not of one voice) on the question of the commercial arrangement enthused patriot opinion and persuaded them of the need to take steps to ensure it continued. Lord Charlemont, for instance, observed that Flood 'spoke admirably' but disapproved of his 'obstinacy' in going 'against the sense of the [opposition] party'. The influential Whig William Ogilvie was more uneasy but, as far as can be established, it was his idea that Forbes should invite Grattan and Flood to co-operate lest any attempt by Grattan to 'defend the rights of Ireland' was undermined by an 'attack from behind by Flood'.[108] What followed next is obscure, but it can be assumed that it was as a result of this that Charlemont and Forbes approached Flood and persuaded him to concert his opposition to the commercial bill with that of Grattan.

The potential value of this intervention was first manifested on Thursday, 11 August, when Flood sought once again to negate the controversial fourth resolution by presenting MPs with a motion affirming the 'clear and undoubted right of the parliament to legislate for Ireland in all cases whatsoever'. Because the bill based on the Westminster resolutions was scheduled to be presented on the following day, Chief Secretary Orde was able to persuade Flood to withdraw his proposal, but this was not before he had reiterated his conviction that 'he thought it impossible to go on with the commercial system without violating the constitution of Ireland', and made it clear that if the bill Orde introduced contained 'the marrow and pith of the resolutions of England' he would oppose it tooth and nail. Grattan was less aggressive. But the fact that he spoke directly after Flood indicated that the patriots in the Irish parliament were more united than they had been at any point since April 1782

---

107 *Parl. Reg. (Irl.)*, v, 309–10; Fitzgibbon to de Vere Hunt, 5 Aug. 1785 (Limerick Archives Office, de Vere Hunt Papers, Letterbook 2 no 126).   108 *Parl. Reg. (Irl.)*, v, 309–16; Charlemont to Stewart, 3 Aug. (P.R.O.N.I., Stewart Papers, D 3167/1/16); Ogilvie to Forbes, Aug. 1785 (N.L.I., Forbes Papers, Ms 10713).

when they joined together in pursuit of the legislative independence they were now united in defending.[109]

The debate of 12/13 August 1785 on whether the House should receive the bill to join Britain and Ireland in a commercial union was one of the epic moments in the eighteenth-century Irish parliament, and the gallery as well as the chamber of the House of Commons was full. Opening the debate on behalf of the government, Thomas Orde did his best to convince MPs that the commercial bill was grounded on the eleven propositions they had ratified in February and that the manifold additions made at Westminster were consistent with them. It was a most difficult brief, and the consensus was that he did not rise to the task. This was in sharp contrast to Henry Grattan, who took the lead for the opposition. Even those who disagreed profoundly with his sentiments acknowledged the 'beautiful eloquence' of his three-hour speech. It was, like all Grattan's orations, more replete with emotional crescendos than compelling logic, but his advocacy of protecting duties and his ringing paean against what he alleged was an 'incipient and ... creeping union' struck precisely the right note as far as the bill's opponents were concerned.[110]

In length as well as scope, Grattan's effusion was more than enough for one debate, but it was followed by a number of further lengthy contributions before Flood received his turn. Given these circumstances, he would have been well-advised to have kept his contribution short. Instead he commenced with a detailed explication as to why the original ten propositions represented an attempt to get Ireland 'to relinquish the two settlements of 1780 and 1782'. As a preliminary to a comparison of the propositions approved at College Green and the twenty resolutions agreed at Westminster this was appropriate, but when he embarked on the exercise his speech soon became wearisome. It was not that Flood was ill-informed. He made a number of factual errors that John Foster delighted in pointing out, but in most respects the speech was a monument to the close study he had given the issue. At the same time, there was little in his speech, even on the controversial fourth resolution which, he argued, made the Westminster parliament superior to its Irish counterpart, to excite his audience, and John Foster had little difficulty upstaging him.[111]

As this suggests, the reaction to Flood's speech was predominantly negative. Most concurred with 'Memory' Woodfall, the parliamentary reporter, that he was 'tedious and uninteresting'. Some went further. Lord Mornington described it as 'a most stupid speech'. A more measured assessment was provided by the visiting English peer, Lord Camden, who concluded that Flood made a 'very sensible' contribution compared with Grattan who had 'borrowed' 'all' his arguments from Richard Brinsley Sheridan. Despite this, Grattan's speech was, Camden acknowledged, 'better calculated' to excite; Flood must, he surmised, 'have wearied the

109 *Parl. Reg.(Irl.)*, v, 320–9. 110 *Parl. Reg.(Irl.)*, v, 329–64; Kelly, *Prelude to Union*, pp 188–9. 111 *Parl. Reg.(Irl.)*, v, 394–414; Woodfall to Eden, 16 Aug. 1785 in *Auckland Corres.*, i, 80–2.

audience'.[112] Wearied or not, Flood was utterly determined to protect the constitutional gains made in 1782–3 against dilution, and following the administration's modest victory on the admission of the commercial bill he gave notice that he would 'move a resolution grounded on the fourth of the British propositions, which he considered as a dereliction of the independence of the parliament of Ireland', asserting the Irish parliament's commitment to 'retain its constitutional legislative rights undiminished', when the House reconvened two days later.[113]

The decision of Dublin Castle not to proceed with the commercial bill, because it did not possess the votes necessary to guarantee its passage, deprived Flood's motion of its urgency. Despite this, there was a widespread expectation in official circles that it would be passed if he pressed it.[114] Flood was eager to do so, and following his welcome for Orde's announcement that he would not take the commercial bill beyond the first reading stage on Monday, 15 August, he rose to make his motion. His purpose, he pronounced, was not to advance sentiments 'inimical to Great Britain' but to pre-empt the introduction and ratification of 'any proposition to take away the right of legislation' from Ireland:

> Such a proposition was inadmissible now; it would be inadmissible to-morrow; it would be inadmissible at any time. The constitution was not a subject of negociation; it was not a commodity for barter; it was not an article of commerce – his resolution was necessary to shew the people of Ireland, to shew the people of England, to shew the world that was too sacred for the hands of the most ruinous and profligate minister to touch; that it was above the power or wickedness of even such – beyond the grasp of depravity or ambition. In his opinion there existed not at this day a subject of commerce between the two countries worth any sort of altercation. We now had a right of trading with any part of the world that chuses to trade with us. No stipulation was therefore necessary; common probity would be sufficient. To think of binding the legislature was foolish and absurd, as the constitution acknowledged, common sense or reason acknowledged, no power to reside in one parliament to bind any future parliament ... The regulation of the commerce and intercourse between the two countries, must be left to their respective legislatures, to be settled from time to time as to them might seem meet. That England could have nothing to fear from leaving this in such a situation, he proved, from the conduct invariably observed by Ireland, since the recovery of a free constitution. Had we since that period, had we since we were permitted to legislate for our own commerce, shewn any indisposition towards that country? Had we not on the contrary gone on very many

112 Woodfall to Eden, 16 Aug. in *Auckland Corres*, i, 80; Mornington to Grenville, 13 Aug. in H.M.C., *Fortescue*, i, 253; Camden to Stewart, 4 Oct. 1785 (K.A.O., Camden Papers, U840/ c173/95). 113 *Parl.Reg. (Irl.)*, v, 443–4. 114 Mornington to Grenville, 13 Aug., Buckingham to Grenville, 18 Aug. 1785 in H.M.C., *Fortescue*, i, 253–4.

occasions farther than the interests of Ireland could well permit? Had we never since sacrificed some of our most important interests, at the shrine of their good pleasure? Arguing with much strength for some time, from the greater influence possessed by England in our parliament, than by Ireland in hers, he said there was no necessity for that kingdom to invade the constitution of this, the only nation that shewed itself friendly to Great Britain, and we could not, ought not, must not, attempt the subversion of the constitution. He said that as the whole business was to be considered only in the light of a bargain between two equal and independent states, as each sought its own advantage, the rejection of their own propositions here could give no offence to the English parliament; nor should any Irishman be chagrined, because the legislature of England did not agree to the propositions of this country. He then proposed the following resolution: 'Resolved, that we hold ourselves bound not to enter into any engagement to give up the sole and exclusive right of the parliament of Ireland to legislate for Ireland in all cases whatever, as well externally as commercially and internally'.[115]

This was as powerful a statement as Flood had offered of his vision of an independent Irish parliament since 1783. The fact that Grattan sat beside him during his speech was welcomed by patriots, but it was noteworthy that Grattan confined his remarks to the commercial bill. Encouraged by this, Chief Secretary Orde sought to prevent debate on Flood's motion by proposing that the House should adjourn following the formal reading of the commercial bill. This discommoded a number of those present, and following assertive speeches in support of Flood's motion by Charles O'Hara, Sir Edward Newenham, John Philpot Curran and others, tempers became frayed. Excepting an exchange with John Fitzgibbon, Flood maintained a cool head initially. But when the Castle interest declined to allow him to withdraw his motion when it was clear it would not be accepted, he accused them of prolonging the debate needlessly and of having recourse to 'inflammatory language' and 'saucy folly' for their own ends. This elicited a further reprimand from John Foster, which Flood wisely let pass. The debate concluded soon afterwards with the rejection of his motion without a division.[116]

This was a disappointing outcome for Flood, but it accurately reflected the disinclination of a majority of MPs to press home the advantage they had gained on 12/13 August. The administration was understandably pleased that it had, Fitzgibbon crowed, 'bullied and abused Mr Flood for an attempt to move an hostile resolution against England'.[117] Despite this, Flood too had good reason to feel content. He had, as he did not hesitate to let it be known, opposed the proposal for a commercial arrangement when it was neither popular nor profitable to do so. He had seen the vote against the arrangement rise from a derisory two in February to a prospective

115 *Parl. Reg. (Irl.)*, v, 447–8.   116 *Parl. Reg. (Irl.)*, v, 444–80; Woodfall to Eden, 16 Aug. 1785 in *Auckland Corres.*, i, 81–2.   117 Fitzgibbon to Eden, 22 Aug.1785 (Sneyd Papers, P.R.O.N.I., T 3229/1/4).

majority in August. He could, though he did not do so, also claim much of the credit for this, but it won him few bouquets with MPs because of his remoteness from most of them. He demonstrated this further in the aftermath of the debate of 15 August by returning immediately to Farmley, which meant he played no part in the campaign to chose a new speaker caused by Edmond Sexten Pery's unexpected resignation.[118]

This contest, which the Castle's candidate, John Foster, won comfortably, indicated that the endemic fissiparousness of the patriot interest, which contributed to its intermittent impact in the Commons during Flood's lifetime, remained as engrained as ever. John Forbes sought to remedy this deficiency in the summer of 1785 by founding an Irish Whig party, but interest among opposition MPs was modest. Flood was certainly not prepared to surrender his independence by participating in such a venture, despite his positive comments on the idea earlier in the session. He spent the remainder of the year in Farmley, where he played host to Lawrence Parsons and Peter Burrowes, a liberal barrister with whom he had become acquainted in England.[119] The fact that he stayed in Ireland encouraged Samuel Haliday of Belfast to hope that Lord Charlemont could persuade him 'to act in concert and upon a system' in 1786 to repulse the expected attempt to advance the commercial bill, but realising the futility of pursuing this, the Volunteer-earl did nothing, and the opposition embarked on the 1786 session, as they had that of 1785, without a plan of action.[120]

Flood approached the 1786 determined to act independently of all interests. He, too, was uneasy lest the administration sought to reanimate the late 'rejected and reprobated' commercial arrangement, so he was pleasantly pleased that the address from the throne was 'very moderately turned'. At the same time, the refusal of the Chief Secretary to state explicitly that the commercial bill would not be pressed worried him. For this reason, he proposed an amendment to the address to the King committing the Commons 'to alleviate the burdens of the people' by abolishing the taxation measures introduced in 1785.[121] This was not taken up but, undeterred, Flood raised it once again on Friday, 20 January, when he offered a persuasive argument in favour of low taxation, and a scathing indictment of the practice of entrusting the administration of Ireland to Englishmen as a preliminary to calling for the repeal of 'the new taxes granted last session to the estimated amount of £140,000 and founded on the commercial arrangement'. It attracted no support and it was rejected without a division.[122]

It is unlikely that Flood expected otherwise. He did receive some public praise

---

118 Kelly, *Prelude to Union*, pp 201–8; *Parl. Reg. (Irl.)*, v, 480–506.   119 Kelly, *Prelude to Union*, p. 165; Sydney to Rutland, 8 Sept. in H.M.C., *Rutland*, iii, 240; Flood to Parsons, 30 Aug. 1785 (Rosse Papers, C/8/30).   120 Haliday to Charlemont, 27 Dec. 1785 in H.M.C., *Charlemont*, ii, 32–3; Kelly, *Prelude to Union*, pp 210–14; *Letters to the people of Ireland on the subject of an union with Great Britain* (Dublin, 1786).   121 *Parl. Reg. (Irl.)*, vi, 12–18.   122 *Parl. Reg. (Irl.)*, vi, 19–25.

for the determined manner in which he pursued the question, but the prospect of a session in which the administration's majority was utterly secure so long as it did not attack the constitutional and commercial concessions agreed in 1780 and 1782 (which it had no intention of doing) was distinctly unappealing. For this reason, Flood was pleased when the possibility of his securing a seat at Westminster demanded he leave immediately for England. He had demonstrated in 1785, without ever showing the oratorical or tactical mastery with which he was once synonymous, that he was not the spent political force many believed him to be in the winter of 1783-84 following his disappointing early contributions at Westminster. Moreover, he was determined to obtain another chance to perform on the imperial stage.

MP FOR SEAFORD

Flood left Ireland for England in early February 1786[123] to attend the hearing of his and Lawrence Parsons' petition against the election in late March 1785 of Sir John Henderson and Sir Peter Parker for Seaford. This poll had followed the decision of the House of Commons to void the return made in 1784. Initially, Parker was joined on the treasury ticket by the Irish peer, Lord Mountmorres, until he was controversially obliged to make way for Sir John Henderson. Their opponents were Sir Godfrey Webster and Thomas Alves, who represented the Pelham interest, and Flood and Parsons, who offered themselves as the candidates of the 'non-rated housekeepers'.[124]

Parsons' candidature was unexpected. It was initially assumed that Flood would stand alone, but because he was otherwise occupied and had such low expectations of success, he invited Peter Burrowes, whom he had met in London in 1784 when he was 'in the last year of [his] preparations for being called to the Irish bar', to canvas Seaford on his behalf. When Burrowes went to Seaford, he 'found that very many of the claimants [non-rated housekeepers] were very anxious to have a candidate for the second seat' and he was invited to stand. He 'could not think of complying', and when Thomas Erskine, a Whig with reformist credentials, also declined, Lawrence Parsons joined Flood instead.

The poll, which took place on 29 March 1785, was eventful. Flood and Parsons had the bulk of public support, but since the returning officer accepted the Treasury candidates' contention that non-rated voters were ineligible, all of Flood's 27 or 28 votes and Parsons' 23 or 24 were rejected. This cleared the way for Henderson

123 Rutland to Sydney, 29 Jan., Pulteney to [Rutland], 9 Feb. 1786 in H.M.C., *Rutland*, iii, 278-9, 281.
124 Flood, *Memoirs*, pp 309-12; Oldfield, *Representative history*, v, 450-56; A.Luders, *Reports of proceedings in committee of the House of Commons upon controverted elections* (3 vols, London, 1785-90), iii, 33-5; Namier and Brooke, eds, *The House of Commons*, ii, 604.

and Parker who were returned with 14 votes each, as against eleven for Webster and Alves; Flood and Parsons were deemed to have received no votes.

Despite this result, Burrowes and Parsons were hopeful that the return would yet be theirs and they recommended an appeal to the Court of King's Bench to secure the legitimation of the 'populacy' from which they derived their support. Flood was less confident, but he had no hesitation in appealing to the law. He directed Parsons to secure 'some able and trusty lawyer ... who has no hostile or secret connexions' and to persuade Thomas Oldfield to travel to London 'with all his documents' so that proceedings could be initiated, and preparations made to appeal the return in the House of Commons. Documentary gaps means it is impossible to describe their strategy fully, but it is clear that Flood did not hold out high hopes of success. He ruled out the idea of a strategic alliance with either the Pelham or Treasury interest and, though he had little expectation of an appeal to the courts, he persisted 'for form's sake' in order to demonstrate 'that rateability is not required' and 'to prove corruption, mendicancy etc on the voters from our adversaries'.[125]

The courts did not, as Flood had anticipated, pronounce in his favour before the House of Commons determined on 22 February 1786 to convene a controverted election committee to determine who should represent the constituency. Four petitions were presented against the return of Parker and Henderson, two by Flood and Parsons and the 'electors in their interest', and two by Webster and Alves and their electors. All contended that they had secured a majority of the legal votes, and accused the returning officer of acting 'with great partiality in favour of the sitting members by rejecting the legal votes of persons tendered for the petitioners and by admitting other persons who had no legal right to vote'. They also alleged that some of the votes registered for Parker and Henderson were invalid because they were acquired by bribery and 'other undue means'.[126] Inevitably, each set of petitioners wanted the committee to proceed in a manner most likely to advantage them. Webster and Alves hoped it would investigate 'the merits of several votes tendered for them and rejected by the bailiff, and ... their objections to voters for the sitting members', whereas Flood and Parsons wanted, in the first instance, 'to establish a more extended right of election'. After some procedural wrangling, it was agreed that the latter point should be determined first.

Flood and Parsons' counsel presented a detailed statement in support of their contention that the Commons' decision of 1670–1 vested the right of election in the populacy, and that 'historically ... the inhabitants at large had the right to vote', whereas counsel for Parker and Henderson maintained that the term 'populacy, applied only to those 'inhabitant housekeepers paying scot and lot' as the Commons had determined in 1761 and 1774. Flood's and Parsons' case was reinforced by their

125 Luders, *Reports upon controverted elections*, iii, 77; Flood to Parsons, 18, 30 Apr., 25 May, 5 June, 23 July, 30 Aug 1785 (Rosse Papers, C/8/25–30).   126 Luders, *Reports ... upon controverted elections*, iii, 33–4.

assertion that the accusation of Webster and Alves that electors in their interest were illegally prohibited from voting because they were prevented from paying the local poor rate also applied in their case. Their claim that the Treasury interest in the borough manipulated this to perpetuate its electoral majority was not new, but it was given added authority by their contention that attempts by residents to pay the poor rate in 1784 had been rejected illegally. This was denied by Parker and Henderson's counsel. They contended that the residents had not followed the correct procedures and that their campaign to be enfranchised was prompted by political ambition rather than civic commitment: 'The principle of scot and lot right of voting is that they who bear the public burthens of the parish shall enjoy the right of choosing members. This must mean a regular, not a temporary or occasional contribution', they argued. This elicited a barrage of counter-claims that the officers of the borough contrived deliberately to non-rate potential voters, but the Commons' committee was not persuaded. They determined that the rate of April 1784 was the 'rate by which this election must be governed', and concluded that none of the petitioners had shown grounds why they should be elected. However, in their report, which was delivered on 13 March, they accepted Alves' and Webster's contention that a number of Parker's and Henderson's voters were ineligible, which meant four candidates 'were brought to an equality', and that there would have to be another election to determine the outcome.[127]

This was not the optimum outcome as far as Flood was concerned, but it did give him the option of offering himself as a candidate once more and, in the estimation of Lord Newhaven, 'a very good chance of ... election'.[128] The fact that the non-rated voters expected their appeal to be rated to be accepted at the next quarter session was obviously significant, but so too was the decision of Thomas Alves, having 'received a complete surfeit' of Seaford, and Lawrence Parsons not to offer themselves as candidates. The advantage accruing from Alves' retirement was vitiated by the fact that all but one of his voters aligned themselves with the Treasury interest, but once Flood joined with Sir Godfrey Webster's Pelham interest he was in a strong position. In the poll, which was held on 21 March, Flood and Webster polled thirty-two votes each and Parker and Henderson sixteen. However, in accordance with precedent, the returning officer struck off twenty-four of Flood's and Webster's votes on the grounds that they were non-rated, and declared Parker and Henderson elected. This obliged Flood and Webster to petition against the return, but the hearing on this occasion was merely a formality. A controverted election committee was chosen on 25 April, and

127 Oldfield, *Representative history*, v, 456–8; Luders, *Reports...upon controverted elections*, iii, 32–114; Namier and Brooke, eds, *House of Commons*, i, 456–7; *D.E.P.*, 18 May. 1786. 128 Newhaven to Rutland, 9 Mar. 1786 in H.M.C., *Rutland*, iii, 287. Sir William Mayne, Lord Newhaven sat in the Irish parliament in the 1770s.

upon the opening of the court, when the petitioners were preparing to state their case, the leading counsel for the sitting members informed the committee that he had found, upon a consideration of the case of her clients, that he shall not be able ... to maintain their return against the petitioners.

This left the way clear for Flood and Webster and they were declared 'duly elected'.[129]

So after an exceptionally prolonged and complex campaign, Flood was finally in a position to take a seat again at Westminster. Surprisingly, he did not speak during the remainder of the 1786 session. Possibly, he concluded that this was the best option because the dominant issue was Warren Hastings' conduct in India, and he had no wish to repeat his experience of December 1783. Moreover, he must have known that his every move was being monitored. Daniel Pulteney, one of the duke of Rutland's political dependents, was briefed 'to acquaint individuals or the House with any state of a case different from his [Flood's] whenever he begins his plot'.[130] He was not to have an early opportunity, because though Flood attended the House of Commons regularly his deportment remained 'languid'. He had determined prior to his re-election to continue to act as an independent, as cartoonists as well as politicians soon noted, and he habitually absented himself prior to divisions being called in order not to give gratuitous offence either to the Whigs or to the government.[131]

Following a break in the debate on Hastings' conduct in early June, Flood returned to Ireland. He arrived in Dublin on Thursday, 15 June, and promptly set out for Farmley. Domestic rather than political matters were uppermost in his minds, and he was not back in Ireland a week when his Dominick Street house was put on the market. This disappointed those who yearned for a return to the glory days of patriotism of the early 1780s, but Flood was disenchanted with what he contemptuously termed the 'drovers' and 'cattle' of College Green. He had now decided that he could apply his abilities more productively at Westminster than he could in Ireland, and it is significant that he did not take up Lord Charlemont's invitation to meet in July.[132]

129 Oldfield, *Representative history*, v, 458–9; Luders, *Reports ... upon controverted elections*, iii, 136–8; Namier and Brooke, *House of Commons*, i, 457; Pulteney to Rutland, 26 Apr. 1786 (2) in H.M.C., *Rutland*, iii, 292.   **130** *Parl.Hist.*, xxv–vi *passim*; Pulteney to Rutland, 26 Apr., 2 June in H.M.C., *Rutland*, iii, 292, 306; *D.E.P.*, 20 Apr. 1786.   **131** Pulteney to [Rutland], 2, 11 June in H.M.C., *Rutland*, iii, 306, 308; Flood, *Memoirs*, p. 372; George, *Catalogue of political and personal satires*, vi, no 7139.   **132** *D.E.P.*, 20, 24 June, 6 July, 3, 19 Oct., 7 Dec.; Flood to Parsons, 30 Aug. (Rosse Papers, C/8/32); Charlemont to Flood, 11 July in R[odd], ed., *Letters to Flood*, pp 166–7; Pulteney to Rutland, 18 Jan., 10 Mar. 1786 in H.M.C., *Rutland*, iii, 366, 377–8.

WESTMINSTER POLITICIAN

Re-invigorated by three months in Farmley, Flood returned to London via Dublin in early October.[133] He travelled in the expectation that the Westminster parliament would meet before Christmas, but on his arrival he found that it was not scheduled to reconvene until the New Year. The tedium of London without parliament was relieved somewhat by rumours that the government intended to effect the legislative union of Britain and Ireland in 1787, and by mounting concern with the Anglo-French commercial treaty currently being negotiated. Flood was so ill-at-ease on both counts, he appealed to Lord Charlemont in November for information. Charlemont was pleased to be contacted, but he was no better informed, though he correctly surmised that speculation about a union was baseless.[134]

Reports of an Anglo-French commercial treaty were not and, like many Irish Protestants, Flood was unhappy that its implementation would mean that France would displace Ireland as Britain's 'most favoured trading partner'. Irish concerns centred on the linen industry – an issue which, one informed commentator observed, 'it is not natural for Ireland to be reasonable'. But there was anxiety too that the negotiation of the treaty would further set back the hopes many in Ireland entertained that the country could develop its economy behind a wall of protective tariffs.[135] There was a strong mercantilist tendency in Britain as well, but the tariff changes agreed by the French were of sufficient liberality to ensure that key sectors of public and political opinion welcomed the treaty. This secured it a relatively trouble-free passage through parliament, but it did not obviate criticism. A number of prominent Whigs sought to use it as a stick with which to beat Pitt, while Flood was determined both to expose what he was convinced were its fundamental economic and political misconceptions and to vindicate his parliamentary reputation with a strong performance.[136]

Flood's primary grounds for opposing the treaty, which he enunciated on 15 February 1787, was that it ran 'contrary' to the 'indispensably leading principle that England and France are naturally and invariably rivals'. This was the position adopted by the earl of Chatham in 1762 'when he refused agreeing to the family compact', and Flood cited this in support of his contention that history and British self-interest offered compelling reasons why it was inappropriate that these longstanding rivals should agree a treaty that must, he argued, 'increase ... rather than extenuate ... animosity':

---

133 *D.E.P.*, 3 Oct.; Flood to Parsons, 30 Aug. 1786 (Rosse Papers, C/8/32).   134 Flood to Charlemont, 6 Nov. in H.M.C., *Charlemont*, ii, 43; Charlemont to Flood, 12 Nov. in R[odd]. ed., *Letters to Flood*; Kelly, 'Origins of the Act of Union', pp 259; Kelly, 'The Anglo-French commercial treaty of 1786: the Irish dimension', *Eighteenth-Century Ireland*, iv (1989), pp 101–2.   135 Kelly, 'The Anglo-French Commercial treaty', pp 96–7.   136 Ibid., pp 102–4; Flood, *Memoirs*, p. 356; Pulteney to Rutland, 16 Jan. in H.M.C., *Rutland*, iii, 365; Orde to Rose, 24 Jan. 1787 (Bolton Papers, Ms 16358 ff 263–5).

To show that the end of this treaty with France, this treaty of friendship, harmony and confidence, was absurd and impracticable, he should state as briefly as possible his reasons ... He should not therefore, repeat, that every attempt to open a commerce with France had proved abortive. He should not press the remark already made that James 2 had opened our ports, and that William had damned them up again. He should not repeat that every treaty we had formed with this rival served but to convince us of its being impracticable to form a permanent intercourse of friendship and mutual reciprocity. But whence came it that we had now this assurance of her affection towards this country? How long had she shown this liberal sentiment towards Great Britain? In what was it displayed? Was it in the usurpation of Corsica, or in her political intrigues against our interest and alliance with Holland? Or was it in her assistance of America, by which we were dismembered of that part of our empire? If she entertained this kind of intention towards a liberal union of commercial interests with Great Britain, it would certainly have been displayed. He saw no signs of friendship in her behaviour towards this or any other country. Her principle of policy was, to hold the sceptre of Europe. And what prevented her from this object of her ambition, but the power of Great Britain? Shall we, then, resign a power which has preserved the liberties of Europe, by controlling her schemes of universal monarchy? Is it consistent with that policy which causes all Europe to depend on us for their protection, against the intrigues, ambition, and encroachments of France, to think of depending on her assumed friendship? This was not the policy of Queen Elizabeth, who raised the power and glory of this country to that height, as to render it the sole arbiter and protector of Europe. She, when our resources were infanine, our commerce but just expanding its various branches, and our national spirit arousing itself from the languor of preceding reigns, did not think of establishing her glory on a commercial alliance with France. She considered this country as her rival in consequence, and therefore sought those means of power in foreign commerce whenever it could be obtained.[137]

Having established that the treaty was not compatible with Britain's strategic interests in Europe and elsewhere, Flood turned to the commercial argument adduced in its favour, and pronounced himself unpersuaded that Britain would benefit economically because the treaty gave it preferential access to a large new market. Britain and France were too alike in their manufacturing and commercial profiles, he contended, for this to happen. Indeed, from his mercantilist perspective, it was more logical for Britain to concentrate on safeguarding its domestic market rather than on making liberal trade treaties with its rivals, and he maintained that it was

137 *Parl. Hist.*, xxvi, 426–7.

'absurd and chimerical' to believe that a treaty which provided for 'mutual and commercial intercourse' could ever be appropriate between 'rival powers' or, fiscally advantageous to Britain:

> Such was the nature of two rival powers, that it was impossible but one must have the advantage of the other in all treaties of this nature. And that nation would have the advantage which was the poorest and the most abstemious. Which was the richest and most luxurious, was too evident to require him to declare. Would not France, he asked, with her wines, brandies, and olives, draw from us our specie in proportion to her wants and our own superiority in wealth? She certainly would, and therefore we should find ourselves not only supplanted in our resources for wealth, but drained of the remaining specie we had to support our credit. With respect to credit, he stated, that France certainly possessed less credit than we did. The trade in which France engaged was not by any means to that extent of capital on which we conducted our commerce. Our paper and credit enabled us to transact such a portion of trade, as was, he believed, unexampled in every other nation. We should, therefore, be very cautious of entering into any negociation which might tend to drain us of that portion of specie indispensably necessary to preserve our credit from being diminished. This was a consequence he was apprehensive would follow from the Treaty. As it was a fact that the poorer nation would always drain from the richest in all commercial intercourses. France must ultimately diminish our specie and increase her own.[138]

Flood conceded that British merchants and manufacturers 'had not given any specific objection to the treaty', but since they had strongly opposed a similar arrangement with Ireland when it was agitated in 1785, they had, he averred with more than a hint of special pleading, in effect 'spoken out in the most emphatic way' because France possessed five time's Ireland credit, eight times its population and forty times its capital. This cleared the way for Flood to express his mercantilist conviction that protecting duties and a nation supplying itself were more advantageous economically and to accuse William Eden, who had negotiated the Anglo-French treaty, of inconsistency for having previously opposed the commercial arrangement with Ireland. He also urged his fellow politicians to bear in mind the likely negative impact of the treaty on traditional British allies like Portugal and Spain.

Drawing the threads of his speech together, Flood concluded his most ambitious and successful Westminster speech to date with an apostrophe to MPs to reject the treaty as contrary to Britain's economic and political interests and traditions:

138 *Parl. Hist.*, xxv, 431–2.

From the war of 1688 until the present period, we had always been successful from our own commercial consumption at home, and our alliances abroad. But these means would by this Treaty, be all forfeited. We should lose all our character and consequences in the opinion of all Europe. No longer should we be considered, as we had been, the guardians of their liberties. Is there any one reason, then, to favour this Treaty? View it in a political, commercial, and relative situation to other countries, and you find it fraught with destruction to all our former glories, and our present greatness. No part of our acquired prosperity but it threatens with rapid and immediate annihilation. It commands you to recede from every other European friend, and to bury yourself in the embraces of France, your unalterable enemy. Who formed this negociation? Would they ask him to withdraw the pillars which had been the support of the nations glory? No! he should answer. Would they ask him to repeal the Revolution? No! The Treaty was hurried through the House. It was fraught with so much danger to the state and constitution, that he begged they would delay the proceeding until the manufacturers of the country could be apprized of its real nature and tendency.[139]

Flood delivered this speech – his most extended commentary on Britain's role in international politics and on Pitt's enthusiasm for economic deregulation – with 'great eloquence', as William Wilberforce acknowledged. It was a confident, powerful display, and his friends and admirers were delighted; Lawrence Parsons described it as 'a better model for pure eloquence than any extant by any of the other public speakers of his time'. As far as he was concerned, Flood had exorcised the ghost of December 1783, and he and others were encouraged in this view by the extensive publicity and positive response accorded his speech in the press.[140] By no means everyone was commendatory, however. There was a strong current of opinion on the government benches that was so hostile to Flood that nothing he did or said was ever regarded in a positive light. Daniel Pulteney is typical; he dismissed both the 'tedious' speech and its author:

It was full of unconnected paradoxes, syllogisms, dilemmas, and of all commonplace pamphlet remarks put into logic, with some upbraidings, well enough put, to the English manufacturers for grudging to Ireland, without capital, industry, &c., and what they were contented to grant to France – the English market ...; but, upon the whole, Flood's language is so barbarous to an English ear, his manner of arguing so abstracted and void of illustration, and his *tout ensemble*

---

139 *Parl. Hist.*, xxv, 437–8.   **140** Rosse Papers, c/14/1–5; *Parl. Hist.*, xxvi, 438; Flood, *Memoirs of Flood*, p. 357; *Annual Register*, 29 (1787), pp 82–9; *The speech of Henry Flood in the House of Commons of Great Britain on February 15, 1787 on the commercial treaty with France* (Dublin, 1787).

somehow or other so disgusting, that ... will never make the slightest impression on our side, I perceive, nor is he likely, from what I saw, to gain much confidence with the Opposition.[141]

Wilberforce was less censorious in his reply on behalf of the government. However, he rejected Flood's request to delay the treaty because his 'speech abounded with false reasoning and unwarrantable conclusions'. He maintained reasonably that there was no reason why Britain and France should continue to regard each other as 'natural and jealous rivals', for though France had traditionally posed a threat to 'our civil and religious liberties' and to the Protestant succession, this was no longer so. This was debateable but Wilberforce was on less contentious grounds when he addressed Flood's claim that British industry was unhappy with the treaty; he trumpeted the commercial concessions made by France and cited the absence of protest in support of his contention that British manufacturers 'were almost universally in favour of it'. Flood denied this, and urged that manufacturers were given an opportunity to express their opinions, but once Charles James Fox interjected with a motion calling for a reduction by one-third in the duties on Portuguese wines, the normal government/opposition dynamic was reestablished and Flood was pushed to the sidelines.[142]

Flood cannot have anticipated any other outcome. At the same time, it is not without significance that he did not participate in the debate on the treaty on 16 February or endorse Richard Brinsley Sheridan's blatant attempt three days later to stir up opposition in Ireland by alleging 'that a new commercial arrangement with Ireland must be set on foot as a consequence of the commercial treaty with France'. As an independent, Flood was determined not to become involved in a quarrel between government and opposition.[143] So, when he took the floor, he continued to target British mercantile opinion and to argue that they could not, with any consistency, oppose the commercial arrangement with Ireland and support a commercial treaty with France.

Flood's predisposition to link the Anglo-French treaty and the Irish commercial arrangement irritated ministers. Their patience snapped when he queried 'what security had Ireland for her share of the advantages or privileges which the treaty held out to Great Britain' and expressed his displeasure that the treaty allowed France preferential access over Ireland to the British market. Demonstrating the 'high' and 'imperative' tone that alienated many, the former Chief Secretary, William Grenville, angrily retorted

that it ill became those who had principally stood forward in the parliament of

141 Pulteney to Rutland, 16 Feb. in H.M.C., *Rutland*, iii, 372. see also ibid., pp 366, 377–8.   **142** *Parl. Hist.*, xxvi, 424–48; *Annual Register*, 29 (1787), p. 84.   **143** *Parl. Hist.*, xxvi, 461–4; *Annual Register*, 29 (1787), pp 86–8; Kelly, *Prelude to Union*, pp 183–4.

Ireland to persuade that assembly to reject the offer [of a commercial arrangement in 1785], to be among the foremost to endeavour to prevent this country from carrying into execution a treaty with France, which was concluded with a view to the benefit of Great Britain. Ireland had been favoured with an early option of solid and substantial advantage, and Ireland had rejected the offer – under circumstances of great delusion, and under artful misrepresentations of the real nature of that offer.[144]

This was a sharp rebuke, but Flood declined to take offence. 'He was', he maintained, 'a friend to both countries' and it was 'the indispensable duty' of the Westminster parliament 'to look to the general interests of the empire, and to see that no injurious consequences followed to the peculiar interests of any part of it'. Arising out of this, he justified his opposition to the commercial arrangement on the grounds that it was a flawed initiative: 'the offer had been insidious', he maintained because 'under colour of commercial advantage, the constitution of Ireland was endeavoured to be bartered away'. These were not sentiments calculated to endear Flood to an English political audience. Conscious of this, he explained that he had been induced to make these remarks by the comments of others. He also observed that he would not be browbeaten into 'an unbecoming silence'. This was an unfortunate observation given his response to his hostile reception in December 1783, and it was greeted by 'a general laugh'. Realising immediately that one poor choice of words had undone much of the good he had done his reputation over the preceding week, Flood 'abruptly' resumed his seat 'in great apparent pique' and left the House soon afterwards. Daniel Pulteney reported that Flood had lost his temper. The *Parliamentary History* does not substantiate this, but there is no doubt but that he was distressed by the incident because he did not participate in any further debates on the treaty or any other matter in the days and weeks that followed.[145]

Meanwhile, Flood's relations with Thomas Oldfield also deteriorated because of his refusal to honour a commitment, Oldfield maintained Lawrence Parsons had made, to pay him £1,000 in return for his acting as their agent in Seaford. Flood was displeased that there should be any cause for disagreement between Oldfield and himself, but he accepted Parsons' assurance that he had not given any such commitment. His wish was that the matter should be resolved amicably, but when this did not prove possible and Oldfield increased his demand to £2,000, his characteristic resolve not to be taken advantage of took over and the dispute dragged on.[146]

Flood was obliged to entrust the representation of his cause in his difference with Oldfield to Lawrence Parsons and Peter Burrowes, because he was indisposed

144 *Parl. Hist.*, xxvi, 466; Jupp, *Grenville*, p. 56.   **145** *Parl. Hist.*, xxvi, 461–8 and *passim*; *Annual Register*, 29 (1787), pp 88–9; Pulteney to Rutland, 20, 22, 24 Feb. 1787 in H.M.C., *Rutland*, iii, 373–7.   **146** Statement about Mr Oldfield's connection with Flood and Seaford, [Spring], Parsons to Flood, [Spring], July, 10, 24, 25 July 1787, 4, 12 May 1788 (Rosse Papers, C/8/33–39, 43, 44).

for much of the second half of 1787 following his return to Ireland. The precise nature of Flood's maladies, which occurred with increasing regularity in the late 1780s is not clear, but the periodic attacks of gout he had long endured were exacerbated in the late 1780s by something altogether different culminating in the summer of 1787 in 'a scorbutic eruption from head to foot' which necessitated attentive care and prolonged recuperation. Indeed, Flood's health was so poor for a time in 1787 that some feared for his life. However, he made a good recovery and he was well enough by October to make his traditional journey to England for the beginning of the new session.[147]

By this time, Flood was an established part of a London intellectual and social circle that included Edmond Malone, William Windham, William Gerard Hamilton, John Courtenay and James Boswell. Flood's acquaintanceship with Malone, Hamilton and Boswell extended over several decades but it was only in the late 1780s that it blossomed into friendship. Flood was a sufficiently warm admirer of Samuel Johnson to fit easily into this milieu. At the same time, he was more at ease politically with an Irish circle that included George Knox, Peter Burrowes, Lawrence Parsons and Wolfe Tone, whose companionship he occasionally shared at this time.[148]

Though he did not contribute to the controversial debate on the impeachment of Warren Hastings, which dominated the opening weeks of the 1788 session, Flood was not willing to allow the session pass without some contribution, and the subject he chose was Pitt's controversial legislation granting power to the Board of Control to charge the cost of raising 20,000 troops to the East India Company. Because of the controversy attached to Charles James Fox's 1783 and Pitt's 1784 India bills, and the reception accorded his observations, Flood was understandably cautious. He confined himself to observing proceedings during the early stage debates when the Whigs sought to exploit the fact that Pitt was conferring additional powers, for which he had abused Fox in 1783, on the Board of Control.[149] However, since he believed the bill infringed the chartered rights of the company, Flood indicated during the report stage on 12 March that he could not support it for the same reasons that he had opposed Fox's East India Bill in 1783 and Pitt's 1784 legislation. It was, he contended, improper and 'unbecoming' for parliament to extend the powers of the Board of Control and the minister at the expense of the Board of Direc-

147 Burrowes to Parsons [July], Flood to Parsons, 25 July (Rosse Papers, C/8/36, 39); Charlemont to Flood, 27 July [Oct./Nov.] 1787 in R[odd], ed., *Letters to Flood*, pp 169–70, 104–5. 148 R.C. Cole, *Irish booksellers and English writers 1740–1800*, pp 96–7; Boswell to Percy, 9 Feb. 1788 in F.W. Hilles, ed., *The correspondence of James Boswell* (3 vols, London, 1966–76), ii, 265–6; I.S. Lustig and F.A. Pottle, eds, *Boswell: the English experiment 1785–89* (London, 1986), pp 185–6; G.B. Hill, ed., *Boswell's life of Johnson* (6 vols, Oxford, 1934–50), ii, 139; F.A. Pottle, *James Boswell: the earlier years 1740–69* (London, 1966), p. 408; Elliott, *Wolfe Tone*, p. 48. 149 L.G. Mitchell, *Charles James Fox and the Whig Party* (Oxford, 1971), p. 113; *Courts and cabinets of George III*, i, 355–6; Flood to Parsons, 14 Feb., 13 Mar. 1788 (Rosse Papers, C/8/40, 42).

tors. Indeed, he alleged that Pitt was 'prostitut[ing]' his 'great name' by doing so. This was neither polite nor tactful. But it reflected Flood's unhappiness with the direction of Crown policy in India:

> He wished to ask if gentlemen were prepared to pronounce it a wise measure, at the expiration of the Company's charter, when it could be done without any violation of justice, to take the territories in India into their own hands, and to annex them to the Crown of Great Britain. He should conceive that such an idea would be not only an inexpedient, but an impolitic and unwise measure in every view of it. The territorial possessions of India had always been considered, and so they sought to remain, as a fortuitous acquisition of commerce, and they were by no means fit either to be made subject to imperial sovereignty, or annexed to the Crown of Great Britain. From the very moment of their being determined to be a part of the British empire, the dearest concerns of this country would be pledged to their preservation. Mr Flood contended that the true meaning of the Acts of 1784 was to institute a board of control and superintendence; with this distinction, that the political part of the Company's affairs ought to be controlled, but the commercial part not; yet, if the Board was admitted to be a board of power, the end of the Act of 1784 would be defeated; the control of parliament, as well as the control of the Court of Directors would be at an end, in the instance in question; and the Board of Control would not prove the best control in the world over themselves.[150]

Flood's speech was, as he knew, not one of his finest. Despite this, it was disheartening that no one on either the government or opposition benches took up the issues he had raised. He was, admittedly, complimented by James Martin, another independent, two days later, but since Martin was a political maverick this carried little weight, as Flood's admission to Lawrence Parsons that he found the experience 'awkward and distressing' bears witness.[151]

Given his continuing failure to establish himself as a voice of consequence at Westminster, it is not surprising that Flood did not speak during the remainder of the session. It is tempting, also, to suggest that it influenced his decision to allow James Martin propose him for membership of the Society for Constitutional Information on 30 May. He certainly did not do so in the expectation that this respectable, but sleepy, body would animate his stuttering English political career, as he returned to Farmley, via Milford Haven and Waterford, in early June.[152]

150 *Parl. Hist.*, xxvii, 181–2; *Annual Register*, 30 (1788), pp 108–10; Pitt to George III, 13 Mar. 1788 in Aspinall, ed., *Later corres. of George III*, i, 368. **151** *Parl. Hist.*, xxvii, 182–90, 193–4; Namier and Brooke, eds, *The House of Commons*, iii, 114–16; Flood to Parsons, 13 Mar. 1788 (Rosse Papers, C/8/42). **152** Society for Constitutional Information minute book, 30 May 1788 (P.R.O., T.S. 11/961/3507 f183); Black, *The association*, p. 202. R.E. Toohey, *Liberty and empire: British radical solutions to the American*

Despite his lack of impact, Flood remained less well-disposed to Irish politics than to British because of the overwhelming dominance exercised by Dublin Castle in the House of Commons in the late mid-1780s. He was kept apprised of developments in Ireland by Lawrence Parsons who possessed a similar disposition to his mentor, and a similar impatience with Henry Grattan whose efforts to advance tithe reform in Ireland was no more successful than Flood's attempt to resist East India reform at Westminster.[153]

Flood's time in Ireland in 1788 was largely taken up with nursing the mounting list of ailments that continued to afflict him. Despite this, he returned to London in time for the new session, but following a tedious, and troublesome, journey he was obliged, by a 'relapse' in his condition, to take to his bed on his arrival in late November. It is ironic that Flood should make such an effort to get to London when he would have been afforded a greater opportunity to display his talents at College Green. However, he let it be known to Lord Charlemont on 27 November that he found life as 'a spectator' at Westminster 'less irksome than to be an actor in a lifeless, useless drama at College Green', though the crisis caused in the winter of 1788–9 by George III's incapacitation does not entirely bear this out.[154]

Illness obliged Flood to miss out on most of the power struggle that took place between Pitt and Fox to determine the terms on which George, Prince of Wales would be made Prince-regent. He did consider leaving his sick-bed on 16 December to observe the attempt by the Whigs, who had not acquitted themselves well up to this, to seize the initiative from Pitt but he sensibly concluded it was not worth the effort:

> To be lifted into a chair and thence into the House; to be silent or to desire to speak sitting, which would be laughed at and disliked; and then to speak as languidly as from weakness I must do, and not to be able to stay (to give even a silent vote) to late in the morning – all this would be to put life into one scale and dishonour only in the other, which would be too much.[155]

He was deeply concerned by the implications of the 'regency crisis', nonetheless, because four days later he wrote to Charlemont to inquire how people in Ireland felt

problem (Kentucky, 1970), pp 108–9; Flood attended none of the society's meetings until November when he, among others, was nominated to act as a steward at the Society's annual December dinner (T.S.11/961/3507 ff 155–7, 184); Flood to Parsons, early June 1788 (Rosse Papers, C/8/46). **153** *Parl.Reg.(Irl.)*, viii, 1 ff; Hobart list of Irish MPs, 1788 (Buckinghamshire R.O., Hobart Papers, (P.R.O.N.I., T2627/ 1/1); Hobart to Buckinghamshire, 25 Jan.in H.M.C., *Lothian*, p. 433); Foster to Sheffield, 15 Mar. (Additional Sheffield Papers, P.R.O.N.I., T 3465/ 36); Parsons to Flood, [May], Flood to Parsons, [May] 1788 (Rosse Papers, C/8/45, 46). **154** *Dublin Chronicle*, 17 June; Flood to Parsons, 18, 26 Nov. (Rosse Papers, C/8/47, 49); Flood to Charlemont, 27 Nov. 1788 in H.M.C., *Charlemont*, ii, 392; the standard account of the regency crisis is J.W. Derry, *The regency crisis and the Whigs 1788–89* (Cambridge, 1963). **155** Flood to Parsons, 16 Dec. 1788 (Rosse Papers, C/8/50).

about the restrictive regency being proposed by Pitt. Charlemont was deeply disquieted that an attempt might be made to compel the Irish parliament to follow the line taken in London and, thereby, to return Ireland to what he termed the 'slavish bondage' it had broken free of in 1782. This was not the government's intention, but Charlemont was so concerned he appealed to Flood to stand forward as a 'vigilant guard' to 'the interests of Ireland'.[156]

This was not a role in which Flood had any interest. He certainly had no intention of joining forces with Grattan, towards whom he had developed a deep antipathy.[157] However, it was not personal animus, but his opposition to the readiness of Grattan, Forbes, Charlemont and others to extend English party divisions to Ireland that proved the main stumbling block. Lord Charlemont wrote encouragingly to him on 19 December that those of 'genuine Whiggish principles' (Foxites), towards whom he wrongly believed Flood was well-disposed, represented no threat to Irish rights. Flood was unpersuaded because he repulsed 'flattering overtures' made by W.G. Hamilton 'tempting him to join the opposition'.[158] In fact, he continued to hold Pitt in higher regard than Fox, which partly explains why he favoured Pitt's plan for a restrictive regency, but his most compelling reason was his belief that it was most likely to stem the rising tide of enthusiasm for the politics of party.

Flood differed fundamentally with Grattan and Irish Whigs who held that the parliamentary opposition in the two kingdoms should converge in anticipation that this would facilitate them secure a regency on favourable terms and ease their route to power. This is why he alerted Parsons, who was in Dublin, in January 1789 to be at the ready to challenge Grattan if he returned to Ireland 'a perfect Foxite' – eager to advance the Whigs' claim that the Prince of Wales had an 'inherent right' to be made regent on unrestricted terms.[159] Like Pitt, Flood was not opposed to a regency in principle, but he shared the Prime Minister's concern that the Whigs would infringe the rights of parliament to ensure a regency upon their terms. This put him at odds with the stand taken by most Irish Whig-patriots, Lord Charlemont included, whom he had hoped would concur with him that the main constitutional point at issue was 'the rights of parliament'. The 'Volunteer earl' was, he concluded, too 'addicted to the [Whig] party' to make a stand on this principle, and it is significant that the break in their correspondence that ensued was at his instigation.[160]

---

156 Flood to Charlemont, 20 Dec. in H.M.C., *Charlemont*, ii, 392–3; Charlemont to Flood, 19 Dec. 1788 in R[odd], ed., *Letters to Flood*, pp 174–5. 157 Flood to Parsons, 13 Mar. 1788 (Rosse Papers, C/8/42). 158 Charlemont to Flood, 19 Dec. 1788 in R[odd], ed., *Letters to Flood*, p. 175; D.R. Schweitzer, 'The Whig political connection in Great Britain and Ireland' (Ph.D. thesis, University of London, 1984), p. 127; Parsons' Memoir (Rosse Papers, C/14/1–5). 159 Kelly, *Grattan*, pp 24–5; Schweitzer, 'The Whig political connection', chapter 2; Mornington to Buckingham, 6 Jan. in *Courts and cabinets of George III*, ii, 89; Grattan to Forbes, [9 Jan.] (N.L.I., Forbes Papers, Ms 978); Flood to Parsons, 11 Jan., Charlemont to Sheridan, 10 Apr. 1789 in H.M.C., *Charlemont*, ii, 123. 160 Majority on the question respecting the regency (Yale University Library, Sterling Library); Flood to Charlemont, 12 Jan. 1789, Charlemont to Sheridan, 10 Apr. 1790 in H.M.C., *Charlemont*, ii, 391–2, 123.

Once Flood's health had recovered sufficiently by early January to allow him to observe the regency crisis personally, his hostility to party intensified. It distressed him that genuine constitutional debate was being subverted by party allegiance and that 'the few independent men' remaining in both kingdoms were being 'dragged into the vortex of those who are not so'. He was particularly incensed by the 'tumultary' nature of the parliamentary exchanges, as his account of the debate prompted by John Rolle's 'attack' on the Prince of Wales on 7 February attests:

> Burke screeched half a dozen speeches and seemed stunned almost to madness at their clamorous inattention. Grey, who is very warm, charged Pitt with insincerity in his pretended civility to the Prince. This inflamed Pitt to the highest degree you can conceive, so that, while Grey was speaking, Pitt shook a roll of paper he had in his hand at Grey, just in the action and with the countenance of a man going to strike another. It was a scene of disorder. Not one word on the great points of the question was spoken, and I saw that I might as well read the psalms and lessons to them as argue the point, and I felt so little of, and could so little partake in, the outrage around me, that it even disgusted me, as a sober man is disgusted with a drunken company.

Flood had planned to speak during this debate, but since what he had to say could not be encompassed within a 'short sparring', he kept his own counsel.[161]

If the disorderly nature of the exchange at Westminster disturbed Flood, reports from Ireland that Grattan secured the ratification of a regency on the unrestricted terms advocated by the Whigs, compounded his unease. He had anticipated that this would happen but he was disappointed by the lack of 'dignity, ... [and] reserve' displayed, and the readiness with which Grattan, or '£50,000' as Flood now dubbed him, allowed himself to become 'a tool of faction'.[162] Had circumstances permitted, he would have travelled to Ireland to assert the independence of the Irish parliament, but this was impossible. And, as the worrying implications of the Irish parliament's decision to offer the Prince of Wales a regency on terms different to those favoured at Westminster legislature sunk in,[163] his animus towards Grattan intensified:

> Fate seems determined to make a certain person's [Grattan] measures always stultify themselves. Simple Repeal, Poynings and the Judges Bill were all blunders. We voted 20,000 seamen to England, though we had no seamen, but because we have landsmen. Yet, of the latter, we could raise but a few thousand ..., and those few thousand were no gain to England, for they would have been got

161 Flood to Parsons, 8, 8–12 Feb. 1789 (Rosse Papers, C/8/53, 54).   162 Flood to Parsons, 8–12 Feb. 1789 (Rosse Papers, C/8/54).   163 See Hastings to Knox, 11 Feb. in H.M.C., *Various collections, vi, Knox Mss*, p. 242; Foster to Sheffield, 12 Feb. 1789 (Stanley of Alderley Papers, P.R.O.N.I.,T 3725/4).

equally and with less expense by the common recruiting service. The Irish propositions were at first supported, and he burdened the public with £140,000 to pay for what he did not understand, and to secure an economy which he has not in [text defective] ... On the contrary, he opposed a resolve in favour of economy after, and opposed my motion either to resume the taxes or to insist on some recompense for them. What was his conduct on the Press Bill, the Riot Act, the Police and the resolve against the liberty of speech or writing?[164]

Given the strength of Flood's feelings, it is hardly surprising that Lawrence Parsons should feel himself obligated to challenge Grattan's strategy by impugning his constitutional knowledge and the value of legislative independence or that they should have a furious row on 3 March which seemed fated to conclude in an exchange of bullets. A duel was avoided, but since Parsons came best out of the exchange in the judgement of most observers, Flood included, he had good reason to feel happier than his antagonist. Flood was certainly pleased, but the incident does not reflect well on him since he had primed Parsons to behave as he did. Flood also took heart from the fact that the regency crisis exposed Grattan's 'folly as well as ... ignorance', and that the round robin some fifty Irish Whigs, Grattan and Charlemont included, signed in late February when the recovery of George III in late February invalidated their whole strategy, was 'vulgar, nauseous and unconstitutional'. Nonetheless, his pleasure at the discomfort of Grattan, whom he alleged, 'has arrogance enough to undo a dozen better men than himself', sits awkwardly alongside his equally haughty description of Parsons and himself as 'high-minded men' because they had not succumbed to the temptations of party.[165]

This blind spot excepted, Flood had behaved honourably and consistently during the regency crisis. It was, of course, easier to do this from his 'independent' position than from within one of the major party groupings he condemned so heartily, but Flood made no allowance for this. In this context, the creation of an Irish Whig party around the Whig Club served to disenchant him further with Irish politics, and he remained in England for the rest of the session. He gave Parsons to understand in May that 'the slave trade question, the East Indian budget, new taxes and a probable regency bill' demanded his presence, but he did not contribute to the debates on any of these issues in the long session that followed.[166]

At some time in the late summer, Flood made his annual visit to Farmley. It is to

164 Flood to Parsons, 20 Feb. 1789 (Rosse Papers, C/8/55). This letter provided the arguments for Parsons' celebrated attack on Grattan on 3 March (*Par. Reg.(Irl.)*, ix, 255). 165 *Clonmel Gazette*, 12 Mar.; Buckingham to Grenville, 4, 9 Mar. in H.M.C., *Fortescue*, i, 425, 428; *Parl.Reg.(Irl.)*, ix, 255–8; Flood to Parsons, 20 Feb., 5, 7, 9 Mar. (Rosse Papers, C/8/55–8); W.E.H.Williams, *The Irish parliament 1782–1800* (London, 1912), p. 110; Preston to [Dundas], 27 Feb. 1789 (Pitt-Pretyman Papers, P.R.O.N.I., T3319/1). 166 Denis Kennedy, 'The Irish Whigs, administrative reform and responsible government 1782–1800', *Eire-Ireland*, viii (1973), pp 62–3; Flood to Parsons, 9 May 1789 (Rosse Papers, C/8/60); *Parl. Hist.*, xxvii-viii, *passim*.

be presumed that the visit fulfilled its practical and therapeutic purposes because he returned to London later in the year to rejoin his familiar social circle which now included James and Thomas Boswell, Joshua Reynolds, Edmond Malone and John Courtenay among its members. Lady Frances and he occasionally hosted 'splendid' dinners at their house in Berners Street, which the bibulous James Boswell deemed 'dull' because of Flood's disinclination to dispense the bottle with sufficient liberality.[167] Flood's abstemiousness may have been a product of his own susceptibility to the gout, and it was not a source of ill-feeling. He was a sufficiently respected member of the circle to contribute generously to the fund established to erect a monument to Dr Johnson and to have his suggestion for an epitaph afforded serious consideration by Boswell and Malone.[168]

Drafting an epitaph for Dr Johnson was a pleasant diversion from Flood's main object in 1790, which was to advance the cause of parliamentary reform. The first inkling most people had of Flood's intentions in this respect was provided on 9 February when he gave notice in the House of Commons of his wish to propose a motion in favour of the reform of the representative system, but he had been contemplating such a step since the outbreak of revolution in France. Flood entertained, as he had demonstrated during the debate on the Anglo-French treaty, deep suspicions of France. However, he recognised more quickly than most that what had happened there in 1789 was pregnant with implications for Britain, and he concluded that it was incumbent on the legislature to take immediate steps to ensure the country did not succumb to the same disorder:

> I am told this is not the time. And why? because, forsooth, there are disturbances in France. Now first I say, that if those disturbances were ten times greater than with every exaggeration they are represented to be, yet that mass of confusion and ruin would only render the argument more completely decisive in favour of a timely and temperate reform here. And why? because it is only from want of timely and temperate reform there, that these evils have fallen upon France. They could not begin with reparation in France: there was nothing to repair: they did not begin with ruin, they found ruin accomplished to their hands. Neither the king nor his ministers knew where to find the constitution. The king called upon his notables (no legal body) to see where the constitution was to be found. Not a vestige of it could be recovered. They had lived so long as slaves, that they had unlearned the constitution; they were driven to speculation because practice had vanished; and hence all those calamities which have excited such tragical exclamations here.

167 M.K. Danziger and Frank Brady, eds, *Boswell: the great biographer* (London, 1990), pp 16–17; Boswell to Temple, 20 Nov. 1789 in Thomas Seccombe, ed., *Letters of James Boswell to the Rev. W.J. Temple* (London, 1908), pp 262–3.   168 Hill, ed., *Boswell's life of Johnson*, iv, 424–5, 470; Seccombe, ed., *Letters of Boswell to Temple*, pp 265–6.

Moreover, since France had embarked on the path to 'improve her constitution', it was essential, Flood contended, if Britain was to remain 'superior' that it 'restored' its own by reforming the representative system.[169]

As this indicates, Flood was deeply activated by the revolution in France. More significantly, in contrast to Edmund Burke, he was convinced that it made reform more rather than less necessary. It is noteworthy, for example, that he dismissed the concept of virtual representation, to which Burke was so attached, as 'the shadow ... of representation' more likely to lead to 'dismemberment' (as it had done in the case of the American colonies) than to political or constitutional harmony. This was not an argument calculated to win over the House of Commons, but Flood was not troubled by this. He took heart from the support he received from the Society for Constitutional Information and from his conviction that 'timely reform renders revolution unnecessary'. If such a course had been pursued by Charles I and Charles II, he informed the House of Commons, it would have averted the need for two revolutions in the seventeenth century; a timely reform would save the 'constitution'.[170]

As this and his exposition of the detail of his proposal on 12 March confirms, Flood's plan of reform had the avoidance of revolution as its *raison d'être*. Appropriately, for what was to be his last major speech, it was one of the best-judged and most lucid of his career. He had contrived, after his spectacular failure in 1783, to forsake the 'emotional display[s] of eloquence' preferred at College Green for the 'grave, argumentative appeals to reason' preferred at Westminster, but it was not until March 1790 that he can be said to have achieved his object. It was, as John Cannon has observed, 'one of the most impressive [speeches] made in support of reform up to then'.[171]

Central to the success of the speech was Flood's 'moderate tone'.[172] He could have supported his plan by indicting the existing system, but realising that persuasion was a more effective tactic, he commenced with an appeal to MPs as the 'legal representatives' of the people to weigh his arguments before they made up their minds on the merits of reform. He was also at pains to set his ideas in their political context by alluding to the plans of reform presented by Lord Chatham, to whom he made a typical genuflection, and William Pitt, towards whom he made a delicate play for support. Pitt was not taken in by this or by further positive references to his ideas. However, like all who were present, he had no difficulty with Flood's statement that even in its unreformed state, the Westminster legislature 'would be a great acquisition' to 'any other government of Europe', while those of more radical

169 S. Maccoby, *English radicalism 1786–1832* (London, 1955); *Parl. Hist.*, xxviii, 455–7.   **170** *Parl. Hist.*, xxviii, 454–8; Minute book for the Society for Constitutional Information, 19 Feb. 1790 (P.R.O., T.S.11/961 /3507 f 209).   **171** Parsons memoir (Rosse Papers, C/ 14/ 1–5); Cannon, *Parliamentary reform*, p. 117; H.T. Dickinson, *Liberty and property: political ideology in eighteenth-century Britain* (London, 1977), p. 237.   **172** Maccoby, *English radicalism*, p. 37.

disposition welcomed his assertion that the Commons had responded 'iniquitously' during the Middlesex election.

Having set the scene and established that he was an opponent of all forms of 'absolute government' – 'monarchy, aristocracy or democracy' – Flood proceeded to argue that the constitution could be improved if 'an adequate' or 'actual representation' was implemented. He explained:

> that as, by the general law of the constitution, the majority is to decide for the whole, the representative must be chosen by a body of constituents, whereof the elective franchise may extend to the majority of the people. For, what can be so evident, as, if the constituent body consisted of but one thousand for the whole nation, the representatives chosen by that thousand could not, in any rational sense, be the actual representatives of the people? It is equally clear in reason, that nothing less than a constituent body, formed on a principle that may extend to the majority, can be constitutionally adequate to the return of an actual representative of the people; and that unless the people be actually represented, they are not constitutionally represented at all.

Flood did not favour the abolition of a franchise property qualification; quite the contrary he deemed it a

> necessary ingredient to the elective power; that is to say, that franchise ought not to go beyond property; but at the same time to say, that it ought to be as nearly commensurate to it as possible. Property by the original principle of the constitution was the source of all power, both elective and legislative.

As this suggests, Flood believed that, as things stood:

> the whole number of electors is infinitely short of what it ought to be, and, what is worse, the majority of the representatives who decide for the whole, are chosen by a number of electors not exceeding six or eight thousand; though these representatives are to act for eight millions of people. A new body of constituents is therefore wanting; and in their appointment two things are to be considered; one, that they should be numerous enough, because numbers are necessary to the spirit of liberty; the other, that they should have a competent degree of property, because that is conducive to the spirit of order.

Flood's specific recommendation was that the electorate would be suitably augmented by the admission of one hundred thousand resident householders who 'being masters, or fathers of families, ... must be sufficiently responsible to be entitled to the franchise'.[173]

173 *Parl. Hist.*, xxviii, 454–5, 460.

This was not all. Flood held fast to the opinion he had first articulated in the 1760s that 'the balance of the constitution is ... gone', because of the increase in the power of the House of Lords and the prerogative of the monarchy, and that 'it must be restored, or the constitution will be undone'. The only way this could be achieved, he maintained, was 'by opening all the boroughs, so as to make them places of popular and constitutional election'. Lord Chatham had previously made such a recommendation, and Flood cited him once more in support of his recommendation that one hundred boroughs should have their right of representation halved from two to one MP. This was controversial, but Flood was convinced that the arguments in its favour were compelling; it would make the House of Commons 'more a public, and less a party assembly; it would, by course, become less tumultuary, and rise in dignity and order'.[174] This was a subject, as his private observations during the regency crisis had indicated, upon which Flood felt very strongly, but his priority was that the constitution at large was seen to work and to work fairly, and it was this which prompted his memorable appeal to MPs to recognize the danger of alienating the population, and to take steps to regain their allegiance if they wanted to stave off revolution:

The people have lost their constitutional influence in the legislature. Instead of having the whole, they are far from having a majority in their own representative; the majority is against them; and the majority decides for the whole. The House is a second rate aristocracy, instead of a popular representation; the pillar of the constitution is undermined; it is nonsense to say that every thing is well, when every thing is in danger; every country in Europe was once as free as England; in every country in Europe it was said that every thing was well, till they found that every thing was otherwise; they went to bed saying they were free, and they awakened bondsmen.

Let us not flatter ourselves that there is a destiny peculiar to England: she has lost her liberty more than once; it is our business to take care that she shall never lose it again. Machiavel says wisely, that no free government can last, that is not often brought back to its first principles – and why? Because the excellence of a free government is, to control the evil passions and practices of rulers. What is the consequence? Those passions and practices are at perpetual war with such a constitution: they make a constant effort to undermine or evade this barrier which is opposed to them. What is perpetually assailed, must be perpetually defended – what is incessantly sapped, must be incessantly repaired. It is nonsense to say that the English constitution, because it was once the best in the world, can never want reformation. A bad government cannot easily become worse; it therefore may not want, and certainly does not deserve reparation. A

174 Ibid., 462–3.

good government does easily become worse; it is with difficulty it can be preserved even by vigilance; and of all things in the world it best deserves to be repaired.[175]

Having brought his address to a close with a few final practical observations (the most striking of which concerned holding polls over one day) Flood requested 'that leave be given to bring in a bill to amend the representation of the people'. It was not received with the sympathy he hoped for.[176] Both William Windham and William Pitt acknowledged the merits of Flood's scheme, but they deemed the moment 'improper'; 'you would not', Windham observed memorably, 'repair your house in the hurricane season'. Charles James Fox was more positive; he observed 'that he thought the outline of the present proposition the best of all which he had yet heard', but he was sure that a 'majority either within or without doors' was hostile. Flood's response to these observations was tactful and non-confrontational. He pronounced himself satisfied that he had reanimated an issue 'considered dead by [its] enemies', and he offered a further witty justification of the need for reform and a vivid illustration of his oratorical prowess by dealing comfortably and decisively with the criticisms of his plan and his motion before acknowledging it stood no chance and withdrawing it.[177]

Despite this outcome, Flood had good reason to be pleased with his own performance and with the response to his plan. He had not pressed the matter to a division (though that was his original intention) because a decisive contrary majority would have setback the plans afoot to launch a reform campaign. Flood was hopeful that the Society for Constitutional Information would spearhead this, but it proved difficult to generate momentum. He chaired the Society's meeting on 19 March at which it was determined to invite all 'sincere friends to a parliamentary reform' to an assembly at the London Tavern on 12 April 'to consider the most constitutional, vigorous and effectual measures for promoting' this object, but this meeting had to be postponed for four days because of the venue's unavailability. The Society took advantage of the delay to agree resolutions with the Revolution Society, but when a further postponement of a week proved necessary, Flood declined to make himself available. The last meeting of the Society for Constitutional Information which he attended took place on 9 April when a number of resolutions in favour of reform were approved. These included statements that the 'present representation of the people in parliament is grossly inadequate', that it was 'a particularly suitable time' to pursue reform and that the franchise should be extended 'to all householders ... paying taxes', and a call on people to attend the meeting of 23

175 *Parl. Hist.*, xxviii, 463–4; Pares, *George III and the politicians*, p. 43 note 6.   176 Flood's speech is in *Parl.Hist.*, xxviii, 451–65, R[odd], ed., *Letters to Flood*, pp 181–94 and Henry Flood, *A speech in March 1790 on the reform of parliament* (London, 1790).   177 *Parl. Hist.*, xxviii, 465–76; Parsons memoir (Rosse Papers, C/ 14/ 1–5); Ryan, *Beauties of Ireland*, ii, 149.

April. Flood gave no reason for his absence from this or further meetings of the Society, but he can hardly have been impressed by the poverty of its organizational capacities.[178] Besides, he had the pressing matter of his parliamentary representation to attend to, as 1790 was an election year in Ireland as well as Britain.

ENFORCED RETIREMENT

Flood's electoral position was very problematic as the 1780s drew to a close. He was in the unusual position of holding insecure seats in two different legislatures. Given his contribution to the undoing of oligarchical control in Seaford in 1786, he retained hopes that he would be returned for this constituency. However, he had broken with Thomas Oldfield, and the emergence of Thomas Harben, an ambitious banker, as a force in the constituency in the mid-1780s had produced a tense struggle for control between Harben and Lancelot Harrison, who had managed the treasury interest since the 1760s. Harben's good tactical sense enabled him to triumph over Harrison's experience, and because his plans for the borough did not include him, Flood stood no chance of re-election.[179]

His prospects of holding on to his seat in Ireland were only a little less unpromising. As the representative by purchase for the borough of Enniskillen, Flood had no entitlement to represent the constituency after 1790. Indeed, the decision of its proprietor, the earl of Enniskillen, to keep it in the family meant that Flood had to look elsewhere, and spurred by atavistic ambition, his thoughts turned once more to Callan. The corporation was the subject of further litigation in 1786, and while it is not clear precisely what the case (which was heard before the Court of King's Bench) was about, it did not pave the way for the restoration of Flood's ascendancy in the borough. At the same time, he contrived to uphold a symbolic claim to control the borough by maintaining a separate corporation. In practice, the borough remained firmly under the control of James Agar (from 1790 Lord Callan) throughout the 1780s and he ensured against revolt by maintaining a minimum number of electors and by entrusting office to non-residents. Matters remained thus until the late 1780s when Flood and he agreed 'a compromise' which finally brought the dispute over the borough which had lasted the length of Flood's adult life to a close. As a result, Flood formally accepted that the Agars controlled the borough while James Agar restored the burgess roll to its 'proper number', following which two Castle nominees were returned to represent the constituency as a *quid pro quo* for his ennoblement.[180]

178 Minute book of the Society for Constitutional Information, 27 Nov. 1789, 19 Feb., 12, 19 Mar.1790 (P.R.O., T.S.11/961/3507 ff 201–2, 204–6, 208–9, 211–6); Black, *The association*, p. 217 n 14.　179 Oldfield, *Representative history*, v, 460–67; Flood to Parsons, 10 Oct. 1789 (Rosse Papers, C/ 8/61); R.Thorne, ed., *A history of parliament: the House of Commons 1790–1820* (5 vols, London, 1986), ii, 475–6.　180 *D.E.P.*, 11 May, 3 Oct. 1786; *Clonmel Gazette*, 8 Dec. 1790; E.M. Johnston, ed., 'State of

Conscious that he stood little chance of being returned either for Enniskillen or for Callan, Flood commenced his search for a safe Irish seat in early November 1788 by requesting Lord Charlemont 'to speak for me to Lord Longford, whose borough I once represented, and should wish to do so again in the usual terms.' His letter went astray, and it was left to Lawrence Parsons to convey Flood's request orally. However, when Charlemont approached Longford he was informed that the peer 'had resolved never more to sell'. Mrs Grenville, who controlled the borough of Granard, was also unforthcoming with the result that Parsons was forced to accelerate his search for a seat as the date of the election approached. He appeared to have succeeded in July 1789 when he concluded an agreement with Lord Aldborough, the patron of the borough of Baltinglass, to nominate Flood to represent the constituency in return for a payment of between £2,500 and £3,000. As evidence of his intentions, Aldborough had both Flood and Parsons appointed to Baltinglass borough corporation.[181]

Relieved that he had solved one of his parliamentary problems, Flood awaited the announcement of the dissolution of the Irish parliament with peace of mind. His plan was to stay in England until the Westminster legislature was dissolved and to pursue his electoral ambitions in England prior to returning to Ireland to take his seat for Baltinglass. However, matters did not proceed according to plan because early in April 1790 he was informed by Lord Aldborough that he could not after all honour his promise to return him because of over-riding family commitments.[182] When Aldborough made his bargain with Parsons in 1789 he was, he claimed, free to do so because his 'family' had 'told' him 'they did not wish to come into parliament'. However, when the general election was called, fourteen corporators approached 'beseeching me not to reject my own family' and making it clear 'that ... a most violent opposition would have been the consequence if I persisted in rejecting them'. Their choice for the constituency was Aldborough's brother, John Stratford, who was also a candidate for Wicklow County, and they were sufficiently numerous to triumph over Flood's supporters, several of whom (Flood included) missed the poll, to ensure that Stratford secured the return when the election was held in late April.[183]

Flood was taken aback by what he regarded as an act of betrayal. His initial response was to refuse 'to relinquish the seat' he believed was his by right since he had agreed to represent it and paid £1,400 to Lord Aldborough. However, since he

the Irish House of Commons in 1791', *P.R.I.A.*, 59C (1957), p. 31; Power, 'Parliamentary representation', p. 331; Falkland, *Parliamentary representation*, p. 47.   181 Flood to Parsons, 18 Nov 1788, Aldborough to Parsons, 4 July 1789 (Rosse Papers, C/8/47, 61); Charlemont to Flood, 25 Nov. in R[odd] ed., *Letters to Flood*, pp 173–4; Crofton to Dundas, 6 Jan., Mahon to [Dundas], 17, 21 Jan. 1789 (North Yorkshire R.O., Zetland Papers (P.R.O.N.I., T 3418/16–8)); *Dublin Chronicle*, 15 Apr. 1790; Namier and Brooke, eds, *The House of Commons*, i, 12.   182 Flood to Parsons, 12, 16, 17 Apr. 1790 (Rosse Papers, C/8/64, 65, 66).   183 Aldborough to Parsons, 3 May, Flood to Parsons, 11 May 1790 (Rosse Papers, C/8/67, 69).

was neither in possession of the seat nor in Ireland, there was little he could do to prevent Aldborough confirming the return. His instinct was to make the matter a dispute of honour, and he would surely have done so if he had been aware that John Stratford had reached an agreement with the Lord Lieutenant, the earl of Westmorland, to deliver two votes and to keep 'Flood out' in return for a pension or employment worth £1,000 p.a.[184] It is likely, given their reputed 'dire enmity', that the earl of Aldborough was unaware of his brother's engagement, as he genuinely desired to aid Flood. Indeed, he professed on 3 May that he was 'on the look out for a seat for you, and shall readily contribute towards it, if you desire it'. Flood was not appeased by Aldborough's offer of help.[185] His suspicious mind detected treachery, and his priority was to put it to right. With this in view, he requested Parsons to seek a commitment from Aldborough that he would secure the vacant Baltinglass seat if John Stratford was elected to sit for County Wicklow. This was a long shot because John Stratford's hopes rested on the outcome of an election petition, but Flood at least had the consolation of an assurance that he should 'certainly ... succeed' if Stratford's petition was successful. In the meantime, he did not let up in his search for a seat elsewhere, but approaches to Lord Granard (concerning Mullingar) and Lord Mornington (concerning Trim) proved fruitless.[186]

As time elapsed, and the opening of the Irish parliament grew closer, Flood's desperation for a seat increased. In the middle of May, he advised Parsons to explore every option, Dublin Castle included. He did not anticipate that the Castle would make a seat available directly, but he expressed a hope that it would 'furnish' Lord Aldborough with the means of fulfilling his engagement to him by providing appropriately for John Stratford. Indeed, he made it known to the press that he would 'consider it as a decisive proof of repeated and unmerited hostility' if his hopes were unanswered. He also calculated that it would bring 'a distinct *éclaircissement*' in the 'smothered war' that was being waged against him.[187] This was not the case, and as time passed without a resolution, Flood's hopes dimmed. His situation was so unpromising by 17 May that he requested Parsons to 'summon my relations' to appeal to them to lobby the Chief Secretary, Robert Hobart, on his behalf. The fact that Flood did not write to his family personally (Sir Frederick Flood excepted) indicates how desperate he was and how large a chasm had grown between him and his cousins since the mid-1770s. Not surprisingly, they ignored the summons. Disappointed by the lack of response, Flood sought to browbeat them by allowing it to be 'explicitly understood that I will not consider that relation as a friend who shirks on this occasion', but this also failed to produce the desired result.[188]

184 Flood to Parsons, 16 Apr., 4, 13 May, Aldborough to Flood, [*c.*13 May) (Rosse Papers, C/8/65, 68, 70, 71); Westmorland to Pitt, 22 Jan. 1790 (N.L.I., Union Corres., Ms 886 f 139). 185 Aldborough to Parsons, 3 May, Flood to Parsons, 11 May 1790 (Rosse Papers, C/8/67, 69). 186 Flood to Parsons, 11 May, Aldborough to Flood [*c.*13 May] (Rosse Papers, C/8/69, 70). 187 Flood to Parsons, 13, [ca 13], 14, 15 May 1790 (Rosse Papers, C/8/71, 80, 72, 73). 188 Flood to Parsons, 17, 31 May [May/June 1790] (Rosse Papers, C/8/74, 76, 81).

Flood now had few options. He instructed Parsons to explore every possibility and refused to accept as final the failure of his family to rally to his side. As this suggests, Flood was allowing his desperation for a seat impede his judgement, and his advice to Parsons on 1 June not to 'let difficulties repress you, only think by what expedient to get round what cannot be directly surmounted' was as hapless as his attempt in early July to commit Lord Aldborough 'to promise a return ... in place of that [for] Baltinglass' and to induce him to make 'common cause' in an approach to Dublin Castle. Flood was in a position personally to assess how bleak his situation really was when he arrived belatedly in Ireland on 4 July, having failed to secure his re-election for Seaford. He determined at the outset to persist with his overtures to Lord Aldborough and Major Hobart, and to seek an amenable borough patron.[189] The interruption of his correspondence with Parsons following his return to Ireland means it is not possible to follow his activities, but his hopes soon rested entirely on the outcome of the petition of John Stratford against the return for County Wicklow. The fact that he did not have a seat distressed some who believed he would be 'a very considerable acquisition to the popular party', but this is how it stayed.[190] Stratford's petition failed, and Flood was left to contemplate a life outside parliamentary politics.

From what one can gather it did not prove an especially difficult adjustment. He spent most of his time at Farmley where he put his affairs in order, read, entertained friends (Lawrence Parsons, Ambrose Smith, Dean Kirwan and Peter Burrowes), managed his estates and supervised the improvement of his family home.[191] At the same time he continued to take an interest in political events. He spent the winter of 1790–1 in London as usual, but because his movements were no longer bound by the parliamentary session he was back in Ireland by the spring of 1791 to support Lawrence Parsons' political aspirations.

Flood now vested his political hopes in Parsons, who was the leading independent voice in the Irish House of Commons, and he was delighted that Parsons bounced back from the rejection of his petition against the return for Trinity College in 1790 with victory in the Kings' County bye-election in May 1791.[192] As this indicates, Flood, in retirement, remained committed to reformist politics. He was also critical of the conservative response to the French Revolution and, in particular, of Edmund Burke's anti-revolutionary crusade:

189 Flood to Parsons, 31 May, 1 June, 2, 4 July 1790 (Rosse Papers, C/8/76–9).   190 *Clonmel Gazette*, 31 July, 4 Dec. 1790.   191 Flood to Parsons, 5, 22 Aug. 1790, 19 May, 23 Sept. 1791 (Rosse Papers, C/8/82–5); Map of Burnchurch, Oct. 1789 (Land Commission, Flood-Hanford Papers, Box 5555 (E.C.10055)).   192 *Dublin Chronicle*, 1 Feb.; Petition of Parsons, 1790–91 (T.C.D., Mun.P/1/967); Flood to Parsons, 27 Mar. (R.I.A., Flood Autograph, 3D8/7); Johnston, ed., 'The Irish House of Commons in 1791', p. 2; Flood to Parsons, 19 May. 1791 (Rosse Papers, C/8/84); Elliott, *Tone*, pp 81–3.

The anti-American, anti-Gallican and anti-Philosophic ideas he [Burke] maintains will be too heavy for him. Boswell in his colloquy with Johnson on Burke says that Burke is an hawk, always falling and in rapid pursuit of his object. But he is a hawk that never catches anything, says Johnson. In his climacteric years he has attempted to choose a stormy and insulated summit which he never dared to occupy when in his vigour. The eagle of Mont Blanc is said to start from his eyry and shriek when he sees a tempest coming on like that by which Burke is likely to be shaken. What will the hawk do?[193]

Flood made no attempt to enter the public debate on the Revolution, however. He occupied himself happily as an 'active builder' and had completed the refurbishment of all but 'the attic storey' of his Farmley residence by the autumn of 1791, but he was not to live to enjoy it.[194] He was just recovering from a 'tedious fit of gout' in November 1791 when he 'caught cold ... exerting himself to extinguish a fire' in his carpenter's workshop. The cold flared into pleurisy, and he died, after a few days illness, at 10 p.m. on Friday, 2 December 1791.[195]

193 Flood to Parsons, 19 May 1791 (Rosse Papers, C/8/84).   194 Flood to Parsons, 23 Sept. 1791 (Rosse Papers, C/8/85); M. Quane, ed., 'Tour in Ireland by John Harden in 1797', *J.C.H.A.S.*, 58(1953), p. 27.   195 *Gentleman's Magazine*, 61 (1791), p. 1225; *Cork Gazette*, 7, 17 Dec.; *Dublin Chronicle*, 6 Dec. 1791; Flood, *Memoirs*, p. 390; Ryan, *Worthies of Ireland*, ii, 149.

Conclusion

Because he had effectively withdrawn from active engagement in Irish politics in the mid-1780s, Flood's death did not prompt a major demonstration of public mourning in Ireland. His passing was reported in the main newspapers and magazines in Britain as well as Ireland and he was accorded the honour of a number of extended positive obituaries but, in sharp contrast to Grattan, some thirty years later, his funeral was private and unreported.[1] However, as news of his last will and testament leaked out, public interest increased and by mid-December Flood in death was to find himself the subject of almost as much attention as he was when his political powers were at their height.

WILL

Flood wrote his will in May 1790 as it emerged that he was unlikely to secure a seat in the Irish parliament, and it reflected his angry state of mind at that point because, in contrast to other family members who died without direct heirs, he sought to leave the bulk of his estate outside the family. This is not to say that Flood was bereft of feeling for his friends or relations. As well as providing well for his servants, he bequeathed his wife's companion, Susanna Cockburn, and his own 'faithful' retainer, George Huson, £1,000 each and Ambrose Smith, his life-long friend and joint executor, an annuity of £300 and his property at Maiden Hall on the sole condition that he (Smith) honoured his request to 'assist ... Lady Frances ... with his best advice and endeavours in the execution of ... my will'. By the same token, he sought to ensure the financial well-being of his 'dear wife' by bequeathing to her 'to hold during her life, all the lands, houses, hereditaments and estates whatsoever lying and being in the said county of Kilkenny and in the city of Kilkenny and liberties thereof, and parish of St Canice ... settled on me upon my marriage' and the leasehold and freehold interests he had inherited from his uncle Charles in 1770.[2] This

---

1 See, for example, *Dublin Chronicle*, 10 Dec. 1791; *Gentleman's Magazine*, 61 (1991), p. 1229. Flood was buried in an unostentatious grave in Burnchurch graveyard.   2 Flood's will is printed in Sir Lawrence

was entirely appropriate since Lady Frances's marriage portion had been used to provide for her sister-in-law. However, because Flood's father had only given him a life interest in the lands and stipulated, in the event of Henry's not producing an heir, they should pass to his 'right heir', the expectation within the family was that the lands at Farmley and in Kilkenny city would pass directly to his estranged cousin John, who was his heir-at-law. Flood was so anxious this should not happen on his death, or on the death of his wife, he ignored his own limited title and bequeathed all the lands in his possession elsewhere. In deference to his Uncle Charles' wishes, he decreed that on his wife's death the parcels of freehold and leasehold in Gowran barony he had inherited from that quarter should pass to Warden Flood of Paulstown, with whom he had remained on reasonable terms. More significantly, he instructed that the Farmley estate, worth an estimated £4,000 per annum, should pass to Trinity College 'to hold in fee' to 'institute and maintain, as a perpetual establishment, a professorship of and for the native Irish or Erse language', to provide 'annual and liberal premium[s]' for the two best compositions in prose or verse in Irish, English, Latin and Greek, and to enable the university to 'purchase ... all printed books and manuscripts in the ... native Irish or Erse' and other 'modern polished languages'. Like the rest of the will, this was vulnerable to legal challenge and, anticipating problems, Flood stipulated that if the bequest to Trinity College did not 'take effect', the lands and properties within the city and liberties of Kilkenny should pass to Ambrose Smith and that the Farmley estate should pass to Hatton Flood, one of the sons of his late Uncle Francis.[3]

Flood's attempt to leave the bulk of his estate to Trinity College was so unexpected that it prompted animated public and private debate. Reaction ranged from the sceptical to the effusive. His brother-in-law John Beresford was 'puzzled', but most of the extensive coverage it was accorded by the press was complimentary. The *Dublin Chronicle*, for example, described Flood's decision as the action of an 'exalted mind'; the *Gentleman's Magazine* deemed it the work 'of a mighty mind and patriotic heart'; while, anticipating a welcome surge in the study of the Irish language, the *Corke Gazette* suggested that a statue should be erected in his honour.[4] Others, inevitably, were more pragmatic. 'Several schoolmasters' were reported to be busily occupied 'collecting all the Irish manuscripts they' could 'find expecting they will soon be bought by the university'. More pertinently, if these enterprising pedagogues were to benefit, Trinity College had to ensure it actually received Flood's legacy. His long-time antagonist, Provost John Hely-Hutchinson, had 'little expectation' that the university would 'profit by [Flood's] intentions', but following con-

Parsons, *Observations on the bequest of Henry Flood esq. to Trinity College, Dublin* ... (Dublin, 1795), pp 7–12.   3 Ibid., pp 9, 13–18; Will of Charles Flood, 11 Oct. 1770 (Land Commission, Keogh Papers, Box 13); *Dublin Chronicle*, 10 Dec. 1791; Flood, *Memoirs*, pp 394–7.   4 Annesley to Downshire, 6 Dec. (P.R.O.N.I., Downshire Papers, D607/B/325); *Dublin Chronicle*, 10, 29 Dec.; *Corke Gazette*, 14, 17, 21, 31 Dec. 1791.

sultation with senior fellows he set about engaging legal counsel to represent the institution 'in the suit', which, he calculated, 'will undoubtedly take place'.[5]

Hely-Hutchinson's conclusion was correct. John Flood, who stood to lose so much if his cousin's will was allowed to stand, did not hesitate to assert his right of inheritance, and he filed a bill at the Court of Exchequer in April 1792 for 'an ejectment on the title ... against Lady Flood, for the recovery of the lands devised to her ... charging the illegitimacy of Henry Flood and the right of succession of John Flood, as heir of Warden Flood'.[6] A battery of family testimony was gathered by both sides, but the evidence pointed conclusively to the fact that Henry Flood was born outside wedlock and a judgement was returned in favour of John Flood. Realising that they had to reverse the decision if they were to have any entitlement to the estate, Lady Flood and Trinity College 'joined in defence' of Henry Flood and of his will in the Court of Chancery in May 1793. The 'only question' for this court to decide was whether Henry Flood 'was born in wedlock or not', because this would determine whether or not John Flood's claim to the disputed property was justified and whether Lady Flood would, as she hoped, 'be quieted in the possession of the estates'. To her disappointment, the Chancery Court upheld the decision of the Exchequer,[7] following which Lady Flood was 'dispossessed of Farmley' and forced to take up residence elsewhere. However, she had not exhausted her legal options and further legal proceedings ensued in the late summer. It is not possible, because of the terseness of contemporary reports to establish precisely what transpired, but it appears that following this

> a compromise was entered into between John Flood and Lady F[rances] M. Flood, which resulted in a deed of the 27th of June 1794; by which it was agreed between them, that the suit and action then pending should be abandoned during the life of Lady F.M. Flood; and that the County Kilkenny estate should be given up to John Flood; while Lady F.M. should retain for her life the city of Kilkenny estate; and her jointure of £600 a year, charged on the county estate by the deed of 1762; and should give up forthwith all title deeds and tenants leases in her possession.[8]

This was a defensible compromise since it offered Lady Flood, who was the innocent party in this saga of greed, deceit and jealousy, a genuine prospect of living out her old age in reasonable physical and financial comfort. It is not clear that she was allowed this, as John Flood sought during the remainder of his life to gain full con-

5 Provost to [ ], *c*.Dec 1791 (T.C.D., MUN/P/1/1383/18); *Dublin Chronicle*, 9 Feb. 1792; Brady, ed., *Catholics in the eighteenth-century press* (Maynooth, 1986), p. 282.   6 Hayes and Jones, *Reports of cases*, p. xxiv; *Dublin Chronicle*, 10 Jan., 26 Apr. 1792; Notes on Flood v Flood, [1792] (N.A., Langrishe Papers, B.R., KK, 38/16).   7 Hayes and Jones, *Reports on cases*, p. xxiv; Case on the part of the College, 12 April 1792 (T.C.D., MUN/P/1/1056); *Clonmel Gazette*, 29 May 1793.   8 Hayes and Jones, *Reports on cases*, pp xxiv-xxv; *Dublin Chronicle*, 25 July 1793.

trol of the family lands. Potentially the biggest obstacle in his way was Trinity College. John Flood contemplated disputing the College's entitlement to benefit under his cousin's will in 1792, but he aborted this strategy on the ground that it would not serve any purpose since its claim to the lands and other property was second to Lady Flood's. Moreover, according to Charles Vallancey, College officials were quietly confident that when Lady Frances (whose health was far from robust) died their claim would be upheld.[9]

Since Lady Frances lived until 1815, they had to wait much longer than they anticipated. Meantime, John Flood contrived to strengthen his position by 'purchas[ing] and obtain[ing] conveyances in 1799 and 1804 ... of the reversionary estates devised to [Hatton Flood and Ambrose Smith] respectively ... in case the devise to the College should not take effect'. He also persuaded Lady Frances to execute a deed in July 1806 'whereby, in consideration of an annuity of similar amount charged on the county of Kilkenny estates, she conveyed to John Flood all her life estate in the premises in the city of Kilkenny'.[10] This meant that when John Flood made his will shortly before his death in 1807, he was in a position to bequeath all the Flood lands to his two sons John and Robert, and that it was they who had to mount a defence when, following Lady Frances' demise eight years later, 'the Trinity lawyers requested that [Henry Flood's] will, as regards the College, be carried into effect' directly or, if the devise to them was void, that proceeding be instituted to vest the estate in trustees who would make the income from the property available to the College. Aware that Trinity had a weak case (they would have moved directly for an ejectment otherwise), John and Robert Flood countered by claiming that Henry Flood's devise was 'altogether ... void' and they secured legal support for their position. Freehold 'devises to corporations ... are void in Ireland', the Master of the Rolls determined, because the law on the subject provided only for alienations in such cases to archbishops and bishops.[11]

This was a serious setback for Trinity College's claim. But encouraged by Lawrence Parsons, who was so anxious to ensure that Henry Flood's intentions were honoured he supplied the College with documents and other matter and published a pamphlet in 1795 defending and explaining his decision to leave his estate to Trinity,[12] they determined to appeal. Their main grounds was their contention that if the judgement was allowed to stand, Trinity, or any other educational institution, would be rendered 'incapable of taking by devise for any purpose connected with the general objects of learning or religion, even with the King's licence'.[13] Their appeal was heard by the Court of Exchequer on Monday 12 May, 1817, but the

9 Vallancey to Yonge, 20 Mar. 1792 (B.L.,O.C.,Vallancey letters).   10 Hayes and Jones, *Reports on cases*, p. xxv. According to Warden Flood (*Memoirs*, p. 395), Hatton Flood was paid £4,000 in return.   11 Hayes and Jones, *Reports on cases*, pp xxvi-xxxviii.   12 Parsons, *Observations on the bequest of Flood*, pp 23–75; Parsons to Waller, 25 Apr. 1793, Rosse to Provost, 14 Oct. 1815 (T.C.D., MUN/P/1/1057, 1383/1).   13 Legal opinions, July-Oct. 1816 (T.C.D., MUN/P/1/1383/3-7).

Lord Chancellor and Lord Chief Justice Downes, whom the Lord Chancellor brought in to assist him in the case, upheld the judgement of the Master of the Rolls.[14] As a result, Trinity was compelled to cede all hopes of obtaining Henry Flood's estates, and John and Robert Flood were confirmed in possession.

With this decision, Henry Flood's attempt to disinherit his cousins and, on his wife's death, to make his estate available to Trinity College for educational purposes had finally come to naught. His was, contemporaries were agreed, an unusual last will and testament, but the surprised comments it elicited reflected the general poverty of understanding of Flood's personality. It is not entirely surprising that it should be so since Henry's family biographer professed not to know why 'John Flood ..., the heir-at-law ..., was overlooked' when Henry made his will, and lamely explained the 'unaccountable' preference shown Ambrose Smith as a manifestation of 'the eccentricities of genius'. He was also puzzled as to why Flood bequeathed an estate he estimated was worth £5,000 a year to Trinity College to fund a professorship of Irish, a number of academic prizes and the purchase of books. But in this instance he could, at least, invoke Flood's affirmation that the study 'of ... great characters ... of ancient or modern nations' would stimulate 'GREAT DEEDS' in the future and Lawrence Parsons' *Observations on the bequest of Henry Flood* in support of the simplified explanation he offered.[15]

In fact, Henry Flood's will is less resistant to explanation than Warden's *Memoirs* suggest, and it is reasonable to conclude that it was fuelled primarily by Henry's wish to ensure that John Flood of Floodhall, with whom he had been at odds since the 1770s, did not benefit in any way by his death. The solution he hit upon failed primarily because he was powerless to alter the circumstances of his birth, or the terms upon which he had been entrusted with the family lands by his father. To complicate matters further, he had gone about attempting to endow Trinity College in a rather crude way. It is unlikely that anything he might have done or said would have prevented litigation by his cousin aimed at overturning his will, but it is significant that he never sought to explain his intentions to him during his lifetime and that he also did not consult with Charles Vallancey to establish how he would respond to the suggestion that he should become 'the first professor' of Irish at Trinity College. Vallancey was understandably flattered by the notice, but he deemed 'the place ... so very incompatible to my profession and rank in the army' that he was unwilling to accept it. His object, he explained to Sir George Yonge in the spring of 1792, was promotion to the military rank of major-general not an academic chair.[16]

Because of their ignorance of Flood's biography, contemporaries interested in fostering antiquarian research interpreted his will reflexively as proof of his 'undeviating patriotism': as one observed 'what can be more characteristic of a

14 Edmund Hayes, *Reports of cases argued and determined in the Court of Exchequer in Ireland* (Dublin, 1837), pp 611–41.   15 Flood, *Memoirs*, pp 395–407.   16 As note 9.

mighty mind and patriotic heart than the whole scheme of this great bequest ... to the people of Ireland ... to draw its ancient records from neglect and oblivion'.[17] People certainly believed that the country possessed the materials, that they needed attention urgently and that Flood's generosity provided the means whereby this could be accomplished and Trinity College became a centre of world learning:

> There are many manuscripts in the Irish language, which are the most ancient and authentic records that any nation in Europe can boast. These are now either scattered and perishing in the possession of individuals in Ireland, or consigned to oblivion in the libraries of France and Rome. To have these venerable memorials deposited in the University of Dublin was his first object. To provide by the establishment of an Irish professor for the development of all the curious and interesting information they contained, the next. After this, the income of his estate is to replenish the library of that University with all valuable books ancient and modern, which must render it in time the most noble repository of literary production in the world.[18]

According to an uncorroborated report, Flood left behind a collection of Irish manuscripts, which he hoped would be published.[19] If this could be substantiated, it would suggest that Flood's personal interest in Irish antiquities and the Irish past was deep and sustained and that the encomia bestowed upon him by enthusiastic antiquarians were well-deserved. The problem is that whereas there is plenty of evidence to demonstrate his life long engagement with English and classical literature,[20] it is less easy to sustain a similar case with regard to the Irish language and 'ancient Irish' past. County Kilkenny, and the Callan area in particular, was rich in antiquities and ruins,[21] but it cannot be shown that Flood afforded them special enquiry either as a youth or as a young adult. It can be suggested that he became interested in pre-Norman Ireland in the 1760s as background to his study of post-conquest Irish history because he described the 'ancient Irish' in his introduction to the 1770 edition of Molyneux's *Case* as

> fierce, active, robust, patient of hunger and of toil, proud in being the posterity of the heroes who chased the prowling Danes from their country, plumed as they were at the time with repeated victories over the prostrate Saxons.[22]

---

17 *Dublin Chronicle*, 10 Dec. 1791; Flood, *Memoirs*, p. 407.   18 *Gentleman's Magazine*, 61 (1791), p. 1229.   19 *Dublin Chronicle*, 10 Dec.; *Cork Gazette*, 14 Dec. 1791.   20 Above pp 175–6; Webb to Flood, 7 Nov. 1783 in R[odd], ed., *Letters to Flood*, p. 122; Grieg, ed., *The Farington diary*, i, 202. It is noteworthy that he also sought to encourage Dermody, the poet (J.C. Beckett, 'Literature in English 1691–1800' in Moody and Vaughan, eds, *A new history*, iv, 455).   21 Carrigan, *Ossory*, ii, 2; Mason, *A statistical ... survey of Ireland*, iii, 530–2.   22 Molyneux, *Case of Ireland ... stated*, p. xv.

The language here is significant because it indicates that Flood accepted the positive portrayal of pre-Norman Ireland that was currently favoured in contemporary antiquarian and historical scholarship. One should not attach too much weight to one sentence, but the fact that Flood should make such a statement and 'bequeath the proceeds of an estate to Trinity College in order to found a chair of Irish philology' does, as Joep Leerssen has argued, represent 'a remarkable indication of the sympathy between Irish antiquarianism and patriot political thought' that developed in the 1770s and 1780s even if it does not of itself demonstrate how deep Flood's interests ran.[23] At the same time, it is highly significant that he and the other prominent patriots (Lord Charlemont, Sir Lucius O'Brien, Hussey Burgh, Henry Grattan) favoured 'the speculative, mystical' conclusions advanced by Vallancey' over 'the rationalist, debunking, cynical' approach espoused by Thomas Campbell and Edward Ledwich because it suggests that his and their interest in Irish history, antiquities and language did not arise out of disinterested scholarship, but out of a political wish to affirm the entitlement of the Protestant interest in Ireland to commercial and constitutional equality with England.[24] This is corroborated by the justification Lucius O'Brien provided the Dublin Society's standing committee on antiquities when he invited Charles O'Conor to become a corresponding member:

> If by shewing that the inhabitants of this islands were all times respectable and often the masters & more often the instructors of Britain we can convince our neighbours that, alltho' Providence has at present given them superior strength, yet ought they not to treat the Irish as a Barbarous, or a contemptible people.[25]

There can be no gainsaying that Henry Flood's comprehension of the Irish past was influenced, if not shaped, by the tradition of historical investigation represented by scholars and controversialists like O'Conor, Walter Harris and John Keogh, whose writings stimulated many of his contemporaries to look positively upon Ireland's Gaelic, and particularly Ireland's pre-Norman, past, and to conclude with them that it was an era of signal achievement.[26] It cannot be proven that Flood read the works of these authors, but it is unlikely that he was not familiar with O'Conor's *Dissertations on the ancient history of Ireland* (1753) since Dr Johnson, whom he so admired and who was eager to learn more about this 'illustrious' phase in Irish history, encouraged O'Conor to research this subject.[27] Johnson's main interest was language, which was not O'Conor's or Flood's speciality, but following the publica-

---

23 J.Th. Leerssen, *Mere Irish and Fíor-Ghael: studies in the idea of Irish nationality, its development and literary expression prior to the nineteenth century* (Amsterdam, 1986), p. 420.   24 T.C.D., Burgh Papers, Ms 9318/4; DeValera, 'Antiquarian investigation' *passim*; Leerssen, *Mere Irish and Fíor-Ghael*, pp 420–1; Leerssen, 'Anglo-Irish patriotism', pp 22–4; Clare O'Halloran, 'Irish recreations of the Gaelic past: the challenge of MacPherson's Ossian', *Past and Present*, no 124 (1989), pp 72–3.   25 Cited in Leerssen, *Mere Irish and Fíor-Ghael*, pp 403–4.   26 Leerssen, *Mere Irish and Fíor-Ghael*, p. 376; de Valera, 'Irish antiquarianism', pp 89–92; Murphy, 'Lucas', pp 98–9, 183   27 Johnson to O'Conor, 9 Apr. 1757, 19

tion in the early 1760s of James MacPherson's controversial *Ossian* epics, the perception that Gaelic was 'a barbaric tongue' was revised and there was a dramatic rise in interest in language and in the appreciation of the importance of the discovery and preparation of editions of old manuscripts.[28] Henry Flood was as intrigued by the Ossian controversy as many of his contemporaries. Indeed, he became a member of the Dublin Society which made antiquarian research a priority, but whereas Lucius O'Brien and William Burton Conyngham actively encouraged scholarship, Flood did not engage so directly.[29] His interest derived from the work of others, and the most formative influence on him was Charles Vallancey. An English officer in the Royal Engineers stationed in Ireland, Vallancey's researches led him to conclude that the aboriginal people of Ireland were Phoenicians (rather than uncivilized northern Europeans or Scandians, which was the main rival theory) who had come to Ireland from Spain, and that therefore pre-Norman Ireland possessed an advanced and sophisticated civilisation. Indeed, the Irish language, Vallancey argued, was related not just to Phoenician, but to Chinese and Persian and was therefore one of the purest and oldest (older than Scots-Gaelic) languages in existence.[30]

Vallancey's speculative conclusions were challenged by the likes of Edward Ledwich, which created deep fissures within Irish antiquarian scholarship. However, Vallancey's supporters, Henry Flood included, were predisposed to accept his assessment because his reinforcement of the image of pre-conquest Ireland as a complex and advanced society challenged the establishment view that civilisation only came to Ireland with the Normans, and reinforced the patriots' contention that the country would profit if it was liberated from its political and economic subordination to Great Britain that had been brought into being since the Tudor conquest.[31] Indeed, it was not long before Vallancey's view that Irish/Erse was not a 'primitive' language was being propounded in Johnson's circle. Flood welcomed this, and he can only have been encouraged further by the attention given to Gaelic literary material in the 1780s.[32] At the same time, he did not become involved personally in

May 1777 in B. Redford, ed., *The letters of Samuel Johnson* (5 vols, Oxford, 1992–4), i, 151–2, iii, 23–4; Leerssen, *Mere Irish and Fíor-Ghael*, p. 382; Jeanne Sheehy, *The discovery of Ireland's past: the Celtic revival 1830–1930* (London, 1980), pp 13–14.   28 O'Halloran, 'Irish recreations', pp 82–4; John Pinkerton, *An enquiry into the history of Scotland preceding ... 1056* (Edinburgh, 1789).   29 R[odd], ed., *Letters to Flood*, p. 172; *The Royal Charter of the Dublin Society*, p. 59; *Dublin Chronicle*, 25 Oct. 1787; C.E.F. Trench, 'William Burton Conyngham', *J.R.S.A.I.*, 115 (1985), pp 42–8.   30 de Valera, 'Antiquarianism', p. 135; Parsons, *Observations*, pp 14, 27–46; O'Halloran, 'Irish recreations', pp 81–2; Walter Love, 'The Hibernian Antiquarian Society', *Studies* (1962), pp 422–3; Love, 'Charles O'Conor of Belanagare and Thomas Leland's 'philosophical' history of Ireland', *I.H.S.*, xiii (1962), pp 18–19; Monica Nevin, 'General Charles Vallancey 1725–1812', *J.R.S.A.I.* 123 (1993), pp 25–7.   31 Love, 'The Hibernian Antiquarian Society', pp 422–3; Love, 'Charles O'Conor', pp 18–19; Flood's speech, Oct. 1765 (Rosse papers, F/21).   32 F.A. Pottle, ed., *Boswell in extremes 1776–8* (London, 1970), pp 236–8; de Valera, 'Antiquarianism', pp 242–3, 247–8; R.A. Breatnach, 'The end of a tradition: a survey of eighteenth-century Gaelic literature', *Studia Hibernica*, i (1961), pp 145–6.

promoting this activity. He became a member of the Royal Irish Academy, which identified the collection and publication of Irish language material among its goals on its foundation in 1785, but he did not respond to the urgings of its president, Lord Charlemont, to contribute to its proceedings.[33] He was, and remained, essentially an observer whose interest in Irish history, Irish language and Irish antiquities derived, as Lawrence Parsons explained, from his intrinsically political object of 'reliev[ing] this country from the most unjust charges of ignorance and barbarism, at a time when it was by far more enlightened and civilized than any of the adjacent nations'.[34] He certainly had no wish 'to bring the Irish language again into general use'. Indeed, one cannot even say that he was at one with Henry Grattan who averred that he 'should be sorry that the Irish language should be forgotten, but glad that the English language should be generally understood'.[35] He bequeathed his estate to Trinity College for the study of Irish and for the collection and study of Irish manuscripts because he believed this was the route to 'the truths of antient history' that would enhance the self-image of the kingdom in its relationship with Britain and thereby enhance the prospect of Irish Protestants enjoying the same rights as Englishmen. Like William Brownlow, Jonathan Swift and George Macartney, who were also interested in the collection and promotion of the study of Irish manuscripts, Flood's engagement had no covert separatist dimension because such aspirations did not enter into his conception of Anglo-Irish relations.[36] Indeed, considering the modest personal priority he gave the subject during his lifetime, it is quite likely that Henry Flood would not have made his celebrated will in favour of Trinity College and the Irish language had he not been childless and had he been on amicable terms with his heir-at-law.

ASSESSMENT

The fact that Flood's estate was not put to the use he directed in his last will and testament could be seen as the *leitmotif* of his whole political career. Indeed, the finest assessment of his political life has been published in a collection devoted to 'losers' in history.[37] It is not surprising that this should be so since generations of

33 R.B. McDowell, 'The main narrative' in T.O'Raifeartaigh, ed., *The Royal Irish Academy: a bicentennial history* (Dublin, 1985), p. 12; de Valera, 'Antiquarianism', pp 149–51; Charlemont to Flood, 2 Aug. 1787 in R[odd], ed., *Letters to Flood*, p. 171.   34 Parsons, *Observations*, pp 24–5.   35 Parsons, *Observations*, p. 24; L.M. Cullen, *The emergence of modern Ireland 1600–1900* (London, 1981), pp 138–9.   36 Parsons, *Observations*, pp 55–6, 58–9; B. Cunningham and R. Gillespie, 'An Ulster settler and his Irish manuscripts', *Eigse*, 21 (1987), pp 27–36; Roebuck, ed., *Macartney of Lissanoure* (Belfast, 1983), pp 288; McGawley to Macartney, 14 Aug. 1790 (P.R.O.N.I., Macartney/Filgate Papers, D2225/7/44); Carole Fabricant, *Swift's landscape* (London, 1982), p. 288.   37 David Dickson, 'Henry Flood and the eighteenth-century Irish patriots' in Ciaran Brady, ed., *Worsted in the game: losers in Irish history* (Dublin, 1989), pp 97–108.

historical commentators have interpreted his life in only slightly less critical terms. However, since by the same token few political careers can be defined as 'successful', one might question the appositeness of such a reductionist approach. In Flood's case, it suggests (though Dickson does not do this) that one should overlook his signal contribution to the definition and articulation of political patriotism in the 1760s, his role in the elaboration of 'the 1782 constitution' and his commitment to the cause of parliamentary reform in Britain as well as Ireland in the 1780s. It suggests also that his attempt both in his politics and in his life to make the patriot aspiration of constitutional equality with Britain a reality and his commanding presence in the Irish House of Commons over two decades were of little consequence, and this is hardly sustainable.

Henry Flood achieved great political renown during his lifetime because he was one of the most talented patriot politicians the eighteenth-century Irish parliament produced. He achieved this despite that fact that he possessed a personality which did not encourage confidence or win trust. He could be 'uncommonly pleasing' in social situations because of his 'very extensive knowledge' and 'gentleness of manners'. He was also capable of acts of great generosity and of winning the devoted loyalty of those in whom he trusted and confided.[38] However, this encompassed only a small percentage of those with whom he came into contact, and the prevailing impression of most others was that he was 'overbearing in council ..., too ardent in debate, [and] ... unyielding to persuasion'. Indeed, according to Lawrence Parsons, Philip Tisdall declined on one occasion to take Flood to task when he was 'animadverting freely on the government' because he did not want to become the target of his vitriol. To compound matters, he was also secretive and disinclined to confide in his political colleagues and, following his acceptance of office in 1775, to act 'in concert' with others.[39]

The reserve, remoteness and singularity which so non-plussed Flood's peers in the 1770s and 1780s was less in evidence when he first attracted political notice in the early 1760s. He was aided then by his physical presence, which was 'tall, erect and graceful'. He had a hare-lip (which only the most malicious ever referred to[40]) but, despite this, he was regarded as good looking until a severe attack of smallpox when he was at the Inns of Court in the 1750s left its mark on his countenance and 'somewhat impaired his speaking'. He overcame this debility, and he enjoyed good health and a 'robust constitution' until his middle years when it was gradually 'impaired and broken down' by increasingly frequent and, from the mid-1780s, by in-

---

38 *Gentleman's Magazine*, 61(1791), p. 1225; *Life of Grattan*, i, 201; R[odd] ed., *Letters to Flood*, introduction. 39 *Gentleman's Magazine*, 61(1791), p. 1164; Rosse Papers, C/15/1; Flood, *Memoirs*, p. 230; R[odd], ed., *Letters to Flood*, introduction; Sayles, ed., 'Irish parliament in 1782', p. 267. 40 Cooke to Eden, 25 July 1782 (B.L., Auckland Papers, Add. Ms 34418 ff 510–11); *Parl. Reg. (Irl)*, ii, 41–2; above pp 352, 391.

creasingly serious afflictions.[41] Despite contrary claims by his opponents, Flood sought not to allow illness restrict him politically though it took an increasing toll as he got older; it certainly did not inhibit his oratorical capacities which had been his passport to eminence in the 1760s.

Oratorical proficiency was highly prized in the Irish parliament in the late eighteenth century, so much so that J.R. Scott used it as his main criterion to assess the skills and abilities of the dozens of politicians that figure in his valuable *Review of the principal characters*. Many of the individuals analyzed in this and other works in eighteenth-century collective political biography are now known only to specialists, but the fact that Hussey Burgh, John Hely-Hutchinson, Isaac Corry, Barry Yelverton, Denis Daly, John Foster, John Philpot Curran, Henry Grattan and Henry Flood, to name only the most eminent, are remembered as exceptional parliamentary orators emphasises the point.[42] Not surprisingly, there is little unanimity as to which was the finest, but all are agreed that Flood's 'splendid talents and superior abilities' entitle him to automatic inclusion among the first rank, and his claim to head this list is reinforced by the fact that, in the words of Henry Grattan junior, it was he 'who introduced oratory into the House of Commons'.[43] Prior to his emergence in the 1760s, debate was staid, dispassionate and undemonstrative; with Flood it became increasingly mannered, energetic and argumentative.

Flood's oratorical impact was first and foremostly the product of hard work and effort. It is significant that he studied public speaking by, among other means, scrutinising 'the expressions and delivery of the best actors' and by learning how to use his voice to best effect. He was enabled by this means to overcome his 'provincial' accent when 'he declaimed', and since set-piece orations were a central feature of political debate throughout his political life this was most advantageous. Like Grattan, Flood prepared all his 'great speeches' in advance and learned them by heart, and if this lent itself to a style of speaking that was at once 'more ... dignified and pompous' than was the fashion at Westminster, it mattered little since he was commonly acknowledged as its finest exponent.[44] More importantly, and in vivid contrast to Grattan whose language was 'lofty, magnificent [and] copious ... always possessing a pleasing warmth, expressive of feeling and imparting spirit',[45] Flood adeptly combined logic, reason and insight with information and oratorical pyrotechnics:

41 Rosse's Life of Flood, 1813 (Rosse Papers, C/12); Donleavy, *Irish dress*, p. 121; R[odd], ed., *Letters to Flood*, p. b; *Life of Grattan*, i, 198, 201.   42 Beckett, 'Literature in English 1691–1800', p. 466; William O'Regan, *Memoirs of the legal, literary and political life of the right honourable John Philpot Curran* (London, 1817), pp xv, 19; *Life of Grattan*, i, 277; Burgh's oratory, c.1820 (B.L., O.C., Flood files); Political recollections of the earl of Rosse (N.L.I., Ms 13841).   43 Scott, *Principal characters*, p. 203; *Life of Grattan*, i, 197; Prior, *Life of Malone*, pp 39, 361.   44 Scott, *Principal characters*, pp 203–9 and *passim*; Rosse Papers, C/12/1, C/15/1; *Life of Grattan*, i, 197–8.   45 MacDougall, *Sketches of Irish political characters*, pp 243–5; Greig, ed., *Farington diary*, ii, 152–3; Flood, *Memoirs*, pp 225–8; Scott, *Principal characters*, pp 203–9, 185–93; Mac Nevin, *History of the Volunteers*, pp 126–8; Drennan to McTier, 5 Feb. 1791 in Chart, ed., *Drennan letters*, p. 53; Burtchaell, *Kilkenny members*, p. 151.

He on every great occasion shewed a great and comprehensive mind replete with knowledge, ardent, vigorous, acute and argumentative. His wit, and sarcasm, and happy allusions (for his mind was replete with imagery) would have highly distinguished any other man; but *convincing* being his *chief* object, and the faculty of reasoning his *principal* power, his adversaries have represented it as his only talent. His classical allusions were never trite, always short, and uncommonly happy; and his metaphors, chaste, pure and unmixed. Powerful as he was in stating, enforcing and illustrating subjects which he propounded in parliament, and on which he always shewed that he had obtained every possible information, he was still more impressive in reply, always preserving his temper, and refuting his opponents with the same perspicuity, precision, correctness and elegance of language, which marked his original speech. His memory was so tenacious that he frequently, at the end of a long debate, answered every member of any weight who had spoken on the opposite side, refuting their arguments *seriatim*, without the aid of a single note;... His admiration of the great Grecian orator [Demosthenes] led him to make, perhaps, too frequent use of enthymemes; a mode of reasoning which, on account of the suppression of one of the propositions of the syllogism, seems not well suited to a mixed assembly, and renders an argument more difficult to be understood by common auditors. He was also perhaps too fond of suspending his adversary on the horns of a dilemma. His English auditors argue he spoke too deliberately, but consistently with his scheme of elocution, neither he nor any other man, could have been a rapid speaker, his extemporaneous effusions being always as correct, energetic and compressed as the premeditated speeches of others. He endeavoured never to use a superfluous word. He never, at any time, permitted himself to be diffusive or inaccurate.[46]

Flood's exceptional oratorical skill ensured him a commanding presence in the House of Commons for most of his political life.[47] He made his first contribution in 1762, but it was not until the 1763–4 session that he stood forward on a regular basis as an independent voice. He made a major impression. This was due in part to the energy and intelligence of his contributions, but of equal significance was his willingness to take controversial stands on sensitive political issues such as Poynings' Law, the pension list, the size of the military establishment and the limitation of the duration of parliament. There was nothing intrinsically novel or especially radical in the positions he took on any of these issues, but his blend of Whig, Commonwealth and patriot arguments won him political as well as popular applause and enabled him within a few years to displace the redoubtable Sexten Pery as the most popular opposition politician.

---

46 *Gentleman's Magazine*, 61 (1791), pp 1226–7.   **47** See *H.J.*, 10 Jan. 1772; Windham to Northington, 16 July 1783 in *Windham Papers*, i, 37.

Flood was a better orator and more radically-minded politician than Pery, but he was less clear on what he wanted to achieve and on how best he might do so. As a result, whereas Pery tactfully sidestepped every attempt to convince him to take government office and, ultimately, secured the prestigious and independent position of Speaker, Flood concluded that the more risky office-holding path chosen by his political hero, William Pitt, earl of Chatham, was the way for him, and he allowed himself to be persuaded that Chatham's accession to power in 1766, by paving the way for the inauguration of rule by a resident executive that would govern that kingdom according to the Whig principles that triumphed during the Glorious Revolution, opened up the prospect of his taking office. However, when he met with Chatham, it quickly became clear that his vision of the government of Ireland did not coincide with Flood's reformist aspirations.

Indeed, instead of the partnership with Chatham he earnestly wished, Flood found himself within two years precipitated into sharp confrontation with Dublin Castle as he vigorously opposed the controversial imperial style of government favoured by Lord Townshend. He did so discreetly at first because he did not wish to rule out his chances of profitable accommodation with the new Lord Lieutenant and because the ratification, in 1768, of octennial legislation he promoted, suggested that there was much he could achieve if he took office in the right administration. However, though Flood figured prominently in the Townshend's calculations in 1768–9, the complications caused by his fateful duel with James Agar in August 1769, and his conclusion that Townshend was embarked on the same despotic course that the English Whigs accused Lord Bute pushed him into unconditional opposition. Indeed, he helped generate opposition among the politicised public as well as his parliamentary colleagues by inaugurating a celebrated exercise in political propaganda which ensured that he spent the rest of Townshend's viceroyalty heading the opposition rather than patrolling the corridors of power. It was a contribution that further enhanced his public reputation and his standing as the country's greatest living patriot. He was lionised by the public and perceived by the small but committed patriot interest in the House of Commons as the figure who was destined to lead them to further triumphs. Another personality would have been content with this, but Flood had concluded that government office alone would allow him the necessary influence he needed if he was to achieve the policy changes that would place the kingdom of Ireland on the same constitutional footing as England and enable him to make the successful entry into British politics that was his ambition.

For a large and growing number of Irish patriots, Flood's belief that it was possible to remain faithful to patriot principles and hold government office was a contradiction in terms. But Flood adhered to the traditional view, famously articulated by Samuel Johnson, that

A patriot is he whose public conduct is regulated by one single motive, the love of his country; who, as an agent in parliament, has for himself neither hope nor fear, neither kindness nor resentment, but refers everything to the common interest'.[48]

Based upon this, Flood could see no reason why an ambitious and able politician, who aspired fervently to improve the way in which the empire at large as well as Ireland was governed, should not take office. Indeed, only office would provide him with the opportunity to achieve these goals since by the early 1770s 'the inefficacy of opposition' to implement its own or to frustrate government measures was commonly acknowledged.[49]

Guided by this realisation, and encouraged by the attempt to advance an absentee tax in 1773, Flood effectively invited the Irish administration to recruit him. He did this in the knowledge that his decision would prove controversial and, possibly, personally costly since he had pointed out as far back as 1763 that

there was scarce one instance upon record of a person having derived popularity from any other source than some advantages which he had procured to his country, and that no man ever preserved his popularity after sacrificing the public interest to his own.[50]

Despite this, Flood did not anticipate that his own reputation would plummet so sharply when he finally took office in 1775 because he underestimated how important opposition was to patriots outside parliament. Moreover, unlike Hely-Hutchinson, Denis Daly, Barry Yelverton, George Ogle, Lucius O'Brien and most of the other patriots, who took the same course during his lifetime, he did not do so for financial or status reasons.[51] He was, at the same time, not prepared to work with the Irish administration unless he was satisfied that the position he was offered met his extremely exigent conditions. And it was only after tortuous negotiation that highlighted for the first time to those outside the confines of his family and the borough of Callan, how difficult he could be,[52] and that, in retrospect, manifested his unsuitability for government, that he accepted the vice-treasurership during King's pleasure with the promise that he would be offered an office for life and supported in Kilkenny. At various points during the negotiation, Flood raised issues that threatened to bring the discussions between him and the Irish administration to a close. However, he appears not to have appreciated that the primary object of

---

48 Samuel Johnson, *Political tracts containing … the Patriot* (London, 1776), p. 146; see *F.J.*, 20 Jan. 1767 for a similar definition.   49 Almon's *Narrative of proceedings …*, p. 80.   50 Caldwell, *Debates*, ii, 644.   51 *Parl. Reg. (Irl.)*, i, 439–40; Burton to Baxter, 11 Dec. 1781 (N.A., Burton Papers, Ms 3249); Sayles, ed., 'Members of the Irish parliament in 1782', p. 237; Johnson, ed., 'Members of the Irish parliament 1784–7', pp 194–5.   52 Hunt, ed., *Irish parliament in 1775*, p. 21.

the Castle was to bring him into office to neutralise the potential threat he posed rather than to allow him to advance reformist and patriot policies. This was a major error of judgement. But then so too was his failure to read public opinion correctly. This flowed from the suspicion with which he (and, it must be added, most of his parliamentary colleagues on the opposition as well as government benches) regarded public opinion. He maintained in the House of Commons in 1781 that the best way 'public men' could respond to the 'illiberal and brutal treatment' they received at the hands of the public and the press 'was by doing justice to the nation' since this 'seldom fails to bestow ... good opinion upon the deserving', but his own experiences (not least his forays into political propagandising) in the late 1760s and early 1770s indicated that political life was more complicated and unpredictable.[53] However, though he contrived to use public acclaim to his own advantage in the early 1780s, he never entirely conquered his suspicion of street politics because, like Grattan, he believed that the business of politics was best conducted by those whose position in society and education prepared them for it.

Though the complex discussions that were a feature of Flood's discussions with government prior to his accepting the vice-treasurership might suggest otherwise, Flood sought and accepted office with the intention of 'doing justice to the nation'. His reputation as a political patriot and the wish of the administration to avoid dramatic constitutional change suggested that it would prove difficult to reconcile these two essentially conflicting aspirations, and it was made more so by the fact that both the middle class patriots and his parliamentary colleagues expected immediate results. They were encouraged in this by the high expectations he generated as well as by the controversy occasioned by the perception that he had abandoned the patriot cause. His *demarche* was seen by many outside parliament as a betrayal because, by the 1770s, the patriot political catechism deemed taking office to be so. However, even had he retained public support and worked closely and cooperatively with the administration, it is improbable that he would have been able to bend government policy in the direction he wanted, because the purpose and function of the Irish executive and its office-holding managers he was seen to have joined did not alter with his recruitment. Given this fact, the reforms Flood desired to make to the operation of the Anglo-Irish nexus and the government of the kingdom of Ireland were destined not to come voluntarily from that quarter despite his presence in office. They could only be brought about by the pressure of public opinion working in concert with patriot sympathizers in the House of Commons. Flood's failure to appreciate this and to anticipate the transformation that was to take place in Irish politics in the late 1770s were factors in consigning him to the political margins at the very time that he might, had he remained in opposition, have been to the fore harrying Dublin Castle and the government in London into conceding the

53 *Parl. Reg. (Irl.)*, i, 34–5.

commercial and constitutional equality that provided political patriotism and him with its *raison d'être*.

Flood spent the bulk of his six years as an officeholder keeping a low profile and behaving, to outward appearances at least, like one of the sinecure officeholders he previously criticised. Had he possessed a less acutely developed sense of honour, he would have manufactured an early reason to resign and set about rebuilding his career and reputation as a patriot politician. However, he was too proud to admit he had made an error,[54] and the fact that the Irish administration failed to implement its part of the exceptionally favourable agreement he had concluded with Lord Harcourt in 1775 provided him with a ready made reason for sitting tight. Flood gave the Irish administration plenty of opportunity to honour its agreement with him because it was an article of faith with him that agreements should be honoured and because he stood to gain so handsomely if it did so. However, Harcourt's successor, the earl of Buckinghamshire, showed little interest in honouring his predecessor's commitment or, even, in discussing the matter with the result that Flood's relations with Dublin Castle were strained throughout the four and a half years that Buckinghamshire was in Ireland. Flood's unwillingness to approach the Castle to explain his position contributed to this. At the same time Buckinghamshire's recalcitrance provided Flood with a perfectly good, and sustainable, reason to claim that they and not he was at fault, because it was their responsibility (as the delivering agency) to implement the terms of the 1775 agreement. The problem for Flood was that while this was so, he and not they was seen to be behaving badly and that his reputation suffered proportionately both with politicians and public alike. Indeed, his difficulties with Dublin Castle only ended when, following Buckinghamshire's recall and the earl of Carlisle's appointment in 1781, Flood determined to push matters to a showdown that must result either in the implementation of the 1775 agreement in full or, as happened, in his dismissal.

Though he refused to concede the point, Flood's dismissal from office saved his political career. Once free of the constraints of office, he was at liberty to articulate the forceful patriotism that was masked in the late 1770s. His return was not welcomed by most of his erstwhile colleagues who now dominated the patriot interest in the House of Commons, but Flood did not allow their hostility cow him into silence. Distrustful of government and opposition, hostile to party alliances and remote from practically everybody, he followed his own star regardless of what people thought.[55] It did not elicit much applause at the outset, but as the prospects for legislative independence improved, Flood's knowledge, parliamentary skill, persistence and disinclination to compromise on matters of constitutional principle won him positive notice with the patriot public.

Some critics maintained that Flood was motivated in the early 1780s by a wish to upstage the younger, more popular voices that had emerged while he was an officeholder, but this is unconvincing because it fails to take Flood's singled-minded character and formidable intellect into account. Flood studied each constitutional grievance closely and arrived at his own independent assessment as to how it should be remedied, and no matter what his diagnosis was (and it tended to be more radical than that favoured by most patriots) he showed no readiness to accommodate his point of view to that of others. This is well illustrated by his resistance to the attempts of Lord Charlemont to reabsorb him into the patriot fold in the early 1780s, and by the fact that Flood was one of the few to criticise the constitutional concessions yielded in 1782. His criticisms (many of which were in the public domain before legislative independence became a possibility on the collapse of the government of Lord North) drew down a torrent of abuse upon his head. But they were articulated with sufficient conviction and reason that others were gradually won over with the result that Flood became the hero once again of the politicised middle classes who were distrustful of British intentions and who were eager to build on the momentum engendered by the campaign for legislative independence to advance their wish to gain direct access to the political process. Flood's insistence that the constitutional concessions obtained by Grattan that constituted 'legislative independence' would not be secure as long as Britain did not renounce its claim to legislate for Ireland was not entirely successful, but the recognition accorded the 'legislative independence' of the Irish parliament by its Westminster equivalent in the spring of 1783 was sufficient to consolidate Flood's reputation among the politicised protestant public who fêted him. It was a quite remarkable political resuscitation given his predicament two years earlier, and it provided Flood with an opportunity to reestablish himself as a patriot politician of real consequence.

Irish politics stood at a crossroads in the spring of 1783. As a consequence of the acceleration in their politicisation in the 1770s and early 1780s, the country's protestant middle classes were eager to reform the representative system in order that they could gain fuller access. Moreover, they needed, as they acknowledged, guidance and support to press their case, but rather than seize the opportunity it offered him to develop and expand on his position as the leading popular politician, Flood held back. It was not, as some commentators suggested, that he was more interested in eclipsing Grattan as the leading patriot of the day.[56] Rather, he could not conceive of himself in the role because Flood, for all his radical patriot rhetoric, shared Grattan's and Charlemont's conviction that politics was the responsibility of the elite. All three were agreed on the desirability of parliamentary reform, but they were not convinced of the need to modify existing constitutional practice fundamentally. Significantly, considering his earlier reserve on the matter, Flood was happy

56 Francis Plowden, *Historical review*, pp 320; H.M.C., *Charlemont*, i, 63.

to work closely with and to consort openly with the Volunteers in 1783–4, but he remained as hostile as ever to the suggestion emanating from radical quarters that Catholics should be admitted to the political process. It was not that he was anti-Catholic *per se*. He maintained throughout his career that 'every individual, in his private capacity, has by the fundamental laws of this country a right of private judgement with respect ... to religion',[57] but he believed that the security of the Protestant interest in Ireland and the Anglo-Irish connection depended on maintaining an exclusively Protestant political system. This was an analysis shared by William Pitt (the younger), but since Flood had become *persona non grata* with the political establishment in Britain as well as Ireland, he was poorly placed to forward Pitt's ideas for a 'Protestant reform' in Ireland when the Prime Minister tried to convince a hostile Irish administration in 1784 of the usefulness of such a programme, and his own attempt to advance a pittite-style reform in 1785 failed abysmally.[58] Had he been in office and in good standing with the British and Irish administrations at this point, there is a good chance that Flood might have been able to advance the sort of progressive legislation he had aspired to nearly twenty years earlier when he contemplated taking office under Pitt's father. However, he was neither. His reputation with those in power on both sides of the Irish Sea had plummeted as a result of his stand on legislative independence.[59]

More consequentially, in a decision almost as pregnant for his reputation as his acceptance of the vice-treasurership, he effectively took the first step on a road that, within a few years, was to see him withdraw from Irish politics when he became a Westminster MP in 1783. This was something Flood had long aspired to, and which, given his conviction that he was entitled to all the rights of Englishmen, did no violence to his political *credo*. But just as 1775 was the wrong time to take office, so 1783 was the wrong time for him to leave Ireland. To compound his problems, he failed to appreciate that it was vital if he was to make an impact at Westminster that he carefully chose the issues and moments at which he spoke.[60] By failing to do this, he contributed to the failure of his maiden speech. He did make a number of more impressive contributions later in the decade, but the negative resonances of his initial and subsequent failures, his disinclination to ally himself with either of the main party interests, personal antipathy and serious electoral complications ensured that his political career blossomed only occasionally in the mid and late 1780s. Indeed, just as his term in office proved a let down after the drama of the 1760s and early 1770s, so his years at Westminster were anti-climactic compared to the drama of the early 1780s.

---

57 Caldwell, *Debates*, ii, 503; *Parl. Reg. (Irl.)*, i, 285.   58 Kelly, *Prelude to Union*, pp 88–90.   59 Above p. 364; Cooke to Eden, 27 July 1782 in *Auckland Corres.*, i, 334–5.   60 See P.J. Jupp, ed., 'Canning's Journal', p. 10.

REPUTATION

The extended and overwhelmingly positive assessments of Flood's political career that followed his death attest, as obituaries tend to do, only to the respect and admiration his eloquence, parliamentary skill and principled conduct brought him during his lifetime:

> his every effort was invariably directed to improve the political constitution, to increase the internal resources, and to promote the general prosperity of Ireland. No despicable plans of private emolument, no paltry schemes of party interest debased the dignity of his character or reduced him to the low level of commonmen.[61]

There is more than a hint of rhapsody in this and other comparable commentaries, because no attempt is made to balance the merited applause with an acknowledgement that his political impact was less than it might have been.

It is probably unreasonable to expect balanced reflection at that moment since it took the events of the 1790s to reveal the full extent of the patriots' failure. In mitigation, it must be pointed out that Flood (unique among patriots) recognized as early as 1785 that 'legislative independence' had failed to give Ireland a parliament that met the aspirations of the politicised Protestant middle classes and that accorded the Irish 'protestant nation' genuine equality of status with England under the crown. This was clearer in 1790 as the first shoots of the radicalism that provided the most cogent and popular alternative to the conservativism then dominant in Irish parliamentary politics manifested themselves, and it is hardly a coincidence that moderates then found good reason to applaud Flood's stand on renunciation.[62] Inevitably, radicals were more forthcoming as the approving citation by the Dublin Society of United Irishmen in 1791 and by W.J. MacNeven in 1799 of his observations on the vulnerability of Ireland in negotiations with English ministers and his advocacy that to 'demand' was more likely to pay dividends than to 'negotiate' indicate. He was also cited approvingly in the United Irish compilation, *The Beauties of the Press*.[63] He was even seen in some quarters to have been right on 'the operation of the corn laws', while the continuing positive publicity in the 1790s arising out of his bequest to Trinity College enhanced his reputation further.[64] Indeed, even his opponents in life were inclined to speak positively of him as Henry Grattan's generous assessment of 1801 bears out:

61 *Gentleman's Magazine*, 61 (1791), p. 1163. The *Annual Register*, (1791), pp 295–303 was complimentary but less effusive.   62 *Dublin Chronicle*, 26 Jan. 1790; *A brief reply to the observations of Ben Bousfield, esq. on Mr Burke's pamphlet, respecting the Revolution in France ...* (Dublin, 1791), p. 46.   63 N.A., Rebellion Papers, 620/19/44; R.B. McDowell, 'Proceedings of the Dublin Society of United Irishmen', *Analecta Hibernica*, xvii (1943), p. 9; [W.J.MacNeven], *An argument for independence in opposition to an union* (Dublin, 1799), p. 20; *Beauties of the press* (Dublin, 1800), pp 200, 306.   64 *D.E.P.*, 13 May

He had his faults; but he had great powers, great public effect; he persuaded the old, he inspired the young; the Castle vanished before him. On a small subject he was miserable: put into his hand a distaff, and, like Hercules, he made sad work of it; but give him a thunderbolt, and he had the arm of a Jupiter.[65]

This positive image was reinforced in the early nineteenth century by the claim of Lawrence Parsons (from 1807 earl of Rosse) and others that Flood had penned the Junius letters,[66] but it was not long before the tide of opinion began to turn.

The most weighty challenge to the preeminently positive image of Flood that prevailed in the quarter century after his death was offered by Francis Hardy in his influential biography of Lord Charlemont, the first edition of which saw print in 1810. Hardy had personal knowledge of Flood from his time as an Irish MP, and he provided a portrait of Flood that was at once more informed and more critical than then prevailed. Flood was, he maintained, a vain, self-preoccupied man who had 'defected' from the ranks of the patriots in 1775 because he

indulged himself with the prospect of an almost entire ascendancy in the cabinet of Ireland. He flattered himself that his talents could easily sway a very amiable, very well bred incurious old nobleman [earl Harcourt], and an active, adroit colonel of dragoons [John Blaquiere].[67]

Hardy's unflattering view of Flood was more in tune with the prevailing conservative world view of the early nineteenth century than the eulogistic reflections offered by radicals in the 1790s. Moreover, it was reinforced by the less than complimentary perspective on his personal life provided by the continuing fall-out arising out of his bequest to Trinity College.

As time passed and those who knew him shrunk in number, and as Catholic emancipation moved to the top of the political agenda, interest in and the accuracy of the anecdotes and memories of Flood's life dipped sharply. Daniel O'Connell even claimed in 1826 that Flood had urged 'the independence of Ireland'; others offered misleading accounts of his supposed 'defection from the cause of liberty and the people'.[68] Clearly, Henry Flood was in urgent need of a biographer by the 1820s if his life was not to become a hostage to partisan and inaccurate recollection.

1794; Parsons, *Observations, passim*; Carr, *The stranger in Ireland* (London, 1806), p. 330. **65** Cited in W.H. Curran, *The life of the right honourable John Philpot Curran* (2 vols, Edinburgh, 1822), i, 156. When he was on his death bed in 1820 he was even more unconditionally magnanimous; then he spoke of Flood's 'great talent and abilities' (*Life of Grattan* , v, 552). **66** Rosse Papers, C/13, 14/1–5, 16; 'Junius and Henry Flood' in *Notes and Queries*, 2nd series, viii (1859), pp 101–3, 189–90; *Life of Grattan*, i, 159; Flood, *Memoirs*, pp 81–3. **67** Francis Hardy, *Memoirs of the political and private life of James Caulfield, Earl of Charlemont* (2 vols, London, 1812), i, 357–8; Flood, *Memoirs*, p. 116. **68** O'Regan, *Curran*, pp xv; *Diary and reminiscences of Henry Crabb Robinson* (2 vols, London, 1872), ii, 27; 'An Irish Patriot's memoirs' in *Blackwood's Magazine*, xix (1826), p. 268.

The earl of Rosse made a number of attempts, but no finished work ever saw the light of day. A select edition of letters rescued from destruction in 1791/2 was published by Thomas Rodd in 1820 and 'a not entirely uncritical' but essentially derivative biography was assembled by his descendant, Warden Flood, in 1838. Neither are without value, but they were slight and uninfluential compared to the carefully edited four volumes of Henry Grattan's speeches (1822), volume of *Miscellaneous works* (1820) and five-volume *Life and times* (1839–46) seen through the press by Grattan's protective family.[69] Grattan's *Life* was one of the most influential books on eighteenth-century Ireland published in the nineteenth century, and whilst its author, Henry Grattan junior, does not set out to be unfair to Flood, the reader is left in no doubt that the author believed he was a lesser figure than his father or that his known prejudices were justified.[70] As a consequence, 'legislative independence' became so closely identified with Grattan that the eighteen years of Irish parliamentary history between its inauguration and the Act of Union became commonly known as 'Grattan's parliament', while Flood was relegated to an honourable but, increasingly, symbolic second place.

Not surprisingly, this tendency to perceive Flood as not 'so great a man, ... so great an orator', nor so successful a politician as Grattan (they were bound so inextricably in the public's mind that images of both were carried side by side on the membership card of the Repeal Association) intensified thereafter.[71] There is, for this reason, little advantage in embarking on a detailed historiographical review of the largely monochromatic, though not always consensual representation of Flood in the historical literature of the late nineteenth and twentieth centuries. Clearly, the truth lies somewhere between the 'corrupt Drawcansir' of some and the 'great statesman' of others,[72] and if the construction of this reality is rendered difficult by the shortage of personal documentation, it is clear that, in many respects, his career as well as his personality epitomises the weaknesses and the strengths of eighteenth-century Irish patriotism. Like the patriots, he appeared to seek power, but when he was given an opportunity to grasp it, he failed to take it; like the patriots, he had an unrealistic expectation of the advantages that would accrue to the protestants and to the kingdom of Ireland if they secured the rights of Englishmen given the continuing perception of British politicians that it was more appropriate that Ireland reconciled itself to political subordination; and, like the generality of patriots, he was unwilling to sacrifice his personal autonomy to the discipline of group action though decades of disappointment in Ireland and the development of party at Westminster indicated that this was the way forward. In short, for all his fine words and

69 Flood, *Memoirs*, p. 233; Kelly, *Henry Grattan*, p. 4.   70 Henry Grattan junior to James Grattan, 30 Nov. 1810 (N.L.I., Grattan Papers, Ms 2111).   71 Sheehy, *The Celtic revival*, p. 28; Mac Nevin, *The Volunteers*, pp 128–9, 131.   72 John Brooke, ed., *Horace Walpole's memoirs of the reign of George II* (3 vols, London, 1985), iii, 89 note 6; Hume-Williams, *The Irish parliament*, p. 93.

defiant stands, Flood did not present a *workable* alternative to the political system he found so problematic and criticised so fluently throughout his political life.

Flood was, as this suggests, first and foremostly an opposition politician. He was more capable and constructive than his great rival Henry Grattan, and more likely to produce workable legislation. However, he was also too single-minded and too outspoken to work for any length of time with those with whom he shared the chambers of the British as well as Irish parliaments. Politically, he defined his ambitions in terms of *restoration* and *improvement* (the watchwords of patriots throughout Europe) because he wanted to preserve the essentials of the Irish political system (its protestantism) and the British link. By failing to embrace Catholic enfranchisement and to deliver on parliamentary reform, Flood, like the political patriotism he espoused, had become something of a political anachronism by 1790 because, like it, he had failed to deliver the changes that could have made both the existing representative system and the Anglo-Irish connection less vulnerable to the exogenous challenge posed by the French Revolution and the United Irishmen. It could be argued, because of this, that Flood's death in 1791 was timely because it saved him from having to negotiate between the politics of protestant ascendancy which, in the 1790s, meant opposing all change, or of embracing the revolutionary ideals of the United Irishmen which involved creating a new system.

Throughout his political career, he had been activated by the wish to extend the rights and privileges enshrined for Englishmen in the system of constitutional monarchy put in place in Britain in the seventeenth century to the protestant nation in Ireland and of creating an equal Anglo-Irish nexus. For this, for the energy and vigour he brought to parliamentary politics, and for the illustration his biography provides of the refinement and ruthlessness, sophistication and sophistry, openness and elitism, erudition and ignorance that co-existed in the political and social world of the eighteenth-century Irish protestant elite, he was, and remains, a tantalising but important figure.

Bibliography

PRIMARY SOURCES

I MANUSCRIPTS

Boston Public Library
Autograph Mss (CH, H.7.1a)

British Library
Auckland Papers (Add. Ms 34417–9)
Dropmore Papers (Add. Ms 59407A)
Entry books for fees on patents (Add. Ms 23711)
Flood Papers (Add. Ms 22930)
Fox Papers (Add. Mss 45580, 47567–8)
Hardwicke Papers (Add. Ms 35892)
Holland House Papers (Add. Ms 51426)
Kings Ms 439
Lansdowne Abstracts (Add. Mss 24137–8)
Lansdowne Mss 733, 1235
Liverpool Papers (Add. Mss 38206, 38306, 38211)
Mackintosh Collection (Add. Ms 34523)
Miscellaneous Mss (Add. Ms 29736)
Mitchell Papers (Add. Mss 6839, 6857)
Northington Letterbook (Add. Ms 38716)
Peel Papers (Add. Ms 40218)
Pelham Papers (Add. Mss 33100, 33117–18, 33128)
Robinson Papers (Add. Ms 37833)
Sloane Ms 4164
Southwell Papers (Add. Mss 34773, 34777)
Valentia Papers (Add. Ms 19349)
Wellesley Papers (Add. Mss 37308, 38103)
Windham Papers (Add. Ms 37873)

Cambridge University Library
Pitt (Pretyman) Papers (P.R.O.N.I., T3319)

Dublin Public Library
Harcourt Papers (Gilbert Mss 93–5)

Durham University Library
Grey/Ponsonby Papers (P.R.O.N.I., T3393)

East Sussex Record Office
Additional Sheffield Papers (P.R.O.N.I., T3465)

Genealogical Office, Dublin
A list of officers in the several regiments and independent troops and companies of militia in Ireland (Ms 608)
Pedigree of Sir Frederick Flood (Ms 112)
Landed families of Co.Kilkenny, 1775 (Ms 443)

Harvard University Library
Orrery Papers (N.L.I., microfilm p 789)

Hampshire Record Office
Normanton Papers (P.R.O.N.I., T3719)

Henry Huntington Library, San Marino, California
Chandos Papers (STB, Box 10)
Jerningham Papers (JE286)
Manuscript account of the Irish parliament in 1782

Ipswich and East Suffolk Record Office
Grafton Papers (P.R.O.N.I., T2959)

Keele University Library
Sneyd Papers (P.R.O.N.I.,T3229)

Kent Archives Office
Camden Papers (U840/C173)

Lambeth Palace Library, London
Secker Papers

Land Registry, Dublin
Land Commission, Bishop Street
  Flood-Hanford estate papers (Box 5555)
  Keogh estate papers (Box 13)
Registry of Deeds, Henrietta Street
  Memorials of deeds registered by Flood
  family

Library of Congress, Washington
Sir Henry Cavendish's parliamentary
  diary, 1776–89 (N.L.I., microfilm p
  7002–10)

Limerick Archives Office
de Vere Hunt Papers

Linenhall Library, Belfast
Joy Papers

National Archives, Dublin
Agar Papers (Ms 3239)
Burton Papers (Ms 3249)
Calendar of departmental correspondence
  1741–59
Calendar of miscellaneous letters and
  papers prior to 1760
Calendar of miscellaneous letters and
  papers 1760–89
Calendar of presentments, affidavits and
  examinations 1698–1813
Clifden Deeds (D20038–150)
Fitzgerald Papers (Ms 2736)
Forfeited estates Ireland: 1641; undisposed
  lands and plus acres
Index to departmental letters and papers
  1760–89
Index to Irish Privy Councillors 1711–1910
Irish correspondence 1697–1798 (Ms 2446)

Irish correspondence 1697–1782 (Ms 2447)
Kenefick donation (Ms 999/355)
Langrishe Papers (BR, K.K.38)
Landed Estates Court records, vols 10 no
  2, 34 no 49
Prim Collection (Ms Pri/36–7, 84, 687)
Rebellion Papers (620/19)
Shelly Papers (Ms 999/462)
Style Papers (Ms 600)
Townshend Papers (Mss 671–3, 724–33,
  5050)

National Library of Ireland
Baker Papers (Ms 21004)
Blaquiere Papers (Ms 877)
Blennerhassett and Eager (Agar) pedigrees
  (Ms 4112)
Bolton Papers (Mss 15877 15958, 16039,
  16350–8)
Buckingham Papers (Joly Ms 39)
Civil establishment list for 1789 (Ms 4109)
Dobbs Papers (Ms 2551)
Fitzgerald Papers (Mss 624, 13022)
Forbes Papers (Mss 978, 10715)
Fownes Papers (Mss 8470)
French Papers (Ms 2745)
Grattan Papers (Ms 2111)
Harcourt Papers (Mss 755, 5161)
Headfort Papers
Heron Papers (Mss 3532, 4135, 5168,
  13034–60)
Lord Halifax's journal, 1761 (Ms 8064/7)
Inchiquin Papers
Gosford Papers (Ms 8018)
A sketch of the political history of Ireland
  (Joly Ms 29)
A list of the Irish parliament in 1783 (Ms
  2098)
Lists of the Lords and Commons who
  dined with Lord Lieutenant, 1761–9
  (Ms 1467–70)
List of the Volunteer companies, Feb. 1782
  (Ms 743)
Melville Papers (Ms 54)
Napier Papers (Ms 683)
O'Hara Papers (microfilm, p1576; Mss
  15368, 20389, 20393–5, 20398, 20402)

Ormonde Papers (Ms 23787)
Political recollections of the Earl of Rosse
(Ms 13841)
Shannon Papers (Ms 13032)
Stratford Papers (Ms 18788–94)
Sydney Papers (Mss 51–2)
Talbot-Crosbie Papers (Ms 2054)
Tighe (Woodstock) Papers (Ms 3889)
Townshend Papers (Mss 394, 8009, 14299, 21129)
Union Correspondence (Ms 886)
Walsh newscuttings (Ms 14023)
Dudley Westropp Papers (Ms 24937)
Wynne Papers (Ms 22252)

National Library of Scotland
Lothian Papers (P.R.O.N.I., T3502)

Norfolk Record Office
Hobart Papers (P.R.O.N.I., T3110)
Walsingham Papers (P.R.O.N.I., T3428)

Northamptonshire Record Office
Fitzwilliam Papers (A.viii)

North Yorkshire Record Office, Northallerton
Wyvill Papers (Ms ZFW/7/2)
Zetland Papers (P.R.O.N.I., T3418)

Oireachtas Library, Dublin
List of the Commons of Ireland (Ms 7:H:37)
Reports on reform meetings, 1784 (Ms 8:H:10)

Pennsylvania Historical Society
Dreer Collection, Letters of English Statesmen

Public Record Office
Chatham Papers (30/8 vols 32, 84, 320–30)
Grenville Papers (30/29)
Home Office Papers (H.O., 100 vols 1–20)
King's Bench Papers: writs of error from Ireland (K.B.,7/7–11)
Privy Council Papers, registers (P.C.2/100–36), unbound papers (P.C.1/7/15–84)

Society for Constitutional Information minute books, 1780s (T.S.11/961/3507)
State Papers, Ireland (S.P.,63 vols 417–80)
State Papers, Ireland (S.P.,67 vols 14–20)
State Papers, Domestic (S.P., 35/44)

Public Record Office of Northern Ireland
Additional Pery Papers (T3052)
Alnwick Papers (T2872)
Babingdon and Croasdaile Papers (D1514)
Bedford Papers (T2915)
Belfast Chamber of Commerce Papers (D1857)
Bristol Papers (T2960)
Chatsworth Papers (T3158)
Conolly Papers (T2825)
Downshire Papers (D607)
Drennan Papers (D765)
Drennan-Bruce Letters (D553)
Emly (Pery) Papers (T3087)
Foster Papers (D562)
Harrowby Papers (T3228)
Hobart Papers (T2627)
Hotham Papers (T3429)
Leinster Papers (D3078)
Macartney Papers (D562)
Macartney/Filgate Papers (D2225)
Pomeroy Papers (T2954)
Shannon Papers (D2707)
Shirley Papers (D3531)
Stanley of Alderley Papers (T3725)
Stewart of Killymoon Papers (D3167)
Villiers-Stuart Papers (T3131)
Willes Papers (T2855)
Wilmot Papers (T3019)

Royal Irish Academy, Dublin
Burrowes Papers (Ms 23/K/53)
Flood autograph (Ms 3D8/7)
J.L.Foster Papers
Knox Papers (Ms G.5.1)

Royal Society of Antiquaries of Ireland, Dublin
Callan Court Book (Ms C7A6)
Corporation book of Gowran 1736–1800 (Ms C7A5)

Minutebooks of Thomastown Corporation
  1720–1840 (Ms C7A1)

Sheffield City Libraries
Wentworth Woodhouse Manuscripts:
  Burke Papers (P1)
  Rockingham Papers (R1)

West Sussex Record Office
Bunbury Papers (P.R.O.N.I., Mic 238)

Trinity College, Dublin
Arran Papers (Ms 7576)
Barker Ponsonby Papers
Burgh Papers (Ms 9318)
Clements Papers (Mss 1742–3, 7302)
Conolly Papers (Ms 3978)
Crosbie Papers (Ms 3821)
Donoughmore Papers
Trinity College Muniments (Mun/V/23,
  27, P/1/967, 1383, 1386)
Stock Papers (Ms 3762)

Yale University
Beinecke Library: Osborn Collection:
  Ballitore Papers
  Buckinghamshire Letters
  Clements Letters
  Deane Letters
  Flood Letter

Grafton Letters
Lifford Letters
Malone Letters
Northington Letterbook
Nugent Letters
Smith-Townshend Letters
Southwell Papers
Townshend Papers (Boxes 1–14)
Vallancey letter
Waite-Macartney Letters
Wyndham Letters
Sterling Library:
  English misc. Mss 1766–72
Lewis Walpole Library, Farmington,
  Connecticut:
  Townshend Papers

Warwickshire Record Office
Willes Papers

Private Collections
Rosse Papers, Birr Castle, Birr, County
  Offaly
Malone Papers (in possession of Mrs A.
  O'Neill, Rathganny, Multyfarnham,
  County Westmeath (N.L.I., microfilm
  p. 1561))
Rutland Papers (Belvoir Castle, Rutland-
  shire)

II PRINTED PRIMARY MATERIAL: DOCUMENTS, MEMOIRS AND CORRESPONDENCE

Abercorn: *An introduction to the Abercorn letters*, ed., J.H. Gebbie (Omagh, 1972).
Auckland: *The journal and correspondence of William, Lord Auckland*, ed., Bishop of Bath
  and Wells (4 vols, London, 1861–2).
Bagshawe: *Colonel Samuel Bagshawe and the army of George II, 1731–62*, ed., J.A. Guy
  (London, 1990).
Bedford: *The correspondence of John, fourth Duke of Bedford*, ed., Lord John Russell (3
  vols, London, 1842–6).
Beresford: *The correspondence of John Beresford*, ed., William Beresford (2 vols, London,
  1854).
Boswell: *The correspondence of James Boswell*, ed., F.W. Hilles (3 vols, London, 1966–
  76).
Boswell: *Letters of James Boswell to Rev. W.J. Temple*, ed., T. Seccombe (London, 1908).

Boswell: *Boswell's life of Johnson*, ed., G.B. Hill (6 vols, Oxford, 1934–64).

Boswell: *Boswell in extremes 1776–8*, ed., F.A. Pottle (London, 1970).

Boswell: *Boswell: the English experiment 1785–89*, eds, I.S. Lustig and F.A. Pottle (London, 1986).

Boswell: *Boswell: the great biographer*, ed., M.K. Danziger and F. Brady (London, 1990).

Bowen: 'Bowen Papers', ed., E.A. MacLysaght in 'Reports on private collections' in *Analecta Hibernica*, xv (1944).

Buckingham: *Memoirs of the courts and cabinets of George III*, ed., duke of Buckingham and Chandos (4 vols, London, 1853–5).

Burke: *The early life, correspondence and writings of Edmund Burke* by A.P.I. Samuels (Cambridge, 1923).

Burke: *Edmund Burke, New York Agent ...*, ed., R.J.S. Hoffman (Philadelphia, 1956).

Burke: *The correspondence of Edmund Burke*, ed., T.W. Copeland (10 vols, Cambridge, 1958–70).

Campbell: *Dr Campbell's diary of a visit to England in 1775*, ed., J.L. Clifford (Cambridge, 1947).

Catholics: *Catholics in the eighteenth-century press*, ed., John Brady (Maynooth, 1966).

Chatham: *The correspondence of William Pitt, Earl of Chatham*, eds, W.S. Taylor and J.H. Pringle (4 vols, London, 1838–40).

Chesterfield: *The letters of Philip Dormer Stanhope ... Earl of Chesterfield*, ed., Bonamy Dobrée (6 vols, London, 1932).

Census: *A census of Ireland in 1659*, ed., S. Pender (Dublin, 1939)

Day: *Mr Justice Day of Kerry* by Ella B. Day (Exeter, 1938).

Delany: *Autobiography and correspondence of Mary Granville, Mrs Delany*, ed., Lady Llanover (6 vols, London, 1861–2).

Devonshire: 'The Devonshire diary 1759–62', eds, P.D. Brown and K.W. Schweizer, *Camden*, 4th series, 27 (1982).

Drennan: *The Drennan Letters*, ed., D.A. Chart (Belfast, 1931).

Farington: *The Farington diary*, ed., John Greig (3 vols, London, 1922–4).

Flood: *Original Letters to Henry Flood*, ed., T[homas] R[odd] (London, 1820).

Flood: *Memoirs of the life and correspondence of Henry Flood* by Warden Flood (Dublin, 1838).

Flood: 'Documents re Flood duel', ed., J. Prim, *Journal of the Historical and Archaeological Society of Ireland*, 3rd series, 10 (1868), pp 234–41.

Flood: 'Flood's bail bond, 1 Sept. 1769', *Journal of the Kilkenny and South-East of Ireland Archaeological Society*, 3 (1854–5), pp 316–17.

Flood: 'A letter on a fatal duel', *Journal of the Royal Historical and Archaeological Society of Ireland*, 4th series, 2 (1870–1), pp 13–14.

Fox: *Memorials and correspondence of the right honourable Charles James Fox*, ed., Lord John Russell (4 vols, London, 1853).

George III: *Letters from George III to Lord Bute*, ed., Romney Sedgwick (London, 1939).

George III: *The correspondence of George III*, ed., Sir John Fortescue (6 vols, London, 1927–8).

George III: *The later correspondence of George III, 1784–1812*, ed., Arthur Aspinall (5 vols, London, 1962–70).

Grafton: *Autobiography and political correspondence of Augustus Henry, third Duke of Grafton*, ed., Sir William Anson (London, 1898).

Grattan: *Memoirs of the life and times of Henry Grattan* by Henry Grattan Jr. (5 vols, London, 1839–46).

Grattan: *The speeches of Henry Grattan*, ed., D.O. Madden (Dublin, 1847).

Grattan: *Miscellaneous works of the right honourable Henry Grattan* (London, 1822).

Gray: *Correspondence of Thomas Gray*, eds, Paget Toynbee and Leonard Whibley (3 vols, Oxford, 1935).

Grenville: *The Grenville Papers*, ed., W.J. Smith (4 vols, London, 1852–3).

Grenville: *Additional Grenville papers 1763-65*, ed., J.R.G. Tomlinson (Manchester, 1962).

Harden, 'Tour in Ireland by John Harden in 1797', ed., Michael Quane, *J.C.H.A.S.*, 58 (1953), pp 26–32, 81–90.

Hardwicke: *The life and correspondence of Philip Yorke, Lord Chancellor Hardwicke* by P.C. Yorke (3 vols, Cambridge, 1913).

Harcourt: *Harcourt papers*, ed., W.E. Harcourt (privately printed, 15 vols, 1876–1903).

Inchiquin: *Inchiquin Manuscripts*, ed., John Ainsworth (Dublin, 1943).

Irish papers: *Eighteenth century Irish official papers in Great Britain*, ed., A.P.W. Malcomson (2 vols, Belfast, 1973–90).

Irish parliament: 'The Irish House of Commons in 1769', ed., David Large in *I.H.S.*, xi (1958), pp 18–45.

Irish parliament: 'The Irish parliament in 1773', ed., M. Bodkin, *R.I.A. proc.*, 48C(1942), pp 145–232.

Irish parliament: *The Irish parliament in 1775*, ed., William Hunt (Dublin, 1907).

Irish parliament: 'The Irish parliament in 1782', ed., G.O. Sayles, *R.I.A. proc.*, 56C (1954), pp 227–86.

Irish parliament: 'Members of the Irish parliament 1784-7', ed., E.M. Johnston, *R.I.A. proc.*, 71C (1971), pp 139–246.

Irish parliament: 'State of the Irish House of Commons in 1791', E.M. Johnston, ed., *R.I.A. proc.*, 59C (1957), pp 1–56.

Johnson: *The letters of Samuel Johnson*, ed., Bruce Redford (5 vols, Oxford, 1992–4).

Johnson: *Boswell's Life of Johnson*, ed., G.B. Hill (6 vols, Oxford, 1934–64).

Junius: *The letters of Junius*, ed., John Cannon (Oxford, 1978).

Kerry: *Old Kerry Records*, ed., M.A. Hickson (2 vols, London, 1872–4).

Leinster: *Correspondence of Emily, Duchess of Leinster*, ed., Brian Fitzgerald (3 vols, Dublin, 1945–57).

Lennox: *The life and letters of Lady Sarah Lennox*, eds, Countess of Ilchester and Lord Stavordale (2 vols, London, 1902).

Longford: 'Letters of Lord Longford and others 1689–1702' ed., Patrick Melvin in *Analecta Hibernica* 32 (1985).

Macartney: *Macartney in Ireland 1768–1772*, ed., Thomas Bartlett (Belfast, 1978).

Macartney, 'The private correspondence of Lord Macartney 1781–85', ed., C. Collin Davies, *Camden*, third series, 77 (1950).

Malone: *Life of Edmond Malone* by James Prior (London, 1860).

O'Conor: *The letters of Charles O'Conor 1731–90*, eds, C.C. Ward and R.E. Ward (2 vols, Ann Arbor, 1980).

O'Hanlon: 'Testamentary records', ed., L.E. O'Hanlon, *Irish Genealogist*, 2 no. 5 (1947), p. 142.

Ordnance Survey: *Letters of the Ordnance Survey: Kilkenny*, ed., Michael O'Flanagan (privately published, 2 vols, Dublin, 1928).

Orrery: *The Orrery papers*, ed., Countess of Cork and Orrery (2 vols, London, 1903).

Oswald: *Memorials of public life of James Oswald* (Edinburgh, 1825).

Pembroke: *Pembroke Papers 1734–94*, ed., Lord Herbert (2 vols, London, 1939–50).

Pitt: *Correspondence between the Right honourable William Pitt and Charles, Duke of Rutland 1781–87*, ed., Lord Mahon (London, 1890).

Pococke: *Richard Pococke's Irish Tours*, ed., John McVeagh (Dublin, 1995).

Portarlington: *Gleanings from an old portfolio containing some correspondence between Lady Louisa Stewart and ... Countess of Portarlington*, ed., Mrs Godfrey Clark (3 vols, privately printed Edinburgh, 1895–8).

Price: *The correspondence of Richard Price* vol 2, ed., D.O. Thomas (Cardiff, 1991).

Reynolds: *The life of Thomas Reynolds* by T. Reynolds (2 vols, London, 1839).

Robinson: *Diary and reminiscences of Henry Crabb Robinson* (2 vols, London, 1872).

Robinson: 'The parliamentary papers of John Robinson', *Camden*, third series, 33 (1922).

Rockingham: *Memoirs of the Marquis of Rockingham and his contemporaries*, ed., Earl of Albemarle (2 vols, London, 1852).

Rowan: *Autobiography of Archibald Hamilton Rowan*, ed., W.H. Drummond (Dublin, 1840).

Sandwich: *The private papers of the Earl of Sandwich 1772–82*, eds, G.R.B. and H.H. Owen (4 vols, London, 1933–8).

Shelburne: *Life of William Earl of Shelburne* by Lord Fitzmaurice (3 vols, London, 1875–6).

Sheridan: *Memoirs of the life of Richard Brinsley Sheridan* by Thomas Moore (2 vols, London, 1825).

Teignmouth, Lord, *Reminiscences of many years* (2 vols, Edinburgh, 1878).

United Irishmen: 'Proceedings of the Dublin Society of United Irishmen', ed., R.B. McDowell, *Analecta Hibernica*, xvii (1949), pp 1–143.

Walpole: *The correspondence of Horace Walpole*, eds, W.S. Lewis et al., (48 vols, New Haven, 1937–83).

Walpole: *Memoirs of the reign of George III*, ed., G.F. Russell-Barker (4 vols, London, 1894).

Walpole: *Horace Walpole's memoirs of the reign of George II*, ed., John Brooke (3 vols, London, 1985).

Walpole: *The last journals of Horace Walpole*, ed., A.F. Steuart (2 vols, London, 1910).

Windham: *The Windham Papers*, ed., L.S. Benjamin (2 vols, London, 1913).

Willes: *The letters of Lord Chief Baron Edward Willes to the Earl of Warwick 1757–62*, ed., James Kelly (Aberystwyth, 1990).

Whiteboys: 'The Whiteboys in 1762: a contemporary account', ed., James Kelly in *J.C.H.A.S.*, 94 (1989), pp 19–26.

III RECORD PUBLICATIONS

A Calendar of the records of the Inner Temple, ed., R.A. Roberts (5 vols, London, 1896–1936).

Calendar of ancient records of Dublin, eds, Sir John and Lady Gilbert (19 vols, Dublin, 1889–1944).

Calendar of Home Office Papers 1760–75 (4 vols, London, 1878–99).
'Catalogue of Nunziatura di Fiandra, parts 6, 7', ed., C. Giblin, *Collectanea Hibernica*, x,
    xi (1967, 1968), pp 72–138, 53–90.
Corporation book of the corporation of Cork, ed., Richard Caulfeild (Guildford, 1876).
Corporation book of Ennis, ed., Sean Ó Dalaigh (Dublin, 1990).
King's Inns admission Papers 1607–1867, eds, E. Keane, P. Beryl Phair and T.U. Sadleir
    (Dublin, 1982)
The records of the Honourable Society of Lincoln's Inns 1420–1799 (London, 1896).
Register of admissions to the honourable Society of the Middle Temple, ed., H.A.C. Sturgess
    (3 vols, London, 1949).

IV PUBLICATIONS OF THE HISTORICAL MANUSCRIPTS COMMISSION

Carlisle Mss (15th Report, appendix 6).
Charlemont Mss (12th Report, appendix 10, and 13th Report, appendix vii).
Donoughmore Mss (12 Report, appendix 9).
Egmont Diary, vol 2.
Emly Mss (14 Report, appendix 9).
Eyre Matcham Mss (Reports on various collections, vi).
Fortescue Mss, vol vi.
Hastings Mss, vol iii.
Knox Mss (Reports on various collections, vi).
Lansdowne Mss (5th report, appendix).
Lothian Mss.
Puleston Mss (15 Report, appendix 7).
Rutland Mss, vols ii and iii.
P.V.Smith Mss (12 Report, appendix 9).
Stopford-Sackville Mss (2 vols).
Townshend Mss (15 Report, appendix 4).
Wood Papers (Reports on various collections, viii).

V PARLIAMENTARY PROCEEDINGS, JOURNALS, SPEECHES ETC.

Irish parliament:
Journals of the House of Commons of the kingdom of Ireland 1613-1800 (19 vols, Dublin,
    1796–1800).
Caldwell, James, *Debates relative to the affairs of Ireland in the years 1763 and 1764* (2
    vols, London, 1766).
[John Almon], *Narrative of proceedings in the parliament of Ireland* (London, 1777).
*Debates in the House of Commons of Ireland on a motion whether the King's most excellent
    majesty and the Lords and Commons of Ireland are the only power competent to bind or
    enact laws in this kingdom* (Dublin, 1780).
A.R. Black, ed., *An edition of the Cavendish Irish parliamentary diary 1776–78* (3 vols.,
    Delavan and Westport, 1984–5).

Callen, R.V., 'The structure of Anglo-Irish politics during the American Revolution: Cavendish's diary of the Irish parliament October 12 1779 to September 2 1780: edition of the partial text and a critical essay' (Ph.D. thesis, University of Notre Dame, 1973).

The parliamentary register, or history of the proceedings and debates of the House of Commons of Ireland (17 vols, Dublin, 1782–1801).

Flood, Henry, *Two celebrated speeches on the repeal of the Declaratory Act of the sixth of George I as delivered in the House of Commons of Ireland on 11 and 14 June 1782* (Dublin, [1782]).

The Statutes at large passed in the parliaments held in Ireland 1310–1800 (20 vols, Dublin, 1789–1800).

British parliament:

The parliamentary History of England from the Norman conquest to 1803 (36 vols, London, 1806–20).

Luders, A., *Reports of proceedings in committee of the House of Commons upon controverted elections* (3 vols, London, 1785–90).

Municipal Corporations Report, 7, 8 (Ireland), 27, 28 (1835).

The speech of Henry Flood in the House of Commons of Great Britain on February 15, 1787 on the commercial treaty with France (Dublin, 1787).

The speech of Henry Flood in March 1790 on the reform of parliament (London, 1790).

VI PAMPHLETS AND OTHER CONTEMPORARY PUBLICATIONS

Barrington, Jonah, *Personal sketches of his own times* (3 vols, London, 1827–32).

——, *Historic memoirs of Ireland* (2 vols, London, 1835).

Beattie, James, *Essays on the nature and immutability of truth in opposition to sophistry and scepticism* (Edinburgh, 1776).

Beauties of the press (Dublin, 1800).

Biographical, literary and political anecdotes of several of the most eminent persons of the present era (3 vols, London, 1797).

A brief reply to the observations of Ben Bousfield, esq., on Mr Burke's pamphlet respecting the Revolution in France (Dublin, 1791).

Bushe, Gervaise Parker, *The case of Great Britain and America addressed to the King and both houses of parliament* (3rd ed., Dublin, 1767).

Campbell, Thomas, *A philosophical survey of the south of Ireland* (Dublin 1777).

A candid review of the most important occurrences that took place in Ireland during the last three years (Dublin, 1787).

Carr, Sir John, *The stranger in Ireland* (London, 1806).

The Case of Henry Flood and John Flood esqrs upon the petition of Thomas Matthew and John Echlin [Dublin, 1768].

The Case of Thomas Matthew and John Echlin esqrs on their petition complaining of an undue election and return ... for ... Callan [Dublin, 1768].

A catalogue of the library of the right honourable Denis Daly ... (Dublin, 1792).

[Chetwood, W.R.] *A tour through Ireland in several entertaining letters wherein the present state of that kingdom is considered* ... (London, 1748).

A critical examination of the sense, style and grammar of Mr Sheridan's printed oration (Dublin, 1758).

Cuffe, Agmondisham, *Petition to the honourable the knights, citizens and burgesses in parliament assembled...on behalf of himself, his tenants and other inhabitants of the County of Kilkenny* [Dublin, 1705].

Cunningham, G.G., *Lives of eminent and illustrious Englishmen* (8 vols, Glasgow, 1837).

[Dennis, Michael], *A second oration to the Hibernian Society* (Dublin, 1758).

Epicedia Oxoniensia (Oxford, 1751).

Falkland [pseud for J.R. Scott] *Parliamentary representation, being a political and critical review of all the counties, cities and boroughs of Ireland* (Dublin, 1790).

Fitzgerald, G.R., *The law of attachments* (Dublin, 1785).

[Flood, Henry], *A letter from Sindercombe and Broghill's answer* (Dublin, 1770).

[Flood, Henry, et al.], *Baratariana: a select collection of fugitive political pieces, published during the administration of Lord Townshend in Ireland* (3rd ed., Dublin, 1777).

Flood, Henry, *Fame: an ode* (privately printed, London, 1775).

[Flood, Henry], *A letter to the people of Ireland on the expediency and necessity of the present associations in Ireland in favour of our own manufactures with some cursory observations on the effects of an union* (Dublin, 1779).

Hardy, Francis, *Memoirs of the political and private life of James Caulfield, Earl of Charlemont* (2 vols, London, 1812).

Hayes, Edward, *Reports of cases argued and determined in the Court of Exchequer in Ireland* (Dublin, 1837).

Hayes, E. and Jones, T., *Reports of cases argued and determined in the Court of Exchequer* (Dublin, 1843).

An Address to the Hibernian Society with a plan of education ... (Dublin, 1758).

The Charter for incorporating the Hibernian Society in Dublin ... (Dublin, 1769).

By-laws agreed to and confirmed by the Hibernian Society according to the rules prescribed by their charter (Dublin 1775).

History of the proceedings of the Volunteer delegates (Dublin, 1783).

[Irwin], *Two translations from the Greek addressed to H[enr]y F[loo]d esq.* (Dublin, 1774).

Johnson, Samuel, *Taxation no tyranny* (London, 1775).

Johnson, Samuel, *Political tracts, containing* ... *the Patriot* (London, 1776).

A letter from a gentleman in the city to a member of parliament in the north of Ireland ([Dublin], 1757).

A letter to Henry Flood on the present state of representation in Ireland (Belfast, 1783).

A letter to a school master in the country from his friend in town relative to Mr Sheridan's scheme of education (Dublin, 1758).

A letter to the right honourable J[ohn] P[onsonby] of the H[ous]e of C[ommon]s of I[relan]d (3rd ed., London, 1767).

Letters of William Russel on the doctrine of constructive contempt with...an report of the judgement of the King's Bench (Dublin, 1786).

Letters to the people of Ireland on the subject of an union with Great Britain (Dublin, 1786).

MacDougall, Henry, *Sketches of Irish political characters* (Dublin, 1799).

[MacNeven, W.J.], *An argument for independence in opposition to an union* (Dublin, 1799).

Mason, W.S., *A statistical account or parochial survey of Ireland* (3 vols, London, 1814–7).

Medland, W.M. and Weobly, Charles, *A collection of remarkable and interesting trials* (London, 1808).

Molyneux, William, *The case of Ireland...stated*, introduction by [Henry Flood] (London, 1770).

Molyneux, William, *The case of Ireland ... stated*, ed., J.G. Simms (Dublin, 1977).

Newport, Sir John, *The state of the borough representation of Ireland in 1783 and 1800* (London, 1832).

O'Conor, Matthew, *The history of the Irish Catholics from the settlement in 1691* (Dublin, 1813).

Oldfield, T.H.B., *The representative history of Great Britain and Ireland* (6 vols, London, 1816).

O'Regan, William, *Memoirs of the legal, literary and political life of ... John Philpot Curran* (London, 1817).

Parsons, Lawrence, *Observations on the bequest of Henry Flood, esq., to Trinity College, Dublin ...* (Dublin, 1795).

Plowden, Francis, *An historical review of the state of Ireland ... to ... 1801* (5 vols, Philadelphia, 1805–6).

Postlethwayt, Malachy, *Britain's commercial interest explained and improved ... also the great advantage which would accrue to this kingdom from an union with Ireland* (2 vols, London, 1757).

Proceedings relative to the Ulster assembly of Volunteer delegates (Belfast, 1783).

The private theatres of Kilkenny with introductory observations on other private theatres in Ireland ([Dublin], 1825).

The proceedings of the Hibernian Society (Dublin, 1758).

The royal charter of the Dublin Society to which are added the Society's by-laws and ordinances (Dublin, 1825).

The Royal register with annotations (9 vols, London, 1779–84).

Ryan, Richard, *A biographical dictionary of the worthies of Ireland* (2 vols, London, 1819).

Sheridan, C.F., *A review of the three great national questions relative to a declaration of right, Poynings' Law and the mutiny bill* (Dublin, 1781).

——, *Letters of a Dungannon and Munster delegate* (Dublin, 1784).

Sheridan, Thomas, *British education; or the source of the disorders of Great Britain* (London, 1756).

——, *An oration pronounced before a numerous body of the nobility and gentry assembled at the Musick Hall in Fishamble street* (Dublin, 1757).

A short account of the affairs of Ireland during the years 1783, 1784 and part of 1785 in a letter from a clergyman in Ireland (Dublin, 1782).

Short history of opposition to the present time in a letter to a member of parliament (Dublin, 1796).

Some authentic minutes of the proceedings of a very respectable assembly on the 20th of December 1779 (Dublin, 1780).

Tighe, William, *Statistical observations relative to the County Kilkenny in 1800 and 1801* (Dublin, 1802).

Vindex, *A treatise on the origin of attachments and information* (Dublin, 1785).

Webb, Daniel, *An enquiry into the beauties of painting ...* (London, 1760, Dublin, 1764).

——, *Remarks on the beauty of poetry* (London, 1762, Dublin, 1764).

——, *Observations on the correspondence between poetry and music* (Dublin, 1769).

Wilson, C.H., *A Compleat collection of the resolutions of the Volunteers ... of Ireland* (Dublin, 1782).
Wraxall, Nathanial, *Historical memoirs of my own time* (3 vols, London, 1818).
Young, Arthur, *A tour in Ireland* (2 vols, London, 1780).

VII   NEWSPAPERS AND PERIODICALS

Annual Register, 1782, 1787–91
Belfast Mercury, 1783–4
Blackwood's Magazine, 1826
The Corke Journal, 1762
Cork Evening Post, 1782
Corke Gazette, 1791
Clonmel Gazette, 1789–93
Dublin Chronicle, 1788–91
Dublin Courant, 1746
Dublin Daily Post, 1740
Dublin Gazette, 1764–5
Dublin Evening Post, 1783–87

Dublin Mercury, 1766
Faulkner's Dublin Journal, 1757–9
Finn's Leinster Journal, 1767–79
Freeman's Journal, 1763–70
Gentleman's Magazine, 1773, 1791
Hibernian Journal, 1771–83
Public Advertizer, 1761
Public Gazetteer, 1761–3
Pue's Occurrences, 1752, 1754–5, 1768–9
Universal Advertizer, 1759–60
Volunteer Evening Post, 1783–5
Volunteer Journal (Dublin), 1783–5

SECONDARY SOURCES

I   PUBLISHED WORKS

Anon., 'An affair of honour a hundred years ago', *Dublin University Magazine*, 78 (1871), pp 376–7.
——, 'Junius and Henry Flood', *Notes and Queries*, 2nd series, 8 (1859), pp 101–3, 189–90.
——, 'Notes on places of antiquarian interest', in *J.R.S.A.I.*, 5th series, 36 (1906), pp 265–75.
Ball, F.E., *The judges in Ireland 1221-1921* (2 vols, London, 1926).
Barry, Kevin, *Language, music and the sign* (Cambridge, 1987).
Bartlett, Thomas, 'Viscount Townshend and the Irish revenue 1767–73' in *R.I.A., proc.*, 79C(1979), pp 153–75.
——, 'The augmentation of the army in Ireland 1767–69' in *E.H.R.*, 96 (1981), pp 540–73.
——, 'The Irish House of Commons' rejection of the 'Privy Council' money bill of 1769: a reassessment', *Studia Hibernica*, 21 (1981), pp 63–77.
——, 'Opposition in late eighteenth-century Ireland: the case of the Townshend viceroyalty', *I.H.S.*, 22(1981), pp 313–30.
——, 'Ireland 1769–72' in *Macartney of Lisanoure 1737–1806*, ed., Peter Roebuck (Belfast, 1983), pp 66–87.

——, 'A people made rather for copies than originals': the Anglo-Irish 1760–1800, *The International History Review*, xii (1990), pp 11–24.

——, *The fall and rise of the Irish nation: the Catholic question 1690–1830* (Dublin, 1992)

Beckett, J.C., 'Literary life in eighteenth century Ireland' in S. Dyrvik, et al., eds, *The satellite states in the seventeenth and eighteenth centuries* (Bergen, 1979), pp 157–68.

——, 'Literature in English 1691–1800', in T.W. Moody and W.E. Vaughan, eds, *A new history of Ireland iv: the eighteenth century* (Oxford, 1986), pp 424–9.

Belmore, Earl of, *Parliamentary memoirs of Fermanagh and Tyrone from 1613–1885* (Dublin, 1887).

Benzie, W., *The Dublin orator: Thomas Sheridan's influence on eighteenth-century rhetoric and belles lettres* (Leeds, 1792).

Bettany, Lewis, *Edward Jerningham and his friends* (London, 1919).

Bill, E.G.W., *Education at Christ Church Oxford 1660–1800* (Oxford, 1988).

Bodkin, M.MacDonnell, *Grattan's parliament: before and after* (London, 1912).

Black, E.C., *The association: British extra parliamentary political organization 1769–93* (London, 1963).

Black, Jeremy, *A system of ambition: British foreign policy 1660–1793* (London, 1991).

Boydell, Brian, *Rotunda music in eighteenth-century Dublin* (Dublin, 1992).

——, *A Dublin musical calendar 1700–60* (Dublin, 1988).

Breatnach, R.A., 'The end of a tradition: a survey of eighteenth-century Gaelic literature', *Studia Hibernica*, 1 (1961).

Brennan, Monica, 'The changing composition of Kilkenny landowners 1641–1700', in W.Nolan and K.Whelan, eds, *Kilkenny: history and society* (Dublin, 1990), pp 161–96.

Brown, P.D, *William Pitt, Earl of Chatham: the great commoner* (London, 1978).

Bullion, J.L., *'A great and necessary measure': George Grenville and the genesis of the Stamp Act* (London, 1982).

Burns, R.E., *Irish parliamentary politics in the eighteenth century* (2 vols, Washington, 1989–90).

——, 'Ireland and British military preparations for war in America in 1775' in *Cithara*, ii (1963), pp 42–61.

Burtchaell, G.D., *Genealogical memoirs of the members of parliament for the county and city of Kilkenny* (Dublin, 1888).

Cannon, John, *Parliamentary reform 1640–1832* (Cambridge, 1973).

——, *The Fox-North coalition: crisis of the constitution* (Cambridge, 1969).

Carrigan, Canon, *History of the diocese of Ossory* (4 vols, Dublin, 1905).

Childe-Pemberton, W.S., *The Earl-Bishop: the life of Frederick, Bishop of Derry, Earl of Bristol* (2 vols, London, 1924).

Christie, I.R., 'William Pitt and American taxation, 1766: a problem of parliamentary reporting', *Studies in Burke and his times*, 17 (1986).

Clark, J.C.D., 'Whigs politics and parliamentary precedent: the English management of Irish politics 1754–56', *Historical Journal*, xxi (1978), pp 275–301.

Clark, W.S., *The Irish stage in the country towns 1720–1800* (Oxford, 1965).

Clarke, Aidan, 'Colonial constitutional attitudes in Ireland 1640–60', *R.I.A. proc.*, 90C(1990), pp 357–75.

Clarke, M.L., 'Classical studies' in L.S. Sutherland and L.G. Mitchell, eds, *The history of the University of Oxford, v: the eighteenth century* (Oxford, 1986), pp 519–33.

Connolly, Sean, *Religion, law and power: the making of Protestant Ireland 1660–1760* (Oxford, 1992).

Craig, M.J., *The Volunteer Earl* (London, 1948).

Curran, W.H., *The life of the right honourable John Philpot Curran* (2 vols, Edinburgh, 1822).

Cullen, L.M., *Anglo-Irish trade 1660–1800* (Manchester, 1968).

——, *An economic history of Ireland since 1660* (London, 1972).

——, 'Economic development 1691–1750' and 'Economic development 1750-1800' in T.W. Moody and W.E. Vaughan, *A New History of Ireland, iv* (Oxford, 1986), pp 146–95.

——, *The emergence of modern Ireland 1600–1900* (London, 1981).

Cummins, S.A., 'Extra-parliamentary agitation in Dublin in the 1760s' in R.V. Comerford, et al., eds, *Religion, conflict and coexistence in Ireland* (Dublin, 1990), pp 118–34.

Curran, William Henry, *The life of John Philpot Curran* (2 vols, Edinburgh, 1822).

Davies, G.L. Herries, 'The Physico-Historical society', *Irish Geography*, 12 (1979), pp 92–8.

Derry, J.W., *The regency crisis and the Whigs 1788–89* (Cambridge, 1963).

Dickinson, H.T., *Liberty and property: political ideology in eighteenth-century Britain* (London, 1977).

Dickson, David, *New foundations: Ireland 1660–1800* (Dublin, 1987).

——, 'Henry Flood and the eighteenth-century Irish Patriots' in Ciaran Brady, ed., *Worsted in the game: losers in Irish history* (Dublin, 1989), pp 97–108.

Donnelly, J.S., 'The Whiteboy movement 1761–65', *I.H.S.*, 21 (1981), pp 20-54.

——, 'The Whiteboys of 1769–76', *R.I.A. proc.*, 83C (1983).

Dunabain, J.P.D., 'College estates and wealth 1660–1815' in L.S. Sutherland and L.G. Mitchell, eds, *The history of the University of Oxford, v: the eighteenth century* (Oxford, 1986), pp 269–307.

Dunleavy, Mairead, *Dress in Ireland* (London, 1981).

Dunlop, Robert, *Ireland under the Commonwealth* (2 vols, Manchester, 1913).

——, 'Ireland in the eighteenth century', *Cambridge Modern History, vi* (Cambridge, 1934), pp 479–505.

Elliott, Marianne, *Wolfe Tone: prophet of Irish independence* (Yale, 1989).

Eshelman, D.H., *Elizabeth Griffith: a biographical and critical study* (Philadelphia, 1949).

Fabricant, Carole, *Swift's landscape* (London, 1982).

Fanning, S.J., 'The King's purse and the absentee's pocket in eighteenth-century Ireland', in G.L. Vincitorio, ed., *Crisis in the 'Great Republic'* (New York, 1969), pp 47–84.

Galloway, Peter, *The most illustrious order of St Patrick* (Chichester, 1983).

Gold, Joel, 'In defence of single-speech Hamilton', *Studies in Burke and his times*, x (1968–9), pp 1144–9.

Green, V.H.H., 'The university and social life' in L.S. Sutherland and L.G. Mitchell, eds, *The history of the University of Oxford, v: the eighteenth century* (Oxford, 1986), pp 309–35.

Healy, William, *History and antiquities of Kilkenny* (Kilkenny, 1893).

Hill, Jacqueline, 'Religious toleration and the relaxation of the Penal Laws: an imperial perspective', *Archivium Hibernicum*, 44 (1989), pp 98–109.

——, *From Patriots to Unionists: Dublin civic politics and Irish Protestant Patriotism 1660–1840* (Oxford, 1997).

Hoffman. R.J.S., *The Marquis: a study of Lord Rockingham* (New York, 1973).

Hogan, I.M., *Anglo-Irish music 1780–1830* (Cork, 1966).

Hume Williams, W.F., *A short history of the Irish parliament from 1782 to 1800* (London, 1912).

Hutchison, W.R., *Tyrone Precinct* (Belfast, 1951).

Ilchester, Earl of, *Henry Fox, first Lord Holland: his family and relations* (2 vols, London, 1920).

James, F.G., 'The Church of Ireland the Patriot movement in the late eighteenth century', *Eire-Ireland*, 17 (1982), pp 47–55.

Johnston, E.M., *Great Britain and Ireland 1760–1800* (Edinburgh, 1963).

Jupp. P.J., 'Earl Temple's viceroyalty and the question of renunciation', *I.H.S.*, xvii (1972), pp 299–317.

——, *Lord Grenville 1759–1834* (Oxford, 1985).

Kelly, James, 'The origins of the Act of Union: an examination of unionist opinion in Britain and Ireland 1650-1800', *I.H.S.*, 25 (1987), pp 236–63.

——, 'The parliamentary reform movement and the Catholic question 1783-85' in *Archivium Hibernicum*, 43(1988), pp 95–117.

——, 'A secret return of the Volunteers in 1784', *I.H.S.*, 26 (1989), pp 268–82.

——, 'The Irish trade dispute with Portugal 1780–87' in *Studia Hibernica*, 25 (1989–90), pp 8–48.

——, 'The Anglo-French Commercial treaty of 1786: the Irish dimension', *Eighteenth-Century Ireland*, iv (1989), pp 93–112.

——, 'Swift and the Irish economy in the 1720s', *Eighteenth-Century Ireland*, 6 (1991), pp 7–36.

——, 'Scarcity and poor relief in eighteenth-century Ireland: the subsistence crisis of 1782-4', *I.H.S.*, 28(1992), pp 38–62.

——, *Prelude to Union: Anglo-Irish politics in the 1780s* (Cork, 1992).

——, 'Parliamentary reform in Irish politics 1760–90', in David Dickson, Daire Keogh and Kevin Whelan, eds, *The United Irishmen* (Dublin, 1993), pp 74–87.

——, *Henry Grattan* (Dundalk, 1993).

——, 'The Glorious and immortal memory: commemoration and Protestant identity 1660–1800', *R.I.A., proc.*, 94C(1994), pp 25–52.

——, *That damn'd thing called honour': duelling in Ireland 1570–1860* (Cork, 1995).

——, 'The politics of Protestant ascendancy: County Galway 1650–1832' in Gerard Moran, ed., *Galway: politics and society* (Dublin, 1996).

Kelly, Patrick, 'William Molyneux and the spirit of liberty in eighteenth-century Ireland', *Eighteenth-Century Ireland*, 3 (1988), pp 133–48.

Kenealy, Mary, 'Henry Flood of Farmley', *Old Kilkenny Review*, 2 (1983), pp 518–26.

Kennedy, Denis, 'The Irish Whigs, administrative reform and responsible government 1782–1800', *Eire-Ireland*, 8 (1973), pp 55–69.

Kennedy, Joe, 'Callan: a corporate town 1700–1800' in William Nolan and Kevin Whelan, eds, *Kilkenny: history and society* (Dublin, 1990), pp 289–304.

Kidd, Colin, 'North Britishness and the nature of eighteenth-century British patriotism' in *Historical Journal*, 39 (1996), pp 361–82.

Langford, Paul, 'Tories and Jacobites 1714–51' in L.S. Sutherland and L.G. Mitchell, eds, *The history of the University of Oxford, v: the eighteenth century* (Oxford, 1986), pp 99–127.

Lecky, W.E.H., *Leaders of public opinion in Ireland* (London, 1871).

Leerssen, J.T., *Mere Irish and Fíor Ghael: studies in the idea of Irish nationality, its development and literary expression* (Amsterdam, 1986).

——,'Anglo-Irish patriotism and its European context: notes towards a reassessment', *Eighteenth-Century Ireland*, 3 (1988), pp 7–21.

Legg, M.L., 'Money and reputation: the effects of the banking crises of 1755 and 1760' in *Eighteenth-Century Ireland*, 11 (1996), pp 74–87.

Liechty, Joseph, 'Testing the depth of Catholic-Protestant enmity: the case of Thomas Leland's *History of Ireland, 1773*' in A.D. Falconer, ed., *Reconciling Memories* (Dublin, 1988), pp 52–67.

Love, Walter, 'Charles O'Conor of Belanagare and Thomas Leland's philosophical *History of Ireland*', *I.H.S.*, 13 (1962), pp 2–25.

——, 'The Hibernian Antiquarian Society', *Studies* 1962

Luce, J.V., *Trinity College Dublin: the first four hundred years* (Dublin, 1984).

Lyons, F.S.L., *Ireland since the famine* (London, 1973).

McAnally, Henry, 'The militia array of 1756', *Irish Sword*, i (1949–53), pp 94–104.

McCracken, J.L., 'The Irish viceroyalty 1760–73' in H. Cronne, et al., eds, *Essays in British and Irish history* (London, 1949), pp 152–68.

——, 'Irish parliamentary elections 1727–68', *I.H.S.*, 5 (1947), pp 209–30.

——, 'The social structure and social life 1714–60' in T.W. Moody and W.E. Vaughan, eds, *A new history of Ireland, iv: eighteenth-century Ireland* (Oxford, 1986), pp 31–56.

McDowell, R.B., *Irish public opinion 1750–1800* (London, 1944).

——, *Ireland in the age of imperialism and revolution 1760–1801* (Oxford, 1979).

——, 'Colonial nationalism and the winning of parliamentary independence 1760–82' in T.W. Moody and W.E.Vaughan, eds, *A new history of Ireland, iv: eighteenth-century Ireland* (Oxford, 1986), pp 196-235.

——, and Webb, D.A., *Trinity College Dublin 1592–1952: an academic history* (Cambridge, 1982).

——, 'The main narrative' in T. Ó Raifeartaigh, ed., *The Royal Irish Academy: a bicentennial history* (Dublin, 1985).

McGuire, James, 'The Irish parliament in 1692' in T. Bartlett and D. Hayton, eds, *Penal era and golden age* (Belfast, 1979), pp 1–31.

MacNevin, Thomas, *The history of the Volunteers of 1782* (Dublin, 1846).

McParland, Edward, *James Gandon: vitruvius Hibernicus* (London, 1985).

Maccoby, S., *English radicalism 1786–1832* (London, 1955).

Malcomson, A.P.W., 'Speaker Pery and the Pery papers', *N.M.A.J.*, 16 (1973–4), pp 33–60.

——, *John Foster: the politics of the Anglo-Irish ascendancy* (Oxford, 1978).

Markham, C.R., *Memoir of Archbishop Markham* (London, 1906).

Maxwell, Constantia, *A history of Trinity College, Dublin 1592–1892* (Dublin, 1946).

Mitchell, J., 'Colonel William Persse', *J.G.A.H.S.*, 30 (1963), pp 49–89.

Mitchell, L.G., *Charles James Fox and the disintegration of the Whig Party 1782–94* (Oxford, 1971).

Mockler, J., 'Mallow district in 1775', *J.C.H.A.S.*, 21 (1915), pp 17–29.

Moran, Mary, 'The Agars of Gowran' in *In the shadows of the steeple*, 2 (1990), pp 110–35.

Moriarty, T.F., 'The Irish absentee tax controversy of 1773', *Proceedings of the American Philosophical Society*, 118 (1974), pp 370–408.

Murphy, Sean, 'The Dublin anti-union riot of 3 December 1759' in G. O'Brien, ed, *Parliament, politics and people* (Dublin, 1989), pp 49–68.

Neely, W.G., 'The Ormonde Butlers of County Kilkenny 1515–1715', in K.Whelan and W.Nolan, eds, *Kilkenny: history and society* (Dublin, 1990), pp 107–26.

Nevin, Monica, 'General Charles Vallancey 1725–1812', *R.S.A.I., Jn.*, 123 (1993), pp 19–58.

O'Brien, Conor Cruise, *The Great Melody: a thematic biography … of Edmund Burke* (London, 1992).

O'Brien, George, 'The Irish free trade agitation of 1779', *E.H.R.*, 38 (1923), pp 564–81, 39 (1924), pp 96–109.

O'Brien, Gerard, *Anglo-Irish politics in the age of Grattan and Pitt* (Dublin, 1987).

——, 'Francophobia in eighteenth-century Ireland' in H. Gough and D. Dickson, eds, *Ireland and the French Revolution* (Dublin 1990), pp 40–51.

O'Connor, T.M., 'The embargo on the export of Irish provisions 1776–79', *I.H.S.*, 2 (1940), pp 4–11.

——, 'The conflict between Flood and Grattan 1782-3' in H.A. Cronne, et al., eds, *Essays in British and Irish history* (London, 1949), pp 169–84.

O'Halloran, Clare, 'Irish recreations of the Gaelic past: the challenge of MacPherson's Ossian', *Past and Present*, no. 124 (1989).

Ó Snodaigh, P., 'Notes on theVolunteers … of County Louth', *County Louth Antiquarian Journal*, 18(1976), pp 279–94.

——, 'TheVolunteers of 1782: a citizen army or armed citizens', *Irish Sword*, 15 (1983), pp 117–88.

——, Notaí ar Óglaigh … Chontae na Gaillimhe', *Galvia* 11 (1979), pp 1–31.

O'Snoddy, P., 'Notes on theVolunteers … of County Roscommon', *Irish Sword*, 12 (1975–6), pp 15–35.

Pares, Richard, *King George III and the politicians* (Oxford, 1953).

Phipps, P.W., *The life of Colonel Pownoll Phipps* (Privately printed, London, 1894).

Pocock, J.G.A., *The Machiavellian moment* (Princeton, 1975).

Ponsonby, Sir John, *The Ponsonby family* (London, 1929).

Pottle, F.A., *James Boswell: the earlier years 1740–69* (London, 1966).

Power, T.P., 'Parliamentary representation in County Kilkenny in the eighteenth century', William Nolan and Kevin Whelan, eds, *Kilkenny: history and society* (Dublin, 1990), pp 305–32.

Prim, J., ' Notes on Kilkenny inns and taverns', *Journal of the Kilkenny and south-east of Ireland Archaeological Society*, vii (1862–3), pp 152–80.

Puirséil, Séamus, *Henry Flood: aiste eolais ar a shaol is a shaother* (Baile Átha Cliath, 1973).

Quane, Michael, 'Aspects of education in Ireland 1695–1795', *J.C.A.H.S.*, 73 (1968), pp 120–36.

Roebuck, Peter, ed., *Macartney of Lisanoure 1737–1806* (Belfast, 1983).

Seagrave, C.W., *The Seagrave family* (London, [1936]).

Sheehy, Jeanne, *The discovery of Ireland's past: the Celtic revival 1830–1930* (London, 1980).

Sheldon, E.K., *Thomas Sheridan of Smock Alley* (Princeton, 1967).

——, 'The Hibernian Academy: an eighteenth century experiment in group education', *Long Room*, 11 (1975), pp 23–34.

Simms, J.G., *Colonial nationalism 1698–1776* (Cork, 1976).

Smyth, Jim, 'Dublin's political underground in the 1790s' in Gerard O'Brien, ed., *Parliament, politics and people: essays in eighteenth-century Irish history* (Dublin, 1989), pp 129–48.

Snoddy, C., 'Some notes on parliament and its Limerick members 1767–71', *N.M.A.J.*, ix (1962-5), pp 165–81.

Stanford, W.B., *Ireland and the classical tradition* (Dublin, 1984).

Stewart, A.T.Q., *A deeper silence: the hidden origins of the United Irishmen* (London, 1993).

Stubbs, J.W., *The history of the University of Dublin from its foundation to the end of the eighteenth century* (Dublin, 1889.

Sutherland, L.S., 'Political respectability 1751–71' in L.S. Sutherland and L.G. Mitchell, eds, *The history of the University of Oxford, v: the eighteenth century* (Oxford, 1986), pp 129–61.

Swift, John, *History of the Dublin bakers and others* (Dublin, [1948]).

Thomas, P.D.G., *British politics and the Stamp Act crisis 1763–67* (Oxford, 1975).

——, 'Two voting lists for the Irish House of Commons in 1773', *Parliamentary History*, 7 (1988), pp 313–27.

Toohey, R.E., *Liberty and empire: British radical solutions to the American problem* (Kentucky, 1970).

Trench. C.E.F., 'William Burton Conyngham', *R.S.A.I. Jn.*, 115 (1985), pp 40–63.

Tyrrell, A.Brooke, 'Homage to Grattan 1746-1820', *Dublin Historical Record*, 37 (1983), pp 31–43.

Williams, Basil, *Life of William Pitt, Earl of Chatham* (2 vols, Oxford, 1915).

II UNPUBLISHED THESES

Bartlett, Thomas, 'The Townshend viceroyalty 1767–72' (Ph.D., Q.U.B., 1976).

Brennan, Monica, 'The making of the Protestant ascendancy in County Kilkenny' (Ph.D., SUNY, 1983).

Cummins, S.A., 'Opposition and the Irish parliament 1759–71' (MA, St Patrick's College, Maynooth, 1978).

Day, J.P., 'The Catholic question in the Irish parliament 1760-82' (MA, U.C.D., 1973).

de la Poer Beresford, Marcus, 'Ireland in French strategy 1691–1789' (M.Litt., T.C.D., 1975).

de Valera, Ann, 'Antiquarianism and historical investigation in Ireland in the eighteenth century', (MA, U.C.D., 1978).

Duncan, A.I.M., 'A study of the life and public career of Frederick Howard, fifth Earl of Carlisle 1748–1825' (Ph.D, Oxford University, 1981).

Hayton, David, 'Ireland and the English ministers 1703–15' (D.Phil., Oxford University, 1975).

Kelly, James, 'The Irish parliamentary reform movement: the administration and popular politics 1783-85' (MA, U.C.D., 1981).

Kelly, Paul, 'The establishment of Pitt's administration 1783-86' (D.Phil., Oxford University, 1971).

Lammey, David 'A study of Anglo-Irish relations between 1772 and 1782 with particular reference to the 'free trade' movement' (Ph.D., Q.U.B., 1984).

Liechty, Joseph, 'Irish evangelicalism, Trinity College Dublin and the mission of the Church of Ireland at the end of the eighteenth century' (Ph.D., St Patrick's College, Maynooth, 1987).

McCoy, J.G., 'Court ideology in mid-eighteenth-century Ireland: an examination of political culture' (MA, St Patrick's College, Maynooth, 1990).

Murphy, Sean, 'The Lucas affair: a study of municipal and electoral politics in Dublin 1742–49' (MA, U.C.D., 1981).

O'Brien, M.G., 'The exercise of legislative power in Ireland 1781–1800' (Ph.D., Cambridge University, 1983).

O'Donoghue, Fergus, 'Parliament in Ireland under Charles II' (MA, U.C.D., 1970).

O'Donovan, Declan, 'The money bill dispute of 1753', (Ph.D., U.C.D., 1973).

O'Flaherty, Eamon, 'The Catholic question in Irish politics, 1772–93 (MA, U.C.D., 1981).

Schweitzer, D.R.,'The Whig political connection Between Britain and Ireland 1784–1801' (Ph.D., University of London, 1982).

Victory, Isolde, 'Colonial nationalism 1692–1725: from common law to natural right' (Ph.D., T.C.D., 1984).

III WORKS OF REFERENCE

Alumni Dublinenses, eds, G.D. Burtchaell and T.U. Sadleir (Dublin, 1935).

Alumni Oxonienses: the members of the University of Oxford 1715–1886, ed., John Foster (6 vols, Oxford, 1888).

Black, R.D.C., Collinson, *A catalogue of pamphlets on economic subjects 1750–1900 in Irish libraries* (Belfast, 1969).

Burke, A.P., *A genealogical and heraldic dictionary of the peerage, baronetage, privy council, knightage and companionage* (London, 1905).

Burke, Sir Bernard, *A genealogical and heraldic history of the landed gentry of Ireland* (London, 1912).

G.E. C[ocayne], *The complete peerage*, Vicary Gibbs, et al., eds. (13 vols, London, 1910–40).

de Burgh, U.U., *Landowners of Ireland* (London, 1878).

Dictionary of National Biography (22 vols, London, 1908–9).

George, M.D., *Catalogue of political and personal satires preserved in ... the British Museum* (vols v-x, London, 1935–54).

Highfell, P.H. et als, eds, *A biographical dictionary of actors, actresses ... and other stage personnel in London 1660–1800* (Carbondale, 1978).

Leslie, J.B., ed., *Ossory clergy and parishes* (Enniskillen, 1933).

Moody, T.W., et al., eds, *A new history of Ireland, ix* (Oxford, 1984).

Namier, Lewis and Brooke, John, eds, *The history of parliament: the House of Commons 1754–90* (3 vols, London, 1964).

O'Hart, John, *The Irish and Anglo-Irish landed gentry* (London, 1884).

Sedgwick, Romney, ed., *The history of parliament: the House of Commons 1715–54* (2 vols, London, 1970).

Thorne, Ronald, ed., *The history of parliament: the House of Commons 1790–1820* (5 vols, London, 1986).

Webb, A.J., *Compendium of Irish biography* (Dublin, 1878).

Index

159; absentee tax, 191; corn export bill, 199; returns money bills, 1775, 227; Flood seeks seat, 227–8; Flood member of, 238; Flood loses place, 281, 302; Yelverton bill, 311; seat offered to Flood, 314; powers attacked, 318–19

Privy Council, Irish, 81, 238, 331; refuses to send money bill, 77–8; money bills, 79, 135–6, 148; decennial bill, 94; corn trade ban, 103; septennial bills, 104, 120; in Philadelphus letters, 124; Mayne dismissed, 145; admission of Flood, 205; Flood member of, 223–4, 226; oath, 244; powers attacked, 269–70, 272, 296–8; Yelverton bill, 298–300; changes discussed, 302

Protestants: role of elite, 15; identity, 68, 76; seek equal status, 69–70; Flood on position of, 141–3; as Volunteers, 230, 250–1, 256–7; firm on British links, 257–8; wider franchise sought, 343, 347, 357; antiquarianism, 434; ascendancy politics, 449

public works, 153, 154

Pulteney, Daniel, 405, 409–10, 411

quarterage, 105, 165

Randalstown, Co., Antrim 193

regency crisis, 414–17

Reilly, Sheriff, 390

renunciation debate; *see* under Poynings' Law

Repeal Association, 448

revenue bill, 150

revenue board; proposal to split, 154–64; Flood on division of, 155–7, 162–4; Osborne dismissed, 178; reunification, 184, 185–6, 188

revenue sources, 165–6, 184, 196, 223, 248; Carlisle administration, 288

Reynolds, Joshua, 418

Rigby, Richard, 72–3, 95, 132

Ringwood, 42, 55

Roberts, John, 22

Robinson, Judge Christopher, 48, 164

Robinson, John, 228, 238

Rochford, Lord, 136, 147

Rockingham, Marquess of, 132, 141; Flood on, 97; prime minister, 108; possible coalition, 147; constitutional change, 255, 312; prime minister, 1782, 311; death of, 331

Rodd, Thomas, 448

Rolles, John, 416

Roscrea, 230

Rosse, earl of; *see* Parsons, Lawrence

Roth, Richard, 58

Rowan, Archibald Hamilton, 385

Rowley, Hercules Langford, 36, 73

Royal Irish Academy, 436

royal prerogative, 89

rum trade, 166

Rutland, duke of, 405; administration, 368–72, 382–402; commercial propositions, 385–402

Ryder, John, Archbishop of Tuam, 71

Savage, Philip, 52

Scott, John, 150, 223, 239, 240, 246, 288, 306, 370; Buckinghamshire administration, 258, 265–6; Carlisle administration, 277; attack on Flood, 293–4; replaced, 313; Northington administration, 368

Scott, J.R., 438

Scott, William, 36

Seaford borough, 378, 380–2, 411, 423, 426; Flood wins, 402–5

secret service list, 90

septennial bills, 78–9, 80, 85, 88, 97, 103, 110, 112; 1763, 94; Flood's bill, 1765, 104, 105; Flood's bill, 1766, 106; Flood supports, 1767, 117, 119–21, 122; and Townshend, 118; in Philadelphus letters, 123; returned, 1768, 125–6

Seven Years War, 65, 80, 93

Shannon river navigation, 92

Sharman, William, 379

Shearman, Robert, 50

Shelburne, earl of, 36, 118, 119, 132, 330, 331, 340

Sheridan, Charles Francis, 312, 316

Sheridan, Richard Brinsley, 398, 410

Sheridan, Thomas, 35–7

Shillelogher, Co. Kilkenny, 257

Shuttle Club, the Coombe, 126

Sindercombe letters, 138–41, 258

Singleton, Sydenham, 242

slave trade, 417

Smith, Ambrose, 28, 36, 235, 285, 349, 426; Flood papers, 13; at Oxford, 31; legal training, 34; duties of sovereign, 60; Flood bequest, 428, 429, 431, 432

Smith, Thomas, 28

Smock Alley theatre, 35